The

NAME
BK

The NAME BK

Over 10,000 Names—Their Meanings, Origins, and *Spiritual Significance*

DOROTHY ASTORIA

BETHANY HOUSE PUBLISHERS

Minneapolis, Minnesota

Published by Bethany House Publishers
11400 Hampshire Avenue South
Minneapolis, Minnesota 55438

Bethany House publishers is a division of
Baker Publishing Group, Grand Rapids, Michigan

Printed in the United States of America

Library of Congress Cataloging-in-Publication Data

Astoria, Dorothy.
    The name book : over 10,000 names—their meanings, origins, and spiritual significance / Dorothy Astoria.
        p.   cm.
    Summary: "A comprehensive list of names that includes the name's cultural origin, meaning, spiritual conotation, and a related Bible verse"—Provided by publisher.
    ISBN 978-0-7642-0566-8 (pbk. ; alk. paper)   1. Names, Personal—Dictionaries.
I. Title.
    CS2367.A95   2008
    929.4'03—dc22

                                                                                2008028761

C●NTENTS

What's in a Name?.. 7

The Deciding Factors..................................... 11

Guide to Using Name Listings 17

Alphabetical Listings of Names.......................... 19

List of Bible Names 301

Birthstones and Flowers................................. 313

Heritage of Names 314

Our Favorite Girl Names................................. 316

Our Favorite Boy Names 317

WHAT'S IN A
NAME

Names have been in existence as long as humanity. God created a timeless tradition when he gave Adam the first name, meaning "formed of earth." In the same manner, humans have been handing out names since the beginning of recorded time.

But why names? Why not labels, symbols, or codes? Part of the answer is found in Genesis 1:27. "So God created human beings in his image. In the image of God he created them. He created them male and female" (NCV). If we were merely another species of God's creation, we would all have one name, such as "lion," "sparrow," or "mole." But because we are a special and unparalleled creation—individuals—we each have a name.

Names are an integral part of who we are. While we are all intrinsically unique, names bestow upon us a tangible way to distinguish one another. God reveals this individuality in Isaiah 43:1 in saying, "I have redeemed you; I have called you by name, you are mine" (NRSV). The names we now bear have meaning to the Lord! Not only this, but in Revelation 2:17 He tells his children that He will give us "a new name that no one knows except the one who receives it" (NLT).

The evolution of names has been shaped by both religious and cultural influences. In ancient times people were generally given one name (called a "given name"). This name often related to a circumstance surrounding a child's birth ("Moses," meaning "drawn from the water") or a trait that parents hoped a child would possess ("Salome," meaning "peaceful"). Also, the name could be connected with a promise or an aspiration ("Isaac," meaning "laughter") or possibly a simple object ("Esther," meaning "star").

In latter ancient history, some utilization of second names (and third, and fourth, et al.) can be observed. These names were usually given to demonstrate a person's identification with a particular family and/or clan (Gaius Julius Caesar) or with a father (Simon bar-Jonah, with "bar" meaning "son of"). This practice was carried into modern times through various tribal societies.

These additional names, however, were not commonplace in Western civilization until about 900 years ago (around A.D. 1100). At first, added names were taken only by the nobility. They became known as "surnames," derived from the literal words "sir names." This practice was gradually embraced by the common people over the centuries until, in 1465, King Edward V of England delivered an edict requiring that surnames be adopted universally for identification purposes. He ordered that the names taken reflect the individual's identity, representing either a town, color, art, or office. Therefore, many new surnames came into being, such as Black, Smith, Miller, and Baker.

Over time, the means by which names were chosen and/or acquired broadened significantly. Some came from physical characteristics. For example, dark-haired Elizabeth became Elizabeth Browne, and blond James became James White. Some also were formed by adding "son" to the father's name (Wilson, Carlson, Johnson, and Anderson). Others came about by adding prefixes meaning "son" to the father's name (Fitzpatrick, Fitzgerald, MacMurray, MacDonald, O'Bannon, and O'Shea). There were also many other means of deriving and obtaining surnames.

The Church had an unparalleled influence over the choosing of names in medieval times. In the twelfth century, it decreed that only children named after saints and martyrs could be baptized. This was an attempt to stop the practice of naming children after pagan gods and entities. It was rather effective, for a priest of the Church had to be present to officiate at a child's baptism and confirmation. Since these practices were generally believed to be integral to salvation, most people honored the edicts. Statistics show that the great majority of women at that time were named Mary, Ann, Elizabeth, or Catherine, while most men were named John, James, William, Charles, or George.

For the most part, additional titles, known to us as "middle names," were not utilized until the eighteenth century. At this time, these new names became a way of further distinguishing an individual and also of honoring deceased relatives or admired persons. These, along with surnames, have emerged with ever-increasing importance as the earth's population has continued to geometrically increase.

While all names have both denotative (inherent) and connotative (implied) meaning(s), this is no longer as important to many parents who are choosing names for their child. Often a child is still named for a characteristic or place, but in many cases names are now selected for the way in which they commemorate someone or something, or simply on the basis of their own various aesthetic qualities.

When inherent meaning *is* important to prospective parents, names are normally chosen on the merits of their positive implications. Parents naming their daughter "Cady" often do so in the expectation and hope that she will be pure. In the same way, parents who choose "Matthew" for their son most likely consider him a gift of God.

So, what's in a name? Names are a celebration not only of our humanity, but also a reminder of our individuality—that we are uniquely made in the image of God. They are wonderful gifts, given second only to the gift of life itself—lasting testimonies to the beauty of personhood. Best of all, *you* now have the opportunity to make these choices for your child. Enjoy your quest.

THE DECIDING
FACT●RS

Associations

While particular names are given for many different reasons, three associations are of primary importance to most people. One, most children are in some way named after at least one relative. Two, they are often named in honor of historical figures and celebrities. Three, the majority of people in the Western hemisphere is named for biblical characters. Naturally, there is a great amount of overlap between these areas. For example, a baby named "Joseph Lincoln Johnson" could be named after both his grandfather Joseph and the Joseph of biblical renown, while also commemorating Abraham Lincoln.

Gender

While there seems to be a vast discrepancy in the ratio of male and female biblical names, since there are over 3,000 men listed in the Bible and less than 200 women, it's not as "unequal" as it might appear. Many of the male names recorded in the Scriptures are now used frequently for females, such as Ariel, Dara, Jada, Neriah, Reba, Susi, and Zina. In the same way, there are many names which were once considered to be exclusively for boys or girls that now are commonly used and considered appropriate for both sexes. Pay attention to name usage around you—you may have more options than you realized! Examples of "gender-neutral" monikers are: Adrian, Audrey, Courtney, Dana, Greer, Jamie, Kelly, Kevin, Lee, Lindsay, Madison, Robin, Sydney, Taylor, Terry, Tierney, and Tony. Even so, it is important to be mindful of the consequences of choosing a traditionally gender-specific name for a child of the opposite sex. Innovation is fun, but try to envision any possible disadvantages as well.

Characteristics

Children are frequently named in celebration of treasured ideals, or given names that intrinsically represent these characteristics (Charity, Hope, or Grace, for example). Also, some are named after commemorative circumstances surrounding the child's birth, such as Spring, Noel, or Joy. In addition, parents often give names which represent elements of character that it is hoped the child will possess. For instance, Ryan (meaning "little ruler"), Alexis (meaning "defender of mankind"), Katrina (meaning "pure"), or Caleb (meaning "bold").

Nicknames

There are two important factors to consider regarding the use of shortened names. One, don't use a longer name that will likely be shortened to a name that is undesirable to you. That is to say, if you cringe at the thought of Josh or Ash, don't name your baby Joshua or Ashleigh. Other people *will* shorten it. Two, in most cases it's preferable to give your child the "long version" of the chosen name. "Allison" and "Jacob" can always be abbreviated by merely using "Allie" and "Jake," if those are the names you happen to prefer. However, if you choose the nickname as the given name, you impose unnecessary limits. As your child matures he or she may desire to put aside the nickname in favor of the full name. This may be difficult if the legality of the situation hinders such change (like altering a birth certificate).

Acronyms

An acronym is a word formed from letters of a set of words that stands for the group of words as a whole (usually the first letter or letters). Some common examples are SCUBA (Self-Contained Underwater Breathing Apparatus), RADAR (RAdio Detection And Ranging), and PANIC (Parents Attempting to Name Imminent Children) (editor's creation). What is not commonly realized, however, is that often the set of names given to a person will lend itself to an acronym. This can be a wonderful thing. For instance, you may want to give your child names which will spell out LUV (Lexi Umaya Vanderberg) or TRU (Tyler Robinson Ulrich). Another enjoyable option has been to create a set of names that will match the standard nickname of the given name. Megan Elizabeth Gander brings out *Meg,* and Nicholas Ian Cortese emits *Nic.*

There are elements of acronyms which are, perhaps, less desirable. First, the gender of the child should be taken into account. *HUG* might seem adorable for a child, but a young man might see it differently, as did one great military officer. Hiram Ulysses Grant (who also became our eighteenth president) was so mortified by the hazing he received at West Point for his acronym that he changed his name to the more commonly recognized Ulysses Simpson Grant. Likewise, *BIG* could be both fun and appropriate for a baby boy who weighs in at 10 lbs., 4 oz., but Brianna Ingrid Gates certainly will someday object.

Second, there are many acronyms which should be avoided altogether. Don't combine names that invite merciless teasing. Most of these can be spotted as soon as they are spelled out. Avoid, for instance, Ferris Alastair Tannen, Zachery Isaac Thatcher, and (for those who prefer longer titles) Brittaney Ariel Rhiannon Frazier.

Humor

Often parents give their children names that evoke concrete images of one thing or another. *Every* name carries connotations, just as every word does. However, if humor is involved, in each case it must be decided how far this will be carried. This is especially true when it comes to rhymes. Conventional wisdom says to forgo combinations that are "overly harmonious." Mild examples are "Sarah Barah" or "Jason Mason." Sometimes these can be fun, although it might not be fun for your child.

Even more consideration should be given to those names which could bring further ridicule. Real-life demonstrations are offered by Robin Banks, Wayne Dwopp, Cinder Eller, Krystal Ball, Flip Side, Otto Graph, Ann Cuff, Iona Mink, Paul Bearer, Candy Barr, and Constance Noring.

Spelling

There are some other points to mull and muse. It's always enjoyable and challenging to look for ways to make the names that you select "stand out." If you're thinking about utilizing a notably unique name or a considerably variant spelling of a name, remember: your child will need to write it out each and every time a full signature is required throughout his or her life. Your darling baby might someday come to resent your creativity if you invent a "Ghennyphur Kolleene" or a "Qristaphir Writcherd."

Pronunciation

No matter what languages underlie the root of the name you choose, there is a fair chance that you have many options available to you in terms of pronunciation. Frequently, notably ethnic and exotic names bring new zest to communication. Sometimes variety is refreshing. Bring to mind, however, this simple maxim: People tend to pronounce a name the way it looks. Ask yourself honestly whether having to repeatedly correct the name's pronunciation and/or spelling will at some point become burdensome to your child (or you!).

Trends

Many people opt for trendy names. This is often regarded as a means to ensure that as children grow up they will "fit in" with others of or near their age. But first consider: which is more important to you—commonality or exclusivity? Tradition or authenticity? Harmony or distinction?

In many cases both can be had. Most of us are given at least three names. Ponder this with special consideration in regard to the first name. Do you want your child to have six others in her class/office/sandbox/committee who share the same name? Or would you rather give him one which will set him apart in one or more ways?

A pair of asides might be examined here. First, you can label your child with an exact era if a name is a falling star (beautiful and thrilling, yes, but burned up in the atmosphere in a flash). Second, while a name's denotative, or official, meaning probably won't change quickly, it's connotative, or implied, meanings often do. It usually takes the passing of three generations for a name to be regenerated from its previously imagined meanings. This is not altogether bad—all names will change to a degree in this sense over the course of a lifetime. Do try to evaluate possible names with the big-picture timeline in mind.

Flow

It has been said that names are either the best or worst gifts a child can be given. That is to say, the implications of a child's given names should be thoroughly considered. In so doing, picture your child having these particular names all of his or her life. One of the most effective means of carrying this out is by saying, out loud, the prospective full name(s) of the child. Also, you might try writing the information out, in index card form. For example:

Name: Danelle Marie Soderstrom

Initials: DMS

First and Middle: Danelle Marie

First and Last: Danelle Soderstrom

Possible Nicknames: Dani, Dee, Nell, Nelly

By working this out, you may possibly avoid an unforeseen disaster. If you don't, you might end up with an Anna Graham or an Evan Gelical.

Surnames

Surnames can be a determining element in deciding first and middle names. The standard factors are how long and how distinguished surnames appear to be. First, if you have a short, easily recognized surname (Chang or Jones), you can be somewhat more "adventurous" in selecting the other names. You might choose longer or more unique names such as Jacqueline, Payton, Savanah, or Madison. Second, if your surname is uncommon or extra long, you may want to choose a simpler or shorter first name to provide contrast.

Phonetics

In many cases you'll want to avoid choosing a given name that ends with the same letter or sound with which the middle or surname begins. If this is not observed, it can be difficult to know where one name ends and the other begins. Some examples are Lauren Newall, Janelle Leeden, Caleb Billings, Joseph Foston, Phillip Pryors, and Bob Block. It would take some thought to process these names. This is particularly noticeable with vowels: Joshua Aling, Cori Easter, or Kayla Underman.

Hyphenation

Many parents today give their child a hyphenated surname in order to preserve the maiden surname of the mother, e.g., Caitlyn Paige Larsen-Wilder, or Austin Cole Jennings-Thurston. Another option would be to use the mother's maiden name as the child's middle name, shortening the surname. In this case, your child might be Haley McDonald Fair or Alexander Brown Hastings.

GUIDE TO USING
NAME LISTINGS

AARON, Aaran, Aaren, Aarin, Aaronn, Aarron, Aron, Arran, Arron (see also Aran, Aren)

Language/Cultural Origin: **Hebrew**

Inherent Meaning: **Light Bringer**

Spiritual Connotation: **Radiating God's Light**

Scripture: **Isaiah 60:1** KJV

Arise, shine; for thy light is come, and the glory of the Lord is risen upon thee.

Primary Name (example: Aaron):

In most cases, this is the form of the name that is most commonly used. Sometimes a more secondary form will be listed first. This is done when, for instance, this form was used in the Bible or in classical literature (i.e., original rendering).

Alternative Spellings (examples: Aaran, Aaren . . .):

These are other ways in which the name has been used. These lists are not meant to be exhaustive. There are many additional possible spellings, renderings, and combinations of names.

(see also . . .):

This indicates that another name which is quite similar to the one listed has its own entry in the book and can be cross-referenced.

📖 This symbol indicates that the primary name listed appears (in that form) in the Bible.

Language/Cultural Origin:

This is the primary cultural and lingual setting from which the name is derived. In most cases, the origin is quite apparent. There are instances, however, in which a word has legitimate roots in two or more languages. In these cases, the focus has been to determine the most common usage of the name and follow it in this book. Bear in mind, as well, that names evolve in form as they cross lingual barriers. Consequently, there may exist several forms of the same name.

Inherent Meaning:

This is the literal, or *denotative*, meaning of the name. Here, also, most of the names listed have a clear heritage. As a result, most of the inherent meanings are readily discoverable. Even so, some may have more than one meaning (again, having crossed languages). In addition, many of the words originate in ancient tongues and have notably changed in meaning. The greatest efforts have been made to ensure that the meaning listed is that which is derived from the original language of the name.

Spiritual Connotation:

This is an implied, or *connotative*, meaning of the name. The goal has been to take connotative meanings and interpret them in a spiritual (or abstract) sense. There is a subjective element here, for almost every name has more than one connotative meaning. However, the goal here is not to exhaustively list the traits or characteristics implied by a given name. Instead, one or two are listed to give a general idea of what are often seen as intrinsic qualities of a particular name, such as would be desired, thought, or hoped for a child given the name to possess.

Scripture:

This is a reference from God's Word which is intended to shed light upon the inherent and implied meanings of the name. Attention has been centered especially upon the promises, encouragements, and exhortations the heavenly Father has given.

A

AARON, Aaran, Aaren, Aarin, Aaronn, Aarron, Aron, Arran, Arron (see also Aran, Aren)
Language/Cultural Origin: **Hebrew**
Inherent Meaning: **Light Bringer**
Spiritual Connotation: **Radiating God's Light**
Scripture: **Isaiah 60:1** KJV
Arise, shine; for thy light is come, and the glory of the LORD is risen upon thee.

ABBOT, Abbott
Language/Cultural Origin: **Aramaic**
Inherent Meaning: **Spiritual Leader**
Spiritual Connotation: **Walks in Truth**
Scripture: **2 Kings 20:3** NKJV
Remember now, O LORD, I pray, how I have walked before You in truth and with a loyal heart, and have done what was good in Your sight.

ABDIEL, Abdeel, Abdeil
Language/Cultural Origin: **Hebrew**
Inherent Meaning: **Servant of God**
Spiritual Connotation: **Worshiper**
Scripture: **Psalm 2:11** TLB
Serve the Lord with reverent fear; rejoice with trembling.

ABDUL, Abdoul
Language/Cultural Origin: **Middle Eastern**
Inherent Meaning: **Servant**
Spiritual Connotation: **Humble**
Scripture: **Matthew 23:12** RSV
Whoever exalts himself will be humbled, and whoever humbles himself will be exalted.

ABEL, Abell
Language/Cultural Origin: **Hebrew**
Inherent Meaning: **Breath**
Spiritual Connotation: **Life of God**
Scripture: **Ephesians 5:2** NLT
Live a life filled with love for others, following the example of Christ, who loved you and gave himself as a sacrifice to take away your sins.

ABI, Abbey, Abbi, Abby (see also Abigail)
Language/Cultural Origin: **Anglo-Saxon**
Inherent Meaning: **God's Will**
Spiritual Connotation: **Secure in God**
Scripture: **Psalm 91:2** NKJV
I will say of the LORD, He is my refuge and my fortress; my God, in Him I will trust.

ABIA, Abiah (see also Habaiah)
Language/Cultural Origin: **Hebrew**
Inherent Meaning: **God Is My Father**
Spiritual Connotation: **Child of God**
Scripture: **Galatians 4:7** NKJV
Therefore you are no longer a slave but a son, and if a son, then an heir of God through Christ.

ABIEL, Abielle (see also Aviel)
Language/Cultural Origin: **Hebrew**
Inherent Meaning: **Child of God**
Spiritual Connotation: **Heir of the Kingdom**
Scripture: **Luke 18:16** NASB
Permit the children to come to Me, and do not hinder them, for the kingdom of God belongs to such as these.

ABIGAIL, Abbigail, Abbigayle, Abbygayle, Abigael, Abigale
Language/Cultural Origin: **Hebrew**
Inherent Meaning: **My Father Rejoices**
Spiritual Connotation: **Cherished of God**
Scripture: **Zephaniah 3:17** NKJV
The LORD your God in your midst, the Mighty One, will save; He will rejoice over you with gladness, He will quiet you

with His love, He will rejoice over you with singing.

ABIJAH, Abija, Abiya, Abiyah
☞ Language/Cultural Origin: **Hebrew**
Inherent Meaning: **Will of God**
Spiritual Connotation: **Eternal**
Scripture: **1 John 2:17** NRSV
And the world and its desire are passing away, but those who do the will of God live forever.

ABNER, Ab, Avner
☞ Language/Cultural Origin: **Hebrew**
Inherent Meaning: **Enlightener**
Spiritual Connotation: **Believer of Truth**
Scripture: **Ephesians 1:18** NASB
I pray that the eyes of your heart may be enlightened, so that you may know what is the hope of His calling, what are the riches of the glory of His inheritance in the saints.

ABRAHAM, Abe, Abrahim, Abram
☞ Language/Cultural Origin: **Hebrew**
Inherent Meaning: **Father of the Nations**
Spiritual Connotation: **Founder**
Scripture: **Genesis 12:2** TLB
I will cause you to become the father of a great nation; I will bless you and make your name famous, and you will be a blessing to many others.

ABRIEL, Abrielle
Language/Cultural Origin: **French**
Inherent Meaning: **Innocent**
Spiritual Connotation: **Tenderhearted**
Scripture: **Ephesians 4:32** RSV
Be kind to one another, tenderhearted, forgiving one another, as God in Christ forgave you.

ACE, Acey, Acie
Language/Cultural Origin: **Latin**
Inherent Meaning: **Unity**
Spiritual Connotation: **One With the Father**
Scripture: **John 6:44** TLB
For no one can come to me unless the Father who sent me draws him to me, and at the Last Day I will cause all such to rise again from the dead.

ACTON, Akton
Language/Cultural Origin: **Old English**

Inherent Meaning: **Oak-Tree Settlement**
Spiritual Connotation: **Agreeable**
Scripture: **Matthew 18:20** NASB
For where two or three have gathered together in My name, there I am in their midst.

ADA, Adah, Adalee, Aida
☞ Language/Cultural Origin: **Hebrew**
Inherent Meaning: **Ornament**
Spiritual Connotation: **One Who Adorns**
Scripture: **1 Peter 3:4** NKJV
Let [your adornment] be the hidden person of the heart, with the incorruptible beauty of a gentle and quiet spirit, which is very precious in the sight of God.

ADAEL, Adayel (see also Adiel)
Language/Cultural Origin: **Hebrew**
Inherent Meaning: **God Is Witness**
Spiritual Connotation: **Vindicated**
Scripture: **Job 16:19** TLB
Yet even now the Witness to my innocence is there in heaven; my Advocate is there on high.

ADALIA, Adala, Adalin, Adelyn (see ☞ also Adeline)
Language/Cultural Origin: **Hebrew**
Inherent Meaning: **Honor**
Spiritual Connotation: **Courageous**
Scripture: **Joshua 1:9** NKJV
Be strong and of good courage; do not be afraid, nor be dismayed, for the LORD your God is with you wherever you go.

ADAM, Addam, Adem
☞ Language/Cultural Origin: **Hebrew**
Inherent Meaning: **Formed of Earth**
Spiritual Connotation: **In God's Image**
Scripture: **Genesis 1:27** KJV
So God created man in his own image, in the image of God created he him; male and female created he them.

ADARA, Adair, Adaira
☞ Language/Cultural Origin: **Hebrew**
Inherent Meaning: **Exalted**
Spiritual Connotation: **Worthy of Praise**
Scripture: **Luke 14:11** NASB
For everyone who exalts himself will be humbled, and he who humbles himself will be exalted.

ADAYA, Adaiah

Language/Cultural Origin: **Hebrew**
Inherent Meaning: **God's Jewel**
Spiritual Connotation: **Valuable**
Scripture: **Matthew 6:26** TLB
Look at the birds! They don't worry about what to eat . . . for your heavenly Father feeds them. And you are far more valuable to him than they are.

ADDI, Addy (see also Adelaide)

Language/Cultural Origin: **Hebrew**
Inherent Meaning: **My Witness**
Spiritual Connotation: **Chosen**
Scripture: **Acts 1:8** NRSV
But you will receive power when the Holy Spirit has come upon you; and you will be my witnesses.

ADDISON, Adison, Adisson

Language/Cultural Origin: **Old English**
Inherent Meaning: **Son of Adam**
Spiritual Connotation: **In God's Image**
Scripture: **Ezekiel 36:27** RSV
And I will put my spirit within you, and cause you to walk in my statutes and be careful to observe my ordinances.

ADELAIDE, Addey, Addie (see also Addi)

Language/Cultural Origin: **Old German**
Inherent Meaning: **Joyful**
Spiritual Connotation: **Spirit of Joy**
Scripture: **Psalm 5:11** NKJV
But let all those rejoice who put their trust in You; Let them ever shout for joy.

ADELINE, Adalina, Adella, Adelle, Adelynn (see also Adalia)

Language/Cultural Origin: **Old German**
Inherent Meaning: **Noble**
Spiritual Connotation: **Under God's Guidance**
Scripture: **Psalm 31:3** NKJV
For You are my rock and my fortress; therefore, for Your name's sake, lead me and guide me.

ADIA, Adiah

Language/Cultural Origin: **African**
Inherent Meaning: **Gift**
Spiritual Connotation: **Gift of Glory**

Scripture: **John 17:22** NASB
And the glory which Thou hast given Me I have given to them; that they may be one, just as We are one.

ADIEL, Addiel, Addielle (see also Adael)

Language/Cultural Origin: **Hebrew**
Inherent Meaning: **Ornament of God**
Spiritual Connotation: **Lovely**
Scripture: **1 Peter 3:4** NLT
You should be known for the beauty that comes from within . . . which is so precious to God.

ADINA, Adeena, Adena

Language/Cultural Origin: **Hebrew**
Inherent Meaning: **Adorned**
Spiritual Connotation: **Clothed With Praise**
Scripture: **Jeremiah 31:4** RSV
Again I will build you. . . . Again you shall adorn yourself with timbrels, and shall go forth in the dance of the merrymakers.

ADLAI, Adley (see also Hadlai)

Language/Cultural Origin: **Hebrew**
Inherent Meaning: **Justice of God**
Spiritual Connotation: **Truthful**
Scripture: **Zechariah 8:16** NKJV
Speak each man the truth to his neighbor; Give judgment in your gates for truth, justice, and peace.

ADLAR, Addler, Adler

Language/Cultural Origin: **Old German**
Inherent Meaning: **Eagle**
Spiritual Connotation: **Youthful**
Scripture: **Psalm 103:2, 5** NKJV
Bless the LORD, O my soul, and forget not all His benefits . . . So that your youth is renewed like the eagle's.

ADONIJAH, Adonia, Adoniah, Adonija, Adoniya, Adoniyah

Language/Cultural Origin: **Hebrew**
Inherent Meaning: **God Is My Lord**
Spiritual Connotation: **Reverent**
Scripture: **Exodus 3:5** NCV
Then God said, "Do not come any closer. Take off your sandals, because you are standing on holy ground."

ADORA, Adoree
Language/Cultural Origin: **Latin**
Inherent Meaning: **Beloved**
Spiritual Connotation: **Gift of God**
Scripture: **Malachi 1:2** NKJV
I have loved you, says the LORD.

ADRIA, Adría, Adriah
Language/Cultural Origin: **Latin**
Inherent Meaning: **Love of Life**
Spiritual Connotation: **Filled With Life**
Scripture: **Psalm 36:7** TLB
How precious is your constant love, O God! All humanity takes refuge in the shadow of your wings.

ADRIAN, Adreian, Adreyan, Adriaan, Adrien, Adrion, Adryan, Adryon
Language/Cultural Origin: **Greek**
Inherent Meaning: **Rich**
Spiritual Connotation: **Prosperous**
Scripture: **Deuteronomy 8:18** RSV
You shall remember the LORD your God, for it is he who gives you power to get wealth; that he may confirm his covenant which he swore to your fathers, as at this day.

ADRIANNA, Adriana
Language/Cultural Origin: **Italian**
Inherent Meaning: **Dark**
Spiritual Connotation: **Guarded of God**
Scripture: **Psalm 121:7-8** NASB
The LORD will protect you from all evil; He will keep your soul. The LORD will guard your going out and your coming in from this time forth and forever.

ADRIEL, Adrial
Language/Cultural Origin: **Hebrew**
Inherent Meaning: **Member of God's Flock**
Spiritual Connotation: **Nurtured of God**
Scripture: **John 10:11** NKJV
I am the good shepherd. The good shepherd gives His life for the sheep.

ADRIENNE, Adriane, Adriann, Adrianne, Adrien, Adriene
Language/Cultural Origin: **Greek**
Inherent Meaning: **Confident**
Spiritual Connotation: **Faith in God**
Scripture: **Mark 9:23** NCV
Jesus said to the father, "All things are possible for the one who believes."

AENEAS, Eneas
Language/Cultural Origin: **Greek**
Inherent Meaning: **Praised**
Spiritual Connotation: **Honored**
Scripture: **Proverbs 12:8** NKJV
A man will be commended according to his wisdom, but he who is of a perverse heart will be despised.

AFONYA, Afonja
Language/Cultural Origin: **Russian**
Inherent Meaning: **Immortal**
Spiritual Connotation: **Eternal**
Scripture: **1 Corinthians 15:54** RSV
When the perishable puts on the imperishable, and the mortal puts on immortality, then shall come to pass the saying that is written: Death is swallowed up in victory.

AFTON, Affton, Aftan, Aftyn
Language/Cultural Origin: **Old English**
Inherent Meaning: **From Afton, England**
Spiritual Connotation: **Righteous**
Scripture: **Matthew 5:10** RSV
Blessed are those who are persecuted for righteousness' sake, for theirs is the kingdom of heaven.

AGATHA, Agata, Aggie
Language/Cultural Origin: **Greek**
Inherent Meaning: **Benevolent**
Spiritual Connotation: **Kind**
Scripture: **Proverbs 21:21** NRSV
Whoever pursues righteousness and kindness will find life and honor.

AGNES, Agness, Agnessa, Agniya
Language/Cultural Origin: **Greek**
Inherent Meaning: **Pure**
Spiritual Connotation: **Innocent**
Scripture: **Matthew 5:8** KJV
Blessed are the pure in heart: for they shall see God.

AGRIPPA
Language/Cultural Origin: **Latin**
Inherent Meaning: **Pain of Childbirth**
Spiritual Connotation: **Promise**

Scripture: **Genesis 17:16** NASB
*And I will bless her . . . and she shall be
a mother of nations; kings of peoples shall
come from her.*

AHAB, Ahabb

Language/Cultural Origin: **Hebrew**
Inherent Meaning: **My Father's Brother**
Spiritual Connotation: **Learned**
Scripture: **Proverbs 2:10** TLB
*For wisdom and truth will enter the very
center of your being, filling your life with
joy.*

AHARAH, Aharhel, Aharia, Aharra, Aharya

Language/Cultural Origin: **Hebrew**
Inherent Meaning: **Brother of Rachel**
Spiritual Connotation: **Loyal**
Scripture: **Proverbs 18:24** NLT
*There are friends who destroy each other,
but a real friend sticks closer than a
brother.*

AHMAD, Ahamad, Ahmaad, Amaud

Language/Cultural Origin: **Middle Eastern**
Inherent Meaning: **Most Highly Praised**
Spiritual Connotation: **Servant**
Scripture: **Mark 10:43** NLT
*Whoever wants to be a leader among
you must be your servant, and whoever
wants to be first must be the slave of all.*

AHMED, Ahamed, Amed

Language/Cultural Origin: **Swahili**
Inherent Meaning: **Praiseworthy**
Spiritual Connotation: **Sincere**
Scripture: **Matthew 10:32** NKJV
*Therefore whoever confesses Me before
men, him I will also confess before My
Father who is in heaven.*

AHSAN, Ahsahn, Ahsán (see also Hasani, Ihsan)

Language/Cultural Origin: **Middle Eastern**
Inherent Meaning: **Charitable**
Spiritual Connotation: **Generous**
Scripture: **2 Corinthians 9:7** NRSV
*Each of you must give as you have made
up your mind, not reluctantly or under
compulsion, for God loves a cheerful giver.*

AIAH, Aija, Aijah, Aiya, Aiyah, Aja, Ajah (see also Aya)

Language/Cultural Origin: **Hebrew**
Inherent Meaning: **Bird of Prey**
Spiritual Connotation: **Strength of God**
Scripture: **Psalm 132:8** NKJV
*Arise, O LORD, to Your resting place,
You and the ark of Your strength.*

AIDEN, Aidan

Language/Cultural Origin: **Irish Gaelic**
Inherent Meaning: **Fire**
Spiritual Connotation: **Full of God's Spirit**
Scripture: **Romans 8:11** NLT
*The Spirit of God, who raised Jesus from
the dead, lives in you.*

AIESHA, Aesha, Aisha, Aishah, Ayashah, Ayishah, Ayshea (see also Asia, Iesha)

Language/Cultural Origin: **Middle Eastern**
Inherent Meaning: **Woman**
Spiritual Connotation: **Companion**
Scripture: **Genesis 2:18** NLT
*And the LORD God said, It is not good
for the man to be alone. I will make a
companion who will help him.*

AILEEN, Ailean, Ailene, Ailina, Aleene (see also Eileen)

Language/Cultural Origin: **English**
Inherent Meaning: **Light Bearer**
Spiritual Connotation: **Messenger of Truth**
Scripture: **Matthew 5:14** NKJV
*You are the light of the world. A city that
is set on a hill cannot be hidden.*

AINSLEY, Ainslee, Anslea, Anslee, Ansleigh, Ansley, Aynslee, Aynsley

Language/Cultural Origin: **Scottish**
Inherent Meaning: **My Own Meadow**
Spiritual Connotation: **Bringer of the Word of Life**
Scripture: **Philippians 2:16** KJV
*Holding forth the word of life; that I may
rejoice in the day of Christ, that I have
not run in vain, neither laboured in vain.*

AJANI, Ayani

Language/Cultural Origin: **Yoruba**

Inherent Meaning: **Victorious in the Struggle**
Spiritual Connotation: **Overcomer**
Scripture: **2 Thessalonians 2:15** NRSV
So then, brothers and sisters, stand firm and hold fast to the traditions that you were taught by us.

AJAY, Aja, Ajai
Language/Cultural Origin: **Indo-Pakistani**
Inherent Meaning: **Immovable**
Spiritual Connotation: **Stable**
Scripture: **1 Corinthians 15:58** NCV
So my dear brothers and sisters, stand strong. Do not let anything change you. Always give yourselves fully to the work of the Lord.

AKIL, Ahkeel, Akeel, Akhil, Akiel
Language/Cultural Origin: **Middle Eastern**
Inherent Meaning: **Intelligent**
Spiritual Connotation: **Wise**
Scripture: **Proverbs 2:6** NKJV
For the LORD gives wisdom; from His mouth come knowledge and understanding.

AKIM, Ackeem, Akeam, Akeem (see also Hakim, Joachim)
Language/Cultural Origin: **Russian**
Inherent Meaning: **God Will Establish**
Spiritual Connotation: **Obedient**
Scripture: **Deuteronomy 28:9** RSV
The LORD will establish you as a people holy to himself . . . if you keep the commandments of the LORD your God, and walk in his ways.

AKSEL, Acksel (see also Axel)
Language/Cultural Origin: **Norwegian**
Inherent Meaning: **Father of Peace**
Spiritual Connotation: **Pleasant**
Scripture: **Proverbs 16:7** NKJV
When a man's ways please the LORD, He makes even his enemies to be at peace with him.

ALADDIN, Alaaddin
Language/Cultural Origin: **Middle Eastern**
Inherent Meaning: **Pinnacle of Faith**
Spiritual Connotation: **Righteous**
Scripture: **Luke 7:9, 50** TLB
Jesus was amazed. . . . He said, "Never

among all the Jews in Israel have I met a man with faith like this." And Jesus said . . . "Your faith has saved you; go in peace."

ALAN, Al, Alen, Allan, Allen, Allin, Allon, Allyn
Language/Cultural Origin: **Irish**
Inherent Meaning: **Harmonious**
Spiritual Connotation: **At One With Creation**
Scripture: **2 Corinthians 13:11** NKJV
Be of good comfort, be of one mind, live in peace; and the God of love and peace will be with you.

ALANNA, Alaina, Alainna, Alainnah, Alana, Alanis, Alannah, Alayna, Allana, Allanah, Allanis, Allayna
Language/Cultural Origin: **Gaelic**
Inherent Meaning: **Cheerful**
Spiritual Connotation: **Effective Witness**
Scripture: **John 13:35** NKJV
By this all will know that you are My disciples, if you have love for one another.

ALASTAIR, Alistair, Alister, Allastair, Allaster, Allastir, Allister, Allyster
Language/Cultural Origin: **Scottish**
Inherent Meaning: **Defender**
Spiritual Connotation: **Courage**
Scripture: **Psalm 27:14** NKJV
Wait on the LORD; be of good courage, and He shall strengthen your heart; wait, I say, on the LORD!

ALBEN, Albain, Alban, Albany, Albein
Language/Cultural Origin: **Latin**
Inherent Meaning: **Of the City on a White Hill**
Spiritual Connotation: **Secure in God's Love**
Scripture: **Isaiah 41:13** KJV
For I the LORD thy God will hold thy right hand, saying unto thee, Fear not; I will help thee.

ALBERT, Al, Alberto, Elbert
Language/Cultural Origin: **Old English**
Inherent Meaning: **Noble**

Spiritual Connotation: **Brilliant**
Scripture: **Psalm 18:28** NKJV
For You will light my lamp; the LORD my God will enlighten my darkness.

ALDA

Language/Cultural Origin: **Old German**
Inherent Meaning: **Prosperous**
Spiritual Connotation: **Under God's Direction**
Scripture: **Joshua 1:8** NKJV
This Book of the Law shall not depart from your mouth, but you shall meditate in it day and night. . . . For then you will make your way prosperous, and then you will have good success.

ALDEN, Aldin, Aldis, Aldous, Aldwin

Language/Cultural Origin: **Anglo-Saxon**
Inherent Meaning: **Wise Protector**
Spiritual Connotation: **Guided of God**
Scripture: **Psalm 73:24** NKJV
You will guide me with Your counsel, and afterward receive me to glory.

ALDRICH, Aldric, Aldrick, Aldridge

Language/Cultural Origin: **Old English**
Inherent Meaning: **Wise Counselor**
Spiritual Connotation: **Strong of Mind**
Scripture: **2 Timothy 1:7** NKJV
For God has not given us a spirit of fear, but of power and of love and of a sound mind.

ALEA, Aleah, Aleea, Aleeah, Alia, Allia (see also Aliah)

Language/Cultural Origin: **Middle Eastern**
Inherent Meaning: **Exalted**
Spiritual Connotation: **Servant**
Scripture: **Luke 14:11** RSV
For every one who exalts himself will be humbled, and he who humbles himself will be exalted.

ALEJANDRA, Alesandra, Alessandra

Language/Cultural Origin: **Spanish/Italian**
Inherent Meaning: **Defender of Mankind**
Spiritual Connotation: **Compassionate**
Scripture: **Colossians 3:12** NIV
Therefore, as God's chosen people . . . clothe yourselves with compassion, kindness, humility, gentleness and patience.

ALEJANDRO, Alesandro, Alessandro

Language/Cultural Origin: **Spanish/Italian**
Inherent Meaning: **Defender of Mankind**
Spiritual Connotation: **Sincere**
Scripture: **James 1:27** NCV
Religion that God accepts as pure and without fault is this: caring for orphans or widows who need help, and keeping yourself free from the world's evil influence.

ALETHA, Alathea, Aleta, Aletha, Alethea, Alithea (see also Althea)

Language/Cultural Origin: **Greek**
Inherent Meaning: **Truthful**
Spiritual Connotation: **Wise**
Scripture: **Luke 7:35** NASB
Yet wisdom is vindicated by all her children.

ALEXA, Aleksa, Aleksia, Alex, Alexia, Allex, Allix, Alyx, Allyx

Language/Cultural Origin: **Hungarian**
Inherent Meaning: **Defender of Mankind**
Spiritual Connotation: **Benefactor**
Scripture: **Isaiah 1:17** RSV
Learn to do good; seek justice, correct oppression; defend the fatherless, plead for the widow.

ALEXANDER, Alax, Alec, Aleck, ☞ Aleksandar, Aleksander, Alex, Alexandar, Alexandros, Alexius, Alexxander, Alic, Alixander, Allax, Allex

Language/Cultural Origin: **Greek**
Inherent Meaning: **Defender of Mankind**
Spiritual Connotation: **Brave Protector**
Scripture: **Jeremiah 22:3** TLB
The Lord says: Be fair-minded. Do what is right! Help those in need of justice!

ALEXANDRA, Aleksandra, Alexandria, Lexandra

Language/Cultural Origin: **Greek**
Inherent Meaning: **Defender of Mankind**
Spiritual Connotation: **Generous**
Scripture: **Jeremiah 7:7** NASB
I will let you dwell in this place, in the land that I gave to your fathers forever and ever.

ALEXIS, Aleksei, Aleksey, Aleksi, Alexes, Alexi, Alexus, Alexys
Language/Cultural Origin: **English**
Inherent Meaning: **Defender of Mankind**
Spiritual Connotation: **Intercessor**
Scripture: **Jeremiah 27:18** NKJV
But if they are prophets, and if the word of the LORD is with them, let them now make intercession to the LORD of hosts.

ALFONSO, see Alphonso

ALFRED, Al, Alf, Alfredo
Language/Cultural Origin: **Old English**
Inherent Meaning: **Benevolent Ruler**
Spiritual Connotation: **Obedient**
Scripture: **Luke 10:27** NKJV
You shall love the LORD your God with all your heart, with all your soul, with all your strength, and with all your mind, and your neighbor as yourself.

ALI, Aly (see also Allie)
Language/Cultural Origin: **Swahili**
Inherent Meaning: **Exalted**
Spiritual Connotation: **Greatest**
Scripture: **Luke 13:30** NCV
There are those who have the lowest place in life now who will have the highest place in the future.

ALIAH, Alia, Aliya, Aliyah (see also ☞ Alea)
Language/Cultural Origin: **Hebrew**
Inherent Meaning: **Exalted**
Spiritual Connotation: **Humble**
Scripture: **1 Peter 5:6** NCV
Be humble under God's powerful hand so he will lift you up when the right time comes.

ALIANNA, Aliana
Language/Cultural Origin: **Scottish**
Inherent Meaning: **Bearer of Light**
Spiritual Connotation: **Ambassador of Truth**
Scripture: **Isaiah 49:6** NASB
I will also make You a light of the nations So that My salvation may reach to the end of the earth.

ALICE, Alis, Allis, Alysse
Language/Cultural Origin: **Greek**
Inherent Meaning: **One of Integrity**
Spiritual Connotation: **Truthful**
Scripture: **Proverbs 11:3, 5** RSV
The integrity of the upright guides them. . . . The righteousness of the blameless keeps his way straight.

ALICIA, Alica, Alicea, Alicya, Aliecia, Alycia, Elicia, Ellicia
Language/Cultural Origin: **Hispanic**
Inherent Meaning: **Truthful**
Spiritual Connotation: **Child of Truth**
Scripture: **1 John 3:18-19** NRSV
Little children, let us love, not in word or speech, but in truth and action. And by this we will know that we are from the truth.

ALIKA, Alikah
Language/Cultural Origin: **Nigerian**
Inherent Meaning: **Most Beautiful**
Spiritual Connotation: **Beauty of God**
Scripture: **Psalm 27:4** RSV
One thing have I asked of the LORD. . . . That I may dwell in the house of the LORD all the days of my life, to behold the beauty of the LORD, and to inquire in his temple.

ALIM, Aleem
Language/Cultural Origin: **Middle Eastern**
Inherent Meaning: **Scholar**
Spiritual Connotation: **Wise**
Scripture: **Proverbs 8:11** NKJV
For wisdom is better than rubies, and all the things one may desire cannot be compared with her.

ALINE, Alene
Language/Cultural Origin: **Old German**
Inherent Meaning: **Noble**
Spiritual Connotation: **Righteous**
Scripture: **2 Chronicles 16:9** TLB
For the eyes of the Lord search back and forth across the whole earth, looking for people whose hearts are perfect toward him, so that he can show his great power in helping them.

ALISA, Alissa, Allissa, Allysa, Alysa, Alyssa, Allyssa (see also Elissa, Elysia, Lissa)
Language/Cultural Origin: **English**
Inherent Meaning: **Noble**

Spiritual Connotation: **Bold**
Scripture: **Hebrews 13:6** NRSV
*So we can say with confidence, The Lord
is my helper; I will not be afraid. What
can anyone do to me?*

**ALISHA, Aleasha, Aleesha, Aleisha,
Alesha, Aliesha, Alishah, Alishia,
Alysha, Alyshia, Alyssha**
Language/Cultural Origin: **English**
Inherent Meaning: **Highborn**
Spiritual Connotation: **Victorious**
Scripture: **Isaiah 25:8** KJV
*He will swallow up death in victory; and
the Lord GOD will wipe away tears from
off all faces.*

ALLARD, Alard (see also Ellard)
Language/Cultural Origin: **Old English**
Inherent Meaning: **Brave**
Spiritual Connotation: **Dedicated**
Scripture: **Psalm 119:38** NKJV
*Establish Your word to Your servant,
Who is devoted to fearing You.*

**ALLEGRA, Alegrea, Allegréa,
Allegria**
Language/Cultural Origin: **Latin**
Inherent Meaning: **Cheerful**
Spiritual Connotation: **Eager to Live**
Scripture: **Psalm 37:4** NRSV
*Take delight in the LORD, and he will give
you the desires of your heart.*

ALLEN, see Alan

ALLIE, Alley, Alli (see also Ali)
Language/Cultural Origin: **Anglo-Saxon**
Inherent Meaning: **Brilliant**
Spiritual Connotation: **Illuminated**
Scripture: **Psalm 18:28** TLB
*You have turned on my light! The Lord my
God has made my darkness turn to light.*

**ALLISON, Alicen, Alicyn, Alison,
Alisson, Alisyn, Allyson**
Language/Cultural Origin: **Old German**
Inherent Meaning: **Truthful**
Spiritual Connotation: **Holy**
Scripture: **1 Chronicles 16:29** KJV
*Give unto the LORD the glory due unto
his name . . . worship the LORD in the
beauty of holiness.*

ALMA, Almah
Language/Cultural Origin: **Latin**
Inherent Meaning: **Loving**
Spiritual Connotation: **Patient**
Scripture: **2 Thessalonians 3:5** NKJV
*Now may the Lord direct your hearts
into the love of God and into the patience
of Christ.*

ALMIRA, Allmira, Almeera, Almeira
Language/Cultural Origin: **Middle Eastern**
Inherent Meaning: **Princess**
Spiritual Connotation: **Fulfillment of Truth**
Scripture: **Psalm 25:10** KJV
*All the paths of the LORD are mercy and
truth unto such as keep his covenant and
his testimonies.*

ALONZO, Alanzo, Almanzo, Alonso
Language/Cultural Origin: **Old German**
Inherent Meaning: **Ready for Battle**
Spiritual Connotation: **Prepared**
Scripture: **Luke 1:17** NKJV
*He will also go before Him in the spirit
and power of Elijah . . . to make ready a
people prepared for the Lord.*

ALOYSIUS
Language/Cultural Origin: **Old German**
Inherent Meaning: **Noble**
Spiritual Connotation: **Great**
Scripture: **John 14:12** NCV
*I tell you the truth, whoever believes in me
will do the same things that I do. Those
who believe will do even greater things than
these, because I am going to the Father.*

ALPHA
Language/Cultural Origin: **Phoenician**
Inherent Meaning: **Ox**
Spiritual Connotation: **Restful**
Scripture: **Matthew 11:29** NKJV
*Take My yoke upon you and learn from
Me, for I am gentle and lowly in heart,
and you will find rest for your souls.*

ALPHAEUS
Language/Cultural Origin: **Greek**
Inherent Meaning: **Traveler**
Spiritual Connotation: **Nourished**
Scripture: **Exodus 33:14** NRSV
*My presence will go with you, and I will
give you rest.*

ALPHONSO, Alfonso, Alfonzo, Alphanso, Alphonzo

Language/Cultural Origin: **Italian**
Inherent Meaning: **Noble**
Spiritual Connotation: **Mighty Protector**
Scripture: **Jeremiah 33:3** KJV
Call unto me, and I will answer thee, and show thee great and mighty things, which thou knowest not.

ALTHEA, Altheya, Althia (see also Aletha)

Language/Cultural Origin: **Greek**
Inherent Meaning: **Healer**
Spiritual Connotation: **Wholesome**
Scripture: **Philippians 4:8** NRSV
Finally, beloved, whatever is true, . . . honorable, . . . just, . . . pure, . . . pleasing, . . . [and] commendable, if there is any excellence and if there is anything worthy of praise, think about these things.

ALTON, see Elton

ALVA (see also Elva)

Language/Cultural Origin: **Latin**
Inherent Meaning: **Brightness**
Spiritual Connotation: **Alive**
Scripture: **Job 33:4** NASB
The Spirit of God has made me, and the breath of the Almighty gives me life.

ALVIN, Al, Alvan, Alven, Alvyn (see also Elvin)

Language/Cultural Origin: **German**
Inherent Meaning: **Friend of All**
Spiritual Connotation: **Sincere**
Scripture: **Proverbs 18:24** RSV
There are friends who pretend to be friends, but there is a friend who sticks closer than a brother.

ALVIS (see also Elvis)

Language/Cultural Origin: **Scandinavian**
Inherent Meaning: **All-Knowing**
Spiritual Connotation: **Conqueror**
Scripture: **Romans 8:37** NKJV
Yet in all these things we are more than conquerors through Him who loved us.

ALYSSA, see Alisa

AMADA, Amadea, Amadia

Language/Cultural Origin: **Spanish**
Inherent Meaning: **Beloved**
Spiritual Connotation: **Cherished**
Scripture: **Ephesians 5:29-30** NRSV
For no one ever hates his own body, but he nourishes and tenderly cares for it, just as Christ does for the church, because we are members of his body.

AMADEUS, Amadeaus, Amadeo, Amado, Amador

Language/Cultural Origin: **Latin**
Inherent Meaning: **Lover of God**
Spiritual Connotation: **Obedient**
Scripture: **Joshua 22:5** TLB
Be sure to continue to obey all of the commandments Moses gave you. Love the Lord and follow his plan for your lives. Cling to him and serve him enthusiastically.

AMADIKA, Amadikah

Language/Cultural Origin: **Rhodesian**
Inherent Meaning: **Beloved**
Spiritual Connotation: **Close to God**
Scripture: **1 John 2:5** RSV
But whoever keeps his word, in him truly love for God is perfected. By this we may be sure that we are in him.

AMAL, Amaal

Language/Cultural Origin: **Hebrew**
Inherent Meaning: **Sorrowful**
Spiritual Connotation: **Productive**
Scripture: **Exodus 35:2** NASB
For six days work may be done, but on the seventh day you shall have a holy day, a sabbath of complete rest to the LORD.

AMANDA, Amandah, Amandalyn, Amandi (see also Mandie)

Language/Cultural Origin: **Latin**
Inherent Meaning: **Worthy of Love**
Spiritual Connotation: **Virtuous**
Scripture: **Ephesians 5:25** NCV
Husbands, love your wives as Christ loved the church and gave himself for it.

AMAR, Amarr

Language/Cultural Origin: **Punjabi**

Inherent Meaning: **Immortal**
Spiritual Connotation: **Unending**
Scripture: **Psalm 121:8** RSV
The LORD will keep your going out and your coming in from this time forth and for evermore.

AMARA, Amarah
Language/Cultural Origin: **Greek**
Inherent Meaning: **Wished-for Child**
Spiritual Connotation: **Precious Gift**
Scripture: **Proverbs 17:6** KJV
Children's children are the crown of old men; and the glory of children are their fathers.

AMARANTHA, Amaranda, Amiranda, Amiranté, Amirantha
Language/Cultural Origin: **Greek**
Inherent Meaning: **Immortal**
Spiritual Connotation: **Everlasting**
Scripture: **Revelation 22:5** NCV
There will never be night again. They will not need the light of a lamp or the light of the sun, because the Lord God will give them light.

AMARIAH, Amaria, Amariya, ☞Amariyah, Amarya, Amaryah
Language/Cultural Origin: **Hebrew**
Inherent Meaning: **Covenant of God**
Spiritual Connotation: **Preserved**
Scripture: **Exodus 23:22** RSV
But if you hearken attentively to his voice and do all that I say, then I will be an enemy to your enemies and an adversary to your adversaries.

AMARIS, Amarissa
Language/Cultural Origin: **Hebrew**
Inherent Meaning: **Promise of God**
Spiritual Connotation: **Promise fulfilled**
Scripture: **Lamentations 3:23** KJV
[His compassions] are new every morning: great is thy faithfulness.

AMASIAH, Amaziah
☞ Language/Cultural Origin: **Hebrew**
Inherent Meaning: **My God Has Strength**
Spiritual Connotation: **Reverent**
Scripture: **Psalm 54:1** NKJV

Save me, O God, by Your name, And vindicate me by Your strength.

AMAYA, Amayah
Language/Cultural Origin: **Japanese**
Inherent Meaning: **Night Rain**
Spiritual Connotation: **Gentle**
Scripture: **2 Timothy 2:24** TLB
God's people must not be quarrelsome; they must be gentle, patient teachers of those who are wrong.

AMBER, Ambur (see also Ember)
Language/Cultural Origin: **Latin**
Inherent Meaning: **Like a Jewel**
Spiritual Connotation: **Cherished**
Scripture: **Psalm 143:8** KJV
Cause me to hear thy lovingkindness in the morning; for in thee do I trust: cause me to know the way wherein I should walk; for I lift up my soul unto thee.

AMBROSE, Ambros, Ambrus
Language/Cultural Origin: **Greek**
Inherent Meaning: **Divine**
Spiritual Connotation: **Immortal**
Scripture: **1 Corinthians 15:54** NKJV
So when . . . this mortal has put on immortality, then shall be brought to pass the saying that is written: Death is swallowed up in victory.

AMELIA, Amaley, Amalia, Amalie, Amaliya, Amallia, Amelee, Amélie (see also Emelia, Emily)
Language/Cultural Origin: **Latin**
Inherent Meaning: **Industrious**
Spiritual Connotation: **Independent**
Scripture: **1 Thessalonians 4:11-12** NASB
Make it your ambition to lead a quiet life and attend to your own business and work with your hands, . . . so that you may behave properly toward outsiders and not be in any need.

AMERY, Aimery, Ameri, Ammerie, Ammery, Amory (see also Emery)
Language/Cultural Origin: **German**
Inherent Meaning: **Divine**
Spiritual Connotation: **Shows the Way**
Scripture: **Job 32:8** KJV
But there is a spirit in man: and the

*inspiration of the Almighty giveth them
understanding.*

AMES, Aimes
Language/Cultural Origin: **French**
Inherent Meaning: **Friend**
Spiritual Connotation: **Faithful**
Scripture: **Amos 3:3** KJV
*Can two walk together, except they be
agreed?*

AMICA, Amicah
Language/Cultural Origin: **Italian**
Inherent Meaning: **Beloved Friend**
Spiritual Connotation: **Valuable**
Scripture: **Proverbs 27:17** NRSV
*Iron sharpens iron, and one person
sharpens the wits of another.*

AMIN, Ameen
Language/Cultural Origin: **Hebrew**
Inherent Meaning: **Trustworthy**
Spiritual Connotation: **Obedient**
Scripture: **Ecclesiastes 12:13** NKJV
*Fear God and keep his commandments,
for this is man's all.*

AMINA, Aminah, Aminda, Amindah
Language/Cultural Origin: **Middle Eastern**
Inherent Meaning: **Peaceful**
Spiritual Connotation: **Secure in Christ**
Scripture: **John 10:28** NLT
*I give [my sheep] eternal life, and they
will never perish. No one will snatch
them away from me.*

AMIR, Ameir
Language/Cultural Origin: **Hebrew**
Inherent Meaning: **Proclaimed**
Spiritual Connotation: **Known of God**
Scripture: **Romans 8:29** NASB
*For whom He foreknew, He also predes-
tined to become conformed to the image
of His Son, that He might be the first-
born among many brethren.*

AMIRA, Ameira
Language/Cultural Origin: **Hebrew**
Inherent Meaning: **Speech**
Spiritual Connotation: **Unhidden**
Scripture: **Luke 12:3** RSV
*Therefore whatever you have said in the
dark shall be heard in the light, and what*

*you have whispered in private rooms shall
be proclaimed upon the housetops.*

AMIRAN, Ameiran, Ameiren
Language/Cultural Origin: **Hebrew**
Inherent Meaning: **My Nation Is Joyful**
Spiritual Connotation: **Chosen of God**
Scripture: **Deuteronomy 28:7** RSV
*The LORD will cause your enemies who
rise against you to be defeated before
you; they shall come out against you one
way, and flee before you seven ways.*

AMITTAI, Ahmitay, Amitai, Amitei
Language/Cultural Origin: **Hebrew**
Inherent Meaning: **Friend**
Spiritual Connotation: **Friend of God**
Scripture: **John 15:15** NRSV
*I have called you friends, because I have
made known to you everything that I
have heard from my Father.*

AMITY, Amitee, Amitie
Language/Cultural Origin: **French**
Inherent Meaning: **Bound by Friendship**
Spiritual Connotation: **Faithful Friend**
Scripture: **Ecclesiastes 4:12** KJV
A threefold cord is not quickly broken.

AMMIEL, Amiel
Language/Cultural Origin: **Hebrew**
Inherent Meaning: **God of My People**
Spiritual Connotation: **My Nation Is God's**
Scripture: **Deuteronomy 32:9** NCV
*The LORD took his people as his share,
the people of Jacob as his very own.*

AMMON, Amon, Amonn
Language/Cultural Origin: **Hebrew**
Inherent Meaning: **Of My Nation**
Spiritual Connotation: **Chosen**
Scripture: **Leviticus 26:12** NKJV
*I will walk among you and be your God,
and you shall be My people.*

AMOS
Language/Cultural Origin: **Hebrew**
Inherent Meaning: **Bearer of a Burden**
Spiritual Connotation: **Compassionate**
Scripture: **Galatians 6:2** RSV
*Bear one another's burdens, and so fulfil
the law of Christ.*

AMY, Aimée, Aimey, Aimi, Aimie, Aimmie, Aimy, Amey, Amie, Ammy
Language/Cultural Origin: **Latin**
Inherent Meaning: **Beloved**
Spiritual Connotation: **Serene Spirit**
Scripture: **Psalm 4:8** NASB
In peace I will both lie down and sleep, For Thou alone, O LORD, dost make me to dwell in safety.

AMYAS, Amias
Language/Cultural Origin: **Latin**
Inherent Meaning: **Beloved**
Spiritual Connotation: **Tenderhearted**
Scripture: **Galatians 5:22-23** RSV
But the fruit of the Spirit is love, joy, peace, patience, kindness, goodness, faithfulness, gentleness, self-control; against such there is no law.

ANAIAH, Anaiya, Aniah, Anijah, ☞Aniya, Aniyah
Language/Cultural Origin: **Hebrew**
Inherent Meaning: **God Has Answered Me**
Spiritual Connotation: **Restored**
Scripture: **Psalm 39:12** NLT
Hear my prayer, O LORD! Listen to my cries for help!

ANANI, Annani, Ananni
☞ Language/Cultural Origin: **Hebrew**
Inherent Meaning: **Covered With God**
Spiritual Connotation: **Guarded**
Scripture: **Psalm 3:3** RSV
But thou, O LORD, art a shield about me, my glory, and the lifter of my head.

ANANIAS, Ananiah
☞ Language/Cultural Origin: **Hebrew**
Inherent Meaning: **God Is Gracious**
Spiritual Connotation: **Witness**
Scripture: **2 Corinthians 6:1** NLT
As God's partners, we beg you not to reject this marvelous message of God's great kindness.

ANASTASIA, Anastasha, Anastashia, Anastassia, Anastassya (see also Tasia)
Language/Cultural Origin: **Greek**
Inherent Meaning: **Resurrection**

Spiritual Connotation: **Awakening**
Scripture: **Romans 8:11** NLT
The Spirit of God, who raised Jesus from the dead, lives in you. And just as God raised Christ Jesus from the dead, he will give life to your mortal bodies by this same Spirit living within you.

ANDREA, Andee, Andi, Andraia, Andraya, Andreah, Andreea, Andreia, Andreya, Andria
Language/Cultural Origin: **Greek**
Inherent Meaning: **Womanly**
Spiritual Connotation: **Filled With Grace**
Scripture: **Proverbs 31:28** NKJV
Her children rise up and call her blessed; her husband also, and he praises her.

ANDREW, Anders, Anderson, ☞Andrae, Andras, Andre, André, Andreas, Andrei, Andrés, Andy, Aundré (see also Drew)
Language/Cultural Origin: **Greek**
Inherent Meaning: **Courageous**
Spiritual Connotation: **Enduring**
Scripture: **Psalm 27:1** KJV
The LORD is my light and my salvation; whom shall I fear? The LORD is the strength of my life; of whom shall I be afraid?

ANEMONE, Anemonee, Anémonie
Language/Cultural Origin: **Greek**
Inherent Meaning: **Breath**
Spiritual Connotation: **Life of God**
Scripture: **Psalm 150:6** KJV
Let every thing that hath breath praise the LORD. Praise ye the LORD.

ANESKA, Aneshka
Language/Cultural Origin: **Czech**
Inherent Meaning: **Pure**
Spiritual Connotation: **Likeness of Christ**
Scripture: **1 John 3:2-3** NRSV
For we will see him as he is. And all who have this hope in him purify themselves, just as he is pure.

ANGELA, Angee, Angel, Angela, Angelee, Angeleigh, Angelena, Angeliana, Angelica, Angelíca,

Angelina, Angeline, Angelique, Angi, Angie, Anjelíka, Anjelina
Language/Cultural Origin: **Greek**
Inherent Meaning: **Angel/Messenger**
Spiritual Connotation: **Bringer of Glad Tidings**
Scripture: **Revelation 22:16** RSV
I Jesus have sent my angel to you with this testimony for the churches. I am the root and the offspring of David, the bright morning star.

ANGELO, Angelos
Language/Cultural Origin: **Italian**
Inherent Meaning: **Angel/Messenger**
Spiritual Connotation: **Bringer of Glad Tidings**
Scripture: **Luke 2:10-11** NKJV
I bring you good tidings of great joy which will be to all people. For there is born to you this day in the city of David a Savior, who is Christ the Lord.

ANGUS
Language/Cultural Origin: **Scottish**
Inherent Meaning: **Unique Strength**
Spiritual Connotation: **Creative Spirit**
Scripture: **Luke 10:7** KJV
And in the same house remain, eating and drinking such things as they give: for the labourer is worthy of his hire. Go not from house to house.

ANI, Anii (see also Ann)
Language/Cultural Origin: **Hawaiian**
Inherent Meaning: **Beautiful**
Spiritual Connotation: **Lovely in Spirit**
Scripture: **Isaiah 52:7** NRSV
How beautiful upon the mountains are the feet of the messenger who announces peace . . . who says to Zion, your God reigns.

ANIA, Aniah (see also Anya)
Language/Cultural Origin: **Polish**
Inherent Meaning: **Compassion**
Spiritual Connotation: **Merciful**
Scripture: **Proverbs 21:21** NASB
He who pursues righteousness and loyalty finds life, righteousness and honor.

ANIKA, Aneka, Anekah, Anica, Anicka, Anikka, Annika
Language/Cultural Origin: **Czech**
Inherent Meaning: **Favor**
Spiritual Connotation: **Grace of God**
Scripture: **1 Samuel 2:26** KJV
And the child Samuel grew on, and was in favour both with the LORD, and also with men.

ANITA, Aneeta, Anetra, Anitra (see also Nita)
Language/Cultural Origin: **Hispanic**
Inherent Meaning: **Gracious**
Spiritual Connotation: **Kindness**
Scripture: **1 Corinthians 13:4** NRSV
Love is patient; love is kind; love is not envious or boastful or arrogant.

ANN, Anne, Annette, Anni, Annie, Anny (see also Ani)
Language/Cultural Origin: **English**
Inherent Meaning: **Graceful**
Spiritual Connotation: **Understanding**
Scripture: **Psalms 111:10** KJV
The fear of the LORD is the beginning of wisdom: a good understanding have all they that do his commandments: his praise endureth for ever.

ANNA, Ana, Anah, Anka
☞ Language/Cultural Origin: **German**
Inherent Meaning: **Gracious**
Spiritual Connotation: **Full of Grace**
Scripture: **Luke 1:28** NKJV
And having come in, the angel said to her, Rejoice, highly favored one, the Lord is with you; blessed are you among women!

ANNABELL, Annabelle
Language/Cultural Origin: **Latin**
Inherent Meaning: **Graceful**
Spiritual Connotation: **Beloved**
Scripture: **Psalm 89:1** KJV
I will sing of the mercies of the LORD for ever: with my mouth will I make known thy faithfulness to all generations.

ANNELISA, Annalisa, Annalise, Annelise
Language/Cultural Origin: **English**
Inherent Meaning: **Oath of God**

Spiritual Connotation: **Gracious Promise**
Scripture: **Genesis 9:9, 11** RSV
Behold, I establish my covenant with you and your descendants after you, . . . and never again shall there be a flood to destroy the earth.

ANNEMARIE, Annamaria, Anna-Maria, Annamarie, Anne-Marie, Annmaria, Annmarie
Language/Cultural Origin: **American**
Inherent Meaning: **Bitter Grace**
Spiritual Connotation: **Faithfulness of God**
Scripture: **Hebrews 13:5** NRSV
Keep your lives free from the love of money, and be content with what you have; for he has said, I will never leave you or forsake you.

ANSEL, Ancell, Ansell
Language/Cultural Origin: **Middle English**
Inherent Meaning: **Noble**
Spiritual Connotation: **Follower of Truth**
Scripture: **Jeremiah 33:6** KJV
Behold, I will bring it health and cure, and I will cure them, and will reveal unto them the abundance of peace and truth.

ANSON, Ansun
Language/Cultural Origin: **Old German**
Inherent Meaning: **Divine**
Spiritual Connotation: **Partaker in Glory**
Scripture: **1 Peter 5:10** RSV
And after you have suffered a little while, the God of all grace, who has called you to his eternal glory in Christ, will himself restore, establish, and strengthen you.

ANTHONY, Anfernee, Anthoney, Anthonie, Antoiné, Antony (see also Antonio, Tony)
Language/Cultural Origin: **Latin**
Inherent Meaning: **Praiseworthy**
Spiritual Connotation: **Prosperous**
Scripture: **Psalm 122:7, 9** KJV
Peace be within thy walls, and prosperity within thy palaces. Because of the house of the LORD our God I will seek thy good.

ANTON, Antonn
Language/Cultural Origin: **Slavic**
Inherent Meaning: **One of Value**

Spiritual Connotation: **Eloquent**
Scripture: **Proverbs 25:11** KJV
A word fitly spoken is like apples of gold in pictures of silver.

ANTONIA, Antoinette, Antonette, Antoñia (see also Tania, Toni)
Language/Cultural Origin: **Latin**
Inherent Meaning: **Priceless**
Spiritual Connotation: **Jewel of Light**
Scripture: **Matthew 5:16** KJV
Let your light so shine before men, that they may see your good works, and glorify your Father which is in heaven.

ANTONIO, Antoñio, Antonius
Language/Cultural Origin: **Italian**
Inherent Meaning: **Priceless**
Spiritual Connotation: **Righteous**
Scripture: **Isaiah 54:14** KJV
In righteousness shalt thou be established: thou shalt be far from oppression; for thou shalt not fear: and from terror; for it shall not come near thee.

ANYA, Annya (see also Ania)
Language/Cultural Origin: **Russian**
Inherent Meaning: **Favor of God**
Spiritual Connotation: **Peace**
Scripture: **Proverbs 16:7** RSV
When a man's ways please the LORD, he makes even his enemies to be at peace with him.

APOLLOS, Apollo
☞ Language/Cultural Origin: **Greek**
Inherent Meaning: **Youthful God of Music**
Spiritual Connotation: **Joyful**
Scripture: **Psalm 33:2** NCV
Praise the LORD on the harp; make music for him on a ten-stringed lyre.

APRIL, Aprill, Apryl
Language/Cultural Origin: **Latin**
Inherent Meaning: **New in Faith**
Spiritual Connotation: **Awakened**
Scripture: **Ezekiel 37:14** KJV
And [I] shall put my spirit in you, and ye shall live.

AQUILLA, Aquila
☞ Language/Cultural Origin: **Latin**
Inherent Meaning: **Eagle**

Spiritual Connotation: **Strong**
Scripture: **Isaiah 40:31** NCV
But the people who trust the LORD will become strong again. They will rise up as an eagle in the sky; they will run and not need rest; they will walk and not become tired.

ARAM, Aramia
Language/Cultural Origin: **Syrian**
Inherent Meaning: **Exalted**
Spiritual Connotation: **Humble**
Scripture: **1 Corinthians 1:28-29** NLT
God chose things despised by the world . . . and used them to bring to nothing what the world considers important, so that no one can ever boast in the presence of God.

ARAN, Aranne, Aronne (see also Aaron, Aren)
Language/Cultural Origin: **Hebrew**
Inherent Meaning: **Firm**
Spiritual Connotation: **Gifted**
Scripture: **Ephesians 4:11** NLT
He is the one who gave these gifts to the church. . . . Their responsibility is to equip God's people to do his work and build up the church, the body of Christ.

ARCHER, Arch, Archie
Language/Cultural Origin: **Latin**
Inherent Meaning: **Bowman**
Spiritual Connotation: **Steadfast**
Scripture: **Isaiah 40:31** KJV
But they that wait upon the LORD shall renew their strength; they shall mount up with wings as eagles; they shall run, and not be weary; and they shall walk, and not faint.

ARDEL, Ardell
Language/Cultural Origin: **Latin**
Inherent Meaning: **Industrious**
Spiritual Connotation: **Creative**
Scripture: **Exodus 23:12** NKJV
Six days you shall do your work, and on the seventh day you shall rest.

ARDELLE, Ardella
Language/Cultural Origin: **Latin**
Inherent Meaning: **Eager**
Spiritual Connotation: **Spirit of Praise**

Scripture: **Psalm 67:5-6** NKJV
Let the peoples praise You, O God; Let all the peoples praise You. Then the earth shall yield her increase; God, our own God, shall bless us.

ARDITH, Ardath, Ardeth, Ardyth
Language/Cultural Origin: **Hebrew**
Inherent Meaning: **Faithful**
Spiritual Connotation: **Dependent Upon God**
Scripture: **Psalm 28:7** KJV
The LORD is my strength and my shield; my heart trusted in him, and I am helped: therefore my heart greatly rejoiceth; and with my song will I praise him.

ARDON, Ardan, Arden, Ardyn
Language/Cultural Origin: **Hebrew**
Inherent Meaning: **Descendant**
Spiritual Connotation: **Promise**
Scripture: **1 Chronicles 16:15** NKJV
Remember His covenant forever, the word which He commanded, for a thousand generations.

ARELI, Arilee, Arileigh, Ariley
Language/Cultural Origin: **Hebrew**
Inherent Meaning: **Heroic**
Spiritual Connotation: **Miraculous**
Scripture: **2 Thessalonians 1:10** NCV
This will happen on the day when the Lord Jesus comes to receive glory because of his holy people. And all the people who have believed will be amazed at Jesus.

AREN, Arenn (see also Aaron, Aran)
Language/Cultural Origin: **Danish**
Inherent Meaning: **Eagle**
Spiritual Connotation: **Perseverance**
Scripture: **Hosea 12:6** NRSV
But as for you, return to your God, hold fast to love and justice, and wait continually for your God.

ARETAS, Areetas, Aritas
Language/Cultural Origin: **Greek**
Inherent Meaning: **Pleasing**
Spiritual Connotation: **Wise**
Scripture: **Proverbs 3:17** NCV
Wisdom will make your life pleasant and will bring you peace.

ARETHA, Areatha, Areetha
Language/Cultural Origin: **American**
Inherent Meaning: **Virtuous**
Spiritual Connotation: **Pure**
Scripture: **Matthew 5:8** NASB
Blessed are the pure in heart, for they shall see God.

ARIADNE, Ari, Ariane, Ariann, Arianne, Arien, Arienne
Language/Cultural Origin: **Greek**
Inherent Meaning: **Holy**
Spiritual Connotation: **Presented to God**
Scripture: **Romans 6:13** TLB
Do not let any part of your bodies . . . to be used for sinning; but give yourselves completely to God.

ARIANA, Aeriana, Arianna, Arieana, Aryanna (see also Irina)
Language/Cultural Origin: **Italian**
Inherent Meaning: **Holy**
Spiritual Connotation: **Pure in Heart**
Scripture: **2 Corinthians 7:1** NIV
Let us purify ourselves from everything that contaminates body and spirit, perfecting holiness out of reverence for God.

ARIC, Aaric, Arick, Arik, Arric, Arrick, Arrik (see also Eric)
Language/Cultural Origin: **Old English**
Inherent Meaning: **Holy Ruler**
Spiritual Connotation: **Just**
Scripture: **Colossians 4:1** NCV
Masters, give what is good and fair to your slaves. Remember that you have a Master in heaven.

ARIEL, Aerial, Aeriell, Arial, Ariale, Arielle, Ariyel, Arrial, Arriel (see also Uriel)
Language/Cultural Origin: **Hebrew**
Inherent Meaning: **Lion or Lioness of God**
Spiritual Connotation: **Royal Servant**
Scripture: **1 Peter 2:18** RSV
Servants, be submissive to your masters with all respect. . . . For one is approved if, mindful of God, he endures pain while suffering unjustly.

ARIN, Arinn, Aryn (see also Erin)
Language/Cultural Origin: **Hebrew**
Inherent Meaning: **Enlightened**
Spiritual Connotation: **Filled With Light**
Scripture: **Ephesians 1:18-19** NRSV
So that, with the eyes of your heart enlightened, you may know what is the hope to which he has called you . . . and what is the immeasurable greatness of his power for us who believe.

ARINA, Areena
Language/Cultural Origin: **Russian**
Inherent Meaning: **Peace**
Spiritual Connotation: **Encourager**
Scripture: **Romans 14:19** NKJV
Therefore let us pursue the things which make for peace and the things by which one may edify another.

ARIOCH, Arioc, Arriok
Language/Cultural Origin: **Hebrew**
Inherent Meaning: **Lionlike**
Spiritual Connotation: **Dependent Upon God**
Scripture: **Psalm 34:10** NLT
Even strong young lions sometimes go hungry, but those who trust in the LORD will never lack any good thing.

ARION, Arian, Ariane, Arien, Arrian (see also Ariadne)
Language/Cultural Origin: **Greek**
Inherent Meaning: **Charming**
Spiritual Connotation: **Captivating**
Scripture: **Song of Songs 4:1** NASB
How beautiful you are, my darling, how beautiful you are!

ARISTOTLE, Ari, Arias, Arie, Aris, Arri
Language/Cultural Origin: **Greek**
Inherent Meaning: **Greatest Achievement**
Spiritual Connotation: **Intelligent**
Scripture: **Proverbs 8:10** NCV
Choose my teachings instead of silver, and knowledge rather than the finest gold.

ARLEN, Arlan, Arland, Arlend, Arlin, Arlyn, Arlynn
Language/Cultural Origin: **Irish**
Inherent Meaning: **Pledge**
Spiritual Connotation: **Truthful**
Scripture: **Psalm 34:1** NRSV

*I will bless the LORD at all times; his
praise shall continually be in my mouth.*

ARLENE, Arlana, Arleen, Arleyne, Arline, Arlis, Arliss, Arlyss
Language/Cultural Origin: **Old English**
Inherent Meaning: **Pledge**
Spiritual Connotation: **Truthful**
Scripture: **Luke 8:15** NASB
*But the seed in the good soil, these are the
ones who have heard the word in an hon-
est and good heart, and hold it fast, and
bear fruit with perseverance.*

ARLEY, Arleigh, Arlie, Arly
Language/Cultural Origin: **Old English**
Inherent Meaning: **Hunter**
Spiritual Connotation: **Pledge**
Scripture: **Genesis 1:28** NKJV
*Then God blessed them, and God said
to them, Be fruitful and multiply; fill the
earth and subdue it; have dominion . . .
over every living thing that moves on the
earth.*

ARMAND, Armando, Armond
Language/Cultural Origin: **Old German**
Inherent Meaning: **Army Man**
Spiritual Connotation: **Strong**
Scripture: **Psalm 37:39** NASB
*But the salvation of the righteous is from
the LORD; He is their strength in time of
trouble.*

ARMON, Arman, Armen, Armin
Language/Cultural Origin: **Hebrew**
Inherent Meaning: **Fortress**
Spiritual Connotation: **Guarded**
Scripture: **Psalm 5:12** TLB
*For you bless the godly man, O Lord;
you protect him with your shield of love.*

ARMONI, Armani, Armonni
Language/Cultural Origin: **Hebrew**
Inherent Meaning: **From the Palace**
Spiritual Connotation: **Blessed**
Scripture: **1 Timothy 6:6** NCV
*Serving God does make us very rich, if
we are satisfied with what we have.*

ARNOLD, Arne, Arney, Arni, Arnie
Language/Cultural Origin: **Old German**
Inherent Meaning: **Strong as an Eagle**

Spiritual Connotation: **Brave**
Scripture: **Psalm 103:1, 5** KJV
*Bless the LORD, O my soul . . . Who
satisfieth thy mouth with good things; so
that thy youth is renewed like the eagle's.*

ARRIO, Ario
Language/Cultural Origin: **Hispanic**
Inherent Meaning: **Warlike**
Spiritual Connotation: **Protector**
Scripture: **Psalm 82:3** NKJV
*Defend the poor and fatherless; Do
justice to the afflicted and needy.*

ARSENIO, Arsenius, Arsinio
Language/Cultural Origin: **Greek**
Inherent Meaning: **Masculine**
Spiritual Connotation: **One of Integrity**
Scripture: **Psalm 119:9** NIV
*How can a young man keep his way
pure? By living according to your word.*

ARSLAN, Aslan
Language/Cultural Origin: **Turkish**
Inherent Meaning: **Lion**
Spiritual Connotation: **Symbol of Christ**
Scripture: **Revelation 10:3** NRSV
*He gave a great shout, like a lion roaring.
And when he shouted, the seven thunders
sounded.*

ARTHUR, Art, Arte, Arther, Arthor, Artie, Artis, Arturo, Artur
Language/Cultural Origin: **Irish**
Inherent Meaning: **Bold**
Spiritual Connotation: **Gracious Ruler**
Scripture: **Exodus 34:6** NLT
*I am the LORD, I am the LORD, the merci-
ful and gracious God. I am slow to anger
and rich in unfailing love and faithfulness.*

ASA, Asah
Language/Cultural Origin: **Hebrew**
Inherent Meaning: **Healer**
Spiritual Connotation: **Healer of the Mind
and of the Body**
Scripture: **Isaiah 33:6** KJV
*And wisdom and knowledge shall be the
stability of thy times, and strength of sal-
vation: the fear of the LORD is his treasure.*

ASAD, Asaad, Asád, Assad (see also Hasad)

Language/Cultural Origin: **Middle Eastern**
Inherent Meaning: **Lion**
Spiritual Connotation: **Strength of God**
Scripture: **Chronicles 29:12** NKJV
In Your hand is power and might; in Your hand it is to make great and to give strength to all.

ASAPH

☞ Language/Cultural Origin: **Hebrew**
Inherent Meaning: **Remover of Reproach**
Spiritual Connotation: **Gentle**
Scripture: **Proverbs 15:1** NKJV
A soft answer turns away wrath, but a harsh word stirs up anger.

ASAREL, Ahsarel, Azarael, Azareel ☞ (see also Asriel, Azarel, Azriel)

Language/Cultural Origin: **Hebrew**
Inherent Meaning: **Upright**
Spiritual Connotation: **Exalted**
Scripture: **Genesis 41:43** NASB
And he had him ride in his second chariot; and they proclaimed before him, "Bow the knee!" And he set him over all the land of Egypt.

ASENATH, Asennath

☞ Language/Cultural Origin: **Egyptian**
Inherent Meaning: **Belonging to the Goddess**
Spiritual Connotation: **Honored**
Scripture: **Genesis 41:50** NKJV
And to Joseph were born two sons . . . whom Asenath . . . bore to him.

ASHA, Ashia

Language/Cultural Origin: **Middle Eastern**
Inherent Meaning: **Vitality**
Spiritual Connotation: **Humble Strength**
Scripture: **Genesis 49:15** TLB
When he saw how good the countryside was, how pleasant the land, he willingly bent his shoulder to the task and served his masters with vigor.

ASHBY, Ashbey

Language/Cultural Origin: **English**
Inherent Meaning: **From the Ash-Tree Farm**

Spiritual Connotation: **Fear of God**
Scripture: **2 Corinthians 7:1** NKJV
Let us cleanse ourselves from all filthiness of the flesh and spirit, perfecting holiness in the fear of God.

ASHER, Ashor, Ashur

☞ Language/Cultural Origin: **Hebrew**
Inherent Meaning: **Blessed**
Spiritual Connotation: **Fortunate**
Scripture: **Psalm 16:11** NKJV
You will show me the path of life; In Your presence is fullness of joy; At Your right hand are pleasures forevermore.

ASHFORD, Ash

Language/Cultural Origin: **English**
Inherent Meaning: **From the Ash-Tree Ford**
Spiritual Connotation: **Victorious**
Scripture: **Revelation 2:7** NKJV
To him who overcomes I will give to eat from the tree of life, which is in the midst of the Paradise of God.

ASHLEY, Ashelee, Asheleigh, Asheley, Ashlea, Ashleah, Ashleay, Ashlee, Ashleigh, Ashly

Language/Cultural Origin: **Old English**
Inherent Meaning: **Of the Ash-Tree Meadow**
Spiritual Connotation: **Harmony**
Scripture: **Psalm 133:1** NRSV
How very good and pleasant it is when kindred live together in unity!

ASHLYNN, Ashlan, Ashlen, Ashlin, Ashling, Ashlyn, Ashlyne, Ashlynne

Language/Cultural Origin: **Irish**
Inherent Meaning: **Dream**
Spiritual Connotation: **Vision of God**
Scripture: **Ezekiel 12:23** NKJV
The days are at hand, and the fulfillment of every vision.

ASHTON, Ashtin

Language/Cultural Origin: **English**
Inherent Meaning: **From the Ash-Tree Farm**
Spiritual Connotation: **Supplicant**
Scripture: **Psalm 57:2** NLT

*I cry out to God Most High, to God who
will fulfill his purpose for me.*

ASIA, Aisia, Asya, Aysia
Language/Cultural Origin: **English**
Inherent Meaning: **Eastern Sunrise**
Spiritual Connotation: **God Is Sovereign**
Scripture: **2 Samuel 7:22** NKJV
*For there is none like You, nor is there
any God besides You, according to all
that we have heard with our ears.*

ASRIEL, Ashrael, Ashreel, Ashrayel, ☞ Ashriel, Asrael, Asreel, Asreyel (see also Asarel, Azarel, Azriel)
Language/Cultural Origin: **Hebrew**
Inherent Meaning: **God Is Joined**
Spiritual Connotation: **Unity**
Scripture: **Psalm 133:1** NRSV
*How very good and pleasant it is when
kindred live together in unity!*

ASTHER, Aster (see also Esther)
Language/Cultural Origin: **English**
Inherent Meaning: **Flower**
Spiritual Connotation: **Righteous**
Scripture: **Isaiah 58:8** NKJV
*Then your light shall break forth like the
morning, Your healing shall spring forth
speedily, and your righteousness shall go
before you; The glory of the LORD shall
be your rear guard.*

ATARAH, Atara, Atarra
☞ Language/Cultural Origin: **Hebrew**
Inherent Meaning: **Crown**
Spiritual Connotation: **Faithful**
Scripture: **Revelation 2:10** NCV
*Do not be afraid of what you are about to
suffer. . . . Be faithful, even if you have to
die, and I will give you the crown of life.*

ATHALIA, Atalya, Athalya
☞ Language/Cultural Origin: **Hebrew**
Inherent Meaning: **Afflicted**
Spiritual Connotation: **Honor**
Scripture: **Isaiah 38:19** TLB
*The living, only the living, can praise
you as I do today. One generation makes
known your faithfulness to the next.*

ATHENA, Athina
Language/Cultural Origin: **Greek**

Inherent Meaning: **Wise**
Spiritual Connotation: **Mind of God**
Scripture: **1 Corinthians 2:16** NKJV
*For who has known the mind of the LORD
that he may instruct Him? But we have
the mind of Christ.*

ATHERTON
Language/Cultural Origin: **Middle English**
Inherent Meaning: **Of the Town by the
Spring**
Spiritual Connotation: **Abundant Life**
Scripture: **John 10:10** NASB
*The thief comes only to steal and kill and
destroy; I came that they may have life,
and have it abundantly.*

ATLEY, Atlea, Atlee, Atleigh, Attley
Language/Cultural Origin: **English**
Inherent Meaning: **From the Meadow**
Spiritual Connotation: **Purchased**
Scripture: **Corinthians 7:23** NLT
*God purchased you at a high price. Don't
be enslaved by the world.*

ATWELL, Attwell
Language/Cultural Origin: **English**
Inherent Meaning: **From the Well**
Spiritual Connotation: **Refreshing**
Scripture: **Song of Songs 4:15** TLB
*You are a garden fountain, a well of liv-
ing water, refreshing as the streams from
the Lebanon mountains.*

AUBREY, Aubray, Aubreigh, Aubrie
Language/Cultural Origin: **Old German**
Inherent Meaning: **Noble**
Spiritual Connotation: **Compassionate**
Scripture: **Proverbs 31:26** NASB
*She opens her mouth in wisdom, and the
teaching of kindness is on her tongue.*

AUBURN, Auburne
Language/Cultural Origin: **English**
Inherent Meaning: **Reddish-Brown**
Spiritual Connotation: **Released**
Scripture: **Isaiah 35:5** NKJV
*Then the eyes of the blind shall be opened,
and the ears of the deaf shall be unstopped.*

AUDIE, Audi
Language/Cultural Origin: **Old English**
Inherent Meaning: **Property Guardian**

Spiritual Connotation: **Strong of Heart**
Scripture: **John 16:33** NASB
These things I have spoken to you, so that in Me you may have peace. In the world you have tribulation, but take courage; I have overcome the world.

AUDREY, Audra, Audray, Audree, Audri, Audrianna, Audrie, Audry
Language/Cultural Origin: **Old English**
Inherent Meaning: **Noble Strength**
Spiritual Connotation: **Overcomer of Many Difficulties**
Scripture: **1 John 2:14** NKJV
I have written to you, young men, because you are strong, and the word of God abides in you, and you have overcome the wicked one.

AUDRIC, Audrich (see also Aldrich)
Language/Cultural Origin: **French**
Inherent Meaning: **Wise Ruler**
Spiritual Connotation: **Chosen**
Scripture: **Revelation 2:10** NKJV
Be faithful until death, and I will give you the crown of life.

AUGUSTA, Agusta, Augustina
Language/Cultural Origin: **Latin**
Inherent Meaning: **Majestic**
Spiritual Connotation: **Queenly**
Scripture: **Proverbs 31:25** NLT
She is clothed with strength and dignity, and she laughs with no fear of the future.

AUGUSTUS, August, Augustine
Language/Cultural Origin: **Latin**
Inherent Meaning: **Venerable**
Spiritual Connotation: **Exalted**
Scripture: **Proverbs 27:18** NCV
Whoever takes care of his master will receive honor.

AUREL, Aurèle, Aurelio
Language/Cultural Origin: **Czech**
Inherent Meaning: **From Aurek**
Spiritual Connotation: **Reverent**
Scripture: **Malachi 4:2** TLB
But for you who fear my name, the Sun of Righteousness will rise with healing in his wings.

AURELIA, Auralia, Aurelea, Aureliana, Aurielle, Aurilia
Language/Cultural Origin: **Latin**
Inherent Meaning: **Golden**
Spiritual Connotation: **Sealed**
Scripture: **Hebrews 5:9** NKJV
And having been perfected, He became the author of eternal salvation to all who obey Him.

AURORA, Auroré
Language/Cultural Origin: **Latin**
Inherent Meaning: **Dawn**
Spiritual Connotation: **Mouthpiece of God**
Scripture: **Psalm 50:1** NKJV
The Mighty One, God the LORD, has spoken and called the earth from the rising of the sun to its going down.

AUSTIN, Austan, Austen, Austyn
Language/Cultural Origin: **Latin**
Inherent Meaning: **Renowned**
Spiritual Connotation: **Guided of God**
Scripture: **Isaiah 58:11** KJV
And the LORD shall guide thee continually, and satisfy thy soul in drought . . . and thou shalt be like a watered garden.

AVA, Avae, Ave (see also Eva)
Language/Cultural Origin: **English**
Inherent Meaning: **Filled With Life**
Spiritual Connotation: **Filled With Praise**
Scripture: **Psalm 106:1** KJV
Praise ye the LORD. O give thanks unto the LORD; for he is good: for his mercy endureth for ever.

AVERY, Averey, Averie
Language/Cultural Origin: **Middle English**
Inherent Meaning: **Ruler**
Spiritual Connotation: **Wise Counselor**
Scripture: **Proverbs 20:5** TLB
Though good advice lies deep within a counselor's heart, the wise man will draw it out.

AVIEL, Avi, Avian, Avion (see also Abiel)
Language/Cultural Origin: **Hebrew**
Inherent Meaning: **God Is My Father**
Spiritual Connotation: **Child of God**
Scripture: **1 John 5:1** NCV

Everyone who believes that Jesus is the Christ is God's child, and whoever loves the Father also loves the Father's children.

AVIS, Avia, Aviana
Language/Cultural Origin: **Latin**
Inherent Meaning: **Refuge**
Spiritual Connotation: **Place of Freedom**
Scripture: **Galatians 5:1** NASB
It was for freedom that Christ set us free; therefore keep standing firm and do not be subject again to a yoke of slavery.

AXEL, Axell, Axil, Axill (see also Aksel)
Language/Cultural Origin: **Scandinavian**
Inherent Meaning: **My Father Is Peace**
Spiritual Connotation: **Victory**
Scripture: **Romans 16:20** NASB
And the God of peace will soon crush Satan under your feet. The grace of our Lord Jesus be with you.

AYA, Ayah (see also Aiah)
Language/Cultural Origin: **Hebrew**
Inherent Meaning: **Bird**
Spiritual Connotation: **Committed**
Scripture: **Proverbs 27:8** NASB
Like a bird that wanders from her nest, so is a man who wanders from his home.

AYANNA, Aiyana, Ayana, Ayania, Ayannah
Language/Cultural Origin: **Cherokee**
Inherent Meaning: **Everlasting Bloom**
Spiritual Connotation: **Blessed**
Scripture: **Genesis 13:15** NKJV
All the land which you see I give to you and your descendants forever.

AYASHA, Ayashah
Language/Cultural Origin: **Middle Eastern**
Inherent Meaning: **Life**
Spiritual Connotation: **Eternal**
Scripture: **John 6:27** NLT
But you shouldn't be so concerned about perishable things like food. Spend your

energy seeking the eternal life that I, the Son of Man, can give you.

AZAREL, Ahzarel, Azarael, Azareel ☞ (see also Asarel, Asriel, Azriel)
Language/Cultural Origin: **Hebrew**
Inherent Meaning: **God Helped**
Spiritual Connotation: **Delivered**
Scripture: **Psalm 34:4** NKJV
I sought the LORD, and He heard me, And delivered me from all my fears.

AZARIAH, Azariyah
☞ Language/Cultural Origin: **Hebrew**
Inherent Meaning: **The Lord Will Keep Us**
Spiritual Connotation: **Preserved**
Scripture: **Numbers 6:24** NASB
The LORD bless you, and keep you.

AZEEM, Aseem
Language/Cultural Origin: **Middle Eastern**
Inherent Meaning: **Defender**
Spiritual Connotation: **God's Warrior**
Scripture: **Zechariah 12:8** NASB
In that day the LORD will defend the inhabitants of Jerusalem.

AZRIEL, Azrayel, Azriela, Azrielle ☞ (see also Asarel, Asriel, Azarel)
Language/Cultural Origin: **Hebrew**
Inherent Meaning: **God Is My Help**
Spiritual Connotation: **Prayerful**
Scripture: **Psalm 77:2** NCV
I look for the Lord on the day of trouble. All night long I reach out my hands, but I cannot be comforted.

AZZAN, Azzán
☞ Language/Cultural Origin: **Hebrew**
Inherent Meaning: **Sharp**
Spiritual Connotation: **Devout**
Scripture: **Proverbs 27:17** NASB
Iron sharpens iron, So one man sharpens another.

B

BAARA, Bara, Baarah
Language/Cultural Origin: **Hebrew**
Inherent Meaning: **Burning**
Spiritual Connotation: **Flame of God**
Scripture: **Hebrews 12:29** NKJV
Our God is a consuming fire.

BAASHA, Basha
Language/Cultural Origin: **Hebrew**
Inherent Meaning: **Boldness**
Spiritual Connotation: **Empowered**
Scripture: **Acts 4:29** NCV
*And now, Lord, listen to their threats.
Lord, help us, your servants, to speak
your word without fear.*

BABBIE, Bab, Babb, Babs
Language/Cultural Origin: **American**
Inherent Meaning: **Stranger**
Spiritual Connotation: **Foreigner**
Scripture: **Philippians 3:20** TLB
*But our homeland is in heaven, where
our Savior, the Lord Jesus Christ, is;
and we are looking forward to his return
from there.*

BADEN, Bayden, Baydon, Beyden, Beydon (see also Bedan)
Language/Cultural Origin: **Old English**
Inherent Meaning: **Bather**
Spiritual Connotation: **Cleansed**
Scripture: **Psalm 51:2** NKJV
*Wash me thoroughly from my iniquity,
and cleanse me from my sin.*

BAILEY, Bailee, Bailey, Bailie, Bali, Baylee, Bayley, Baylie
Language/Cultural Origin: **Old French**
Inherent Meaning: **Stewardship**
Spiritual Connotation: **Protector**
Scripture: **1 Peter 4:10** NASB
*As each one has received a special gift,
employ it in serving one another, as good
stewards of the manifold grace of God.*

BAIN, Baine (see also Bane)
Language/Cultural Origin: **Gaelic**
Inherent Meaning: **Fair**
Spiritual Connotation: **Cleansed**
Scripture: **1 Corinthians 6:11** TLB
*Now your sins are washed away, and
you are set apart for God; and he has
accepted you because of what the Lord
Jesus Christ and the Spirit of our God
have done for you.*

BAIRD, Bairde, Bard
Language/Cultural Origin: **Irish**
Inherent Meaning: **Traveling Singer of Ballads**
Spiritual Connotation: **Song of Harmony**
Scripture: **Psalm 81:1** NLT
*Sing praises to God, our strength. Sing to
the God of Israel.*

BAKER, see Baxter

BALAAM, Balam, Balám
Language/Cultural Origin: **Hebrew**
Inherent Meaning: **Lord of the People**
Spiritual Connotation: **Vessel of God**
Scripture: **Numbers 23:8** NASB
*How shall I curse whom God has not
cursed? And how can I denounce whom
the LORD has not denounced?*

BALDWIN, Baldwyn
Language/Cultural Origin: **Old German**
Inherent Meaning: **Bold Friend**
Spiritual Connotation: **Courageous**
Scripture: **1 Chronicles 28:20** NASB
*Be strong and courageous, and act; do
not fear nor be dismayed, for the LORD*

*God, my God, is with you. He will not
fail you nor forsake you.*

BALIN, Baylin (see also Valin)
Language/Cultural Origin: **Indo-Pakistani**
Inherent Meaning: **Mighty Warrior**
Spiritual Connotation: **Successful**
Scripture: **Jeremiah 50:9** NKJV
*And they shall array themselves against
her; from there she shall be captured.
Their arrows shall be like those of an
expert warrior; none shall return in vain.*

BAMBI, Bambee, Bambie
Language/Cultural Origin: **Italian**
Inherent Meaning: **Child**
Spiritual Connotation: **Innocent**
Scripture: **Mark 9:37** NKJV
*Whoever receives one of these little
children in My name receives Me; and
whoever receives Me, receives not Me
but Him who sent Me.*

BANE, Bayne (see also Bain)
Language/Cultural Origin: **Hawaiian**
Inherent Meaning: **Child of Exhortation**
Spiritual Connotation: **Heir**
Scripture: **Hebrews 12:5** NRSV
*My child, do not regard lightly the disci-
pline of the Lord, or lose heart when you
are punished by him.*

BANI, Baani, Banni, Bannie
☞ Language/Cultural Origin: **Hebrew**
Inherent Meaning: **Built**
Spiritual Connotation: **Honorable**
Scripture: **Psalms 127:1** NKJV
*Unless the LORD builds the house, they
labor in vain who build it.*

BANNER, Bannor
Language/Cultural Origin: **Scottish**
Inherent Meaning: **Flag Follower**
Spiritual Connotation: **God's Soldier**
Scripture: **Isaiah 31:9** NCV
*They will panic, and their protection will
be destroyed. Their commanders will be
terrified when they see God's battle flag.*

BANNING, Baning
Language/Cultural Origin: **Irish**
Inherent Meaning: **Small and Fair**
Spiritual Connotation: **Cleansed of God**

Scripture: **John 17:19** KJV
*And for their sakes I sanctify myself, that
they also might be sanctified through the
truth.*

**BARBARA, Barb, Barbe, Barbie,
Barbora, Barbra, Barby**
Language/Cultural Origin: **Greek**
Inherent Meaning: **Stranger**
Spiritual Connotation: **Purchased**
Scripture: **Ephesians 2:19** NKJV
*Now, therefore, you are no longer stran-
gers and foreigners, but fellow citizens
with the saints and members of the
household of God.*

**BARCLAY, Barkley, Berkeley,
Berkley**
Language/Cultural Origin: **Scottish**
Inherent Meaning: **From the Meadow of
the Birch Trees**
Spiritual Connotation: **Renewed in Spirit**
Scripture: **John 6:63** NASB
*It is the Spirit who gives life; the flesh
profits nothing; the words that I have
spoken to you are spirit and are life.*

**BARIAH, Bariya, Bariyah, Barriah
☞ (see also Beraiah)**
Language/Cultural Origin: **Hebrew**
Inherent Meaning: **Fugitive**
Spiritual Connotation: **Seeker of Truth**
Scripture: **Psalms 39:12** NLT
*Hear my prayer, O LORD! Listen to my
cries for help! Don't ignore my tears.
For I am your guest—a traveler passing
through.*

BARKER, Barcker
Language/Cultural Origin: **Old English**
Inherent Meaning: **Shepherd**
Spiritual Connotation: **Guide**
Scripture: **Ecclesiastes 12:11** NLT
*A wise teacher's words spur students to
action and emphasize important truths.
The collected sayings of the wise are like
guidance from a shepherd.*

**BARNABAS, Barnaby, Barney,
☞ Barnie**
Language/Cultural Origin: **Hebrew**
Inherent Meaning: **Son of Exhortation**

Spiritual Connotation: **Praise to God**
Scripture: **Psalm 25:1** KJV
Unto thee, O LORD, do I lift up my soul.

BARRIE, Bari, Barri
Language/Cultural Origin: **Old English**
Inherent Meaning: **Markswoman**
Spiritual Connotation: **Brave**
Scripture: **Judges 4:9** NKJV
There will be no glory for you in the journey you are taking, for the LORD will sell Sisera into the hand of a woman.

BARRY, Barrey, Bary
Language/Cultural Origin: **Irish**
Inherent Meaning: **Marksman**
Spiritual Connotation: **Strong**
Scripture: **Luke 10:27** NKJV
You shall love the LORD your God with all your heart, with all your soul, with all your strength, and with all your mind, and your neighbor as yourself.

BARTHOLOMEW, Bart, Bartlet
☞ Language/Cultural Origin: **Aramaic**
Inherent Meaning: **Son of Tolmai**
Spiritual Connotation: **Heir**
Scripture: **Colossians 1:12** NASB
Giving thanks to the Father, who has qualified us to share in the inheritance of the saints in light.

BARUCH, Boruch
☞ Language/Cultural Origin: **Hebrew**
Inherent Meaning: **Blessed**
Spiritual Connotation: **Righteous**
Scripture: **James 1:12** NRSV
Blessed is anyone who endures temptation. Such a one has stood the test and will receive the crown of life that the Lord has promised to those who love him.

BARUSHKA, Baruska
Language/Cultural Origin: **Czech**
Inherent Meaning: **Stranger**
Spiritual Connotation: **Approved**
Scripture: **Proverbs 27:2** NKJV
Let another man praise you, and not your own mouth; a stranger, and not your own lips.

BASIA, Basha, Basya, Batia, Batya
Language/Cultural Origin: **Hebrew**

Inherent Meaning: **Daughter of God**
Spiritual Connotation: **Valued**
Scripture: **Matthew 21:5** NRSV
Tell the daughter of Zion, Look, your king is coming to you.

BASIL, Bazil
Language/Cultural Origin: **Greek**
Inherent Meaning: **Kingly**
Spiritual Connotation: **Magnificent**
Scripture: **1 Chronicles 29:12** NASB
Both riches and honor come from You, and You rule over all, and in Your hand is power and might.

BAXTER, Baker
Language/Cultural Origin: **Middle English**
Inherent Meaning: **Provider**
Spiritual Connotation: **Industrious**
Scripture: **2 Corinthians 9:10** NASB
Now He who supplies seed to the sower and bread for food will supply and multiply your seed for sowing and increase the harvest of your righteousness.

BAY, Baye
Language/Cultural Origin: **Vietnamese**
Inherent Meaning: **Born on Saturday/Born in the Month of July**
Spiritual Connotation: **Forgiven**
Scripture: **Romans 4:8** TLB
Yes, what joy there is for anyone whose sins are no longer counted against him by the Lord.

BEATRICE, Bea, Beatricia, Bee
Language/Cultural Origin: **Italian**
Inherent Meaning: **Bringer of Joy**
Spiritual Connotation: **Love of Life**
Scripture: **Deuteronomy 27:7** KJV
And thou shalt offer peace offerings, and shalt eat there, and rejoice before the LORD thy God.

BEAU (see also Bo)
Language/Cultural Origin: **French**
Inherent Meaning: **Handsome**
Spiritual Connotation: **Peacemaker**
Scripture: **Psalm 133:1** NASB
Behold, how good and how pleasant it is for brothers to dwell together in unity!

BEBE, Babe (see also Bibi)
Language/Cultural Origin: **Spanish**
Inherent Meaning: **Baby**
Spiritual Connotation: **Faith**
Scripture: **Luke 18:17** NASB
Truly I say to you, whoever does not receive the kingdom of God like a child shall not enter it at all.

BECK, Beckett
Language/Cultural Origin: **Middle English**
Inherent Meaning: **From the Stream**
Spiritual Connotation: **Satisfied**
Scripture: **Psalm 36:8** NLT
You feed them from the abundance of your own house, letting them drink from your rivers of delight.

BECKY, Becca, Becka, Becki, Beckie, Beka, Bekka, Bekki, Bekkie (see also Rebecca)
Language/Cultural Origin: **English**
Inherent Meaning: **Bound by Love**
Spiritual Connotation: **Loving**
Scripture: **1 Corinthians 13:4** NCV
Love is patient and kind. Love is not jealous, it does not brag, and it is not proud.

BEDAN, Baedan, Baedán, Bédan, ☞ Bedán (see also Baden)
Language/Cultural Origin: **Hebrew**
Inherent Meaning: **Son of Judgment**
Spiritual Connotation: **Encourager**
Scripture: **James 5:9** NLT
Don't grumble about each other, my brothers and sisters, or God will judge you. For look! The great Judge is coming. He is standing at the door!

BELA, Béla, Belah
Language/Cultural Origin: **Hebrew**
Inherent Meaning: **Devouring**
Spiritual Connotation: **Godly Example**
Scripture: **Isaiah 60:3** NRSV
Nations shall come to your light, and kings to the brightness of your dawn.

BELDON, Belden
Language/Cultural Origin: **Old English**
Inherent Meaning: **From the Beautiful Valley**
Spiritual Connotation: **Sanctified**
Scripture: **Isaiah 40:4** NKJV
Every valley shall be exalted and every mountain and hill brought low.

BELINDA, Belynda
Language/Cultural Origin: **Spanish**
Inherent Meaning: **Lovely**
Spiritual Connotation: **Beauty of Soul**
Scripture: **Ephesians 4:7** NASB
But to each one of us grace was given according to the measure of Christ's gift.

BELLE, Bell, Bellina
Language/Cultural Origin: **French**
Inherent Meaning: **Beautiful**
Spiritual Connotation: **Blessed**
Scripture: **Psalm 104:33** NCV
I will sing to the LORD all my life; I will sing praises to my God as long as I live.

BENAIAH, Benaiya, Beniyah
☞ Language/Cultural Origin: **Hebrew**
Inherent Meaning: **The Lord Has Built**
Spiritual Connotation: **Foundation**
Scripture: **1 Samuel 12:24** NKJV
Only fear the LORD, and serve Him in truth with all your heart; for consider what great things He has done for you.

BEN-AMMI, Ben Ami, BenAmi, ☞ Ben-Ami, Benn-Ami
Language/Cultural Origin: **Hebrew**
Inherent Meaning: **Son of My People**
Spiritual Connotation: **Ancestor**
Scripture: **Genesis 17:6** NKJV
I will make you exceedingly fruitful; and I will make nations of you, and kings shall come from you.

BEN-HANAN, BenHanan, Ben-☞ Hannan, Benn-Hanan
Language/Cultural Origin: **Hebrew**
Inherent Meaning: **Son of Kindness**
Spiritual Connotation: **Loving**
Scripture: **Ephesians 4:32** NKJV
And be kind to one another, tenderhearted, forgiving one another, just as God in Christ forgave you.

BENITA, Benitta
Language/Cultural Origin: **Spanish**
Inherent Meaning: **Blessed**
Spiritual Connotation: **Cherished**

Scripture: **Numbers 6:25** NRSV
*The LORD make his face to shine upon
you, and be gracious to you.*

**BENJAMIN, Ben, Benjaman,
☞Benjamen, Benji, Benjie, Benn,
Bennie, Benny, Benyamin**
Language/Cultural Origin: **Hebrew**
Inherent Meaning: **Son of My Right Hand**
Spiritual Connotation: **Mighty**
Scripture: **Psalm 18:35** NKJV
*You have also given me the shield of Your
salvation; Your right hand has held me
up, Your gentleness has made me great.*

BENNET, Bennett
Language/Cultural Origin: **English**
Inherent Meaning: **Blessed**
Spiritual Connotation: **Walks With God**
Scripture: **Romans 8:14** NASB
*For all who are being led by the Spirit of
God, these are sons of God.*

BENOIT, Benoît
Language/Cultural Origin: **French**
Inherent Meaning: **Blessed**
Spiritual Connotation: **Received**
Scripture: **Exodus 20:24** NKJV
*In every place where I record My name I
will come to you, and I will bless you.*

BENSON, Bensen
Language/Cultural Origin: **English**
Inherent Meaning: **Son of Ben**
Spiritual Connotation: **Honor of God**
Scripture: **Psalm 127:1** NCV
*If the LORD doesn't build the house, the
builders are working for nothing. If the
LORD doesn't guard the city, the guards
are watching for nothing.*

BENTLEY, Bentlea, Bentlee
Language/Cultural Origin: **Old English**
Inherent Meaning: **From the Grassy
Meadow**
Spiritual Connotation: **Peaceful**
Scripture: **Psalm 121:8** NLT
*The LORD keeps watch over you as you
come and go, both now and forever.*

**BERAIAH, Beraiyah (see also
☞Bariah)**
Language/Cultural Origin: **Hebrew**

Inherent Meaning: **The Lord Has Created**
Spiritual Connotation: **Joyful**
Scripture: **Job 1:21** NASB
*The LORD gave and the LORD has taken
away. Blessed be the name of the LORD.*

BERGEN, Bergan, Bergin
Language/Cultural Origin: **Scandinavian**
Inherent Meaning: **From the Hill**
Spiritual Connotation: **Made Righteous**
Scripture: **Psalm 15:1-2** NKJV
*LORD . . . Who may dwell in Your holy
hill? He who walks uprightly, and works
righteousness, and speaks the truth in his
heart.*

BERNADETTE, Bernadine
Language/Cultural Origin: **French**
Inherent Meaning: **Courageous**
Spiritual Connotation: **Valiant**
Scripture: **1 Corinthians 15:57** NKJV
*But thanks be to God, who gives us the
victory through our Lord Jesus Christ.*

**BERNARD, Barnard, Bernardo,
Berndt, Berney, Bernhard, Berni,
Bernie, Birnee, Birney, Burney**
Language/Cultural Origin: **Old German**
Inherent Meaning: **Brave as a Bear**
Spiritual Connotation: **Wise**
Scripture: **Proverbs 17:12** NCV
*It is better to meet a bear robbed of her
cubs than to meet a fool doing foolish
things.*

**BERNICE, Berenice, Berni, Bernise
☞** Language/Cultural Origin: **Greek**
Inherent Meaning: **Bringer of Victory**
Spiritual Connotation: **Victorious**
Scripture: **Mark 9:23** NLT
Anything is possible if a person believes.

BERTRAM, Bartram, Bert
Language/Cultural Origin: **Old English**
Inherent Meaning: **Brilliant**
Spiritual Connotation: **Magnificent**
Scripture: **Isaiah 62:3** RSV
*You shall be a crown of beauty in the
hand of the LORD, and a royal diadem in
the hand of your God.*

BERTRAND, Bertran
Language/Cultural Origin: **French**

Inherent Meaning: **Bright Shield**
Spiritual Connotation: **Protected of God**
Scripture: **2 Samuel 22:31** NKJV
As for God, His way is perfect; the word of the LORD is proven; He is a shield to all who trust in Him.

BESSIE, Bess, Bessi, Bessy
Language/Cultural Origin: **English**
Inherent Meaning: **Oath of God**
Spiritual Connotation: **Loyal**
Scripture: **Isaiah 30:29** NRSV
You shall have a song as in the night when a holy festival is kept; and gladness of heart.

BETH, Bethe, Bethel, Bethell (see also Bethany, Elizabeth)
Language/Cultural Origin: **Hebrew**
Inherent Meaning: **Oath of God**
Spiritual Connotation: **Wise**
Scripture: **Isaiah 48:17** TLB
I am the Lord your God, who punishes you for your own good and leads you along the paths that you should follow.

BETH ANN, Bethann, Beth-Ann, Beth Anne, Beth-Anne
Language/Cultural Origin: **English**
Inherent Meaning: **Gracious Oath of God**
Spiritual Connotation: **Promise**
Scripture: **Acts 2:39** NASB
For the promise is for you and your children, and for all who are far off, as many as the Lord our God shall call to Himself.

BETHANY, Bethanney, Bethani, Bethanie, Bethanney, Betheny
Language/Cultural Origin: **Aramaic**
Inherent Meaning: **House of Figs**
Spiritual Connotation: **Productive**
Scripture: **Matthew 7:16** NASB
You will know them by their fruits. Grapes are not gathered from thorn bushes nor figs from thistles, are they?

BETHUEL, Bethuelle
Language/Cultural Origin: **Hebrew**
Inherent Meaning: **Dwells in God**
Spiritual Connotation: **Secure**
Scripture: **Psalm 23:6** RSV

Surely goodness and mercy shall follow me all the days of my life; and I shall dwell in the house of the LORD for ever.

BETSY, Betsey, Betsi, Betsie
Language/Cultural Origin: **English**
Inherent Meaning: **Oath of God**
Spiritual Connotation: **Confirmed**
Scripture: **Hebrews 7:21** RSV
The Lord has sworn and will not change his mind, "Thou art a priest forever."

BETTY, Bett, Bette, Betti, Bettie
Language/Cultural Origin: **English**
Inherent Meaning: **Oath of God**
Spiritual Connotation: **Reverent**
Scripture: **Psalm 119:39** NRSV
Turn away the disgrace that I dread, for your ordinances are good.

BEVAN, Bevann, Beven, Bevin, Bevon
Language/Cultural Origin: **Welsh**
Inherent Meaning: **Son of the Young Warrior**
Spiritual Connotation: **Youthful**
Scripture: **Psalm 71:17** NKJV
O God, You have taught me from my youth; and to this day I declare Your wondrous works.

BEVERLY, Bev, Beverlee, Beverley
Language/Cultural Origin: **English**
Inherent Meaning: **Peace and Harmony**
Spiritual Connotation: **Enlightened**
Scripture: **James 1:17** KJV
Every good gift and every perfect gift is from above, and cometh down from the Father of lights, with whom is no variableness, neither shadow of turning.

BEVIS, Bevys
Language/Cultural Origin: **Old French**
Inherent Meaning: **Bull**
Spiritual Connotation: **Powerful**
Scripture: **Isaiah 10:13** NRSV
I have removed the boundaries of peoples, and have plundered their treasures; like a bull I have brought down those who sat on thrones.

BIANCA, Biancha, Bionca, Bioncha
Language/Cultural Origin: **Italian**

Inherent Meaning: **Fair**
Spiritual Connotation: **Wisdom**
Scripture: **Job 5:8-9** NASB
But as for me, I would seek God, and I would place my cause before God; Who does great and unsearchable things, wonders without number.

BIBI, Beebee (see also Bebe)

Language/Cultural Origin: **Middle Eastern**
Inherent Meaning: **Honored**
Spiritual Connotation: **Praised**
Scripture: **Mark 10:43** NCV
But it should not be that way among you. Whoever wants to become great among you must serve the rest of you like a servant.

BILL, see William

BING

Language/Cultural Origin: **German**
Inherent Meaning: **From the Kettle-Shaped Hollow**
Spiritual Connotation: **Blessed**
Scripture: **Luke 3:5** RSV
Every valley shall be filled, and every mountain and hill shall be brought low, and the crooked shall be made straight, and the rough ways shall be made smooth.

BIRDIE, see Roberta

BIRNEY, Birnie, Birny

Language/Cultural Origin: **Middle English**
Inherent Meaning: **From the Island With the Stream**
Spiritual Connotation: **One of Integrity**
Scripture: **Romans 8:28** NKJV
And we know that all things work together for good to those who love God, to those who are the called according to His purpose.

BJORN, Bjarn, Bjarne, Bjorne

Language/Cultural Origin: **Scandinavian**
Inherent Meaning: **Bear**
Spiritual Connotation: **Voice of God**
Scripture: **Joel 2:11** RSV
The LORD utters his voice before his army, for his host is exceedingly great.

BLADE, Blayde

Language/Cultural Origin: **Middle English**
Inherent Meaning: **Knife**
Spiritual Connotation: **Weapon**
Scripture: **Matthew 10:34** NKJV
Do not think that I came to bring peace on earth. I did not come to bring peace but a sword.

BLAINE, Blain, Blane, Blayne

Language/Cultural Origin: **Gaelic**
Inherent Meaning: **Lean**
Spiritual Connotation: **Trusting**
Scripture: **Isaiah 42:16** NRSV
I will turn the darkness before them into light, the rough places into level ground. . . . I will not forsake them.

BLAIR, Blaire

Language/Cultural Origin: **Irish**
Inherent Meaning: **Field Worker**
Spiritual Connotation: **Diligent**
Scripture: **Ephesians 6:7** NLT
Work with enthusiasm, as though you were working for the Lord rather than for people.

BLAISE, Blaize, Blayze, Blaze

Language/Cultural Origin: **French**
Inherent Meaning: **Flame/One Who Stammers**
Spiritual Connotation: **Flame of God**
Scripture: **Hebrews 12:29** NRSV
Indeed our God is a consuming fire.

BLAKE, Blakelee, Blakeleigh, Blakeley, Blakely

Language/Cultural Origin: **English**
Inherent Meaning: **Attractive**
Spiritual Connotation: **Forgiven**
Scripture: **Ephesians 2:4-5** NASB
But God, being rich in mercy, because of His great love with which He loved us . . . made us alive together with Christ.

BLANCHE, Blanch

Language/Cultural Origin: **French**
Inherent Meaning: **Pure**
Spiritual Connotation: **Gentle**
Scripture: **Psalm 49:3** RSV
My mouth shall speak wisdom; the

meditation of my heart shall be under-standing.

BLOSSOM, Blossum
Language/Cultural Origin: **Old English**
Inherent Meaning: **Flower**
Spiritual Connotation: **Joyful**
Scripture: **Isaiah 35:1-2** NKJV
And the desert shall rejoice and blossom as the rose; it shall blossom abundantly and rejoice, even with joy and singing.

BLYTHE, Blithe, Blyth
Language/Cultural Origin: **English**
Inherent Meaning: **Joyful**
Spiritual Connotation: **Cheerful**
Scripture: **John 16:33** NKJV
These things I have spoken to you, that in Me you may have peace. In the world you will have tribulation; but be of good cheer, I have overcome the world.

BO, Boe (see also Beau)
Language/Cultural Origin: **Chinese**
Inherent Meaning: **Precious**
Spiritual Connotation: **Honored**
Scripture: **Isaiah 43:4** TLB
Others died that you might live; I traded their lives for yours because you are precious to me and honored, and I love you.

BOAZ, Boas, Boz
☞ Language/Cultural Origin: **Hebrew**
Inherent Meaning: **Swift**
Spiritual Connotation: **Bearer of the Covenant**
Scripture: **Isaiah 16:5** NRSV
A throne shall be established in steadfast love in the tent of David, and on it shall sit in faithfulness a ruler who seeks justice and is swift to do what is right.

BOB, see Robert

BOBBIE, Bobbi
Language/Cultural Origin: **American**
Inherent Meaning: **Foreigner**
Spiritual Connotation: **Stranger**
Scripture: **1 Peter 2:11** NASB
Beloved, I urge you as aliens and strangers to abstain from fleshly lusts, which wage war against the soul.

BODAN, Bohdan
Language/Cultural Origin: **Ukranian**
Inherent Meaning: **World Leader**
Spiritual Connotation: **Orchestrator of Peace**
Scripture: **Isaiah 60:17** NIV
I will make peace your governor and righteousness your ruler.

BODANA, Bodanna, Bogdana, Bohdana
Language/Cultural Origin: **Polish**
Inherent Meaning: **Heavenly Presence**
Spiritual Connotation: **Keenly Aware**
Scripture: **Psalm 89:7** TLB
The highest of angelic powers stand in dread and awe of him. Who is as revered as he by those surrounding him?

BODEN, Bodee, Bodie, Bodin
Language/Cultural Origin: **French**
Inherent Meaning: **Messenger/Herald**
Spiritual Connotation: **Ready for Service**
Scripture: **Isaiah 6:8** NLT
Then I heard the Lord asking, Whom should I send as a messenger to my people? Who will go for us? And I said, Lord, I'll go! Send me.

BODHAN, Bodhun
Language/Cultural Origin: **Russian**
Inherent Meaning: **Mighty**
Spiritual Connotation: **Devoted**
Scripture: **Deuteronomy 6:5** NKJV
You shall love the LORD your God with all your heart, with all your soul, and with all your strength.

BONNIE, Bonita, Bonne, Bonni, Bonnita, Bonny
Language/Cultural Origin: **French**
Inherent Meaning: **Beautiful**
Spiritual Connotation: **Pure in Heart**
Scripture: **Matthew 5:8** NKJV
Blessed are the pure in heart, for they shall see God.

BOONE, Boon, Boonie
Language/Cultural Origin: **French**
Inherent Meaning: **Good**
Spiritual Connotation: **Obedient**
Scripture: **Psalm 119:2** RSV
Blessed are those who keep his

*testimonies, who seek him with their
whole heart.*

BORDEN, Bordan
Language/Cultural Origin: **French**
Inherent Meaning: **From the Cottage**
Spiritual Connotation: **Righteous**
Scripture: **Proverbs 3:33** NASB
*The curse of the LORD is on the house of
the wicked, but He blesses the dwelling of
the righteous.*

BORIS, Boriss, Borris
Language/Cultural Origin: **Slavic**
Inherent Meaning: **Warrior**
Spiritual Connotation: **Trusting**
Scripture: **Psalm 36:7** NRSV
*How precious is your steadfast love,
O God! All people may take refuge
in the shadow of your wings.*

BOTAN, Botán
Language/Cultural Origin: **Japanese**
Inherent Meaning: **Blossom**
Spiritual Connotation: **Youthful**
Scripture: **Ezekiel 16:7** NKJV
*I made you thrive like a plant in the field;
and you grew, matured, and became very
beautiful.*

BOWEN, Bowie
Language/Cultural Origin: **Gaelic**
Inherent Meaning: **Small**
Spiritual Connotation: **Victorious**
Scripture: **Psalm 20:5** NASB
*We will sing for joy over your victory,
and in the name of our God we will set
up our banners. May the LORD fulfill all
your petitions.*

BOYCE, Boice, Boise, Boycee, Boycie
Language/Cultural Origin: **French**
Inherent Meaning: **From the Forest**
Spiritual Connotation: **Joyful**
Scripture: **Psalm 96:12** TLB
*Praise him for the growing fields, for they
display his greatness. Let the trees of the
forest rustle with praise.*

BOYD, Boid
Language/Cultural Origin: **Scottish**
Inherent Meaning: **Golden-Haired**
Spiritual Connotation: **Quiet Spirit**

Scripture: **Proverbs 15:33** NCV
*Respect for the LORD will teach you
wisdom. If you want to be honored, you
must be humble.*

BRADEN, Bradan, Bradin, Bradon, Braeden, Braedon, Braydon, Brayden
Language/Cultural Origin: **English**
Inherent Meaning: **From the Broad
Clearing**
Spiritual Connotation: **Redeemed**
Scripture: **Romans 5:9** NLT
*And since we have been made right in
God's sight by the blood of Christ, he will
certainly save us from God's judgment.*

BRADFORD, Brad, Braddford
Language/Cultural Origin: **English**
Inherent Meaning: **From the Water
Crossing**
Spiritual Connotation: **Delivered of God**
Scripture: **Mark 14:24** NKJV
*And He said to them, "This is My blood
of the new covenant, which is shed for
many."*

BRADLEY, Brad, Bradd, Braddlee, Bradlay, Bradlee
Language/Cultural Origin: **Old English**
Inherent Meaning: **From the Broad Meadow**
Spiritual Connotation: **Joyful**
Scripture: **Proverbs 15:13** NASB
A joyful heart makes a cheerful face.

BRADY, Bradey (see also Brede)
Language/Cultural Origin: **Irish**
Inherent Meaning: **Spirited**
Spiritual Connotation: **Gentle**
Scripture: **Galatians 5:22-23** NASB
*But the fruit of the Spirit is love, joy,
peace, patience, kindness, goodness,
faithfulness, gentleness, self-control;
against such things there is no law.*

BRANDON, Brandan, Branddon, Branden, Brandin, Brandyn, Brannan, Brannon
Language/Cultural Origin: **Old English**
Inherent Meaning: **From the Flaming Hill**
Spiritual Connotation: **Fervent**
Scripture: **Romans 12:11** NLT

Never be lazy in your work, but serve the Lord enthusiastically.

BRANDY, Brandee, Brandi, Brandie
Language/Cultural Origin: **Middle Dutch**
Inherent Meaning: **Distilled Wine**
Spiritual Connotation: **Filled With Joy**
Scripture: **Psalms 4:7** NKJV
You have put gladness in my heart, more than in the season that their grain and wine increased.

BRANT, Brandt, Brannt, Brantley
Language/Cultural Origin: **Czech**
Inherent Meaning: **Proud**
Spiritual Connotation: **Focused**
Scripture: **2 Timothy 2:4** TLB
And as Christ's soldier, do not let yourself become tied up in worldly affairs, for then you cannot satisfy the one who has enlisted you in his army.

BRAXTON, Braxtun
Language/Cultural Origin: **Old English**
Inherent Meaning: **From Brock's Town**
Spiritual Connotation: **Faithful**
Scripture: **1 Corinthians 7:20** NKJV
Let each one remain in the same calling in which he was called.

BREANNE, Breann, Bre-Ann, Bre-Anne, Breeann, Breeanne, Breighann, Briann, Brianne, Brieann, Briene, Brienne, Bryanne (see also Brenna, Brianna)
Language/Cultural Origin: **Celtic**
Inherent Meaning: **Strong**
Spiritual Connotation: **Dependent**
Scripture: **Psalm 68:34** NRSV
Ascribe power to God, whose majesty is over Israel; and whose power is in the skies.

BRECK, Brec, Brek, Brekk
Language/Cultural Origin: **Irish**
Inherent Meaning: **Freckled**
Spiritual Connotation: **Approved**
Scripture: **Job 5:17** NKJV
Behold, happy is the man whom God corrects; therefore do not despise the chastening of the Almighty.

BREDE, Braede, Bréde (see also Brady)
Language/Cultural Origin: **Scandinavian**
Inherent Meaning: **Glacier**
Spiritual Connotation: **Immovable**
Scripture: **Job 38:29-30** NLT
Who is the mother of the ice? Who gives birth to the frost from the heavens? For the water turns to ice as hard as rock, and the surface of the water freezes.

BRENDA, Brendie
Language/Cultural Origin: **Old Norse**
Inherent Meaning: **Sword**
Spiritual Connotation: **Glory of God**
Scripture: **Psalms 70:4** NASB
Let all who seek You rejoice and be glad in You; and let those who love Your salvation say continually, let God be magnified.

BRENDAN, Brenden, Brendin, Brendon, Brenndan
Language/Cultural Origin: **Irish**
Inherent Meaning: **Stinking Hair**
Spiritual Connotation: **Devout**
Scripture: **1 Timothy 1:5** NASB
But the goal of our instruction is love from a pure heart and a good conscience and a sincere faith.

BRENNA, Brena, Brenin, Brennah, Brennaugh, Brynna
Language/Cultural Origin: **Irish**
Inherent Meaning: **Little Raven**
Spiritual Connotation: **Faithful Friend**
Scripture: **Philippians 2:13** NCV
God is working in you to help you want to do and be able to do what pleases him.

BRENNAN, Brennen, Brennon
Language/Cultural Origin: **Irish**
Inherent Meaning: **Little Raven**
Spiritual Connotation: **Gift of God**
Scripture: **Romans 6:23** NKJV
For the wages of sin is death, but the gift of God is eternal life in Christ Jesus our Lord.

BRENTON, Brendt, Brent, Brentan,

Brenten, Brentin, Brentton, Brentyn
Language/Cultural Origin: English
Inherent Meaning: From the Steep Hill
Spiritual Connotation: Wise
Scripture: Ecclesiastes 4:13 RSV
Better is a poor and wise youth than an old and foolish king, who will no longer take advice.

BRETT, Bret, Brette
Language/Cultural Origin: Scottish
Inherent Meaning: Gifted
Spiritual Connotation: Blessed
Scripture: Proverbs 18:16 NRSV
A gift opens doors; it gives access to the great.

BRIAN, Briant, Brien, Brient, Brion, Bryan, Bryant, Bryen, Bryent, Bryon
Language/Cultural Origin: Celtic
Inherent Meaning: Virtue and Honor
Spiritual Connotation: Follower of God
Scripture: Isaiah 48:17 NRSV
I am the LORD your God, who teaches you for your own good, who leads you in the way you should go.

BRIANNA, Breana, Breanna, Breeana, Breeanna, Bria, Briana, Brianda, Briannah, Briannon, Bryana, Bryanna, Bryannah (see also Breanne, Brenna)
Language/Cultural Origin: Celtic
Inherent Meaning: Honorable
Spiritual Connotation: Virtuous
Scripture: Ruth 3:11 NASB
And now, my daughter, do not fear. I will do for you whatever you ask, for all my people in the city know that you are a woman of excellence.

BRIAR, Brear, Brier, Briet, Brietta, Bryar, Bryer
Language/Cultural Origin: French
Inherent Meaning: Heather
Spiritual Connotation: Child of God
Scripture: Job 29:12 NLT
For I helped the poor in their need and the orphans who had no one to help them.

BRIDGET, Bridgete, Bridgett, Bridgette, Bridgot, Briget, Brigette, , Brigitta, Brigitte
Language/Cultural Origin: Irish
Inherent Meaning: Strength
Spiritual Connotation: Enduring Spirit
Scripture: Psalm 27:1 NKJV
The LORD is my light and my salvation; whom shall I fear? The LORD is the strength of my life; of whom shall I be afraid?

BRIGHAM, Briggs
Language/Cultural Origin: English
Inherent Meaning: From the Covered Bridge
Spiritual Connotation: Challenger of Apostasy
Scripture: Ecclesiastes 12:1 NRSV
Remember your creator in the days of your youth, before the days of trouble come.

BRINA, Breena, Breina, Brin, Brinan, Brindy, Brinn, Brinnan, Bryn, Brynan, Brynn, Brynne
Language/Cultural Origin: Irish
Inherent Meaning: From the Fairy Palace
Spiritual Connotation: God's Salvation
Scripture: Psalm 9:14 NCV
Then, at the gates of Jerusalem, I will praise you; I will rejoice because you saved me.

BRINLEY, Brindlee, Brindley, Brinlee, Brinly, Brynley
Language/Cultural Origin: Old English
Inherent Meaning: Burnt Wood
Spiritual Connotation: Sacrifice
Scripture: Psalms 54:6 NRSV
With a freewill offering I will sacrifice to you; I will give thanks to your name, O LORD, for it is good.

BRIONA, Breeon, Breona, Briele, Brielle, Brieon, Brieona, Brione, Brionne, Briony, Bryoni
Language/Cultural Origin: Irish
Inherent Meaning: Mighty
Spiritual Connotation: God's Power
Scripture: Exodus 9:1 NKJV
Thus says the LORD God of the

Hebrews: "Let My people go, that they may serve Me."

BRIT, Brita, Britt, Britte
Language/Cultural Origin: **Swedish**
Inherent Meaning: **Strong**
Spiritual Connotation: **Prayerful**
Scripture: **Numbers 14:17** NASB
But now, I pray, let the power of the Lord be great, just as You have declared.

BRITTANY, Britain, Britane, Britaney, Britani, Britanny, Britlee, Britley, Britlyn, Britlynn, Britnee, Britney, Britni, Britnie, Britny, Brittain, Brittanee, Brittaney, Brittani, Brittania, Britteney, Brittiney, Brittiny, Brittnay, Brittnee, Brittneigh, Brittney, Brittni, Brittnie, Brittoni, Brittony, Brityn, Bryttani, Bryttany, Bryttney, Bryttni, Bryttny
Language/Cultural Origin: **English**
Inherent Meaning: **From Britain**
Spiritual Connotation: **Stranger**
Scripture: **Ruth 2:10** NKJV
Why have I found favor in your eyes, that you should take notice of me, since I am a foreigner?

BROCK, Broc, Brocke, Brok, Broque
Language/Cultural Origin: **Old English**
Inherent Meaning: **Badger**
Spiritual Connotation: **Full of Praise**
Scripture: **Psalm 3:4** NKJV
I cried to the LORD with my voice, and He heard me from His holy hill.

BRODERICK, Broadrick, Broderic, Brodric, (see also Roderick)
Language/Cultural Origin: **Norse**
Inherent Meaning: **Brother**
Spiritual Connotation: **True Friend**
Scripture: **Psalm 18:24** NASB
Therefore the LORD has recompensed me according to my righteousness, according to the cleanness of my hands in His eyes.

BRODIE, Brodee, Brodey, Brodi
Language/Cultural Origin: **Irish**
Inherent Meaning: **Canal Builder**

Spiritual Connotation: **God Is My Foundation**
Scripture: **Psalm 127:1** NKJV
Unless the LORD builds the house, they labor in vain who build it; unless the LORD guards the city, the watchman stays awake in vain.

BROÑA, Bronja, Bronya
Language/Cultural Origin: **Czech**
Inherent Meaning: **Bringer of Victory**
Spiritual Connotation: **Revered**
Scripture: **1 Corinthians 15:55** TLB
O death, where then your victory? Where then your sting?

BRONSON, Bronnson, Bronsen, Bronsin, Bronsson
Language/Cultural Origin: **English**
Inherent Meaning: **Son of the Dark-Skinned**
Spiritual Connotation: **Great Ruler**
Scripture: **Psalm 100:2** NRSV
Worship the LORD with gladness; come into his presence with singing.

BROOK, Brooke, Brooks, Broox
Language/Cultural Origin: **Old English**
Inherent Meaning: **Peaceful**
Spiritual Connotation: **Refreshed**
Scripture: **Zechariah 2:10** NASB
Sing for joy and be glad, O daughter of Zion; for behold I am coming and I will dwell in your midst.

BROOKLYN, Brooklin, Brooklynn
Language/Cultural Origin: **American**
Inherent Meaning: **Stream of the Waterfall**
Spiritual Connotation: **Praise**
Scripture: **Psalm 74:15** NLT
You caused the springs and streams to gush forth, and you dried up rivers that never run dry.

BROWNING, Bronwyn, Brownyn
Language/Cultural Origin: **Middle English**
Inherent Meaning: **Dark**
Spiritual Connotation: **Enlightened**
Scripture: **Matthew 4:16** NKJV
The people who sat in darkness have seen a great light, and upon those who sat in the region and shadow of death Light has dawned.

BRUCE, Bruse
Language/Cultural Origin: **Scottish**
Inherent Meaning: **From the Woods**
Spiritual Connotation: **Dignity**
Scripture: **Ephesians 2:10** NASB
For we are His workmanship, created in Christ Jesus for good works, which God prepared beforehand, that we should walk in them.

BRUNO, Brûno
Language/Cultural Origin: **Old German**
Inherent Meaning: **Brown**
Spiritual Connotation: **Rich in God's Grace**
Scripture: **Philippians 4:19** KJV
But my God shall supply all your need according to his riches in glory by Christ Jesus.

BRYAN, see Brian

BRYCE, Brice
Language/Cultural Origin: **Welsh**
Inherent Meaning: **Responsive**
Spiritual Connotation: **Ambitious**
Scripture: **Ecclesiastes 9:1** NKJV
For I considered all this in my heart . . . that the righteous and the wise and their works are in the hand of God.

BRYNA, BRYNN, see Brina

BUCKLEY, Bucklea, Bucklee
Language/Cultural Origin: **Middle English**
Inherent Meaning: **From the Deer Meadow**
Spiritual Connotation: **Worshiper**
Scripture: **Psalm 111:1** NKJV
Praise the LORD! I will praise the LORD with my whole heart, in the assembly of the upright and in the congregation.

BUDDY, Bud, Budd, Buddie
Language/Cultural Origin: **Old English**
Inherent Meaning: **Companion**
Spiritual Connotation: **Godly**
Scripture: **Psalm 119:63** NKJV
I am a companion of all who fear You, and of those who keep Your precepts.

BURGESS, Burges, Burgiss
Language/Cultural Origin: **English**
Inherent Meaning: **From the Town**
Spiritual Connotation: **Steadfast**
Scripture: **1 John 2:10** TLB
But whoever loves his fellow man is walking in the light and can see his way without stumbling around in darkness and sin.

BURKE, Berke, Birk, Burk
Language/Cultural Origin: **Old French**
Inherent Meaning: **From the Fortress**
Spiritual Connotation: **Courageous**
Scripture: **Deuteronomy 31:6** NKJV
Be strong and of good courage, do not fear nor be afraid of them; for the LORD your God, He is the One who goes with you. He will not leave you nor forsake you.

BURTON, Berton, Burt
Language/Cultural Origin: **Middle English**
Inherent Meaning: **From the Fortified Town**
Spiritual Connotation: **Amply Supplied**
Scripture: **Psalm 23:1-2** NKJV
The LORD is my shepherd; I shall not want. He makes me to lie down in green pastures; He leads me beside the still waters.

BYRAM, Byramm
Language/Cultural Origin: **Middle English**
Inherent Meaning: **From the Fields**
Spiritual Connotation: **Freedom**
Scripture: **Psalm 146:7** NCV
He does what is fair for those who have been wronged. He gives food to the hungry. The LORD sets the prisoners free.

BYRON, Bieran, Biran, Biren, Biron, Byran, Byrann, Byren
Language/Cultural Origin: **Old English**
Inherent Meaning: **From the Barn**
Spiritual Connotation: **Forgiving**
Scripture: **Mark 11:25** NKJV
And whenever you stand praying, if you have anything against anyone, forgive him, that your Father in heaven may also forgive you your trespasses.

C

CACHET, Cache, Cachea, Cachée
Language/Cultural Origin: **French**
Inherent Meaning: **Prestigious**
Spiritual Connotation: **Blessed**
Scripture: **Matthew 25:34** NASB
Come, you who are blessed of My Father, inherit the kingdom prepared for you from the foundation of the world.

CADELL, Cadel, Cadelle
Language/Cultural Origin: **Welsh**
Inherent Meaning: **Battler**
Spiritual Connotation: **Attentive**
Scripture: **1 Corinthians 14:8** RSV
And if the bugle gives an indistinct sound, who will get ready for battle?

CADENCE, Cadenze, Kadence
Language/Cultural Origin: **Latin**
Inherent Meaning: **Rhythmic Flow**
Spiritual Connotation: **Symphony**
Scripture: **Psalm 98:5-6** NLT
Sing your praise to the LORD with the harp . . . and trumpets and the sound of the ram's horn. Make a joyful symphony before the LORD, the King!

CADY, Cadee, Cadey, Cadi, Cadie (see also Kadee, Katy)
Language/Cultural Origin: **English**
Inherent Meaning: **Pure**
Spiritual Connotation: **Blameless**
Scripture: **Proverbs 2:21** NASB
For the upright will live in the land, and the blameless will remain in it.

CAELAN, Caelin, Cailan, Cailean, Cailen, Caillin, Calan, Calin, Callan, Callen, Callon, Calon, Caylan (see also Cailin, Kaylyn)
Language/Cultural Origin: **Scottish**
Inherent Meaning: **Victorious**
Spiritual Connotation: **Defended of God**
Scripture: **Isaiah 54:17** NKJV
No weapon formed against you shall prosper, And every tongue which rises against you in judgment You shall condemn.

CAELEY, Caelee, Caelie, Cailee, Cailey, Cailie, Caley, Caylee, Cayley, Caylie (see also Kaylee)
Language/Cultural Origin: **American**
Inherent Meaning: **Crowned**
Spiritual Connotation: **Temperate**
Scripture: **1 Corinthians 9:25** NLT
All athletes practice strict self-control. They do it to win a prize that will fade away, but we do it for an eternal prize.

CAESAR, Ceasar, César, Cesare, Cesareo, Cesario, Ceseare, Cezar, Czar, Kaiser, Sezare
Language/Cultural Origin: **Latin**
Inherent Meaning: **Long-Haired**
Spiritual Connotation: **Friend of Many**
Scripture: **Matthew 7:12** NKJV
Therefore, whatever you want men to do to you, do also to them, for this is the Law and the Prophets.

CAILIN, Caelyn, Caelynn, Cailyn, Cailynn, Cailynne, Caylin, Caylyn (see also Caelan, Kaylyn)
Language/Cultural Origin: **American**
Inherent Meaning: **Genuine**
Spiritual Connotation: **Godly**
Scripture: **2 Peter 1:7** NLT
Godliness leads to love for other Christians, and finally you will grow to have genuine love for everyone.

CAIN, Caine (see also Kane)
Language/Cultural Origin: **Hebrew**
Inherent Meaning: **Spear**
Spiritual Connotation: **Weapon**
Scripture: **2 Corinthians 6:7** TLB
We have been truthful, with God's power helping us in all we do. All of the godly man's arsenal . . . have been ours.

CAITLIN, Caitlan, Caitland, Caitlen, Caitlinn, Caitlyn, Caitlynn, Catlin (see also Kaitlin)
Language/Cultural Origin: **Irish**
Inherent Meaning: **Pure**
Spiritual Connotation: **Innocent**
Scripture: **Daniel 6:22** NKJV
My God sent His angel and shut the lions mouths, so that they have not hurt me, because I was found innocent before Him.

CALA, Calah, Calla, Callah (see also Kala)
Language/Cultural Origin: **Middle Eastern**
Inherent Meaning: **Fortress**
Spiritual Connotation: **Protected**
Scripture: **Psalm 59:9** NCV
God, my strength, I am looking to you, because God is my defender.

CALANDRA, Calandria, Calendra, Kalandra, Kalandria
Language/Cultural Origin: **Greek**
Inherent Meaning: **Lark**
Spiritual Connotation: **Created of God**
Scripture: **Genesis 1:21** TLB
So God created great sea animals, and every sort of fish and every kind of bird.

CALEB, Caeleb, Cale, Kaleb
Language/Cultural Origin: **Hebrew**
Inherent Meaning: **Faithful**
Spiritual Connotation: **Great Spiritual Potential**
Scripture: **Numbers 13:30** NKJV
Then Caleb quieted the people before Moses, and said, "Let us go up at once and take possession, for we are well able to overcome it."

CALHOUN, Colhoun
Language/Cultural Origin: **Scottish**
Inherent Meaning: **Strong Warrior**
Spiritual Connotation: **Great in Spirit**
Scripture: **Psalm 33:16** NKJV
No king is saved by the multitude of an army; a mighty man is not delivered by great strength.

CALLAHAN, Calahan, Callaghan
Language/Cultural Origin: **Irish**
Inherent Meaning: **Saint**
Spiritual Connotation: **Faithful**
Scripture: **1 Samuel 2:9** NRSV
He will guard the feet of his faithful ones, but the wicked shall be cut off in darkness; for not by might does one prevail.

CALLIE, Caleigh, Cali, Callee, Calleigh, Calli, Cally (see also Kalei, Kali, Kalli)
Language/Cultural Origin: **Middle Eastern**
Inherent Meaning: **Fortress**
Spiritual Connotation: **Guarded of God**
Scripture: **Psalm 46:7** NLT
The LORD Almighty is here among us; the God of Israel is our fortress.

CALLISTA, Calesta, Calista, Calysta, Kalesta, Kalista, Kallista, Kalysta
Language/Cultural Origin: **Greek**
Inherent Meaning: **Most Beautiful**
Spiritual Connotation: **Lovely**
Scripture: **Song of Songs 2:14** NKJV
O my dove . . . Let me see your face, let me hear your voice; for your voice is sweet, and your face is lovely.

CALLON, see Caelen

CALLUM, Callam, Calum
Language/Cultural Origin: **Irish**
Inherent Meaning: **Dove**
Spiritual Connotation: **Free**
Scripture: **Psalm 55:6** NKJV
So I said, "Oh, that I had wings like a dove! I would fly away and be at rest."

CALVERT
Language/Cultural Origin: **Old English**
Inherent Meaning: **Cattle Herder**
Spiritual Connotation: **Lover of All Creatures**
Scripture: **Psalm 9:2** NKJV
I will be glad and rejoice in You; I will sing praise to Your name, O Most High.

CALVIN, Cal

Language/Cultural Origin: **Latin**
Inherent Meaning: **Bald**
Spiritual Connotation: **Favored**
Scripture: **Proverbs 22:20-21** NKJV
Have I not written to you excellent things of counsels and knowledge . . . that you may answer words of truth to those who send to you?

CAMBRIA, Camberlee, Camberleigh, Camberly, Cambrea, Cambrya, Kamberly, Kambria, Kambriea

Language/Cultural Origin: **Latin**
Inherent Meaning: **From Wales**
Spiritual Connotation: **Delivered**
Scripture: **Colossians 1:13** NRSV
He has rescued us from the power of darkness and transferred us into the kingdom of his beloved Son.

CAMDEN, Camdan

Language/Cultural Origin: **Old English**
Inherent Meaning: **From the Winding Valley**
Spiritual Connotation: **Freedom**
Scripture: **John 8:32** NKJV
And you shall know the truth, and the truth shall make you free.

CAMELLIA, Camala, Camalia, Camelia, Camella, Kamalia, Kamelia, Kamellia

Language/Cultural Origin: **Italian**
Inherent Meaning: **Evergreen**
Spiritual Connotation: **Persistent**
Scripture: **1 Thessalonians 2:8** NRSV
So deeply do we care for you that we are determined to share with you not only the gospel of God but also our own selves, because you have become very dear to us.

CAMERON, Cam, Cameran, Camren, Camron, Kam, Kameron, Kamron

Language/Cultural Origin: **Scottish**
Inherent Meaning: **From the Crooked Stream**
Spiritual Connotation: **Spiritual Potential**
Scripture: **Psalm 36:9** NKJV
For with You is the fountain of life; in Your light we see light.

CAMI, Cammi, Cammie, Cammy (see also Kami)

Language/Cultural Origin: **French**
Inherent Meaning: **Ceremonial Attendant**
Spiritual Connotation: **Helper**
Scripture: **Hebrews 13:6** NKJV
So we may boldly say: The LORD is my helper; I will not fear. What can man do to me?

CAMILLE, Camila, Camill, Camilla, Cammille, Chamelle, Chamille

Language/Cultural Origin: **Latin**
Inherent Meaning: **Devoted**
Spiritual Connotation: **Loving**
Scripture: **1 John 4:7** NCV
Dear friends, we should love each other, because love comes from God. Everyone who loves has become God's child and knows God.

CAMPBELL, Cambell

Language/Cultural Origin: **French**
Inherent Meaning: **Beautiful Field**
Spiritual Connotation: **Consistent**
Scripture: **Proverbs 24:21** NRSV
My child, fear the LORD and the king, and do not disobey either of them.

CANAAN, Caenan, Caynon

Language/Cultural Origin: **Hebrew**
Inherent Meaning: **Lowland**
Spiritual Connotation: **Covenant**
Scripture: **Hebrews 11:9** NCV
It was by faith that he lived like a foreigner in the country God promised to give him.

CANDACE, Candice, Candy, Candyce, Kandace, Kandise, Kandy

Language/Cultural Origin: **Greek**
Inherent Meaning: **Unblemished**
Spiritual Connotation: **Shining**
Scripture: **Isaiah 62:3** NKJV
You shall also be a crown of glory In the hand of the LORD, and a royal diadem in the hand of your God.

CANDRA, Candrea, Candria, Kandra

Language/Cultural Origin: **Latin**
Inherent Meaning: **Incandescent**

Spiritual Connotation: **Reflection of Christ**
Scripture: **Matthew 5:15** NRSV
*No one after lighting a lamp puts it under
the bushel basket, but on the lampstand,
and it gives light to all in the house.*

**CANNON, Cannan, Cannen,
Canning, Canon (see also
Kannon)**
Language/Cultural Origin: **French**
Inherent Meaning: **Church Official**
Spiritual Connotation: **Esteemed**
Scripture: **1 Timothy 5:17** NASB
*Let the elders who rule well be considered
worthy of double honor, especially those
who work hard at preaching and teaching.*

CANUTE, see Knute

**CARA, Caragh, Carah, Carra (see
also Kara, Kerani)**
Language/Cultural Origin: **Latin**
Inherent Meaning: **Beloved**
Spiritual Connotation: **Chosen**
Scripture: **Matthew 25:34** NKJV
*Come, you blessed of My Father, inherit
the kingdom prepared for you from the
foundation of the world.*

**CAREY, Caray, Carrey (see also
Caryn, Kerry)**
Language/Cultural Origin: **Welsh**
Inherent Meaning: **Castle**
Spiritual Connotation: **Dependent**
Scripture: **Psalm 91:2** NKJV
*I will say of the LORD, He is my refuge
and my fortress; My God, in Him I will
trust.*

**CARI, Carie, Carii (see also Carrie,
Kari)**
Language/Cultural Origin: **Turkish**
Inherent Meaning: **Flowing Like Water**
Spiritual Connotation: **Filled With Life**
Scripture: **Psalm 104:10** TLB
*He placed springs in the valleys and
streams that gush from the mountains.*

CARIANNE, see Karianne

**CARINA, Carena (see also Corina,
Kaarina, Karena, Karina, Korina)**
Language/Cultural Origin: **Italian**

Inherent Meaning: **Dear Little One**
Spiritual Connotation: **Precious**
Scripture: **Mark 9:37** NKJV
*Whoever receives one of these little
children in My name receives Me; and
whoever receives Me, receives not Me
but Him who sent Me.*

**CARISSA, Cariisa, Carisa, Carrissa,
Charisa, Charissa, Kariisa, Karisa,
Karissa, Karrisa, Karrissa, Karyssa
(see also Corissa)**
Language/Cultural Origin: **Latin**
Inherent Meaning: **Ingenious**
Spiritual Connotation: **Creative**
Scripture: **Hebrews 13:20** NCV
*I pray that the God of peace will give you
every good thing you need so you can do
what he wants.*

CARITA, Caritta, Karita, Karitta
Language/Cultural Origin: **Latin**
Inherent Meaning: **Loving**
Spiritual Connotation: **Preserved**
Scripture: **Isaiah 42:6** NASB
*I am the LORD, I have called you in
righteousness, I will also hold you by the
hand and watch over you.*

**CARL, Carel, Carle, Carlis, Karal,
Karel, Karl, Karle, Karlis**
Language/Cultural Origin: **German**
Inherent Meaning: **Tiller of the Soil**
Spiritual Connotation: **Strong in Spirit**
Scripture: **Isaiah 40:31** NKJV
*But those who wait on the LORD shall
renew their strength; they shall mount
up with wings like eagles, they shall run
and not be weary, they shall walk and
not faint.*

CARLA, Carlia, Karla, Karlia
Language/Cultural Origin: **Italian**
Inherent Meaning: **Endearing**
Spiritual Connotation: **Ransomed**
Scripture: **Isaiah 49:15** NKJV
*Can a woman forget her nursing child,
and not have compassion on the son of
her womb? Surely they may forget, yet I
will not forget you.*

CARLANA, Carlæna, Karlana
Language/Cultural Origin: Irish
Inherent Meaning: Little Heroine
Spiritual Connotation: Conscientious
Scripture: Judges 4:9 NLT
The Lord's victory over Sisera will be at the hands of a woman.

CARLENE, Carleen, Karlene, Karleen
Language/Cultural Origin: Old English
Inherent Meaning: Womanly
Spiritual Connotation: Respectful
Scripture: Titus 2:3 NASB
Older women likewise are to be reverent in their behavior.

CARLIN, Carlan, Carlen, Carlii, Carling, Carlyn, Karlan, Karleigh, Karlen, Karlii, Karling (see also Carly)
Language/Cultural Origin: Irish
Inherent Meaning: Champion
Spiritual Connotation: Protected
Scripture: Isaiah 42:6 NKJV
I, the LORD, have called you in righteousness, and will hold your hand; I will keep you and give you as a covenant to the people, as a light to the Gentiles.

CARLINA, Carleena, Carliana, Karleena, Karlina, Karliana (see also Carlana)
Language/Cultural Origin: English
Inherent Meaning: Little Champion
Spiritual Connotation: Victor
Scripture: Romans 8:37 NKJV
Yet in all these things we are more than conquerors through Him who loved us.

CARLISLE, Carlyle, Carlysle
Language/Cultural Origin: Old English
Inherent Meaning: Brave
Spiritual Connotation: Defender of Wisdom
Scripture: Proverbs 4:7 NKJV
Wisdom is the principal thing; therefore get wisdom. And in all your getting, get understanding.

CARLISSA, Carlisa, Carlise, Carlisha, Carlissia, Karlisa, Karlissa, Karlise, Karlisha, Karlissia
Language/Cultural Origin: American
Inherent Meaning: Endeared
Spiritual Connotation: Consecrated to God
Scripture: Romans 8:33 NCV
Who can accuse the people God has chosen? No one, because God is the One who makes them right.

CARLOS, Carlo, Karlo, Karlos
Language/Cultural Origin: Spanish
Inherent Meaning: Noble Spirit
Spiritual Connotation: Spiritual Discernment
Scripture: Hebrews 5:14 NASB
But solid food is for the mature, who because of practice have their senses trained to discern good and evil.

CARLOTTA, Karlotta
Language/Cultural Origin: Italian
Inherent Meaning: Womanly
Spiritual Connotation: Godly Heroine
Scripture: 1 Peter 3:4 NCV
No, your beauty should come from within you—the beauty of a gentle and quiet spirit that will never be destroyed and is very precious to God.

CARLTON, Carleton, Carltonn (see also Charlton)
Language/Cultural Origin: Middle English
Inherent Meaning: From the Gathering of the Farmers
Spiritual Connotation: Industrious
Scripture: Ezekiel 34:27 NKJV
Then the trees of the field shall yield their fruit, and the earth shall yield her increase. They shall be safe in their land; and they shall know that I am the LORD.

CARLY, Carlee, Carley, Carli, Carlie, Karlee, Karley, Karli, Karlie, Karly (see also Carlin)
Language/Cultural Origin: English
Inherent Meaning: Little Woman/Little Man
Spiritual Connotation: Innocent
Scripture: Matthew 11:25 NLT
O Father, Lord of heaven and earth, thank you for hiding the truth from those

who think themselves so wise and clever,
and for revealing it to the childlike.

CARMELA, Carmalla, Carmelia, Carmelita, Carmella, Carmellina
Language/Cultural Origin: **Italian**
Inherent Meaning: **Garden**
Spiritual Connotation: **Nurtured of God**
Scripture: **Isaiah 58:11** TLB
And the Lord will guide you continually,
and satisfy you with all good things, and
keep you healthy too; and you will be
like a well-watered garden, like an ever-
flowing spring.

CARMEN, Carmaine, Carman, Carmene, Carmon, Karman, Karmen, Karmin, Karmon
Language/Cultural Origin: **Latin**
Inherent Meaning: **Voice Like Soft Music**
Spiritual Connotation: **Joyful**
Scripture: **Psalm 149:1** NRSV
Praise the LORD! Sing to the LORD a new
song, his praise in the assembly of the
faithful.

CARMI, Carmee, Carmey, Carmie, ☞ Karmey, Karmie
Language/Cultural Origin: **Hebrew**
Inherent Meaning: **My Vineyard**
Spiritual Connotation: **Responsible**
Scripture: **Proverbs 31:16** NKJV
She considers a field and buys it; from
her profits she plants a vineyard.

CARMICHAEL, Charmikael
Language/Cultural Origin: **Latin**
Inherent Meaning: **Follower of Michael**
Spiritual Connotation: **Abundant Power**
Scripture: **Philippians 4:13** KJV
I can do all things through Christ which
strengtheneth me.

CARMIEL, Carmiah, Carmiela, Carmielle, Carmiya, Karmiah, Karmiel, Karmiela, Karmielle
Language/Cultural Origin: **Hebrew**
Inherent Meaning: **God Is My Wisdom**
Spiritual Connotation: **Secure**
Scripture: **Proverbs 28:26** TLB
A man is a fool to trust himself! But
those who use God's wisdom are safe.

CARNEY, Karney
Language/Cultural Origin: **Irish**
Inherent Meaning: **Victorious**
Spiritual Connotation: **Preserved**
Scripture: **Psalm 32:7** NASB
You are my hiding place; You preserve
me from trouble; You surround me with
songs of deliverance.

CAROL, Carel, Carole, Karole, Karrole (see also Carrol)
Language/Cultural Origin: **French**
Inherent Meaning: **Song of Joy**
Spiritual Connotation: **Joy of God**
Scripture: **John 15:11** KJV
These things have I spoken unto you,
that my joy might remain in you, and
that your joy might be full.

CAROLEE, Carolea, Caroleigh
Language/Cultural Origin: **American**
Inherent Meaning: **Little Beloved**
Spiritual Connotation: **Just**
Scripture: **John 7:24** NCV
Stop judging by the way things look, but
judge by what is really right.

CAROLINE, Caralin, Caraline, Carolin, Carolina, Carolyn, Carrolin, Carroline (see also Carlin, Karilynn, Karolyn)
Language/Cultural Origin: **French**
Inherent Meaning: **Womanly**
Spiritual Connotation: **Filled With Praise**
Scripture: **Psalm 150:6** NKJV
Let everything that has breath praise the
LORD. Praise the LORD!

CARON, Carron, Carrone
Language/Cultural Origin: **Welsh**
Inherent Meaning: **Loving**
Spiritual Connotation: **Witness**
Scripture: **John 13:34** NASB
A new commandment I give to you, that
you love one another.

CARRICK, Karrick (see also Garrick)
Language/Cultural Origin: **Irish**
Inherent Meaning: **Surrounded by Sea**
Spiritual Connotation: **Child of God**
Scripture: **Jeremiah 31:33** NKJV

But this is the covenant that I will make with the house of Israel after those days, says the LORD. . . . I will be their God, and they shall be My people.

CARRIE, Carree, Carri, Karrie, Karry (see also Cari, Kari)
Language/Cultural Origin: **English**
Inherent Meaning: **Beloved**
Spiritual Connotation: **Redeemed**
Scripture: **Romans 5:8** NKJV
But God demonstrates His own love toward us, in that while we were still sinners, Christ died for us.

CARROL, Carell, Caroll, Carroll (see also Carol)
Language/Cultural Origin: **Gaelic**
Inherent Meaning: **Champion**
Spiritual Connotation: **Steadfast**
Scripture: **Hebrews 12:1** NRSV
Therefore . . . let us also lay aside every weight and the sin that clings so closely, and let us run with perseverance the race that is set before us.

CARSON, Carrson
Language/Cultural Origin: **English**
Inherent Meaning: **Son of the Marsh-Dweller**
Spiritual Connotation: **Loyal**
Scripture: **John 15:16** NKJV
You did not choose Me, but I chose you and appointed you that you should go and bear fruit, and that your fruit should remain.

CARTER, Cartar
Language/Cultural Origin: **Old English**
Inherent Meaning: **Driver of a Cart**
Spiritual Connotation: **Privileged**
Scripture: **Revelation 3:8** NASB
I know your deeds. Behold, I have put before you an open door which no one can shut.

CARY, Caree, Carree, Carry (see also Carey, Kerry)
Language/Cultural Origin: **Latin**
Inherent Meaning: **Beloved**
Spiritual Connotation: **Divine**
Scripture: **2 Peter 1:4** NRSV

Thus he has given us . . . his precious and very great promises, so that through them you may . . . become participants of the divine nature.

CARYN, Caren, Carin, Carran, Carren, Carrin, Carynn (see also Karen, Karin)
Language/Cultural Origin: **Danish**
Inherent Meaning: **Unblemished**
Spiritual Connotation: **Blameless**
Scripture: **Job 8:20** NKJV
Behold, God will not cast away the blameless, Nor will He uphold the evildoers.

CARYS, Caris, Carissa, Carris, Caryss (see also Karis)
Language/Cultural Origin: **Welsh**
Inherent Meaning: **Loving**
Spiritual Connotation: **Respectful**
Scripture: **Matthew 19:19** NKJV
"Honor your father and your mother," and, "you shall love your neighbor as yourself."

CASEY, Cacey, Cacy, Case, Casie, Casy, Caysee, Caysey, Caysie, K.C., Kace, Kacee, Kacey, Kaci, Kacie, Kacy, Kaicey, Kasee, Kasey, Kasie, Kaycee, Kaycie, Kaysea, Kaysee, Kaysey
Language/Cultural Origin: **Irish**
Inherent Meaning: **Valorous**
Spiritual Connotation: **Leader**
Scripture: **1 John 5:4** NKJV
For whatever is born of God overcomes the world. And this is the victory that has overcome the world; our faith.

CASIMIR, Cachie, Cash, Cashmere, Cashmir, Kashmere, Kasimir, Kasmir, Kasmira, Kazmir, Kazmira
Language/Cultural Origin: **Old Slavic**
Inherent Meaning: **Peacemaker**
Spiritual Connotation: **Flexible**
Scripture: **Matthew 5:9** NRSV
Blessed are the peacemakers, for they will be called children of God.

CASPER, Caspar
Language/Cultural Origin: **Persian**

Inherent Meaning: **Treasurer**
Spiritual Connotation: **Watchful**
Scripture: **Matthew 25:21** NKJV
I will make you ruler over many things.
Enter into the joy of your lord.

CASSANDRA, Casandera, Casandra, Casandria, Casaundra, Casaundria, Casondra, Cassaundra, Cassey, Cassi, Cassie, Cassondra, Cassondria, Cassundra, Cassy, Kasandra, Kasaundra, Kasondra, Kasoundra, Kassandra, Kassaundra, Kassey, Kassi, Kassie, Kassy, Krisandra, Krissandra

Language/Cultural Origin: **Greek**
Inherent Meaning: **Helper of Mankind**
Spiritual Connotation: **Hostess**
Scripture: **Hebrews 13:2** NASB
Do not neglect to show hospitality to strangers, for by this some have entertained angels without knowing it.

CASSIA, Casia, Casiya, Cassya, Casya, Kasia, Kasiya, Kassia, Kasya

Language/Cultural Origin: **Greek**
Inherent Meaning: **Spicy Cinnamon**
Spiritual Connotation: **Treasured**
Scripture: **Song of Songs 4:10** NCV
Your love is so sweet, my sister, my bride. Your love is better than wine, and your perfume smells better than any spice.

CASSIDY, Cass, Cassady, Kass, Kassady, Kassidy

Language/Cultural Origin: **Irish**
Inherent Meaning: **Clever**
Spiritual Connotation: **Wise**
Scripture: **1 Corinthians 10:15** TLB
You are intelligent people. Look now and see for yourselves whether what I am about to say is true.

CASSIUS, Caz, Cazzie

Language/Cultural Origin: **Latin**
Inherent Meaning: **Protective Cover**
Spiritual Connotation: **Guarded**
Scripture: **Psalm 3:3** NASB

But You, O LORD, are a shield about me, My glory, and the One who lifts my head.

CASSON, Cassón, Kasson

Language/Cultural Origin: **English**
Inherent Meaning: **Helper of Mankind**
Spiritual Connotation: **Protected of God**
Scripture: **Proverbs 30:5** NKJV
Every word of God is pure; He is a shield to those who put their trust in Him.

CATALINA, Catalena, Katalena, Katalina

Language/Cultural Origin: **Spanish**
Inherent Meaning: **Unblemished**
Spiritual Connotation: **Refined**
Scripture: **Daniel 12:10** NASB
Many will be purged, purified and refined, but the wicked will act wickedly; and none of the wicked will understand, but those who have insight will understand.

CATAVA, Catavah, Katava

Language/Cultural Origin: **African**
Inherent Meaning: **Restful**
Spiritual Connotation: **Bringer of Peace**
Scripture: **Zechariah 1:11** NRSV
We have patrolled the earth, and lo, the whole earth remains at peace.

CATERINA, see Katerina

CATHERINE, Cat, Catharina, Catharine, Catheren, Catherin, Catherina, Catheryn, Cathrine, Cathryn (see also Katherine)

Language/Cultural Origin: **Greek**
Inherent Meaning: **Pure**
Spiritual Connotation: **Accountable**
Scripture: **Psalm 119:15-16** NKJV
I will meditate on Your precepts, and contemplate Your ways. I will delight myself in Your statutes; I will not forget Your word.

CATHLEEN, Cathaleen, Cathlene (see also Kathleen)

Language/Cultural Origin: **Irish**
Inherent Meaning: **Unblemished**
Spiritual Connotation: **Spotless**
Scripture: **Romans 6:16** NASB

*You are slaves of the one whom you
obey, either of sin resulting in death, or of
obedience resulting in righteousness.*

CATHY, Cathee, Cathey, Cathi, Cathie, Kathee, Kathey, Kathi, Kathie, Kathy
Language/Cultural Origin: **English**
Inherent Meaning: **Spotless**
Spiritual Connotation: **Sanctified**
Scripture: **Philippians 1:6** NASB
*For I am confident of this very thing, that
He who began a good work in you will
perfect it until the day of Christ Jesus.*

CATO, Catón (see also Kato)
Language/Cultural Origin: **Latin**
Inherent Meaning: **Wise**
Spiritual Connotation: **Servant**
Scripture: **Romans 12:16** NRSV
*Live in harmony with one another; do not
be haughty, but associate with the lowly;
do not claim to be wiser than you are.*

CATRINA, see Katrina

CATRIONA, Katriona
Language/Cultural Origin: **Irish**
Inherent Meaning: **Flawless**
Spiritual Connotation: **Perfect**
Scripture: **Matthew 5:48** NKJV
*Therefore you shall be perfect, just as
your Father in heaven is perfect.*

CAVAN, Caven, Cavin, Kavan (see also Kevin)
Language/Cultural Origin: **Irish**
Inherent Meaning: **Handsome**
Spiritual Connotation: **Blessed**
Scripture: **Psalm 45:2** TLB
*You are the fairest of all; your words are
filled with grace; God himself is blessing
you forever.*

CAVANAUGH
Language/Cultural Origin: **Irish**
Inherent Meaning: **Caring**
Spiritual Connotation: **Discerning**
Scripture: **Galatians 6:2** NKJV
*Bear one another's burdens, and so fulfill
the law of Christ.*

CAYLA, Caela, Caila, Cailah, Caylah (see also Kaela, Kaila, Kayla, Kyla)
Language/Cultural Origin: **Hebrew**
Inherent Meaning: **Empowered**
Spiritual Connotation: **Spirit-Filled**
Scripture: **Acts 1:8** NKJV
*But you shall receive power when the
Holy Spirit has come upon you; and you
shall be witnesses to Me in Jerusalem,
and in all Judea and Samaria, and to the
end of the earth.*

CECIL, Cecile, Cécile, Cecill
Language/Cultural Origin: **Latin**
Inherent Meaning: **Blind**
Spiritual Connotation: **Illuminated**
Scripture: **Ephesians 5:8** NKJV
*For you were once darkness, but now
you are light in the Lord. Walk as
children of light.*

CECILIA, Cacelia, Caecilia, Cece, Cecelia, Cecilea, Cecillia, CeeCee
Language/Cultural Origin: **Latin**
Inherent Meaning: **Blind**
Spiritual Connotation: **Of the Spirit**
Scripture: **1 Corinthians 2:12** NCV
*Now we did not receive the spirit of the
world, but we received the Spirit that is
from God so that we can know all that
God has given us.*

CEDRIC, Cedrec, Cédric, Cedrik
Language/Cultural Origin: **English**
Inherent Meaning: **Battle Chieftain**
Spiritual Connotation: **Courageous Defender**
Scripture: **Galatians 6:4** NKJV
*But let each one examine his own work,
and then he will have rejoicing in himself
alone, and not in another.*

CEELEY, Ceelee, Ceeleigh, Ceelie, Ceely, Seelee, Seeleigh, Seeley, Seelie, Seely
Language/Cultural Origin: **Old English**
Inherent Meaning: **Blessed**
Spiritual Connotation: **Favored**
Scripture: **Hebrews 13:9** NLT
*So do not be attracted by strange, new
ideas. Your spiritual strength comes from
God's special favor.*

CELENA, see Selena

CELESTE, Celesta, Celestia, Celestial, Celestine
Language/Cultural Origin: **French**
Inherent Meaning: **Heavenly**
Spiritual Connotation: **Blessed**
Scripture: **Ephesians 1:3** NKJV
Blessed be the God and Father of our Lord Jesus Christ, who has blessed us with every spiritual blessing in the heavenly places in Christ.

CELINE, Celene, Celinda, Céline
Language/Cultural Origin: **English**
Inherent Meaning: **Fair as the Moon**
Spiritual Connotation: **Lovely**
Scripture: **Song of Songs 5:9** NKJV
What is your beloved more than another beloved, O fairest among women? What is your beloved more than another beloved, that you so charge us?

CEPHAS, Cephus
☞ Language/Cultural Origin: **Aramaic**
Inherent Meaning: **Rock**
Spiritual Connotation: **Foundation**
Scripture: **Matthew 16:18** NLT
Now I say to you that you are Peter, and upon this rock I will build my church, and all the powers of hell will not conquer it.

CERELLA, Cerelisa
Language/Cultural Origin: **Latin**
Inherent Meaning: **Springtime**
Spiritual Connotation: **Gentle**
Scripture: **Psalm 72:6** TLB
May the reign of this son of mine be as gentle and fruitful as the springtime rains upon the grass—like showers that water the earth!

CÉRISE, Cerese, Ceri, Cerice, Cerissa, Cerrice, Cerrina, Ceryce (see also Cherise)
Language/Cultural Origin: **French**
Inherent Meaning: **Cherry**
Spiritual Connotation: **Ageless**
Scripture: **Psalm 92:14** NCV
When they are old, they will still produce fruit; they will be healthy and fresh.

CHADWICK, Chad, Chadd, Chadley, Chadrick, Chadron, Chadwyck
Language/Cultural Origin: **Middle English**
Inherent Meaning: **From the Warrior's Town**
Spiritual Connotation: **Privileged**
Scripture: **Revelation 22:1** RSV
Then he showed me the river of the water of life, bright as crystal, flowing from the throne of God and of the Lamb.

CHAI, Chae (see also Chay)
Language/Cultural Origin: **Hebrew**
Inherent Meaning: **Healthy**
Spiritual Connotation: **Eternal**
Scripture: **John 6:27** NKJV
Do not labor for the food which perishes, but for the food which endures to everlasting life.

CHAIM, Khaim
Language/Cultural Origin: **Hebrew**
Inherent Meaning: **Life**
Spiritual Connotation: **Discerning**
Scripture: **John 12:25** NLT
Those who love their life in this world will lose it. Those who despise their life in this world will keep it for eternal life.

CHALICE, Chalace, Chalcie, Chalise, Chalissa, Challis, Challisse, Chalsey
Language/Cultural Origin: **French**
Inherent Meaning: **Goblet**
Spiritual Connotation: **Cheerful**
Scripture: **Proverbs 15:15** NRSV
All the days of the poor are hard, but a cheerful heart has a continual feast.

CHALINA, Chaleena, Chara, Charah
Language/Cultural Origin: **Hispanic**
Inherent Meaning: **Rose**
Spiritual Connotation: **Joy**
Scripture: **Isaiah 35:1** NKJV
The wilderness and the wasteland shall be glad for them, And the desert shall rejoice and blossom as the rose.

CHALMERS, Chalmer, Chamar
Language/Cultural Origin: **Scottish**
Inherent Meaning: **Head of the Household**
Spiritual Connotation: **Prosperous Protector**

Scripture: **Isaiah 55:11** NKJV
So shall My word be that goes forth from My mouth; It shall not return to Me void.

CHAMADYA, Chamadaea, Chamadia
Language/Cultural Origin: **Hebrew**
Inherent Meaning: **Desired**
Spiritual Connotation: **Blessed**
Scripture: **Psalm 45:2** TLB
You are the fairest of all; Your words are filled with grace; God himself is blessing you forever.

CHAN, Chanae, Chann, Chayo
Language/Cultural Origin: **Cambodian**
Inherent Meaning: **Sweet-Smelling Tree**
Spiritual Connotation: **Image of God**
Scripture: **Ephesians 5:2** NCV
Live a life of love just as Christ loved us and gave himself for us as a sweet-smelling offering and sacrifice to God.

CHANAH, Chana, Channa
Language/Cultural Origin: **Hebrew**
Inherent Meaning: **Favor of God**
Spiritual Connotation: **Prayerful**
Scripture: **Malachi 1:9** NKJV
But now entreat God's favor, that He may be gracious to us.

CHANAN, Chanen
Language/Cultural Origin: **Hebrew**
Inherent Meaning: **Cloud**
Spiritual Connotation: **Provision**
Scripture: **Exodus 13:22** NKJV
He did not take away the pillar of cloud by day or the pillar of fire by night from before the people.

CHANDELLE, Chandal, Chandel, Shandal, Shandel, Shandelle
Language/Cultural Origin: **French**
Inherent Meaning: **Candle**
Spiritual Connotation: **Witness**
Scripture: **Matthew 5:14** NCV
You are the light that gives light to the world. A city that is built on a hill cannot be hidden.

CHANDLER, Chandan, Chandlan, Chandon, Chanlan
Language/Cultural Origin: **English**
Inherent Meaning: **Candle Maker**
Spiritual Connotation: **Bearer of Light**
Scripture: **John 8:12** NKJV
I am the light of the world. He who follows Me shall not walk in darkness, but have the light of life.

CHANDRA, Chanda, Chandea, Chandee, Chandre, Chandrelle, Chandria, Shandra, Shandee, Shandrelle, Shandria
Language/Cultural Origin: **Indo-Pakistani**
Inherent Meaning: **Fair as the Moon**
Spiritual Connotation: **Lovely**
Scripture: **Song of Songs 1:8** NCV
You are the most beautiful of women.

CHANEL, Chanell, Chanelle, Channel, Shanel, Shanell, Shanelle, Shannel
Language/Cultural Origin: **English**
Inherent Meaning: **Channel**
Spiritual Connotation: **Abundance**
Scripture: **Psalm 78:16** RSV
He made streams come out of the rock, and caused waters to flow down like rivers.

CHANEY, Chayne, Chayney, Cheney, Cheyne, Cheyney
Language/Cultural Origin: **Old French**
Inherent Meaning: **Oak Wood**
Spiritual Connotation: **Sealed**
Scripture: **1 Chronicles 16:33** NASB
Then the trees of the forest will sing for joy before the LORD; for He is coming to judge the earth.

CHANNING, Chane, Chaning, Chann
Language/Cultural Origin: **English**
Inherent Meaning: **Wise**
Spiritual Connotation: **Obedient**
Scripture: **Deuteronomy 4:6** NCV
Obey these laws carefully, in order to show the other nations that you have wisdom and understanding.

CHANTAL, Chantael, Chantalle, Chantara, Chantay, Chantée, Chantel, Chantell, Chantiel, Chantielle, Chantil, Chantill,

Chantoya, Chantrel, Chantrell, Chauntay, Chauntel, Chauntell, Chauntelle, (see also Shantel)
Language/Cultural Origin: **French**
Inherent Meaning: **Song**
Spiritual Connotation: **Healed**
Scripture: **Isaiah 49:13** NKJV
Sing, O heavens! Be joyful, O earth!
And break out in singing, O mountains!
For the LORD has comforted His people,
and will have mercy on His afflicted.

CHANTE, Chánte, Chanté, Chantha, Chantra (see also Shantae)
Language/Cultural Origin: **French**
Inherent Meaning: **Singer**
Spiritual Connotation: **Treasured**
Scripture: **Zephaniah 3:17** NKJV
The LORD your God in your midst, the
Mighty One, will save; He will rejoice
over you with gladness, He will quiet you
with His love, He will rejoice over you
with singing.

CHANTREA, Chantria
Language/Cultural Origin: **Cambodian**
Inherent Meaning: **Moonbeam**
Spiritual Connotation: **Symbol**
Scripture: **Psalm 136:9** NCV
He made the moon and stars to rule the
night. His love continues forever.

CHANTRICE, Chantreese, Shantreece, Shantrice
Language/Cultural Origin: **French**
Inherent Meaning: **Singer**
Spiritual Connotation: **Joyful**
Scripture: **Psalm 126:2** NKJV
Then our mouth was filled with laughter,
and our tongue with singing. Then they
said among the nations, the LORD has
done great things for them.

CHAPMAN, Chapmann
Language/Cultural Origin: **English**
Inherent Meaning: **Merchant**
Spiritual Connotation: **Wise**
Scripture: **Matthew 13:45-46** NKJV
Again, the kingdom of heaven is like a
merchant seeking beautiful pearls, who,
when he had found one pearl of great

price, went and sold all that he had and
bought it.

CHARISSA, Charesa, Charis, Charisa, Charisse, Charista, Sharesa, Sharese, Sharis, Sharisa, Sharissa, Sharisse, Sharista, Sheresa, Sherisa, Sherise, Sherissa, Sherisse, Sherista
Language/Cultural Origin: **English**
Inherent Meaning: **Kindness**
Spiritual Connotation: **Virtuous**
Scripture: **Proverbs 31:26** NKJV
She opens her mouth with wisdom, and
on her tongue is the law of kindness.

CHARITY, Charitee, Chariti
Language/Cultural Origin: **English**
Inherent Meaning: **Benevolent**
Spiritual Connotation: **Compassionate**
Scripture: **Psalm 23:6** KJV
Surely goodness and mercy shall follow
me all the days of my life: and I will
dwell in the house of the LORD for ever.

CHARLEEN, Charlaine, Charlanna, Charlena, Charlene, Charline, Sharlaina, Sharlanna, Sharleen, Sharlena, Sharlene
Language/Cultural Origin: **English**
Inherent Meaning: **Valiant**
Spiritual Connotation: **Courageous**
Scripture: **1 Chronicles 28:20** NKJV
Be strong and of good courage, and do
it; do not fear nor be dismayed, for the
LORD God; my God; will be with you.

CHARLES, Charle, Charley, Charlie
Language/Cultural Origin: **English**
Inherent Meaning: **Manly**
Spiritual Connotation: **Valiant**
Scripture: **Joshua 1:9** NKJV
Be strong and of good courage; do not
be afraid, nor be dismayed, for the LORD
your God is with you wherever you go.

CHARLOTTE, Charlette, Sharlotte
Language/Cultural Origin: **French**
Inherent Meaning: **Womanly**
Spiritual Connotation: **Joy to the Lord**
Scripture: **Zephaniah 3:17** RSV
The LORD, your God, is in your midst, a

warrior who gives victory; he will rejoice over you with gladness.

CHARLTON, Charleton, Charltonn (see also Carlton)
Language/Cultural Origin: **English**
Inherent Meaning: **From the Dwelling of the Free Peasants**
Spiritual Connotation: **Servant**
Scripture: **Matthew 23:11** NKJV
But he who is greatest among you shall be your servant. . . . He who humbles himself will be exalted.

CHARMAIN, Charmaine, Charmane, Charmayne, Charmian, Sharmain
Language/Cultural Origin: **Latin**
Inherent Meaning: **Singer**
Spiritual Connotation: **Joyful**
Scripture: **Jeremiah 15:16** NKJV
Your word was to me the joy and rejoicing of my heart; for I am called by Your name, O LORD God of hosts.

CHASADYA, Chasádia, Chasádya
Language/Cultural Origin: **Hebrew**
Inherent Meaning: **Mercy of God**
Spiritual Connotation: **Chosen**
Scripture: **Romans 9:16** NLT
So receiving God's promise is not up to us. We can't get it by choosing it or working hard for it. God will show mercy to anyone he chooses.

CHASE, Chaise
Language/Cultural Origin: **Old French**
Inherent Meaning: **Hunter**
Spiritual Connotation: **Pursuer of Truth**
Scripture: **Amos 5:8** TLB
Seek him who . . . turns darkness into morning and day into night, who calls forth the water from the ocean and pours it out as rain upon the land.

CHASTITY, Chasady, Chasiti, Chassady, Chassey, Chassidy, Chassie, Chassity, Chastady, Chastidy, Chastin, Chastney
Language/Cultural Origin: **Latin**
Inherent Meaning: **Pure**
Spiritual Connotation: **Virtuous**
Scripture: **Luke 11:34** NLT
Your eye is a lamp for your body. A pure eye lets sunshine into your soul.

CHASYA, Châsia
Language/Cultural Origin: **Hebrew**
Inherent Meaning: **Shield**
Spiritual Connotation: **Protected by God**
Scripture: **Psalm 2:12** NKJV
Blessed are all those who put their trust in Him.

CHAUNCEY, Chancey, Chauncy
Language/Cultural Origin: **Middle English**
Inherent Meaning: **Chancellor**
Spiritual Connotation: **Worthy of Trust**
Scripture: **Romans 8:16** NKJV
The Spirit Himself bears witness with our spirit that we are children of God.

CHAVA, Chavah, Chavalah, Chavarra, Chavé, Chavel, Chavvis, Kava
Language/Cultural Origin: **Yiddish**
Inherent Meaning: **Bird**
Spiritual Connotation: **Joyful**
Scripture: **Psalm 50:11** NASB
I know every bird of the mountains, and everything that moves in the field is Mine.

CHAVON, Chavonn, Chavonna, Chavonne, Chevon, Chevonn, Chevonna, Shavon, Shavón
Language/Cultural Origin: **Hebrew**
Inherent Meaning: **God Is Gracious**
Spiritual Connotation: **Cherished**
Scripture: **Psalm 103:8** NKJV
The LORD is merciful and gracious, slow to anger, and abounding in mercy.

CHAY, Cháy, Ché (see also Chai)
Language/Cultural Origin: **Spanish**
Inherent Meaning: **God Will Add**
Spiritual Connotation: **Dependent**
Scripture: **Philippians 4:19** NASB
And my God shall supply all your needs according to His riches in glory in Christ Jesus.

CHAYA, Chayka, Chayla, Chaylah, Chaylea, Chayley, Chayra
Language/Cultural Origin: **Hebrew**

Inherent Meaning: **Alive**
Spiritual Connotation: **Heavenly Treasure**
Scripture: **Matthew 19:29** NKJV
And everyone who has left houses or brothers or sisters or father or mother or wife or children or lands, for My name's sake, shall . . . inherit eternal life.

CHAYANNA, Chaeanna, Chayana
Language/Cultural Origin: **American**
Inherent Meaning: **Alive**
Spiritual Connotation: **Childlike**
Scripture: **John 1:4** TLB
Eternal life is in him, and this life gives light to all mankind.

CHAZ, Chazz
Language/Cultural Origin: **English**
Inherent Meaning: **Strong**
Spiritual Connotation: **Reverent**
Scripture: **Luke 12:5** NKJV
But I will show you whom you should fear: Fear Him who, after He has killed, has power to cast into hell.

CHAZAYA, Chazaia, Chazial, Chaziel, Chazielle
Language/Cultural Origin: **Hebrew**
Inherent Meaning: **God Has Seen**
Spiritual Connotation: **Remembered**
Scripture: **Genesis 31:42** NKJV
Unless the God of my father . . . had been with me, surely now you would have sent me away empty-handed.

CHAZON, Chazón
Language/Cultural Origin: **Hebrew**
Inherent Meaning: **Revelation**
Spiritual Connotation: **Disciple**
Scripture: **Galatians 1:12** NLT
For my message came by a direct revelation from Jesus Christ himself. No one else taught me.

CHELSEA, Chelcie, Chelcy, Chellsie, Chelsa, Chelsae, Chelsay, Chelsee, Chelsey, Chelsia, Chelsie, Chelsy, Cheslee, Chesley, Cheslie, Shelsea, Shelsee, Shelsie, Shelsey
Language/Cultural Origin: **Old English**
Inherent Meaning: **Seaport**
Spiritual Connotation: **Shield**

Scripture: **Psalm 65:5** NRSV
By awesome deeds you answer us with deliverance, O God of our salvation; you are the hope of all the ends of the earth and of the farthest seas.

CHELUB, Chélub, Cheylub
Language/Cultural Origin: **Hebrew**
Inherent Meaning: **Wicker Basket**
Spiritual Connotation: **Creative**
Scripture: **Exodus 31:3** NLT
I have filled him with the Spirit of God, giving him great wisdom, intelligence, and skill in all kinds of crafts.

CHERAN, Cherran, Cheranne (see also Sharon)
Language/Cultural Origin: **Hebrew**
Inherent Meaning: **Union**
Spiritual Connotation: **Harmonious**
Scripture: **Psalm 133:1** NRSV
How very good and pleasant it is when kindred live together in unity!

CHERIE, Cheri, Cherí, Chérie (see also Shari)
Language/Cultural Origin: **French**
Inherent Meaning: **Sweetheart**
Spiritual Connotation: **Valuable**
Scripture: **Proverbs 20:15** RSV
There is gold, and abundance of costly stones; but the lips of knowledge are a precious jewel.

CHERISE, Chareese, Charese, Charice, Charise, Cher, Cherice, Cherrise, Shareese, Sharese, Sharice, Sharise, Sher, Shereece, Sherese, Sherice, Sherrice (see also Cerise, Charissa)
Language/Cultural Origin: **French**
Inherent Meaning: **Treasured**
Spiritual Connotation: **Beloved**
Scripture: **Psalm 62:5** NKJV
My soul, wait silently for God alone, for my expectation is from Him.

CHERISH
Language/Cultural Origin: **English**
Inherent Meaning: **Precious**
Spiritual Connotation: **Inestimable**
Scripture: **Proverbs 31:10** NASB

An excellent wife, who can find? For her worth is far above jewels.

CHEROKEE, Cherika, Sherokee
Language/Cultural Origin: **Native American**
Inherent Meaning: **Tribe**
Spiritual Connotation: **Worshiper**
Scripture: **2 Chronicles 20:6** NLT
He prayed, O LORD, God of our ancestors, you alone are the God who is in heaven.

CHERYL, Charelle, Charil, Charrell, Charyl, Chereen, Chereena, Cherelle, Cherrelle, Cheryle (see also Sheryl)
Language/Cultural Origin: **French**
Inherent Meaning: **Filled With Grace**
Spiritual Connotation: **Beloved**
Scripture: **Zephaniah 3:17** RSV
The LORD, your God, is in your midst, a warrior who gives victory; he will rejoice over you with gladness.

CHESNA, Chesnee, Chesney, Chesnie
Language/Cultural Origin: **Slavic**
Inherent Meaning: **Peaceful**
Spiritual Connotation: **Regal Servant**
Scripture: **Isaiah 9:7** NASB
There will be no end to the increase of His government or of peace, on the throne of David and over his kingdom.

CHESTER, Ches, Cheston, Chet
Language/Cultural Origin: **Old English**
Inherent Meaning: **From the Campsite**
Spiritual Connotation: **Valiant Defender**
Scripture: **Psalm 31:3** NKJV
For You are my rock and my fortress; therefore, for Your name's sake, lead me and guide me.

CHEVY, Chev, Chevi, Chevie, Chevvy
Language/Cultural Origin: **American**
Inherent Meaning: **Knight**
Spiritual Connotation: **Victor**
Scripture: **Isaiah 9:3** NLT
Israel will again be great, and its people will rejoice. . . . They will shout with joy like warriors dividing the plunder.

CHEYENNE, Cheyan, Cheyana, Cheyann, Cheyanne, Cheyene, Cheyenna, Chi-Anna, Chyann, Chyanna, Chyanne, Sheyenne, Shiana, Shiane, Shianna, Shianne, Shyana, Shyanne, Shyenna
Language/Cultural Origin: **Native American**
Inherent Meaning: **Tribe**
Spiritual Connotation: **Creative**
Scripture: **Exodus 35:10** NKJV
All who are gifted artisans among you shall come and make all that the LORD has commanded.

CHIARA, Chiarah
Language/Cultural Origin: **Italian**
Inherent Meaning: **Clear**
Spiritual Connotation: **Sealed**
Scripture: **Revelation 21:21** NKJV
And the street of the city was pure gold, like transparent glass.

CHICKARA, Chickarra, Chikona
Language/Cultural Origin: **Japanese**
Inherent Meaning: **Near and Dear**
Spiritual Connotation: **Loving**
Scripture: **Romans 13:10** NLT
Love does no wrong to anyone, so love satisfies all of God's requirements.

CHIKO, Chikora
Language/Cultural Origin: **Japanese**
Inherent Meaning: **Pledge**
Spiritual Connotation: **Promise**
Scripture: **Acts 2:39** NKJV
For the promise is to you and to your children, and to all who are afar off, as many as the Lord our God will call.

CHILTON, Chiltonn
Language/Cultural Origin: **English**
Inherent Meaning: **From the Farm by the Spring**
Spiritual Connotation: **Refreshed**
Scripture: **Psalm 104:10** NKJV
He sends the springs into the valleys, they flow among the hills.

CHINARAH, Chinara, Chinika
Language/Cultural Origin: **Swahili**
Inherent Meaning: **God Receives**
Spiritual Connotation: **Offering to God**

Scripture: **Hebrews 7:8** NKJV
Here mortal men receive tithes, but there
he receives them, of whom it is witnessed
that he lives.

CHIP, Chipper
Language/Cultural Origin: **English**
Inherent Meaning: **Strong**
Spiritual Connotation: **Power of God**
Scripture: **Exodus 10:2** NLT
You will be able to tell wonderful stories
to your children and grandchildren about
the marvelous things I am doing . . . to
prove that I am the LORD.

CHISLON, Cheslin, Cheslon, ☞ Cheslyn, Chislan, Chislyn
Language/Cultural Origin: **Hebrew**
Inherent Meaning: **Trust**
Spiritual Connotation: **Dependent**
Scripture: **Proverbs 3:5-6** NASB
Trust in the LORD with all your heart,
and do not lean on your own understand-
ing. In all your ways acknowledge Him,
and He will make your paths straight.

CHLOE, Chloé, Chlöe, Chloee, Cloe, ☞ Cloey, Kloe, Klöe
Language/Cultural Origin: **Greek**
Inherent Meaning: **Vibrant**
Spiritual Connotation: **One Who Searches**
Scripture: **Psalm 105:4** NKJV
Seek the LORD and His strength; seek His
face evermore!

CHLORIS, Cloris, Clorissa
Language/Cultural Origin: **Greek**
Inherent Meaning: **Pale**
Spiritual Connotation: **Fair**
Scripture: **Psalm 45:2** NASB
You are fairer than the sons of men;
grace is poured upon Your lips; there-
fore God has blessed You forever.

CHONI, Chonee, Choney, Chonia, Chonie, Choniya, Chonya
Language/Cultural Origin: **Hebrew**
Inherent Meaning: **Gracious**
Spiritual Connotation: **Mercy of God**
Scripture: **Deuteronomy 4:31** RSV
The LORD your God is a merciful God;
he will not fail you or destroy you or

forget the covenant with your fathers
which he swore to them.

CHORESH, Choresch
Language/Cultural Origin: **Hebrew**
Inherent Meaning: **Thicket**
Spiritual Connotation: **God's Sacrifice**
Scripture: **Genesis 22:14** NASB
And Abraham called the name of that
place The LORD Will Provide.

CHOSEN, Chosan, Chósen
Language/Cultural Origin: **Hebrew**
Inherent Meaning: **Power**
Spiritual Connotation: **Immunity**
Scripture: **Mark 16:18** TLB
They will be able to place their hands on
the sick and heal them.

CHRISTA, Chris, Chrisa, Chrisie, Chrissey, Chrissi, Chrissie, Chrissy, Christi, Christie, Christy, Chrys, Chryssa, Chrysta, Chrysti, Chrystie, Chrysty, Cris, Crissa, Crissie, Crista, Cristee, Cristey, Cristi, Cristie, Cryssa, Crysta, Crysti, Crystie (see also Kirsty, Krista)
Language/Cultural Origin: **German**
Inherent Meaning: **Follower of Christ**
Spiritual Connotation: **God's Reflection**
Scripture: **John 13:35** NKJV
By this all will know that you are My dis-
ciples, if you have love for one another.

CHRISTEN, Christan, Christin, Christyn, Chrystan, Chrysten, Chrystin, Cristan, Cristen, Cristin, Cristyn, Crystan, Crysten, Crystin (see also Kristen)
Language/Cultural Origin: **English**
Inherent Meaning: **Follower of Christ**
Spiritual Connotation: **Obedient**
Scripture: **John 8:31** NCV
If you continue to obey my teaching, you
are truly my followers.

CHRISTIAN, Christiaan, Christianos, Christion, Christon, Christos, Christyan, Chrystian, Cristian, Cristiano, Cristón,

Khristian, Kristar, Krister, Kristjan, Krystian
Language/Cultural Origin: **Greek**
Inherent Meaning: **Follower of Christ**
Spiritual Connotation: **Anointed**
Scripture: **Acts 10:38** NASB
You know of Jesus of Nazareth, how God anointed Him with the Holy Spirit and with power, and how He went about doing good.

CHRISTINA, Christeena, Christena, Christiana, Christiane, Christiann, Christianna, Christinna, Christy-Anna, Cristeena, Cristina, Cristiona Crystina (see also Kristina)
Language/Cultural Origin: **Greek**
Inherent Meaning: **Follower of Christ**
Spiritual Connotation: **Awareness of Christ**
Scripture: **2 Corinthians 4:5** NRSV
For we do not proclaim ourselves; we proclaim Jesus Christ as Lord and ourselves as your slaves for Jesus' sake.

CHRISTINE, Christeen, Christene, Chrystine, Cristeen, Cristine, Crystine (see also Kristine)
Language/Cultural Origin: **French**
Inherent Meaning: **Follower of Christ**
Spiritual Connotation: **True Disciple**
Scripture: **Luke 9:23** NLT
If any of you wants to be my follower, you must put aside your selfish ambition, shoulder your cross daily, and follow me.

CHRISTOPHER, Chris, Chriss, Christepher, Christobal, Christofer, Christoff, Christoffer, Christophe, Christopherr, Christophor, Chrys, Cris, Cristóbal, Cristofer, Cristopher, Khris, Khriss, Khristofer, Khristoffer, Khristopher, Kris, Kriss, Kristofer, Kristophe, Kristopher, Kristophor, Krys
Language/Cultural Origin: **Greek**
Inherent Meaning: **Bearer/Carrier of Christ**
Spiritual Connotation: **Anointed**
Scripture: **Galatians 6:17** NIV
Finally, let no one cause me trouble, for I bear on my body the marks of Jesus.

CHUCK, Chuckie, Chucky
Language/Cultural Origin: **American**
Inherent Meaning: **Strong**
Spiritual Connotation: **Genuine**
Scripture: **Mark 12:30** NKJV
And you shall love the LORD your God with all your heart, with all your soul, with all your mind, and with all your strength.

CHUMA, Chumah
Language/Cultural Origin: **Rhodesian**
Inherent Meaning: **Wealthy**
Spiritual Connotation: **Heavenly Treasure**
Scripture: **Luke 6:20** NASB
Blessed are you who are poor, for yours is the kingdom of God.

CIAN, Cianán, Ciannan
Language/Cultural Origin: **Irish**
Inherent Meaning: **Ancient**
Spiritual Connotation: **Persistent Faith**
Scripture: **Mark 11:22** NKJV
Have faith in God.

CID, Cyd (see also Sidney)
Language/Cultural Origin: **Spanish**
Inherent Meaning: **Master**
Spiritual Connotation: **Discreet**
Scripture: **Romans 14:4** NASB
Who are you to judge the servant of another? To his own master he stands or falls; and stand he will, for the Lord is able to make him stand.

CIERRA, see Sierra

CINDY, see Cynthia

CIPRIANNA, Cipriana, Cypriana, Cyprianna, Cyprianne
Language/Cultural Origin: **Greek**
Inherent Meaning: **From Cyprus**
Spiritual Connotation: **Bold Witness**
Scripture: **Romans 1:16** NIV
I am not ashamed of the gospel, because it is the power of God for the salvation of everyone who believes: first for the Jew, then for the Gentile.

CISSY, Cissee
Language/Cultural Origin: **American**
Inherent Meaning: **Blind**
Spiritual Connotation: **Discerning**
Scripture: **Ephesians 5:17** RSV
Therefore do not be foolish, but understand what the will of the Lord is.

CLAIRE, Clair, Clara, Clarette, Clarina, Clarinda, Clarita
Language/Cultural Origin: **French**
Inherent Meaning: **Brilliant**
Spiritual Connotation: **Shining Light**
Scripture: **Psalm 36:9** NKJV
For with You is the fountain of life; in Your light we see light.

CLANCY, Clancey
Language/Cultural Origin: **Irish**
Inherent Meaning: **Red-Haired Fighter**
Spiritual Connotation: **Christlike**
Scripture: **Philippians 2:3** NKJV
Let nothing be done through selfish ambition or conceit, but in lowliness of mind let each esteem others better than himself.

CLARENCE, Clarance, Clare, Clarrance, Clarrence
Language/Cultural Origin: **Latin**
Inherent Meaning: **Victorious**
Spiritual Connotation: **Pure**
Scripture: **Philippians 4:8** NKJV
Finally, brethren, whatever things are true, . . . noble, . . . just, . . . pure, . . . lovely, . . . [or] praiseworthy; meditate on these things.

CLARISSA, Claresa, Claressa, Clarice, Clarisa, Clarisse, Clarrisa, Clarrissa, Clerissa (see also Klarissa)
Language/Cultural Origin: **Italian**
Inherent Meaning: **Brilliant**
Spiritual Connotation: **Wise Discerner**
Scripture: **Hosea 14:9** NKJV
Who is wise? Let him understand these things. Who is prudent? Let him know them.

CLARK, Clarke
Language/Cultural Origin: **Old French**
Inherent Meaning: **Scholar**

Spiritual Connotation: **Enlightened Spirit**
Scripture: **James 3:17** NKJV
But the wisdom that is from above is first pure, then peaceable, gentle, willing to yield, full of mercy and good fruits, without partiality and without hypocrisy.

CLAUDIA, Claudeen, Claudette
Language/Cultural Origin: **Latin**
Inherent Meaning: **Lame**
Spiritual Connotation: **Loved**
Scripture: **1 Peter 5:7** NKJV
[Cast] all your care upon Him, for He cares for you.

CLAUDIUS, Claude, Claudell, Claudio
Language/Cultural Origin: **Latin**
Inherent Meaning: **Lame**
Spiritual Connotation: **Strong in Victory**
Scripture: **Isaiah 40:29** NKJV
He gives power to the weak, and to those who have no might He increases strength.

CLAUS, see Klaus

CLAY, Clae
Language/Cultural Origin: **English**
Inherent Meaning: **Malleable Earth**
Spiritual Connotation: **Adaptable**
Scripture: **2 Corinthians 4:7** NKJV
But we have this treasure in earthen vessels, that the excellence of the power may be of God and not of us.

CLAYBORNE, Claeborne
Language/Cultural Origin: **Middle English**
Inherent Meaning: **From the Clay Brook**
Spiritual Connotation: **Molded by God**
Scripture: **Jeremiah 18:6** NKJV
Look, as the clay is in the potter's hand, so are you in My hand, O house of Israel!

CLAYTON, Clayten
Language/Cultural Origin: **Old English**
Inherent Meaning: **From the Clay Estate**
Spiritual Connotation: **Molded by God**
Scripture: **Isaiah 64:8** NKJV
But now, O LORD, You are our Father; we are the clay, and You our potter; and all we are the work of Your hand.

CLEMENT, Clem, Clemens, Clément, Clemente, Klem, Klemens, Klement
Language/Cultural Origin: **Latin**
Inherent Meaning: **Mild, Merciful**
Spiritual Connotation: **Benevolent**
Scripture: **Leviticus 19:34** NKJV
You shall love [the stranger who lives among you] as yourself; for you were strangers in the land of Egypt: I am the LORD your God.

CLEMENTINE, Clementia, Clementina, Clemette
Language/Cultural Origin: **English**
Inherent Meaning: **Merciful**
Spiritual Connotation: **Charitable**
Scripture: **John 13:34** NKJV
A new commandment I give to you, that you love one another.

CLEO, Clio
Language/Cultural Origin: **English**
Inherent Meaning: **One of Eminence**
Spiritual Connotation: **Understanding Spirit**
Scripture: **Psalm 36:9** NKJV
For with You is the fountain of life; In Your light we see light.

CLEON, Kleon
Language/Cultural Origin: **Greek**
Inherent Meaning: **Famous**
Spiritual Connotation: **Bold**
Scripture: **Philippians 1:20** NRSV
I will not be put to shame in any way, but that by my speaking with all boldness, Christ will be exalted now as always in my body, whether by life or by death.

CLEOPATRA, Cliopatra
Language/Cultural Origin: **Greek**
Inherent Meaning: **Fame of Her Father**
Spiritual Connotation: **Cherished**
Scripture: **Zephaniah 3:17** RSV
The LORD, your God, is in your midst, a warrior who gives victory; he will rejoice over you with gladness.

CLIFFORD, Cliff, Cliford, Clyff
Language/Cultural Origin: **Old English**
Inherent Meaning: **From the River's Heights**

Spiritual Connotation: **Vigilant**
Scripture: **Psalm 18:32** NKJV
It is God who arms me with strength, and makes my way perfect.

CLIFTON, Cliffton, Clift
Language/Cultural Origin: **Old English**
Inherent Meaning: **From the Cliff Estate**
Spiritual Connotation: **Prosperous**
Scripture: **Psalm 91:11** NKJV
For He shall give His angels charge over you, to keep you in all your ways.

CLINTON, Clint, Clinten
Language/Cultural Origin: **Old English**
Inherent Meaning: **From the Hill Town**
Spiritual Connotation: **Honorable**
Scripture: **Malachi 3:10** NKJV
I will . . . open for you the windows of heaven and pour out for you such blessing that there will not be room enough to receive it.

CLIVE, Cleve, Clyve
Language/Cultural Origin: **English**
Inherent Meaning: **From Upon the Cliff**
Spiritual Connotation: **Enduring**
Scripture: **Jeremiah 33:11** NKJV
Praise the LORD of hosts, for the LORD is good, for His mercy endures forever.

CLUNY, Clooney
Language/Cultural Origin: **Irish**
Inherent Meaning: **Meadow**
Spiritual Connotation: **Restful**
Scripture: **John 10:9** NRSV
I am the gate. Whoever enters by me will be saved, and will come in and go out and find pasture.

CLYDE, Clide
Language/Cultural Origin: **Welsh**
Inherent Meaning: **Loving**
Spiritual Connotation: **Rewarded**
Scripture: **Luke 12:32** NKJV
Do not fear, little flock, for it is your Father's good pleasure to give you the kingdom.

COBY, Cobe, Cobey, Cobi, Cobie, Kobe, Kobee, Kobi, Kobie, Koby
Language/Cultural Origin: **American**
Inherent Meaning: **Successor**

Spiritual Connotation: **Wise**
Scripture: **Hebrews 6:12** NLT
You will follow the example of those who are going to inherit God's promises because of their faith and patience.

COCO, Cocco, Coccoa (see also Koko)
Language/Cultural Origin: **Spanish**
Inherent Meaning: **Coconut**
Spiritual Connotation: **Sacrifice**
Scripture: **Ephesians 5:2** NKJV
And walk in love, as Christ also has loved us and given Himself for us, an offering and a sacrifice to God for a sweet-smelling aroma.

CODY, Codee, Codey, Codi, Codie, Kodee, Kodey, Kodi, Kodie, Kody
Language/Cultural Origin: **English**
Inherent Meaning: **Cushion**
Spiritual Connotation: **Joyful Witness**
Scripture: **Mark 5:19** NASB
Go home to your people and report to them what great things the Lord has done for you, and how He had mercy on you.

COLBERT, Culbert
Language/Cultural Origin: **English**
Inherent Meaning: **Brilliant Seafarer**
Spiritual Connotation: **Anchored in God**
Scripture: **Psalm 46:1** NKJV
God is our refuge and strength, a very present help in trouble.

COLBY, Colbey, Colbi, Colby, Collby, Kolby, Kollby
Language/Cultural Origin: **Old English**
Inherent Meaning: **From the Coal Farm**
Spiritual Connotation: **Dependent**
Scripture: **1 Peter 5:7** NKJV
[Cast] all your care upon Him, for He cares for you.

COLE, Kole
Language/Cultural Origin: **English**
Inherent Meaning: **Victory of the People**
Spiritual Connotation: **Granted Success**
Scripture: **1 Thessalonians 4:16** NKJV
For the Lord Himself will descend from heaven . . . and the dead in Christ will rise first.

COLETTE, Coletta, Collette, Kolette, Kollette (see also Nicole)
Language/Cultural Origin: **French**
Inherent Meaning: **Victorious**
Spiritual Connotation: **Faithful**
Scripture: **Galatians 5:22-23** NKJV
But the fruit of the Spirit is love, joy, peace, longsuffering, kindness, goodness, faithfulness, gentleness, self-control.

COLEY, Colee, Coleigh, Koley
Language/Cultural Origin: **English**
Inherent Meaning: **Victorious**
Spiritual Connotation: **Bold**
Scripture: **1 Corinthians 15:57** NKJV
But thanks be to God, who gives us the victory through our Lord Jesus Christ.

COLIN, Colan, Colen, Colyn
Language/Cultural Origin: **Irish**
Inherent Meaning: **Victorious**
Spiritual Connotation: **Destined**
Scripture: **1 Corinthians 2:9** NKJV
Eye has not seen, nor ear heard, nor have entered into the heart of man the things which God has prepared for those who love Him.

COLLEEN, Coleen, Colene, Colleene, Collene, Colline, Koleen, Kolleen
Language/Cultural Origin: **Gaelic**
Inherent Meaning: **Maiden**
Spiritual Connotation: **Excellent Virtue**
Scripture: **Psalm 107:9** NKJV
For He satisfies the longing soul, and fills the hungry soul with goodness.

COLLIER, Collyer
Language/Cultural Origin: **Welsh**
Inherent Meaning: **Merchant or Miner**
Spiritual Connotation: **Guided of God**
Scripture: **2 Samuel 22:33** NKJV
God is my strength and power, and He makes my way perfect.

COLLIN, Collen, Collins, Collyn
Language/Cultural Origin: **Scottish**
Inherent Meaning: **Victorious**
Spiritual Connotation: **Pressured**
Scripture: **Matthew 12:20-21** NKJV
A bruised reed He will not break, and

smoking flax He will not quench, till He sends forth justice to victory.

COLSON, Coleson
Language/Cultural Origin: **English**
Inherent Meaning: **Son of the Victor**
Spiritual Connotation: **Generously Gifted**
Scripture: **Ephesians 4:8** NRSV
Therefore it is said, "When he ascended on high he made captivity itself a captive; he gave gifts to his people."

COLTER, Colt
Language/Cultural Origin: **English**
Inherent Meaning: **Lover of Animals**
Spiritual Connotation: **Gentle**
Scripture: **Romans 13:10** NASB
Love does no wrong to a neighbor; therefore love is the fulfillment of the law.

COLTON, Colten, Coltin, Kolten, Koltin, Kolton
Language/Cultural Origin: **Anglo-Saxon**
Inherent Meaning: **From the Coal Town**
Spiritual Connotation: **Resourceful**
Scripture: **Romans 5:5** NKJV
Now hope does not disappoint, because the love of God has been poured out in our hearts by the Holy Spirit who was given to us.

CONAN, Connan
Language/Cultural Origin: **Celtic**
Inherent Meaning: **Intelligent**
Spiritual Connotation: **Spiritual Discernment**
Scripture: **Exodus 31:3** NKJV
And I have filled him with the Spirit of God, in wisdom, in understanding, in knowledge, and in all manner of workmanship.

CONCETTA, Conchita, Conciana, Concianna, Concieta
Language/Cultural Origin: **Italian**
Inherent Meaning: **Pure**
Spiritual Connotation: **Undefiled**
Scripture: **Titus 1:15** NKJV
To the pure all things are pure.

CONIAH, Coniyah
Language/Cultural Origin: **Hebrew**
Inherent Meaning: **God-Appointed**
Spiritual Connotation: **Destined**

Scripture: **James 4:10** NASB
Humble yourselves in the presence of the Lord, and He will exalt you.

CONLAN, Conlen, Conley, Conlin
Language/Cultural Origin: **Irish**
Inherent Meaning: **Hero**
Spiritual Connotation: **Gifted**
Scripture: **Proverbs 2:6** NKJV
For the LORD gives wisdom; from His mouth come knowledge and understanding.

CONNERY, Connary
Language/Cultural Origin: **Irish**
Inherent Meaning: **Exalted**
Spiritual Connotation: **Humble**
Scripture: **Luke 14:11** NKJV
For whoever exalts himself will be humbled, and he who humbles himself will be exalted.

CONNIE, Connee, Conni, Conny, Konnie
Language/Cultural Origin: **English**
Inherent Meaning: **Consistent**
Spiritual Connotation: **Unwavering**
Scripture: **1 Peter 5:9** TLB
Stand firm when he attacks. Trust the Lord; and remember that other Christians all around the world are going through these sufferings too.

CONNOR, Conner, Konner, Konnor
Language/Cultural Origin: **Irish**
Inherent Meaning: **Lofty Desire**
Spiritual Connotation: **Stronghold of God**
Scripture: **2 Corinthians 10:5** NASB
We are taking every thought captive to the obedience of Christ.

CONRAD, Conrade, Konrad, Konrade
Language/Cultural Origin: **German**
Inherent Meaning: **Bold Counselor**
Spiritual Connotation: **Discerner of Excellence**
Scripture: **Colossians 3:16** NKJV
Let the word of Christ dwell in you richly in all wisdom . . . singing with grace in your hearts to the Lord.

CONROY, Conroye
Language/Cultural Origin: **Irish**
Inherent Meaning: **Wise**
Spiritual Connotation: **Strong Leader**
Scripture: **Ecclesiastes 2:26** NKJV
For God gives wisdom and knowledge and joy to a man who is good in His sight.

CONSTANCE, Constanze, Konstance, Konstanze (see also Connie)
Language/Cultural Origin: **Latin**
Inherent Meaning: **Steadfast**
Spiritual Connotation: **Consecrated**
Scripture: **Romans 8:16** NKJV
The Spirit Himself bears witness with our spirit that we are children of God.

CONSUELA, Konsuela
Language/Cultural Origin: **Spanish**
Inherent Meaning: **Consoling Friend**
Spiritual Connotation: **Compassionate**
Scripture: **Proverbs 27:9** NLT
The heartfelt counsel of a friend is as sweet as perfume and incense.

COOPER, Couper
Language/Cultural Origin: **English**
Inherent Meaning: **Barrel Maker**
Spiritual Connotation: **Servant**
Scripture: **1 Corinthians 16:16** TLB
Please follow their instructions and do everything you can to help them as well as all others like them who work hard at your side with such real devotion.

CORA, Corra, Kora, Korra
Language/Cultural Origin: **Greek**
Inherent Meaning: **Maiden**
Spiritual Connotation: **Abiding in God**
Scripture: **1 John 4:16** NKJV
And we have known and believed the love that God has for us. God is love, and he who abides in love abides in God, and God in him.

CORAL, Corral, Koral
Language/Cultural Origin: **Latin**
Inherent Meaning: **Coral**
Spiritual Connotation: **Joyful Praise**
Scripture: **Psalm 69:34** NKJV
Let heaven and earth praise Him, the seas and everything that moves in them.

CORALEE, Coralea, Cora-Lee, Coralie, Coraline, Coralyn, Corilee, Koralee, Koralie, Koralyn
Language/Cultural Origin: **English**
Inherent Meaning: **Maiden From the Sea**
Spiritual Connotation: **Beloved**
Scripture: **Psalm 139:9-10** NASB
If I take the wings of the dawn, if I dwell in the remotest part of the sea, even there Thy hand will lead me, and Thy right hand will lay hold of me.

CORBETT, Corbet, Corbitt
Language/Cultural Origin: **Irish**
Inherent Meaning: **Raven**
Spiritual Connotation: **Attractive**
Scripture: **Song of Songs 5:11** NRSV
His head is the finest gold; his locks are wavy, black as a raven.

CORBIN, Corban, Corben, Korban, Korben, Korbin
Language/Cultural Origin: **Latin**
Inherent Meaning: **Raven**
Spiritual Connotation: **For Whom the Lord Will Provide**
Scripture: **Job 38:41** NKJV
Who provides food for the raven, when its young ones cry to God, and wander about for lack of food?

CORDELIA, Cordey, Cordia, Cordie
Language/Cultural Origin: **Welsh**
Inherent Meaning: **Jewel of the Sea**
Spiritual Connotation: **Precious**
Scripture: **Psalm 139:17** NKJV
How precious also are Your thoughts to me, O God! How great is the sum of them!

CORDELL, Cordelle, Kordell
Language/Cultural Origin: **French**
Inherent Meaning: **Rope Maker**
Spiritual Connotation: **Laborer**
Scripture: **Exodus 20:10** NKJV
The seventh day is the Sabbath of the LORD your God. In it you shall do no work.

COREY, Coree, Correy, Corry, Cory (see also Korey)
Language/Cultural Origin: **Irish**
Inherent Meaning: **From the Hollow**
Spiritual Connotation: **Prosperous**
Scripture: **Psalm 1:3** NKJV
He shall be like a tree planted by the rivers of water. . . . Whatever he does shall prosper.

CORI, Coriann, Corianne, Cori-Anne, Corie, Corri, Corrie, Corrienne (see also Cora, Korah)
Language/Cultural Origin: **Irish**
Inherent Meaning: **From the Hollow**
Spiritual Connotation: **Empowered Spirit**
Scripture: **James 4:7** NKJV
Therefore submit to God. Resist the devil and he will flee from you.

CORIN, Coren, Corian, Corien, Corinn, Corren, Corrian, Corrin, Corryn, Coryn, Corynn
Language/Cultural Origin: **English**
Inherent Meaning: **Little One**
Spiritual Connotation: **Trusting**
Scripture: **Hebrews 13:5** NRSV
Keep your lives free from the love of money, and be content with what you have; for he has said, I will never leave you or forsake you.

CORINA, Coreena, Corinna, Corrina (see also Carina, Cori, Korina)
Language/Cultural Origin: **English**
Inherent Meaning: **Little Damsel**
Spiritual Connotation: **Innocent**
Scripture: **Titus 1:15** NKJV
To the pure all things are pure.

CORINNE, Coreen, Corine, Corinne, Correen, Corrinne
Language/Cultural Origin: **Greek**
Inherent Meaning: **Fair Maiden**
Spiritual Connotation: **Illuminated**
Scripture: **Job 22:28** NKJV
You will also declare a thing, and it will be established for you; so light will shine on your ways.

CORISSA, Corisa, Korissa (see also Carissa)
Language/Cultural Origin: **English**
Inherent Meaning: **Most Maidenly**
Spiritual Connotation: **Filled With Praise**
Scripture: **Psalm 145:3** RSV
Great is the LORD, and greatly to be praised, and his greatness is unsearchable.

CORLISS, Corlisa, Corlise, Corlissa, Korlisa, Korlise, Korliss
Language/Cultural Origin: **English**
Inherent Meaning: **Good-Hearted**
Spiritual Connotation: **Sanctified**
Scripture: **2 Corinthians 3:18** RSV
And we all, with unveiled face, beholding the glory of the Lord, are being changed into his likeness from one degree of glory to another.

CORNELIUS
Language/Cultural Origin: **Latin**
Inherent Meaning: **Sunbeam**
Spiritual Connotation: **Praise**
Scripture: **Psalm 113:3** RSV
From the rising of the sun to its setting the name of the LORD is to be praised!

CORRIGAN, Korrigan
Language/Cultural Origin: **Irish**
Inherent Meaning: **Spearman**
Spiritual Connotation: **Proud Father**
Scripture: **Psalm 127:4** RSV
Like arrows in the hand of a warrior are the sons of one's youth.

CORT, see Courtney

CORTEZ, Courtez
Language/Cultural Origin: **Spanish**
Inherent Meaning: **Conqueror**
Spiritual Connotation: **Valiant**
Scripture: **Revelation 6:2** NASB
And I looked, and behold, a white horse, and he who sat on it had a bow; and a crown was given to him; and he went out conquering, and to conquer.

CORWIN, Corwyn
Language/Cultural Origin: **Latin**
Inherent Meaning: **Heart's Delight**
Spiritual Connotation: **Brilliant Countenance**
Scripture: **2 Corinthians 4:6** NKJV

For it is the God who commanded light to shine out of darkness, who has shone in our hearts.

CORY, see Corey

COSETTE, Cosetta, Cossetta, Cossette
Language/Cultural Origin: **French**
Inherent Meaning: **Victorious**
Spiritual Connotation: **Confident Spirit**
Scripture: **Isaiah 42:16** NKJV
I will bring the blind by a way they did not know; I will lead them in paths they have not known.

COSMO, Cozmo, Kosmo
Language/Cultural Origin: **Greek**
Inherent Meaning: **Orderly**
Spiritual Connotation: **Peaceful**
Scripture: **1 Thessalonians 4:11** TLB
This should be your ambition: to live a quiet life, minding your own business and doing your own work.

COURTLAND, Courtlin, Courtlyn
Language/Cultural Origin: **English**
Inherent Meaning: **From the Farmstead**
Spiritual Connotation: **Truthful**
Scripture: **Psalm 19:14** NKJV
Let the words of my mouth and the meditation of my heart be acceptable in Your sight, O LORD, my strength and my Redeemer.

COURTNEY, Cort, Cortnay, Cortne, Cortnee, Cortney, Cortni, Cortnie, Corttney, Court, Courtenay, Courteney, Courtnae, Courtnay, Courtnee, Courtnée, Courtni, Courtnie, Courtny, Courtonie, Kort, Kortnay, Kortnee, Kortney, Kortni, Kortnie, Kortny, Kourtinee, Kourtney, Kourtni, Kourtny
Language/Cultural Origin: **Old French**
Inherent Meaning: **From the Court**
Spiritual Connotation: **Amidst God's Love**
Scripture: **1 John 4:16** NKJV
And we have known and believed the love that God has for us. God is love,

and he who abides in love abides in God, and God in him.

COWAN, Cowey
Language/Cultural Origin: **Irish**
Inherent Meaning: **From the Hillside**
Spiritual Connotation: **Generous**
Scripture: **Luke 6:38** NKJV
Give, and it will be given to you. . . . For with the same measure that you use, it will be measured back to you.

COY, Coi, Koy
Language/Cultural Origin: **English**
Inherent Meaning: **From the Woods**
Spiritual Connotation: **Focused**
Scripture: **1 Corinthians 2:2** NLT
For I decided to concentrate only on Jesus Christ and his death on the cross.

COYLE, Coyel
Language/Cultural Origin: **Irish**
Inherent Meaning: **Courageous Leader**
Spiritual Connotation: **God's Warrior**
Scripture: **1 Timothy 6:12** NKJV
Fight the good fight of faith, lay hold on eternal life, to which you were also called.

COZBI, Cosbey, Cosbie, Cosby, Coz, ☞Cozbee, Cozbie, Cozby
Language/Cultural Origin: **Canaanite**
Inherent Meaning: **Deceiver**
Spiritual Connotation: **Loving**
Scripture: **1 John 4:7** NKJV
Beloved, let us love one another, for love is of God; and everyone who loves is born of God and knows God.

CRAIG, Cregg, Crieg, Kraig
Language/Cultural Origin: **Scottish**
Inherent Meaning: **From the Steep Rock**
Spiritual Connotation: **Enduring Spirit**
Scripture: **Matthew 7:24** NKJV
Therefore whoever hears these sayings of Mine, and does them, I will liken him to a wise man who built his house on the rock.

CRANDELL, Crandall
Language/Cultural Origin: **English**
Inherent Meaning: **From the Valley**
Spiritual Connotation: **Freedom**
Scripture: **2 Corinthians 3:17** NKJV

Now the Lord is the Spirit; and where the Spirit of the Lord is, there is liberty.

CREED, Creedon
Language/Cultural Origin: **Latin**
Inherent Meaning: **Belief**
Spiritual Connotation: **Power in Faith**
Scripture: **Matthew 8:10** NRSV
Truly I tell you, in no one in Israel have I found such faith.

CREIGHTON, Cray, Crayton
Language/Cultural Origin: **English**
Inherent Meaning: **From the Rocky Place**
Spiritual Connotation: **Humble Spirit**
Scripture: **3 John 2** NKJV
Beloved, I pray that you may prosper in all things and be in health, just as your soul prospers.

CROSBY, Crosbie
Language/Cultural Origin: **Scandinavian**
Inherent Meaning: **Shrine of the Cross**
Spiritual Connotation: **Reminder of Christ**
Scripture: **Luke 23:33** NASB
And when they came to the place called The Skull, there they crucified Him and the criminals, one on the right and the other on the left.

CRUZ, Kruz
Language/Cultural Origin: **Portuguese**
Inherent Meaning: **Cross**
Spiritual Connotation: **Symbol**
Scripture: **Philippians 2:8** NKJV
And being found in appearance as a man, He humbled Himself and became obedient to the point of death, even the death of the cross.

CRYSTAL, Christal, Christalin, Christall, Christalyn, Christel, Chrystal, Chrystel, Cristal, Cristel, Cristelle, Crystalee, Crystall, Crystallin, Crystallynn, Crystel, Crystilin, Crystol, Crystyl (see also Krystal)
Language/Cultural Origin: **Latin**
Inherent Meaning: **Sparkling**
Spiritual Connotation: **Pure**
Scripture: **1 Timothy 4:12** NCV
Do not let anyone treat you as if you

are unimportant because you are young. Instead, be an example to the believers with . . . your pure life.

CULLEN, Cullan, Cullin, Cully
Language/Cultural Origin: **Irish**
Inherent Meaning: **Pleasing to Look Upon**
Spiritual Connotation: **Loving**
Scripture: **Romans 13:10** NKJV
Love does no harm to a neighbor; therefore love is the fulfillment of the law.

CURRAN, Curan
Language/Cultural Origin: **Irish**
Inherent Meaning: **Hero**
Spiritual Connotation: **Example**
Scripture: **1 Corinthians 11:1** NKJV
Imitate me, just as I also imitate Christ.

CURTIS, Curt, Curtiss, Kurtis, Kurtiss (see also Kurt)
Language/Cultural Origin: **Old French**
Inherent Meaning: **Courteous**
Spiritual Connotation: **Just and Honorable**
Scripture: **Zechariah 7:9** NKJV
Thus says the LORD of hosts: "Execute true justice, show mercy and compassion everyone to his brother."

CUSH, Kush
☞ Language/Cultural Origin: **Hebrew**
Inherent Meaning: **Black**
Spiritual Connotation: **Forgiven**
Scripture: **1 John 3:3** NCV
Christ is pure, and all who have this hope in Christ keep themselves pure like Christ.

CYBIL, see Sybil

CYNTHIA, Cindee, Cindi, Cindie, Cindy, Cydna, Cynda, Cyndee, Cyndi, Cyndie, Cyndy
Language/Cultural Origin: **Greek**
Inherent Meaning: **Moon**
Spiritual Connotation: **Celestial Light**
Scripture: **Psalm 27:1** NKJV
The LORD is my light and my salvation; whom shall I fear? The LORD is the strength of my life; of whom shall I be afraid?

CYRIL, Cyrill, Cyrille
Language/Cultural Origin: **Greek**

Inherent Meaning: **Lordly**

Spiritual Connotation: **Great Spiritual Potential**

Scripture: **Malachi 3:10** NKJV

I will . . . open for you the windows of heaven and pour out for you such blessing that there will not be room enough to receive it.

CYRUS, Cy, Cyris

☞ Language/Cultural Origin: **Persian**

Inherent Meaning: **Sun**

Spiritual Connotation: **Spiritual Enlightenment**

Scripture: **Ephesians 1:18** NASB

I pray that the eyes of your heart may be enlightened, so that you may know . . . what are the riches of the glory of His inheritance in the saints.

CZARINA, Czareena, Czariana, Czarianna (see also Zorina)

Language/Cultural Origin: **Russian**

Inherent Meaning: **Empress**

Spiritual Connotation: **Regal**

Scripture: **Psalm 45:9** NKJV

Kings' daughters are among Your honorable women; at Your right hand stands the queen in gold.

D

DACEY, Dacee, Daci, Dacie, Dacy, Daicee, Daycee, Daycie
Language/Cultural Origin: **Gaelic**
Inherent Meaning: **Southerner**
Spiritual Connotation: **Friend of Christ**
Scripture: **Hebrews 2:7** NKJV
You have made him a little lower than the angels; you have crowned him with glory and honor, and set him over the works of Your hands.

DACIA, Dacya
Language/Cultural Origin: **Latin**
Inherent Meaning: **Southerner**
Spiritual Connotation: **Divine Perspective**
Scripture: **Isaiah 65:17** NKJV
For behold, I create new heavens and a new earth; and the former shall not be remembered or come to mind.

DACIAN, Dacien
Language/Cultural Origin: **Latin**
Inherent Meaning: **Southerner**
Spiritual Connotation: **Divine Perspective**
Scripture: **Isaiah 55:8** NKJV
"For My thoughts are not your thoughts, nor are your ways My ways," says the LORD.

DAGAN, Dagon
Language/Cultural Origin: **Hebrew**
Inherent Meaning: **Grain**
Spiritual Connotation: **Wise**
Scripture: **Ecclesiastes 7:19** NKJV
Wisdom strengthens the wise more than ten rulers of the city.

DAGANA, Dagania, Daganna
Language/Cultural Origin: **Hebrew**
Inherent Meaning: **Grain**
Spiritual Connotation: **Chosen**
Scripture: **Deuteronomy 33:28** NKJV
Then Israel shall dwell in safety, the fountain of Jacob alone, in a land of grain and new wine; His heavens shall also drop dew.

DAGMAR
Language/Cultural Origin: **Old German**
Inherent Meaning: **Glorious Day**
Spiritual Connotation: **Redeemed**
Scripture: **Romans 8:2** NKJV
For the law of the Spirit of life in Christ Jesus has made me free from the law of sin and death.

DAHLIA, Dahliana, Dahlianna (see also Daliah)
Language/Cultural Origin: **Scandinavian**
Inherent Meaning: **From the Valley**
Spiritual Connotation: **Example**
Scripture: **Job 21:33** NKJV
The clods of the valley shall be sweet to him; everyone shall follow him, as countless have gone before him.

DAISY, Daisee
Language/Cultural Origin: **Old English**
Inherent Meaning: **Vision of the Day**
Spiritual Connotation: **Cleansed**
Scripture: **Ephesians 1:4** NKJV
He chose us in Him before the foundation of the world, that we should be holy and without blame before Him in love.

DAJUAN, Dawan, Dawon, Dejuan, Dewaun, Dijuan, D'Juan, Dujuan
Language/Cultural Origin: **American**
Inherent Meaning: **God Is Gracious**
Spiritual Connotation: **Promise**
Scripture: **2 Chronicles 30:9** NKJV
For if you return to the LORD, your brethren and your children will . . . come

back to this land; for the LORD your God is gracious and merciful.

DAKOTA, Dakotah
Language/Cultural Origin: **Sioux**
Inherent Meaning: **Friend**
Spiritual Connotation: **Sincere**
Scripture: **Proverbs 22:11** NCV
Whoever loves pure thoughts and kind words will have even the king as a friend.

DALE, Dayle
Language/Cultural Origin: **Old English**
Inherent Meaning: **From the Valley**
Spiritual Connotation: **Peaceful**
Scripture: **Psalm 85:11** NKJV
Truth shall spring out of the earth, and righteousness shall look down from heaven.

DALIAH, Dalia, Daliyah (see also Dahlia)
Language/Cultural Origin: **Hebrew**
Inherent Meaning: **Branch**
Spiritual Connotation: **Destined**
Scripture: **Isaiah 4:2** NKJV
In that day the Branch of the LORD shall be beautiful and glorious; and the fruit of the earth shall be excellent and appealing.

DALLAN, Daelan, Daelen, Daelin, Dalian, Daylan, Daylen, Daylin
Language/Cultural Origin: **English**
Inherent Meaning: **From the Dale**
Spiritual Connotation: **Secure**
Scripture: **Joel 2:21** NASB
Do not fear, O land, rejoice and be glad, for the LORD has done great things.

DALLAS, Dallis, Dallys
Language/Cultural Origin: **Scottish**
Inherent Meaning: **Gentle**
Spiritual Connotation: **Efficient**
Scripture: **Deuteronomy 15:10** NKJV
You shall surely give to him, and your heart should not be grieved . . . because for this thing the LORD your God will bless you.

DALTON, Dalten
Language/Cultural Origin: **Old English**
Inherent Meaning: **From the Valley Town**
Spiritual Connotation: **Filled With Peace**

Scripture: **Luke 6:45** NKJV
A good man out of the good treasure of his heart brings forth good.

DALY, Daley
Language/Cultural Origin: **Irish**
Inherent Meaning: **Assembly**
Spiritual Connotation: **Bringer of Light**
Scripture: **Isaiah 52:7** NKJV
How beautiful upon the mountains are the feet of him who brings good news . . . Who says to Zion, Your God reigns!

DAMARA, Damarrah
Language/Cultural Origin: **Czech**
Inherent Meaning: **Glory of the Day**
Spiritual Connotation: **Promised Result**
Scripture: **Isaiah 29:18** NKJV
In that day the deaf shall hear the words of the book, and the eyes of the blind shall see out of obscurity and out of darkness.

DAMARIS, Damarius, Damarys, ☞ Demaras, Demaris, Demarius
Language/Cultural Origin: **Greek**
Inherent Meaning: **Gentle**
Spiritual Connotation: **Forgiving**
Scripture: **Hosea 11:4** NRSV
I led them with cords of human kindness, with bands of love. I was to them like those who lift infants to their cheeks. I bent down to them and fed them.

DAMIAN, Daemien, Daimyan, Dameion, Dameon, Damián, Damien, Damion, Daymian
Language/Cultural Origin: **Russian**
Inherent Meaning: **Soother**
Spiritual Connotation: **One Who Restores**
Scripture: **Isaiah 40:1** NKJV
Comfort, yes, comfort My people! Says your God.

DAMIANA, Damianna
Language/Cultural Origin: **Greek**
Inherent Meaning: **Soother**
Spiritual Connotation: **Healer**
Scripture: **Jeremiah 31:13** NRSV
Then shall the young women rejoice in the dance, and the young men and

the old shall be merry. I will turn their mourning into joy.

DAMICA, Damika, Damikah, Demeeka, Demica, Demicah
Language/Cultural Origin: French
Inherent Meaning: Friendly
Spiritual Connotation: Seeker of Truth
Scripture: Psalm 25:14 RSV
The friendship of the LORD is for those who fear him, and he makes known to them his covenant.

DAMITA, Dametia, Dametra
Language/Cultural Origin: Spanish
Inherent Meaning: Noble Lady
Spiritual Connotation: Gracious Spirit
Scripture: Psalm 97:11 NKJV
Light is sown for the righteous, and gladness for the upright in heart.

DAMON, Daemon, Daman, Damen, Damonn, Daymon
Language/Cultural Origin: Greek
Inherent Meaning: Loyal
Spiritual Connotation: Walks With God
Scripture: Zechariah 8:16 NKJV
These are the things you shall do: speak each man the truth to his neighbor; give judgment in your gates for truth, justice, and peace.

DANA, Daina, Danah, Dayna, Daynah
Language/Cultural Origin: Scandinavian
Inherent Meaning: Bright as Day
Spiritual Connotation: Obedient
Scripture: Deuteronomy 16:20 NASB
Justice, and only justice, you shall pursue, that you may live and possess the land which the LORD your God is giving you.

DANAE, Danaë, Danay, Dannae (see also Denae)
Language/Cultural Origin: English
Inherent Meaning: God Is My Judge
Spiritual Connotation: Just
Scripture: 1 Kings 10:9 NKJV
Blessed be the LORD your God, who delighted in you, setting you on the throne of Israel!

DANE, Daine, Dayne, Dhane
Language/Cultural Origin: Old English
Inherent Meaning: Trickling Stream
Spiritual Connotation: Blessed
Scripture: Psalm 104:10 NKJV
He sends the springs into the valleys, they flow among the hills.

DANELLE, Danel, Danele, Danell, Dannell (see also Danielle)
Language/Cultural Origin: French
Inherent Meaning: God Is My Judge
Spiritual Connotation: Discerning
Scripture: Psalm 36:6 NCV
Your goodness is as high as the mountains. Your justice is as deep as the great ocean. LORD, you protect both people and animals.

DANETTE, Danett
Language/Cultural Origin: American
Inherent Meaning: God Is My Judge
Spiritual Connotation: Perceptive
Scripture: Psalm 45:6 TLB
Your throne, O God, endures forever. Justice is your royal scepter.

DANIA, Danee, Dani, Daniah, Danie, Danni, Danya
Language/Cultural Origin: Hebrew
Inherent Meaning: God Is My Judge
Spiritual Connotation: Intuitive
Scripture: Psalm 146:7 NCV
He does what is fair for those who have been wronged. He gives food to the hungry. The LORD sets the prisoners free.

DANICA, Daneeka, Danika, Dannika
Language/Cultural Origin: Slavic
Inherent Meaning: Morning Star
Spiritual Connotation: Attentive
Scripture: 2 Peter 1:19 NRSV
You will do well to be attentive to this as to a lamp shining in a dark place, until the day dawns and the morning star rises in your hearts.

DANIEL, Dan, Dániel, Daniël, ☞Daniyel, Danny, Donyel, Donyell
Language/Cultural Origin: Hebrew
Inherent Meaning: God Is My Judge

Spiritual Connotation: **Discerning**
Scripture: **Psalm 119:142** NKJV
Your righteousness is an everlasting righteousness, and Your law is truth.

DANIELLE, Danialle, Daniela, Daniele, Daniell, Daniella, Dannielle, Danyel, Danyele, Danyelle (see also Danelle)
Language/Cultural Origin: **French**
Inherent Meaning: **God Is My Judge**
Spiritual Connotation: **Perceptive**
Scripture: **Psalm 119:112** NKJV
I have inclined my heart to perform Your statutes forever, to the very end.

DANNON, Danaan, Danen, Danon
Language/Cultural Origin: **American**
Inherent Meaning: **God Is My Judge**
Spiritual Connotation: **Preserved**
Scripture: **Numbers 6:24** NKJV
The LORD bless you and keep you; the LORD make His face shine upon you, and be gracious to you.

DANTE, Danté, Dauntay, Dauntaye, Daunte (see also Deon, Dontae)
Language/Cultural Origin: **Latin**
Inherent Meaning: **Enduring**
Spiritual Connotation: **Loving**
Scripture: **1 Corinthians 13:7** RSV
Love bears all things, believes all things, hopes all things, endures all things.

DANYA, Danyah, Donya (see also Dawn, Donna)
Language/Cultural Origin: **Russian**
Inherent Meaning: **God Is My Judge**
Spiritual Connotation: **Vindicated**
Scripture: **Hebrews 13:10** TLB
We have an altar—the cross where Christ was sacrificed—where those who continue to seek salvation by obeying Jewish laws can never be helped.

DAPHNE, Daphaney, Daphanie, Daphany, Daphnee, Daphney
Language/Cultural Origin: **Greek**
Inherent Meaning: **Laurel Tree**
Spiritual Connotation: **Victorious**
Scripture: **1 Kings 3:12** NKJV
I have given you a wise and understanding heart, so that there has not been anyone like you before you, nor shall any like you arise after you.

DARA, Darah, Darra, Darrah
Language/Cultural Origin: **Hebrew**
Inherent Meaning: **Compassionate**
Spiritual Connotation: **Bearer of Mercy**
Scripture: **Matthew 25:40** NKJV
Assuredly, I say to you, inasmuch as you did it to one of the least of these My brethren, you did it to Me.

DARBY, Darbey, Darbi, Darbie
Language/Cultural Origin: **Irish**
Inherent Meaning: **Freedom**
Spiritual Connotation: **Free Spirit**
Scripture: **Romans 8:21** NLT
All creation anticipates the day when it will join God's children in glorious freedom from death and decay.

DARCY, Darcee, Darcey, Darcie, Darsey, Darsie
Language/Cultural Origin: **French**
Inherent Meaning: **Fortress**
Spiritual Connotation: **Established in Strength**
Scripture: **Psalm 25:10** NKJV
All the paths of the LORD are mercy and truth, to such as keep His covenant and His testimonies.

DARIA, Darria, Darya
Language/Cultural Origin: **Greek**
Inherent Meaning: **Wealthy**
Spiritual Connotation: **Gracious**
Scripture: **Psalm 9:1** NKJV
I will praise You, O LORD, with my whole heart; I will tell of all Your marvelous works.

DARIELLE, Dariel, Darriel, Darrielle
Language/Cultural Origin: **French**
Inherent Meaning: **Little Darling**
Spiritual Connotation: **Cherished**
Scripture: **Psalm 108:6** TLB
Hear the cry of your beloved child— come with mighty power and rescue me.

DARIUS, Darian, Dariann, Darias, Darien, Darion, Dárion
Language/Cultural Origin: **Persian**

Inherent Meaning: **Prosperous**
Spiritual Connotation: **Preserved**
Scripture: **Isaiah 42:6** NKJV
I, the LORD, have called you in righteousness, and will hold your hand; I will keep you.

DARLENE, Darla, Darleen, Darling
Language/Cultural Origin: **French**
Inherent Meaning: **Darling**
Spiritual Connotation: **Beloved**
Scripture: **Proverbs 4:23** NKJV
Keep your heart with all diligence, for out of it spring the issues of life.

DARNELLE, Darnall, Darnell
Language/Cultural Origin: **Irish**
Inherent Meaning: **Magnificent**
Spiritual Connotation: **Loving**
Scripture: **1 Peter 4:8** NRSV
Above all, maintain constant love for one another, for love covers a multitude of sins.

DARON, Darron, Daryn, Darynn, Darynne, Derrion, Derron, Diron (see also Darius, Darren, Deron)
Language/Cultural Origin: **English**
Inherent Meaning: **Rocky Hill**
Spiritual Connotation: **Obedient**
Scripture: **1 John 2:28** NKJV
And now, little children, abide in Him, that when He appears, we may have confidence and not be ashamed before Him at His coming.

DARRELL, Darelle, Daril, Darral, Darrel, Darril, Darryl, Darryll, Daryl, Derell, Derrel, Derril
Language/Cultural Origin: **French**
Inherent Meaning: **Beloved**
Spiritual Connotation: **Blessed**
Scripture: **Psalm 18:32** NKJV
It is God who arms me with strength, and makes my way perfect.

DARREN, Daran, Daren, Darin, Darran, Darrian, Darrien, Darrin, Deren, Derran, Derren, Derrin (see also Daron, Darius, Deron)
Language/Cultural Origin: **Irish**
Inherent Meaning: **Great**

Spiritual Connotation: **Esteemed**
Scripture: **2 Corinthians 9:8** NKJV
And God is able to make all grace abound toward you, that you . . . may have an abundance for every good work.

DARWIN, Darwyn
Language/Cultural Origin: **Old English**
Inherent Meaning: **Beloved**
Spiritual Connotation: **Treasured**
Scripture: **2 Corinthians 4:7** NIV
But we have this treasure in jars of clay to show that this all-surpassing power is from God and not from us.

DASAN, Dassan
Language/Cultural Origin: **Pomo**
Inherent Meaning: **Leader**
Spiritual Connotation: **Chosen**
Scripture: **Jeremiah 30:21** NASB
Their leader shall be one of them, and their ruler shall come forth from their midst.

DASHA, Dashah, Dasya
Language/Cultural Origin: **Russian**
Inherent Meaning: **Divine Display**
Spiritual Connotation: **Miracle**
Scripture: **Joel 2:30** NLT
I will cause wonders in the heavens and on the earth—blood and fire and pillars of smoke.

DASHAWNA, Deshandra, Deshaundra, Deshawna, Deshawnda, Deshonda, Deshonna
Language/Cultural Origin: **American**
Inherent Meaning: **God Is Gracious**
Spiritual Connotation: **Pardoned**
Scripture: **Isaiah 63:9** NLT
In all their suffering he also suffered, and he personally rescued them. In his love and mercy he redeemed them.

DATHAN, Dathon, Daythan, ☞ Daython
Language/Cultural Origin: **Hebrew**
Inherent Meaning: **Belonging to the Law**
Spiritual Connotation: **Redeemed**
Scripture: **Ephesians 2:5** NCV
Though we were spiritually dead because of the things we did against God, he gave

us new life with Christ. You have been saved by God's grace.

DATIA, Datiah, Datiya, Datya
Language/Cultural Origin: **Hebrew**
Inherent Meaning: **Faith in God**
Spiritual Connotation: **Strength**
Scripture: **Matthew 9:22** RSV
Take heart, daughter; your faith has made you well.

DAVID, Dave, Daved, Daveed, ☞ Davey, Davíde, Davy, Dayvid
Language/Cultural Origin: **Hebrew**
Inherent Meaning: **Beloved**
Spiritual Connotation: **Lover of All**
Scripture: **1 John 4:16** NKJV
And we have known and believed the love that God has for us. God is love, and he who abides in love abides in God, and God in him.

DAVIN, Daevin, Daevon, Davohn, Davon, Davonn, Davontay, Davonte, Dayvin (see also Devin)
Language/Cultural Origin: **Scandinavian**
Inherent Meaning: **Brilliant**
Spiritual Connotation: **Heavenly Light**
Scripture: **Psalm 148:3** NRSV
Praise him, sun and moon; praise him, all you shining stars!

DAVINA, Dava, Daveena, Davi, Daviana, Davine, Davinia, Davria, Devona, Devonda, Devonna, Devina
Language/Cultural Origin: **Scottish**
Inherent Meaning: **Beloved**
Spiritual Connotation: **Enlightened**
Scripture: **Zechariah 4:6** NKJV
Not by might nor by power, but by My Spirit, says the LORD of hosts.

DAVIS, Davidson, Davies, Davison
Language/Cultural Origin: **English**
Inherent Meaning: **Honorable**
Spiritual Connotation: **Loving**
Scripture: **1 John 4:8** NKJV
He who does not love does not know God, for God is love.

DAWN, Dawana, Dawna, Dawne,

Dawnn, Dawnna, Dawnya (see also Danya, Donna)
Language/Cultural Origin: **Old English**
Inherent Meaning: **Beginning Anew**
Spiritual Connotation: **Joy and Praise**
Scripture: **Psalm 113:2-3** NKJV
Blessed be the name of the LORD from this time forth and forevermore! From the rising of the sun to its going down the Lord's name is to be praised.

DAWSON, Dawsen
Language/Cultural Origin: **English**
Inherent Meaning: **Son of the Beloved**
Spiritual Connotation: **Victorious**
Scripture: **Psalm 60:5** RSV
That thy beloved may be delivered, give victory by thy right hand and answer us!

DAYA, Daeya, Daia
Language/Cultural Origin: **Hebrew**
Inherent Meaning: **Bird**
Spiritual Connotation: **Secure**
Scripture: **Psalm 84:3** RSV
Even the sparrow finds a home, and the swallow a nest for herself, where she may lay her young, at thy altars, O LORD of hosts, my King and my God.

DAYANA, Dayahna
Language/Cultural Origin: **Middle Eastern**
Inherent Meaning: **Divine**
Spiritual Connotation: **Warrior**
Scripture: **2 Corinthians 10:4** NCV
We fight with weapons that are different from those the world uses. Our weapons have power from God that can destroy the enemy's strong places.

DEACON, Deke, Diakonos
☞ Language/Cultural Origin: **Greek**
Inherent Meaning: **One Who Serves**
Spiritual Connotation: **Honored**
Scripture: **1 Timothy 3:8** NLT
In the same way, deacons must be people who are respected and have integrity. They must not be heavy drinkers and must not be greedy for money.

DEAN, Deane, Dene
Language/Cultural Origin: **Old English**
Inherent Meaning: **Valley**

Spiritual Connotation: **Prosperous**
Scripture: **Matthew 12:35** NKJV
A good man out of the good treasure of his heart brings forth good things.

DEANDRA, Deandrá, Deandrea, Deandria, Deanndra, Diandre
Language/Cultural Origin: **American**
Inherent Meaning: **Courageous**
Spiritual Connotation: **Heir**
Scripture: **Deuteronomy 31:7** NASB
Be strong and courageous, for you shall go with this people into the land which the LORD has sworn to their fathers to give them.

DEANDRE, D'Andre, Dandrae, Dandray, Dandré, De Andre, Deandré, Deaundre, Deondré
Language/Cultural Origin: **French**
Inherent Meaning: **Courageous**
Spiritual Connotation: **Submissive**
Scripture: **1 Chronicles 19:13** NRSV
Be strong, and let us be courageous for our people and for the cities of our God.

DEANNA, Deana, Deann, Déanne, Deeann, Deeanna
Language/Cultural Origin: **Latin**
Inherent Meaning: **Divine**
Spiritual Connotation: **Brightness of the Dawn**
Scripture: **Psalm 143:8** NKJV
Cause me to hear Your lovingkindness in the morning, for in You do I trust.

DEBORAH, Deb, Debb, Debbi, ☞Debbie, Debbora, Debborah, Debby, Debi, Debora, Deborrah, Debra
Language/Cultural Origin: **Hebrew**
Inherent Meaning: **Honey Bee**
Spiritual Connotation: **New Era of Leadership**
Scripture: **Isaiah 65:17** NKJV
For behold, I create new heavens and a new earth; and the former shall not be remembered or come to mind.

DEE, Dede, Deedee
Language/Cultural Origin: **Welsh**
Inherent Meaning: **Dark**

Spiritual Connotation: **Loving**
Scripture: **2 John 1:6** NRSV
And this is love, that we walk according to his commandments.

DEENA, see Dena

DEIRDRE, Dedra, Deedra, Deidra, Deidre, Dierdra, Dierdre, Diérdre
Language/Cultural Origin: **Irish**
Inherent Meaning: **Wanderer**
Spiritual Connotation: **Seeker of Righteousness and Truth**
Scripture: **Psalm 119:35** NKJV
Make me walk in the path of Your commandments, for I delight in it.

DEITRA, Deetra, Detria
Language/Cultural Origin: **Greek**
Inherent Meaning: **Abundant**
Spiritual Connotation: **Refreshed**
Scripture: **Psalm 68:9** TLB
You sent abundant rain upon your land, O God, to refresh it in its weariness!

DEJA, Daija, Daja, Déja
Language/Cultural Origin: **French**
Inherent Meaning: **Before**
Spiritual Connotation: **Compassionate**
Scripture: **Romans 12:15** NKJV
Rejoice with those who rejoice, and weep with those who weep.

DEJUAN, see Dajuan

DELAIAH, Dalaiah
☞ Language/Cultural Origin: **Hebrew**
Inherent Meaning: **God Is the Deliverer**
Spiritual Connotation: **Redeemed**
Scripture: **Romans 11:26** NKJV
The Deliverer will come out of Zion.

DELANA, Dalanna, Dalayna, Dalena, Dalina, Delaina, Delena, Delina
Language/Cultural Origin: **German**
Inherent Meaning: **Noble Protector**
Spiritual Connotation: **Example**
Scripture: **Psalm 71:7** NLT
My life is an example to many, because you have been my strength and protection.

DELANO, Dellano
Language/Cultural Origin: **French**
Inherent Meaning: **Nut Tree**

Spiritual Connotation: **Anchored**
Scripture: **Psalm 1:3** RSV
He is like a tree planted by streams of water, that yields its fruit in its season, and its leaf does not wither. In all that he does, he prospers.

DELANY, Dalaney, Delainey, Delanny, Delaynie, Dellaney
Language/Cultural Origin: **Irish**
Inherent Meaning: **Of the Champion**
Spiritual Connotation: **Victorious**
Scripture: **Psalm 98:2** NIV
The LORD has made his salvation known and revealed his righteousness to the nations.

DELIA, Dehlia, Deleah, Dellia, Delya
Language/Cultural Origin: **Greek**
Inherent Meaning: **Visible**
Spiritual Connotation: **Divine Reflection**
Scripture: **1 Corinthians 13:12** TLB
We can see and understand only a little about God now, as if we were peering at his reflection in a poor mirror; but someday we are going to see him . . . face to face.

DELICIA, Deleesha, Delisha, Delysia
Language/Cultural Origin: **Latin**
Inherent Meaning: **Delightful**
Spiritual Connotation: **Joyous Spirit**
Scripture: **Psalm 16:11** NKJV
You will show me the path of life; in Your presence is fullness of joy; At Your right hand are pleasures forevermore.

DELLA, Dellie
Language/Cultural Origin: **Old German**
Inherent Meaning: **Noble Maiden**
Spiritual Connotation: **Excellent Virtue**
Scripture: **1 Corinthians 13:13** NKJV
And now abide faith, hope, love, these three; but the greatest of these is love.

DELMAR, Dalmar
Language/Cultural Origin: **Latin**
Inherent Meaning: **By the Sea**
Spiritual Connotation: **Filled With Praise**
Scripture: **Psalm 69:34** NRSV
Let heaven and earth praise him, the seas and everything that moves in them.

DELORES, Deloria, Deloris, Dolores
Language/Cultural Origin: **Spanish**
Inherent Meaning: **Sorrowful**
Spiritual Connotation: **Compassionate**
Scripture: **Psalm 121:1** NKJV
I will lift up my eyes to the hills; from whence comes my help?

DELSIE, Delcee, Delcie, Delsee
Language/Cultural Origin: **English**
Inherent Meaning: **Oath of God**
Spiritual Connotation: **Promise**
Scripture: **Genesis 17:4** NRSV
As for me, this is my covenant with you: you shall be the ancestor of a multitude of nations.

DELTA, Deltra
Language/Cultural Origin: **Greek**
Inherent Meaning: **Door**
Spiritual Connotation: **Seeker of Truth**
Scripture: **Revelation 3:20** NKJV
Behold, I stand at the door and knock. If anyone hears My voice and opens the door, I will come in to him and dine with him, and he with Me.

DEMAS, Deemas, Deimas
☞ Language/Cultural Origin: **Greek**
Inherent Meaning: **Ruler of People**
Spiritual Connotation: **Powerful**
Scripture: **Psalm 105:21** NKJV
He made him lord of his house, and ruler of all his possessions.

DEMETRIA, Demetra, Demitra
Language/Cultural Origin: **Greek**
Inherent Meaning: **Plentiful**
Spiritual Connotation: **Fruitful**
Scripture: **John 10:10** NKJV
I have come that they may have life, and that they may have it more abundantly.

DEMETRIUS, Demetreus, ☞Demetrias, Demetric, Demetrik, Demitrias, Dimitrios, Dimitrius, Dmetrius (see also Dimitri)
Language/Cultural Origin: **Greek**
Inherent Meaning: **Lover of the Earth**
Spiritual Connotation: **Fruitful Increase**
Scripture: **Luke 11:10** NKJV
For everyone who asks receives, and he

*who seeks finds, and to him who knocks
it will be opened.*

DEMI, Demee, Demiah
Language/Cultural Origin: **French**
Inherent Meaning: **Half**
Spiritual Connotation: **Dependent**
Scripture: **Zechariah 4:6** NASB
*Not by might nor by power, but by My
Spirit, says the LORD of hosts.*

DEMPSEY, Dempsie
Language/Cultural Origin: **Irish**
Inherent Meaning: **Proud**
Spiritual Connotation: **Honorable**
Scripture: **Galatians 5:1** NKJV
*Stand fast therefore in the liberty by
which Christ has made us free, and do
not be entangled again with a yoke of
bondage.*

DENA, Deena
Language/Cultural Origin: **Native American**
Inherent Meaning: **From the Valley**
Spiritual Connotation: **Peaceful**
Scripture: **John 16:33** NASB
*These things I have spoken to you, so
that in Me you may have peace. In the
world you have tribulation, but take
courage; I have overcome the world.*

**DENAE, Denaé, Denay, Deneé (see
also Danae)**
Language/Cultural Origin: **Hebrew**
Inherent Meaning: **Vindicated**
Spiritual Connotation: **Example**
Scripture: **Ezekiel 39:27** RSV
*Through them I have vindicated my holi-
ness in the sight of many nations.*

DENHAM, Denhem
Language/Cultural Origin: **English**
Inherent Meaning: **From the Valley Village**
Spiritual Connotation: **One of Integrity**
Scripture: **Acts 24:16** NRSV
*Therefore I do my best always to have
a clear conscience toward God and all
people.*

**DENISE, Danice, Deni, Dení,
Denice, Deniece, Dennise**
Language/Cultural Origin: **French**
Inherent Meaning: **Favored**

Spiritual Connotation: **Reborn**
Scripture: **Isaiah 65:17** NKJV
*For behold, I create new heavens and a
new earth; and the former shall not be
remembered or come to mind.*

**DENNIS, Dénes, Denis, Dennes,
Denny**
Language/Cultural Origin: **Greek**
Inherent Meaning: **Happy**
Spiritual Connotation: **Effective**
Scripture: **Isaiah 55:11** NKJV
*So shall My word be that goes forth from
My mouth; it shall not return to Me void.*

DENTON, Dentin
Language/Cultural Origin: **English**
Inherent Meaning: **From a Happy Home**
Spiritual Connotation: **Trusting Spirit**
Scripture: **Romans 8:28** KJV
*And we know that all things work
together for good to them that love God,
to them who are the called according to
his purpose.*

**DENZEL, Danzel, Danzell, Dennzel,
Denzell, Denzil**
Language/Cultural Origin: **English**
Inherent Meaning: **From Cornwall, England**
Spiritual Connotation: **Forgiven**
Scripture: **1 John 3:20** NKJV
*For if our heart condemns us, God is
greater than our heart, and knows all
things.*

**DEON, Deion, Deone, Deontée,
Deontre, Dion, Diontae, Dionte
(see also Dante, Dontae)**
Language/Cultural Origin: **English**
Inherent Meaning: **Joyful**
Spiritual Connotation: **Praise**
Scripture: **Habakkuk 3:18** NASB
*Yet I will exult in the LORD, I will rejoice
in the God of my salvation.*

**DEREK, Darek, Darik, Darrick,
Darrik, Dereck, Derikk, Derreck,
Derrek, Derric, Derrick, Derrik**
Language/Cultural Origin: **German**
Inherent Meaning: **Ruler**
Spiritual Connotation: **Gifted**
Scripture: **Ecclesiastes 2:26** NKJV

For God gives wisdom and knowledge and joy to a man who is good in His sight.

DERIKA, Dereka, Derica, Dericka, Derrica, Derrika
Language/Cultural Origin: **German**
Inherent Meaning: **Ruler of the People**
Spiritual Connotation: **Generous**
Scripture: **Luke 11:13** TLB
Don't you realize that your heavenly Father will . . . give the Holy Spirit to those who ask for him?

DERON, De-Ron, Deronne, Derronn, Diron, Durron (see also Darius, Daron, Darren)
Language/Cultural Origin: **Welsh**
Inherent Meaning: **Freedom**
Spiritual Connotation: **Spirit-Filled**
Scripture: **2 Corinthians 3:17** NKJV
Now the Lord is the Spirit; and where the Spirit of the Lord is, there is liberty.

DESHAWNA, see Dashawna

DESHAY, Deshae, Deshea
Language/Cultural Origin: **American**
Inherent Meaning: **Courteous**
Spiritual Connotation: **Kind**
Scripture: **Psalm 57:10** TLB
Your kindness and love are as vast as the heavens. Your faithfulness is higher than the skies.

DESI, Dési, Dezi
Language/Cultural Origin: **French**
Inherent Meaning: **Longed-For**
Spiritual Connotation: **Faithful**
Scripture: **Philippians 4:1** NRSV
Therefore, my brothers and sisters, whom I love and long for, my joy and crown, stand firm in the Lord in this way, my beloved.

DESIREE, Desarae, Desaray, Desaré, Deserae, Deseray, Desirae, Desiray, Desirée, Désirée, Dezirae, Dezirée
Language/Cultural Origin: **French**
Inherent Meaning: **Desired**
Spiritual Connotation: **Likeness of God**
Scripture: **Isaiah 55:12** NKJV
The mountains and the hills shall break

forth into singing before you, and all the trees of the field shall clap their hands.

DESMOND, Des, Desmon, Desmund, Dezmond
Language/Cultural Origin: **Irish**
Inherent Meaning: **Youthful**
Spiritual Connotation: **Refreshing**
Scripture: **Ecclesiastes 3:17** NKJV
God shall judge the righteous and the wicked, for there is a time there for every purpose and for every work.

DESTIN, Deston, Destry
Language/Cultural Origin: **French**
Inherent Meaning: **Fate**
Spiritual Connotation: **Confirmed**
Scripture: **Isaiah 11:10** NLT
The nations will rally to him, for the land where he lives will be a glorious place.

DESTINY, Destanee, Destanie, Destany, Destinee, Destinée, Destiney, Destinie
Language/Cultural Origin: **Old French**
Inherent Meaning: **Fate**
Spiritual Connotation: **Fulfilled**
Scripture: **Psalm 132:14** NASB
This is My resting place forever; here I will dwell, for I have desired it.

DEVA, see Diva

DEVANY, Devaney, Devoney, Devony
Language/Cultural Origin: **Gaelic**
Inherent Meaning: **Dark-Haired**
Spiritual Connotation: **Sacrifice**
Scripture: **Romans 12:1** NRSV
I appeal to you therefore, brothers and sisters . . . to present your bodies as a living sacrifice, holy and acceptable to God.

DEVIN, Devan, Deven, Devine, Devyn
Language/Cultural Origin: **Irish**
Inherent Meaning: **Poet**
Spiritual Connotation: **Seeker of Wisdom**
Scripture: **Hebrews 13:16** NKJV
But do not forget to do good and to share, for with such sacrifices God is well pleased.

DEVON, Devonlee, Devonleigh, Devonn, Devonne (see also Davon)
Language/Cultural Origin: **English**
Inherent Meaning: **From Devonshire**
Spiritual Connotation: **Obedient**
Scripture: **Exodus 19:5** NKJV
Now therefore, if you will indeed obey My voice and keep My covenant, then you shall be a special treasure to Me above all people.

DEWEY, Dewie
Language/Cultural Origin: **Welsh**
Inherent Meaning: **Prized**
Spiritual Connotation: **Prosperous**
Scripture: **3 John 1:2** NLT
Dear friend, I am praying that all is well with you and that your body is as healthy as I know your soul is.

DEXTER, Dextor
Language/Cultural Origin: **Latin**
Inherent Meaning: **Skilled in Workmanship**
Spiritual Connotation: **Industrious**
Scripture: **Exodus 31:3** NLT
I have filled him with the Spirit of God, giving him great wisdom, intelligence, and skill in all kinds of crafts.

DIAMOND, Diamonique, Diamonté
Language/Cultural Origin: **Latin**
Inherent Meaning: **Precious Gem**
Spiritual Connotation: **Carefully Guarded**
Scripture: **Isaiah 54:12** NCV
I will use rubies to build your walls and shining jewels for the gates and precious jewels for all your outer walls.

DIANA, Daiana, Daianna, Di, Diahann, Dianah, Diandra, Diane, Diann, Dianna, Dianne, Dyan, Dyana, Dyane, Dyann, Dyanna, Dyanne
Language/Cultural Origin: **Latin**
Inherent Meaning: **Divine**
Spiritual Connotation: **Glorious**
Scripture: **Psalm 40:5** NKJV
Many, O LORD my God, are Your wonderful works which You have done. . . . They are more than can be numbered.

DIBRI, Díbri
Language/Cultural Origin: **Hebrew**
Inherent Meaning: **God's Promise**
Spiritual Connotation: **Reverent**
Scripture: **Psalm 25:14** NASB
The secret of the LORD is for those who fear Him, and He will make them know His covenant.

DICK, Dic, Dickenson, Dickie, Dik, Dikk (see also Richard)
Language/Cultural Origin: **English**
Inherent Meaning: **Powerful Ruler**
Spiritual Connotation: **Refuge**
Scripture: **Isaiah 32:2** NASB
And each will be like a refuge from the wind, and a shelter from the storm, like streams of water in a dry country, like the shade of a huge rock in a parched land.

DIEGO, Diaz
Language/Cultural Origin: **Spanish**
Inherent Meaning: **Supplanter**
Spiritual Connotation: **Wise**
Scripture: **Proverbs 9:9** NRSV
Give instruction to the wise, and they will become wiser still; teach the righteous and they will gain in learning.

DIETER, Deiter
Language/Cultural Origin: **German**
Inherent Meaning: **Army of the People**
Spiritual Connotation: **God's Warrior**
Scripture: **Isaiah 13:3** NASB
I have commanded My consecrated ones, I have even called My mighty warriors, My proudly exulting ones, to execute My anger.

DIETRICH, Dedric, Dedrick, Detrick, Didrik, Diedrick
Language/Cultural Origin: **German**
Inherent Meaning: **Ruler of the People**
Spiritual Connotation: **Respected**
Scripture: **Hebrews 13:17** NKJV
Obey those who rule over you, and be submissive, for they watch out for your souls. . . . Let them do so with joy and not with grief.

DILBERT, Dalbert, Del, Delbert
Language/Cultural Origin: **English**

Inherent Meaning: **Bright as Day**
Spiritual Connotation: **Obedient**
Scripture: **Deuteronomy 5:33** NKJV
*You shall walk in all the ways which the
LORD your God has commanded you . . .
that you may prolong your days in the
land which you shall possess.*

DILLON, Dillan, Dillen, Dillin (see also Dylan)
Language/Cultural Origin: **Irish**
Inherent Meaning: **Faithful**
Spiritual Connotation: **Steadfast in Christ**
Scripture: **1 John 3:18** NKJV
*My little children, let us not love in word
or in tongue, but in deed and in truth.*

DIMITRI, Demetri, Demitré, Dimitrie, Dmitri, Dymitri (see also Demetrius)
Language/Cultural Origin: **Russian**
Inherent Meaning: **Immeasurable**
Spiritual Connotation: **Gracious**
Scripture: **Jonah 4:2** NLT
*I knew that you were a gracious and
compassionate God, slow to get angry
and filled with unfailing love.*

DINAH, Dina, Dyna, Dynah
Language/Cultural Origin: **Hebrew**
Inherent Meaning: **God Has Vindicated**
Spiritual Connotation: **Righteous**
Scripture: **1 John 4:16** NKJV
*God is love, and he who abides in love
abides in God, and God in him.*

DINO, Deeno
Language/Cultural Origin: **German**
Inherent Meaning: **Little Sword**
Spiritual Connotation: **Covenant**
Scripture: **1 Kings 3:14** RSV
*And if you will walk in my ways, keeping
my statutes and my commandments . . .
then I will lengthen your days.*

DION, see Deon

DIONNE, Deondra, Deonna, Deonne, Dione, Dionna, Dionté, Diontée
Language/Cultural Origin: **Greek**
Inherent Meaning: **Divine Queen**
Spiritual Connotation: **Promise**

Scripture: **2 Peter 1:4** NRSV
*Thus he has given us . . . his precious
and very great promises, so that through
them you . . . may become participants
of the divine nature.*

DIOR, Diora, Diore, Diorra
Language/Cultural Origin: **French**
Inherent Meaning: **Golden**
Spiritual Connotation: **Seeker of Wisdom**
Scripture: **Colossians 2:3** NLT
*In him lie hidden all the treasures of wis-
dom and knowledge.*

DIRK, Derk
Language/Cultural Origin: **German**
Inherent Meaning: **Ruler**
Spiritual Connotation: **Perceptive Leadership**
Scripture: **Psalm 91:2** NKJV
*I will say of the LORD, He is my refuge
and my fortress; my God, in Him I will
trust.*

DIVA, Deva
Language/Cultural Origin: **Indo-Pakistani**
Inherent Meaning: **Blessed**
Spiritual Connotation: **Praise**
Scripture: **Psalm 8:1** NKJV
*O LORD, our Lord, how excellent is Your
name in all the earth, Who have set Your
glory above the heavens!*

DIVINA, Divinia
Language/Cultural Origin: **English**
Inherent Meaning: **Beloved**
Spiritual Connotation: **Humble**
Scripture: **Galatians 6:14** NKJV
*But God forbid that I should boast except
in the cross of our Lord Jesus Christ, by
whom the world has been crucified to me,
and I to the world.*

DIXIE, Dixee, Dixi, Dixy
Language/Cultural Origin: **French**
Inherent Meaning: **Tenth**
Spiritual Connotation: **Blessing**
Scripture: **2 Corinthians 4:15** NKJV
*For all things are for your sakes, that
grace, having spread through the many,
may cause thanksgiving to abound to the
glory of God.*

DIXON, Dickson
Language/Cultural Origin: **English**
Inherent Meaning: **Son of the Ruler**
Spiritual Connotation: **Youthful Courage**
Scripture: **Psalm 92:4** NKJV
*For You, LORD, have made me glad
through Your work; I will triumph in the
works of Your hands.*

DOLAN, Dolin, Dolyn
Language/Cultural Origin: **Irish**
Inherent Meaning: **Dark-Haired**
Spiritual Connotation: **Full of Life**
Scripture: **Psalm 145:10** NKJV
*All Your works shall praise You, O
LORD, and Your saints shall bless You.*

DOLLY, Dollee, Dolli, Dollie
Language/Cultural Origin: **American**
Inherent Meaning: **Compassionate**
Spiritual Connotation: **Christlike**
Scripture: **Psalm 116:5** NASB
*Gracious is the LORD, and righteous; yes,
our God is compassionate.*

DOLPH, Dolf
Language/Cultural Origin: **Slavic**
Inherent Meaning: **Famous**
Spiritual Connotation: **Great**
Scripture: **Ruth 4:14** NASB
*Then the women said to Naomi,
"Blessed is the LORD who has not left you
without a redeemer today."*

**DOMINIC, Dom, Domenick,
Domenico, Domingo, Dominitric**
Language/Cultural Origin: **Latin**
Inherent Meaning: **Belonging to the Lord**
Spiritual Connotation: **Faithful Disciple**
Scripture: **John 6:39** NLT
*And this is the will of God, that I should
not lose even one of all those he has given
me, but that I should raise them to eter-
nal life at the last day.*

DOMINIQUE, Dominica, Dominika
Language/Cultural Origin: **Latin**
Inherent Meaning: **Belonging to the Lord**
Spiritual Connotation: **Consecrated**
Scripture: **Isaiah 58:11** NKJV
*The LORD will guide you continually,
and satisfy your soul in drought, and*

*strengthen your bones; you shall be like a
watered garden.*

**DONALD, Don, Donn, Donnie,
Donny**
Language/Cultural Origin: **Gaelic**
Inherent Meaning: **World Leader**
Spiritual Connotation: **Faithful**
Scripture: **James 2:22** NKJV
*Do you see that faith was working
together with his works, and by works
faith was made perfect?*

DONATA, Donatta
Language/Cultural Origin: **Latin**
Inherent Meaning: **Gift of God**
Spiritual Connotation: **Contemplative**
Scripture: **Psalm 25:5** NKJV
*Lead me in Your truth and teach me, for
You are the God of my salvation; on You
I wait all the day.*

DONATO, Donatello
Language/Cultural Origin: **Italian**
Inherent Meaning: **Gift of God**
Spiritual Connotation: **Kind**
Scripture: **Proverbs 16:24** NKJV
*Pleasant words are like a honeycomb,
sweetness to the soul and health to the
bones.*

**DONNA, Dona, Doña, Doni, Donia,
Donica, Donie, Donika, Donni,
Donya (see also Danya, Dawn)**
Language/Cultural Origin: **Italian**
Inherent Meaning: **Refined Lady**
Spiritual Connotation: **Dependent**
Scripture: **Matthew 4:4** NKJV
*Man shall not live by bread alone, but by
every word that proceeds from the mouth
of God.*

**DONNELL, Donell, Donelle, Donnel,
Donnelle**
Language/Cultural Origin: **Irish**
Inherent Meaning: **Brave**
Spiritual Connotation: **Vigilant**
Scripture: **1 Corinthians 16:13** NKJV
*Watch, stand fast in the faith, be brave,
be strong.*

DONOVAN, Donavan, Donavon, Donoven, Donovon
Language/Cultural Origin: **Irish**
Inherent Meaning: **Dark Warrior**
Spiritual Connotation: **Refreshed**
Scripture: **Colossians 3:10** NKJV
Put on the new man who is renewed in knowledge according to the image of Him who created him.

DONTAE, Dontai, Dontay, Dontáy, Dontaye, Donté, Dontée
Language/Cultural Origin: **American**
Inherent Meaning: **Persevering**
Spiritual Connotation: **Steadfast**
Scripture: **1 Thessalonians 3:8** TLB
We can bear anything as long as we know that you remain strong in him.

DONYEL, see Daniel

DORA, Doralia, Doralie
Language/Cultural Origin: **Greek**
Inherent Meaning: **Gift of God**
Spiritual Connotation: **Wise**
Scripture: **Isaiah 33:6** NKJV
Wisdom and knowledge will be the stability of your times, and the strength of salvation; the fear of the LORD is His treasure.

DORAN, Dorin, Doron, Dorran, Dorren
Language/Cultural Origin: **Hebrew**
Inherent Meaning: **God's Gift**
Spiritual Connotation: **Sacrifice**
Scripture: **1 Corinthians 9:23** NASB
And I do all things for the sake of the gospel, that I may become a fellow partaker of it.

DORCAS
☞ Language/Cultural Origin: **Greek**
Inherent Meaning: **Filled With Grace**
Spiritual Connotation: **Heir**
Scripture: **Psalm 37:18** NKJV
The LORD knows the days of the upright, and their inheritance shall be forever.

DOREEN, Dorene, Dorey, Dori, Dorie, Dorri, Dorrie, Dureen
Language/Cultural Origin: **Gaelic**
Inherent Meaning: **Acrimonious**
Spiritual Connotation: **Peerless**
Scripture: **Psalm 100:5** NKJV
For the LORD is good; His mercy is everlasting, and His truth endures to all generations.

DORIAN, Doriana, Doriann, Dorianna, Dorien, Dorion, Dorrian, Dorrien
Language/Cultural Origin: **Greek**
Inherent Meaning: **Gift**
Spiritual Connotation: **Gracious**
Scripture: **1 John 3:2** NKJV
Beloved, now we are children of God . . . when He is revealed, we shall be like Him, for we shall see Him as He is.

DORIS, Dorice, Dorise, Dorris
Language/Cultural Origin: **Greek**
Inherent Meaning: **From the Ocean**
Spiritual Connotation: **Strong**
Scripture: **Isaiah 33:6** NKJV
Wisdom and knowledge will be the stability of your times, and the strength of salvation; the fear of the LORD is His treasure.

DOROTHEA, Dorotheé, Dorothy, Dotti, Dottie, Dotty
Language/Cultural Origin: **Greek**
Inherent Meaning: **Gift of God**
Spiritual Connotation: **Blessed**
Scripture: **Isaiah 52:7** NKJV
How beautiful upon the mountains are the feet of him who brings good news . . . who says to Zion, "Your God reigns!"

DOUGLAS, Doug, Douglass
Language/Cultural Origin: **Scottish**
Inherent Meaning: **From the Dark Stream**
Spiritual Connotation: **Adventurous**
Scripture: **1 Corinthians 2:7** NKJV
But we speak the wisdom of God in a mystery, the hidden wisdom which God ordained before the ages for our glory.

DOYLE, Doyal
Language/Cultural Origin: **Irish**
Inherent Meaning: **Dark Stranger**
Spiritual Connotation: **Guided by the Spirit**
Scripture: **2 Corinthians 3:17** NKJV

Now the Lord is the Spirit; and where the Spirit of the Lord is, there is liberty.

DRAKE, Drago
Language/Cultural Origin: **Latin**
Inherent Meaning: **Dragon**
Spiritual Connotation: **Symbol**
Scripture: **Psalm 104:25** NKJV
[In] this great and wide sea . . . the ships sail about; there is that Leviathan which You have made to play there.

DREW, Drewe, Dru, Drue
Language/Cultural Origin: **Welsh**
Inherent Meaning: **Wise**
Spiritual Connotation: **Esteemed**
Scripture: **Romans 12:10** NKJV
Be kindly affectionate to one another with brotherly love, in honor giving preference to one another.

DRISANA, Drisanna
Language/Cultural Origin: **Sanskrit**
Inherent Meaning: **Daughter of the Sun**
Spiritual Connotation: **Loyal**
Scripture: **Ruth 1:16** NLT
I will go wherever you go and live wherever you live. Your people will be my people, and your God will be my God.

DRUSILLA, Drucilla, Druscilla
☞ Language/Cultural Origin: **Latin**
Inherent Meaning: **Strong**
Spiritual Connotation: **Strong in Spirit**
Scripture: **John 15:7** NKJV
If you abide in Me, and My words abide in you, you will ask what you desire, and it shall be done for you.

DRYDEN, Drieden
Language/Cultural Origin: **English**
Inherent Meaning: **From the Arid Valley**
Spiritual Connotation: **Trusting**
Scripture: **Proverbs 3:5-6** NKJV
Trust in the LORD with all your heart, and lean not on your own understanding; in all your ways acknowledge Him, and He shall direct your paths.

DUANA, Duanna
Language/Cultural Origin: **Irish**
Inherent Meaning: **Cheerful Song**
Spiritual Connotation: **Harmonious**

Scripture: **Psalm 92:4** NKJV
For You, LORD, have made me glad through Your work; I will triumph in the works of Your hands.

DUANE, see Dwayne

DUDLEY, Dudly
Language/Cultural Origin: **English**
Inherent Meaning: **From the Common Field**
Spiritual Connotation: **Free in Christ**
Scripture: **John 8:32** KJV
And ye shall know the truth, and the truth shall make you free.

DUGAN, Doogan, Duggan
Language/Cultural Origin: **Scottish**
Inherent Meaning: **Dark**
Spiritual Connotation: **Gifted**
Scripture: **Psalm 150:4** NCV
Praise him with tambourines and dancing; praise him with stringed instruments and flutes.

DULCINEA, Dulcia, Dulciana, Dulcie
Language/Cultural Origin: **Spanish**
Inherent Meaning: **Sweet**
Spiritual Connotation: **Delights in God's Grace**
Scripture: **Psalm 37:5** NKJV
Commit your way to the LORD, trust also in Him, and He shall bring it to pass.

DUNCAN, Duncon
Language/Cultural Origin: **Scottish**
Inherent Meaning: **Steadfast Warrior**
Spiritual Connotation: **Strong in Faith**
Scripture: **Romans 10:8** NKJV
The word is near you, in your mouth and in your heart.

DUNSTAN, Dunsten
Language/Cultural Origin: **English**
Inherent Meaning: **From the Stony Hill**
Spiritual Connotation: **Victorious**
Scripture: **John 5:26** NKJV
For as the Father has life in Himself, so He has granted the Son to have life in Himself.

DURANT, Durand, Durante, Durrant

Language/Cultural Origin: Latin
Inherent Meaning: Enduring
Spiritual Connotation: Protected
Scripture: Psalm 34:7 NKJV
The angel of the LORD encamps all around those who fear Him, and delivers them.

DUSTIN, Dustan, Dusten, Duston, Dusty, Dustyn

Language/Cultural Origin: German
Inherent Meaning: Valiant Warrior
Spiritual Connotation: Brave
Scripture: Acts 27:22 NLT
But take courage! None of you will lose your lives, even though the ship will go down.

DUSYA, Dusyanna

Language/Cultural Origin: Russian
Inherent Meaning: Hope
Spiritual Connotation: Steadfast
Scripture: Hebrews 3:6 NRSV
Christ, however, was faithful over God's house as a son, and we are his house if we hold firm the confidence and the pride that belong to hope.

DWAYNE, DeWayne, Duaine, Duane, Dwane

Language/Cultural Origin: Irish
Inherent Meaning: Dark
Spiritual Connotation: Transformed Heart
Scripture: Job 22:28 NKJV
You will also declare a thing, and it will be established for you; so light will shine on your ways.

DWIGHT, Dweight

Language/Cultural Origin: English
Inherent Meaning: Fair
Spiritual Connotation: Diligent Leader
Scripture: Psalm 91:1 NKJV
He who dwells in the secret place of the Most High shall abide under the shadow of the Almighty.

DYLAN, Dyllan, Dyllon, Dylon (see also Dillon)

Language/Cultural Origin: Welsh
Inherent Meaning: From the Sea
Spiritual Connotation: Resolute Courage
Scripture: Deuteronomy 20:4 NKJV
The LORD your God is He who goes with you, to fight for you against your enemies, to save you.

DYLANA, Dylanna

Language/Cultural Origin: Welsh
Inherent Meaning: From the Sea
Spiritual Connotation: Devoted
Scripture: John 21:7 NASB
And so when Simon Peter heard that it was the Lord, he put his outer garment on . . . and threw himself into the sea.

E

EAGAN, see Egan

EAN, see Ian

EARL, Earle
Language/Cultural Origin: **English**
Inherent Meaning: **Noble**
Spiritual Connotation: **Reflected Image**
Scripture: **Genesis 1:26** NKJV
Let Us make man in Our image, according to Our likeness.

EASTER, Eastre
Language/Cultural Origin: **Old German**
Inherent Meaning: **Spring Festival**
Spiritual Connotation: **Celebration**
Scripture: **Matthew 28:6** NASB
He is not here, for He has risen, just as He said.

EASTON, Eason
Language/Cultural Origin: **English**
Inherent Meaning: **From the Eastern Town**
Spiritual Connotation: **Christlike**
Scripture: **2 Corinthians 4:6** NASB
Light shall shine out of darkness . . . to give the light of the knowledge of the glory of God in the face of Christ.

EBONY, Ebanee, Ebany, Ebonee, Eboney, Eboni, Ebonie
Language/Cultural Origin: **American**
Inherent Meaning: **Hard, Dark Wood**
Spiritual Connotation: **Shining**
Scripture: **John 8:12** NRSV
I am the light of the world. Whoever follows me will never walk in darkness but will have the light of life.

ECHO, Ecko, Ekko
Language/Cultural Origin: **Greek**
Inherent Meaning: **Repeated Sound**
Spiritual Connotation: **Constant Prayer**
Scripture: **1 Thessalonians 5:17** NASB
Pray without ceasing; in everything give thanks; for this is God's will for you in Christ Jesus.

EDA, Edah
Language/Cultural Origin: **Irish**
Inherent Meaning: **Loyal**
Spiritual Connotation: **Faithful**
Scripture: **Psalm 77:14** NKJV
You are the God who does wonders; You have declared Your strength among the peoples.

EDANA, Edanna, Edena
Language/Cultural Origin: **Irish**
Inherent Meaning: **Ardent Flame**
Spiritual Connotation: **Unending Love**
Scripture: **Song of Songs 8:6** RSV
Set me as a seal upon your heart, as a seal upon your arm; for love is strong as death.

EDEN, Eaden, Eadin, Edin, Edyn
Language/Cultural Origin: **Hebrew**
Inherent Meaning: **Delightful**
Spiritual Connotation: **Pleasing**
Scripture: **Zephaniah 3:17** NKJV
The LORD your God in your midst, the Mighty One, will save; He will rejoice over you with gladness, He will quiet you with His love.

EDGAR, Ed
Language/Cultural Origin: **English**
Inherent Meaning: **Prosperous**
Spiritual Connotation: **Gifted**
Scripture: **1 Corinthians 12:4** NKJV
There are diversities of gifts, but the same Spirit.

EDIE, Eadie, Edy, Eydie
Language/Cultural Origin: **English**
Inherent Meaning: **Wealthy**
Spiritual Connotation: **Obedient**
Scripture: **1 Kings 2:3** TLB
Obey the laws of God and follow all his ways; keep each of his commands written in the law of Moses so that you will prosper in everything you do.

EDITH, Edythe
Language/Cultural Origin: **Old English**
Inherent Meaning: **Valuable Gift**
Spiritual Connotation: **Wise**
Scripture: **Proverbs 3:15** RSV
She is more precious than jewels, and nothing you desire can compare with her.

EDMUND, Edmon, Edmond, Edmonde, Esmond
Language/Cultural Origin: **Old English**
Inherent Meaning: **Blessed Peace**
Spiritual Connotation: **Prosperous Protector**
Scripture: **John 14:27** NKJV
Peace I leave with you, My peace I give to you; not as the world gives do I give to you. Let not your heart be troubled, neither let it be afraid.

EDNA, Ednah
Language/Cultural Origin: **Hebrew**
Inherent Meaning: **Rejuvenated**
Spiritual Connotation: **Filled With Pleasure**
Scripture: **John 3:6** NASB
That which is born of the flesh is flesh, and that which is born of the Spirit is spirit.

EDOM
Language/Cultural Origin: **Hebrew**
Inherent Meaning: **Red Earth**
Spiritual Connotation: **Strong**
Scripture: **Genesis 36:8** NCV
So Esau lived in the mountains of Edom. (Esau is also named Edom.)

EDRIC, Eddrick, Ederick, Edrick
Language/Cultural Origin: **Old English**
Inherent Meaning: **Powerful With Property**
Spiritual Connotation: **Blessed**
Scripture: **Deuteronomy 30:9** RSV
The LORD your God will make you abundantly prosperous in all the work of your hand.

EDWARD, Ed, Eddie, Eddy, Eduardo, Edwardo, Edwards
Language/Cultural Origin: **Old English**
Inherent Meaning: **Appointed to Protect**
Spiritual Connotation: **Guardian of Happiness**
Scripture: **John 14:13** NKJV
And whatever you ask in My name, that I will do, that the Father may be glorified in the Son.

EDWIN, Edwyn
Language/Cultural Origin: **Old English**
Inherent Meaning: **Prosperous Friend**
Spiritual Connotation: **Belonging to God**
Scripture: **John 17:10** NKJV
And all Mine are Yours, and Yours are Mine, and I am glorified in them.

EDWINA (Ed-ween-a)
Language/Cultural Origin: **English**
Inherent Meaning: **Rich in Friendship**
Spiritual Connotation: **A Friend of God**
Scripture: **John 15:14** NIV
You are my friends if you do what I command.

EGAN, Eagan, Egann, Egen
Language/Cultural Origin: **Irish**
Inherent Meaning: **Ardent**
Spiritual Connotation: **Filled With Zeal**
Scripture: **Psalm 69:9** NLT
Passion for your house burns within me, so those who insult you are also insulting me.

EILEEN, Eilean, Eilene, Eilleen (see also Aileen)
Language/Cultural Origin: **English**
Inherent Meaning: **Bright Light**
Spiritual Connotation: **Glorious**
Scripture: **Psalm 23:6** KJV
Surely goodness and mercy shall follow me all the days of my life: and I will dwell in the house of the LORD for ever.

EINAR, Ejnar
Language/Cultural Origin: **Old Norse**
Inherent Meaning: **Individualist**
Spiritual Connotation: **Free**
Scripture: **Galatians 5:1** NASB

*It was for freedom that Christ set us free;
therefore keep standing firm and do not
be subject again to a yoke of slavery.*

EIRA, Eirah
Language/Cultural Origin: **Welsh**
Inherent Meaning: **Snow**
Spiritual Connotation: **Pure**
Scripture: **Psalm 51:7** NLT
*Purify me from my sins, and I will be
clean; wash me, and I will be whiter
than snow.*

EIRENA, Eirana, Eiranna, Eirenna
Language/Cultural Origin: **English**
Inherent Meaning: **Peace**
Spiritual Connotation: **Contentment**
Scripture: **Psalm 119:165** NASB
*Those who love Your law have great
peace, and nothing causes them to
stumble.*

ELADAH, Eilada, Eláda, Elahdah
Language/Cultural Origin: **Hebrew**
Inherent Meaning: **Adorned of God**
Spiritual Connotation: **Lovely**
Scripture: **Psalm 45:11** NCV
*The king loves your beauty. Because he
is your master, you should obey him.*

ELAINE, Elain, Elane, Elayne, Eliane
Language/Cultural Origin: **Old French**
Inherent Meaning: **Brilliant**
Spiritual Connotation: **Admirable**
Scripture: **Psalm 84:11** NKJV
*For the LORD God is a sun and shield;
the LORD will give grace and glory; no
good thing will He withhold from those
who walk uprightly.*

ELAN, Elann
Language/Cultural Origin: **Native American**
Inherent Meaning: **Friendly**
Spiritual Connotation: **Servant**
Scripture: **John 15:13** NKJV
*Greater love has no one than this, than
to lay down one's life for his friends.*

ELANA, Elaina, Elainna, Elani, Elania, Elanna
Language/Cultural Origin: **English**
Inherent Meaning: **Shining**
Spiritual Connotation: **Standard**

Scripture: **Isaiah 60:3** NCV
*Nations will come to your light; kings will
come to the brightness of your sunrise.*

ELASAH, Elasa, Elása, Elasia, Elasya
Language/Cultural Origin: **Hebrew**
Inherent Meaning: **God Has Created**
Spiritual Connotation: **Image of God**
Scripture: **Genesis 5:2** NKJV
*He created them male and female, and
blessed them and called them Mankind in
the day they were created.*

ELDEN, Eldin
Language/Cultural Origin: **Old English**
Inherent Meaning: **Wise Guardian**
Spiritual Connotation: **Good Judgment**
Scripture: **Hebrews 13:20** NKJV
*Now may the God of peace who brought
up our Lord Jesus from the dead . . .
make you complete in every good work to
do His will.*

ELDON, Elldon
Language/Cultural Origin: **English**
Inherent Meaning: **From the Holy Hill**
Spiritual Connotation: **Enlightened**
Scripture: **Isaiah 30:29** NKJV
*You shall have a song as in the night
when a holy festival is kept, and gladness
of heart.*

ELDRED, Eldrid
Language/Cultural Origin: **Old English**
Inherent Meaning: **Elderly Counsel**
Spiritual Connotation: **Friend of God**
Scripture: **1 John 2:13** NRSV
*I am writing to you, fathers, because you
know him who is from the beginning. I
am writing to you, young people, because
you have conquered the evil one.*

ELDRIDGE, Eldredge
Language/Cultural Origin: **German**
Inherent Meaning: **Mature Counselor**
Spiritual Connotation: **Godly**
Scripture: **Romans 12:2** NKJV
*And do not be conformed to this world,
but be transformed by the renewing of
your mind.*

ELEANOR, Eleanore, Elinor, Ellenora, Elynora

Language/Cultural Origin: **Greek**
Inherent Meaning: **Bright as the Sun**
Spiritual Connotation: **Kindhearted**
Scripture: **Ephesians 4:32** NKJV
And be kind to one another, tenderhearted, forgiving one another, just as God in Christ forgave you.

ELEAZAR, Eléazar, Eliazar

Language/Cultural Origin: **Hebrew**
Inherent Meaning: **God Has Helped**
Spiritual Connotation: **Set Apart**
Scripture: **Numbers 4:16** NCV
Eleazar son of Aaron, the priest, will be responsible for the Holy Tent and for everything in it, for all the holy things.

ELECTRA, Elektra

Language/Cultural Origin: **Greek**
Inherent Meaning: **Brilliant**
Spiritual Connotation: **Eternal Hope**
Scripture: **Isaiah 60:19** NRSV
The sun shall no longer be your light by day . . . but the LORD will be your everlasting light, and your God will be your glory.

ELENA, Eleena, Elina, Ellena

Language/Cultural Origin: **Russian**
Inherent Meaning: **Radiant**
Spiritual Connotation: **Illuminated**
Scripture: **Psalm 16:11** NKJV
You will show me the path of life; in Your presence is fullness of joy; at Your right hand are pleasures forevermore.

ELGIN, Elgen

Language/Cultural Origin: **English**
Inherent Meaning: **Noble**
Spiritual Connotation: **Responsible**
Scripture: **Ezra 10:4** NASB
Arise! For this matter is your responsibility, but we will be with you; be courageous and act.

ELI, Ely

Language/Cultural Origin: **Hebrew**
Inherent Meaning: **Uplifted**
Spiritual Connotation: **Delivered**
Scripture: **Psalm 50:15** NKJV
Call upon Me in the day of trouble; I will deliver you, and you shall glorify Me.

ELIAB

Language/Cultural Origin: **Hebrew**
Inherent Meaning: **God Is My Father**
Spiritual Connotation: **God's Child**
Scripture: **Exodus 3:6** NCV
I am the God of your ancestors—the God of Abraham, the God of Isaac, and the God of Jacob.

ELIADA, Eliadah, Elliada, Elyada

Language/Cultural Origin: **Hebrew**
Inherent Meaning: **God Knows**
Spiritual Connotation: **Revealed**
Scripture: **Luke 16:15** NKJV
You are those who justify yourselves before men, but God knows your hearts.

ELIAH, Eliyah

Language/Cultural Origin: **Hebrew**
Inherent Meaning: **The Lord Is God**
Spiritual Connotation: **Believer**
Scripture: **Deuteronomy 4:39** NCV
Know and believe today that the LORD is God. He is God in heaven above and on the earth below. There is no other god!

ELIANA, Elianna, Ellianna (see also Iliana, Liana)

Language/Cultural Origin: **Hebrew**
Inherent Meaning: **God Has Answered Me**
Spiritual Connotation: **Fulfilled Promise**
Scripture: **1 Samuel 1:20** NKJV
Hannah conceived and bore a son, and called his name Samuel, saying, "Because I have asked for him from the LORD."

ELIAS, Ellis

Language/Cultural Origin: **Greek**
Inherent Meaning: **God Is My Salvation**
Spiritual Connotation: **Mouthpiece of God**
Scripture: **Luke 12:11** NKJV
Do not worry about how or what you should answer, or what you should say. For the Holy Spirit will teach you in that very hour what you ought to say.

ELIJAH, Elija, Eliyahu

Language/Cultural Origin: **Hebrew**
Inherent Meaning: **The Lord Is My God**

Spiritual Connotation: **Spiritual Champion**
Scripture: **Proverbs 3:6** KJV
In all thy ways acknowledge him, and he shall direct thy paths.

ELIORA, Eliaura, Eliorra, Eliyora
Language/Cultural Origin: **Hebrew**
Inherent Meaning: **My God Is Light**
Spiritual Connotation: **Beloved**
Scripture: **Isaiah 12:2** NRSV
Surely God is my salvation; I will trust, and will not be afraid, for the LORD GOD is my strength and my might; he has become my salvation.

ELISE, Élise, Elisse, Ellice, Ellise, Ellyce, Ellyse, Elyce, Elyse
Language/Cultural Origin: **French**
Inherent Meaning: **Oath of God**
Spiritual Connotation: **Dedicated**
Scripture: **Acts 11:23** NRSV
When he came and saw the grace of God, he rejoiced, and he exhorted them all to remain faithful to the Lord with steadfast devotion.

ELISHA, Elishah, Elishia, Elishua
Language/Cultural Origin: **Hebrew**
Inherent Meaning: **God Will Save Me**
Spiritual Connotation: **Protected**
Scripture: **Psalm 62:7** TLB
My protection and success come from God alone. He is my refuge, a Rock where no enemy can reach me.

ELISSA, Elisia, Ellisa, Ellissa, Ellisia, Ellyssa, Elysa, Elyssa (see also Alisa, Elysia, Lissa)
Language/Cultural Origin: **Italian**
Inherent Meaning: **Oath of God**
Spiritual Connotation: **Devoted**
Scripture: **Psalm 89:1** NRSV
I will sing of your steadfast love, O LORD, forever; with my mouth I will proclaim your faithfulness to all generations.

ELIZA, Aliza, Elizah
Language/Cultural Origin: **Polish**
Inherent Meaning: **Oath of God**
Spiritual Connotation: **Pledged**
Scripture: **2 Corinthians 11:2** NLT
I am jealous for you with the jealousy of God himself. For I promised you as a pure bride to one husband, Christ.

ELIZABETH, Elisabeth, Elisabethe
Language/Cultural Origin: **Hebrew**
Inherent Meaning: **Oath of God**
Spiritual Connotation: **Consecrated**
Scripture: **Romans 6:23** NKJV
But the gift of God is eternal life in Christ Jesus our Lord.

ELKANAH, Elkana
Language/Cultural Origin: **Hebrew**
Inherent Meaning: **God Is Jealous**
Spiritual Connotation: **Pure**
Scripture: **Deuteronomy 5:9** NLT
You must never worship or bow down to them, for I, the LORD your God, am a jealous God who will not share your affection with any other god!

ELKE, Elki
Language/Cultural Origin: **German**
Inherent Meaning: **Nobility**
Spiritual Connotation: **Approved**
Scripture: **1 Thessalonians 2:4** NLT
For we speak as messengers who have been approved by God to be entrusted with the Good News.

ELLA, Ellah
Language/Cultural Origin: **Old German**
Inherent Meaning: **Beautiful**
Spiritual Connotation: **Sustained**
Scripture: **Psalm 91:11** KJV
For he shall give his angels charge over thee, to keep thee in all thy ways.

ELLEN, Elen, Ellan, Ellin
Language/Cultural Origin: **English**
Inherent Meaning: **Bright**
Spiritual Connotation: **Heir**
Scripture: **Matthew 4:16** NKJV
The people who sat in darkness have seen a great light, and upon those who sat in the region and shadow of death Light has dawned.

ELLERY, Elleree, Ellerey
Language/Cultural Origin: **English**
Inherent Meaning: **From Elder Tree Island**
Spiritual Connotation: **Creative Worker**
Scripture: **Psalm 31:23** NKJV

Oh, love the LORD, *all you His saints!
For the* LORD *preserves the faithful, and
fully repays the proud person.*

ELLIE, Elie, Elli

Language/Cultural Origin: **Estonian**
Inherent Meaning: **Illuminated**
Spiritual Connotation: **Shining Light**
Scripture: **Luke 11:36** TLB
*If you are filled with light within, with no
dark corners, then your face will be radi-
ant too, as though a floodlight is beamed
upon you.*

ELLIOT, Eliot, Eliott, Elliott

Language/Cultural Origin: **Hebrew**
Inherent Meaning: **The Lord Is My God**
Spiritual Connotation: **Consecrated**
Scripture: **Isaiah 51:16** NASB
*And I have put My words in your
mouth, and have covered you with the
shadow of My hand. . . . You are My
people.*

ELLIS, see Elias

ELLISON, Elison, Ellyson

Language/Cultural Origin: **English**
Inherent Meaning: **Son of the Redeemed
One**
Spiritual Connotation: **Near to God's Heart**
Scripture: **Psalm 32:7** NASB
*You are my hiding place; You preserve
me from trouble; You surround me with
songs of deliverance.*

ELMER, Ellmer

Language/Cultural Origin: **Old English**
Inherent Meaning: **Famous**
Spiritual Connotation: **Trusting**
Scripture: **Psalm 36:7** NKJV
*How precious is Your lovingkindness, O
God! Therefore the children of men put
their trust under the shadow of Your wings.*

ELMO, Almo

Language/Cultural Origin: **Latin**
Inherent Meaning: **Vigilant**
Spiritual Connotation: **Secure**
Scripture: **John 14:1** NKJV
*Let not your heart be troubled; you
believe in God, believe also in Me.*

ELOISE

Language/Cultural Origin: **Old German**
Inherent Meaning: **Wise**
Spiritual Connotation: **Sustained**
Scripture: **Psalms 121:5** NKJV
The LORD *is your keeper; the* LORD *is
your shade at your right hand.*

ELROY

Language/Cultural Origin: **Latin**
Inherent Meaning: **Majestic**
Spiritual Connotation: **Noble**
Scripture: **Proverbs 17:24** NKJV
*Wisdom is in the sight of him who has
understanding, but the eyes of a fool are
on the ends of the earth.*

ELSA, Ellsa

Language/Cultural Origin: **Swedish**
Inherent Meaning: **Royal**
Spiritual Connotation: **Honorable**
Scripture: **Philippians 4:8** RSV
*Finally, brethren, whatever is true, . . .
honorable, . . . just, whatever is
pure, . . . lovely, . . . gracious, if there is
any excellence, . . . [or] anything worthy
of praise, think about these things.*

ELSIE, Ellsey, Ellsie, Elsi, Elsy

Language/Cultural Origin: **German**
Inherent Meaning: **Noble**
Spiritual Connotation: **Priceless Friend**
Scripture: **John 15:13** NKJV
*Greater love has no one than this, than
to lay down one's life for his friends.*

ELSTON, Ellston

Language/Cultural Origin: **Old English**
Inherent Meaning: **From the Old Farm**
Spiritual Connotation: **Believer**
Scripture: **John 11:25** NKJV
*He who believes in Me, though he may
die, he shall live.*

ELTON, Alten, Alton, Ellton

Language/Cultural Origin: **English**
Inherent Meaning: **From the Old Town**
Spiritual Connotation: **Steadfast**
Scripture: **Hebrews 4:14** NKJV
*Seeing then that we have a great High
Priest who has passed through the heav-
ens, Jesus the Son of God, let us hold
fast our confession.*

ELVA, Elvia (see also Alva)
Language/Cultural Origin: **Old English**
Inherent Meaning: **Delicate**
Spiritual Connotation: **Enlightened**
Scripture: **Psalm 54:2** NKJV
Hear my prayer, O God; Give ear to the words of my mouth.

ELVIN, Elvyn (see also Alvin)
Language/Cultural Origin: **Old English**
Inherent Meaning: **Friend of All**
Spiritual Connotation: **Joyous**
Scripture: **Matthew 9:15** NKJV
Can the friends of the bridegroom mourn as long as the bridegroom is with them?

ELVIRA, Elvera
Language/Cultural Origin: **Spanish**
Inherent Meaning: **Fair**
Spiritual Connotation: **Wise**
Scripture: **James 3:17** NKJV
But the wisdom that is from above is first pure, then peaceable, gentle, . . . [and] without partiality and without hypocrisy.

ELVIS, Elvys
Language/Cultural Origin: **Old Norse**
Inherent Meaning: **All-Wise**
Spiritual Connotation: **Righteous**
Scripture: **Isaiah 58:8** NKJV
Then your light shall break forth like the morning, your healing shall spring forth speedily, and your righteousness shall go before you.

ELYA, Elja, Elyah (see also Ilya)
Language/Cultural Origin: **Hebrew**
Inherent Meaning: **The Lord Is My God**
Spiritual Connotation: **Filled With Praise**
Scripture: **Exodus 15:2** RSV
The LORD is my strength and my song, and he has become my salvation; this is my God, and I will praise him, my father's God, and I will exalt him.

ELYNN, Elinn, Elyne, Ellynn
Language/Cultural Origin: **American**
Inherent Meaning: **Clear Pool**
Spiritual Connotation: **Cleansed**
Scripture: **Hebrews 10:22** NCV
We have been made free from a guilty conscience, and our bodies have been washed with pure water.

ELYSIA (see also Alisa, Elissa, Lissa)
Language/Cultural Origin: **Latin**
Inherent Meaning: **Sweetly Blissful**
Spiritual Connotation: **Strong Faith**
Scripture: **Matthew 17:20** NKJV
If you have faith as a mustard seed, you will say to this mountain, Move from here to there, and it will move; and nothing will be impossible for you.

EMANUEL, Emanual, Emanuell, Emmanuel, Immanuel
Language/Cultural Origin: **Hebrew**
Inherent Meaning: **God With Us**
Spiritual Connotation: **Gift of God**
Scripture: **John 3:16** NKJV
For God so loved the world that He gave His only begotten Son, that whoever believes in Him should not perish but have everlasting life.

EMANUELA, Emmanuella, Emmanuelle, Imanuela
Language/Cultural Origin: **Hebrew**
Inherent Meaning: **God With Us**
Spiritual Connotation: **Gift of God**
Scripture: **Isaiah 7:14** NKJV
Therefore the Lord Himself will give you a sign: Behold, the virgin shall conceive and bear a Son, and shall call His name Immanuel.

EMBER, Embur (see also Amber)
Language/Cultural Origin: **Old English**
Inherent Meaning: **Ashes**
Spiritual Connotation: **Confirmed Faith**
Scripture: **Acts 10:40** NASB
God raised Him up on the third day, and granted that He should become visible.

EMELIA, Amilia, Emalia, Emilia (see also Amelia, Emily)
Language/Cultural Origin: **Latin**
Inherent Meaning: **Industrious**
Spiritual Connotation: **Blessed**
Scripture: **Zephaniah 3:17** NKJV
The LORD your God in your midst, the Mighty One, will save; He will rejoice over you with gladness.

EMERALD, Emeralde
Language/Cultural Origin: **French**

Inherent Meaning: **Green Gem**
Spiritual Connotation: **Breathtaking**
Scripture: **Revelation 4:3** NCV
The One who sat on the throne looked like precious stones. . . . All around the throne was a rainbow the color of an emerald.

EMERSON, Emmerson
Language/Cultural Origin: **English**
Inherent Meaning: **Son of the Leader**
Spiritual Connotation: **Victorious**
Scripture: **Psalm 20:5** RSV
May we shout for joy over your victory, and in the name of our God set up our banners! May the LORD fulfil all your petitions!

EMERY, Emeri, Emmery, Emmory, Emory (see also Amery, Emre)
Language/Cultural Origin: **German**
Inherent Meaning: **Industrious Leader**
Spiritual Connotation: **Authority Under God**
Scripture: **Proverbs 29:2** NKJV
When the righteous are in authority, the people rejoice.

EMIL, Emill
Language/Cultural Origin: **German**
Inherent Meaning: **Industrious**
Spiritual Connotation: **Diligent Seeker**
Scripture: **Jeremiah 29:12** NKJV
Then you will call upon Me and go and pray to Me, and I will listen to you. And you will seek Me and find Me, when you search for Me with all your heart.

EMILIAN, Emille, Emillé, Emils
Language/Cultural Origin: **Polish**
Inherent Meaning: **Eager**
Spiritual Connotation: **Purified**
Scripture: **2 Corinthians 7:11** NRSV
For see what earnestness this godly grief has produced in you. . . . At every point you have proved yourselves guiltless in the matter.

EMILIANNA, Emiliana, Emiliann, Emilianne, Emilyann, Emilyanne
Language/Cultural Origin: **American**
Inherent Meaning: **Gracious**
Spiritual Connotation: **Thoughtful**

Scripture: **Ruth 3:10** NKJV
Blessed are you of the LORD, my daughter! For you have shown more kindness at the end than at the beginning.

EMILIO, Emillio
Language/Cultural Origin: **Italian**
Inherent Meaning: **Glorifier**
Spiritual Connotation: **Obedient**
Scripture: **Isaiah 26:8** NLT
LORD, we love to obey your laws; our heart's desire is to glorify your name.

EMILY, Emalee, Emelie, Emile, Emilee, Emiley, Emilie, Emillie, Emilly, Emmélie, Emylee (see also Amelia, Emelia)
Language/Cultural Origin: **German**
Inherent Meaning: **Industrious**
Spiritual Connotation: **Diligent Worker**
Scripture: **Matthew 5:16** NKJV
Let your light so shine before men, that they may see your good works and glorify your Father in heaven.

EMMA, Ema
Language/Cultural Origin: **Old German**
Inherent Meaning: **All-Embracing**
Spiritual Connotation: **Absolute Faith**
Scripture: **Mark 11:24** NKJV
Therefore I say to you, whatever things you ask when you pray, believe that you receive them, and you will have them.

EMMET, Emitt, Emmett, Emmit, Emmitt, Emmot, Emmott
Language/Cultural Origin: **Old English**
Inherent Meaning: **Earnest**
Spiritual Connotation: **Genuine Devotion**
Scripture: **Philippians 4:4** NKJV
Rejoice in the Lord always. Again I will say, rejoice!

EMMY, Emee, Emi, Emmi, Emmie
Language/Cultural Origin: **English**
Inherent Meaning: **Striving**
Spiritual Connotation: **Attentive**
Scripture: **Hebrews 2:1** NRSV
Therefore we must pay greater attention to what we have heard, so that we do not drift away from it.

EMRE, Emra, Emrah, Emree (see also Amery, Emery)
Language/Cultural Origin: **Turkish**
Inherent Meaning: **Brother**
Spiritual Connotation: **God's Servant**
Scripture: **Mark 3:35** NKJV
For whoever does the will of God is My brother and My sister and mother.

ENID, Ennid
Language/Cultural Origin: **Welsh**
Inherent Meaning: **Soul of Life**
Spiritual Connotation: **Obedient**
Scripture: **Hebrews 5:9** NASB
And having been made perfect, He became to all those who obey Him the source of eternal salvation.

ENNIS, Enis (see also Innes)
Language/Cultural Origin: **Irish**
Inherent Meaning: **Chosen**
Spiritual Connotation: **Enduring**
Scripture: **Psalm 51:12** NRSV
Restore to me the joy of your salvation, and sustain in me a willing spirit.

ENOCH, Enoc, Enock
☞ Language/Cultural Origin: **Hebrew**
Inherent Meaning: **Consecrated**
Spiritual Connotation: **Dedicated to God**
Scripture: **Exodus 32:29** NKJV
Consecrate yourselves today to the LORD, that He may bestow on you a blessing this day, for every man has opposed his son and his brother.

ENOS, Enosh
☞ Language/Cultural Origin: **Hebrew**
Inherent Meaning: **Man**
Spiritual Connotation: **Expectant**
Scripture: **Jude 1:20** NCV
But dear friends, use your most holy faith to build yourselves up, praying in the Holy Spirit.

ENRICA, Enrikka
Language/Cultural Origin: **French**
Inherent Meaning: **Home Ruler**
Spiritual Connotation: **Righteous**
Scripture: **Psalm 33:5** NKJV
He loves righteousness and justice; the earth is full of the goodness of the LORD.

ENRIQUE, Enrico, Enrikos, Enriqué
Language/Cultural Origin: **Spanish**
Inherent Meaning: **Head of the Home**
Spiritual Connotation: **Servant**
Scripture: **Matthew 25:21** NIV
Well done, good and faithful servant! You have been faithful with a few things, I will put you in charge of many things.

ENYA, Eina, Einya, Enyah
Language/Cultural Origin: **Hebrew**
Inherent Meaning: **God's Eye**
Spiritual Connotation: **Beloved**
Scripture: **Psalm 17:8** NKJV
Keep me as the apple of Your eye; hide me under the shadow of Your wings.

EPHRAIM, Efraim, Efrayim, Ephrem
☞ Language/Cultural Origin: **Hebrew**
Inherent Meaning: **Fruitful**
Spiritual Connotation: **Prosperous**
Scripture: **John 6:35** NKJV
I am the bread of life. He who comes to Me shall never hunger, and he who believes in Me shall never thirst.

EPHRON
☞ Language/Cultural Origin: **Hebrew**
Inherent Meaning: **Strong**
Spiritual Connotation: **Thankful**
Scripture: **Psalm 21:13** RSV
Be exalted, O LORD, in thy strength! We will sing and praise thy power.

ERASMUS
Language/Cultural Origin: **Greek**
Inherent Meaning: **Lovable**
Spiritual Connotation: **Endearing**
Scripture: **Psalm 116:15** NKJV
Precious in the sight of the LORD is the death of His saints.

ERHARD, Erhardt, Erhart
Language/Cultural Origin: **German**
Inherent Meaning: **Resolute**
Spiritual Connotation: **Efficient**
Scripture: **Job 14:5** NCV
Our time is limited. You have given us only so many months to live and have set limits we cannot go beyond.

ERIC, Aric, Arick, Arik, Arrict,

Erek, Erich, Erick, Erik, Ériq, Erric, Errick, Errict, Eryk
Language/Cultural Origin: Old Norse
Inherent Meaning: Powerful
Spiritual Connotation: Unifier
Scripture: John 13:34 NKJV
A new commandment I give to you, that you love one another; as I have loved you, that you also love one another.

ERICA, Arica, Aricka, Arika, Arikka, Ericca, Ericka, Erika, Erikka, Errica, Errika, Eryka, Erykka
Language/Cultural Origin: Old Norse
Inherent Meaning: Brave
Spiritual Connotation: Victorious
Scripture: Isaiah 60:1 NKJV
Arise, shine; for your light has come! And the glory of the LORD is risen upon you.

ERIN, Erine, Erinn, Erinne, Errin, Eryn, Erynn, Erynne (see also Arin)
Language/Cultural Origin: Irish
Inherent Meaning: Bringer of Peace
Spiritual Connotation: Benevolent
Scripture: Psalm 121:8 NKJV
The LORD shall preserve your going out and your coming in from this time forth, and even forevermore.

ERNEST, Ernesto, Ernie, Ernst
Language/Cultural Origin: English
Inherent Meaning: Sincere
Spiritual Connotation: Free in Spirit
Scripture: John 8:31 NKJV
If you abide in My word, you are My disciples indeed. And you shall know the truth, and the truth shall make you free.

ERROL, Erol, Erroll, Erryl
Language/Cultural Origin: Turkish
Inherent Meaning: Courageous
Spiritual Connotation: God's Messanger
Scripture: Acts 23:11 RSV
Take courage, for as you have testified about me at Jerusalem, so you must bear witness also at Rome.

ERVING, see Irving

ERWIN, see Irwin

ESAU, Esaw
Language/Cultural Origin: Hebrew
Inherent Meaning: Hairy
Spiritual Connotation: Strength
Scripture: Genesis 25:25 NASB
Now the first came forth red, all over like a hairy garment; and they named him Esau.

ESDRAS, Ezdras
Language/Cultural Origin: French
Inherent Meaning: Help
Spiritual Connotation: Supported
Scripture: Psalm 121:2 RSV
My help comes from the LORD, who made heaven and earth.

ESHBAN, Eshbán
Language/Cultural Origin: Hebrew
Inherent Meaning: Man of Understanding
Spiritual Connotation: Wise
Scripture: Proverbs 15:21 NCV
A person without wisdom enjoys being foolish, but someone with understanding does what is right.

ESHTON, Eshtonn
Language/Cultural Origin: Hebrew
Inherent Meaning: Rest
Spiritual Connotation: Humble
Scripture: Matthew 11:28 NLT
Come to me, all of you who are weary and carry heavy burdens, and I will give you rest.

ESMÉ, Esme, Esmée
Language/Cultural Origin: French
Inherent Meaning: Overcomer
Spiritual Connotation: Victor
Scripture: Romans 8:37 NRSV
No, in all these things we are more than conquerors through him who loved us.

ESMERALDA, Esmerelda, Esmiralda
Language/Cultural Origin: Spanish
Inherent Meaning: Victory
Spiritual Connotation: Triumphant Spirit
Scripture: Luke 12:32 NKJV
Do not fear, little flock, for it is your

Father's good pleasure to give you the kingdom.

ESMOND, Esmonde, Esmunde
Language/Cultural Origin: **Old English**
Inherent Meaning: **Rich Protector**
Spiritual Connotation: **Gracious**
Scripture: **2 Corinthians 3:17** NKJV
Now the Lord is the Spirit; and where the Spirit of the Lord is, there is liberty.

ESTE, Estes
Language/Cultural Origin: **Italian**
Inherent Meaning: **East**
Spiritual Connotation: **Armed**
Scripture: **Ephesians 6:13** NLT
Use every piece of God's armor to resist the enemy in the time of evil, so that after the battle you will still be standing firm.

ESTEBAN, Estéban
Language/Cultural Origin: **Spanish**
Inherent Meaning: **Crowned**
Spiritual Connotation: **Wise**
Scripture: **Proverbs 14:18** TLB
The simpleton is crowned with folly; the wise man is crowned with knowledge.

ESTEE, Estée
Language/Cultural Origin: **English**
Inherent Meaning: **Star**
Spiritual Connotation: **Fulfillment**
Scripture: **Numbers 24:17** NCV
I see someone who will come some day, someone who will come, but not soon. A star will come from Jacob; a ruler will rise from Israel.

ESTELLE, Estele
Language/Cultural Origin: **French**
Inherent Meaning: **Star**
Spiritual Connotation: **Infinite Potential**
Scripture: **Matthew 9:29** NKJV
According to your faith let it be to you.

ESTHER, Ester, Esthur (see also ☞ Asther, Hester)
Language/Cultural Origin: **Persian**
Inherent Meaning: **Star**
Spiritual Connotation: **Victorious**
Scripture: **Esther 2:17** NKJV
The king loved Esther more than all the other women, and she obtained grace and favor in his sight.

ESTRELLA, Estelina, Estelita, Estella, Estrela, Estrellita, Estrietta
Language/Cultural Origin: **Spanish**
Inherent Meaning: **Child of the Star**
Spiritual Connotation: **Witness**
Scripture: **Matthew 10:32** NASB
Everyone therefore who shall confess Me before men, I will also confess him before My Father who is in heaven.

ETHAN, Eathan, Ethen, Eythan
☞ Language/Cultural Origin: **Hebrew**
Inherent Meaning: **Firmness**
Spiritual Connotation: **Steadfast in Truth**
Scripture: **Romans 8:28** NKJV
And we know that all things work together for good to those who love God, to those who are the called according to His purpose.

ETHEL, Ethyl
Language/Cultural Origin: **Old English**
Inherent Meaning: **One of High Regard**
Spiritual Connotation: **Noble**
Scripture: **Matthew 7:7** KJV
Ask, and it shall be given you; seek, and ye shall find; knock, and it shall be opened unto you.

ETHNI, Ethnee, Ethney
☞ Language/Cultural Origin: **Hebrew**
Inherent Meaning: **My Gift**
Spiritual Connotation: **Secure**
Scripture: **John 14:27** NASB
Peace I leave with you; My peace I give to you. . . . Do not let your heart be troubled, nor let it be fearful.

ETIENNE, Etiene
Language/Cultural Origin: **French**
Inherent Meaning: **Enthroned**
Spiritual Connotation: **Humble**
Scripture: **Psalm 113:5** NLT
Who can be compared with the LORD our God, who is enthroned on high?

EUCLID
Language/Cultural Origin: **Greek**
Inherent Meaning: **Brilliant**
Spiritual Connotation: **Creative**

Scripture: **Psalm 19:2** RSV
*Day to day pours forth speech, and night
to night declares knowledge.*

EUDORA, Eldora, Eudorra
Language/Cultural Origin: **Greek**
Inherent Meaning: **Honorable Gift**
Spiritual Connotation: **Invaluable**
Scripture: **John 4:10** NCV
*If you only knew the free gift of God and
who it is that is asking you for water,
you would have asked him, and he would
have given you living water.*

EUGENE, Eugéne, Gene
Language/Cultural Origin: **Greek**
Inherent Meaning: **Born to Nobility**
Spiritual Connotation: **Vivacious**
Scripture: **Isaiah 58:8** NKJV
*Then your light shall break forth like the
morning, your healing shall spring forth
speedily, and your righteousness shall go
before you.*

EULALIA, Eulalie
Language/Cultural Origin: **French**
Inherent Meaning: **Sweetly Speaking**
Spiritual Connotation: **Mouthpiece of God**
Scripture: **Matthew 10:20** NRSV
*Do not worry about how you are to
speak or what you are to say; for it is not
you who speak, but the Spirit of your
Father speaking through you.*

EUNICE, Eunique, Eunise
Language/Cultural Origin: **Greek**
Inherent Meaning: **Joyous**
Spiritual Connotation: **Victorious**
Scripture: **Psalm 40:5** NKJV
*Many, O LORD my God, are Your won-
derful works which You have done.*

EUSTACE, Eustasius, Eustis
Language/Cultural Origin: **Greek**
Inherent Meaning: **Productive**
Spiritual Connotation: **Diligent**
Scripture: **2 Timothy 2:15** NASB
*Be diligent to present yourself approved
to God as a workman who does not need
to be ashamed, handling accurately the
word of truth.*

EVE, Eva, Evah, Evie
Language/Cultural Origin: **Hebrew**
Inherent Meaning: **Mother of Life**
Spiritual Connotation: **Full of Life**
Scripture: **Psalm 16:11** NKJV
*You will show me the path of life; in Your
presence is fullness of joy; at Your right
hand are pleasures forevermore.*

EVAN, Evann, Evans, Evin, Evyn
Language/Cultural Origin: **Irish**
Inherent Meaning: **Young Warrior**
Spiritual Connotation: **Noble Protector**
Scripture: **Philippians 4:13** KJV
*I can do all things through Christ which
strengtheneth me.*

EVANGELINE, Evangelina
Language/Cultural Origin: **Greek**
Inherent Meaning: **Bringer of Good News**
Spiritual Connotation: **Happy Messenger**
Scripture: **Psalm 37:6** NKJV
*He shall bring forth your righteousness
as the light, And your justice as the
noonday.*

EVELYN, Evalina, Evaline, Evelynne
Language/Cultural Origin: **English**
Inherent Meaning: **Hazelnut**
Spiritual Connotation: **Radiant**
Scripture: **1 John 2:8** NASB
*The darkness is passing away and the
true Light is already shining.*

EVERETT, Everet, Everette, Everitt
Language/Cultural Origin: **German**
Inherent Meaning: **Courageous**
Spiritual Connotation: **Unending Praise**
Scripture: **Psalm 96:1** NKJV
*Oh, sing to the LORD a new song! Sing to
the LORD, all the earth.*

EVERLEY, Everlea, Everlee, Everleigh
Language/Cultural Origin: **English**
Inherent Meaning: **From the Boar Meadow**
Spiritual Connotation: **Faithful**
Scripture: **1 Timothy 6:12** NCV
*Fight the good fight of faith, grabbing hold
of the life that continues forever.*

EVETTE, see Yvette

EVITA, Evéeta
Language/Cultural Origin: **Hispanic**
Inherent Meaning: **Youthful Life**
Spiritual Connotation: **Childlike**
Scripture: **Job 33:25** NLT
Then his body will become as healthy as a child's, firm and youthful again.

EVONNE, see Yvonne

EWING, Ewin, Ewynn
Language/Cultural Origin: **English**
Inherent Meaning: **Friend of Justice**
Spiritual Connotation: **Benevolent Protector**
Scripture: **Psalm 28:7** NKJV
The LORD is my strength and my shield; my heart trusted in Him, and I am helped.

EYOTA, Eyotah
Language/Cultural Origin: **Native American**
Inherent Meaning: **Greatest**
Spiritual Connotation: **Servant**
Scripture: **Matthew 23:11** NRSV
The greatest among you will be your servant.

EZEKIEL, Ezekial, Zeke
↙ Language/Cultural Origin: **Hebrew**
Inherent Meaning: **Whom God Makes Strong**
Spiritual Connotation: **God Is My Strength**
Scripture: **1 Corinthians 2:12** NKJV
Now we have received, not the spirit of the world, but the Spirit who is from God.

EZRA, Esera, Esra, Ezera, Ezri (see ↙ also Izri)
Language/Cultural Origin: **Hebrew**
Inherent Meaning: **Helper**
Spiritual Connotation: **Strong**
Scripture: **Luke 12:12** NKJV
For the Holy Spirit will teach you in that very hour what you ought to say.

EZRELA, Ezraela
Language/Cultural Origin: **Hebrew**
Inherent Meaning: **God Is My Strength**
Spiritual Connotation: **Adoration**
Scripture: **Psalm 18:1** NLT
I love you, LORD; you are my strength.

F

FABIA, Fabiana, Fabianna, Fabianne, Fabria, Fabriana, Fabrianne
Language/Cultural Origin: **English**
Inherent Meaning: **Bean Grower**
Spiritual Connotation: **Laborer**
Scripture: **Psalm 33:4** NKJV
For the word of the LORD is right, and all His work is done in truth.

FABIAN, Fabayan, Fabiano, Fabien, Fabio, Faybian
Language/Cultural Origin: **Latin**
Inherent Meaning: **Bean Grower**
Spiritual Connotation: **Nourishing Spirit**
Scripture: **Jeremiah 31:16** NRSV
Thus says the LORD: "Keep your voice from weeping, and your eyes from tears; for there is a reward for your work."

FADEY, Faidee
Language/Cultural Origin: **Ukrainian**
Inherent Meaning: **Father**
Spiritual Connotation: **Gentle**
Scripture: **Ephesians 6:4** NASB
And, fathers, do not provoke your children to anger; but bring them up in the discipline and instruction of the Lord.

FAITH, Fayth, Faythe
Language/Cultural Origin: **English**
Inherent Meaning: **Firm Believer**
Spiritual Connotation: **Faith**
Scripture: **Mark 9:23** NCV
All things are possible for the one who believes.

FALINA, Falena, Faylina, Felina
Language/Cultural Origin: **Latin**
Inherent Meaning: **Catlike**
Spiritual Connotation: **Upright**
Scripture: **Psalm 17:2** NASB
Let my judgment come forth from Your presence; let Your eyes look with equity.

FALKNER, Faulkner
Language/Cultural Origin: **Old English**
Inherent Meaning: **Trainer of Falcons**
Spiritual Connotation: **One Who Disciples**
Scripture: **Philippians 1:21** KJV
For to me to live is Christ, and to die is gain.

FALLON, Falan, Falen, Falin, Fallan, Fallyn, Falyn
Language/Cultural Origin: **Irish**
Inherent Meaning: **Grandchild of the Ruler**
Spiritual Connotation: **Heir**
Scripture: **Exodus 20:6** NRSV
But showing steadfast love to the thousandth generation of those who love me and keep my commandments.

FANNY, Fanney, Fanni, Fannie
Language/Cultural Origin: **English**
Inherent Meaning: **French**
Spiritual Connotation: **Dedicated**
Scripture: **Psalm 62:1** NASB
My soul waits in silence for God only; from Him is my salvation.

FANYA, Fania, Fannia
Language/Cultural Origin: **Russian**
Inherent Meaning: **Free**
Spiritual Connotation: **Vindicated**
Scripture: **Psalm 146:7** NCV
He does what is fair for those who have been wronged. He gives food to the hungry. The LORD sets the prisoners free.

FARLEY, Fairleigh, Farlay, Farrley
Language/Cultural Origin: **English**
Inherent Meaning: **From the Sheep Meadow**
Spiritual Connotation: **Serene**

Scripture: **Exodus 14:14** NASB
*The LORD will fight for you while you
keep silent.*

FARRAH, Fara, Farah, Farra
Language/Cultural Origin: **English**
Inherent Meaning: **Beautiful**
Spiritual Connotation: **Favored**
Scripture: **Esther 2:9** NASB
*Now the young lady pleased him and
found favor with him.*

FARREL, Farrel, Ferel, Ferell, Ferryl
Language/Cultural Origin: **Irish**
Inherent Meaning: **Valiant**
Spiritual Connotation: **Servant**
Scripture: **2 Samuel 17:10** NKJV
*For all Israel knows that your father is a
mighty man, and those who are with him
are valiant men.*

**FARREN, Faran, Farin, Farrahn,
Farran, Farrin, Farron, Farryn,
Faryn (see also Ferran)**
Language/Cultural Origin: **English**
Inherent Meaning: **Wanderer**
Spiritual Connotation: **Foreigner**
Scripture: **Ruth 2:10** NKJV
*Why have I found favor in your eyes,
that you should take notice of me, since I
am a foreigner?*

FAUSTINA, Faustana
Language/Cultural Origin: **Latin**
Inherent Meaning: **Fortunate**
Spiritual Connotation: **Blessed**
Scripture: **Genesis 1:28** NKJV
*Then God blessed them, and God said to
them, "Be fruitful and multiply."*

FAWN, Faun, Fauna, Fawna, Fawne
Language/Cultural Origin: **Old French**
Inherent Meaning: **Young Deer**
Spiritual Connotation: **Innocent**
Scripture: **Psalm 42:1** NRSV
*As a deer longs for flowing streams, so
my soul longs for you, O God.*

FAXON, Faxan
Language/Cultural Origin: **Old German**
Inherent Meaning: **Long-Haired**
Spiritual Connotation: **Devotion**
Scripture: **Judges 13:7** NKJV

*Behold, you shall conceive and bear a
son . . . for the child shall be a Nazirite
to God from the womb to the day of his
death.*

FAYE, Fae, Fay, Fayanna, Fayla
Language/Cultural Origin: **Latin**
Inherent Meaning: **Raven**
Spiritual Connotation: **Remembered**
Scripture: **Isaiah 65:24** NKJV
*It shall come to pass that before they call,
I will answer; and while they are still
speaking, I will hear.*

**FELICIA, Falesha, Falisha, Felecia,
Feleesha, Felesha, Felicya, Felisha**
Language/Cultural Origin: **Latin**
Inherent Meaning: **Fortunate**
Spiritual Connotation: **Joyful**
Scripture: **John 10:10** NKJV
*The thief does not come except to steal,
and to kill, and to destroy. I have come
that they may have life, and that they
may have it more abundantly.*

**FELICITY, Felicianna, Félicité,
Felisianna, Felissa, Feliza, Felysse**
Language/Cultural Origin: **English**
Inherent Meaning: **Joyful**
Spiritual Connotation: **Content**
Scripture: **Philippians 4:4** NKJV
*Rejoice in the Lord always. Again I will
say, rejoice!*

FELIPE, see Phillip

FELIX, Feliks, Félix
Language/Cultural Origin: **Latin**
Inherent Meaning: **Fortunate**
Spiritual Connotation: **Blessed**
Scripture: **Isaiah 40:31** NKJV
*But those who wait on the LORD shall
renew their strength; they shall mount
up with wings like eagles, they shall run
and not be weary, they shall walk and
not faint.*

FELTON, Felten
Language/Cultural Origin: **English**
Inherent Meaning: **From the Field Town**
Spiritual Connotation: **Hopeful**
Scripture: **Psalm 42:5** NKJV
Why are you cast down, O my soul?

And why are you disquieted within me?
Hope in God, for I shall yet praise Him
for the help of His countenance.

FENTON, Fenny
Language/Cultural Origin: **English**
Inherent Meaning: **From the Marshland Farm**
Spiritual Connotation: **Spirit of Life**
Scripture: **Galatians 6:8** NKJV
For he who sows to his flesh will of the flesh
reap corruption, but he who sows to the
Spirit will of the Spirit reap everlasting life.

FERDINAND, Ferdinánd, Fernand
Language/Cultural Origin: **Gothic**
Inherent Meaning: **Adventurous**
Spiritual Connotation: **Seeker of Truth**
Scripture: **Psalm 33:3-4** NKJV
Sing to Him a new song; play skillfully
with a shout of joy. For the word of the
LORD is right, and all His work is done
in truth.

FERGUS, Ferguson
Language/Cultural Origin: **Irish**
Inherent Meaning: **Very Choice One**
Spiritual Connotation: **Esteemed**
Scripture: **Psalm 18:2** NKJV
The LORD is my rock and my fortress and
my deliverer; my God, my strength, in
whom I will trust; my shield and the horn
of my salvation, my stronghold.

FERN, Ferne, Fernleigh
Language/Cultural Origin: **Old English**
Inherent Meaning: **Sincere**
Spiritual Connotation: **Loving**
Scripture: **1 John 4:11** KJV
Beloved, if God so loved us, we ought
also to love one another.

FERNANDO, Fernandez
Language/Cultural Origin: **Spanish**
Inherent Meaning: **Fearless**
Spiritual Connotation: **Redeemed**
Scripture: **Matthew 28:5-6** NKJV
Do not be afraid, for I know that you
seek Jesus who was crucified. He is not
here; for He is risen, as He said.

FERRAN, Feran, Feron, Ferren,

Ferrin, Ferron, Ferryn (see also Farran)
Language/Cultural Origin: **Middle Eastern**
Inherent Meaning: **Baker**
Spiritual Connotation: **Laborer for Souls**
Scripture: **Luke 10:2** NLT
The harvest is so great, but the workers are
so few. Pray to the Lord . . . and ask him
to send out more workers for his fields.

FERRAND, Farrand
Language/Cultural Origin: **French**
Inherent Meaning: **Iron-Haired**
Spiritual Connotation: **Believer**
Scripture: **Ephesians 1:19** NCV
And you will know that God's power is
very great for us who believe. That power
is the same as the great strength.

FERRIS, Faris, Farris, Feris
Language/Cultural Origin: **Middle Eastern**
Inherent Meaning: **Horseman**
Spiritual Connotation: **Fearsome**
Scripture: **Jeremiah 4:29** NASB
At the sound of the horseman and bow-
man every city flees.

FIDEL, Fidele, Fidéle, Fidelis
Language/Cultural Origin: **Latin**
Inherent Meaning: **Faithful**
Spiritual Connotation: **Secure**
Scripture: **Romans 8:38-39** NKJV
For I am persuaded that neither death nor
life . . . nor any other . . . thing, shall be
able to separate us from the love of God
which is in Christ Jesus our Lord.

FIDELITY, Fidelia
Language/Cultural Origin: **Latin**
Inherent Meaning: **Faithful**
Spiritual Connotation: **Received**
Scripture: **Isaiah 26:2** NASB
Open the gates, that the righteous nation
may enter, the one that remains faithful.

FIEVEL, Feivel, Fivel
Language/Cultural Origin: **Yiddish**
Inherent Meaning: **Bright**
Spiritual Connotation: **Attentive**
Scripture: **2 Peter 1:19** NRSV
You will do well to be attentive to this as
to a lamp shining in a dark place, until

the day dawns and the morning star rises in your hearts.

FINDLAY, Finlay, Finley
Language/Cultural Origin: **Irish**
Inherent Meaning: **Valorous Soldier**
Spiritual Connotation: **Victorious Life**
Scripture: **Proverbs 12:28** NKJV
In the way of righteousness is life, and in its pathway there is no death.

FINIAN, Phinean
Language/Cultural Origin: **Irish**
Inherent Meaning: **Fair Hero**
Spiritual Connotation: **Servant**
Scripture: **Proverbs 27:18** NASB
He who tends the fig tree will eat its fruit; and he who cares for his master will be honored.

FIONA, Fionna
Language/Cultural Origin: **Irish**
Inherent Meaning: **Fair**
Spiritual Connotation: **Persevering**
Scripture: **Isaiah 66:22** RSV
For as the new heavens and the new earth which I will make shall remain before me, says the LORD; so shall your descendants and your name remain.

FISK, Fiske
Language/Cultural Origin: **Middle English**
Inherent Meaning: **Fisherman**
Spiritual Connotation: **Witness**
Scripture: **Matthew 4:19** NKJV
Follow Me, and I will make you fishers of men.

FITZGERALD, Fitz
Language/Cultural Origin: **Old English**
Inherent Meaning: **Son of the Mighty One**
Spiritual Connotation: **Hopeful**
Scripture: **Colossians 1:27** NKJV
To them God willed to make known what are the riches of the glory of this mystery among the Gentiles: which is Christ in you, the hope of glory.

FLAIR, Flaire, Flare
Language/Cultural Origin: **English**
Inherent Meaning: **Vivacious**
Spiritual Connotation: **Glorified**
Scripture: **Psalm 64:10** RSV

Let the righteous rejoice in the LORD, and take refuge in him! Let all the upright in heart glory!

FLANA, Flanna
Language/Cultural Origin: **Latin**
Inherent Meaning: **Blonde**
Spiritual Connotation: **Satisfied**
Scripture: **Psalm 90:14** NASB
O satisfy us in the morning with Thy lovingkindness, that we may sing for joy and be glad all our days.

FLANNERY, Flann
Language/Cultural Origin: **Irish**
Inherent Meaning: **Redhead**
Spiritual Connotation: **Accountable**
Scripture: **Ecclesiastes 11:9** NCV
Young people, enjoy yourselves while you are young. . . . But remember that God will judge you for everything you do.

FLAVIA, Flavian, Flaviar, Flavio
Language/Cultural Origin: **Latin**
Inherent Meaning: **Blond**
Spiritual Connotation: **Redeemed**
Scripture: **Isaiah 61:10** NASB
I will rejoice greatly in the LORD . . . For He has clothed me with garments of salvation, He has wrapped me with a robe of righteousness.

FLEMING, Flemming
Language/Cultural Origin: **English**
Inherent Meaning: **From Denmark**
Spiritual Connotation: **Obedient**
Scripture: **Romans 16:19** NKJV
For your obedience has become known to all. Therefore I am glad on your behalf.

FLETCHER, Flecher, Fletch
Language/Cultural Origin: **Anglo-Saxon**
Inherent Meaning: **Arrow Featherer**
Spiritual Connotation: **Ingenious**
Scripture: **John 14:12** NKJV
He who believes in Me, the works that I do he will do also; and greater works than these he will do, because I go to My Father.

FLEUR, Flure
Language/Cultural Origin: **French**
Inherent Meaning: **Flower**

Spiritual Connotation: **Efficient**
Scripture: **Isaiah 40:6** NKJV
All flesh is grass, and all its loveliness is like the flower of the field.

FLINT, Flynt
Language/Cultural Origin: **Old English**
Inherent Meaning: **Stream**
Spiritual Connotation: **Praise**
Scripture: **Psalm 78:16** RSV
He made streams come out of the rock, and caused waters to flow down like rivers.

FLIP, Flipp
Language/Cultural Origin: **American**
Inherent Meaning: **Lover of Horses**
Spiritual Connotation: **Joyful**
Scripture: **Psalm 45:15** NRSV
With joy and gladness they are led along as they enter the palace of the king.

FLORA, Floria, Floriana, Florianna
Language/Cultural Origin: **Latin**
Inherent Meaning: **Flower**
Spiritual Connotation: **Nurtured**
Scripture: **Isaiah 49:13** NASB
Shout for joy, O heavens! And rejoice, O earth! . . . For the LORD has comforted His people And will have compassion on His afflicted.

FLORENCE, Flo, Florance, Florann, Floren, Florida, Florrie, Flossie
Language/Cultural Origin: **Latin**
Inherent Meaning: **Flourishing**
Spiritual Connotation: **Prosperous**
Scripture: **Psalm 91:1** NKJV
He who dwells in the secret place of the Most High shall abide under the shadow of the Almighty.

FLORIAN, Florien, Florrian
Language/Cultural Origin: **English**
Inherent Meaning: **Blooming**
Spiritual Connotation: **Nourished**
Scripture: **Isaiah 35:1** NKJV
And the desert shall rejoice and blossom as the rose.

FLOYD, Floydd
Language/Cultural Origin: **Welsh**
Inherent Meaning: **White- or Gray-Haired**
Spiritual Connotation: **Wise**

Scripture: **1 Samuel 10:6** NKJV
Then the Spirit of the LORD will come upon you, and you will prophesy with them and be turned into another man.

FLYNN, Flinn, Flyn
Language/Cultural Origin: **Gaelic**
Inherent Meaning: **Son of the Redhead**
Spiritual Connotation: **Blessed**
Scripture: **1 Kings 8:56** NKJV
Blessed be the LORD, who has given rest to His people Israel. . . . There has not failed one word of all His good promise.

FONTANNA, Fontaine, Fontana
Language/Cultural Origin: **French**
Inherent Meaning: **Fountain**
Spiritual Connotation: **Sustained**
Scripture: **Psalm 36:9** NKJV
For with You is the fountain of life; in Your light we see light.

FONZIE, Fonsie, Fonz
Language/Cultural Origin: **German**
Inherent Meaning: **Zealous**
Spiritual Connotation: **Righteous**
Scripture: **Proverbs 23:17** NKJV
Do not let your heart envy sinners, but be zealous for the fear of the LORD all the day.

FORBES, Forbe
Language/Cultural Origin: **Gaelic**
Inherent Meaning: **Prosperous**
Spiritual Connotation: **Blessed**
Scripture: **Proverbs 16:20** NLT
Those who listen to instruction will prosper; those who trust the LORD will be happy.

FORREST, Forest, Forster, Foster
Language/Cultural Origin: **Latin**
Inherent Meaning: **Guardian of the Forest**
Spiritual Connotation: **Preserved**
Scripture: **Psalm 138:8** NKJV
The LORD will perfect that which concerns me; Your mercy, O LORD, endures forever; do not forsake the works of Your hands.

FRANCES, Fran, Francesca, Francess, Franchelle, Franchesca,

Franchette, Francine, Frann, Frannie
Language/Cultural Origin: Latin
Inherent Meaning: Free
Spiritual Connotation: Triumphant
Scripture: Isaiah 65:24 NKJV
It shall come to pass that before they call, I will answer; and while they are still speaking, I will hear.

FRANCIS, Fran, Francesco, Franchot, Francisco, Franco, Francois, Franz
Language/Cultural Origin: Latin
Inherent Meaning: Free
Spiritual Connotation: Victorious
Scripture: John 5:24 NKJV
He who hears my word and believes in Him who sent Me has everlasting life, and shall not come into judgment, but has passed from death into life.

FRANK, Franc, Frankie, Franky
Language/Cultural Origin: English
Inherent Meaning: Free Man
Spiritual Connotation: Shining
Scripture: Matthew 5:14 NKJV
You are the light of the world. A city that is set on a hill cannot be hidden.

FRANKLIN, Francklin, Franklinn, Franklyn, Franklynn
Language/Cultural Origin: Old English
Inherent Meaning: Free Holder of Land
Spiritual Connotation: Joyful
Scripture: Nehemiah 8:10 NKJV
This day is holy to our LORD. Do not sorrow, for the joy of the LORD is your strength.

FRASER, Fraizer, Frasier, Frazer, Frazier
Language/Cultural Origin: French
Inherent Meaning: Strawberry
Spiritual Connotation: Filled With Life
Scripture: 2 Peter 1:4 NKJV
By which have been given to us exceedingly great and precious promises, that through these you may be partakers of the divine nature.

FRAYNE, Fraine, Freyne
Language/Cultural Origin: Old English
Inherent Meaning: Stranger
Spiritual Connotation: Accepting
Scripture: Deuteronomy 23:7 NRSV
You shall not abhor any of the Edomites, for they are your kin. You shall not abhor any of the Egyptians, because you were an alien residing in their land.

FREDERICA, Freddi, Fredericka, Frederina, Frederique, Fredrika
Language/Cultural Origin: Old German
Inherent Meaning: Peaceful Ruler
Spiritual Connotation: Compassionate
Scripture: Psalm 112:4 NKJV
Unto the upright there arises light in the darkness; He is gracious, and full of compassion, and righteous.

FREDERICK, Fred, Fredd, Freddi, Freddrick, Freddy, Frederic, Frederich, Frederico, Frederik, Frederric, Fredric, Fredrich, Fredrik, Freéderic, Fritz
Language/Cultural Origin: German
Inherent Meaning: Peaceful Ruler
Spiritual Connotation: Perceptive
Scripture: Proverbs 20:12 NKJV
The hearing ear and the seeing eye, the LORD has made them both.

FREEDOM
Language/Cultural Origin: Old German
Inherent Meaning: Freedom
Spiritual Connotation: Released
Scripture: James 2:12 NASB
So speak and so act, as those who are to be judged by the law of liberty.

FREEMAN, Freedman, Freemon
Language/Cultural Origin: English
Inherent Meaning: Free
Spiritual Connotation: Witness
Scripture: 1 Corinthians 10:31 NRSV
So, whether you eat or drink, or whatever you do, do everything for the glory of God.

FREIDA, Freda, Freeda, Freia, Frieda
Language/Cultural Origin: German
Inherent Meaning: Serene

Spiritual Connotation: **Victorious**
Scripture: **Revelation 2:7** NKJV
To him who overcomes I will give to eat from the tree of life, which is in the midst of the Paradise of God.

FREJA, Fraya, Freya
Language/Cultural Origin: **Swedish**
Inherent Meaning: **Virtuous Woman**
Spiritual Connotation: **Valuable**
Scripture: **Proverbs 31:10** NASB
An excellent wife, who can find? For her worth is far above jewels.

FREEMONT, Freemondt
Language/Cultural Origin: **German**
Inherent Meaning: **Protector of Freedom**
Spiritual Connotation: **Righteous**
Scripture: **Psalm 146:7-8** NASB
The LORD sets the prisoners free. The LORD opens the eyes of the blind; the LORD raises up those who are bowed down; the LORD loves the righteous.

FRITZI, Fritzie, Fritzy
Language/Cultural Origin: **German**
Inherent Meaning: **Restful**

Spiritual Connotation: **Righteous**
Scripture: **Hebrews 12:11** RSV
For the moment all discipline seems painful rather than pleasant; later it yields the peaceful fruit of righteousness.

FULLER, Fullar
Language/Cultural Origin: **English**
Inherent Meaning: **Cloth Worker**
Spiritual Connotation: **Diligent**
Scripture: **Psalm 103:1-4** NKJV
Bless the LORD, O my soul; and all that is within me, bless His holy name!

FULTON, Fultan
Language/Cultural Origin: **English**
Inherent Meaning: **From Near the Town**
Spiritual Connotation: **Spirit-Filled Life**
Scripture: **Galatians 5:22-23** NKJV
But the fruit of the Spirit is love, joy, peace, longsuffering, kindness, goodness, faithfulness, gentleness, self-control.

G

GABOR, Gábor

Language/Cultural Origin: **Hungarian**
Inherent Meaning: **God Is My Strength**
Spiritual Connotation: **Grounded in Faith**
Scripture: **Isaiah 12:2** NASB
Behold, God is my salvation, I will trust and not be afraid; for the LORD GOD is my strength and song, and He has become my salvation.

GABRIEL, Gab, Gabe, Gabriël, ☞ Gabriell, Gabrielli, Gabriello, Gibbee, Gibbie

Language/Cultural Origin: **Hebrew**
Inherent Meaning: **Devoted to God**
Spiritual Connotation: **Brave**
Scripture: **Joshua 1:9** NKJV
Have I not commanded you? Be strong and of good courage; do not be afraid, nor be dismayed, for the LORD your God is with you wherever you go.

GABRIELLE, Gabbey, Gabbi, Gabbie, Gabrial, Gabriala, Gabrialla, Gabriana, Gabrianna, Gabriela, Gabriele, Gabriella

Language/Cultural Origin: **Hebrew**
Inherent Meaning: **Devoted to God**
Spiritual Connotation: **Confident**
Scripture: **2 Corinthians 7:16** RSV
I rejoice, because I have perfect confidence in you.

GAETAN, Gaetano

Language/Cultural Origin: **Italian**
Inherent Meaning: **From Southern Italy**
Spiritual Connotation: **Redeemed**
Scripture: **Romans 5:2** RSV
Through him we have obtained access to this grace in which we stand, and we rejoice in our hope of sharing the glory of God.

GAGE, Gaege

Language/Cultural Origin: **French**
Inherent Meaning: **Promise**
Spiritual Connotation: **Vision**
Scripture: **Zechariah 9:9** NRSV
Rejoice greatly, O daughter Zion! . . . Lo, your king comes to you; triumphant and victorious is he, humble and riding on a donkey.

GAIL, Gael, Gaila, Gale, Gayle

Language/Cultural Origin: **Old English**
Inherent Meaning: **My Father Rejoices**
Spiritual Connotation: **Lively**
Scripture: **Zephaniah 3:17** NKJV
The LORD your God in your midst, the Mighty One, will save; He will rejoice over you with gladness.

GAIUS, Caius

☞ Language/Cultural Origin: **Latin**
Inherent Meaning: **One Who Rejoices**
Spiritual Connotation: **Bold**
Scripture: **Joel 2:21** TLB
Fear not, my people; be glad now and rejoice, for he has done amazing things for you.

GALA, Galla

Language/Cultural Origin: **Old Norse**
Inherent Meaning: **Singer**
Spiritual Connotation: **Filled With Praise**
Scripture: **Psalm 84:4** RSV
Blessed are those who dwell in thy house, ever singing thy praise!

GALATIA

Language/Cultural Origin: **Greek**
Inherent Meaning: **Pure**

Spiritual Connotation: **Courageous**
Scripture: **Psalm 27:1** NKJV
*The LORD is my light and my salvation;
whom shall I fear? The LORD is the
strength of my life; of whom shall I be
afraid?*

GALEN, Gaelen, Gaylen
Language/Cultural Origin: **Greek**
Inherent Meaning: **Healer**
Spiritual Connotation: **Established in Truth**
Scripture: **Psalm 37:5** NKJV
*Commit your way to the LORD, trust also
in Him, and He shall bring it to pass.*

GALENA, Galeena
Language/Cultural Origin: **Greek**
Inherent Meaning: **Calm**
Spiritual Connotation: **Amiable**
Scripture: **Proverbs 15:18** NRSV
*Those who are hot-tempered stir up
strife, but those who are slow to anger
calm contention.*

GALIANA, Galianna, Galiena, Galienna
Language/Cultural Origin: **Old German**
Inherent Meaning: **Supreme**
Spiritual Connotation: **Respectful**
Scripture: **1 Timothy 5:2** NLT
*Treat the older women as you would your
mother, and treat the younger women
with all purity as your own sisters.*

GALINA, Gailina
Language/Cultural Origin: **Russian**
Inherent Meaning: **Shining**
Spiritual Connotation: **Glorified**
Scripture: **Isaiah 60:1** NKJV
*Arise, shine; for your light has come! And
the glory of the LORD is risen upon you.*

GALLIO, Galio
Language/Cultural Origin: **Hebrew**
Inherent Meaning: **He That Sucks**
Spiritual Connotation: **Mighty**
Scripture: **Isaiah 54:17** NKJV
*No weapon formed against you shall
prosper.*

GALVIN, Galvan, Galven
Language/Cultural Origin: **Gaelic**
Inherent Meaning: **Glowing**

Spiritual Connotation: **Blessed**
Scripture: **Isaiah 49:4** NKJV
*I have labored in vain, I have spent my
strength for nothing and in vain; yet
surely my just reward is with the LORD,
and my work with my God.*

GALYA, Galia, Gallia
Language/Cultural Origin: **Russian**
Inherent Meaning: **Illuminated**
Spiritual Connotation: **Untainted**
Scripture: **Luke 11:36** NRSV
*If then your whole body is full of light,
with no part of it in darkness, it will be as
full of light as when a lamp gives you light
with its rays.*

GAMALIEL, Gaméliel
Language/Cultural Origin: **Hebrew**
Inherent Meaning: **God Is My Reward**
Spiritual Connotation: **Blessed**
Scripture: **Ruth 2:12** NASB
*May the LORD reward your work, and
your wages be full from the LORD, the
God of Israel, under whose wings you
have come to seek refuge.*

GAMARYA, Gamara, Gamária, Gamariya
Language/Cultural Origin: **Hebrew**
Inherent Meaning: **Act of God**
Spiritual Connotation: **Pledged**
Scripture: **Micah 7:15** NASB
*As in the days when you came out
from the land of Egypt, I will show you
miracles.*

GANNON, Gannan, Gannen
Language/Cultural Origin: **Irish**
Inherent Meaning: **White**
Spiritual Connotation: **Devout**
Scripture: **Matthew 4:10** NKJV
*Away with you, Satan! For it is written,
"You shall worship the LORD your God,
and Him only you shall serve."*

GANYA, Gania, Ganyah
Language/Cultural Origin: **Hebrew**
Inherent Meaning: **Garden of God**
Spiritual Connotation: **Refreshed**
Scripture: **Isaiah 51:3** NLT
*The LORD will comfort Israel again and
make her deserts blossom. Her barren*

wilderness will become as beautiful as Eden—the garden of the LORD.

GARETH, Garith, Garreth
Language/Cultural Origin: **Welsh**
Inherent Meaning: **Gentle**
Spiritual Connotation: **Peaceful**
Scripture: **Proverbs 15:1** RSV
A soft answer turns away wrath, but a harsh word stirs up anger.

GARNER, Garnier
Language/Cultural Origin: **French**
Inherent Meaning: **Guard**
Spiritual Connotation: **One of Integrity**
Scripture: **1 Timothy 6:20** NCV
Timothy, guard what God has trusted to you. Stay away from foolish, useless talk and from the arguments of what is falsely called knowledge.

GARNET, Garnette
Language/Cultural Origin: **Latin**
Inherent Meaning: **Precious Stone**
Spiritual Connotation: **Invaluable**
Scripture: **Isaiah 49:8** NKJV
In an acceptable time I have heard You, and in the day of salvation I have helped You; I will preserve You.

GARNETT, Garnatt
Language/Cultural Origin: **Anglo-Saxon**
Inherent Meaning: **Protection**
Spiritual Connotation: **Obedient**
Scripture: **Deuteronomy 11:1** NKJV
Therefore you shall love the LORD your God, and keep His charge, His statutes, His judgments, and His commandments always.

GARRETT, Garett, Garret, Gerrett (see also Jarrett)
Language/Cultural Origin: **Irish**
Inherent Meaning: **Warrior**
Spiritual Connotation: **Free**
Scripture: **Galatians 5:1** NKJV
Stand fast therefore in the liberty by which Christ has made us free, and do not be entangled again with a yoke of bondage.

GARRICK, Garick, Garreck, Garrik (see also Carrick)
Language/Cultural Origin: **English**
Inherent Meaning: **Ruler**
Spiritual Connotation: **Champion**
Scripture: **Psalm 24:3** NKJV
Who may ascend into the hill of the LORD? Or who may stand in His holy place? He who has clean hands and a pure heart.

GARRIN, Garran, Garren, Garron
Language/Cultural Origin: **Old English**
Inherent Meaning: **Spearman**
Spiritual Connotation: **Preserved**
Scripture: **Philippians 4:7** RSV
And the peace of God, which passes all understanding, will keep your hearts and your minds in Christ Jesus.

GARRISON, Garris
Language/Cultural Origin: **Old French**
Inherent Meaning: **Fortress**
Spiritual Connotation: **Guided of God**
Scripture: **Psalm 31:3** NRSV
You are indeed my rock and my fortress; for your name's sake lead me and guide me.

GARTH, Gar
Language/Cultural Origin: **Old Norse**
Inherent Meaning: **From the Garden**
Spiritual Connotation: **Wise**
Scripture: **Job 28:28** NKJV
Behold, the fear of the Lord, that is wisdom, and to depart from evil is understanding.

GARVEY, Garrvey
Language/Cultural Origin: **Irish**
Inherent Meaning: **Rugged Place**
Spiritual Connotation: **Increasing Faithfulness**
Scripture: **Ephesians 5:8** NKJV
For you were once darkness, but now you are light in the Lord. Walk as children of light.

GARVIN, Garvan, Garvyn
Language/Cultural Origin: **English**
Inherent Meaning: **Friend in Battle**
Spiritual Connotation: **Peaceful**

Scripture: **Colossians 3:15** NKJV
And let the peace of God rule in your
hearts, to which also you were called in
one body; and be thankful.

GARY, Garry
Language/Cultural Origin: **German**
Inherent Meaning: **Mighty**
Spiritual Connotation: **Regenerated**
Scripture: **2 Corinthians 5:17** NKJV
Therefore, if anyone is in Christ, he is
a new creation; old things have passed
away; behold, all things have become new.

GASTON, Gascon, Gastón
Language/Cultural Origin: **French**
Inherent Meaning: **From Gascony**
Spiritual Connotation: **Protected**
Scripture: **2 Samuel 22:2** NCV
The LORD is my rock, my protection,
my Savior.

GAVIN, Gavan, Gaven, Gavyn
Language/Cultural Origin: **Welsh**
Inherent Meaning: **White Hawk**
Spiritual Connotation: **Content**
Scripture: **Psalm 119:34** NKJV
Give me understanding, and I shall keep
Your law; Indeed, I shall observe it with
my whole heart.

GAYLORD, Gayler, Gaylor
Language/Cultural Origin: **Old French**
Inherent Meaning: **Lively**
Spiritual Connotation: **Gifted**
Scripture: **Psalm 84:11** NKJV
For the LORD God is a sun and shield;
the LORD will give grace and glory; no
good thing will He withhold From those
who walk uprightly.

GEARY, Gearey
Language/Cultural Origin: **English**
Inherent Meaning: **Changeable**
Spiritual Connotation: **Courageous**
Scripture: **Psalm 16:8** NKJV
I have set the LORD always before me;
because He is at my right hand I shall not
be moved.

GEMINI, Gemelle, Gemina,
Gemmina
Language/Cultural Origin: **Greek**

Inherent Meaning: **Twin**
Spiritual Connotation: **Righteous**
Scripture: **Isaiah 61:1** RSV
The Spirit of the Lord GOD is upon me,
because the LORD has anointed me to
bring good tidings to the afflicted.

GENA, see Gina

GENE, see Eugene

GENEEN, see Jeanine

GENEVA, Jeneva
Language/Cultural Origin: **French**
Inherent Meaning: **Juniper Tree**
Spiritual Connotation: **Wise**
Scripture: **Psalm 111:10** NKJV
The fear of the LORD is the beginning of
wisdom; a good understanding have all
those who do His commandments. His
praise endures forever.

GENEVIEVE, Genavieve, Geneviéve,
Jenavieve
Language/Cultural Origin: **French**
Inherent Meaning: **Fair**
Spiritual Connotation: **Inner Beauty**
Scripture: **Proverbs 31:10** RSV
A good wife who can find? She is far
more precious than jewels.

GENNA, see Jenna

GENNIFER, see Jennifer

GEOFFREY, Geffery, Geffrey, Geoff,
Geoffery, Giotto, Gottfried (see
also Godfrey, Jeffrey)
Language/Cultural Origin: **Old German**
Inherent Meaning: **Perfectly Tranquil**
Spiritual Connotation: **Restful**
Scripture: **Isaiah 32:18** NRSV
My people will abide in a peaceful habita-
tion, in secure dwellings, and in quiet
resting places.

GEORGE, Georges, Georgio,
Gheorghe, Giorgio, Giorgios
Language/Cultural Origin: **Greek**
Inherent Meaning: **Land Worker**
Spiritual Connotation: **Walks With God**
Scripture: **Genesis 5:24** NRSV

Enoch walked with God; then he was no more, because God took him.

GEORGIA, Georgeann, Georgeanna, Georgene, Georgette, Georgie
Language/Cultural Origin: **Greek**
Inherent Meaning: **Farmer**
Spiritual Connotation: **Promise of God**
Scripture: **Hebrews 8:10** NKJV
I will put My laws in their mind and write them on their hearts; and I will be their God, and they shall be My people.

GERALD, Geraldo, Gerrald, Gerrold, Gerry, Jerald, Jeraldo, Jeri, Jerrald, Jerri, Jerrold, Jerry
Language/Cultural Origin: **Old German**
Inherent Meaning: **Mighty**
Spiritual Connotation: **Loyal**
Scripture: **Psalm 25:5** NKJV
Lead me in Your truth and teach me, for You are the God of my salvation; on You I wait all the day.

GERALDINE, Geraldina, Geralyn, Geri, Gerianna, Gerry, Jeraldine
Language/Cultural Origin: **Old German**
Inherent Meaning: **Powerful**
Spiritual Connotation: **Victorious**
Scripture: **Psalm 118:14** NKJV
The LORD is my strength and song, and He has become my salvation.

GERARD, Gérard, Gerardo, Gerrard, Gerry, Girard
Language/Cultural Origin: **Old German**
Inherent Meaning: **Strong, Powerful**
Spiritual Connotation: **Trusting Heart**
Scripture: **Psalm 138:8** NKJV
The LORD will perfect that which concerns me; Your mercy, O LORD, endures forever; do not forsake the works of Your hands.

GERMAIN, Germaine, Germana, Germane, Germaya, Germayne (see also Jermaine)
Language/Cultural Origin: **French**
Inherent Meaning: **From Germany**
Spiritual Connotation: **Bringer of Unity**
Scripture: **2 Timothy 2:22** NKJV
Flee also youthful lusts; but pursue

righteousness, faith, love, peace with those who call on the Lord out of a pure heart.

GERSHOM, Gershon
Language/Cultural Origin: **Hebrew**
Inherent Meaning: **Stranger**
Spiritual Connotation: **Visitor**
Scripture: **John 8:23** NKJV
You are from beneath; I am from above. You are of this world; I am not of this world.

GIANNA, Giana, Gianella, Giannella, Gianni, Jiana, Jianna, Jianella
Language/Cultural Origin: **Italian**
Inherent Meaning: **God Is Gracious**
Spiritual Connotation: **Sanctified**
Scripture: **1 Corinthians 1:4** RSV
I give thanks to God always for you because of the grace of God which was given you in Christ Jesus.

GIBBAR, Gibbár
Language/Cultural Origin: **Hebrew**
Inherent Meaning: **Mighty Man**
Spiritual Connotation: **Empowered**
Scripture: **Judges 6:12** NRSV
The LORD is with you, you mighty warrior.

GIBSON, Gilson
Language/Cultural Origin: **English**
Inherent Meaning: **Son of the Honest Man**
Spiritual Connotation: **Fruitful**
Scripture: **Luke 8:15** NASB
And the seed in the good soil, these are the ones who have heard the word in an honest and good heart . . . and bear fruit with perseverance.

GIDEON, Gedeon, Gideón
Language/Cultural Origin: **Hebrew**
Inherent Meaning: **Tree Cutter**
Spiritual Connotation: **Victorious**
Scripture: **Judges 8:28** NRSV
So Midian was subdued before the Israelites, and they lifted up their heads no more. So the land had rest forty years in the days of Gideon.

GIGI, G.G., Geegee
Language/Cultural Origin: **French**
Inherent Meaning: **Trustworthy**

Spiritual Connotation: **True Friend**
Scripture: **Proverbs 11:13** NLT
*A gossip goes around revealing secrets,
but those who are trustworthy can keep a
confidence.*

GILANA, Gilanna

Language/Cultural Origin: **Hebrew**
Inherent Meaning: **Hill of the Monument**
Spiritual Connotation: **Testimony**
Scripture: **Matthew 10:8** NKJV
*Heal the sick, cleanse the lepers, raise the
dead, cast out demons. Freely you have
received, freely give.*

GILBERT, Gibb, Gibbs, Gil, Guilbert

Language/Cultural Origin: **Old German**
Inherent Meaning: **Bright Pledge**
Spiritual Connotation: **Devoted**
Scripture: **Psalm 119:38** NLT
*Reassure me of your promise, which is
for those who honor you.*

GILDA, Gildé

Language/Cultural Origin: **Anglo-Saxon**
Inherent Meaning: **Covered With Gold**
Spiritual Connotation: **Blessed**
Scripture: **Psalm 68:13** NLT
*Though they lived among the sheepfolds,
now they are covered with silver and
gold, as a dove is covered by its wings.*

GILEAD, Giliad

Language/Cultural Origin: **Hebrew**
Inherent Meaning: **Mass of Testimony**
Spiritual Connotation: **Witness**
Scripture: **Matthew 10:18** NKJV
*You will be brought before governors and
kings for my sake, as a testimony to them
and to the Gentiles.*

GILEN, Gilan

Language/Cultural Origin: **Basque**
Inherent Meaning: **Notable Promise**
Spiritual Connotation: **Protected**
Scripture: **Psalm 18:30** RSV
*This God—his way is perfect; the prom-
ise of the LORD proves true; he is a shield
for all those who take refuge in him.*

GILES, Gilles, Gyles

Language/Cultural Origin: **French**
Inherent Meaning: **Shield**

Spiritual Connotation: **Strength**
Scripture: **Psalm 66:1-2** NKJV
*Make a joyful shout to God, all the
earth! Sing out the honor of His name;
make His praise glorious.*

GILLIAN, see Jillian

GILMORE, Gilmour

Language/Cultural Origin: **Irish**
Inherent Meaning: **Devout**
Spiritual Connotation: **Dependent**
Scripture: **Job 10:12** NKJV
*You have granted me life and favor, and
Your care has preserved my spirit.*

GILSEY, Gilsea, Gilsee

Language/Cultural Origin: **English**
Inherent Meaning: **Flower**
Spiritual Connotation: **Flourishing**
Scripture: **Psalm 92:12** TLB
*But the godly shall flourish like palm trees
and grow tall as the cedars of Lebanon.*

GINA, Geena, Gena, Ginah, Ginia (see also Jean)

Language/Cultural Origin: **Italian**
Inherent Meaning: **Queen**
Spiritual Connotation: **Full of Love**
Scripture: **Colossians 3:12** NRSV
*Above all, clothe yourselves with love,
which binds everything together in perfect
harmony.*

GINGER, Gingata

Language/Cultural Origin: **English**
Inherent Meaning: **Pure**
Spiritual Connotation: **Respectful**
Scripture: **1 Timothy 5:2** NLT
*Treat the older women as you would your
mother, and treat the younger women
with all purity as your own sisters.*

GINNY, Gini, Ginni, Ginnie, Jinnee, Jinney, Jinni, Jinnie, Jinny (see also Jina)

Language/Cultural Origin: **English**
Inherent Meaning: **Unblemished**
Spiritual Connotation: **Spotless**
Scripture: **Matthew 5:48** NKJV
*Therefore you shall be perfect, just as
your Father in heaven is perfect.*

GINO, Geno
Language/Cultural Origin: **Greek**
Inherent Meaning: **Of Noteworthy Birth**
Spiritual Connotation: **Delivered**
Scripture: **Ezekiel 34:29** NRSV
I will provide for them a splendid vegetation so that they shall no more be consumed with hunger in the land.

GIOVANNA, Giovana (see also Jovanna)
Language/Cultural Origin: **Italian**
Inherent Meaning: **God Is Gracious**
Spiritual Connotation: **Blessed**
Scripture: **Titus 2:11** NRSV
For the grace of God has appeared, bringing salvation to all.

GIOVANNI, Geovani, Geovanni, Gian, Giani, Gianni, Giavani, Giovanno (see also Jovan)
Language/Cultural Origin: **Italian**
Inherent Meaning: **God Is Gracious**
Spiritual Connotation: **Servant**
Scripture: **1 Peter 4:10** NCV
Each of you has received a gift to use to serve others. Be good servants of God's various gifts of grace.

GIUSEPPE, Giusepe
Language/Cultural Origin: **Italian**
Inherent Meaning: **God Will Increase**
Spiritual Connotation: **Joyful**
Scripture: **Isaiah 29:19** NKJV
The humble also shall increase their joy in the LORD, And the poor among men shall rejoice In the Holy One of Israel.

GIZELLE, Gissell, Giselle, Jiselle, Jizella, Jizelle
Language/Cultural Origin: **Old German**
Inherent Meaning: **Pledge**
Spiritual Connotation: **Approved**
Scripture: **2 Corinthians 1:22** NCV
He put his mark on us to show that we are his, and he put his Spirit in our hearts to be a guarantee for all he has promised.

GLADYS, Gladis
Language/Cultural Origin: **Irish**
Inherent Meaning: **Princess**
Spiritual Connotation: **Spiritual Understanding**
Scripture: **1 Peter 2:5** NKJV
You also, as living stones, are being built up a spiritual house, a holy priesthood, to offer up spiritual sacrifices.

GLENDON, Glenden
Language/Cultural Origin: **Scottish**
Inherent Meaning: **From the Valley Fortress**
Spiritual Connotation: **Secure**
Scripture: **2 Samuel 22:33** TLB
God is my strong fortress; He has made me safe.

GLENN, Glen
Language/Cultural Origin: **Irish**
Inherent Meaning: **From the Valley**
Spiritual Connotation: **Excellent Worth**
Scripture: **Psalm 84:4** NKJV
Blessed are those who dwell in Your house; they will still be praising You.

GLENNA, Glenda
Language/Cultural Origin: **Irish**
Inherent Meaning: **From the Valley**
Spiritual Connotation: **Blooming**
Scripture: **Psalm 52:8** NKJV
But I am like a green olive tree in the house of God; I trust in the mercy of God forever and ever.

GLORIA, Gloriela, Gloriella, Glorielle, Glory, Glorya
Language/Cultural Origin: **Latin**
Inherent Meaning: **Glory**
Spiritual Connotation: **Glorious**
Scripture: **2 Corinthians 3:18** NRSV
And all of us . . . are being transformed into the same image from one degree of glory to another; for this comes from the Lord, the Spirit.

GLYN, Glynn
Language/Cultural Origin: **Scottish**
Inherent Meaning: **From the Ravine**
Spiritual Connotation: **Protected**
Scripture: **Psalm 3:3** NASB
But Thou, O LORD, art a shield about me, my glory, and the One who lifts my head.

GODFREY, Godfry (see also Geoffrey)

Language/Cultural Origin: **Irish**
Inherent Meaning: **Man of God's Peace**
Spiritual Connotation: **Divinely Peaceful**
Scripture: **John 7:38** NKJV
He who believes in Me, as the Scripture has said, out of his heart will flow rivers of living water.

GOLDA, Golden, Goldi, Goldie

Language/Cultural Origin: **English**
Inherent Meaning: **Golden**
Spiritual Connotation: **Divine Perspective**
Scripture: **Psalms 119:127** NLT
Truly, I love your commands more than gold, even the finest gold.

GOMER

Language/Cultural Origin: **Hebrew**
Inherent Meaning: **Completion**
Spiritual Connotation: **Preserved**
Scripture: **Philippians 1:6** NCV
God began doing a good work in you, and I am sure he will continue it until it is finished when Jesus Christ comes again.

GORDON, Gordan, Gordie, Gordy

Language/Cultural Origin: **Anglo-Saxon**
Inherent Meaning: **From the Round Hill**
Spiritual Connotation: **Shining**
Scripture: **Matthew 5:14** NKJV
You are the light of the world. A city that is set on a hill cannot be hidden.

GORMAN, Gormon

Language/Cultural Origin: **Gaelic**
Inherent Meaning: **Blue-eyed**
Spiritual Connotation: **Walks With God**
Scripture: **Psalm 84:11** NKJV
For the LORD God is a sun and shield; the LORD will give grace and glory; no good thing will He withhold From those who walk uprightly.

GOWON, Gowan

Language/Cultural Origin: **Tiv**
Inherent Meaning: **Born During a Storm**
Spiritual Connotation: **Rainmaker**
Scripture: **Joel 2:23** TLB
Rejoice, O people of Jerusalem, rejoice in the Lord your God! For the rains he sends are tokens of forgiveness.

GRACE, Gracey, Graci, Gracia, Graciana, Gracianna, Gracie

Language/Cultural Origin: **Latin**
Inherent Meaning: **Patient**
Spiritual Connotation: **Full of Grace**
Scripture: **1 Corinthians 16:14** TLB
And whatever you do, do it with kindness and love.

GRADY, Gradey

Language/Cultural Origin: **Gaelic**
Inherent Meaning: **Noble**
Spiritual Connotation: **Strong**
Scripture: **Joshua 1:9** NKJV
Be strong and of good courage; do not be afraid, nor be dismayed, for the LORD your God is with you wherever you go.

GRAHAM, Graeham, Graeme

Language/Cultural Origin: **English**
Inherent Meaning: **From a Grand Home**
Spiritual Connotation: **Generous**
Scripture: **1 Corinthians 13:13** NKJV
And now abide faith, hope, love, these three; but the greatest of these is love.

GRANGER, Grainger, Grange

Language/Cultural Origin: **French**
Inherent Meaning: **Farmer**
Spiritual Connotation: **God's Follower**
Scripture: **Isaiah 48:17** NKJV
I am the LORD your God, who teaches you to profit, who leads you by the way you should go.

GRANT, Grantham, Grantley

Language/Cultural Origin: **French**
Inherent Meaning: **Tall**
Spiritual Connotation: **Assurance**
Scripture: **Psalm 18:2** NKJV
The LORD is my rock and my fortress and my deliverer; my God, my strength, in whom I will trust; my shield and the horn of my salvation, my stronghold.

GRANTLAND, Grantlund

Language/Cultural Origin: **Old English**
Inherent Meaning: **From the Great Plains**
Spiritual Connotation: **Strength in God**
Scripture: **Proverbs 3:5-6** NKJV

*Trust in the LORD with all your heart,
and lean not on your own understanding;
in all your ways acknowledge Him, and
He shall direct your paths.*

GRANVILLE, Grenville
Language/Cultural Origin: **French**
Inherent Meaning: **From the Large Village**
Spiritual Connotation: **Righteous**
Scripture: **Psalm 37:6** NKJV
*He shall bring forth your righteousness
as the light, and your justice as the
noonday.*

GRAYSON, Greyson
Language/Cultural Origin: **Middle English**
Inherent Meaning: **Son of the Bailiff**
Spiritual Connotation: **One of Knowledge**
Scripture: **Proverbs 13:14** NKJV
*The law of the wise is a fountain of life, to
turn one away from the snares of death.*

GREER, Grier
Language/Cultural Origin: **English**
Inherent Meaning: **Watchful**
Spiritual Connotation: **Vigilant**
Scripture: **1 Peter 5:8-9** NKJV
*Be sober, be vigilant; because your
adversary the devil walks about like
a roaring lion, seeking whom he may
devour. Resist him, steadfast in the faith.*

**GREGORY, Greg, Gregg, Greggory,
Gregori, Greig, Grigori**
Language/Cultural Origin: **Greek**
Inherent Meaning: **Guardian**
Spiritual Connotation: **God's Trustee**
Scripture: **1 Corinthians 16:13** NKJV
*Watch, stand fast in the faith, be brave,
be strong. Let all that you do be done
with love.*

GRESHAM, Grisham
Language/Cultural Origin: **English**
Inherent Meaning: **From the Village by
the Pasture**
Spiritual Connotation: **Peaceful**
Scripture: **Psalm 23:2** NKJV
*He makes me to lie down in green pas-
tures; He leads me beside the still waters.*

GRETA, Gretal, Grethal, Gretta
Language/Cultural Origin: **English**

Inherent Meaning: **Pearl**
Spiritual Connotation: **Eternal Hope**
Scripture: **Revelation 21:21** NKJV
*The twelve gates were twelve pearls: each
individual gate was of one pearl. And
the street of the city was pure gold, like
transparent glass.*

GRETCHEN, Gretchin
Language/Cultural Origin: **German**
Inherent Meaning: **Pearl**
Spiritual Connotation: **Invaluable**
Scripture: **Psalm 36:7** NIV
*How priceless is your unfailing love!
Both high and low among men find ref-
uge in the shadow of your wings.*

GRIFFITH, Griffey
Language/Cultural Origin: **Welsh**
Inherent Meaning: **Great Strength**
Spiritual Connotation: **Blessed of God**
Scripture: **Psalm 8:5-6** NKJV
*You have crowned him with glory and
honor. You have made him to have
dominion over the works of Your hands;
You have put all things under his feet.*

GROVER, Grove
Language/Cultural Origin: **German**
Inherent Meaning: **Gardener**
Spiritual Connotation: **Consecrated**
Scripture: **Psalm 37:37** NKJV
*Mark the blameless man, and observe the
upright; for the future of that man is peace.*

GUADALUPE, Guadulupe
Language/Cultural Origin: **Spanish**
Inherent Meaning: **From the Valley of
Wolves**
Spiritual Connotation: **Wondrous**
Scripture: **Psalm 29:4** NASB
*The voice of the LORD is powerful, the
voice of the LORD is majestic.*

GUILLAUME, Guillermo
Language/Cultural Origin: **French**
Inherent Meaning: **Strong Guardian**
Spiritual Connotation: **Shielded**
Scripture: **Psalm 5:11** NASB
*But let all who take refuge in You be
glad, let them ever sing for joy; and may
You shelter them, that those who love
Your name may exult in You.*

GUINEVERE, Guenevere

Language/Cultural Origin: **Welsh**
Inherent Meaning: **Unstained**
Spiritual Connotation: **Ransomed**
Scripture: **1 Peter 1:19** TLB
But he paid for you with the precious lifeblood of Christ, the sinless, spotless Lamb of God.

GUNNAR, Gunner, Gunthar, Gunther, Günther

Language/Cultural Origin: **Old Norse**
Inherent Meaning: **Warrior-King**
Spiritual Connotation: **Obedient**
Scripture: **Psalm 119:34** NKJV
Give me understanding, and I shall keep Your law; Indeed, I shall observe it with my whole heart.

GURION, Guri, Guriel

Language/Cultural Origin: **Hebrew**
Inherent Meaning: **Young Lion**
Spiritual Connotation: **Righteous**
Scripture: **Proverbs 28:1** NKJV
The wicked flee when no one pursues, but the righteous are bold as a lion.

GUSTAVE, Gus, Guss, Gustaf, Gustáv, Gustavus

Language/Cultural Origin: **Scandinavian**
Inherent Meaning: **God's Staff**
Spiritual Connotation: **Blessed**
Scripture: **Psalm 24:5** NKJV
He shall receive blessing from the LORD, and righteousness from the God of his salvation.

GUTHRIE, Gutherie, Guthrey

Language/Cultural Origin: **German**
Inherent Meaning: **War Hero**
Spiritual Connotation: **Great**
Scripture: **Colossians 3:16** NKJV
Let the word of Christ dwell in you richly in all wisdom.

GUY, Guido, Gui

Language/Cultural Origin: **French**
Inherent Meaning: **Director**
Spiritual Connotation: **Peaceful**
Scripture: **James 3:18** NKJV
Now the fruit of righteousness is sown in peace by those who make peace.

GWENDOLYN, Gwen, Gwendalyn, Gwendolin, Gwendolynn, Gwenn

Language/Cultural Origin: **Welsh**
Inherent Meaning: **Fair**
Spiritual Connotation: **Full of Honor**
Scripture: **Psalm 18:35** NKJV
You have also given me the shield of Your salvation; Your right hand has held me up, Your gentleness has made me great.

GWYNN, Gwinn, Gwyn, Gwynne

Language/Cultural Origin: **Welsh**
Inherent Meaning: **Spotless**
Spiritual Connotation: **Seeker of Wisdom**
Scripture: **Isaiah 58:14** NKJV
Then you shall delight yourself in the LORD; and I will cause you to ride on the high hills of the earth.

H

HABAIAH, Habiyah (see also Abia)
Language/Cultural Origin: **Hebrew**
Inherent Meaning: **God Has Hidden**
Spiritual Connotation: **Preserved**
Scripture: **Isaiah 49:2** NKJV
And He has made My mouth like a sharp sword; in the shadow of His hand He has hidden Me.

HADAD, Haddad
Language/Cultural Origin: **Hebrew**
Inherent Meaning: **Mighty**
Spiritual Connotation: **Strength of God**
Scripture: **Psalm 66:3** NRSV
How awesome are your deeds! Because of your great power, your enemies cringe before you.

HADASSAH, Hadása, Hadassa
Language/Cultural Origin: **Hebrew**
Inherent Meaning: **Star**
Spiritual Connotation: **Precious**
Scripture: **Genesis 1:16** NASB
God made the two great lights, the greater light to govern the day, and the lesser light to govern the night; He made the stars also.

HADDEN, Haddan, Haddon (see also Hayden)
Language/Cultural Origin: **English**
Inherent Meaning: **From the Hill of Heather**
Spiritual Connotation: **Great Confidence**
Scripture: **Jeremiah 32:17** NKJV
Ah, Lord GOD! Behold, You have made the heavens and the earth by Your great power and outstretched arm. There is nothing too hard for You.

HADLAI, Haddlai (see also Adlai)
Language/Cultural Origin: **Hebrew**
Inherent Meaning: **Frail**
Spiritual Connotation: **Child of God**
Scripture: **2 Corinthians 12:9** NCV
My grace is enough for you. When you are weak, my power is made perfect in you.

HADLEY, Hadlee, Hadleigh
Language/Cultural Origin: **Anglo-Saxon**
Inherent Meaning: **From the Field of Heather**
Spiritual Connotation: **Peaceful Spirit**
Scripture: **Psalm 25:21** NKJV
Let integrity and uprightness preserve me, for I wait for You.

HADRIAN, Hadrien
Language/Cultural Origin: **Swedish**
Inherent Meaning: **Dark**
Spiritual Connotation: **Just**
Scripture: **Colossians 4:1** NKJV
Masters, give your bondservants what is just and fair, knowing that you also have a Master in heaven.

HAGAN, Haggan
Language/Cultural Origin: **German**
Inherent Meaning: **Strong Defense**
Spiritual Connotation: **Immovable**
Scripture: **Psalm 62:6** NRSV
He alone is my rock and my salvation, my fortress; I shall not be shaken.

HAGAR, Haggar
Language/Cultural Origin: **Hebrew**
Inherent Meaning: **Fugitive**
Spiritual Connotation: **Assurance**
Scripture: **Genesis 21:18** NASB
Arise, lift up the lad, and hold him by the hand, for I will make a great nation of him.

HAGEN, Haggen
Language/Cultural Origin: **Irish**
Inherent Meaning: **Youthful**
Spiritual Connotation: **Accountable**

Scripture: **Ecclesiastes 12:1** KJV
Remember now thy Creator in the days of thy youth, while the evil days come not.

HAI, Haian
Language/Cultural Origin: **Vietnamese**
Inherent Meaning: **Sea**
Spiritual Connotation: **Filled With Praise**
Scripture: **Psalm 69:34** NKJV
Let heaven and earth praise Him, the seas and everything that moves in them.

HAIDAR, Haidor
Language/Cultural Origin: **Middle Eastern**
Inherent Meaning: **Lion**
Spiritual Connotation: **Warrior of God**
Scripture: **Isaiah 31:4** KJV
Like as the lion and the young lion roaring on its prey . . . so shall the LORD of hosts come down to fight for Mount Zion.

HAIDEE, Haiday, Haydee (see also Heidi)
Language/Cultural Origin: **English**
Inherent Meaning: **Modest**
Spiritual Connotation: **Humble**
Scripture: **Ezra 8:21** NKJV
Then I proclaimed a fast . . . that we might humble ourselves before our God, to seek from Him the right way for us and our little ones and all our possessions.

HAKIM, Hakeem, Hákeem (see also Akim, Joachim)
Language/Cultural Origin: **Ethiopian**
Inherent Meaning: **Doctor**
Spiritual Connotation: **Healer**
Scripture: **Psalm 147:3** NKJV
He heals the brokenhearted and binds up their wounds.

HAL, see Harold

HALE, Haile
Language/Cultural Origin: **Hawaiian**
Inherent Meaning: **Military Power**
Spiritual Connotation: **Act of God**
Scripture: **Psalm 106:8** RSV
Yet he saved them for his name's sake, that he might make known his mighty power.

HALEN, Haylan
Language/Cultural Origin: **Swedish**

Inherent Meaning: **Hall**
Spiritual Connotation: **Gracious**
Scripture: **Romans 12:14** NKJV
Bless those who persecute you; bless and do not curse.

HALEY, Haeley, Hailee, Hailey, Hailie, Halee, Haleigh, Halie, Haylee, Hayleigh, Hayley, Haylie
Language/Cultural Origin: **Scandinavian**
Inherent Meaning: **Heroine**
Spiritual Connotation: **Creative**
Scripture: **Colossians 3:23-24** NKJV
And whatever you do, do it heartily, as to the Lord and not to men . . . for you serve the Lord Christ.

HALIA, Halianna, Hallia, Halliana
Language/Cultural Origin: **Hawaiian**
Inherent Meaning: **In Remembrance of a Loved One**
Spiritual Connotation: **Reflective**
Scripture: **Luke 22:19** NKJV
And He took bread, gave thanks and broke it, and gave it to them, saying, "This is My body which is given for you; do this in remembrance of Me."

HALIAN, Halien
Language/Cultural Origin: **Zuni**
Inherent Meaning: **Young**
Spiritual Connotation: **Righteous**
Scripture: **2 Timothy 2:2** NKJV
And the things that you have heard from me among many witnesses, commit these to faithful men who will be able to teach others also.

HALIM, Haleem
Language/Cultural Origin: **Middle Eastern**
Inherent Meaning: **Patient**
Spiritual Connotation: **Persistent**
Scripture: **2 Timothy 4:2** NLT
Preach the word of God. Be persistent, whether the time is favorable or not. Patiently correct, rebuke, and encourage your people with good teaching.

HALINA, Halinah (see also Helena)
Language/Cultural Origin: **Russian**
Inherent Meaning: **Glowing**
Spiritual Connotation: **Godly Example**

Scripture: **Matthew 5:14** NLT
You are the light of the world—like a city on a mountain, glowing in the night for all to see.

HALLAN, Hallin
Language/Cultural Origin: **English**
Inherent Meaning: **From the Manor**
Spiritual Connotation: **Generous**
Scripture: **2 Corinthians 9:9** TLB
The godly man gives generously to the poor. His good deeds will be an honor to him forever.

HALLE, Halla, Halley, Halli, Hally
Language/Cultural Origin: **Nigerian**
Inherent Meaning: **Unexpected Gift**
Spiritual Connotation: **Blessing**
Scripture: **2 Corinthians 9:13** TLB
Those you help . . . will praise God for this proof that your deeds are as good as your doctrine.

HALONA, Halonah
Language/Cultural Origin: **Native American**
Inherent Meaning: **Fortunate**
Spiritual Connotation: **Blessed**
Scripture: **Proverbs 3:18** NKJV
She is a tree of life to those who take hold of her, and happy are all who retain her.

HALSEY, Halsee, Halseigh, Halzee
Language/Cultural Origin: **English**
Inherent Meaning: **From the Ruler's Island**
Spiritual Connotation: **Righteous**
Scripture: **3 John 11** NKJV
Beloved, do not imitate what is evil, but what is good. He who does good is of God, but he who does evil has not seen God.

HAMAL, Hamaal
Language/Cultural Origin: **Middle Eastern**
Inherent Meaning: **Lamb**
Spiritual Connotation: **Hopeful**
Scripture: **Isaiah 11:6** NKJV
The wolf also shall dwell with the lamb, the leopard shall lie down with the young goat. . . . And a little child shall lead them.

HAMAN, Hayman
Language/Cultural Origin: **Hebrew**
Inherent Meaning: **Well Disposed**
Spiritual Connotation: **Blessed**

Scripture: **Deuteronomy 30:5** NLT
He will make you even more prosperous and numerous than your ancestors!

HAMILTON, Hamelton
Language/Cultural Origin: **Old English**
Inherent Meaning: **From the Fortified Castle**
Spiritual Connotation: **Faithful**
Scripture: **Proverbs 20:6** RSV
Many a man proclaims his own loyalty, but a faithful man who can find?

HAMLET, Hamlett
Language/Cultural Origin: **Old Norse**
Inherent Meaning: **From the Village**
Spiritual Connotation: **Compassionate**
Scripture: **Luke 6:36** NKJV
Therefore be merciful, just as your Father also is merciful.

HAMLIN, Hamelin, Hamlyn
Language/Cultural Origin: **Old German**
Inherent Meaning: **Loves His Home**
Spiritual Connotation: **Godly Example**
Scripture: **Ephesians 5:25** NKJV
Husbands, love your wives, just as Christ also loved the church and gave Himself for her.

HAMMOND, Hamond
Language/Cultural Origin: **English**
Inherent Meaning: **From the Village**
Spiritual Connotation: **Witness**
Scripture: **1 Peter 2:21** NASB
For you have been called for this purpose, since Christ also suffered for you, leaving you an example for you to follow in His steps.

HAMUEL, Hammuel
Language/Cultural Origin: **Hebrew**
Inherent Meaning: **Warmth of God**
Spiritual Connotation: **Loving**
Scripture: **Isaiah 60:3** NLT
All nations will come to your light. Mighty kings will come to see your radiance.

HANA, Hanita
Language/Cultural Origin: **Japanese**
Inherent Meaning: **Flower**
Spiritual Connotation: **Joyful**
Scripture: **Psalm 96:12-13** NCV
Let the fields and everything in them

rejoice. Then all the trees of the forest will sing for joy before the LORD, because he is coming.

HANAN, Hannan, Hannen, Hannon
Language/Cultural Origin: **Hebrew**
Inherent Meaning: **Merciful**
Spiritual Connotation: **Compassionate**
Scripture: **Matthew 9:13** NRSV
I desire mercy, not sacrifice. For I have come to call not the righteous but sinners.

HANANI, Hananni, Hannani
Language/Cultural Origin: **Hebrew**
Inherent Meaning: **God Has Shown Mercy**
Spiritual Connotation: **Promised**
Scripture: **Deuteronomy 4:31** TLB
For the Lord your God is merciful—he will not abandon you.

HANANIAH, Hananiyah
Language/Cultural Origin: **Hebrew**
Inherent Meaning: **God Is Gracious**
Spiritual Connotation: **Blessed**
Scripture: **Numbers 6:24** NKJV
The LORD bless you and keep you; the LORD make His face shine upon you, and be gracious to you.

HANIA, Hanja, Hanya
Language/Cultural Origin: **Hebrew**
Inherent Meaning: **Resting Place**
Spiritual Connotation: **Peaceful**
Scripture: **Psalm 132:14** NLT
This is my home where I will live forever, he said. I will live here, for this is the place I desired.

HANIEL, Hanniel
Language/Cultural Origin: **Hebrew**
Inherent Meaning: **Grace of God**
Spiritual Connotation: **Restored**
Scripture: **Joel 2:13** NLT
Return to the LORD your God, for he is gracious and merciful.

HANLEY, Hanlee, Hanleigh, Henlee, Henleigh, Henley, Hensley
Language/Cultural Origin: **English**
Inherent Meaning: **From the High Pasture**
Spiritual Connotation: **Protector, Shepherd**
Scripture: **Isaiah 49:10** NKJV
They shall neither hunger nor thirst,

neither heat nor sun shall strike them; for He who has mercy on them will lead them.

HANNAH, Hanna
Language/Cultural Origin: **Hebrew**
Inherent Meaning: **Gracious**
Spiritual Connotation: **Compassionate**
Scripture: **Psalm 145:8** NKJV
The LORD is gracious and full of compassion, Slow to anger and great in mercy.

HANNIBAL, Hanibal
Language/Cultural Origin: **Phoenician**
Inherent Meaning: **Grace**
Spiritual Connotation: **Merciful**
Scripture: **Psalm 18:25** NKJV
With the merciful You will show Yourself merciful; with a blameless man You will show Yourself blameless.

HANS, Hansel, Hansen, Hanz
Language/Cultural Origin: **Swedish**
Inherent Meaning: **God Is Gracious**
Spiritual Connotation: **Discerning Spirit**
Scripture: **1 Corinthians 15:10** NKJV
But by the grace of God I am what I am, and His grace toward me was not in vain.

HARAN, Harran
Language/Cultural Origin: **Hebrew**
Inherent Meaning: **Enlightened**
Spiritual Connotation: **Sanctified**
Scripture: **Ephesians 1:18** NASB
I pray that the eyes of your heart may be enlightened.

HARBIN, Harbyn
Language/Cultural Origin: **German**
Inherent Meaning: **Little Warrior**
Spiritual Connotation: **Obedient**
Scripture: **Matthew 8:9** NKJV
For I also am a man under authority, having soldiers under me. And I say to this one, "Go," and he goes; and to another, "Come," and he comes.

HARDIN, Hardan
Language/Cultural Origin: **English**
Inherent Meaning: **From the Hares' Valley**
Spiritual Connotation: **Righteous**
Scripture: **Philippians 3:17** NCV
Brothers and sisters, all of you should try

to follow my example and to copy those
who live the way we showed you.

HARDY, Hardey
Language/Cultural Origin: **English**
Inherent Meaning: **Bold**
Spiritual Connotation: **Confident**
Scripture: **Hebrews 4:16** NKJV
*Let us therefore come boldly to the throne
of grace, that we may obtain mercy and
find grace to help in time of need.*

HAREL, Hariel, Harrel
Language/Cultural Origin: **Hebrew**
Inherent Meaning: **Mountain of God**
Spiritual Connotation: **Holy**
Scripture: **Exodus 3:1** NKJV
*Now Moses . . . led the flock to the back
of the desert, and came to Horeb, the
mountain of God.*

HARLAN, Harland, Harlon
Language/Cultural Origin: **Old English**
Inherent Meaning: **From the Land**
Spiritual Connotation: **Resolute**
Scripture: **Deuteronomy 31:6** NKJV
*Be strong and of good courage, do not fear
nor be afraid of them; for the LORD your
God, He is the One who goes with you.
He will not leave you nor forsake you.*

HARLEY, Harlee, Harleigh
Language/Cultural Origin: **Old English**
Inherent Meaning: **From the Rabbit Pasture**
Spiritual Connotation: **Chosen of God**
Scripture: **John 15:19** NCV
*If you belonged to the world, it would love
you as it loves its own. But I have chosen
you out of the world, so you don't belong
to it. That is why the world hates you.*

HARMONY, Harmoni, Harmonie
Language/Cultural Origin: **Latin**
Inherent Meaning: **Oneness**
Spiritual Connotation: **Unifier**
Scripture: **Colossians 3:14** NCV
*Do all these things; but most important,
love each other. Love is what holds you
all together in perfect unity.*

HAROLD, Hal, Herald, Herold
Language/Cultural Origin: **Old English**
Inherent Meaning: **Army Leader**

Spiritual Connotation: **Born of God**
Scripture: **Acts 17:28** NKJV
*For in Him we live and move and have
our being, as also some of your own poets
have said, for we are also His offspring.*

HARPER, Harpo
Language/Cultural Origin: **English**
Inherent Meaning: **Harp Player**
Spiritual Connotation: **Instrument of Praise**
Scripture: **Psalm 33:2** NKJV
*Praise the LORD with the harp; make
melody to Him with an instrument of
ten strings.*

HARRIET, Harriett, Hattie
Language/Cultural Origin: **Old German**
Inherent Meaning: **Ruler of the Household**
Spiritual Connotation: **Discerner of
Excellence**
Scripture: **Philippians 4:8** NASB
*Finally, brethren, whatever is true, . . .
honorable, . . . right, . . . pure, . . .
lovely, . . . [or] of good repute, if there is
any excellence and if anything worthy of
praise, let your mind dwell on these things.*

HARRIS, Harrison
Language/Cultural Origin: **Old English**
Inherent Meaning: **Son of the Strong Man**
Spiritual Connotation: **Courageous**
Scripture: **Proverbs 24:5** NKJV
*A wise man is strong, yes, a man of
knowledge increases strength.*

HARRY, Harray, Harrey
Language/Cultural Origin: **Old German**
Inherent Meaning: **Home Ruler**
Spiritual Connotation: **Integrity**
Scripture: **Ephesians 6:8** NKJV
*Whatever good anyone does, he will
receive the same from the Lord, whether
he is a slave or free.*

HARTLEY, Hartlee, Hartleigh
Language/Cultural Origin: **Anglo-Saxon**
Inherent Meaning: **From the Deer Meadow**
Spiritual Connotation: **Victorious**
Scripture: **Psalm 50:15** NKJV
*Call upon Me in the day of trouble; I will
deliver you, and you shall glorify Me.*

HARVEY, Harv (see also Hervé)
Language/Cultural Origin: **Celtic**
Inherent Meaning: **Noble**
Spiritual Connotation: **Brave**
Scripture: **Psalm 100:3** NKJV
Know that the LORD, He is God; it is He who has made us, and not we ourselves; we are His people and the sheep of His pasture.

HASAD, Hasád, Hasaad (see also Asad)
Language/Cultural Origin: **Turkish**
Inherent Meaning: **Harvester**
Spiritual Connotation: **Evangelist**
Scripture: **John 4:35** NCV
You have a saying, "Four more months till harvest." But I tell you, open your eyes and look at the fields ready for harvest now.

HASANA, Haseina
Language/Cultural Origin: **Swahili**
Inherent Meaning: **Firstborn**
Spiritual Connotation: **Follower of Christ**
Scripture: **Colossians 1:15** NKJV
He is the image of the invisible God, the firstborn over all creation.

HASANI, Hasaan, Hasán, Hashaan (see also Ahsan, Ihsan)
Language/Cultural Origin: **Swahili**
Inherent Meaning: **Handsome**
Spiritual Connotation: **Chosen**
Scripture: **1 Samuel 16:12** NKJV
He was ruddy, with bright eyes, and good-looking. And the LORD said, "Arise, anoint him; for this is the one!"

HASRAH, Hazrah
☞ Language/Cultural Origin: **Hebrew**
Inherent Meaning: **Splendor**
Spiritual Connotation: **Praise**
Scripture: **Exodus 15:11** RSV
Who is like thee, majestic in holiness, terrible in glorious deeds, doing wonders?

HATIPHA, Hateefa, Hateepha, ☞ Hatifa
Language/Cultural Origin: **Hebrew**
Inherent Meaning: **Captive**
Spiritual Connotation: **Obedient**
Scripture: **2 Corinthians 10:5** NRSV
We take every thought captive to obey Christ.

HAVEN, Havan, Havin
Language/Cultural Origin: **Dutch**
Inherent Meaning: **Harbor**
Spiritual Connotation: **Preserved**
Scripture: **Leviticus 25:18** NKJV
So you shall observe My statutes and keep My judgments, and perform them; and you will dwell in the land in safety.

HAYDEN, Haden, Haydn, Haydon (see also Hadden)
Language/Cultural Origin: **English**
Inherent Meaning: **From the Hedged Valley**
Spiritual Connotation: **Victorious**
Scripture: **2 Corinthians 6:2** NKJV
In the day of salvation I have helped you. Behold, now is the accepted time; behold, now is the day of salvation.

HAYES, Hays
Language/Cultural Origin: **English**
Inherent Meaning: **From the Hedged Valley**
Spiritual Connotation: **Moderate**
Scripture: **1 Corinthians 6:12** NCV
I am allowed to do all things, but all things are not good for me to do. I am allowed to do all things, but I will not let anything make me its slave.

HAYLEY, see Haley

HAYWARD, Heyward
Language/Cultural Origin: **English**
Inherent Meaning: **Guardian/Protector of the Hedged Area**
Spiritual Connotation: **Secure**
Scripture: **Isaiah 26:3** NLT
You will keep in perfect peace all who trust in you, whose thoughts are fixed on you!

HAYWOOD, Heywood
Language/Cultural Origin: **English**
Inherent Meaning: **From the Hedged Forest**
Spiritual Connotation: **Chosen**
Scripture: **Acts 13:48** NKJV
And as many as had been appointed to eternal life believed.

HAZEL, Hazyl
Language/Cultural Origin: **English**

Inherent Meaning: **Commander of Authority**
Spiritual Connotation: **Cleansed**
Scripture: **1 John 1:7** NKJV
But if we walk in the light as He is in the light, we have fellowship with one another, and the blood of Jesus Christ His Son cleanses us from all sin.

HAZIEL, Hazael

Language/Cultural Origin: **Hebrew**
Inherent Meaning: **God Sees**
Spiritual Connotation: **Witness**
Scripture: **John 8:38** NRSV
I declare what I have seen in the Father's presence.

HEATH, Heathe

Language/Cultural Origin: **English**
Inherent Meaning: **Shrub**
Spiritual Connotation: **Protector**
Scripture: **Ephesians 6:16** NKJV
Above all, taking the shield of faith with which you will be able to quench all the fiery darts of the wicked one.

HEATHER, Heatherlee

Language/Cultural Origin: **Middle English**
Inherent Meaning: **Flowering, Blooming**
Spiritual Connotation: **Cover of Beauty**
Scripture: **Matthew 6:28-29** NKJV
So why do you worry about clothing? Consider the lilies of the field. . . . I say to you that even Solomon in all his glory was not arrayed like one of these.

HEBRON

Language/Cultural Origin: **Hebrew**
Inherent Meaning: **Company**
Spiritual Connotation: **Inheritance**
Scripture: **Joshua 14:14** RSV
So Hebron became the inheritance of Caleb.

HECTOR, Hectar

Language/Cultural Origin: **Greek**
Inherent Meaning: **Steadfast**
Spiritual Connotation: **One of Integrity**
Scripture: **Luke 6:38** NKJV
Give, and it will be given to you. . . . For with the same measure that you use, it will be measured back to you.

HEIDI, Heide, Heidee, Hidee, Hiedi (see also Haidee)

Language/Cultural Origin: **Old German**
Inherent Meaning: **Honored**
Spiritual Connotation: **Blessed**
Scripture: **Psalm 29:11** KJV
The LORD will give strength unto his people; the LORD will bless his people with peace.

HEINRICH, Heinrick, Heinrik

Language/Cultural Origin: **German**
Inherent Meaning: **Household Ruler**
Spiritual Connotation: **Just**
Scripture: **1 Chronicles 18:14** NRSV
So David reigned over all Israel; and he administered justice and equity to all his people.

HELEN, Hellen

Language/Cultural Origin: **Greek**
Inherent Meaning: **Light**
Spiritual Connotation: **Righteous**
Scripture: **Psalm 37:6** NKJV
He shall bring forth your righteousness as the light, and your justice as the noonday.

HELENA, Haleena, Halena, Helana, Heleana, Heleena (see also Halina)

Language/Cultural Origin: **English**
Inherent Meaning: **Brightness**
Spiritual Connotation: **Testimony**
Scripture: **Isaiah 60:3** NRSV
Nations shall come to your light, and kings to the brightness of your dawn.

HENLEY, see Hanley

HENRIETTA, Henrieta

Language/Cultural Origin: **English**
Inherent Meaning: **Household Ruler**
Spiritual Connotation: **Strong**
Scripture: **Psalm 18:32** NKJV
It is God who arms me with strength, and makes my way perfect.

HENRY, Hank, Henri, Henrí

Language/Cultural Origin: **Old German**
Inherent Meaning: **Ruler of the Household**
Spiritual Connotation: **Trusted**
Scripture: **Psalm 37:23** NKJV
The steps of a good man are ordered by the LORD, and He delights in his way.

HERBERT, Herb, Herbie

Language/Cultural Origin: **Old German**
Inherent Meaning: **Shining Soldier**
Spiritual Connotation: **Powerful Protector**
Scripture: **Psalm 37:31** NKJV
The law of his God is in his heart; none of his steps shall slide.

HERCULES

Language/Cultural Origin: **Greek**
Inherent Meaning: **Glorious Gift**
Spiritual Connotation: **Enduring**
Scripture: **Jude 1:24,25** NRSV
Now to him who is able to keep you from falling, be glory, majesty, power, and authority, before all time and now and forever. Amen.

HERMAN, Hermann, Hermon

Language/Cultural Origin: **Old German**
Inherent Meaning: **Noble Soldier**
Spiritual Connotation: **Righteous**
Scripture: **Psalm 37:37** NKJV
Mark the blameless man, and observe the upright; for the future of that man is peace.

HERICK, Herrik

Language/Cultural Origin: **German**
Inherent Meaning: **War Ruler**
Spiritual Connotation: **Chosen**
Scripture: **2 Thessalonians 2:13** RSV
But we are bound to give thanks to God always for you, brethren beloved by the Lord, because God chose you from the beginning to be saved.

HERSHEL, Herschel, Hershell

Language/Cultural Origin: **Hebrew**
Inherent Meaning: **Deer**
Spiritual Connotation: **Promise**
Scripture: **Isaiah 35:6** NKJV
Then the lame shall leap like a deer, and the tongue of the dumb sing. For waters shall burst forth in the wilderness, and streams in the desert.

HERVÉ, Hervay (see also Harvey)

Language/Cultural Origin: **French**
Inherent Meaning: **Warrior**
Spiritual Connotation: **Steadfast**
Scripture: **1 Timothy 6:12** NASB
Fight the good fight of faith; take hold of the eternal life to which you were called.

HESED, Heséd

☞ Language/Cultural Origin: **Hebrew**
Inherent Meaning: **Kindness**
Spiritual Connotation: **Gentle**
Scripture: **Proverbs 3:3** NASB
Do not let kindness and truth leave you.

HESTER, Hestar (see also Esther)

Language/Cultural Origin: **English**
Inherent Meaning: **Star**
Spiritual Connotation: **Gift of God**
Scripture: **Psalm 139:9-10** NKJV
If I take the wings of the morning, and dwell in the uttermost parts of the sea, even there Your hand shall lead me, and Your right hand shall hold me.

HEZEKIAH

☞ Language/Cultural Origin: **Hebrew**
Inherent Meaning: **God Has Strengthened**
Spiritual Connotation: **Hopeful**
Scripture: **2 Thessalonians 3:3** NRSV
But the Lord is faithful; he will strengthen you and guard you from the evil one.

HEZRAI, Hezrael

☞ Language/Cultural Origin: **Hebrew**
Inherent Meaning: **Beautiful**
Spiritual Connotation: **Testimony**
Scripture: **Romans 10:15** RSV
How beautiful are the feet of those who preach good news!

HILDA, Hilde

Language/Cultural Origin: **Old German**
Inherent Meaning: **Battle Maid**
Spiritual Connotation: **Courageous**
Scripture: **Psalm 73:26** NKJV
My flesh and my heart fail; but God is the strength of my heart and my portion forever.

HILLARY, Hilaree, Hilari, Hilary, Hillaree, Hillarie, Hilleree, Hillory

Language/Cultural Origin: **English**
Inherent Meaning: **Cheerful**
Spiritual Connotation: **Blessed**
Scripture: **James 1:17** NKJV
Every good gift and every perfect gift is from above, and comes down from the Father of lights, with whom there is no variation or shadow of turning.

HILLEL, Hillal
Language/Cultural Origin: **Hebrew**
Inherent Meaning: **Greatly Praised**
Spiritual Connotation: **Humble**
Scripture: **Psalm 109:30** NKJV
I will greatly praise the LORD with my mouth; yes, I will praise Him among the multitude.

HILTON, Hillton
Language/Cultural Origin: **English**
Inherent Meaning: **From the Hill Town**
Spiritual Connotation: **Obedient**
Scripture: **Revelation 22:7** NASB
And behold, I am coming quickly. Blessed is he who heeds the words of the prophecy of this book.

HIRAH, Hierah
Language/Cultural Origin: **Hebrew**
Inherent Meaning: **Noble**
Spiritual Connotation: **Holy**
Scripture: **Romans 6:18** NLT
Now you are free from sin, your old master, and you have become slaves to your new master, righteousness.

HIRAM, Hi, Hirom
Language/Cultural Origin: **Hebrew**
Inherent Meaning: **Most Noble**
Spiritual Connotation: **Righteous**
Scripture: **Psalm 84:11** NKJV
For the LORD God is a sun and shield; the LORD will give grace and glory; no good thing will He withhold from those who walk uprightly.

HIROKO, Hirokoh
Language/Cultural Origin: **Japanese**
Inherent Meaning: **Self-Sacrificing**
Spiritual Connotation: **Glorified**
Scripture: **Hebrews 9:26** NASB
Otherwise, He would have needed to suffer often since the foundation of the world; but now once at the consummation of the ages He has been manifested to put away sin by the sacrifice of Himself.

HIROSHI, Hirashi
Language/Cultural Origin: **Japanese**
Inherent Meaning: **Generous**
Spiritual Connotation: **Cheerful**
Scripture: **2 Corinthians 9:7** NCV
Each one should give as you have decided in your heart to give. You should not be sad when you give, and you should not give because you feel forced to give.

HISA, Hisae, Hisayo
Language/Cultural Origin: **Japanese**
Inherent Meaning: **Long-Lasting**
Spiritual Connotation: **Wise**
Scripture: **John 6:27** NKJV
Do not labor for the food which perishes, but for the food which endures to everlasting life.

HODIAH, Hodiyah
Language/Cultural Origin: **Hebrew**
Inherent Meaning: **Splendor of God**
Spiritual Connotation: **Majestic**
Scripture: **Psalm 29:2** NRSV
Ascribe to the LORD the glory of his name; worship the LORD in holy splendor.

HOGAN, Hogen
Language/Cultural Origin: **Gaelic**
Inherent Meaning: **Youthful**
Spiritual Connotation: **Generous Soul**
Scripture: **2 Corinthians 9:12** NCV
This service you do not only helps the needs of God's people, it also brings many more thanks to God.

HOLBROOK, Holbrooke
Language/Cultural Origin: **Old English**
Inherent Meaning: **From the Brook**
Spiritual Connotation: **Peaceful**
Scripture: **Psalm 122:7** NKJV
Peace be within your walls, prosperity within your palaces.

HOLDEN, Holdin
Language/Cultural Origin: **English**
Inherent Meaning: **From the Valley Hollow**
Spiritual Connotation: **Fearless**
Scripture: **Joel 2:21** NKJV
Fear not, O land; be glad and rejoice, for the LORD has done marvelous things!

HOLLIS, Hollyss
Language/Cultural Origin: **Old English**
Inherent Meaning: **From the Holly Trees**
Spiritual Connotation: **Righteous**
Scripture: **Isaiah 58:8** NKJV
Then your light shall break forth like the

morning, your healing shall spring forth speedily, and your righteousness shall go before you.

HOLLY, Hollee, Holley, Holli, Hollie
Language/Cultural Origin: **Old English**
Inherent Meaning: **Holly Tree**
Spiritual Connotation: **Peaceful**
Scripture: **Philippians 4:7** NKJV
And the peace of God, which surpasses all understanding, will guard your hearts and minds through Christ Jesus.

HOLLYANN, Hollianna, Hollyanne
Language/Cultural Origin: **English**
Inherent Meaning: **Gracious**
Spiritual Connotation: **Kind**
Scripture: **Ephesians 4:32** NKJV
And be kind to one another, tender-hearted, forgiving one another, just as God in Christ forgave you.

HOMER
Language/Cultural Origin: **Greek**
Inherent Meaning: **Covenant**
Spiritual Connotation: **Doer of God's Word**
Scripture: **Jeremiah 32:40** NKJV
And I will make an everlasting covenant with them, that I will not turn away from doing them good.

HONORIA, Honor, Honora, Honoré
Language/Cultural Origin: **Latin**
Inherent Meaning: **Honorable Woman**
Spiritual Connotation: **Thankful**
Scripture: **Psalm 100:4** NKJV
Enter into His gates with thanksgiving, and into His courts with praise. Be thankful to Him, and bless His name.

HOPE, Hopie
Language/Cultural Origin: **Old English**
Inherent Meaning: **Trust in the Future**
Spiritual Connotation: **Understanding Heart**
Scripture: **Psalm 37:4** NKJV
Delight yourself also in the LORD, and He shall give you the desires of your heart.

HOPHNI, Hophnee, Hophney
☞ Language/Cultural Origin: **Hebrew**
Inherent Meaning: **Strong**
Spiritual Connotation: **Arm of God**
Scripture: **2 Corinthians 12:9** RSV

My grace is sufficient for you, for my power is made perfect in weakness.

HORACE, Horacio, Horatio, Horatius
Language/Cultural Origin: **Latin**
Inherent Meaning: **Keeper of Time**
Spiritual Connotation: **Efficient**
Scripture: **Ephesians 5:15-16** NKJV
See then that you walk circumspectly, not as fools but as wise, redeeming the time, because the days are evil.

HORTON, Horten
Language/Cultural Origin: **Old English**
Inherent Meaning: **From the Garden Estate**
Spiritual Connotation: **Faithful Steward**
Scripture: **1 Peter 4:10** NRSV
Like good stewards of the manifold grace of God, serve one another with whatever gift each of you has received.

HOSANNA, Hosana (see also ☞ Osanna)
Language/Cultural Origin: **Hebrew**
Inherent Meaning: **God Has Heard**
Spiritual Connotation: **Praise the Lord**
Scripture: **John 12:13** NRSV
Hosanna! Blessed is the one who comes in the name of the Lord—the King of Israel!

HOSEA, Hoshea
☞ Language/Cultural Origin: **Hebrew**
Inherent Meaning: **Deliverance**
Spiritual Connotation: **Strength**
Scripture: **2 Corinthians 12:9** NKJV
My grace is sufficient for you, for My strength is made perfect in weakness.

HOSHAMA, Hoshamma
☞ Language/Cultural Origin: **Hebrew**
Inherent Meaning: **God Has Heard**
Spiritual Connotation: **Godly**
Scripture: **1 John 5:14** NRSV
If we ask anything according to his will, he hears us.

HOWARD, Howie
Language/Cultural Origin: **English**
Inherent Meaning: **Chief Guardian**
Spiritual Connotation: **Discerning**
Scripture: **Psalm 37:23** NKJV

*The steps of a good man are ordered by
the LORD, and He delights in his way.*

HOWE, Howey
Language/Cultural Origin: **German**
Inherent Meaning: **Eminent**
Spiritual Connotation: **Protected**
Scripture: **Job 36:4** NKJV
*For truly my words are not false; One
who is perfect in knowledge is with you.*

HOWELL, Howel
Language/Cultural Origin: **Welsh**
Inherent Meaning: **Remarkable**
Spiritual Connotation: **Reconciled**
Scripture: **2 Corinthians 5:18** NKJV
*Now all things are of God, who has
reconciled us to Himself through Jesus
Christ, and has given us the ministry of
reconciliation.*

HOYT, Hoyte
Language/Cultural Origin: **Irish**
Inherent Meaning: **Spirited**
Spiritual Connotation: **Zealous**
Scripture: **Titus 2:14** NCV
*He gave himself for us so he might pay the
price to free us from all evil and to make
us pure people who belong only to him.*

HUBERT, Hubbard, Hubie
Language/Cultural Origin: **Old German**
Inherent Meaning: **Clear-Minded**
Spiritual Connotation: **Obedient**
Scripture: **Deuteronomy 6:5** NKJV
*You shall love the LORD your God with
all your heart, with all your soul, and
with all your strength.*

HUGH, Huey, Hughes, Hugo
Language/Cultural Origin: **Old German**
Inherent Meaning: **Thoughtful**
Spiritual Connotation: **Wise**
Scripture: **James 3:17** NKJV
*But the wisdom that is from above is first
pure, then peaceable, gentle, willing to
yield, full of mercy and good fruits, with-
out partiality and without hypocrisy.*

HUMPHREY, Humfrey
Language/Cultural Origin: **Old German**
Inherent Meaning: **Protector**

Spiritual Connotation: **Peaceful Strength**
Scripture: **Ecclesiastes 7:12** NKJV
*For wisdom is a defense as money is a
defense, but the excellence of knowledge is
that wisdom gives life to those who have it.*

HUNTER, Huntar
Language/Cultural Origin: **Old English**
Inherent Meaning: **Hunter**
Spiritual Connotation: **Pursuer of Truth**
Scripture: **Lamentations 4:19** NRSV
*Our pursuers were swifter than the eagles
in the heavens; they chased us on the
mountains, they lay in wait for us in the
wilderness.*

HUR, Hurr
Language/Cultural Origin: **Hebrew**
Inherent Meaning: **Noble**
Spiritual Connotation: **Purified**
Scripture: **Ephesians 4:24** NLT
*You must display a new nature because
you are a new person, created in God's
likeness—righteous, holy, and true.*

HURLEY, Hurlee, Hurleigh
Language/Cultural Origin: **Gaelic**
Inherent Meaning: **Lover of the Sea**
Spiritual Connotation: **Blessed**
Scripture: **James 1:17** NKJV
*Every good gift and every perfect gift is
from above, and comes down from the
Father of lights, with whom there is no
variation or shadow of turning.*

HUXLEY, Huxlee
Language/Cultural Origin: **Old English**
Inherent Meaning: **From the Wise Man's
Meadow**
Spiritual Connotation: **Tranquil Spirit**
Scripture: **Romans 8:14** NKJV
*For as many as are led by the Spirit of
God, these are sons of God.*

HYATT, Hyett
Language/Cultural Origin: **English**
Inherent Meaning: **From the High Gate**
Spiritual Connotation: **Righteous**
Scripture: **Psalm 55:22** NASB
*Cast your burden upon the LORD, and
He will sustain you; He will never allow
the righteous to be shaken.*

I

IAGO, Jago, Yago
Language/Cultural Origin: **Welsh**
Inherent Meaning: **Supplanter**
Spiritual Connotation: **Replacement**
Scripture: **Isaiah 9:10** NKJV
The bricks have fallen down, but we will rebuild with hewn stones; the sycamores are cut down, but we will replace them with cedars.

IAN, Ean, Iain
Language/Cultural Origin: **Scottish**
Inherent Meaning: **God Is Gracious**
Spiritual Connotation: **Discreet**
Scripture: **Matthew 6:6** NKJV
When you pray, go into your room, and . . . pray to your Father who is in the secret place; and your Father who sees in secret will reward you openly.

IANOS, Iano, Iános
Language/Cultural Origin: **Czech**
Inherent Meaning: **God Is Gracious**
Spiritual Connotation: **Divine Vision**
Scripture: **Acts 14:20** NLT
But as the believers stood around him, he got up and went back into the city. The next day he left with Barnabas for Derbe.

IANTHE, Iantha, Yantha
Language/Cultural Origin: **Greek**
Inherent Meaning: **Violet Flower**
Spiritual Connotation: **Restored**
Scripture: **Isaiah 35:2** TLB
Yes, there will be an abundance of flowers and singing and joy! The deserts will become as green as the Lebanon mountains.

IBRI, Ibree
Language/Cultural Origin: **Hebrew**
Inherent Meaning: **Passes Over**
Spiritual Connotation: **Symbol**
Scripture: **Exodus 12:13** NRSV
When I see the blood, I will pass over you, and no plague shall destroy you when I strike the land of Egypt.

ICHABOD
Language/Cultural Origin: **Hebrew**
Inherent Meaning: **The Glory Has Departed**
Spiritual Connotation: **Grief**
Scripture: **1 Samuel 4:22** RSV
The glory has departed from Israel, for the ark of God has been captured.

IDA, Idaleena, Idarina
Language/Cultural Origin: **German**
Inherent Meaning: **Youthful**
Spiritual Connotation: **Industrious**
Scripture: **Psalm 16:11** NKJV
You will show me the path of life; In Your presence is fullness of joy; at Your right hand are pleasures forevermore.

IDALIA, Idalis, Idalys
Language/Cultural Origin: **American**
Inherent Meaning: **Creative**
Spiritual Connotation: **Gifted**
Scripture: **Psalm 19:1** NCV
The heavens tell the glory of God, and the skies announce what his hands have made.

IESHA, Ieasha, Ieesha, Ieisha, Ieshia (see also Aiesha)
Language/Cultural Origin: **American**
Inherent Meaning: **Woman**
Spiritual Connotation: **Blessed**
Scripture: **Exodus 3:22** TLB
Every woman will ask for jewels, silver, gold, and the finest of clothes from her Egyptian master's wife and neighbors.

*You will clothe your sons and daughters
with the best of Egypt!*

IGNATIA, Ignacia, Ignashia
Language/Cultural Origin: **Latin**
Inherent Meaning: **Ardent**
Spiritual Connotation: **Full of Honor**
Scripture: **Psalm 51:10** KJV
*Create in me a clean heart, O God; and
renew a right spirit within me.*

IGNATIUS, Ignacius, Ignashus
Language/Cultural Origin: **Latin**
Inherent Meaning: **Ardent**
Spiritual Connotation: **Diligent**
Scripture: **Romans 12:11** NRSV
*Do not lag in zeal, be ardent in spirit,
serve the Lord.*

IGOR, Igorr
Language/Cultural Origin: **Russian**
Inherent Meaning: **Protected**
Spiritual Connotation: **Preserved**
Scripture: **Psalm 20:1** NKJV
*May the LORD answer you in the day
of trouble; may the name of the God of
Jacob defend you.*

IHSAN, Ihsaan, Ihsán (see also Ahsan, Hasani)
Language/Cultural Origin: **Turkish**
Inherent Meaning: **Compassionate**
Spiritual Connotation: **Loving**
Scripture: **Psalm 63:3** RSV
*Because thy steadfast love is better than
life, my lips will praise thee.*

ILAN, Illan
Language/Cultural Origin: **Hebrew**
Inherent Meaning: **Youth**
Spiritual Connotation: **Pride of the Father**
Scripture: **Psalm 127:4** NCV
*Children who are born to a young man
are like arrows in the hand of a warrior.*

ILANA, Ilani, Illana, Illanda, Illani
Language/Cultural Origin: **Hebrew**
Inherent Meaning: **Tree**
Spiritual Connotation: **Firmly Rooted**
Scripture: **Psalm 1:3** NLT
*They are like trees planted along the river-
bank . . . and in all they do, they prosper.*

ILIANA, Ileana, Illiana (see also Eliana, Liana)
Language/Cultural Origin: **Greek**
Inherent Meaning: **From Troy**
Spiritual Connotation: **Believer**
Scripture: **Romans 1:16** NKJV
*For I am not ashamed of the gospel of
Christ, for it is the power of God to sal-
vation for everyone who believes, for the
Jew first and also for the Greek.*

ILONA, Ileena, Ilina
Language/Cultural Origin: **Hungarian**
Inherent Meaning: **Light**
Spiritual Connotation: **Disciple of Christ**
Scripture: **John 15:8** NRSV
*My Father is glorified by this, that you
bear much fruit and become my disciples.*

ILYA, Ilias, Iljah (see also Elya)
Language/Cultural Origin: **Russian**
Inherent Meaning: **The Lord Is My God**
Spiritual Connotation: **Confessor**
Scripture: **Matthew 27:54** NKJV
*So when the centurion . . . saw the
earthquake and the things that had hap-
pened, [he] feared greatly, saying, "Truly
this was the Son of God!"*

IMAN, Imani
Language/Cultural Origin: **Middle Eastern**
Inherent Meaning: **Believer**
Spiritual Connotation: **Illuminated**
Scripture: **John 12:46** NASB
*I have come as light into the world, that
everyone who believes in Me may not
remain in darkness.*

IMELDA, Imalda
Language/Cultural Origin: **Swiss**
Inherent Meaning: **All-Encompassing Battle**
Spiritual Connotation: **Victorious**
Scripture: **Nehemiah 1:10** NASB
*They are Your servants and Your people
whom You redeemed by Your great power
and by Your strong hand.*

IMLA, Imlah
Language/Cultural Origin: **Hebrew**
Inherent Meaning: **Fulfilling**
Spiritual Connotation: **Prosperous**
Scripture: **John 10:10** NKJV

I have come that they may have life, and that they may have it more abundantly.

IMMANUEL, IMMANUELA, see Emanuel, Emanuela

IMOGENE, Imogenia
Language/Cultural Origin: **Latin**
Inherent Meaning: **Image**
Spiritual Connotation: **Likeness of God**
Scripture: **Hebrews 8:10** NKJV
I will put My laws in their mind and write them on their hearts; and I will be their God, and they shall be My people.

IMRA, Imrah
☞ Language/Cultural Origin: **Hebrew**
Inherent Meaning: **Stubborn**
Spiritual Connotation: **Learner of Obedience**
Scripture: **Hosea 4:16** TLB
Don't be like Israel, stubborn as a heifer, resisting the Lord's attempts to lead her in green pastures.

IMRAN, Imrand
Language/Cultural Origin: **Hebrew**
Inherent Meaning: **Host**
Spiritual Connotation: **Gracious**
Scripture: **Romans 16:23** NCV
Gaius is letting me and the whole church here use his home. He also sends greetings to you.

IMRI, Imree, Imrée
☞ Language/Cultural Origin: **Hebrew**
Inherent Meaning: **Speech**
Spiritual Connotation: **Empowered**
Scripture: **Acts 11:15** RSV
As I began to speak, the Holy Spirit fell on them just as on us at the beginning.

INA, Inah
Language/Cultural Origin: **Irish**
Inherent Meaning: **Pure**
Spiritual Connotation: **Divine Inspiration**
Scripture: **Job 22:28** NKJV
You will also declare a thing, and it will be established for you; so light will shine on your ways.

INDIA, Indya
Language/Cultural Origin: **English**
Inherent Meaning: **From India**

Spiritual Connotation: **Gift of Faith**
Scripture: **Job 19:25** NRSV
For I know that my Redeemer lives, and that at the last he will stand upon the earth.

INDIGO
Language/Cultural Origin: **Latin**
Inherent Meaning: **Dark Blue**
Spiritual Connotation: **Strengthened**
Scripture: **Psalm 42:5** RSV
Why are you cast down, O my soul, and why are you disquieted within me? Hope in God.

INDIRA, Indra
Language/Cultural Origin: **Indo-Pakistani**
Inherent Meaning: **Splendid**
Spiritual Connotation: **Miraculous**
Scripture: **1 Chronicles 16:24** NKJV
Declare His glory among the nations, His wonders among all peoples.

INESSA, Innessa
Language/Cultural Origin: **Russian**
Inherent Meaning: **Innocent**
Spiritual Connotation: **Cleansed**
Scripture: **Psalm 36:6** NKJV
Your righteousness is like the great mountains; Your judgments are a great deep; O LORD.

INGEMAR, Ingeborg
Language/Cultural Origin: **Old Norse**
Inherent Meaning: **Famous Son**
Spiritual Connotation: **Adventurous**
Scripture: **Job 23:14** NKJV
For He performs what is appointed for me, And many such things are with Him.

INGER, Ing, Inga, Inge
Language/Cultural Origin: **Old Norse**
Inherent Meaning: **Army of the Son**
Spiritual Connotation: **Kind**
Scripture: **Matthew 25:40** NKJV
Assuredly, I say to you, inasmuch as you did it to one of the least of these My brethren, you did it to Me.

INGERLISA, Ingerlise
Language/Cultural Origin: **Norwegian**
Inherent Meaning: **Praised Daughter**
Spiritual Connotation: **Consecrated to God**
Scripture: **Romans 12:1** NCV

*So brothers and sisters, since God has
shown us great mercy, I beg you to offer
your lives as a living sacrifice to Him.*

INGRAM, Ingraham, Ingrim
Language/Cultural Origin: **Old Norse**
Inherent Meaning: **King's Raven**
Spiritual Connotation: **Wise**
Scripture: **Psalm 121:1** NKJV
*I will lift up my eyes to the hills; from
whence comes my help?*

INGRID, Ingela
Language/Cultural Origin: **Old Norse**
Inherent Meaning: **Hero's Daughter**
Spiritual Connotation: **Cherished**
Scripture: **1 Corinthians 2:9** NKJV
*Eye has not seen, nor ear heard, nor
have entered into the heart of man the
things which God has prepared for those
who love Him.*

INIKO, Ineeko
Language/Cultural Origin: **Ibo**
Inherent Meaning: **Born During Hard
Times**
Spiritual Connotation: **Forever Preserved**
Scripture: **Psalm 27:5** NRSV
*For he will hide me in his shelter in the
day of trouble; he will conceal me under
the cover of his tent; he will set me high
on a rock.*

INKA, Inkah
Language/Cultural Origin: **Russian**
Inherent Meaning: **Heavenly**
Spiritual Connotation: **Image of God**
Scripture: **Matthew 5:48** NKJV
*Therefore you shall be perfect, just as
your Father in heaven is perfect.*

INNIS, Innes, Inness (see also Ennis)
Language/Cultural Origin: **Gaelic**
Inherent Meaning: **From the Island**
Spiritual Connotation: **Obedient**
Scripture: **Psalm 119:30** NKJV
*I have chosen the way of truth; Your
judgments I have laid before me.*

IOAN, Ioann
Language/Cultural Origin: **Romanian**
Inherent Meaning: **God Is Gracious**
Spiritual Connotation: **Cherished**

Scripture: **Titus 2:11** NRSV
*For the grace of God has appeared,
bringing salvation to all.*

IOANNA, Ioana
Language/Cultural Origin: **Russian**
Inherent Meaning: **God Is Gracious**
Spiritual Connotation: **Set Apart**
Scripture: **Ephesians 3:2** NCV
*Surely you have heard that God gave me
this work through his grace to help you.*

IOLA, Iolia
Language/Cultural Origin: **Greek**
Inherent Meaning: **Dawn of Day**
Spiritual Connotation: **One Made Worthy**
Scripture: **Revelation 2:7** NKJV
*To him who overcomes I will give to eat
from the tree of life, which is in the midst
of the Paradise of God.*

IOLANA, Iolanna
Language/Cultural Origin: **Hawaiian**
Inherent Meaning: **Soaring Like a Hawk**
Spiritual Connotation: **Steadfast**
Scripture: **Isaiah 40:31** RSV
*But they who wait for the LORD shall
renew their strength, they shall mount
up with wings like eagles, they shall run
and not be weary, they shall walk and
not faint.*

IONA, Ione, Ionia
Language/Cultural Origin: **Greek**
Inherent Meaning: **Violet Flower**
Spiritual Connotation: **Inner Beauty**
Scripture: **Psalm 119:34** NKJV
*Give me understanding, and I shall keep
Your law; indeed, I shall observe it with
my whole heart.*

IRA, Irah
Language/Cultural Origin: **Hebrew**
Inherent Meaning: **Watchful**
Spiritual Connotation: **Led by the Spirit**
Scripture: **Galatians 5:22-23** NKJV
*But the fruit of the Spirit is love, joy,
peace, longsuffering, kindness, goodness,
faithfulness, gentleness, self-control.*

IRAM, Irram
Language/Cultural Origin: **Hebrew**
Inherent Meaning: **Brightness**

Spiritual Connotation: **Profound**
Scripture: **Psalm 18:12** NLT
*The brilliance of his presence broke
through the clouds, raining down hail and
burning coals.*

IRENE, Irena, Iryna
Language/Cultural Origin: **Greek**
Inherent Meaning: **Messenger of Peace**
Spiritual Connotation: **Victorious Spirit**
Scripture: **Job 22:28** NIV
*What you decide on will be done, and
light will shine on your ways.*

IRI, Iree, Ireigh
☞ Language/Cultural Origin: **Hebrew**
Inherent Meaning: **God Watches**
Spiritual Connotation: **In the Light**
Scripture: **John 2:25** NIV
*He did not need man's testimony about
man, for he knew what was in a man.*

IRIJAH, Irija, Iriya, Iriyah
☞ Language/Cultural Origin: **Hebrew**
Inherent Meaning: **God Sees**
Spiritual Connotation: **One of Integrity**
Scripture: **Job 31:4** NASB
*Does He not see my ways, and number
all my steps?*

IRINA, Irana, Iriana, Irianna (see also Ariana)
Language/Cultural Origin: **Russian**
Inherent Meaning: **Serenity**
Spiritual Connotation: **Absolute Peace**
Scripture: **Exodus 11:7** NASB
*But against any of the sons of Israel a
dog shall not even bark . . . that you may
understand how the LORD makes a dis-
tinction between Egypt and Israel.*

IRIS, Irisa, Irisha, Irissa, Irusya
Language/Cultural Origin: **Greek**
Inherent Meaning: **Rainbow**
Spiritual Connotation: **God's Promise**
Scripture: **Psalm 104:24** NKJV
*O LORD, how manifold are Your works!
In wisdom You have made them all. The
earth is full of Your possessions.*

IRMA, Erma, Irmina
Language/Cultural Origin: **Latin**
Inherent Meaning: **Exalted**

Spiritual Connotation: **Excellent Virtue**
Scripture: **Acts 2:28** NKJV
*You have made known to me the ways of
life; You will make me full of joy in Your
presence.*

IRVING, Earvin, Erv, Ervin, Ervine, Erving, Irv, Irvin, Irvine
Language/Cultural Origin: **Irish**
Inherent Meaning: **Handsome**
Spiritual Connotation: **Trusting Spirit**
Scripture: **Isaiah 26:3** NKJV
*You will keep him in perfect peace,
Whose mind is stayed on You, Because
he trusts in You.*

IRWIN, Erwin, Erwyn, Irwyn
Language/Cultural Origin: **Old English**
Inherent Meaning: **Friend**
Spiritual Connotation: **Triumphant Spirit**
Scripture: **Zechariah 4:6** NKJV
*This is the word of the LORD to Zerubba-
bel: "Not by might nor by power, but by
My Spirit," says the LORD of hosts.*

ISAAC, Ike, Isaak, Isac, Isak, Ishaq, Itzak, Izaac, Izaak, Izac, Izak, Izák, Izakk, Izzy, Yitzak, Yitzhak
☞ Language/Cultural Origin: **Hebrew**
Inherent Meaning: **Laughter**
Spiritual Connotation: **Child of Promise**
Scripture: **Genesis 21:6** NASB
*God has made laughter for me; everyone
who hears will laugh with me.*

ISABEL, Isabela, Isabella, Isabelle, Izabel, Izabele, Izabella
Language/Cultural Origin: **Spanish**
Inherent Meaning: **Consecrated to God**
Spiritual Connotation: **Discerning Spirit**
Scripture: **Isaiah 60:1** NKJV
*Arise, shine; for your light has come! And
the glory of the LORD is risen upon you.*

ISADORA, Isidora
Language/Cultural Origin: **Greek**
Inherent Meaning: **Gift of the Goddess**
Spiritual Connotation: **Inspired**
Scripture: **John 5:30** NKJV
*I can of Myself do nothing. . . . I do
not seek My own will but the will of the
Father who sent Me.*

ISAIAH, Isaia, Isiah, Izaiah
Language/Cultural Origin: **Hebrew**
Inherent Meaning: **God Is My Salvation**
Spiritual Connotation: **Steadfast**
Scripture: **Matthew 17:20** NKJV
If you have faith as a mustard seed, you will say to this mountain, Move from here to there, and it will move; and nothing will be impossible for you.

ISHMAEL, Ishmeil, Ishmaiah, Ismael, Ismail
Language/Cultural Origin: **Hebrew**
Inherent Meaning: **God Will Hear**
Spiritual Connotation: **Blessed**
Scripture: **Genesis 17:20** NCV
As for Ishmael, I have heard you. I will bless him and give him many descendants. . . . I will make him into a great nation.

ISHMAELA, Ismaela
Language/Cultural Origin: **Hebrew**
Inherent Meaning: **God Will Hear**
Spiritual Connotation: **Trusting**
Scripture: **Philemon 1:22** NCV
One more thing—prepare a room for me in which to stay, because I hope God will answer your prayers and I will be able to come to you.

ISRAEL, Izrael, Yisrael
Language/Cultural Origin: **Hebrew**
Inherent Meaning: **Wrestled With God**
Spiritual Connotation: **Reminder**
Scripture: **Genesis 32:25** NKJV
Now when He saw that He did not prevail against him, He touched the socket of his hip; and the socket of Jacob's hip was out of joint as He wrestled with him.

ISSACHAR
Language/Cultural Origin: **Hebrew**
Inherent Meaning: **Reward**
Spiritual Connotation: **Righteous**
Scripture: **1 Samuel 24:19** NKJV
Therefore may the LORD reward you with good for what you have done to me this day.

ITALIA, Italie, Italya
Language/Cultural Origin: **Italian**

Inherent Meaning: **From Italy**
Spiritual Connotation: **Flexible**
Scripture: **Isaiah 64:8** NKJV
But now, O LORD, You are our Father; we are the clay, and You our potter; and all we are the work of Your hand.

IVAN, Iven
Language/Cultural Origin: **Russian**
Inherent Meaning: **God Is Gracious**
Spiritual Connotation: **Triumphant**
Scripture: **Luke 6:38** NKJV
Give, and it will be given to you. . . . For with the same measure that you use, it will be measured back to you.

IVANA, Ivania, Ivanna
Language/Cultural Origin: **Slavic**
Inherent Meaning: **God Is Gracious**
Spiritual Connotation: **Thankful**
Scripture: **Galatians 2:21** NKJV
I do not set aside the grace of God; for if righteousness comes through the law, then Christ died in vain.

IVAR, Iver, Ivor
Language/Cultural Origin: **Old Norse**
Inherent Meaning: **Noble**
Spiritual Connotation: **Peaceful**
Scripture: **John 14:27** NKJV
Peace I leave with you, My peace I give to you; not as the world gives do I give to you. Let not your heart be troubled, neither let it be afraid.

IVES, see Yves

IVONNE, Ivete, Ivette, Ivonn (see also Yvonne)
Language/Cultural Origin: **Scandinavian**
Inherent Meaning: **Yew Wood**
Spiritual Connotation: **Devout**
Scripture: **Luke 7:50** TLB
Your faith has saved you; go in peace.

IVORY, Ivori
Language/Cultural Origin: **American**
Inherent Meaning: **Made of Ivory**
Spiritual Connotation: **Fearless**
Scripture: **Matthew 14:27** NASB
Take courage, it is I; do not be afraid.

IVRIA, Ivriah
Language/Cultural Origin: **Hebrew**
Inherent Meaning: **From the Far Side of the Euphrates River**
Spiritual Connotation: **Fruitful**
Scripture: **John 7:38** NRSV
Out of the believer's heart shall flow rivers of living water.

IVY, Ivey, Ivie
Language/Cultural Origin: **English**
Inherent Meaning: **Ivy Plant**
Spiritual Connotation: **Trusting**
Scripture: **Isaiah 26:3** NKJV
You will keep him in perfect peace, whose mind is stayed on You, because he trusts in You.

IWAN, Iwann
Language/Cultural Origin: **Polish**
Inherent Meaning: **God Is Gracious**
Spiritual Connotation: **Grateful**
Scripture: **1 Corinthians 15:10** NCV
But God's grace has made me what I am, and his grace to me was not wasted.

IZRI, Izree (see also Ezra)
Language/Cultural Origin: **Hebrew**
Inherent Meaning: **Creative**
Spiritual Connotation: **Skilled**
Scripture: **Exodus 31:3** NKJV
And I have filled him with the Spirit of God . . . in all manner of workmanship.

IZUSA, Izussa
Language/Cultural Origin: **Native American**
Inherent Meaning: **White Stone**
Spiritual Connotation: **Overcomer**
Scripture: **Revelation 2:17** NRSV
To everyone who conquers I will give . . . a white stone, and on the white stone is written a new name that no one knows except the one who receives it.

J

JAAKAN, Jaekan, Jakan, Jaikan (see also Jachan)
Language/Cultural Origin: **Hebrew**
Inherent Meaning: **Intelligent**
Spiritual Connotation: **Discerning**
Scripture: **Proverbs 4:5** NASB
Acquire wisdom! Acquire understanding! Do not forget, nor turn away from the words of my mouth.

JAALA, Jala
Language/Cultural Origin: **Hebrew**
Inherent Meaning: **Doe**
Spiritual Connotation: **Loving**
Scripture: **Psalm 42:1** NRSV
As a deer longs for flowing streams, so my soul longs for you, O God.

JAALAM, Jalam
Language/Cultural Origin: **Hebrew**
Inherent Meaning: **Hidden**
Spiritual Connotation: **Guardian of Wisdom**
Scripture: **1 Corinthians 1:27** NKJV
But God has chosen the foolish things of the world to put to shame the wise.

JAAN, Jaann, Jaano, JayAnn, Yaan
Language/Cultural Origin: **Estonian**
Inherent Meaning: **Disciple of Christ**
Spiritual Connotation: **Anointed**
Scripture: **John 8:31** NRSV
If you continue in my word, you are truly my disciples.

JAASIEL, Jasiel
Language/Cultural Origin: **Hebrew**
Inherent Meaning: **God Is My Maker**
Spiritual Connotation: **Thankful**
Scripture: **Psalm 139:14** NASB
I will give thanks to Thee, for I am fearfully and wonderfully made.

JAAZIEL, Jaziel
Language/Cultural Origin: **Hebrew**
Inherent Meaning: **God Is My Comfort**
Spiritual Connotation: **Nurtured**
Scripture: **Isaiah 66:13** NRSV
As a mother comforts her child, so I will comfort you; you shall be comforted in Jerusalem.

JABARI, Jabaar, Jabar, Jabbar, Jabier
Language/Cultural Origin: **Swahili**
Inherent Meaning: **Fearless**
Spiritual Connotation: **Leader**
Scripture: **Matthew 28:5-6** NKJV
Do not be afraid, for I know that you seek Jesus who was crucified. He is not here; for He is risen, as He said.

JABEZ, Jabe, Jabesh
Language/Cultural Origin: **Hebrew**
Inherent Meaning: **Born in Pain**
Spiritual Connotation: **Blessed**
Scripture: **Joel 2:25** NKJV
So I will restore to you the years that the swarming locust has eaten.

JABIN, Jaban
Language/Cultural Origin: **Hebrew**
Inherent Meaning: **God Has Formed**
Spiritual Connotation: **Chosen**
Scripture: **Psalm 139:13** NCV
You made my whole being; you formed me in my mother's body.

JACHAN, Jacan, Jachon, Jacon (see also Jaakan)
Language/Cultural Origin: **Hebrew**
Inherent Meaning: **Trouble**
Spiritual Connotation: **Victorious**
Scripture: **John 16:33** NASB
These things I have spoken to you, that in Me you may have peace. In the world

you have tribulation, but take courage;
I have overcome the world.

JACEY, J.C., Jace, Jacee, Jacie, Jaciel, Jayce, Jaycee, Jaycey, Jaycie (see also Jacy)
Language/Cultural Origin: **American**
Inherent Meaning: **Prestigous**
Spiritual Connotation: **Blessed**
Scripture: **Ezekiel 34:29** RSV
And I will provide for them prosperous plantations so that they shall no more be consumed with hunger in the land.

JACINDA, Jacenda, Jacinta
Language/Cultural Origin: **Hispanic**
Inherent Meaning: **Beautiful**
Spiritual Connotation: **Cherished**
Scripture: **Song of Songs 1:15** NASB
How beautiful you are, my darling, How beautiful you are! Your eyes are like doves.

JACK, Jackie, Jacky, Jax
Language/Cultural Origin: **English**
Inherent Meaning: **God Is Gracious**
Spiritual Connotation: **Redeemed**
Scripture: **Colossians 1:6** TLB
The same Good News that came to you is going out all over the world and changing lives everywhere.

JACKSON, Jakson, Jaxon
Language/Cultural Origin: **English**
Inherent Meaning: **Son of Jack**
Spiritual Connotation: **Gracious**
Scripture: **Psalm 111:4** NKJV
He has made His wonderful works to be remembered; the LORD is gracious and full of compassion.

JACOB, Jacobb, Jacobs, Jakab, Jakiv, Jakov, Jakub (see also Yakov)
Language/Cultural Origin: **Hebrew**
Inherent Meaning: **Supplanter**
Spiritual Connotation: **Benevolent**
Scripture: **1 John 2:17** NKJV
And the world is passing away, and the lust of it; but he who does the will of God abides forever.

JACOBI, Jackobi
Language/Cultural Origin: **Scottish**
Inherent Meaning: **Replacement**

Spiritual Connotation: **Joyous**
Scripture: **Isaiah 9:10** NASB
The bricks have fallen down, but we will rebuild with smooth stones; the sycamores have been cut down, but we will replace them with cedars.

JACQUELINE, Jacalyn, Jackalyn, Jackee, Jacki, Jackie, Jacklyn, Jacqué, Jacquelyn, Jacquelynn, Jacqui, Jakki, Jaquelynn, Jaqui
Language/Cultural Origin: **French**
Inherent Meaning: **Substitute**
Spiritual Connotation: **Renewal**
Scripture: **Job 33:4** NKJV
The Spirit of God has made me, and the breath of the Almighty gives me life.

JACQUES, Jacquan, Jacque, Jacquees, Jacquez, Jaques
Language/Cultural Origin: **French**
Inherent Meaning: **Supplanter**
Spiritual Connotation: **Redeemed**
Scripture: **Titus 3:5** NASB
He saved us . . . according to His mercy, by the washing of regeneration and renewing by the Holy Spirit.

JACY, Jaicy (see also Jacey)
Language/Cultural Origin: **Guarani**
Inherent Meaning: **Moon**
Spiritual Connotation: **Reverent**
Scripture: **Psalm 72:5** NIV
He will endure as long as the sun, as long as the moon, through all generations.

JADA, Jaeda, Jaida, Jayda
Language/Cultural Origin: **Hebrew**
Inherent Meaning: **Wise**
Spiritual Connotation: **Blessed**
Scripture: **Proverbs 4:7** NIV
Wisdom is supreme; therefore get wisdom. Though it cost all you have, get understanding.

JADE, Jadah, Jadi, Jadie, Jady, Jaide, Jayde
Language/Cultural Origin: **Spanish**
Inherent Meaning: **Precious Gem**
Spiritual Connotation: **Priceless**
Scripture: **James 1:17** NKJV
Every good gift and every perfect gift is

from above, and comes down from the Father of lights, with whom there is no variation or shadow of turning.

JADON, Jaden, Jadin, Jaeden, Jaedon
Language/Cultural Origin: **Hebrew**
Inherent Meaning: **God Has Heard**
Spiritual Connotation: **Seeker of the Truth**
Scripture: **Psalm 5:3** NIV
In the morning, O LORD, you hear my voice; in the morning I lay my requests before you and wait in expectation.

JAE, see Jaye

JAEGAR, Jaager
Language/Cultural Origin: **German**
Inherent Meaning: **Hunter**
Spiritual Connotation: **Increase**
Scripture: **Genesis 1:22** NKJV
Be fruitful and multiply, and fill the waters in the seas, and let birds multiply on the earth.

JAE-HWA, Jaewah
Language/Cultural Origin: **Korean**
Inherent Meaning: **Prosperous**
Spiritual Connotation: **Blessed**
Scripture: **Jeremiah 29:11** NLT
For I know the plans I have for you, says the LORD. They are plans for good and not for disaster, to give you a future and a hope.

JAEL, Jaela, Jaelle (see also Yael)
Language/Cultural Origin: **Hebrew**
Inherent Meaning: **Mountain Climber**
Spiritual Connotation: **God's Servant**
Scripture: **Psalm 90:2** NRSV
Before the mountains were brought forth, or ever you had formed the earth and the world, from everlasting to everlasting you are God.

JA'FAR, Jafar, Jaffar
Language/Cultural Origin: **Sanskrit**
Inherent Meaning: **Little Stream**
Spiritual Connotation: **Refreshing**
Scripture: **Psalm 46:4** NASB
There is a river whose streams make glad the city of God, the holy dwelling places of the Most High.

JAFFA, see Yaffa

JAGA, Yaga
Language/Cultural Origin: **Polish**
Inherent Meaning: **Innocent**
Spiritual Connotation: **Cleansed**
Scripture: **2 Chronicles 29:18** RSV
We have cleansed all the house of the LORD.

JAGO, see Iago

JAHDIEL, Jadiel, Yadiel
Language/Cultural Origin: **Hebrew**
Inherent Meaning: **God Gladdens**
Spiritual Connotation: **Cheerful**
Scripture: **Nehemiah 8:10** NKJV
Do not sorrow, for the joy of the LORD is your strength.

JAHZEEL, Jahziel, Jazeel, Jaziel
Language/Cultural Origin: **Hebrew**
Inherent Meaning: **God Distributes**
Spiritual Connotation: **Righteousness of Christ**
Scripture: **Zechariah 3:4** NKJV
See, I have removed your iniquity from you, and I will clothe you with rich robes.

JAIME, Jaimey, Jaimee, Jaimmie, Jaimy, Jayme (see also Jamie)
Language/Cultural Origin: **French**
Inherent Meaning: **I Love**
Spiritual Connotation: **Devoted**
Scripture: **Psalm 18:1** NKJV
I will love You, O LORD, my strength.

JAIRUS, Jairo, Jarius
Language/Cultural Origin: **Hebrew**
Inherent Meaning: **God Enlightens**
Spiritual Connotation: **Wise**
Scripture: **Isaiah 5:16** NKJV
But the LORD of hosts shall be exalted in judgment, and God who is holy shall be hallowed in righteousness.

JAJUAN, Jauan, Jawaan, Jawan, Jawann, Jawaun, Jawon, Jawuan, Jujuan, Juwaan, Juwan, Juwann, Juwaun, Juwon, Juwuan
Language/Cultural Origin: **American**
Inherent Meaning: **God Is Gracious**
Spiritual Connotation: **Blessed**

Scripture: **Jonah 4:2** NKJV
For I know that You are a gracious and merciful God, slow to anger and abundant in lovingkindness, One who relents from doing harm.

JAKE, Jayke
Language/Cultural Origin: **English**
Inherent Meaning: **Substitute**
Spiritual Connotation: **New Covenant**
Scripture: **Colossians 3:11** TLB
In this new life one's nationality or race or education or social position is unimportant. . . . Whether a person has Christ is what matters.

JAKIM, Jakeem
Language/Cultural Origin: **Hebrew**
Inherent Meaning: **Uplifted**
Spiritual Connotation: **Chosen**
Scripture: **John 12:32** NRSV
And I, when I am lifted up from the earth, will draw all people to myself.

JALILA, Jalile
Language/Cultural Origin: **Middle Eastern**
Inherent Meaning: **Great**
Spiritual Connotation: **Humble**
Scripture: **Matthew 20:16** NKJV
So the last will be first, and the first last. For many are called, but few chosen.

JAMAAL, Jamar, see Jhamil

JAMARCUS, Jamarco, Jemarcus
Language/Cultural Origin: **American**
Inherent Meaning: **Aggressive**
Spiritual Connotation: **Zealous**
Scripture: **1 Corinthians 14:12** NKJV
Even so you, since you are zealous for spiritual gifts, let it be for the edification of the church that you seek to excel.

JAMARIO, Jamari, Jamariel, Jamarius, Jemarus
Language/Cultural Origin: **American**
Inherent Meaning: **Of the Sea**
Spiritual Connotation: **Filled With Praise**
Scripture: **Psalm 69:34** NKJV
Let heaven and earth praise Him, the seas and everything that moves in them.

JAMES, Jaimes, Jaymes, Jim, Jimi, ☞Jimmee, Jimmie, Jimmy, Jimy
Language/Cultural Origin: **Hebrew**
Inherent Meaning: **Supplanter**
Spiritual Connotation: **Nurtured**
Scripture: **Psalm 23:4** KJV
Yea, though I walk through the valley of the shadow of death, I will fear no evil: for thou art with me; thy rod and thy staff they comfort me.

JAMESON, Jamerson, Jamison, Jemisian
Language/Cultural Origin: **English**
Inherent Meaning: **Son of James**
Spiritual Connotation: **Persevering**
Scripture: **Jude 1:21** NKJV
Keep yourselves in the love of God, looking for the mercy of our Lord Jesus Christ unto eternal life.

JAMIE, Jama, Jamee, Jamey, Jami, Jamia, Jamian, Jamii, Jammie, Jamya, Jaymee, Jaymie (see also Jaime)
Language/Cultural Origin: **English**
Inherent Meaning: **Replacement**
Spiritual Connotation: **Wise**
Scripture: **Matthew 13:28-29** NASB
Do you want us, then, to go and gather them up? No, lest while you are gathering up the tares, you may root up the wheat with them.

JAMILA, Jahmela, Jahmelia, Jameela, Jamelia, Jamelle, Jamelya, Jamilia, Jamillia, Yamila, Yamilla
Language/Cultural Origin: **Middle Eastern**
Inherent Meaning: **Beautiful**
Spiritual Connotation: **Loving**
Scripture: **Philippians 4:8** NKJV
Finally, brethren, whatever things are true, . . . noble, . . . just, . . . pure, . . . lovely, . . . of good report, if there is any virtue and if there is anything praiseworthy; meditate on these things.

JAMIN, Jaman, Jamial, Jamian, Jamiel, Jamien, Jaymin
Language/Cultural Origin: **Hebrew**
Inherent Meaning: **Favored**
Spiritual Connotation: **Triumphant**

Scripture: **Psalm 44:3** NASB
*Their own arm did not save them, but
Your right hand and Your arm and the light
of Your presence, for You favored them.*

**JAMOND, Jamand, Jamon, Jamón
(see also Jemond)**
Language/Cultural Origin: **American**
Inherent Meaning: **Mighty Protector**
Spiritual Connotation: **Exalted**
Scripture: **Psalm 25:20** NRSV
*O guard my life, and deliver me; do not
let me be put to shame, for I take refuge
in you.*

JAN, Jani, Jania, Jann
Language/Cultural Origin: **German**
Inherent Meaning: **God's Gift**
Spiritual Connotation: **Cherished**
Scripture: **Psalm 70:4** NKJV
*Let all those who seek You rejoice and be
glad in You; and let those who love Your
salvation say continually, let God be
magnified!*

JANA, Janna (See also Yana)
Language/Cultural Origin: **Slavic**
Inherent Meaning: **Gift of God**
Spiritual Connotation: **Cherished**
Scripture: **Deuteronomy 6:11** NKJV
*Houses full of all good things, which you
did not fill, hewn-out wells which you did
not dig, vineyards and olive trees which
you did not plant.*

**JANAE, Janaé, Janay, Janaya, Janea,
Janée, Jannay, Jenay, Jenaya,
Jennae, Jennay, Jennaya**
Language/Cultural Origin: **American**
Inherent Meaning: **God Is Gracious**
Spiritual Connotation: **Treasured**
Scripture: **Numbers 6:24-25** NKJV
*The LORD bless you and keep you; the
LORD make His face shine upon you, and
be gracious to you.*

JANAN, Janani, Janann
Language/Cultural Origin: **Middle Eastern**
Inherent Meaning: **Tenderhearted**
Spiritual Connotation: **Gentle**
Scripture: **Ephesians 4:32** NASB
*And be kind to one another, tender-
hearted, forgiving each other, just as God
in Christ also has forgiven you.*

**JANE, Jaine, Janet, Janett, Janey,
Janie, Janice, Janis, Jannie, Jayna,
Jayne, Jaynee**
Language/Cultural Origin: **English**
Inherent Meaning: **God Is Gracious**
Spiritual Connotation: **Beloved**
Scripture: **Romans 12:2** NKJV
*And do not be conformed to this world,
but be transformed by the renewing of
your mind.*

**JANELLE, Janel, Janele, Janell,
Janella, Janiel, Janielle, Jannel,
Jannell, Jannelle, Jenell, Jenelle,
Jennell, Jennelle, Jonell, Jonelle**
Language/Cultural Origin: **English**
Inherent Meaning: **God Is Gracious**
Spiritual Connotation: **Blessed**
Scripture: **Psalm 138:8** NKJV
*The LORD will perfect that which con-
cerns me; your mercy, O LORD, endures
forever; do not forsake the works of
Your hands.*

**JANESSA, Janiesha, Janissa,
Jannisha, Jannissa, Jenisa, Jenisha,
Jenissa, Jennisha, Jennisse**
Language/Cultural Origin: **American**
Inherent Meaning: **God Is Gracious**
Spiritual Connotation: **Delivered**
Scripture: **Nehemiah 9:31** RSV
*Nevertheless in thy great mercies thou didst
not make an end of them or forsake them;
for thou art a gracious and merciful God.*

**JANSON, Jansen, Janssen, Jantzen,
Janzen, Jensen**
Language/Cultural Origin: **Scandinavian**
Inherent Meaning: **Son of Jan**
Spiritual Connotation: **Joyful**
Scripture: **1 Peter 1:8** NRSV
*Although you have not seen him, you
love him; and even though you do not see
him now, you believe in him and rejoice
with an indescribable and glorious joy.*

JAPHETH, Japeth, Yaphet, Yapheth
Language/Cultural Origin: **Hebrew**
Inherent Meaning: **May He Expand**

Spiritual Connotation: **Ancestor**
Scripture: **Genesis 9:27** NASB
*May God enlarge Japheth, and let
him dwell in the tents of Shem; and let
Canaan be his servant.*

JARAH, Jarrah (see also Jerah)
Language/Cultural Origin: **Hebrew**
Inherent Meaning: **Sweet as Honey**
Spiritual Connotation: **Discerner**
Scripture: **Revelation 10:10** NKJV
*Then I took the little book out of the
angel's hand and ate it, and it was as
sweet as honey in my mouth.*

JARDAN, Jarden, Jardena, Jardina (see also Jordan)
Language/Cultural Origin: **Hebrew**
Inherent Meaning: **Descender**
Spiritual Connotation: **Aide**
Scripture: **Psalm 10:14** NKJV
*The helpless commits himself to You;
You are the helper of the fatherless.*

JARED, Jarad, Ja'red, Jarod, Jarrad, Jarred, Jarrod, Jarryd, Jerad, Jerod, Jerrad, Jerrod, Jerryd, Yarod, Yarrod
Language/Cultural Origin: **Hebrew**
Inherent Meaning: **Descendent**
Spiritual Connotation: **Favored**
Scripture: **Matthew 21:22** NKJV
*And whatever things you ask in prayer,
believing, you will receive.*

JAREK, Jarrek
Language/Cultural Origin: **Slavic**
Inherent Meaning: **Born in January**
Spiritual Connotation: **Promised Assurance**
Scripture: **1 Timothy 1:14** NKJV
*And the grace of our Lord was exceed-
ingly abundant, with faith and love which
are in Christ Jesus.*

JARELL, Jarel, Jarelle, Jarrell, Jerall, Jerel, Jerral, Jerell, Jerrel, Jerrell
Language/Cultural Origin: **Scandinavian**
Inherent Meaning: **Mighty**
Spiritual Connotation: **Power of God**
Scripture: **Exodus 9:16** NKJV
*But indeed for this purpose I have raised
you up, that I may show My power in*

*you, and that My name may be declared
in all the earth.*

JAROAH, Jaroha, Jaroyah
Language/Cultural Origin: **Hebrew**
Inherent Meaning: **New Moon**
Spiritual Connotation: **Festive**
Scripture: **Psalm 81:3** RSV
*Blow the trumpet at the new moon, at
the full moon, on our feast day.*

JARON, Jaaron, Jairon, Jaren, Jarón, Jarone (see also Jeron, Yaron)
Language/Cultural Origin: **Hebrew**
Inherent Meaning: **He Will Sing; He Will Cry Out**
Spiritual Connotation: **Joyful**
Scripture: **Job 8:21** NKJV
*He will yet fill your mouth with laughing,
and your lips with rejoicing.*

JARRETT, Jaret, Jareth, Jarratt, Jarret, Jarrot, Jarrott, Jerrat, Jerrett, Jerott (see also Garrett)
Language/Cultural Origin: **English**
Inherent Meaning: **Warrior**
Spiritual Connotation: **Brave**
Scripture: **1 Corinthians 16:13** NRSV
*Keep alert, stand firm in your faith, be
courageous, be strong.*

JARVIS, Jarvas, Javares, Javaris, Javarius, Javaron, Javarus
Language/Cultural Origin: **German**
Inherent Meaning: **Skilled**
Spiritual Connotation: **Inspired**
Scripture: **2 Corinthians 6:2** NKJV
*And in the day of salvation I have helped
you. Behold, now is the accepted time;
behold, now is the day of salvation.*

JASIA, Jasha, Jasio, Jasya, Jazya
Language/Cultural Origin: **Polish**
Inherent Meaning: **God Is Gracious**
Spiritual Connotation: **Forgiven**
Scripture: **Joel 2:13** TLB
*Return to the Lord your God, for he is
gracious and merciful. He is not easily
angered; he is full of kindness and anx-
ious not to punish you.*

JASMINE, Jas, Jasmain, Jasmaine, Jasman, Jasmin, Jasmon, Jasmyn,

Jass, Jassmin, Jassmine, Jassmyn, Jaz, Jazmin, Jazmine, Jazminn, Jazmon, Jazmyne, Jazz, Jazze, Jazzman, Jazzmin, Jazzmon, Jazzmyn (see also Yasmine)
Language/Cultural Origin: **Persian**
Inherent Meaning: **Jasmine Flower**
Spiritual Connotation: **Messenger of Love**
Scripture: **Isaiah 55:11** NKJV
So shall My word be that goes forth from My mouth; it shall not return to Me void.

JASON, Jacen, Jaeson, Jaison, Jasan, ☞ Jasen, Jasun, Jaysen, Jayson
Language/Cultural Origin: **Greek**
Inherent Meaning: **Healer**
Spiritual Connotation: **Benevolent**
Scripture: **Luke 6:45** NKJV
A good man out of the good treasure of his heart brings forth good. . . . For out of the abundance of the heart his mouth speaks.

JASPER, Jaspar
Language/Cultural Origin: **English**
Inherent Meaning: **Treasure-Holder**
Spiritual Connotation: **Richly Blessed**
Scripture: **Matthew 25:29** NKJV
For to everyone who has, more will be given, and he will have abundance; but from him who does not have, even what he has will be taken away.

JAVAN, Jaavon, Jahvon, Javaughn, ☞ Javon, Javoni, Javonn (see also Jevan, Jovan)
Language/Cultural Origin: **Hebrew**
Inherent Meaning: **Clay**
Spiritual Connotation: **Example**
Scripture: **Deuteronomy 4:10** NASB
Assemble the people to Me, that I may let them hear My words so they . . .may teach their children.

JAVANA, Javanna, Javonna, Javonne, Javonya
Language/Cultural Origin: **Malayan**
Inherent Meaning: **From Java**
Spiritual Connotation: **Honest**
Scripture: **Joshua 24:14** NKJV
Now therefore, fear the LORD, serve Him in sincerity and in truth.

JAVIER, Javiare
Language/Cultural Origin: **Spanish**
Inherent Meaning: **Owner of a New House**
Spiritual Connotation: **Prosperous**
Scripture: **Zechariah 8:12** NLT
For I am planting seeds of peace and prosperity among you.

JAWAUN, see Jajuan

JAY, Jai, Jey
Language/Cultural Origin: **Old French**
Inherent Meaning: **Vivacious**
Spiritual Connotation: **Adventurous**
Scripture: **Psalm 139:3** NKJV
You comprehend my path and my lying down, and are acquainted with all my ways.

JAYA, Jaea, Jaia, Jayla, Jaylah
Language/Cultural Origin: **Indo-Pakistani**
Inherent Meaning: **Victory**
Spiritual Connotation: **Overcomer**
Scripture: **Romans 8:37** NRSV
No, in all these things we are more than conquerors through him who loved us.

JAYE, Jae, Jaela, Jaelin, Jaelynn, Jalen, Jalin, Jaylan, Jaylee, Jayleen, Jaylene, Jaylin, Jaylyn
Language/Cultural Origin: **Latin**
Inherent Meaning: **Jaybird**
Spiritual Connotation: **Source of Joy**
Scripture: **Acts 8:39** NCV
When they came up out of the water, the Spirit of the Lord took Philip away. . . . And the officer continued on his way home, full of joy.

JEAN, Jéan, Jeana, Jeane, Jeanee, Jeanie, Jeanna, Jeanne, Jene (see also Gina)
Language/Cultural Origin: **Scottish**
Inherent Meaning: **God Is Gracious**
Spiritual Connotation: **Gifted**
Scripture: **2 Chronicles 1:12** NKJV
Wisdom and knowledge are granted to you; and I will give you riches and wealth and honor.

JEANETTE, Janeen, Janette,

Jannine, Jeaneen, Jeanett, Jeanine, Jeannette, Jeannine, Jenine
Language/Cultural Origin: **French**
Inherent Meaning: **God Is Gracious**
Spiritual Connotation: **Preserved**
Scripture: **Isaiah 33:2** NRSV
O LORD, be gracious to us; we wait for you. Be our arm every morning, our salvation in the time of trouble.

JEDAIAH, Jedaia, Jediah
☞ Language/Cultural Origin: **Hebrew**
Inherent Meaning: **Hand of God**
Spiritual Connotation: **Guided**
Scripture: **2 Chronicles 30:12** NASB
The hand of God was also on Judah to give them one heart to do what the king and the princes commanded by the word of the LORD.

JEDIDIAH, Jeb, Jebadiah, Jebediah, ☞ Jed, Jedediah
Language/Cultural Origin: **Hebrew**
Inherent Meaning: **Beloved of God**
Spiritual Connotation: **Perceptive**
Scripture: **Psalm 145:10** NKJV
All Your works shall praise You, O LORD, and Your saints shall bless You.

JEFFERSON, Jeferson
Language/Cultural Origin: **English**
Inherent Meaning: **Son of the Peaceful Man**
Spiritual Connotation: **Contemplative**
Scripture: **Genesis 25:27** NKJV
So the boys grew. And Esau was a skillful hunter, a man of the field; but Jacob was a mild man, dwelling in tents.

JEFFREY, Jefery, Jeff, Jefferay, Jefferey, Jefferie, Jefferies, Jeffery, Jeffrie, Jeffries, Jeffry (see also Geoffrey)
Language/Cultural Origin: **English**
Inherent Meaning: **Divine Peace**
Spiritual Connotation: **Wise**
Scripture: **Proverbs 3:13** NKJV
Happy is the man who finds wisdom, and the man who gains understanding.

JEHAN, Jehahn, Jehann
Language/Cultural Origin: **French**
Inherent Meaning: **God Is Gracious**

Spiritual Connotation: **Godly Example**
Scripture: **Isaiah 30:18** NRSV
Therefore the LORD waits to be gracious to you; therefore he will rise up to show mercy to you.

JEHOHANAN
☞ Language/Cultural Origin: **Hebrew**
Inherent Meaning: **God Is Gracious**
Spiritual Connotation: **Contrite**
Scripture: **Joel 2:13** NASB
Now return to the LORD your God, for He is gracious and compassionate.

JEHONATHAN
☞ Language/Cultural Origin: **Hebrew**
Inherent Meaning: **God Has Given**
Spiritual Connotation: **Blessed**
Scripture: **2 Timothy 1:7** NCV
God did not give us a spirit that makes us afraid but a spirit of power and love and self-control.

JEHORAM
☞ Language/Cultural Origin: **Hebrew**
Inherent Meaning: **God Is Exalted**
Spiritual Connotation: **Majestic**
Scripture: **Psalm 118:16** NLT
The strong right arm of the LORD is raised in triumph.

JEHU, Jaehu, Jayhue, Yayhu, Yayhue
☞ Language/Cultural Origin: **Hebrew**
Inherent Meaning: **God Is**
Spiritual Connotation: **Divine Perspective**
Scripture: **Exodus 3:6** NKJV
I am the God of your father; the God of Abraham, the God of Isaac, and the God of Jacob.

JEKAMIAH, Jekamiyah
☞ Language/Cultural Origin: **Hebrew**
Inherent Meaning: **God Will Gather**
Spiritual Connotation: **Blessed Promise**
Scripture: **Nehemiah 1:9** NCV
I will gather your people from the far ends of the earth.

JELANI, Jelanee, Jeláni, Jelanni, Jellani
Language/Cultural Origin: **Swahili**
Inherent Meaning: **Mighty**
Spiritual Connotation: **Strength of God**

Scripture: **Psalm 21:13** NKJV
*Be exalted, O LORD, in Your own
strength! We will sing and praise Your
power.*

JELENA, Jelina (see also Yelina)
Language/Cultural Origin: **Russian**
Inherent Meaning: **Shining**
Spiritual Connotation: **Filled With Praise**
Scripture: **Psalm 148:3** RSV
*Praise him, sun and moon, praise him,
all you shining stars!*

JEMAL, see Jhamil

**JEMIMA, Jamima, Jemimah, Jemma,
☞ Jemmia, Jemmiah**
Language/Cultural Origin: **Hebrew**
Inherent Meaning: **Dove**
Spiritual Connotation: **Serene**
Scripture: **Isaiah 32:18** NASB
*Then my people will live in a peaceful
habitation, and in secure dwellings and in
undisturbed resting places.*

**JEMOND, Jemon, Jémond, Jemonde,
Jemone (see also Jamond)**
Language/Cultural Origin: **French**
Inherent Meaning: **Temporal**
Spiritual Connotation: **Mind of Christ**
Scripture: **Colossians 3:2** NRSV
*Set your minds on things that are above,
not on things that are on earth.*

JEMUEL, Jemuél
☞ Language/Cultural Origin: **Hebrew**
Inherent Meaning: **God Is Light**
Spiritual Connotation: **Set Apart**
Scripture: **John 8:12** NRSV
*I am the light of the world. Whoever
follows me will never walk in darkness.*

JENDAYA, Jenndaya
Language/Cultural Origin: **Shona**
Inherent Meaning: **Give Thanks**
Spiritual Connotation: **Adoration**
Scripture: **Revelation 7:12** NKJV
*Amen! Blessing and glory and wisdom,
thanksgiving and honor and power and
might, be to our God forever and ever.
Amen.*

JENEVIEVE, see Genevieve

JENKIN, Jenkins, Jenkyn, Jenkyns
Language/Cultural Origin: **Flemish**
Inherent Meaning: **Little John**
Spiritual Connotation: **Reverent**
Scripture: **Psalm 2:11** NKJV
*Serve the LORD with fear, and rejoice
with trembling.*

JENNA, Jena, Jenah, Jennah, Jennay
Language/Cultural Origin: **Middle Eastern**
Inherent Meaning: **Small Bird**
Spiritual Connotation: **Nurtured**
Scripture: **Matthew 10:29** RSV
*Are not two sparrows sold for a penny?
And not one of them will fall to the
ground without your Father's will.*

**JENNIFER, Jen, Jenefer, Jeni, Jenifer,
Jeniffer, Jenn, Jennafer, Jennee,
Jenney, Jennie, Jenniffer, Jenny**
Language/Cultural Origin: **Welsh**
Inherent Meaning: **Fair**
Spiritual Connotation: **Trusting**
Scripture: **Psalm 28:7** NKJV
*The LORD is my strength and my shield;
my heart trusted in Him, and I am
helped. . . . With my song I will praise
Him.*

JERAH, Jerrah (see also Jarah)
☞ Language/Cultural Origin: **Hebrew**
Inherent Meaning: **Moon**
Spiritual Connotation: **Glorious Hope**
Scripture: **Isaiah 30:26** NASB
*And the light of the moon will be as the
light of the sun.*

**JEREMIAH, Jaramiah, Jeramaya,
☞ Jeremai, Jeremia, Jeremias,
Yermiya, Yirmaya**
Language/Cultural Origin: **Hebrew**
Inherent Meaning: **God Is Exalted**
Spiritual Connotation: **Seeker of Truth**
Scripture: **Luke 12:31** NKJV
*But seek the kingdom of God, and all
these things shall be added to you.*

**JEREMY, Jeramee, Jerami, Jeramy,
☞ Jéréme, Jeremee, Jeremey, Jeremii**
Language/Cultural Origin: **English**
Inherent Meaning: **God Is Exalted**

Spiritual Connotation: **Humble**
Scripture: **James 4:10** NKJV
*Humble yourselves in the sight of the
Lord, and He will lift you up.*

JERENI, Jerani, Jeraney, Jerenee
Language/Cultural Origin: **Russian**
Inherent Meaning: **Peace**
Spiritual Connotation: **Filled With the Spirit**
Scripture: **Luke 1:79** NCV
*It will shine on those who live in dark-
ness, in the shadow of death. It will guide
us into the path of peace.*

JERIAH, Jariah, Jariya, Jeriya
Language/Cultural Origin: **Hebrew**
Inherent Meaning: **God Has Seen**
Spiritual Connotation: **Proven**
Scripture: **Psalm 33:14-15** NRSV
*From where he sits enthroned he watches
all the inhabitants of the earth—he who
fashions the hearts of them all, and
observes all their deeds.*

JERIEL, Jerriel (see also Yeriel)
Language/Cultural Origin: **Hebrew**
Inherent Meaning: **God's Foundation**
Spiritual Connotation: **Reflection of Christ**
Scripture: **Ephesians 2:20** NLT
*We are his house. . . . And the corner-
stone is Christ Jesus himself.*

JERMAINE, Jermain, Jermane, Jermayne, Jhirmaine (see also Germain)
Language/Cultural Origin: **English**
Inherent Meaning: **Sprout**
Spiritual Connotation: **Constant Growth**
Scripture: **Isaiah 45:8** NKJV
*Rain down, you heavens, from
above . . . let them bring forth salvation,
and let righteousness spring up together.
I, the LORD, have created it.*

JEROHAM, Jeroam
Language/Cultural Origin: **Hebrew**
Inherent Meaning: **Loved**
Spiritual Connotation: **Treasured**
Scripture: **1 John 4:7** NASB
*Beloved, let us love one another, for love
is from God.*

JEROME, Jérome, Jerôme, Jerrome
Language/Cultural Origin: **Latin**
Inherent Meaning: **Sacred**
Spiritual Connotation: **Holy**
Scripture: **Leviticus 11:45** NASB
*For I am the LORD, who brought you up
from the land of Egypt, to be your God;
thus you shall be holy for I am holy.*

JERON, Jéron, Jerone, Jerron (see also Jaron)
Language/Cultural Origin: **English**
Inherent Meaning: **Set Apart**
Spiritual Connotation: **Chosen**
Scripture: **Psalm 4:3** RSV
*But know that the LORD has set apart the
godly for himself; the LORD hears when I
call to him.*

JESAIAH, Jeshaiah
Language/Cultural Origin: **Hebrew**
Inherent Meaning: **God Is Wealthy**
Spiritual Connotation: **Eternal Perspective**
Scripture: **Luke 12:34** TLB
*Wherever your treasure is, there your
heart and thoughts will also be.*

JESSE, Jesee, Jess, Jessé, Jessee, Jessey, Jessie
Language/Cultural Origin: **Hebrew**
Inherent Meaning: **God Exists**
Spiritual Connotation: **Upright**
Scripture: **Job 19:25** NIV
*I know that my Redeemer lives, and that
in the end he will stand upon the earth.*

JESSENIA, Jeseenya
Language/Cultural Origin: **Middle Eastern**
Inherent Meaning: **Flower**
Spiritual Connotation: **Spiritual Maturity**
Scripture: **Mark 4:27** NCV
*Night and day, whether the person is
asleep or awake, the seed still grows, but
the person does not know how it grows.*

JESSICA, Jesi, Jesica, Jesika, Jess, Jessa, Jessaca, Jesseca, Jessi, Jessie, Jessika, Jessy, Jessyca, Yessica, Yessika
Language/Cultural Origin: **Hebrew**
Inherent Meaning: **Wealthy**
Spiritual Connotation: **Blessed**

Scripture: **1 Corinthians 13:13** NKJV
And now abide faith, hope, love, these three; but the greatest of these is love.

JETHRO, Jethroe
Language/Cultural Origin: **Hebrew**
Inherent Meaning: **Excellence**
Spiritual Connotation: **Abundant Praise**
Scripture: **Psalm 98:4** NKJV
Shout joyfully to the LORD, all the earth; break forth in song, rejoice, and sing praises.

JEVAN, Jevaughn, Jevaun, Jevohn, Jevon, Jevoni, Jevonn, Jevonne (see also Javan, Jovan)
Language/Cultural Origin: **English**
Inherent Meaning: **Abundance**
Spiritual Connotation: **Heir**
Scripture: **Psalm 37:11** NKJV
But the meek shall inherit the earth, and shall delight themselves in the abundance of peace.

JEWEL, Jewell, Jewelle
Language/Cultural Origin: **French**
Inherent Meaning: **Gem**
Spiritual Connotation: **Precious**
Scripture: **Psalm 16:11** NKJV
You will show me the path of life; in Your presence is fullness of joy; at Your right hand are pleasures forevermore.

JEZANIAH, Jezánia, Jezzania
Language/Cultural Origin: **Hebrew**
Inherent Meaning: **God Determines**
Spiritual Connotation: **In God's Hands**
Scripture: **Job 14:5** NLT
You have decided the length of our lives. You know how many months we will live, and we are not given a minute longer.

JEZIEL, Jezziel
Language/Cultural Origin: **Hebrew**
Inherent Meaning: **Assembly of God**
Spiritual Connotation: **Restored**
Scripture: **Ezra 5:15** NCV
Put them back in the Temple in Jerusalem and rebuild the Temple of God where it was.

JEZREEL, Jezriel
Language/Cultural Origin: **Hebrew**
Inherent Meaning: **God Sows**
Spiritual Connotation: **Proclaimer of the Word**
Scripture: **Matthew 13:3** NKJV
Behold, a sower went out to sow.

JHAMIL, Jahmal, Jahmel, Jamaal, Jamaar, Jamaari, Jamahl, Jamail, Jamal, Jamall, Jamar, Jamara, Jamarr, Jameel, Jamel, Jamell, Jamelle, Jamiel, Jamil, Jamill, Jamille, Jammal, Jammel, Jemaal, Jemal, Jemar, Jemel, Jhamaal, Jhamal, Jhamar, Jhameel, Jhamel, Jhamell, Jhamelle, Jhamiel, Jhamielle, Jimaal, Jimell, Jimelle
Language/Cultural Origin: **Hebrew**
Inherent Meaning: **Handsome**
Spiritual Connotation: **Image of Christ**
Scripture: **Titus 2:10** NCV
They . . . should show their masters they can be fully trusted so that in everything they do they will make the teaching of God our Savior attractive.

JIANNA, see Gianna

JILLIAN, Gillian, Jil, Jilaine, Jilayne, Jileesa, Jilian, Jiliana, Jiliann, Jilianna, Jill, Jillana, Jillene, Jilliana, Jillianne, Jillisa
Language/Cultural Origin: **Latin**
Inherent Meaning: **Youthful**
Spiritual Connotation: **Regenerated**
Scripture: **Psalm 103:5** TLB
He fills my life with good things! My youth is renewed like the eagle's!

JIN, Jinn
Language/Cultural Origin: **Chinese**
Inherent Meaning: **Gold**
Spiritual Connotation: **True Worth**
Scripture: **Proverbs 3:14** NLT
For the profit of wisdom is better than silver, and her wages are better than gold.

JINA, Jinna (see also Ginny)
Language/Cultural Origin: **Swahili**
Inherent Meaning: **Name**
Spiritual Connotation: **Destined**

Scripture: **Revelation 2:17** NRSV
To everyone who conquers I will . . .
give a white stone, and on the white stone
is written a new name that no one knows
except the one who receives it.

JINDRICH, Jindrick
Language/Cultural Origin: **Czech**
Inherent Meaning: **Head of the Household**
Spiritual Connotation: **Trusted**
Scripture: **Psalm 105:21** NKJV
He made him lord of his house, and ruler
of all his possessions.

JINNY, see Ginny

JIRI, Jirian
Language/Cultural Origin: **Czech**
Inherent Meaning: **Farmer**
Spiritual Connotation: **Skilled**
Scripture: **2 Samuel 9:10** NASB
And you and your sons and your ser-
vants shall cultivate the land for him. . . .

JIRINA, Jirana, Jiranna, Jireena
Language/Cultural Origin: **Czech**
Inherent Meaning: **Farmer**
Spiritual Connotation: **Expectant**
Scripture: **James 5:7** NLT
Dear brothers and sisters, you must be
patient as you wait for the Lord's return.

JIZELLE, see Gizelle

JOAB, Joäb, Yoab, Yoav
Language/Cultural Origin: **Hebrew**
Inherent Meaning: **Praise the Lord**
Spiritual Connotation: **Adoration**
Scripture: **Psalm 34:1** NKJV
I will bless the LORD at all times; His
praise shall continually be in my mouth.

JOACHIM, Joakim, Joaquim (see also ☞ Akim, Hakim, Joaquin)
Language/Cultural Origin: **Hebrew**
Inherent Meaning: **God Will Establish**
Spiritual Connotation: **Enthroned**
Scripture: **1 Chronicles 17:12** NKJV
He shall build Me a house, and I will
establish his throne forever.

JOAH, Yoah
☞ Language/Cultural Origin: **Hebrew**
Inherent Meaning: **God Is Father**

Spiritual Connotation: **Secure**
Scripture: **Psalm 89:26** NKJV
You are my Father, My God, and the
rock of my salvation.

JOAN, Joane, Joanelle, Joanie, Joann, Jo-Anne, Joanne, Joni
Language/Cultural Origin: **English**
Inherent Meaning: **God Is Gracious**
Spiritual Connotation: **Wise**
Scripture: **Proverbs 4:7** NKJV
Wisdom is the principal thing; therefore
get wisdom. And in all your getting, get
understanding.

JOANNA, Jo, Joana, Jo-Anna, ☞ Joannah, Joey, Johana, Johannah, Yoana, Yoanna, Yohana, Yohanna
Language/Cultural Origin: **German**
Inherent Meaning: **God Is Gracious**
Spiritual Connotation: **Delivered**
Scripture: **1 Corinthians 15:10** RSV
But by the grace of God I am what I am,
and his grace toward me was not in vain.

JOAQUIN, Joaquín, Jocquin, Juquin
Language/Cultural Origin: **Portuguese**
Inherent Meaning: **God Is My Salvation**
Spiritual Connotation: **Filled With Praise**
Scripture: **Isaiah 12:2** NASB
Behold, God is my salvation, I will trust
and not be afraid; for the LORD GOD
is my strength and song, and He has
become my salvation.

JOASH
☞ Language/Cultural Origin: **Hebrew**
Inherent Meaning: **God Hastens to Help**
Spiritual Connotation: **Delivered**
Scripture: **2 Kings 17:39** NLT
You must worship only the LORD your
God. He is the one who will rescue you
from all your enemies.

JOB, Jobe
☞ Language/Cultural Origin: **Hebrew**
Inherent Meaning: **Afflicted**
Spiritual Connotation: **Delivered**
Scripture: **Job 36:15** NLT
But by means of their suffering, he res-
cues those who suffer. For he gets their
attention through adversity.

JOBEN, Joban
Language/Cultural Origin: **Japanese**
Inherent Meaning: **Cleanliness**
Spiritual Connotation: **White as Snow**
Scripture: **Acts 15:9** TLB
He made no distinction between them and us, for he cleansed their lives through faith, just as he did ours.

JOCELYN, Jocelin, Jocelynn, Josalene, Joscelyn, Joscelynn, Joselyn
Language/Cultural Origin: **Old German**
Inherent Meaning: **Joyous**
Spiritual Connotation: **Righteous**
Scripture: **Ezekiel 36:26** NKJV
I will give you a new heart and put a new spirit within you; I will take the heart of stone out of your flesh and give you a heart of flesh.

JODY, Jodee, Jodene, Jodey, Jodi, Jodie, Jodine
Language/Cultural Origin: **American**
Inherent Meaning: **Praised**
Spiritual Connotation: **Humble**
Scripture: **1 Chronicles 16:25** NKJV
For the LORD is great and greatly to be praised; He is also to be feared above all gods.

JOEL, Jôel, Joël, Jole
☞ Language/Cultural Origin: **Hebrew**
Inherent Meaning: **The Lord Is God**
Spiritual Connotation: **God's Messenger**
Scripture: **Romans 12:2** NKJV
And do not be conformed to this world, but be transformed by the renewing of your mind.

JOELLE, Joella, Joëlle
Language/Cultural Origin: **French**
Inherent Meaning: **The Lord Is God**
Spiritual Connotation: **Beloved**
Scripture: **Psalm 100:3** NKJV
Know that the LORD, He is God; it is He who has made us, and not we ourselves; we are His people and the sheep of His pasture.

JOERGEN, Jergen, Jöergen, Jörgen, Jürgen
Language/Cultural Origin: **Danish**
Inherent Meaning: **Farmer**
Spiritual Connotation: **Persevering**
Scripture: **2 Timothy 2:6** NASB
The hard-working farmer ought to be the first to receive his share of the crops.

JOHANN, Joannes, Johan, Johanan, Johannas, Johannes, Yohan, Yohann, Yohannes
Language/Cultural Origin: **German**
Inherent Meaning: **God Is Gracious**
Spiritual Connotation: **Generosity of Spirit**
Scripture: **Galatians 5:22-23** NKJV
But the fruit of the Spirit is love, joy, peace, longsuffering, kindness, goodness, faithfulness, gentleness, self-control.

JOHANNA, see Joanna

JOHN, Jahn, Jhan, Jhon, Johnnie,
☞ **Johnny, Jon, Jonn, Jonnie, Jonny (see also Jonathan)**
Language/Cultural Origin: **Greek**
Inherent Meaning: **God Is Gracious**
Spiritual Connotation: **Strength of God**
Scripture: **Psalm 118:14** NKJV
The LORD is my strength and song, and He has become my salvation.

JOLAN, Jolán, Jolánda, Jolánta
Language/Cultural Origin: **Hungarian**
Inherent Meaning: **Violet Flower**
Spiritual Connotation: **Steady Growth**
Scripture: **Hosea 14:5** NKJV
I will be like the dew to Israel; he shall grow like the lily, and lengthen his roots like Lebanon.

JOLENE, Jolayne, Jolean, Joleane, Joleen, Joline, Jolinn, Jolynn
Language/Cultural Origin: **English**
Inherent Meaning: **God Will Increase**
Spiritual Connotation: **Reborn**
Scripture: **Isaiah 38:5** NASB
I have heard your prayer, I have seen your tears; behold, I will add fifteen years to your life.

JONAH, Jona, Jonas, Yona, Yonah
☞ Language/Cultural Origin: **Hebrew**

Inherent Meaning: **Dove**
Spiritual Connotation: **Declarer of Joy and Salvation**
Scripture: **Acts 4:20** NLT
We cannot stop telling about the wonderful things we have seen and heard.

JONATHAN, Johnathan, Johnathon, ☞Jonathon, Jonnathan (see also John)
Language/Cultural Origin: **Hebrew**
Inherent Meaning: **Gift of the Lord**
Spiritual Connotation: **God's Precious Gift**
Scripture: **Psalm 92:4** NKJV
For You, LORD, have made me glad through Your work; I will triumph in the works of Your hands.

JONINA, Jeneena, Joneena, Jonika, Joniqua, Jonita, Jonnina, Jontaya
Language/Cultural Origin: **Hebrew**
Inherent Meaning: **Dove**
Spiritual Connotation: **Reflection of God**
Scripture: **Luke 3:22** NKJV
And the Holy Spirit descended in bodily form like a dove upon Him, and a voice came from heaven which said, "You are My beloved Son; in You I am well pleased."

JONTAE, see Shantae

JORAH, Jora, Yora, Yorah
☞ Language/Cultural Origin: **Hebrew**
Inherent Meaning: **Autumn Rain**
Spiritual Connotation: **Blessing**
Scripture: **Joel 2:23** NIV
Rejoice in the LORD your God, for he has given you the autumn rains in righteousness. He sends you abundant showers, both autumn and spring rains, as before.

JORAM, Jorim
☞ Language/Cultural Origin: **Hebrew**
Inherent Meaning: **God Is Exalted**
Spiritual Connotation: **Reverent**
Scripture: **Isaiah 25:1** NKJV
O LORD, You are my God. I will exalt You, I will praise Your name.

JORDAN, Jordaan, Jordain, Jordane, ☞Jorden, Jordenn, Jordenne, Jordin,

Jordon, Jordyn, Joree, Jorée, Jori, Jorie, Jorii, Jorin, Jorrdan, Jorrie, Jorrín, Jorry, Jory, Jourdan
Language/Cultural Origin: **Hebrew**
Inherent Meaning: **Descender**
Spiritual Connotation: **Wise in Judgment**
Scripture: **Proverbs 21:30** NCV
There is no wisdom, understanding, or advice that can succeed against the LORD.

JORDANA, see Yordana

JORELL, Jorel, Jorrel, Jorrell
Language/Cultural Origin: **American**
Inherent Meaning: **He Preserves**
Spiritual Connotation: **Witness**
Scripture: **Isaiah 42:6** RSV
I am the LORD, I have called you in righteousness, I have taken you by the hand and kept you.

JORGEN, see Joergen

JORIANNA, Joriann, Jori-Anna, Jorianne, Jorrianna, Yoriann, Yorianna, Yorianne
Language/Cultural Origin: **American**
Inherent Meaning: **Increasing in Grace**
Spiritual Connotation: **Blessed**
Scripture: **Joel 2:13** NASB
Now return to the LORD your God, for He is gracious and compassionate, slow to anger, abounding in lovingkindness, and relenting of evil.

JOSEPH, Joe, Joeseph, Joey, José, ☞Josée, Josef, Joseff, Josephe, Josephus, Jozef, Yosef, Yoseff, Yosif, Yousef, Yusif
Language/Cultural Origin: **Hebrew**
Inherent Meaning: **God Will Add**
Spiritual Connotation: **Wise and Understanding**
Scripture: **Proverbs 28:5** NKJV
Evil men do not understand justice, but those who seek the LORD understand all.

JOSEPHINE, Jo, Joey, Josée, Joselle, Josephina, Josetta, Josette, Josey, Josie
Language/Cultural Origin: **French**

Inherent Meaning: **She Shall Increase in Wisdom**
Spiritual Connotation: **Spiritual Understanding**
Scripture: **Romans 12:2** NKJV
And do not be conformed to this world, but be transformed by the renewing of your mind.

JOSHUA, Jeshua, Jeshuah, Josh, ☞ Joshe, Joshuah, Joshuwa, Jozua
Language/Cultural Origin: **Hebrew**
Inherent Meaning: **God Is My Salvation**
Spiritual Connotation: **Bringer of Truth**
Scripture: **James 1:25** NKJV
But he who looks into the perfect law of liberty and continues in it . . . this one will be blessed in what he does.

JOSIAH, Josia, Josias
☞ Language/Cultural Origin: **Hebrew**
Inherent Meaning: **Fire of the Lord**
Spiritual Connotation: **Intuitive Perception**
Scripture: **1 Corinthians 2:7** NKJV
But we speak the wisdom of God in a mystery, the hidden wisdom which God ordained before the ages for our glory.

JOVAN, Jeovani, Jeovanni, Jiovani, Jiovanni, Jovaan, Jovani, Jovann, Jovanni, Jovonn, Yovaan, Yovan, Yovani, Yovann, Yovanni (see also Giovanni, Javan, Jevan)
Language/Cultural Origin: **Latin**
Inherent Meaning: **Majestic**
Spiritual Connotation: **Delightful**
Scripture: **Psalm 16:3** NASB
As for the saints who are in the earth, they are the majestic ones in whom is all my delight.

JOVANNA, Jeovana, Jeovanna, Jovana, Jovena, Jovonna (see also Giovanna)
Language/Cultural Origin: **Latin**
Inherent Meaning: **Majestic**
Spiritual Connotation: **Lovely**
Scripture: **Psalm 76:4** NASB
You are resplendent, more majestic than the mountains of prey.

JOY, Joya, Joyanna, Joye
Language/Cultural Origin: **Latin**
Inherent Meaning: **Joyful**
Spiritual Connotation: **Follower of Truth**
Scripture: **Psalm 119:105** NKJV
Your word is a lamp to my feet and a light to my path.

JOYCE, Joice, Joyous
Language/Cultural Origin: **Latin**
Inherent Meaning: **Vivacious**
Spiritual Connotation: **God's Gracious Gift**
Scripture: **Psalm 16:11** NKJV
You will show me the path of life; in Your presence is fullness of joy; at Your right hand are pleasures forevermore.

JUAN, Juanito, Juaun
Language/Cultural Origin: **Spanish**
Inherent Meaning: **God Is Gracious**
Spiritual Connotation: **Righteous**
Scripture: **Psalm 97:11** NKJV
Light is sown for the righteous, and gladness for the upright in heart.

JUANITA, Juana, Juanequa, Juanesha, Juanna
Language/Cultural Origin: **Spanish**
Inherent Meaning: **God Is Gracious**
Spiritual Connotation: **Famous**
Scripture: **Ezekiel 16:14** NRSV
Your fame spread among the nations on account of your beauty, for it was perfect because of my splendor that I had bestowed on you.

JUBAL, Jubel
☞ Language/Cultural Origin: **Hebrew**
Inherent Meaning: **Ram's Horn**
Spiritual Connotation: **Victorious**
Scripture: **Joshua 6:5** NRSV
When they make a long blast with the ram's horn . . . then all the people shall shout with a great shout; and the wall of the city will fall down flat.

JUDAH, Jud, Juda, Judas, Judd, Jude
☞ Language/Cultural Origin: **Hebrew**
Inherent Meaning: **Praised**
Spiritual Connotation: **Full of Love**
Scripture: **John 13:34** NKJV
A new commandment I give to you,

*that you love one another; as I have
loved you, that you also love one
another.*

JUDSON, Judsen
Language/Cultural Origin: **English**
Inherent Meaning: **Son of the Praised One**
Spiritual Connotation: **Glory to God**
Scripture: **Daniel 4:34** NKJV
*I blessed the Most High and praised and
honored Him who lives forever: for His
dominion is an everlasting dominion,
and His kingdom is from generation to
generation.*

JUDITH, Judi, Judie, Judy
Language/Cultural Origin: **Hebrew**
Inherent Meaning: **She Who Praises**
Spiritual Connotation: **Righteous**
Scripture: **Isaiah 58:8** NKJV
*Then your light shall break forth like the
morning, your healing shall spring forth
speedily, and your righteousness shall go
before you.*

**JULIA, Julee, Juleen, Juli, Juliana,
Juliane, Juliann, Julianna, Julie,
Julieann, Juliene, Julienne, Julila,
Julilla, Julina, Juline, Julisa,
Julissa, Julliana, Jullianna**
Language/Cultural Origin: **Latin**
Inherent Meaning: **Youthful**
Spiritual Connotation: **Guided by Faith**
Scripture: **Matthew 9:29** NKJV
According to your faith let it be to you.

**JULIET, Julieta, Juliete, Julietta,
Juliette, Julliet, Jullietta**
Language/Cultural Origin: **French**
Inherent Meaning: **Youthful**
Spiritual Connotation: **Immovable**
Scripture: **Psalm 16:8** NKJV
*I have set the LORD always before me;
because He is at my right hand I shall not
be moved.*

**JULIUS, Jule, Jules, Julian, Juliano,
Julias, Julien, Julio, Jullian**
Language/Cultural Origin: **Latin**
Inherent Meaning: **Youthful**
Spiritual Connotation: **Regenerated**
Scripture: **Ephesians 4:23-24** NKJV

*And be renewed in the spirit of your mind,
and that you put on the new man . . . in
true righteousness and holiness.*

JUNE, Junelle, Junia
Language/Cultural Origin: **Latin**
Inherent Meaning: **Born in the Fourth
Month**
Spiritual Connotation: **Loving**
Scripture: **Romans 13:10** NKJV
*Love does no harm to a neighbor; there-
fore love is the fulfillment of the law.*

JURI, see Yuri

JURRIEN, Jurian, Jurien, Jurrian
Language/Cultural Origin: **Dutch**
Inherent Meaning: **God Will Uplift**
Spiritual Connotation: **Humble**
Scripture: **James 4:10** NKJV
*Humble yourselves in the sight of the
Lord, and He will lift you up.*

**JUSTIN, Justan, Justen, Justinn,
Justinus, Juston, Justun, Justyn**
Language/Cultural Origin: **Latin**
Inherent Meaning: **Upright**
Spiritual Connotation: **Righteous**
Scripture: **Psalm 138:8** NKJV
*The LORD will perfect that which con-
cerns me; your mercy, O LORD, endures
forever; do not forsake the works of Your
hands.*

JUSTINA, Justeen, Justine, Justinna
Language/Cultural Origin: **French**
Inherent Meaning: **Upright**
Spiritual Connotation: **Righteous**
Scripture: **Psalm 139:17** NKJV
*How precious also are Your thoughts to me,
O God! How great is the sum of them!*

JUSTUS, Justas, Justice, Justis
Language/Cultural Origin: **Hebrew**
Inherent Meaning: **Just**
Spiritual Connotation: **Righteous**
Scripture: **Isaiah 26:7** NIV
*O upright One, you make the way of the
righteous smooth.*

JUWAN, see Jajuan

K

KAARINA, Kaariana, Kaarianna (see also Carina, Karena, Karina)
Language/Cultural Origin: **Finnish**
Inherent Meaning: **Pure**
Spiritual Connotation: **Spotless**
Scripture: **2 Peter 3:14** RSV
Therefore, beloved, since you wait for these, be zealous to be found by him without spot or blemish, and at peace.

KACEY, see Casey

KACHINA, Kachéna
Language/Cultural Origin: **Native American**
Inherent Meaning: **Sacred Dancer**
Spiritual Connotation: **Pleasant Offering**
Scripture: **Exodus 15:20** NASB
And Miriam the prophetess, Aaron's sister, took the timbrel in her hand, and all the women went out after her with timbrels and with dancing.

KACIA, Cacia, Casia, Kaycia, Kaysia
Language/Cultural Origin: **Greek**
Inherent Meaning: **Thorny**
Spiritual Connotation: **Holy**
Scripture: **2 Corinthians 7:1** NASB
Therefore, having these promises, beloved, let us cleanse ourselves from all defilement of flesh and spirit, perfecting holiness in the fear of God.

KADEE, K.D., Kadey, Kadie, Kady, Kaydee, Kaydi, Kaydie, Kaydy (see also Cady, Katy)
Language/Cultural Origin: **English**
Inherent Meaning: **Stainless**
Spiritual Connotation: **Sanctified**
Scripture: **Ephesians 5:27** NCV
He died so that he could give the church to himself like a bride in all her beauty.

He died so that the church could be pure and without fault.

KADIM, Kadeem, Kadím, Khadeem (see also Qadim)
Language/Cultural Origin: **Middle Eastern**
Inherent Meaning: **Servant**
Spiritual Connotation: **Messenger**
Scripture: **Matthew 12:18** NRSV
Here is my servant, whom I have chosen, my beloved, with whom my soul is well pleased. . . . He will proclaim justice to the Gentiles.

KADIN, Kaden, Kadeen, Kaiden, Kadon
Language/Cultural Origin: **Middle Eastern**
Inherent Meaning: **Confidant**
Spiritual Connotation: **Peacemaker**
Scripture: **Proverbs 21:14** NKJV
A gift in secret pacifies anger.

KADMIEL, Kadmielle
Language/Cultural Origin: **Hebrew**
Inherent Meaning: **God Is of Old**
Spiritual Connotation: **Eternal**
Scripture: **Matthew 22:32** NKJV
God is not the God of the dead, but of the living.

KAELA, Kaelah, Kahla, Kahlah, Keila, Keilah, Keyla, Keylah (see also Cayla, Kaila, Kayla, Kyla)
Language/Cultural Origin: **Middle Eastern**
Inherent Meaning: **Cherished**
Spiritual Connotation: **Adored**
Scripture: **Song of Songs 6:3** NKJV
I am my beloved's, and my beloved is mine.

KAELYN, see Kaylyn

KAHLIL, Kahleil, Kahlíl (see also Kalil)
Language/Cultural Origin: **Turkish**
Inherent Meaning: **Young**
Spiritual Connotation: **Accountable**
Scripture: **Ecclesiastes 11:9** NRSV
Rejoice, young man, while you are young . . . but know that for all these things God will bring you into judgment.

KAI
Language/Cultural Origin: **Navaho**
Inherent Meaning: **Willow Tree**
Spiritual Connotation: **Firmly Rooted**
Scripture: **Psalm 1:3** NKJV
He shall be like a tree planted by the rivers of water, that brings forth its fruit in its season.

KAIJA, Kaijah, Kaiya, Kaiyah
Language/Cultural Origin: **Russian**
Inherent Meaning: **Life**
Spiritual Connotation: **Eternal**
Scripture: **Psalm 23:6** RSV
Surely goodness and mercy shall follow me all the days of my life; and I shall dwell in the house of the LORD for ever.

KAILA, Kailah, Kailla, Kaillah (see also Cayla, Kaela, Kayla, Kyla)
Language/Cultural Origin: **Hebrew**
Inherent Meaning: **Crowned**
Spiritual Connotation: **Wise**
Scripture: **Proverbs 14:18** NASB
The naive inherit foolishness, but the sensible are crowned with knowledge.

KAILEE, KAILEY, see Kaylee

KAITLIN, Kaatlan, Kaetlin, Kaetlynn, Kaitlan, Kaitland, Kaitlen, Kaitlinn, Kaitlyn, Kaitlynn, Kateland, Katelin, Katelyn, Katlyn, Kaytlin, Kaytlynn (see also Caitlin)
Language/Cultural Origin: **Irish**
Inherent Meaning: **Virtuous**
Spiritual Connotation: **Favored**
Scripture: **Ruth 3:11** NKJV
And now, my daughter, do not fear. I will do for you all that you request, for all the people of my town know that you are a virtuous woman.

KALA, Kalah, Kalla, Kallah (see also Cala)
Language/Cultural Origin: **American**
Inherent Meaning: **Refuge**
Spiritual Connotation: **Guarded of God**
Scripture: **Psalm 91:2** NKJV
He is my refuge and my fortress; My God, in Him I will trust.

KALAMA, Kalam, Kallam, Kallama
Language/Cultural Origin: **Hawaiian**
Inherent Meaning: **Flaming Torch**
Spiritual Connotation: **Testimony**
Scripture: **2 Kings 1:12** NKJV
If I am a man of God, let fire come down from heaven and consume you and your fifty men. And the fire of God came down from heaven and consumed him and his fifty.

KALANI, Kailana, Kailani, Kalan, Kalana, Kalanee, Kalanna, Kalanie (see also Keilani)
Language/Cultural Origin: **Hawaiian**
Inherent Meaning: **Chieftain**
Spiritual Connotation: **Guardian**
Scripture: **Psalm 61:2** NASB
From the end of the earth I call to Thee, when my heart is faint; lead me to the rock that is higher than I.

KALE, Kayle
Language/Cultural Origin: **Hawaiian**
Inherent Meaning: **Farmer**
Spiritual Connotation: **Sower of Truth**
Scripture: **Mark 4:14** NCV
The farmer is like a person who plants God's message in people.

KALEA, Kahlea, Kahleah, Kallea, Khalea, Khaleah
Language/Cultural Origin: **Hawaiian**
Inherent Meaning: **Clear**
Spiritual Connotation: **Righteous**
Scripture: **John 3:21** NRSV
But those who do what is true come to the light, so that it may be clearly seen that their deeds have been done in God.

KALEENA, Kalena (see also Kalina)
Language/Cultural Origin: **Hawaiian**
Inherent Meaning: **Spotless**
Spiritual Connotation: **Respectful**
Scripture: **1 Timothy 5:2** NLT
Treat the older women as you would your mother, and treat the younger women with all purity as your own sisters.

KALEI, Kahléi, Kallei, Khalei (see also Callie, Kali, Kalli)
Language/Cultural Origin: **Hawaiian**
Inherent Meaning: **Wreath of Flowers**
Spiritual Connotation: **Adorned**
Scripture: **Revelation 12:1** NASB
And a great sign appeared in heaven: a woman clothed with the sun, and the moon under her feet, and on her head a crown of twelve stars.

KALEY, see Kaylee

KALI (see also Callie, Kalli)
Language/Cultural Origin: **Hawaiian**
Inherent Meaning: **Hesitating**
Spiritual Connotation: **Examiner of Truth**
Scripture: **Acts 17:11** NASB
For they received the word with great eagerness, examining the Scriptures daily, to see whether these things were so.

KALIANA, See Kaulana

KALIL, Kahleel, Kaleel, Kaléel (see also Kahlil)
Language/Cultural Origin: **Hebrew**
Inherent Meaning: **Complete**
Spiritual Connotation: **Righteous**
Scripture: **Philippians 1:6** NRSV
I am confident of this, that the one who began a good work among you will bring it to completion by the day of Jesus Christ.

KALILA, Kahlila, Kaleela, Kalilla, Kaylila, Khalilah, Kylila, Kylilah
Language/Cultural Origin: **Middle Eastern**
Inherent Meaning: **Sweetheart**
Spiritual Connotation: **Beloved**
Scripture: **Genesis 24:67** TLB
And Isaac brought Rebekah into his mother's tent, and she became his wife. He loved her very much.

KALIN, KALYN, see Kaylyn

KALINA, Kalinna (see also Kaleena)
Language/Cultural Origin: **Slavic**
Inherent Meaning: **Flower**
Spiritual Connotation: **Nurtured**
Scripture: **Isaiah 35:2** NKJV
It shall blossom abundantly and rejoice, even with joy and singing.

KALISA, Kalissa, Kalysa, Kalyssa
Language/Cultural Origin: **American**
Inherent Meaning: **Pure Offering**
Spiritual Connotation: **Sweet Sacrifice**
Scripture: **Exodus 29:18** NKJV
And you shall burn the whole ram on the altar. It is a burnt offering to the LORD; it is a sweet aroma, an offering made by fire to the LORD.

KALLAN, Kallen, Kallin, Kallon, Kallun, Kallyn (see also Kellen)
Language/Cultural Origin: **Slavic**
Inherent Meaning: **River**
Spiritual Connotation: **Joyful**
Scripture: **Psalm 98:8** NASB
Let the rivers clap their hands; let the mountains sing together for joy.

KALLI, Kaleigh, Kallee, Kalley, Kallie, Kally
Language/Cultural Origin: **English**
Inherent Meaning: **Lark**
Spiritual Connotation: **Cheerful**
Scripture: **Psalm 100:2** NKJV
Serve the LORD with gladness; come before His presence with singing.

KALYCA, Kaleecia, Kalica, Kalicia, Kalicya
Language/Cultural Origin: **Greek**
Inherent Meaning: **Rosebud**
Spiritual Connotation: **Promise**
Scripture: **Isaiah 35:1** NKJV
The wilderness and the wasteland shall be glad for them, and the desert shall rejoice and blossom as the rose.

KAMA, Kamah, Khama
Language/Cultural Origin: **Hebrew**
Inherent Meaning: **Ripe Harvest**
Spiritual Connotation: **Reaper**
Scripture: **Revelation 14:15** NKJV

Thrust in Your sickle and reap, for the time has come for You to reap, for the harvest of the earth is ripe.

KAMAL, Kamaal, Kamâl, Kamîl
Language/Cultural Origin: **Middle Eastern**
Inherent Meaning: **Perfect**
Spiritual Connotation: **Power of God**
Scripture: **2 Samuel 22:33** NKJV
God is my strength and power, and He makes my way perfect.

KAMALI, Kamalaya, Kamalee, Kamaleah, Kamaleigh
Language/Cultural Origin: **Mahona**
Inherent Meaning: **Protector**
Spiritual Connotation: **Chosen**
Scripture: **Nehemiah 13:22** NKJV
Remember me, O my God, concerning this also, and spare me according to the greatness of Your mercy!

KAMARIA, Kamara, Kamari
Language/Cultural Origin: **Swahili**
Inherent Meaning: **Moonlight**
Spiritual Connotation: **Deliverance**
Scripture: **Isaiah 30:26** NKJV
Moreover the light of the moon will be as the light of the sun. . . . In the day that the LORD binds up the bruise of His people and heals the stroke of their wound.

KAMEA, Kameah
Language/Cultural Origin: **Hawaiian**
Inherent Meaning: **Precious**
Spiritual Connotation: **Honored**
Scripture: **Isaiah 43:4** NKJV
Since you were precious in My sight, You have been honored, and I have loved you; therefore I will give men for you, and people for your life.

KAMEKO, Kameka, Kamika, Kamiko
Language/Cultural Origin: **Japanese**
Inherent Meaning: **Turtle Child**
Spiritual Connotation: **Humble**
Scripture: **Proverbs 15:33** NRSV
The fear of the LORD is instruction in wisdom, and humility goes before honor.

KAMI, Kamee, Kámi, Kahmi (see also Cami)
Language/Cultural Origin: **Japanese**

Inherent Meaning: **Divine Aura**
Spiritual Connotation: **Gifted**
Scripture: **2 Peter 1:4** NASB
For by these He has granted to us His precious and magnificent promises, in order that by them you might become partakers of the divine nature.

KAMILAH, Kameela, Kameelah, Kamila, Kamilla, Kamillah
Language/Cultural Origin: **Middle Eastern**
Inherent Meaning: **Perfect**
Spiritual Connotation: **Holy**
Scripture: **Hebrews 10:14** NCV
With one sacrifice he made perfect forever those who are being made holy.

KANA, Kána, Kaena, Kaina, Kayna
Language/Cultural Origin: **Japanese**
Inherent Meaning: **Powerful**
Spiritual Connotation: **Strength of God**
Scripture: **Psalm 106:8** NKJV
Nevertheless He saved them for His name's sake, that He might make His mighty power known.

KANANI, Kananee, Kananie
Language/Cultural Origin: **Hawaiian**
Inherent Meaning: **Beautiful**
Spiritual Connotation: **Obedient**
Scripture: **Psalm 45:11** NCV
The king loves your beauty. Because he is your master, you should obey him.

KANE, Kané (see also Cain)
Language/Cultural Origin: **Celtic**
Inherent Meaning: **Beautiful**
Spiritual Connotation: **Hopeful**
Scripture: **Psalm 31:24** NKJV
Be of good courage, and He shall strengthen your heart, all you who hope in the LORD.

KANGE, Kainge, Kangé
Language/Cultural Origin: **Lakota**
Inherent Meaning: **Raven**
Spiritual Connotation: **Genuine**
Scripture: **Song of Songs 5:11** NCV
His head is like the finest gold; his hair is wavy and black like a raven.

KANIEL, Kahniel, Kahnyell, Kanyel
Language/Cultural Origin: **Hebrew**

Inherent Meaning: **God Is My Reed**
Spiritual Connotation: **God Has Bought Me**
Scripture: **1 Corinthians 6:20** NASB
For you have been bought with a price:
therefore glorify God in your body.

KANIKA, Kanicka, Kaneeka, Kanikah

Language/Cultural Origin: **Kenyan**
Inherent Meaning: **Black Cloth**
Spiritual Connotation: **Reverent**
Scripture: **Hebrews 12:29** NKJV
For our God is a consuming fire.

KANNON, Kanen, Kannen, Kanon (see also Cannon)

Language/Cultural Origin: **Polynesian**
Inherent Meaning: **Unchained**
Spiritual Connotation: **Free**
Scripture: **Psalm 107:14** NKJV
He brought them out of darkness and the
shadow of death, And broke their chains
in pieces.

KANYA, Kania, Kanyah

Language/Cultural Origin: **Thai**
Inherent Meaning: **Young Lady**
Spiritual Connotation: **Prosperous**
Scripture: **Zechariah 9:17** NKJV
For how great is its goodness and how
great its beauty! Grain shall make the
young men thrive, and new wine the
young women.

KAORI, Kaory

Language/Cultural Origin: **Japanese**
Inherent Meaning: **Strong**
Spiritual Connotation: **Majestic**
Scripture: **1 Chronicles 16:27** NKJV
Honor and majesty are before Him;
strength and gladness are in His place.

KARA, Kaira, Kairah, Karah, Karrah (see also Cara, Kerani)

Language/Cultural Origin: **Danish**
Inherent Meaning: **Pure**
Spiritual Connotation: **Cherished**
Scripture: **Psalm 36:9** NKJV
For with You is the fountain of life; in
Your light we see light.

KARAL, KAREL, see Carl

KARALEE, Karalea, Karaleah, Karaleigh, Karalie

Language/Cultural Origin: **English**
Inherent Meaning: **Innocent**
Spiritual Connotation: **Righteous**
Scripture: **Job 33:9** NKJV
I am pure, without transgression; I am
innocent, and there is no iniquity in me.

KARE, Kåre, Kareé

Language/Cultural Origin: **Norwegian**
Inherent Meaning: **Enormous**
Spiritual Connotation: **Saved by Faith**
Scripture: **Psalm 33:16** TLB
The best-equipped army cannot save a
king—for great strength is not enough to
save anyone.

KAREAH, Kareeah

Language/Cultural Origin: **Hebrew**
Inherent Meaning: **Bald**
Spiritual Connotation: **Forgiven**
Scripture: **Romans 5:8** NRSV
But God proves his love for us in that while
we still were sinners Christ died for us.

KAREEM, see Karim

KAREN, Kaaren, Karan, Karon, Karren, Karron, Karryn, Karyn, Karynn (see also Caryn, Karin)

Language/Cultural Origin: **German**
Inherent Meaning: **Pure**
Spiritual Connotation: **Beloved**
Scripture: **Nehemiah 8:10** NKJV
Do not sorrow, for the joy of the LORD is
your strength.

KARENA, Kareena, Karyna, Karynna (see also Corina, Kaarina, Karina)

Language/Cultural Origin: **Norwegian**
Inherent Meaning: **Spotless**
Spiritual Connotation: **Purchased**
Scripture: **1 Peter 1:19** NLT
He paid for you with the precious
lifeblood of Christ, the sinless, spotless
Lamb of God.

KARI, Karee, Karie, Karri (see also Cari, Carrie)

Language/Cultural Origin: **Greek**

Inherent Meaning: **Pure**
Spiritual Connotation: **Righteous**
Scripture: **2 Timothy 2:22** NKJV
Flee also youthful lusts; but pursue righteousness, faith, love, peace with those who call on the Lord out of a pure heart.

KARIANNE, Cariana, Cariann, Carianne, Carrianna, Kariana, Kariann, Karianna, Karriana (see also Kerianne)

Language/Cultural Origin: **English**
Inherent Meaning: **Virtuous**
Spiritual Connotation: **Godly**
Scripture: **2 Peter 1:3** NRSV
His divine power has given us everything needed for life and godliness, through the knowledge of him who called us by his own glory and goodness.

KARIF, Kareef

Language/Cultural Origin: **Middle Eastern**
Inherent Meaning: **Born in the Fall**
Spiritual Connotation: **Prosperous**
Scripture: **Jeremiah 33:9** NKJV
They shall fear and tremble for all the goodness and all the prosperity that I provide for it.

KARILYNN, Karilin, Karilyne, Karilynne, Karylin, Karylynn (see also Caroline, Karolyn)

Language/Cultural Origin: **American**
Inherent Meaning: **Clear, Pure Water**
Spiritual Connotation: **Cleansed**
Scripture: **Hebrews 10:22** NKJV
Let us draw near with a true heart in full assurance of faith, having our hearts sprinkled from an evil conscience and our bodies washed with pure water.

KARIM, Kareem, Karém, Karriem

Language/Cultural Origin: **Middle Eastern**
Inherent Meaning: **Distinguished**
Spiritual Connotation: **Chosen**
Scripture: **Psalm 4:3** NKJV
But know that the LORD has set apart for Himself him who is godly; the LORD will hear when I call to Him.

KARIN, Kaarin, Kárin, Karrin (see also Caryn, Karen)

Language/Cultural Origin: **Scandinavian**
Inherent Meaning: **Unblemished**
Spiritual Connotation: **Righteous**
Scripture: **Psalm 18:2** NCV
The LORD is my rock, my protection, my Savior. My God is my rock. I can run to him for safety. He is my shield and my saving strength, my defender.

KARINA, Karine, Karinna, Karrina, Karrine, Karyna (see also Carina, Kaarina, Karena)

Language/Cultural Origin: **Russian**
Inherent Meaning: **Innocent**
Spiritual Connotation: **Pure**
Scripture: **Psalm 26:6** NKJV
I will wash my hands in innocence; so I will go about Your altar, O LORD.

KARIS, Kariss, Karris, Karys, Karyss (see also Carys)

Language/Cultural Origin: **Greek**
Inherent Meaning: **Graceful**
Spiritual Connotation: **Discreet**
Scripture: **Proverbs 3:21-22** NKJV
Keep sound wisdom and discretion; So they will be life to your soul and grace to your neck.

KARISSA, see Carissa

KARL, see Carl

KARLA, see Carla

KARLANA, see Carlana

KARLENE, see Carlene

KARLIN, KARLEE, see Carlin

KARLINA, see Carlina

KARLISSA, see Carlissa

KARLYNN, Karlyn

Language/Cultural Origin: **Slavic**
Inherent Meaning: **Womanly**
Spiritual Connotation: **Valuable**
Scripture: **Proverbs 31:10** NKJV
Who can find a virtuous wife? For her worth is far above rubies.

KARMEN, see Carmen

KAROLYN, Karalyn, Karalynn, Karilyn, Karilynn, Karrolyn (see also Caroline, Karilynn)
Language/Cultural Origin: **American**
Inherent Meaning: **Womanly**
Spiritual Connotation: **Cherished**
Scripture: **Ephesians 5:25** NKJV
Husbands, love your wives, just as Christ also loved the church and gave Himself for her.

KARSTEN, Karstan, Kärsten, Karstin, Karstine
Language/Cultural Origin: **Swedish**
Inherent Meaning: **Anointed**
Spiritual Connotation: **Chosen**
Scripture: **1 Samuel 16:13** NKJV
Then Samuel took the horn of oil and anointed him . . . and the Spirit of the LORD came upon David from that day forward.

KASEM, Casem
Language/Cultural Origin: **Thai**
Inherent Meaning: **Joy**
Spiritual Connotation: **Fulfilled**
Scripture: **John 15:11** NRSV
I have said these things to you so that my joy may be in you, and that your joy may be complete.

KASEY, see Casey

KASHA, Kahasha, Kahsha, Kasa
Language/Cultural Origin: **Native American**
Inherent Meaning: **Fur Robe**
Spiritual Connotation: **Righteous**
Scripture: **Isaiah 61:10** NKJV
He has clothed me with the garments of salvation, He has covered me with the robe of righteousness.

KASHAWNA, Kashana, Kashaun, Kashauna, Kashawn, Kashonda
Language/Cultural Origin: **American**
Inherent Meaning: **Pure Promise**
Spiritual Connotation: **Eternal Gift**
Scripture: **Joshua 23:14** NKJV
Not one thing has failed of all the good things which the LORD your God spoke

concerning you. All have come to pass for you; not one word of them has failed.

KASIM, Kaseem, Kazeem
Language/Cultural Origin: **Middle Eastern**
Inherent Meaning: **Divided**
Spiritual Connotation: **Holy**
Scripture: **Philippians 1:23-24** NRSV
I am hard pressed between the two: my desire is to depart and be with Christ, for that is far better; but to remain in the flesh is more necessary for you.

KASIMIR, see Casimir

KASSANDRA, see Cassandra

KASSIDY, see Cassidy

KATARINA, Catarina, Caterina, Ecatarina, Ecaterina, Ekatarina, Ekaterina, Katareena, Katerina (see also Katrina)
Language/Cultural Origin: **Czech/Russian**
Inherent Meaning: **Unblemished**
Spiritual Connotation: **Purified**
Scripture: **Hebrews 9:14** NRSV
How much more will the blood of Christ . . . purify our conscience from dead works to worship the living God!

KATE, Cait, Cate, Kait
Language/Cultural Origin: **English**
Inherent Meaning: **Innocent**
Spiritual Connotation: **Godly Example**
Scripture: **Philippians 2:15** NASB
So that you will prove yourselves to be blameless and innocent, children of God above reproach.

KATHERINE, Katharin, Katharine, Katheren, Kathereen, Katherin, Katheryn, Kathren, Kathryn (see also Catherine)
Language/Cultural Origin: **Greek**
Inherent Meaning: **Pure**
Spiritual Connotation: **Perceptive**
Scripture: **Jeremiah 33:3** NKJV
Call to Me, and I will answer you, and show you great and mighty things, which you do not know.

KATHLEEN, Katheleen, Kathlynn, Katleen (see also Cathleen)

Language/Cultural Origin: **Irish**
Inherent Meaning: **Pure**
Spiritual Connotation: **Treasured**
Scripture: **Psalm 115:15** NKJV
May you be blessed by the LORD, who made heaven and earth.

KATO, Katón (see also Cato)

Language/Cultural Origin: **English**
Inherent Meaning: **Wise**
Spiritual Connotation: **Humble**
Scripture: **Proverbs 13:10** RSV
By insolence the heedless make strife, but with those who take advice is wisdom.

KATONE, Katóne

Language/Cultural Origin: **Hungarian**
Inherent Meaning: **The Lord Exalts**
Spiritual Connotation: **Obedient**
Scripture: **Isaiah 42:21** NKJV
The LORD is well pleased for His righteousness' sake; He will exalt the law and make it honorable.

KATRIEL, Catriel, Catrielle, Cattriel, Katrielle, Kattriel

Language/Cultural Origin: **Hebrew**
Inherent Meaning: **God Is My Crown**
Spiritual Connotation: **Redeemed**
Scripture: **Hebrews 2:9** NKJV
But we see Jesus, who was . . . for the suffering of death crowned with glory and honor, that He, by the grace of God, might taste death for everyone.

KATRINA, Cateena, Catina, Catreen, Catreena, Catrien, Catrién, Catrin, Catrina, Catrine, Catrinia, Catriona, Catryn, Catryna, Cattrina, Cattrinna, Cattryna, Ecatrinna, Ekatrinna, Kateena, Katina, Katreen, Katreena, Katrene, Katrien, Katrién, Katrin, Katrine, Katrinia, Katriona, Katryn, Katryna, Kattrina, Kattryna

Language/Cultural Origin: **Russian/German**
Inherent Meaning: **Spotless**
Spiritual Connotation: **Cleansed**
Scripture: **1 Peter 1:19** NKJV
But with the precious blood of Christ, as of a lamb without blemish and without spot.

KATURAH, Katura (see also Keturah)

Language/Cultural Origin: **Rhodesian**
Inherent Meaning: **Relieved**
Spiritual Connotation: **Righteous**
Scripture: **Psalm 119:142** NKJV
Your righteousness is an everlasting righteousness, and Your law is truth.

KATY, Catey, Caytee, Caytie, Katey, Kati, Katie, Kaytee, Kaytie (see also Cady, Kadee)

Language/Cultural Origin: **Estonian**
Inherent Meaning: **Spotless**
Spiritual Connotation: **Unblemished**
Scripture: **Ephesians 5:27** NLT
He did this to present her to himself as a glorious church without a spot or wrinkle or any other blemish.

KATYA, Cata, Catia, Catja, Catka, Cattiah, Catya, Kata, Katia, Katica, Katja, Katka, Kattiah

Language/Cultural Origin: **Russian**
Inherent Meaning: **Pure**
Spiritual Connotation: **Righteous**
Scripture: **Psalm 119:1** NRSV
Happy are those whose way is blameless, who walk in the law of the LORD.

KAULANA, Kaliana, Kalianna

Language/Cultural Origin: **Hawaiian**
Inherent Meaning: **Famous**
Spiritual Connotation: **Strength of God**
Scripture: **Psalm 89:13** NKJV
You have a mighty arm; strong is Your hand, and high is Your right hand.

KAY, Kae, Kaye

Language/Cultural Origin: **Latin**
Inherent Meaning: **Rejoicer**
Spiritual Connotation: **Joyful**
Scripture: **Proverbs 15:23** NRSV
To make an apt answer is a joy to anyone, and a word in season, how good it is!

KAYA, Kayah

Language/Cultural Origin: **Hopi**
Inherent Meaning: **Child of Wisdom**

Spiritual Connotation: **Youthful Example**
Scripture: **Luke 2:49** NKJV
*Why did you seek Me? Did you not
know that I must be about My Father's
business?*

KAYLA, Kaylia, Kayliah (see also Cayla, Kaela, Kaila, Kyla)

Language/Cultural Origin: **Middle Eastern**
Inherent Meaning: **Crowned**
Spiritual Connotation: **Exalted**
Scripture: **Psalm 8:5** NKJV
*For You have made him a little lower
than the angels, and You have crowned
him with glory and honor.*

KAYLEE, Kaeleah, Kaelee, Kaeleigh, Kaelie, Kailee, Kaileigh, Kailey, Kalee, Kaleigh, Kaley, Kayleah, Kayleigh, Kayley, Kaylie (see also Caeley)

Language/Cultural Origin: **American**
Inherent Meaning: **Crowned**
Spiritual Connotation: **Wise**
Scripture: **Proverbs 14:18** NASB
*The naive inherit foolishness, but the
sensible are crowned with knowledge.*

KAYLEEN, Caeleen, Caileen, Cayleen, Caylene, Kaeleen, Kaileen, Kaylene

Language/Cultural Origin: **Middle Eastern**
Inherent Meaning: **Sweetheart**
Spiritual Connotation: **Beloved**
Scripture: **Song of Songs 2:14** NKJV
*Let me see your face, let me hear your
voice; for your voice is sweet, and your
face is lovely.*

KAYLYN, Kaelan, Kaelen, Kaelin, Kaelyn, Kaelynn, Kailyn, Kalan, Kalen, Kalin, Kalyn, Kaylan, Kaylin, Kaylon, Kaylynn (see also Caelan, Cailin)

Language/Cultural Origin: **American**
Inherent Meaning: **Crowned**
Spiritual Connotation: **Delivered**
Scripture: **Hebrews 2:9** NKJV
*But we see Jesus who was . . . for the
suffering of death crowned with glory
and honor, that He, by the grace of God,
might taste death for everyone.*

KAYSA, Kajsa

Language/Cultural Origin: **Swedish**
Inherent Meaning: **Clean**
Spiritual Connotation: **Innocent**
Scripture: **2 Samuel 22:21** NLT
*The LORD rewarded me for doing right; he
compensated me because of my innocence.*

KEANDRE, Kendre, Keondre (see also Kendre)

Language/Cultural Origin: **American**
Inherent Meaning: **Manly**
Spiritual Connotation: **Gentle**
Scripture: **Philippians 4:5** NRSV
*Let your gentleness be known to
everyone. The Lord is near.*

KEANE, Kean, Keano, Keanu

Language/Cultural Origin: **Irish**
Inherent Meaning: **Commander**
Spiritual Connotation: **Steadfast**
Scripture: **Psalm 16:8** NKJV
*I have set the LORD always before me;
because He is at my right hand I shall not
be moved.*

KEARA, Kearra, Keera, Keira, Keirra, Kera (see also Kiera, Kira, Kyrie)

Language/Cultural Origin: **Irish**
Inherent Meaning: **Dark**
Spiritual Connotation: **Obedient**
Scripture: **Isaiah 50:10** NKJV
*Who among you fears the LORD? . . .
Who walks in darkness and has no light?
Let him trust in the name of the LORD
and rely upon his God.*

KEARNEY, Kearn, Kearny

Language/Cultural Origin: **Irish**
Inherent Meaning: **Victorious**
Spiritual Connotation: **Thankful**
Scripture: **Psalm 20:5** NASB
*We will sing for joy over your victory,
and in the name of our God we will set
up our banners. May the LORD fulfill all
your petitions.*

KEATON, Keaten, Keeton

Language/Cultural Origin: **English**
Inherent Meaning: **From Where Hawks Fly**
Spiritual Connotation: **Reverent**

Scripture: **Exodus 3:5** NRSV
*Come no closer! Remove the sandals
from your feet, for the place on which
you are standing is holy ground.*

KEEGAN, Kaegan, Keagan, Kegan, Keghan

Language/Cultural Origin: **Gaelic**
Inherent Meaning: **Fiery**
Spiritual Connotation: **Righteous**
Scripture: **Psalm 37:37** NKJV
*Mark the blameless man, and observe
the upright; for the future of that man is
peace.*

KEELAN, Kealyn, Keelen, Keelin, Keelyn, Kielan, Kielyn

Language/Cultural Origin: **Irish**
Inherent Meaning: **Slender**
Spiritual Connotation: **Holy**
Scripture: **Leviticus 26:12** NKJV
*I will walk among you and be your God,
and you shall be My people.*

KEELY, Kealey, Kealy, Keelee, Keeleigh, Keelie, Keely, Keilee, Kieley

Language/Cultural Origin: **Gaelic**
Inherent Meaning: **Beautiful**
Spiritual Connotation: **Trusting**
Scripture: **Proverbs 30:5** NKJV
*Every word of God is pure; He is a shield
to those who put their trust in Him.*

KEENA, Kina

Language/Cultural Origin: **Irish**
Inherent Meaning: **Brave**
Spiritual Connotation: **Given Strength**
Scripture: **Acts 28:15** NKJV
*When Paul saw them, he thanked God
and took courage.*

KEENAN, Keanan, Keenen, Keenon, Kienan, Kienon

Language/Cultural Origin: **Irish**
Inherent Meaning: **Little Commander**
Spiritual Connotation: **Honored**
Scripture: **Isaiah 12:2** NKJV
*Behold, God is my salvation, I will trust
and not be afraid; for YAH, the LORD,
is my strength and song; He also has
become my salvation.*

KEIANNA, Kayana, Kayanna, Keiana (see also Kiana, Kiona, Quiana)

Language/Cultural Origin: **Japanese**
Inherent Meaning: **Reverent**
Spiritual Connotation: **Heir**
Scripture: **Hebrews 12:28** NKJV
*Therefore, since we are receiving a
kingdom which cannot be shaken, let us
have grace, by which we may serve God
acceptably with reverence and godly fear.*

KEIFFER, Keefer, Kieffer

Language/Cultural Origin: **German**
Inherent Meaning: **Barrel Maker**
Spiritual Connotation: **Beloved**
Scripture: **John 14:23** NKJV
*If anyone loves Me, he will keep My
word; and My Father will love him,
and We will come to him and make Our
home with him.*

KEIKO, Keiki

Language/Cultural Origin: **Japanese**
Inherent Meaning: **Happy Child**
Spiritual Connotation: **Chosen**
Scripture: **Psalm 65:4** NRSV
*Happy are those whom you choose and
bring near to live in your courts. We shall
be satisfied with the goodness of your
house, your holy temple.*

KEILA, see Kaela

KEILANI, Keilana, Keilanna (see also Kalani)

Language/Cultural Origin: **Hawaiian**
Inherent Meaning: **Glorious**
Spiritual Connotation: **Likeness of God**
Scripture: **2 Corinthians 3:18** NLT
*As the Spirit of the Lord works within us,
we become more and more like him and
reflect his glory even more.*

KEISHA, Keesha, Keeshawna, Keisha, Kesha, Keshia, Keshonda, Keysha, Kiesha, Kisha (see also Queisha)

Language/Cultural Origin: **American**
Inherent Meaning: **Beautiful Woman**
Spiritual Connotation: **Gentle**
Scripture: **1 Peter 3:4** TLB

*Be beautiful inside, in your hearts, with
the lasting charm of a gentle and quiet
spirit that is so precious to God.*

KEITA, Keeta
Language/Cultural Origin: **Scottish**
Inherent Meaning: **Enclosed Place**
Spiritual Connotation: **Joyful**
Scripture: **Zechariah 2:10** RSV
*Sing and rejoice, O daughter of Zion; for
lo, I come and I will dwell in the midst of
you, says the LORD.*

KEITH, Keath
Language/Cultural Origin: **Scottish**
Inherent Meaning: **From the Place of Battle**
Spiritual Connotation: **Brave**
Scripture: **Galatians 5:25** NKJV
*If we live in the Spirit, let us also walk in
the Spirit.*

KELBY, Kelbee, Kelbey, Kellby
Language/Cultural Origin: **Old German**
Inherent Meaning: **From the Spring Farm**
Spiritual Connotation: **Petition**
Scripture: **Matthew 18:20** NKJV
*For where two or three are gathered
together in My name, I am there in the
midst of them.*

KELISSA, Kalisa, Kalissa, Kelisa
Language/Cultural Origin: **English**
Inherent Meaning: **Fighter**
Spiritual Connotation: **Witness**
Scripture: **1 Timothy 6:12** NKJV
*Fight the good fight of faith, lay hold
on eternal life, to which you were also
called.*

KELITA, Kelitta, Kellita
✎ Language/Cultural Origin: **Hebrew**
Inherent Meaning: **Poverty**
Spiritual Connotation: **Unselfish**
Scripture: **John 12:8** NCV
*You will always have the poor with you,
but you will not always have me.*

KELLEN, Kellan, Kellin, Kellon, Kellyn (see also Kallen)
Language/Cultural Origin: **English**
Inherent Meaning: **Mighty Warrior**
Spiritual Connotation: **Triumphant**
Scripture: **Jeremiah 50:9** NKJV

*Their arrows shall be like those of an
expert warrior; none shall return in vain.*

KELLER, Keler
Language/Cultural Origin: **Irish**
Inherent Meaning: **Little Friend**
Spiritual Connotation: **Selfless**
Scripture: **John 15:13** NASB
*Greater love has no one than this, that
one lay down his life for his friends.*

KELLY, Keli, Kelia, Keliana, Kelianna, Kellee, Kelley, Kelli, Kellia, Kelliana, Kellie
Language/Cultural Origin: **Irish**
Inherent Meaning: **Warrior**
Spiritual Connotation: **Loyal and Brave**
Scripture: **Proverbs 2:7** NKJV
*He stores up sound wisdom for the
upright; He is a shield to those who walk
uprightly.*

KELSEY, Kelcea, Kelcee, Kelcey, Kelcie, Kelcy, Kellsea, Kellsee, Kellsie, Kelsee, Kelsi, Kelsie, Kelsy
Language/Cultural Origin: **Old Norse**
Inherent Meaning: **From Ship Island**
Spiritual Connotation: **Malleable**
Scripture: **Jeremiah 18:6** NKJV
*Look, as the clay is in the potter's hand,
so are you in My hand, O house of
Israel!*

KELVIN, Kelvan, Kelvyn
Language/Cultural Origin: **Celtic**
Inherent Meaning: **From the Narrow River**
Spiritual Connotation: **Reasonable**
Scripture: **Psalm 119:130** NKJV
*The entrance of Your words gives light; it
gives understanding to the simple.*

KEMP, Khemp
Language/Cultural Origin: **English**
Inherent Meaning: **Champion**
Spiritual Connotation: **Zealous**
Scripture: **Psalm 19:5** NCV
*The sun comes out like a bridegroom
from his bedroom. It rejoices like an
athlete eager to run a race.*

KENDA, Kendi, Kendie, Kennda, Kindi, Kinnda, Kynda
Language/Cultural Origin: **English**
Inherent Meaning: **Water Baby**
Spiritual Connotation: **Pure**
Scripture: **2 Corinthians 11:2** NLT
I am jealous for you with the jealousy of God himself. For I promised you as a pure bride to one husband, Christ.

KENDALL, Kendahl, Kendal, Kendel, Kendell, Kindal, Kindall, Kyndal, Kyndall
Language/Cultural Origin: **English**
Inherent Meaning: **From the Clear Valley**
Spiritual Connotation: **Thankful**
Scripture: **Psalm 126:3** NKJV
The LORD has done great things for us, and we are glad.

KENDRA, Kenndra, Kindra, Kyndra
Language/Cultural Origin: **English**
Inherent Meaning: **Understanding**
Spiritual Connotation: **Filled With Wisdom**
Scripture: **Proverbs 24:3** NKJV
Through wisdom a house is built, and by understanding it is established.

KENDRE, Kendrae, Kendré, Kendrei (see also Keandre)
Language/Cultural Origin: **American**
Inherent Meaning: **Strong**
Spiritual Connotation: **Victorious**
Scripture: **Joshua 10:25** NKJV
Do not be afraid, nor be dismayed; be strong and of good courage, for thus the LORD will do to all your enemies against whom you fight.

KENDRICK, Kendric, Kendrik (see also Kenrick)
Language/Cultural Origin: **Celtic**
Inherent Meaning: **Royal Chief**
Spiritual Connotation: **Subject of God**
Scripture: **Deuteronomy 11:1** NKJV
Therefore you shall love the LORD your God, and keep His charge, His statutes, His judgments, and His commandments always.

KENEESE, Kenese, Keniece, Keniese, Kennise
Language/Cultural Origin: **English**
Inherent Meaning: **Fair**
Spiritual Connotation: **Companion**
Scripture: **Psalm 55:14** NASB
We who had sweet fellowship together, walked in the house of God in the throng.

KENEISHA, Kaneisha, Kaneshia, Keneesha, Keneshia, Kenishia, Kennesha, Kennisha, Kineesha, Kineisha, Kinesha, Kineshia (see also Quaneisha)
Language/Cultural Origin: **American**
Inherent Meaning: **Beautiful Woman**
Spiritual Connotation: **Promise**
Scripture: **Isaiah 4:2** NKJV
In that day the Branch of the LORD shall be beautiful and glorious; and the fruit of the earth shall be excellent and appealing.

KENNAN, Kenan, Kennen, Kennon
Language/Cultural Origin: **Scottish**
Inherent Meaning: **Little Ken**
Spiritual Connotation: **Encourager**
Scripture: **1 Thessalonians 3:2** NKJV
To establish you and encourage you concerning your faith.

KENNEDY, Kenadee, Kenedy, Kennady
Language/Cultural Origin: **Irish**
Inherent Meaning: **Ugly-Headed**
Spiritual Connotation: **Obedient**
Scripture: **2 John 1:9** NCV
But whoever continues to follow the teaching of Christ has both the Father and the Son.

KENNETH, Ken, Keneth, Kenney, Kennith, Kenny
Language/Cultural Origin: **Old English**
Inherent Meaning: **Royal Oath**
Spiritual Connotation: **Trustworthy**
Scripture: **Luke 19:17** NRSV
Well done, good slave! Because you have been trustworthy in a very small thing, take charge of ten cities.

KENRICK, Kenric, Kenrik (see also Kendrick)
Language/Cultural Origin: Old English
Inherent Meaning: Bold Ruler
Spiritual Connotation: Loyal
Scripture: Psalms 119:112 NKJV
I have inclined my heart to perform Your statutes forever, to the very end.

KENT, Khent
Language/Cultural Origin: Welsh
Inherent Meaning: Radiant
Spiritual Connotation: Wise
Scripture: Colossians 3:16 NKJV
Let the word of Christ dwell in you richly in all wisdom.

KENYA, Kenia, Kenja
Language/Cultural Origin: Hebrew
Inherent Meaning: Animal Horn
Spiritual Connotation: Accountable
Scripture: Hebrews 10:24 NKJV
And let us consider one another in order to stir up love and good works, but exhorting one another.

KENYON, Kenyan
Language/Cultural Origin: Irish
Inherent Meaning: Blond/White-Haired
Spiritual Connotation: Righteous
Scripture: Philippians 1:27 NRSV
Only, live your life in a manner worthy of the gospel of Christ.

KENZIE, Kensie, Kenzy, Kinzie (see also Mackenzie)
Language/Cultural Origin: English
Inherent Meaning: Child of the Wise Leader
Spiritual Connotation: Destined
Scripture: Isaiah 11:2 NASB
The Spirit of the LORD will rest on Him, the spirit of wisdom and understanding, the spirit of counsel and strength, the spirit of knowledge and the fear of the LORD.

KEON, Keion, Keionne, Keón, Keyon
Language/Cultural Origin: Irish
Inherent Meaning: God Is Gracious
Spiritual Connotation: Blessed
Scripture: 1 Corinthians 1:4 RSV
I give thanks to God always for you because of the grace of God which was given you in Christ Jesus.

KERANI, Kera, Kura, Kurani
Language/Cultural Origin: Indo-Pakistani
Inherent Meaning: Sacred Bells
Spiritual Connotation: Protected
Scripture: Psalm 23:5 NKJV
You prepare a table before me in the presence of my enemies; You anoint my head with oil; my cup runs over.

KERENSA, Karensa, Karenza, Kerenza
Language/Cultural Origin: Cornish
Inherent Meaning: Loving
Spiritual Connotation: Beloved
Scripture: Isaiah 43:4 NCV
Because you are precious to me, because I give you honor and love you . . . I will give other nations to save your life.

KERMIT, Kermet, Kermie
Language/Cultural Origin: Irish
Inherent Meaning: Free of Envy
Spiritual Connotation: Steadfast
Scripture: Isaiah 33:5-6 NKJV
The LORD is exalted, for He dwells on high; He has filled Zion with justice and righteousness. Wisdom and knowledge will be the stability of your times.

KERN, Kerne
Language/Cultural Origin: Irish
Inherent Meaning: Dark
Spiritual Connotation: Righteous
Scripture: Romans 12:21 NKJV
Do not be overcome by evil, but overcome evil with good.

KEROS, Karos
Language/Cultural Origin: Hebrew
Inherent Meaning: Reed of a Weaver's Beam
Spiritual Connotation: Gifted
Scripture: Exodus 35:35 NRSV
He has filled them with skill to do every kind of work done . . . by any sort of artisan or skilled designer.

KERRIANNE, Karriann, Karrianne, Keriann, Kerianne, Kerriann,

Kerryann, Kerryanne (see also Karianne)

Language/Cultural Origin: English
Inherent Meaning: Grace of the People
Spiritual Connotation: Child of Grace
Scripture: Romans 9:8 NCV
Abraham's true children are those who become God's children because of the promise God made to Abraham.

KERRY, Kearie, Keary, Keree, Kerey, Keri, Kerrey, Kerri, Kerrick, Kerrie (see also Carey, Cary)

Language/Cultural Origin: Irish
Inherent Meaning: Dark-Haired
Spiritual Connotation: Diligent
Scripture: Colossians 3:23 NKJV
And whatever you do, do it heartily, as to the Lord and not to men.

KERSEN, Kersan, Kersun

Language/Cultural Origin: Indonesian
Inherent Meaning: Cherry
Spiritual Connotation: Destined
Scripture: Isaiah 27:6 NASB
In the days to come Jacob will take root, Israel will blossom and sprout; and they will fill the whole world with fruit.

KERSTEN, see Kirsten

KESHAWN, Keshaun, Keshon, Keyshaun, Keyshawn

Language/Cultural Origin: American
Inherent Meaning: God Is Gracious
Spiritual Connotation: Forgiven
Scripture: Psalm 116:5 RSV
Gracious is the LORD, and righteous; our God is merciful.

KESHIA, see Keisha

KESSIE, Kessa, Kessey, Kessi, Kessia, Kessiah

Language/Cultural Origin: Ashanti
Inherent Meaning: Chubby Baby
Spiritual Connotation: Nourished
Scripture: 1 Peter 2:2 NRSV
Like newborn infants, long for the pure, spiritual milk, so that by it you may grow into salvation.

KESTER, Kesster

Language/Cultural Origin: English
Inherent Meaning: Bearer of Christ
Spiritual Connotation: Servant
Scripture: Mark 8:34 NRSV
If any want to become my followers, let them deny themselves and take up their cross and follow me.

KETURAH, Keturia, Keturyah (see also Katurah)

Language/Cultural Origin: Hebrew
Inherent Meaning: Incense
Spiritual Connotation: Holy
Scripture: Psalm 141:2 NCV
Let my prayer be like incense placed before you, and my praise like the evening sacrifice.

KEVIN, Kev, Keven, Kévin, Kevinn, Kevon (see also Cavan)

Language/Cultural Origin: Irish
Inherent Meaning: Handsome
Spiritual Connotation: Honored
Scripture: Psalm 91:15 NKJV
He shall call upon Me, and I will answer him; I will be with him in trouble; I will deliver him and honor him.

KEVYN, Kevan, Kevynn

Language/Cultural Origin: Irish
Inherent Meaning: Beautiful
Spiritual Connotation: Attractive
Scripture: Song of Songs 2:14 NASB
Let me see your form, let me hear your voice; for your voice is sweet, and your form is lovely.

KEZIA, Kazia, Kaziah, Ketzia, Ketziah, Keziah, Kizzie, Kizzy

Language/Cultural Origin: Hebrew
Inherent Meaning: Cinnamonlike Bark
Spiritual Connotation: Valuable
Scripture: Luke 12:24 NKJV
Consider the ravens. . . . God feeds them. Of how much more value are you than the birds?

KHALID, Khaled, Khälid

Language/Cultural Origin: Middle Eastern
Inherent Meaning: Eternal
Spiritual Connotation: Divine

Scripture: **John 6:51** NRSV
*I am the living bread that came down
from heaven.*

KHAN, Khanh (see also Quanah)
Language/Cultural Origin: **Turkish**
Inherent Meaning: **Prince**
Spiritual Connotation: **Promise**
Scripture: **Psalm 45:16** NASB
*In place of your fathers will be your sons;
You shall make them princes in all the
earth.*

**KHRISTIAN, KHRISTOPHER, see
Christian, Christopher**

KIA, Kiah
Language/Cultural Origin: **Nigerian**
Inherent Meaning: **Beginning of the Season**
Spiritual Connotation: **Sign**
Scripture: **Psalm 104:19** NRSV
*You have made the moon to mark the sea-
sons; the sun knows its time for setting.*

**KIANA, Keanna, Keiana, Kianna,
Kiauna, Kiaunna (see also
Keianna, Kiona, Quiana)**
Language/Cultural Origin: **American**
Inherent Meaning: **Grace of God**
Spiritual Connotation: **Restored**
Scripture: **Isaiah 30:18** NKJV
*Therefore the LORD will wait, that He
may be gracious to you; and therefore He
will be exalted, that He may have mercy
on you.*

KIARIA, Kiariah, Kiariana, Kiarianna
Language/Cultural Origin: **Japanese**
Inherent Meaning: **Fortunate**
Spiritual Connotation: **Blessed**
Scripture: **Ruth 3:10** NKJV
Blessed are you of the LORD, my daughter!

KIELE, Kiela, Kieli
Language/Cultural Origin: **Hawaiian**
Inherent Meaning: **Fragrant Blossom**
Spiritual Connotation: **Sacrifice**
Scripture: **2 Corinthians 2:15** NKJV
*For we are to God the fragrance of
Christ among those who are being saved
and among those who are perishing.*

KIERA, Kiara, Kiarra, Kierlyn,

**Kierlynn, Kierra (see also Keara,
Kira, Kyrie)**
Language/Cultural Origin: **Irish**
Inherent Meaning: **Little and Dark**
Spiritual Connotation: **Contemplative**
Scripture: **Psalm 46:10** NKJV
*Be still, and know that I am God; I will
be exalted among the nations, I will be
exalted in the earth!*

**KIERAN, Keiran, Kernan, Kiernan,
Kieron**
Language/Cultural Origin: **Irish**
Inherent Meaning: **Little**
Spiritual Connotation: **Blessed**
Scripture: **Proverbs 3:13** NKJV
*Happy is the man who finds wisdom, and
the man who gains understanding.*

KILEY, Kilee, Kileigh (see also Kylie)
Language/Cultural Origin: **Irish**
Inherent Meaning: **Attractive**
Spiritual Connotation: **Desirable**
Scripture: **Zechariah 9:17** NLT
*How wonderful and beautiful they will be!
The young men and women will thrive on
the abundance of grain and new wine.*

KILLIAN, Kilian
Language/Cultural Origin: **Irish**
Inherent Meaning: **Little Warrior**
Spiritual Connotation: **Attentive**
Scripture: **1 Corinthians 14:8** NLT
*And if the bugler doesn't sound a clear
call, how will the soldiers know they are
being called to battle?*

KIMANA, Kimanna
Language/Cultural Origin: **Shushone**
Inherent Meaning: **Butterfly**
Spiritual Connotation: **Unchained**
Scripture: **Galatians 5:1** NASB
*It was for freedom that Christ set us free;
therefore keep standing firm and do not
be subject again to a yoke of slavery.*

KIMBALL, Kim, Kimbal, Kimble
Language/Cultural Origin: **Celtic**
Inherent Meaning: **Ruler**
Spiritual Connotation: **Subject of God**
Scripture: **Psalm 29:2** NKJV
Give unto the LORD the glory due to His

name; worship the LORD in the beauty of holiness.

KIMBERLY, Kim, Kimba, Kimber, Kimberlea, Kimberlee, Kimberleigh, Kimberley, Kimberli, Kimberlyn, Kimberlynn, Kimbria, Kym, Kymberlee, Kymberly
Language/Cultural Origin: **Old English**
Inherent Meaning: **From the Royal Meadow**
Spiritual Connotation: **Seeker of Truth**
Scripture: **Psalm 119:2** NKJV
Blessed are those who keep His testimonies, who seek Him with the whole heart!

KIMI, Kimia, Kimie, Kimika, Kimiko
Language/Cultural Origin: **Japanese**
Inherent Meaning: **Peerless**
Spiritual Connotation: **Honored**
Scripture: **Hebrews 8:11** NRSV
And they shall not teach one another or say to each other, know the Lord, for they shall all know me, from the least of them to the greatest.

KINEISHA, see Keneisha

KINSEY, Kingsley, Kingsly, Kinsea, Kinsee, Kinslea, Kinslee, Kinsleigh
Language/Cultural Origin: **Old English**
Inherent Meaning: **Relative**
Spiritual Connotation: **Protected**
Scripture: **Ruth 3:13** NASB
Remain this night, and when morning comes, if he will redeem you, good; let him redeem you.

KIOKO, Kiyoko (see also Kyoko)
Language/Cultural Origin: **Japanese**
Inherent Meaning: **Happy Child**
Spiritual Connotation: **Respectful**
Scripture: **Proverbs 29:18** NASB
Where there is no vision, the people are unrestrained, but happy is he who keeps the law.

KIONA, Kionia, Kionna, Kionya (see also Keianna, Kiana, Quiana)
Language/Cultural Origin: **Native American**
Inherent Meaning: **Dark Hills**
Spiritual Connotation: **Preserved**
Scripture: **Psalm 121:1-2** NASB
I will lift up my eyes to the mountains;

from whence shall my help come? My help comes from the LORD, who made heaven and earth.

KIPP, Kip, Kippar, Kipper, Kippie, Kippy
Language/Cultural Origin: **English**
Inherent Meaning: **From the Pointed Hill**
Spiritual Connotation: **Near the Heart of God**
Scripture: **Exodus 24:13** RSV
So Moses rose with his servant Joshua, and Moses went up into the mountain of God.

KIRA, Kiri, Kiria, Kiriana (see also Keara, Kiera, Kyrie)
Language/Cultural Origin: **Bulgarian**
Inherent Meaning: **Throne**
Spiritual Connotation: **Temple of God**
Scripture: **Isaiah 37:16** NRSV
O LORD of hosts, God of Israel, who are enthroned above the cherubim, you are God, you alone.

KIRAL, Kieral
Language/Cultural Origin: **Turkish**
Inherent Meaning: **King**
Spiritual Connotation: **Obedient**
Scripture: **1 Samuel 13:4** TLB
Saul sounded the call to arms throughout Israel. He announced that he had destroyed the Philistine garrison.

KIRBY, Kerbey, Kerbie, Kerby, Kirbey, Kirbie
Language/Cultural Origin: **Anglo-Saxon**
Inherent Meaning: **From the Church Village**
Spiritual Connotation: **Follower of God**
Scripture: **Psalm 1:3** NKJV
He shall be like a tree planted by the rivers of water, that brings forth its fruit in its season.

KIRIMA, Kireema
Language/Cultural Origin: **Eskimo**
Inherent Meaning: **Hill**
Spiritual Connotation: **Joyful Praise**
Scripture: **Psalm 98:8** NASB
Let the rivers clap their hands, let the mountains sing together for joy.

KIRI, Kiree, Kirie, Kirey (see also Kuri)

Language/Cultural Origin: **Cambodian**
Inherent Meaning: **Mountain**
Spiritual Connotation: **Abundance**
Scripture: **Amos 9:13** NCV
The time is coming when there will be all kinds of food. People will still be harvesting crops when it's time to plow again.

KIRK, Kerk

Language/Cultural Origin: **Old Norse**
Inherent Meaning: **From the Church**
Spiritual Connotation: **Glad in Heart**
Scripture: **Psalm 4:7** TLB
Yes, the gladness you have given me is far greater than their joys at harvest time as they gaze at their bountiful crops.

KIRSI, Kirsea, Kirsee

Language/Cultural Origin: **Indo-Pakistani**
Inherent Meaning: **Blossoming Flower**
Spiritual Connotation: **Blessed**
Scripture: **Hosea 14:5** NCV
I will be like the dew to Israel, and they will blossom like a lily.

KIRSTEN, Keirstan, Kersten, Kerstin, Kerstine, Kerston, Kerstyn, Kiersten, Kirstan, Kirstien, Kirstin, Kirstine, Kirston, Kirstyn, Kjersten, Kurstan, Kursten, Kurstyn (see also Karsten)

Language/Cultural Origin: **Greek**
Inherent Meaning: **Follower of Christ**
Spiritual Connotation: **Anointed**
Scripture: **2 Chronicles 6:42** NLT
O LORD God, do not reject your anointed one. Remember your unfailing love for your servant David.

KIRSTY, Kersta, Kerstee, Kersti, Kerstie, Kersty, Kirsta, Kirstee, Kirsti, Kirstie, Kjersti

Language/Cultural Origin: **Scandinavian**
Inherent Meaning: **Follower of Christ**
Spiritual Connotation: **Anointed**
Scripture: **Psalm 28:8** RSV
The LORD is the strength of his people, he is the saving refuge of his anointed.

KISA, Keesa, Keeson, Kison, Kissa

Language/Cultural Origin: **Russian**
Inherent Meaning: **Kitten**
Spiritual Connotation: **Formed of God**
Scripture: **Genesis 2:20** NCV
The man gave names to all the tame animals, to the birds in the sky, and to all the wild animals.

KISH

☞ Language/Cultural Origin: **Hebrew**
Inherent Meaning: **Straw**
Spiritual Connotation: **Faithful**
Scripture: **1 Corinthians 3:14** NRSV
If what has been built on the foundation survives, the builder will receive a reward.

KJELL, Kjele

Language/Cultural Origin: **Swedish**
Inherent Meaning: **Landworker**
Spiritual Connotation: **Blessed**
Scripture: **Psalm 80:9** TLB
You cleared the ground and tilled the soil, and we took root and filled the land.

KLARISSA, Klaresa, Klaressa, Klarisa, Klarissc, Klarrisa, Klarrissa, Klerissa (see also Clarissa)

Language/Cultural Origin: **German**
Inherent Meaning: **Bright**
Spiritual Connotation: **Glorious Reflection**
Scripture: **Psalm 148:3** NRSV
Praise him, sun and moon; praise him, all you shining stars!

KLAUS, Claas, Clas, Claus, Klaas, Klas, Klause

Language/Cultural Origin: **German**
Inherent Meaning: **Victory of the People**
Spiritual Connotation: **Triumphant**
Scripture: **Deuteronomy 20:4** NLT
For the LORD your God is going with you! He will fight for you against your enemies, and he will give you victory!

KNOX, Knoxx

Language/Cultural Origin: **Old English**
Inherent Meaning: **From the Hills**
Spiritual Connotation: **Peaceful**
Scripture: **Psalm 72:3** NASB

Let the mountains bring peace to the people, and the hills in righteousness.

KNUTE, Canute, Knut
Language/Cultural Origin: **Old Norse**
Inherent Meaning: **Knot**
Spiritual Connotation: **Victorious**
Scripture: **Psalm 18:32** NKJV
It is God who arms me with strength, and makes my way perfect.

KOBI, see Coby

KODY, see Cody

KOHANA, Kohanna
Language/Cultural Origin: **Lakota**
Inherent Meaning: **Speedy**
Spiritual Connotation: **Efficient**
Scripture: **Psalm 147:15** NRSV
He sends out his command to the earth; his word runs swiftly.

KOKO, Kokko (see also Coco)
Language/Cultural Origin: **Japanese**
Inherent Meaning: **Stork**
Spiritual Connotation: **Created**
Scripture: **Genesis 1:20** NASB
Let the waters teem with swarms of living creatures, and let birds fly above the earth in the open expanse of the heavens.

KOLEY, see Coley

KOLYA, Kollya
Language/Cultural Origin: **Russian**
Inherent Meaning: **Victory of the People**
Spiritual Connotation: **Exalted**
Scripture: **Psalm 44:7** NLT
It is you who gives us victory over our enemies; it is you who humbles those who hate us.

KONA, Konia, Konya
Language/Cultural Origin: **Hawaiian**
Inherent Meaning: **Lady**
Spiritual Connotation: **Loving**
Scripture: **2 John 1:5** NASB
And now I ask you, lady, not as writing to you a new commandment, but the one which we have had from the beginning, that we love one another.

KONSTANCE, see Constance

KORAH, Korrah
Language/Cultural Origin: **Hebrew**
Inherent Meaning: **Baldness**
Spiritual Connotation: **Covenant**
Scripture: **Genesis 9:15** NIV
Never again will the waters become a flood to destroy all life.

KORDELL, see Cordell

KOREN, Coren, Corren, Korren
Language/Cultural Origin: **Hebrew**
Inherent Meaning: **Shining**
Spiritual Connotation: **Image of Christ**
Scripture: **1 John 2:8** NKJV
The darkness is passing away, and the true light is already shining.

KOREY, Koree, Korrey, Korry, Kory (see also Corey)
Language/Cultural Origin: **English**
Inherent Meaning: **From the Hollow**
Spiritual Connotation: **Heir**
Scripture: **Psalm 2:8** NKJV
Ask of Me, and I will give you the nations for your inheritance, and the ends of the earth for your possession.

KORINA, Koreen, Koreena, Koren, Korey, Kori, Korianna, Korie, Korine, Korri, Korrie, Korrin, Korrina, Korrine, Koryn (see also Cora, Cori, Corina, Corinne, Kaarina, Karina, Korah)
Language/Cultural Origin: **Greek**
Inherent Meaning: **Maiden**
Spiritual Connotation: **Pure**
Scripture: **1 Peter 1:22** NASB
Since you have in obedience to the truth purified your souls for a sincere love of the brethren, fervently love one another from the heart.

KORISSA, see Corissa

KORTNEY, see Courtney

KRISSY, Khris, Kris, Krissey, Krissi
Language/Cultural Origin: **American**
Inherent Meaning: **Follower of Christ**
Spiritual Connotation: **Disciple**
Scripture: **Matthew 28:19** NKJV

*Go therefore and make disciples of all
the nations, baptizing them in the name
of the Father and of the Son and of the
Holy Spirit.*

**KRISTA, Khrissa, Khrista, Khryssa,
Khrysta, Krisa, Kriska, Krissa,
Kristia, Kryssa, Krysta (see also
Christa, Kirsty)**
Language/Cultural Origin: **Latvian**
Inherent Meaning: **Follower of Christ**
Spiritual Connotation: **Disciple**
Scripture: **Luke 6:20** RSV
*And he lifted up his eyes on his disciples,
and said: "Blessed are you poor, for
yours is the kingdom of God."*

**KRISTEN, Kristan, Kristi, Kristie,
Kristii, Kristin, Kristy, Kristyn,
Krysten, Krysti, Krystin (see also
Christen, Karsten, Kirsten)**
Language/Cultural Origin: **Scandinavian**
Inherent Meaning: **Follower of Christ**
Spiritual Connotation: **Anointed**
Scripture: **Psalm 84:9** NRSV
*Behold our shield, O God; look on the
face of your anointed.*

KRISTIAN, see Christian

**KRISTIANA, Kristi-Ann,
Kristianna, Kristi-Anna,
Kristianne, Kristyana, Kristyanna,
Krystiana, Krystianna**
Language/Cultural Origin: **Greek**
Inherent Meaning: **Follower of Christ**
Spiritual Connotation: **Joyful**
Scripture: **Luke 11:37** NASB
*Now when He had spoken, a Pharisee
asked Him to have lunch with him; and
He went in, and reclined at the table.*

**KRISTINA, Khristina, Kristeena,
Krysteena, Krystina, Krystyna
(see also Christina)**
Language/Cultural Origin: **Swedish**
Inherent Meaning: **Follower of Christ**
Spiritual Connotation: **Near to God**
Scripture: **John 6:3** NKJV
*And Jesus went up on the mountain, and
there He sat with His disciples.*

**KRISTINE, Kristeen, Kristene,
Krystine (see also Christine)**
Language/Cultural Origin: **Norwegian**
Inherent Meaning: **Follower of Christ**
Spiritual Connotation: **Chosen**
Scripture: **John 8:31-32** NRSV
*If you continue in my word, you are
truly my disciples; and you will know the
truth, and the truth will make you free.*

KRISTOPHER, see Christopher

KRUIN, Kruan
Language/Cultural Origin: **Afrikaans**
Inherent Meaning: **Mountain Top**
Spiritual Connotation: **Sacred**
Scripture: **Ezekiel 43:12** RSV
*This is the law of the temple: the whole
territory round about upon the top of the
mountain shall be most holy.*

KRUZ, see Cruz

**KRYSTAL, Kristal, Kristalin, Kristall,
Kristalyn, Krisstal, Kristal,
Kristalee, Kristel, Kristelle,
Krystall, Krystallin, Krystel,
Krystell, Krystilin, Krystol,
Krystylyn (see also Crystal)**
Language/Cultural Origin: **American**
Inherent Meaning: **Clear, Sparkling**
Spiritual Connotation: **Blessed**
Scripture: **Isaiah 54:12** NASB
*Moreover, I will make your battlements
of rubies, and your gates of crystal, and
your entire wall of precious stones.*

**KRYSTALYNN, Krystaleen,
Krystalina, Kristalyn, Kristilynn,
Krystalin**
Language/Cultural Origin: **English**
Inherent Meaning: **Perfectly Clear Water**
Spiritual Connotation: **Symbol**
Scripture: **Revelation 21:21** NASB
*And the twelve gates were twelve pearls;
each one of the gates was a single pearl.
And the street of the city was pure gold,
like transparent glass.*

KUMI, Kumie, Kumika, Kumiko
Language/Cultural Origin: **Japanese**
Inherent Meaning: **Braided Hair**
Spiritual Connotation: **Lovely Sacrifice**

Scripture: **Luke 7:38** TLB
Going in, she knelt behind him at his feet, weeping, with her tears falling down upon his feet; and she wiped them off with her hair and kissed them and poured the perfume on them.

KURI, Kuree, Kurie, Kurii, Kurri (see also Kiri)
Language/Cultural Origin: **Japanese**
Inherent Meaning: **Chestnut**
Spiritual Connotation: **Expectant**
Scripture: **Song of Songs 6:11** NCV
I went down into the orchard of nut trees to see the blossoms of the valley, to look for buds on the vines, to see if the pomegranate trees had bloomed.

KURT, Kort (see also Curtis)
Language/Cultural Origin: **German**
Inherent Meaning: **Bold Counselor**
Spiritual Connotation: **Wise and Just**
Scripture: **Colossians 2:3** NLT
In him lie hidden all the treasures of wisdom and knowledge.

KWAN, Kwanan
Language/Cultural Origin: **Korean**
Inherent Meaning: **Strong**
Spiritual Connotation: **Upright**
Scripture: **1 Corinthians 10:13** NLT
But remember that the temptations that come into your life are no different from what others experience. And God is faithful.

KYLA, Kylah, Kylla, Kyllah (see also Cayla, Kaela, Kaila, Keila)
Language/Cultural Origin: **Yiddish**
Inherent Meaning: **Crowned**
Spiritual Connotation: **Purchased**
Scripture: **Hebrews 2:9** NASB

But we do see . . . Jesus, because of the suffering of death crowned with glory and honor, that by the grace of God He might taste death for everyone.

KYLE, Kile, Kylan, Kylen, Kyler
Language/Cultural Origin: **Gaelic**
Inherent Meaning: **From the Strait**
Spiritual Connotation: **Perceptive Insight**
Scripture: **Proverbs 15:33** NKJV
The fear of the LORD is the instruction of wisdom, and before honor is humility.

KYLIE, Kylee, Kyleigh, Kylen, Kylyn (see also Kiley)
Language/Cultural Origin: **Aboriginal**
Inherent Meaning: **Boomerang**
Spiritual Connotation: **Generous**
Scripture: **Ecclesiastes 11:1** NASB
Cast your bread on the surface of the waters, for you will find it after many days.

KYRIE, Kyra, Kyrah, Kyria, Kyriah (see also Keara, Kiera, Kira)
Language/Cultural Origin: **Greek**
Inherent Meaning: **Feminine, Ladylike**
Spiritual Connotation: **Tenderhearted**
Scripture: **2 John 1:5** NRSV
But now, dear lady, I ask you, not as though I were writing you a new commandment, but one we have had from the beginning, let us love one another.

KYOKO, Kyokoh (see also Kioko)
Language/Cultural Origin: **Japanese**
Inherent Meaning: **Mirror**
Spiritual Connotation: **Reflection**
Scripture: **1 Corinthians 13:12** NRSV
For now we see in a mirror, dimly, but then we will see face to face.

L

LABAN, Laben, Labon
Language/Cultural Origin: **Hebrew**
Inherent Meaning: **White**
Spiritual Connotation: **Glorious**
Scripture: **Matthew 28:3** NASB
And his appearance was like lightning, and his garment as white as snow.

LACEY, Lacee, Laci, Lacie, Lacy
Language/Cultural Origin: **Latin**
Inherent Meaning: **Joyful**
Spiritual Connotation: **Filled With Praise**
Scripture: **Psalm 98:4** RSV
Make a joyful noise to the LORD, all the earth; break forth into joyous song and sing praises!

LACHELLE, Lachele, Lachell
Language/Cultural Origin: **American/French**
Inherent Meaning: **Lock**
Spiritual Connotation: **Steadfast**
Scripture: **Revelation 2:17** NRSV
To everyone who conquers I will give . . . a white stone, and on the white stone is written a new name that no one knows except the one who receives it.

LACHLAN, Lachlann, Lochlan, Lochlann
Language/Cultural Origin: **Scottish**
Inherent Meaning: **From the Land of Lakes**
Spiritual Connotation: **Reverent**
Scripture: **Mark 4:41** NCV
The followers were very afraid and asked each other, "Who is this? Even the wind and the waves obey him!"

LACHLANA, Lachlanna, Lochlanna, Lochlanne
Language/Cultural Origin: **Scottish**
Inherent Meaning: **From the Land of Lakes**
Spiritual Connotation: **Strength Through Faith**
Scripture: **Mark 11:23** NASB
Whoever says to this mountain, Be taken up and cast into the sea, and does not doubt in his heart, but believes that what he says is going to happen, it shall be granted him.

LADA, Ladah
Language/Cultural Origin: **Russian**
Inherent Meaning: **Beauty**
Spiritual Connotation: **Useful**
Scripture: **Romans 10:15** NKJV
How beautiful are the feet of those who preach the gospel of peace, who bring glad tidings of good things!

LADONNA, La Donna, Ladona, Ladonia, Ladonya
Language/Cultural Origin: **American**
Inherent Meaning: **Refined Lady**
Spiritual Connotation: **Loving**
Scripture: **2 John 1:5** NRSV
But now, dear lady, I ask you, not as though I were writing you a new commandment, but one we have had from the beginning, let us love one another.

LAELA, see Layla

LAHELA, Lahaela, Lahaila
Language/Cultural Origin: **Hawaiian**
Inherent Meaning: **Lamb**
Spiritual Connotation: **Redeemed**
Scripture: **1 Peter 1:19** NLT
He paid for you with the precious lifeblood of Christ, the sinless, spotless Lamb of God.

LAINE, Laina, Lainee, Lainey (see also Lane)
Language/Cultural Origin: **French**
Inherent Meaning: **Brilliant**
Spiritual Connotation: **Righteous**
Scripture: **Proverbs 4:18** RSV
But the path of the righteous is like the light of dawn, which shines brighter and brighter until full day.

LAIRD, Layrd
Language/Cultural Origin: **Scottish**
Inherent Meaning: **Wealthy Landowner**
Spiritual Connotation: **Prosperous**
Scripture: **Proverbs 4:7** NKJV
Wisdom is the principal thing; therefore get wisdom. And in all your getting, get understanding.

LAKEISHA, Lakaisha, Lakasha, Lakecia, Lakeesha, Lakesha, Lakeshia, Lakesia, Lakeysha, Lakicia, Lakisha, Laqueisha, Laquesha, Laquiesha, Laquisha, Lekasha, Lekeesha, Lekeisha, Lekesha, Lekeshia, Lekicia, Lekisha
Language/Cultural Origin: **American**
Inherent Meaning: **Lovely**
Spiritual Connotation: **Thankful**
Scripture: **Psalm 27:4** NASB
One thing . . . I shall seek: That I may dwell in the house of the LORD all the days of my life, to behold the beauty of the LORD, and to meditate in His temple.

LAKENYA, Lakeena, Lakeenya, Lakena, Lakenia, Lakinya, Lekenya
Language/Cultural Origin: **American**
Inherent Meaning: **Horn**
Spiritual Connotation: **Symbol of Strength**
Scripture: **Psalm 89:17** NKJV
For You are the glory of their strength, and in Your favor our horn is exalted.

LAKIA, Lakita, Lakiya, Lakya
Language/Cultural Origin: **Middle Eastern**
Inherent Meaning: **Treasure Discovered**
Spiritual Connotation: **Wise**
Scripture: **Isaiah 33:6** NASB

And He will be the stability of your times, a wealth of salvation, wisdom and knowledge; the fear of the LORD is his treasure.

LAKRESHA, see Lucretia

LALA, Lalla
Language/Cultural Origin: **Slavic**
Inherent Meaning: **Tulip**
Spiritual Connotation: **Enduring**
Scripture: **Isaiah 40:8** NKJV
The grass withers, the flower fades, but the word of our God stands forever.

LAMAR, Lamarr, Lemar, Lemarr
Language/Cultural Origin: **Latin**
Inherent Meaning: **From the Sea**
Spiritual Connotation: **Preserved**
Scripture: **Psalm 139:9-10** NKJV
If I take the wings of the morning, and dwell in the uttermost parts of the sea, even there Your hand shall lead me, and Your right hand shall hold me.

LAMBERT, Lambard
Language/Cultural Origin: **Old German**
Inherent Meaning: **From the Bright Land**
Spiritual Connotation: **Protected**
Scripture: **Psalm 121:8** NKJV
The LORD shall preserve your going out and your coming in from this time forth, and even forevermore.

LAMOND, Lammond, Lemond
Language/Cultural Origin: **French**
Inherent Meaning: **From the Earth**
Spiritual Connotation: **Blessed**
Scripture: **Acts 3:25** NRSV
You are the descendants of the prophets and of the covenant that God gave to your ancestors.

LAMONT, Lamonte, Lemont
Language/Cultural Origin: **Old Norse**
Inherent Meaning: **Lawman**
Spiritual Connotation: **Fearless**
Scripture: **Haggai 2:5** NKJV
According to the word that I covenanted with you when you came out of Egypt, so My Spirit remains among you; do not fear!

LANA, Lanna, Lannah
Language/Cultural Origin: **Irish**

Inherent Meaning: **Attractive**
Spiritual Connotation: **Peaceful**
Scripture: **Psalm 37:3** NKJV
Trust in the LORD, and do good; dwell in the land, and feed on His faithfulness.

LANAE, Lanai, Lanay, Lannay
Language/Cultural Origin: **Hawaiian**
Inherent Meaning: **Buoyant**
Spiritual Connotation: **Full of Faith**
Scripture: **Matthew 14:31** RSV
Jesus immediately reached out his hand and caught him.

LANCE, Lantz, Launce
Language/Cultural Origin: **German**
Inherent Meaning: **From the Land**
Spiritual Connotation: **Witness**
Scripture: **Acts 13:47** NLT
For this is as the Lord commanded us when he said, I have made you a light to the Gentiles, to bring salvation to the farthest corners of the earth.

LANCELOT, Launcelot
Language/Cultural Origin: **Old French**
Inherent Meaning: **Attendant**
Spiritual Connotation: **God's Helper**
Scripture: **Ezekiel 18:31** NKJV
Get yourselves a new heart and a new spirit. For why should you die, O house of Israel?

LANDER, Landers
Language/Cultural Origin: **Basque**
Inherent Meaning: **Like a Lion**
Spiritual Connotation: **Powerful**
Scripture: **Genesis 49:9** NCV
Judah is like a young lion. . . . Like a lion, he stretches out and lies down to rest, and no one is brave enough to wake him.

LANDO, Landro
Language/Cultural Origin: **Portuguese**
Inherent Meaning: **From the Famous Land**
Spiritual Connotation: **Destined**
Scripture: **Acts 17:26** NLT
From one man he created all the nations throughout the whole earth.

LANDON, Landan, Landin
Language/Cultural Origin: **Old English**

Inherent Meaning: **From the Grassy Meadow**
Spiritual Connotation: **Comforted**
Scripture: **John 10:9** NRSV
I am the gate. Whoever enters by me will be saved, and will come in and go out and find pasture.

LANDRY, Landré
Language/Cultural Origin: **French**
Inherent Meaning: **Ruler**
Spiritual Connotation: **Subject of God**
Scripture: **Luke 1:33** NKJV
And He will reign over the house of Jacob forever, and of His kingdom there will be no end.

LANE, Laney, Lanie, Layne (see also Laine)
Language/Cultural Origin: **English**
Inherent Meaning: **Road**
Spiritual Connotation: **Eternal**
Scripture: **Matthew 7:14** NLT
But the gateway to life is small, and the road is narrow, and only a few ever find it.

LANG, Lange
Language/Cultural Origin: **Old Norse**
Inherent Meaning: **Tall**
Spiritual Connotation: **Lifted Up**
Scripture: **Psalm 18:33** NRSV
He made my feet like the feet of a deer, and set me secure on the heights.

LANGLEY, Langlee
Language/Cultural Origin: **Old English**
Inherent Meaning: **From the Long Meadow**
Spiritual Connotation: **Peaceful**
Scripture: **Psalm 147:8** RSV
He covers the heavens with clouds, he prepares rain for the earth, he makes grass grow upon the hills.

LANGSTON, Langsdon
Language/Cultural Origin: **Old English**
Inherent Meaning: **From the Tall Man's Town**
Spiritual Connotation: **Rescued**
Scripture: **Isaiah 49:9** NCV
You will tell the prisoners, "Come out of your prison." You will tell those in darkness, "Come into the light."

LANI, Lanata, Lanita
Language/Cultural Origin: **Hawaiian**
Inherent Meaning: **Heavenly**
Spiritual Connotation: **Thankful**
Scripture: **Psalm 111:3** NCV
*What he does is glorious and splendid,
and his goodness continues forever.*

LANNY, see Lawrence

LAQUISHA, see Lakeisha

LARA, Larah (see also Laura)
Language/Cultural Origin: **Latin**
Inherent Meaning: **Famous**
Spiritual Connotation: **God's Gracious Gift**
Scripture: **Romans 8:28** NKJV
*And we know that all things work
together for good to those who love God,
to those who are the called according to
His purpose.*

**LARAINE, Larain, Larayne, Larine,
Lauraine (see also Lorraine)**
Language/Cultural Origin: **Latin**
Inherent Meaning: **Freedom**
Spiritual Connotation: **Free Spirit**
Scripture: **Malachi 3:1** NKJV
*Behold, I send My messenger, and he
will prepare the way before Me.*

LARAMIE, Laramee
Language/Cultural Origin: **French**
Inherent Meaning: **Tears of Love**
Spiritual Connotation: **Vital**
Scripture: **Ecclesiastes 3:4** NKJV
*A time to weep, and a time to laugh; a
time to mourn, and a time to dance.*

LARI, Laree, Larey, Larii
Language/Cultural Origin: **English**
Inherent Meaning: **Bay**
Spiritual Connotation: **Protected**
Scripture: **Isaiah 4:6** NLT
*It will be a shelter from daytime heat and
a hiding place from storms and rain.*

LARINA, Larena
Language/Cultural Origin: **Greek**
Inherent Meaning: **Sea Bird**
Spiritual Connotation: **Free**
Scripture: **Matthew 6:26** NRSV
Look at the birds of the air; they neither

*sow nor reap . . . and yet your heavenly
Father feeds them. Are you not of more
value than they?*

LARISSA, Larisa, Laryssa
Language/Cultural Origin: **Greek**
Inherent Meaning: **Cheerful**
Spiritual Connotation: **Grateful**
Scripture: **James 5:13** NRSV
*Are any among you suffering? They should
pray. Are any cheerful? They should sing
songs of praise.*

LARK, Larke
Language/Cultural Origin: **English**
Inherent Meaning: **Skylark**
Spiritual Connotation: **Spiritual Freedom**
Scripture: **Galatians 5:1** NASB
*It was for freedom that Christ set us free;
therefore keep standing firm and do not
be subject again to a yoke of slavery.*

LARKIN, Larkan
Language/Cultural Origin: **Irish**
Inherent Meaning: **Fierce**
Spiritual Connotation: **Strength of God**
Scripture: **Psalm 29:4** NASB
*The voice of the LORD is powerful, the
voice of the LORD is majestic.*

LARRY, see Lawrence

LARS, Larsen, Larson, Larss, Larsson
Language/Cultural Origin: **Scandinavian**
Inherent Meaning: **Crowned With Honor**
Spiritual Connotation: **Redeemed**
Scripture: **Hebrews 2:9** NRSV
*But we do see Jesus, who . . . was . . .
now crowned with glory and honor
because of the suffering of death, so that
by the grace of God he might taste death
for everyone.*

**LASHONDA, Lashana, Lashandra,
Lashanna, Lashannon, Lashauna,
Lashaunda, Lashaundra,
Lashawnda, Lashawndra,
Lashawnia, Lashona, Lashondia,
Lashondra, Lashonna, Lashunda,
Lashundra, Leshandra, Leshondra,
Leshundra, Leshawna**
Language/Cultural Origin: **American**
Inherent Meaning: **God Is Gracious**

Spiritual Connotation: **Victorious**
Scripture: **Romans 16:20** NLT
The God of peace will soon crush Satan under your feet. May the grace of our Lord Jesus Christ be with you.

LATANYA, Latana, Latania, Latanja, Latanna, Latona, Latonia, Latonna, Latonya (see also Litonya)
Language/Cultural Origin: **American**
Inherent Meaning: **Queen**
Spiritual Connotation: **Righteous**
Scripture: **Psalm 45:6** NKJV
Your throne, O God, is forever and ever; a scepter of righteousness is the scepter of Your kingdom.

LATASHA, Latacia, Latashia, Lataysha, Letasha, Letashia
Language/Cultural Origin: **American**
Inherent Meaning: **Christmas Child**
Spiritual Connotation: **Witness of Christ**
Scripture: **Revelation 1:18** NCV
I am the One who lives; I was dead, but look, I am alive forever and ever! And I hold the keys to death and to the place of the dead.

LATAVIA, Latavya
Language/Cultural Origin: **Middle Eastern**
Inherent Meaning: **Pleasant**
Spiritual Connotation: **Wise**
Scripture: **Proverbs 2:10** NCV
Wisdom will come into your mind, and knowledge will be pleasing to you.

LATEEFAH, Latifa, Latifah
Language/Cultural Origin: **Hebrew**
Inherent Meaning: **Caress**
Spiritual Connotation: **Tender**
Scripture: **Matthew 5:5** NASB
Blessed are the gentle, for they shall inherit the earth.

LATHAM, Laith, Lathe
Language/Cultural Origin: **Old Norse**
Inherent Meaning: **From the Farmstead**
Spiritual Connotation: **Strong**
Scripture: **Micah 3:8** NKJV
But truly I am full of power by the Spirit of the LORD, and of justice and might, to declare to Jacob his transgression and to Israel his sin.

LATISHA, Latecia, Lateesha, Lateisha, Latishia, Latissa
Language/Cultural Origin: **Latin**
Inherent Meaning: **Gladness**
Spiritual Connotation: **Joyful**
Scripture: **Psalm 4:7** NLT
You have given me greater joy than those who have abundant harvests of grain and wine.

LATORIA, Latora, Latorya
Language/Cultural Origin: **American**
Inherent Meaning: **Victorious**
Spiritual Connotation: **Faithful**
Scripture: **1 John 5:4** NKJV
For whatever is born of God overcomes the world. And this is the victory that has overcome the world; our faith.

LATOYA, Latoiya, LaToya
Language/Cultural Origin: **American**
Inherent Meaning: **Victorious**
Spiritual Connotation: **Exalted**
Scripture: **Matthew 12:20** NLT
He will not crush those who are weak, or quench the smallest hope, until he brings full justice with his final victory.

LAURA, Lauralee, Laureana, Lauret, Laurette, Lauriana, Lauriane, Laurianna, Laurina, Lora, Lorah, Loretta, Lorra, Lorrah, Lorreta (see also Lara, Lori)
Language/Cultural Origin: **Latin**
Inherent Meaning: **Crowned With Honor**
Spiritual Connotation: **Victorious**
Scripture: **1 Thessalonians 4:4** NLT
Then each of you will control your body and live in holiness and honor.

LAUREL, Laural, Laurell, Laurelle
Language/Cultural Origin: **Latin**
Inherent Meaning: **Laurel**
Spiritual Connotation: **Faithful**
Scripture: **John 15:5** NRSV
I am the vine, you are the branches. Those who abide in me and I in them bear much fruit, because apart from me you can do nothing.

LAUREN, Lauran, Laurene, Laurin, Lauryn, Laurynn (see also Loren)
Language/Cultural Origin: **English**
Inherent Meaning: **Bay**
Spiritual Connotation: **Guarded of God**
Scripture: **Isaiah 25:4** TLB
But to the poor, O Lord, you are a refuge from the storm, a shadow from the heat.

LAURIE, see Lori

LAVEDA, Lavedia
Language/Cultural Origin: **Latin**
Inherent Meaning: **Purified**
Spiritual Connotation: **Blessed**
Scripture: **Psalm 84:11** NKJV
For the LORD God is a sun and shield; the LORD will give grace and glory; no good thing will He withhold from those who walk uprightly.

LAVERNE, LaVerne, Laverna
Language/Cultural Origin: **Latin**
Inherent Meaning: **Springtime**
Spiritual Connotation: **Peaceful**
Scripture: **Isaiah 9:7** NKJV
Of the increase of His government and peace there will be no end.

LAVINIA, Lavenia, Lavina
Language/Cultural Origin: **Latin**
Inherent Meaning: **Pure**
Spiritual Connotation: **Priceless**
Scripture: **Job 22:26** NKJV
For then you will have your delight in the Almighty, and lift up your face to God.

LAVONNE, Lavanna, Lavonda, Lavondria, LaVonne, Lavonya
Language/Cultural Origin: **Latin**
Inherent Meaning: **Warm, Cheerful**
Spiritual Connotation: **Fruitful**
Scripture: **Psalm 8:6** NKJV
You have made him to have dominion over the works of Your hands; You have put all things under his feet.

LAWRENCE, Lanny, Larrance, Larrence, Larry, Laurant, Laurence, Laurens, Laurent, Lauris, Lauritz, Lawrance,

Lorence, Lorentz, Lorenzo, Lorinzo, Lorrenzo (see also Loren)
Language/Cultural Origin: **Latin**
Inherent Meaning: **Crowned With Laurel**
Spiritual Connotation: **Joyful**
Scripture: **Psalm 118:24** NKJV
This is the day the LORD has made; We will rejoice and be glad in it.

LAWTON, Laughton
Language/Cultural Origin: **English**
Inherent Meaning: **From the Hill Town**
Spiritual Connotation: **Seeker of Truth**
Scripture: **Matthew 6:33** NKJV
But seek first the kingdom of God and His righteousness, and all these things shall be added to you.

LAYLA, Laela, Laylah, Laylee, Laylie (see also Leala, Leila, Lila)
Language/Cultural Origin: **Middle Eastern**
Inherent Meaning: **Born at Night**
Spiritual Connotation: **Cause for Joy**
Scripture: **Luke 2:11** TLB
The Savior—yes, the Messiah, the Lord— has been born tonight in Bethlehem!

LAZARUS, Lazaros
Language/Cultural Origin: **Greek**
Inherent Meaning: **He Whom God Helps**
Spiritual Connotation: **Friend of God**
Scripture: **John 16:13** NKJV
When He, the Spirit of truth, has come, He will guide you into all truth.

LEAH, Lea, Léa, Leeah, Leia (see also Leigh, Lia, Liya)
Language/Cultural Origin: **Hebrew**
Inherent Meaning: **Gazelle**
Spiritual Connotation: **Beauty and Grace**
Scripture: **Psalm 18:32-33** NKJV
It is God who arms me with strength, and makes my way perfect. He makes my feet like the feet of deer, and sets me on my high places.

LEALA, Lealia, Leial, Leiala (see also Layla, Leila, Lila)
Language/Cultural Origin: **French**
Inherent Meaning: **Loyal**
Spiritual Connotation: **Faithful**
Scripture: **Proverbs 3:3** RSV

Let not loyalty and faithfulness forsake you; bind them about your neck, write them on the tablet of your heart.

LEANDER, Léandre
Language/Cultural Origin: **Greek**
Inherent Meaning: **Brave as a Lion**
Spiritual Connotation: **Strong in Spirit**
Scripture: **John 15:4** NCV
Remain in me, and I will remain in you. . . . You cannot produce fruit alone but must remain in me.

LEANDRA, Leandrea, Leandria, Leeandra
Language/Cultural Origin: **English**
Inherent Meaning: **Brave as a Lion**
Spiritual Connotation: **Steadfast**
Scripture: **Psalm 86:15** NASB
But You, O Lord, are a God merciful and gracious, slow to anger and abundant in lovingkindness and truth.

LEANN, Leanne, Leean, Leeanne, Leiann, Leianne (see also Lian)
Language/Cultural Origin: **English**
Inherent Meaning: **Youthful**
Spiritual Connotation: **Righteous**
Scripture: **2 Timothy 2:22** NIV
Flee the evil desires of youth, and pursue righteousness, faith, love and peace, along with those who call on the Lord out of a pure heart.

LEANNA, see Liana

LEANORE, Lanore, Leanora, Lenora, Lenore, Leonora, Leonorah
Language/Cultural Origin: **English**
Inherent Meaning: **Bright Like the Sun**
Spiritual Connotation: **Reflection of Christ**
Scripture: **Revelation 1:16** NASB
His face was like the sun shining in its strength.

LEE
Language/Cultural Origin: **German**
Inherent Meaning: **From the Sheltered Place**
Spiritual Connotation: **Gracious**
Scripture: **Romans 8:16** NKJV
The Spirit Himself bears witness with our spirit that we are children of God.

LEEANN, see Leann

LEEDON, Leydon, Lidon, Liedon
Language/Cultural Origin: **Hebrew**
Inherent Meaning: **Justice Is Mine**
Spiritual Connotation: **Defended**
Scripture: **Deuteronomy 32:35** NLT
I will take vengeance; I will repay those who deserve it.

LEESHA, Lecia, Leecia, Leesia, Lesha, Leshia
Language/Cultural Origin: **English**
Inherent Meaning: **Happy**
Spiritual Connotation: **Obedient**
Scripture: **Psalm 119:35** NLT
Make me walk along the path of your commands, for that is where my happiness is found.

LEEZA, Leza (see also Lisa, Liza)
Language/Cultural Origin: **American**
Inherent Meaning: **Surrendered to God**
Spiritual Connotation: **Sacrifice**
Scripture: **Luke 23:46** RSV
Then Jesus, crying with a loud voice, said, "Father, into thy hands I commit my spirit!"

LEIF, Léif, Lief
Language/Cultural Origin: **Old Norse**
Inherent Meaning: **Beloved**
Spiritual Connotation: **Chosen**
Scripture: **Matthew 3:17** RSV
And lo, a voice from heaven, saying, "This is my beloved Son, with whom I am well pleased."

LEIGH, Leigha, Leighann, Leighanna (see also Leah, Lia, Liya)
Language/Cultural Origin: **American**
Inherent Meaning: **Meadow**
Spiritual Connotation: **Guided of God**
Scripture: **Psalm 95:7** RSV
For he is our God, and we are the people of his pasture, and the sheep of his hand. O that today you would hearken to his voice!

LEIGHTON, Layton, Leyton
Language/Cultural Origin: **Old English**
Inherent Meaning: **From the Meadow Farm**
Spiritual Connotation: **Rescued**

Scripture: **Isaiah 49:9** TLB
Come out! I am giving you your freedom! They will be my sheep, grazing in green pastures and on the grassy hills.

LEILA, Laila, Leala, Lela (see also Layla, Leala, Lila)
Language/Cultural Origin: **Hebrew**
Inherent Meaning: **Dark Beauty**
Spiritual Connotation: **Bringer of Light**
Scripture: **Ecclesiastes 3:11** NKJV
He has made everything beautiful in its time. Also He has put eternity in their hearts.

LEILANI, Lelani, Lelania
Language/Cultural Origin: **Hawaiian**
Inherent Meaning: **Heavenly Flower**
Spiritual Connotation: **Priceless**
Scripture: **Luke 12:32** NKJV
Do not fear, little flock, for it is your Father's good pleasure to give you the kingdom.

LEITH, Léith
Language/Cultural Origin: **Scottish**
Inherent Meaning: **From the Broad River**
Spiritual Connotation: **Blessed**
Scripture: **Acts 3:19-20** NRSV
Repent therefore, and turn to God so that your sins may be wiped out, so that times of refreshing may come from the presence of the Lord.

LEKEISHA, see Lakeisha

LELAND, Leeland, Leyland
Language/Cultural Origin: **English**
Inherent Meaning: **From the Meadowland**
Spiritual Connotation: **Prosperous**
Scripture: **Deuteronomy 30:9** NASB
Then the LORD your God will prosper you abundantly in all the work of your hand.

LEMUEL, Lem
Language/Cultural Origin: **Hebrew**
Inherent Meaning: **Consecrated to God**
Spiritual Connotation: **Holy**
Scripture: **2 Timothy 1:7** NKJV
For God has not given us a spirit of fear, but of power and of love and of a sound mind.

LENA, Leena, Lenah, Lina
Language/Cultural Origin: **Greek**
Inherent Meaning: **Gentle**
Spiritual Connotation: **Blessed Peacemaker**
Scripture: **Matthew 7:12** NKJV
Therefore, whatever you want men to do to you, do also to them, for this is the Law and the Prophets.

LENITA, Leneisha, Lenice, Lenis, Lenise, Lenisha
Language/Cultural Origin: **Latin**
Inherent Meaning: **White Lily**
Spiritual Connotation: **Discerning Spirit**
Scripture: **Proverbs 16:20** NLT
Those who listen to instruction will prosper; those who trust the LORD will be happy.

LENNON, Lennan, Lennen
Language/Cultural Origin: **Irish**
Inherent Meaning: **Small Cloak**
Spiritual Connotation: **Selfless**
Scripture: **Luke 6:29** NKJV
To him who strikes you on the one cheek, offer the other also. And from him who takes away your cloak, do not withhold your tunic either.

LENNOX, Lenox
Language/Cultural Origin: **Scottish**
Inherent Meaning: **Placid Stream**
Spiritual Connotation: **God Is All-Sufficient**
Scripture: **Jeremiah 32:27** TLB
I am the Lord, the God of all mankind; is there anything too hard for me?

LENORE, see Leanore

LEO, Léo
Language/Cultural Origin: **Latin**
Inherent Meaning: **Lionhearted**
Spiritual Connotation: **Courageous**
Scripture: **Deuteronomy 31:6** NASB
Be strong and courageous, do not be afraid or tremble at them, for the LORD your God is the one who goes with you. He will not fail you or forsake you.

LEON, Léon, Leone
Language/Cultural Origin: **English**
Inherent Meaning: **Brave as a Lion**
Spiritual Connotation: **Brave**

Scripture: **Joshua 1:7** NASB
*Only be strong and very courageous;
be careful to do according to all the law
which Moses My servant commanded
you . . . so that you may have success
wherever you go.*

LEONA, Leone, Leonia, Liona
Language/Cultural Origin: **Latin**
Inherent Meaning: **Lioness**
Spiritual Connotation: **Courageous Spirit**
Scripture: **Psalm 25:5** RSV
*Lead me in thy truth, and teach me, for
thou art the God of my salvation; for
thee I wait all the day long.*

**LEONARD, Len, Lenard, Lennard,
Lennie, Lenno, Lenny, Leno,
Léonard, Leonardo**
Language/Cultural Origin: **Old German**
Inherent Meaning: **Strong as a Lion**
Spiritual Connotation: **Fearless Spirit**
Scripture: **Proverbs 8:14** NKJV
*Counsel is mine, and sound wisdom; I
am understanding, I have strength.*

LEORA, see Liora

LEROY, Leeroy, LeeRoy, LeRoy
Language/Cultural Origin: **Old French**
Inherent Meaning: **Royal**
Spiritual Connotation: **Esteemed**
Scripture: **1 Corinthians 2:10** NKJV
*But God has revealed them to us through
His Spirit. For the Spirit searches all
things, yes, the deep things of God.*

**LESLIE, Leslea, Leslee, Lesley, Lesli,
Lesslie, Lezlee, Lezley, Lezlie**
Language/Cultural Origin: **Scottish**
Inherent Meaning: **From the Low Meadow**
Spiritual Connotation: **Remembered**
Scripture: **Isaiah 42:16** NKJV
*I will bring the blind by a way they did
not know; I will lead them in paths they
have not known. I will make darkness
light before them.*

LESTER, Les
Language/Cultural Origin: **English**
Inherent Meaning: **From the Chosen Camp**
Spiritual Connotation: **Shining Spirit**
Scripture: **2 Corinthians 5:17** NKJV

*Therefore, if anyone is in Christ, he is
a new creation; old things have passed
away; behold, all things have become new.*

**LEVANA, Lévana, Levanna, Livana,
Livanna**
Language/Cultural Origin: **Hebrew**
Inherent Meaning: **Moon**
Spiritual Connotation: **Symbol**
Scripture: **Psalm 89:37** NRSV
*It shall be established forever like the
moon, an enduring witness in the skies.*

**LEVANON, Levanan, Levanen,
Levannon**
Language/Cultural Origin: **Hebrew**
Inherent Meaning: **Moon**
Spiritual Connotation: **Blessed**
Scripture: **Psalm 136:9** NCV
*He made the moon and stars to rule the
night. His love continues forever.*

LEVI, Leevi, Levey, Levy
☞ Language/Cultural Origin: **Hebrew**
Inherent Meaning: **Harmonious**
Spiritual Connotation: **Enlightened**
Scripture: **Psalm 18:28** NKJV
*For You will light my lamp; the LORD my
God will enlighten my darkness.*

LEVIA, Levya
Language/Cultural Origin: **Hebrew**
Inherent Meaning: **Attached**
Spiritual Connotation: **One With God**
Scripture: **Zechariah 2:11** NKJV
*Many nations shall be joined to the LORD
in that day, and they shall become My
people. And I will dwell in your midst.*

LEVINA, Leveena
Language/Cultural Origin: **Latin**
Inherent Meaning: **Flash of Lightning**
Spiritual Connotation: **Ardent Praise**
Scripture: **Psalm 36:7** NLT
*How precious is your unfailing love, O
God! All humanity finds shelter in the
shadow of your wings.*

LEVONA, Livona
Language/Cultural Origin: **Hebrew**
Inherent Meaning: **Incense**
Spiritual Connotation: **Sacrifice**
Scripture: **Psalm 141:2** NRSV

Let my prayer be counted as incense before you, and the lifting up of my hands as an evening sacrifice.

LEWIS, Lew, Lewie
Language/Cultural Origin: **Old English**
Inherent Meaning: **Safeguard of the People**
Spiritual Connotation: **Righteous**
Scripture: **Matthew 12:35** NLT
A good person produces good words from a good heart, and an evil person produces evil words from an evil heart.

LEX, Lexx
Language/Cultural Origin: **English**
Inherent Meaning: **Defender of Mankind**
Spiritual Connotation: **Protector**
Scripture: **Psalm 9:9** TLB
All who are oppressed may come to him. He is a refuge for them in their times of trouble.

LEXI, Leksa, Lexa, Lexee, Lexey, Lexia, Lexie, Lexxa, Lexxia, Lexxie, Lexy
Language/Cultural Origin: **Czech**
Inherent Meaning: **Defender of Mankind**
Spiritual Connotation: **Stronghold**
Scripture: **Isaiah 4:6** NASB
There will be a shelter to give shade from the heat by day, and refuge and protection from the storm and the rain.

LIA, Liah (see also Leah, Leigh, Liya)
Language/Cultural Origin: **Greek**
Inherent Meaning: **Bringer of Good News**
Spiritual Connotation: **Messenger**
Scripture: **Luke 2:10** NASB
And the angel said to them, "Do not be afraid; for behold, I bring you good news of a great joy which shall be for all the people."

LIAN, Liane, Lianne (see also Leann)
Language/Cultural Origin: **Chinese**
Inherent Meaning: **Willow**
Spiritual Connotation: **Eternal**
Scripture: **Jeremiah 17:8** NRSV
They shall be like a tree planted by water, sending out its roots by the stream. It shall not . . . cease to bear fruit.

LIANA, Leana, Leanna, Leeanna, Leiana, Leianna, Lianna (see also Iliana, Eliana)
Language/Cultural Origin: **Hebrew**
Inherent Meaning: **My God Has Answered Me**
Spiritual Connotation: **Important**
Scripture: **Genesis 21:17** NRSV
Do not be afraid; for God has heard the voice of the boy where he is.

LIBBY, Libbee, Libbey, Libbie
Language/Cultural Origin: **English**
Inherent Meaning: **Promise of God**
Spiritual Connotation: **Preserved**
Scripture: **Isaiah 59:21** NASB
My Spirit which is upon you, and My words which I have put in your mouth shall not depart from your mouth.

LIBERTY, Libertee
Language/Cultural Origin: **Latin**
Inherent Meaning: **Freedom**
Spiritual Connotation: **Unchained**
Scripture: **Galatians 5:1** NASB
It was for freedom that Christ set us free; therefore keep standing firm and do not be subject again to a yoke of slavery.

LIDA, Leeda, Lita
Language/Cultural Origin: **Slavic**
Inherent Meaning: **Love**
Spiritual Connotation: **Beloved**
Scripture: **Ephesians 4:32** NASB
Be kind to one another, tender-hearted, forgiving each other, just as God in Christ also has forgiven you.

LIESEL, Leisel, Liesl, Liezel, Liezl, Lisel
Language/Cultural Origin: **German**
Inherent Meaning: **Oath of God**
Spiritual Connotation: **Promise**
Scripture: **Zechariah 9:11** NASB
As for you also, because of the blood of My covenant with you, I have set your prisoners free from the waterless pit.

LILA, Lilah, Lyla, Lylah (see also Layla, Leala, Leila)
Language/Cultural Origin: **Persian**
Inherent Meaning: **Lilac**
Spiritual Connotation: **Lovely Aroma**

Scripture: **2 Corinthians 2:15** NKJV
*For we are to God the fragrance of
Christ among those who are being saved
and among those who are perishing.*

LILITH, Lillith
Language/Cultural Origin: **Hebrew**
Inherent Meaning: **Night Owl**
Spiritual Connotation: **Wise**
Scripture: **Proverbs 8:9** NKJV
*They are all plain to him who understands,
and right to those who find knowledge.*

LILLIAN, Lili, Lilia, Lilian, Liliana, Liliane, Liljana, Lilliana, Lillianna, Lillyan, Lily
Language/Cultural Origin: **Latin**
Inherent Meaning: **Purity**
Spiritual Connotation: **Shining Light**
Scripture: **Zechariah 2:10** NKJV
*Sing and rejoice, O daughter of Zion!
For behold, I am coming and I will dwell
in your midst.*

LIN, Linh, Linn (see also Lynn)
Language/Cultural Origin: **Chinese**
Inherent Meaning: **Jade**
Spiritual Connotation: **Beautiful**
Scripture: **Revelation 4:3** NKJV
*And He who sat there was like a jasper
and a sardius stone in appearance; and
there was a rainbow around the throne,
in appearance like an emerald.*

LINCOLN, Lincon
Language/Cultural Origin: **Old English**
Inherent Meaning: **From the Pool Town**
Spiritual Connotation: **Victorious**
Scripture: **1 John 5:4** RSV
*For whatever is born of God overcomes
the world; and this is the victory that
overcomes the world, our faith.*

LINDA, Linnea, Linnie, Lynda
Language/Cultural Origin: **Spanish**
Inherent Meaning: **Beautiful**
Spiritual Connotation: **Excellent Virtue**
Scripture: **James 5:16** NRSV
*Therefore confess your sins to one
another, and pray for one another, so
that you may be healed. The prayer of
the righteous is powerful and effective.*

LINDEE, Lindey, Lindi, Lindie, Lindy
Language/Cultural Origin: **American**
Inherent Meaning: **Lovely**
Spiritual Connotation: **Witness**
Scripture: **Romans 10:15** NLT
*How beautiful are the feet of those who
bring good news!*

LINDELL, Lendell, Lindall, Lindel, Lyndel, Lyndell
Language/Cultural Origin: **Anglo-Saxon**
Inherent Meaning: **From the Linden Trees**
Spiritual Connotation: **Inheritor**
Scripture: **Luke 12:32** NASB
*Do not be afraid, little flock, for your
Father has chosen gladly to give you the
kingdom.*

LINDSEY, Lindsay, Lindsee, Lindsi, Lindsie, Lindsy, Lindzee, Linsay, Linsey, Linsi, Linsie, Linzee, Linzey, Lyndsay, Lyndsee, Lyndsey, Lynnsey, Lynnzey, Lynsay, Lynsee, Lynsey, Lynzey, Lynzi, Lynzie
Language/Cultural Origin: **English**
Inherent Meaning: **From the Pool Island**
Spiritual Connotation: **Peaceful**
Scripture: **Hebrews 12:11** RSV
*For the moment all discipline seems pain-
ful rather than pleasant; later it yields the
peaceful fruit of righteousness.*

LINFORD, Lynford
Language/Cultural Origin: **Middle English**
Inherent Meaning: **From the Lime-Tree Ford**
Spiritual Connotation: **Gentle**
Scripture: **Matthew 11:29** NRSV
*Take my yoke upon you, and learn from
me; for I am gentle and humble in heart,
and you will find rest for your souls.*

LINLEY, Lindlee, Linlea, Linlee
Language/Cultural Origin: **Old English**
Inherent Meaning: **From the Flax Meadow**
Spiritual Connotation: **Abiding in God**
Scripture: **Acts 17:28** NRSV
*For in him we live and move and have
our being; as even some of your own
poets have said . . . we too are his off-
spring.*

LINUS, Linas

Language/Cultural Origin: **Greek**
Inherent Meaning: **Fair-Haired**
Spiritual Connotation: **Treasurer of Wisdom and Knowledge**
Scripture: **Colossians 2:2** NRSV
I want their hearts to . . . have the knowledge of God's mystery, that is, Christ himself, in whom are hidden all the treasures of wisdom and knowledge.

LIONEL, Lional, Lionell, Lyonel

Language/Cultural Origin: **Latin**
Inherent Meaning: **Little Lion**
Spiritual Connotation: **Strong in Faith**
Scripture: **Psalm 26:3** RSV
For thy steadfast love is before my eyes, and I walk in faithfulness to thee.

LIORA, Leora

Language/Cultural Origin: **Hebrew**
Inherent Meaning: **Glowing Light**
Spiritual Connotation: **Brilliance**
Scripture: **Revelation 21:11** NCV
It was shining with the glory of God and was bright like a very expensive jewel, like a jasper, clear as crystal.

LISA, Leesa, Liesa, Liisa, Lisana, Lisann, Lisanna, Lisanne, Lise (see also Leeza, Liza)

Language/Cultural Origin: **English**
Inherent Meaning: **Consecrated to God**
Spiritual Connotation: **Redeemed**
Scripture: **Romans 11:27** NKJV
For this is My covenant with them, when I take away their sins.

LISETTE, Lissette

Language/Cultural Origin: **French**
Inherent Meaning: **Promise of God**
Spiritual Connotation: **One With Christ**
Scripture: **Romans 8:38-39** NKJV
For I am persuaded that neither death nor life . . . nor anything else in all creation, will be able to separate us from the love of God in Christ Jesus our Lord.

LISSA, Lissee, Lissey, Lissi, Lissie, Lissy, Lyssa (see also Alisa, Elissa, Elysia)

Language/Cultural Origin: **English**
Inherent Meaning: **Honeybee**
Spiritual Connotation: **Servant**
Scripture: **1 Corinthians 16:16** NRSV
I urge you to put yourselves at the service of such people, and of everyone who works and toils with them.

LITA, see Lida

LITONYA, Litania, Litanya, Litonia (see also Latanya)

Language/Cultural Origin: **Moquelumnan**
Inherent Meaning: **Darting Hummingbird**
Spiritual Connotation: **Child of God**
Scripture: **Matthew 6:26** RSV
Look at the birds of the air: they neither sow nor reap . . . and yet your heavenly Father feeds them. Are you not of more value than they?

LIVIA, Levia, Leviya, Levya, Livie, Liviya, Livy, Livya (see also Olivia)

Language/Cultural Origin: **Hebrew**
Inherent Meaning: **Royal Crown**
Spiritual Connotation: **Exalted**
Scripture: **Psalm 89:19** NRSV
Then you spoke in a vision to your faithful one, and said: I have set the crown on one who is mighty, I have exalted one chosen from the people.

LIVINGSTON, Livingstone

Language/Cultural Origin: **Old English**
Inherent Meaning: **From Leif's Town**
Spiritual Connotation: **Chosen**
Scripture: **Isaiah 55:5** NKJV
Surely you shall call a nation you do not know, and nations who do not know you shall run to you, because of the LORD your God . . . for He has glorified you.

LIYA, Leeya (see also Leah, Leigh, Lia)

Language/Cultural Origin: **Hebrew**
Inherent Meaning: **Belonging to God**
Spiritual Connotation: **Trusting**
Scripture: **John 1:12** TLB
But to all who received him, he gave the right to become children of God. All they needed to do was to trust him to save them.

LIZA, Liz, Lizann, Lizanne, Lizbeth, Lizina, Lizzey, Lizzie, Lizzy, Lyza (see also Leeza, Lisa)
Language/Cultural Origin: American
Inherent Meaning: Covenant of God
Spiritual Connotation: Established
Scripture: Psalm 132:12 NCV
If your sons keep my agreement and the rules that I teach them, then their sons after them will rule on your throne forever and ever.

LLEWELLYN, Lewellyn
Language/Cultural Origin: Celtic
Inherent Meaning: Ruler
Spiritual Connotation: Peaceful
Scripture: 1 John 4:18 NASB
There is no fear in love; but perfect love casts out fear, because fear involves punishment, and the one who fears is not perfected in love.

LLOYD, Loyd
Language/Cultural Origin: Welsh
Inherent Meaning: Wise
Spiritual Connotation: Seeker of Holiness
Scripture: Proverbs 12:28 NKJV
In the way of righteousness is life, and in its pathway there is no death.

LOCKE, Lock
Language/Cultural Origin: Old English
Inherent Meaning: From the Forest
Spiritual Connotation: Wise
Scripture: Proverbs 23:24 NKJV
The father of the righteous will greatly rejoice, and he who begets a wise child will delight in him.

LOGAN, Logen
Language/Cultural Origin: Celtic
Inherent Meaning: From the Little Hollow
Spiritual Connotation: Devoted to God
Scripture: Philippians 4:6 NCV
Do not worry about anything, but pray and ask God for everything you need, always giving thanks.

LOIS
Language/Cultural Origin: Greek
Inherent Meaning: Desired
Spiritual Connotation: Established in Truth

Scripture: 2 Samuel 22:29 NKJV
For You are my lamp, O LORD; the LORD shall enlighten my darkness.

LOLA, Lolita
Language/Cultural Origin: Latin
Inherent Meaning: Crowned With Compassion and Grace
Spiritual Connotation: Perceptive Insight
Scripture: Psalm 16:11 NKJV
You will show me the path of life; in Your presence is fullness of joy; at Your right hand are pleasures forevermore.

LOMAN, Lomán
Language/Cultural Origin: Serbian
Inherent Meaning: Delicate
Spiritual Connotation: Loving
Scripture: Ephesians 4:32 NKJV
And be kind to one another, tenderhearted, forgiving one another, just as God in Christ forgave you.

LOMAS, Lomás
Language/Cultural Origin: English
Inherent Meaning: From Lomas
Spiritual Connotation: Reverent
Scripture: Psalm 33:8 NKJV
Let all the earth fear the LORD; let all the inhabitants of the world stand in awe of Him.

LONDON, Londan, Londen, Londyn
Language/Cultural Origin: English
Inherent Meaning: Castle of the Moon
Spiritual Connotation: Unique
Scripture: 1 Corinthians 15:41 NCV
The sun has one kind of beauty, the moon has another beauty, and the stars have another. And each star is different in its beauty.

LONNA, Lona, Loni, Lonie
Language/Cultural Origin: German
Inherent Meaning: Lioness
Spiritual Connotation: Courageous
Scripture: Joshua 1:9 RSV
Be strong and of good courage; be not frightened, neither be dismayed; for the LORD your God is with you wherever you go.

LONNIE, Lon, Lonn, Lonny
Language/Cultural Origin: **English**
Inherent Meaning: **Ready for Battle**
Spiritual Connotation: **God's Soldier**
Scripture: **Exodus 13:18** RSV
But God led the people . . . and the people of Israel went up out of the land of Egypt equipped for battle.

LORA, see Laura

LORELEI, Loralee, Loralie, Lorilee
Language/Cultural Origin: **Old German**
Inherent Meaning: **Alluring**
Spiritual Connotation: **Witness**
Scripture: **Titus 2:10** NCV
They . . . should show their masters they can be fully trusted so that in everything they do they will make the teaching of God our Savior attractive.

LOREN, Larian, Larien, Laurin, Lawren, Lorin, Loring, Lorne, Lorren, Lorrin, Loryn (see also Lauren, Lawrence)
Language/Cultural Origin: **Basque**
Inherent Meaning: **Son of the Famous Warrior**
Spiritual Connotation: **God's Warrior**
Scripture: **Ephesians 6:17** NKJV
And take the helmet of salvation, and the sword of the Spirit, which is the word of God.

LORI, Lari, Laure, Lauré, Lauri, Laurie, Loree, Lorey, Lorianna, Lorie, Lorrie (see also Laura)
Language/Cultural Origin: **English**
Inherent Meaning: **Crowned With Honor**
Spiritual Connotation: **Hopeful**
Scripture: **Isaiah 28:5** NASB
In that day the LORD of hosts will become a beautiful crown and a glorious diadem to the remnant of His people.

LORITZ, Lauritz
Language/Cultural Origin: **Danish**
Inherent Meaning: **Evergreen**
Spiritual Connotation: **Promise**
Scripture: **Isaiah 55:13** NIV
Instead of the thornbush will grow the pine tree, and instead of briers the myrtle will grow. This will be for . . . an everlasting sign.

LORRAINE, Loraine, Lorayne, Lorrayne (see also Laraine)
Language/Cultural Origin: **German**
Inherent Meaning: **Warrior**
Spiritual Connotation: **Strength of God**
Scripture: **Isaiah 45:2** NKJV
I will go before you and make the crooked places straight; I will break in pieces the gates of bronze and cut the bars of iron.

LORRETA, see Laura

LOT, Lott
Language/Cultural Origin: **Hebrew**
Inherent Meaning: **Covered**
Spiritual Connotation: **Protected**
Scripture: **Isaiah 32:2** NASB
And each will be like a refuge from the wind, and a shelter from the storm, . . . like the shade of a huge rock in a parched land.

LOUIS, Lou, Louie, Luigi, Luis
Language/Cultural Origin: **Old German**
Inherent Meaning: **Famous Warrior**
Spiritual Connotation: **Declarer of God**
Scripture: **Isaiah 43:19** NASB
Behold, I will do something new, now it will spring forth. . . . I will even make a roadway in the wilderness, rivers in the desert.

LOUISE, Louisa, Luisa, Luiza
Language/Cultural Origin: **Old German**
Inherent Meaning: **Protectress**
Spiritual Connotation: **Watchful**
Scripture: **1 Peter 2:25** NRSV
For you were going astray like sheep, but now you have returned to the shepherd and guardian of your souls.

LOURDES, Lordes
Language/Cultural Origin: **French**
Inherent Meaning: **From Lourdes**
Spiritual Connotation: **Redeemed**
Scripture: **Romans 5:8** RSV
But God shows his love for us in that while we were yet sinners Christ died for us.

LOWELL, Lovell, Lowel
Language/Cultural Origin: **Latin**
Inherent Meaning: **Little Wolf**
Spiritual Connotation: **Peaceful**
Scripture: **Colossians 3:15** NKJV
And let the peace of God rule in your hearts, to which also you were called in one body; and be thankful.

LUANN, Luana, Luanna, Luanne
Language/Cultural Origin: **Hebrew**
Inherent Meaning: **Graceful Warrior**
Spiritual Connotation: **Righteous**
Scripture: **Psalm 55:22** NASB
Cast your burden upon the LORD, and He will sustain you; He will never allow the righteous to be shaken.

LUCILE, Luci, Lucia, Luciann, Lucie, Lucienne, Lucile, Lucille, Lucina, Lucinda, Lucy
Language/Cultural Origin: **English**
Inherent Meaning: **Light Bringer**
Spiritual Connotation: **Chosen of God**
Scripture: **Romans 8:28** NKJV
And we know that all things work together for good to those who love God, to those who are the called according to His purpose.

LUCIUS, Lucas, Lucian, Luciano, Lucien (see also Luke)
Language/Cultural Origin: **Latin**
Inherent Meaning: **Bringer of Light**
Spiritual Connotation: **Enlightened**
Scripture: **Psalm 139:9-10** NRSV
If I take the wings of the morning and settle at the farthest limits of the sea, even there your hand shall lead me, and your right hand shall hold me fast.

LUCRETIA, Lacresha, Lacreshia, Lacretia, Lakresha, Lakreshia, Lucresha, Lucreshia
Language/Cultural Origin: **Latin**
Inherent Meaning: **Riches, Rewards**
Spiritual Connotation: **Prosperous**
Scripture: **2 Chronicles 20:20** KJV
Believe in the LORD your God, so shall ye be established; believe his prophets, so shall ye prosper.

LUDWIG, Ludvig
Language/Cultural Origin: **German**
Inherent Meaning: **Famous Warrior**
Spiritual Connotation: **Gifted**
Scripture: **Psalm 89:18** NKJV
For our shield belongs to the LORD, and our king to the Holy One of Israel.

LUKE, Luc, Luk (see also Lucius)
Language/Cultural Origin: **Greek**
Inherent Meaning: **Luminous**
Spiritual Connotation: **Talented**
Scripture: **Exodus 31:3** NKJV
And I have filled him with the Spirit of God, in wisdom, in understanding, in knowledge, and in all manner of workmanship.

LUPE, Lupé
Language/Cultural Origin: **Spanish**
Inherent Meaning: **Wolf**
Spiritual Connotation: **Courageous**
Scripture: **Psalm 91:11** NKJV
For He shall give His angels charge over you, to keep you in all your ways.

LUTHER, Lothar, Luthor
Language/Cultural Origin: **Old German**
Inherent Meaning: **Famous Warrior**
Spiritual Connotation: **Honored**
Scripture: **Isaiah 41:13** RSV
For I, the LORD your God, hold your right hand. . . . Fear not, I will help you.

LYDIA, Lidi, Lidia, Lidiya
Language/Cultural Origin: **Greek**
Inherent Meaning: **Womanly**
Spiritual Connotation: **Beautiful Light**
Scripture: **2 Corinthians 4:6** NASB
For God . . . is the One who has shone in our hearts to give the Light of the knowledge of the glory of God in the face of Christ.

LYLE, Lisle, Lysle
Language/Cultural Origin: **Old French**
Inherent Meaning: **From the Island**
Spiritual Connotation: **Joyous Spirit**
Scripture: **Psalm 32:11** NASB
Be glad in the LORD and rejoice, you righteous ones; and shout for joy, all you who are upright in heart.

LYNDON, Lindan, Linden, Lindon, Lynden
Language/Cultural Origin: **English**
Inherent Meaning: **From the Lime Tree Hill**
Spiritual Connotation: **Excellent Worth**
Scripture: **Luke 12:7** NASB
Indeed, the very hairs of your head are all numbered. Do not fear; you are of more value than many sparrows.

LYNELLE, Linell, Linnell, Lynell, Lynnell, Lynnelle
Language/Cultural Origin: **English**
Inherent Meaning: **Pretty**
Spiritual Connotation: **Virtuous**
Scripture: **Proverbs 31:30** RSV
Charm is deceitful, and beauty is vain, but a woman who fears the LORD is to be praised.

LYNN, Linette, Lyn, Lynetta, Lynette, Lynne (see also Lin)
Language/Cultural Origin: **English**
Inherent Meaning: **Clear Pool**

Spiritual Connotation: **Holy**
Scripture: **Proverbs 9:10** NKJV
The fear of the LORD is the beginning of wisdom, and the knowledge of the Holy One is understanding.

LYSANDER, Lisander
Language/Cultural Origin: **Greek**
Inherent Meaning: **Liberator**
Spiritual Connotation: **Freedom**
Scripture: **John 8:32** NASB
And you shall know the truth, and the truth shall make you free.

LYSANDRA, Lisandra
Language/Cultural Origin: **Greek**
Inherent Meaning: **Liberator**
Spiritual Connotation: **Freedom**
Scripture: **Galatians 5:1** NKJV
Stand fast therefore in the liberty by which Christ has made us free, and do not be entangled again with a yoke of bondage.

M

MAAYAN, Maayana, Maeanna, Maion, Mayani, Mayon (see also Mahon, Maon)
Language/Cultural Origin: **Hebrew**
Inherent Meaning: **Water Source**
Spiritual Connotation: **Fountain of Life**
Scripture: **John 4:14** NRSV
But those who drink of the water that I will give them will never be thirsty. The water that I will give will become in them a spring of water gushing up to eternal life.

MABEL, Mable
Language/Cultural Origin: **Latin**
Inherent Meaning: **Lovable**
Spiritual Connotation: **Beautiful in Spirit**
Scripture: **John 15:5** NKJV
I am the vine, you are the branches. He who abides in Me, and I in him, bears much fruit; for without Me you can do nothing.

MACABEE, Maccabee, Mákabi
Language/Cultural Origin: **Hebrew**
Inherent Meaning: **Who Is Like God?**
Spiritual Connotation: **Reverent**
Scripture: **Exodus 15:11** NASB
Who is like Thee among the gods, O LORD? Who is like Thee, majestic in holiness, awesome in praises, working wonders?

MACARTHUR, MacArthur, McArthur
Language/Cultural Origin: **Scottish**
Inherent Meaning: **Child of the Brave Man**
Spiritual Connotation: **Forgiven**
Scripture: **Matthew 9:2** NASB
Take courage, My son, your sins are forgiven.

MACAULAY, Macauley, McCauley
Language/Cultural Origin: **Scottish**
Inherent Meaning: **Child of Righteousness**
Spiritual Connotation: **Mature**
Scripture: **Proverbs 22:6** NKJV
Train up a child in the way he should go, and when he is old he will not depart from it.

MACDONALD, McDonald, McDonnell
Language/Cultural Origin: **Scottish**
Inherent Meaning: **Child of the Great Ruler**
Spiritual Connotation: **Honest**
Scripture: **Proverbs 20:11** TLB
The character of even a child can be known by the way he acts—whether what he does is pure and right.

MACIA, Macya
Language/Cultural Origin: **Polish**
Inherent Meaning: **Wished-for**
Spiritual Connotation: **Blameless**
Scripture: **Psalm 37:4** NASB
Delight yourself in the LORD; and He will give you the desires of your heart.

MACKAY, MacKay, McKay
Language/Cultural Origin: **Scottish**
Inherent Meaning: **Son of the Rejoicer**
Spiritual Connotation: **Received With Glory**
Scripture: **Zephaniah 3:17** RSV
The LORD, your God, is in your midst, a warrior who gives victory; he will rejoice over you with gladness.

MACKENZIE, Mackensie, Mackenzee, McKensi, McKenzee, McKenzie
Language/Cultural Origin: **Scottish Gaelic**

Inherent Meaning: **Child of the Wise Leader**
Spiritual Connotation: **Witness**
Scripture: **Proverbs 23:24** NKJV
The father of the righteous will greatly rejoice, and he who begets a wise child will delight in him.

MACKINNLEY, MacKinnley, Mckinnlee, McKinnley
Language/Cultural Origin: **Irish**
Inherent Meaning: **Child of the Scholarly Ruler**
Spiritual Connotation: **Peaceful**
Scripture: **Isaiah 11:6** RSV
The wolf shall dwell with the lamb . . . and a little child shall lead them.

MACNAIR, McNair
Language/Cultural Origin: **Scottish**
Inherent Meaning: **Child of the Heir**
Spiritual Connotation: **Favored**
Scripture: **Galatians 3:29** NLT
And now that you belong to Christ, you are the true children of Abraham. . . . All the promises God gave to him belong to you.

MACY, Macee, Macey, Maci, Macie
Language/Cultural Origin: **French**
Inherent Meaning: **From Matthew's Estate**
Spiritual Connotation: **Enlightened**
Scripture: **John 1:29** NKJV
The next day John saw Jesus coming toward him, and said, Behold! The Lamb of God who takes away the sin of the world!

MADDOX, Madox
Language/Cultural Origin: **Welsh**
Inherent Meaning: **Son of the Benefactor**
Spiritual Connotation: **Promise**
Scripture: **Hebrews 11:11** RSV
By faith Sarah herself received power to conceive, even when she was past the age, since she considered him faithful who had promised.

MADELINE, Mada, Madalaina, Madaline, Madalyn, Madalynn, Maddi, Maddie, Maddy, Madelaine, Madeleine, Madelene, Madelynn, Madelynne, Madlen, Madlin, Madoline
Language/Cultural Origin: **Greek**
Inherent Meaning: **Magnificent**
Spiritual Connotation: **Prayerful**
Scripture: **1 Corinthians 14:15** NKJV
I will pray with the spirit, and I will also pray with the understanding. I will sing with the spirit, and I will also sing with the understanding.

MADISON, Maddison, Madisen, Madissen, Madisson
Language/Cultural Origin: **Old English**
Inherent Meaning: **Child of the Valiant Warrior**
Spiritual Connotation: **Brave**
Scripture: **Luke 18:27** NKJV
The things which are impossible with men are possible with God.

MADONNA, Madona
Language/Cultural Origin: **Latin**
Inherent Meaning: **My Lady**
Spiritual Connotation: **Pure**
Scripture: **1 Timothy 5:2** NLT
Treat the older women as you would your mother, and treat the younger women with all purity as your own sisters.

MAE, see May

MAGDALENE, Magdalen, ☞Magdalina, Magdaline, Magdalyn, Magdelana, Magdelena, Magdelene, Magdelina, Magdeline, Magdelyn, Magdelynn
Language/Cultural Origin: **Greek**
Inherent Meaning: **High Fortress**
Spiritual Connotation: **Protected**
Scripture: **Psalm 144:2** NLT
He is my loving ally and my fortress, my tower of safety, my deliverer. He stands before me as a shield, and I take refuge in him.

MAGGIE, Maggee, Maggi
Language/Cultural Origin: **Greek**
Inherent Meaning: **Pearl**
Spiritual Connotation: **Of Great Value**
Scripture: **Revelation 21:21** NKJV
The twelve gates were twelve pearls: each

*individual gate was of one pearl. And
the street of the city was pure gold, like
transparent glass.*

MAGNUS, Magnes
Language/Cultural Origin: **Latin**
Inherent Meaning: **Great**
Spiritual Connotation: **Privileged**
Scripture: **Jeremiah 33:3** NKJV
*Call to Me, and I will answer you, and
show you great and mighty things, which
you do not know.*

MAGUIRE, MacGuire, McGwire
Language/Cultural Origin: **Irish**
Inherent Meaning: **Child of the Fair One**
Spiritual Connotation: **Trustworthy**
Scripture: **James 2:5** NRSV
*Has not God chosen the poor in the
world to be rich in faith and to be heirs of
the kingdom that he has promised to those
who love him?*

MAHALAH, Mahala, Mahalia, ☞ Mahaliah, Mahalla, Mahlah, Mehalia, Mehalla
Language/Cultural Origin: **Hebrew**
Inherent Meaning: **Tenderness**
Spiritual Connotation: **Gentle**
Scripture: **Ephesians 4:32** RSV
*And be kind to one another, tender-
hearted, forgiving one another, as God in
Christ forgave you.*

MAHINA, Maheina
Language/Cultural Origin: **Hawaiian**
Inherent Meaning: **Moon**
Spiritual Connotation: **Testimony**
Scripture: **Psalm 89:37** NRSV
*It shall be established forever like the
moon, an enduring witness in the skies.*

MAHIRA, Maheira
Language/Cultural Origin: **Hebrew**
Inherent Meaning: **Industrious**
Spiritual Connotation: **Diligent**
Scripture: **Matthew 9:37** RSV
*Then he said to his disciples, the harvest
is plentiful, but the laborers are few.*

MAHON, Mahan (see also Maayan, Maon)
Language/Cultural Origin: **Irish**

Inherent Meaning: **Bear**
Spiritual Connotation: **Favored**
Scripture: **Ephesians 1:5** NRSV
*He destined us for adoption as his chil-
dren through Jesus Christ, according to
the good pleasure of his will.*

MAIA, Maiah (see also Maija, Maya, Mia, Miya)
Language/Cultural Origin: **Greek**
Inherent Meaning: **Nurse**
Spiritual Connotation: **Healer**
Scripture: **Psalm 147:3** RSV
*He heals the brokenhearted, and binds up
their wounds.*

MAIJA, Maja, Majalyn (see also Maia, Maya, Mia, Miya)
Language/Cultural Origin: **Middle Eastern**
Inherent Meaning: **Splendid**
Spiritual Connotation: **Wondrous**
Scripture: **Micah 7:15** RSV
*As in the days when you came out of the
land of Egypt I will show them marvelous
things.*

MAITLAND, Maitlan, Maitlen
Language/Cultural Origin: **English**
Inherent Meaning: **From the Meadowland**
Spiritual Connotation: **Blessed**
Scripture: **Isaiah 30:23** NASB
*Then He will give you rain . . . and
bread from the yield of the ground, and
it will be rich and plenteous; on that
day your livestock will graze in a roomy
pasture.*

MAJOR, Majar, Majer
Language/Cultural Origin: **Latin**
Inherent Meaning: **Greater**
Spiritual Connotation: **Selfless**
Scripture: **John 15:13** NKJV
*Greater love has no one than this, than
to lay down one's life for his friends.*

MAKANA, Makanna
Language/Cultural Origin: **Hawaiian**
Inherent Meaning: **Present**
Spiritual Connotation: **Priceless Gift**
Scripture: **Romans 6:23** NKJV
For the wages of sin is death, but the gift

of God is eternal life in Christ Jesus our Lord.

MAKANI, Makánee
Language/Cultural Origin: **Hawaiian**
Inherent Meaning: **Wind**
Spiritual Connotation: **Mysterious**
Scripture: **John 3:8** TLB
Just as you can hear the wind but can't tell where it comes from or where it will go next, so it is with the Spirit.

MALA, Malea (see also Malaya, Malia)
Language/Cultural Origin: **English**
Inherent Meaning: **High Fortress**
Spiritual Connotation: **Child of God**
Scripture: **Joel 3:16** NKJV
The heavens and earth will shake; but the LORD will be a shelter for His people, and the strength of the children of Israel.

MALACHI, Malakai
☞ Language/Cultural Origin: **Hebrew**
Inherent Meaning: **Messenger of the Lord**
Spiritual Connotation: **Trustworthy**
Scripture: **Proverbs 25:13** RSV
Like the cold of snow in the time of harvest is a faithful messenger to those who send him, he refreshes the spirit of his masters.

MALANA, Malanna
Language/Cultural Origin: **Hawaiian**
Inherent Meaning: **Buoyant**
Spiritual Connotation: **Preserved**
Scripture: **John 10:9** NRSV
I am the gate. Whoever enters by me will be saved, and will come in and go out and find pasture.

MALAYA, Malaea (see also Mala, Malia)
Language/Cultural Origin: **Filipino**
Inherent Meaning: **Free**
Spiritual Connotation: **Liberated**
Scripture: **John 8:32** NKJV
And you shall know the truth, and the truth shall make you free.

MALCOLM, Malcom
Language/Cultural Origin: **Scottish**
Inherent Meaning: **Diligent Servant**

Spiritual Connotation: **Teachable Spirit**
Scripture: **Isaiah 42:16** NRSV
I will lead the blind by a road they do not know, by paths they have not known I will guide them. I will turn the darkness before them into light.

MALI, Malee, Maley, Malí (see also Malley)
Language/Cultural Origin: **Thai**
Inherent Meaning: **Flower**
Spiritual Connotation: **Joyful**
Scripture: **Isaiah 35:2** NKJV
It shall blossom abundantly and rejoice, even with joy and singing.

MALIA, Maleah, Maleia, Maliea (see also Mala, Malaya)
Language/Cultural Origin: **Irish**
Inherent Meaning: **Bitterness**
Spiritual Connotation: **Forgiven**
Scripture: **1 John 2:12** NRSV
I am writing to you, little children, because your sins are forgiven on account of his name.

MALIK, Maalik, Málik, Maliq, Malique
Language/Cultural Origin: **Middle Eastern**
Inherent Meaning: **The Lord's Messenger**
Spiritual Connotation: **Forerunner**
Scripture: **Mark 1:2** RSV
As it is written in Isaiah the prophet, "Behold, I send my messenger before thy face, who shall prepare thy way."

MALIKA, Maleeka, Maleka
Language/Cultural Origin: **Hungarian**
Inherent Meaning: **Industrious**
Spiritual Connotation: **Committed**
Scripture: **Colossians 3:23** TLB
Work hard and cheerfully at all you do, just as though you were working for the Lord and not merely for your masters.

MALIN, Mallin, Mallon, Maylin
Language/Cultural Origin: **Old English**
Inherent Meaning: **Little Warrior**
Spiritual Connotation: **Champion**
Scripture: **Matthew 5:6** NKJV
Blessed are those who hunger and thirst for righteousness, for they shall be filled.

MALINA, Malena (see also Milana, Milena)

Language/Cultural Origin: **Hebrew**
Inherent Meaning: **Tower**
Spiritual Connotation: **Secure**
Scripture: **Proverbs 18:10** NKJV
*The name of the LORD is a strong tower;
the righteous run to it and are safe.*

MALINDA, Malinde, Malynda (see also Melinda)

Language/Cultural Origin: **Greek**
Inherent Meaning: **Gentle**
Spiritual Connotation: **Tenderhearted**
Scripture: **1 Corinthians 3:16** NKJV
*Do you not know that you are the temple
of God and that the Spirit of God dwells
in you?*

MALLEY, Malli, Mallie (see also Mali)

Language/Cultural Origin: **English**
Inherent Meaning: **Bitterness**
Spiritual Connotation: **Peaceful**
Scripture: **Isaiah 38:17** NKJV
*Indeed it was for my own peace that I
had great bitterness; but You have lov-
ingly delivered my soul . . . for You have
cast all my sins behind Your back.*

MALLORY, Malerie, Mallari, Mallary, Mallerie, Mallery, Malloree, Mallorey, Mallori, Mallorie, Malori, Malorie, Malory

Language/Cultural Origin: **German**
Inherent Meaning: **Counselor**
Spiritual Connotation: **Joyful**
Scripture: **John 15:11** NKJV
*These things I have spoken to you, that
My joy may remain in you, and that
your joy may be full.*

MAMIE, Maymee

Language/Cultural Origin: **English**
Inherent Meaning: **Desired**
Spiritual Connotation: **Righteous**
Scripture: **Psalm 27:4** NCV
*I ask only one thing from the LORD. . . .
Let me live in the LORD's house all my
life. Let me see the LORD's beauty and
look with my own eyes at his temple.*

MANASSEH, Manassah

Language/Cultural Origin: **Hebrew**
Inherent Meaning: **Cause to Forget**
Spiritual Connotation: **Restored**
Scripture: **Psalm 103:12** NASB
*As far as the east is from the west, so
far has He removed our transgressions
from us.*

MANDEL, Mandell

Language/Cultural Origin: **German**
Inherent Meaning: **Almond**
Spiritual Connotation: **Sign**
Scripture: **Numbers 17:8** NCV
*[Moses] saw that Aaron's stick (which
stood for the family of Levi) had grown
leaves. It had even budded, blossomed,
and produced almonds.*

MANDIE, Manda, Mandaline, Mandalyn, Mandee, Mandi, Mandy (see also Amanda)

Language/Cultural Origin: **Latin**
Inherent Meaning: **Lovable**
Spiritual Connotation: **Eternal**
Scripture: **John 3:16** NKJV
*For God so loved the world that He gave
His only begotten Son, that whoever
believes in Him should not perish but
have everlasting life.*

MANLEY, Manlea, Manleigh

Language/Cultural Origin: **Irish**
Inherent Meaning: **Heroic**
Spiritual Connotation: **Victorious Spirit**
Scripture: **Isaiah 58:8** NKJV
*Then your light shall break forth like the
morning, your healing shall spring forth
speedily, and your righteousness shall go
before you.*

MANNING, Maning

Language/Cultural Origin: **English**
Inherent Meaning: **Child of the Hero**
Spiritual Connotation: **Obedient**
Scripture: **Proverbs 1:8** RSV
*Hear, my son, your father's instruction,
and reject not your mother's teaching.*

MANON, Mannon

Language/Cultural Origin: **French**
Inherent Meaning: **Wished-For**

Spiritual Connotation: **Fulfilled**

Scripture: **Psalm 132:14** NLT

This is my home where I will live forever,
he said. I will live here, for this is the
place I desired.

MANOR, Mannor

Language/Cultural Origin: **Hebrew**

Inherent Meaning: **Weaver's Beam**

Spiritual Connotation: **Creative**

Scripture: **Exodus 39:29** NIV

The sash was of finely twisted linen and
blue, purple and scarlet yarn—the work
of an embroiderer—as the LORD *com-*
manded Moses.

MANSEL, Mansell

Language/Cultural Origin: **Old English**

Inherent Meaning: **From the Pastor's House**

Spiritual Connotation: **Discerning**

Scripture: **1 John 2:14** RSV

I write to you, fathers, because you know
him who is from the beginning.

MANSIE, Mancey, Manci, Mancie, Mansey, Mansy

Language/Cultural Origin: **Hopi**

Inherent Meaning: **Pruned Blossom**

Spiritual Connotation: **Fruitful**

Scripture: **Hebrews 12:6** NLT

For the Lord disciplines those he loves,
and he punishes those he accepts as his
children.

MANTON, Manten

Language/Cultural Origin: **Old English**

Inherent Meaning: **From the Hero's Town**

Spiritual Connotation: **Wise**

Scripture: **Titus 2:6** TLB

In the same way, urge the young men to
behave carefully, taking life seriously.

MANUEL, Manni, Mannuel, Manny (see also Emanuel)

Language/Cultural Origin: **Spanish**

Inherent Meaning: **God With Us**

Spiritual Connotation: **Consecrated to God**

Scripture: **Isaiah 9:6** NKJV

For unto us a Child is born, unto us a
Son is given; and the government will be
upon His shoulder.

MANUELA, Manuelle (see also Emanuela)

Language/Cultural Origin: **Spanish**

Inherent Meaning: **God With Us**

Spiritual Connotation: **Consecrated to God**

Scripture: **Isaiah 7:14** NKJV

Therefore the Lord Himself will give you
a sign: Behold, the virgin shall conceive
and bear a Son, and shall call His name
Immanuel.

MANYA, Manyah

Language/Cultural Origin: **Russian**

Inherent Meaning: **Wished-For**

Spiritual Connotation: **Faithful**

Scripture: **Proverbs 19:22** NRSV

What is desirable in a person is loyalty,
and it is better to be poor than a liar.

MAON, Maeon, Mayon, Meion, Meyon (see also Maayan, Mahon)

Language/Cultural Origin: **Hebrew**

Inherent Meaning: **Habitation**

Spiritual Connotation: **Beautiful**

Scripture: **Psalm 84:1** RSV

How lovely is thy dwelling place, O
LORD *of hosts!*

MARA, Marah, Marra (see also ☞ Maria)

Language/Cultural Origin: **Hebrew**

Inherent Meaning: **Bitterness**

Spiritual Connotation: **Blessed**

Scripture: **Matthew 5:4** NKJV

Blessed are those who mourn, for they
shall be comforted.

MARCEL, Marcele, Marcelis, Marcelius, Marcell, Marcello, Marcellus, Marsel, Marsello

Language/Cultural Origin: **Latin**

Inherent Meaning: **Industrious Worker**

Spiritual Connotation: **Strong in Spirit**

Scripture: **Proverbs 4:23** NKJV

Keep your heart with all diligence, for out
of it spring the issues of life.

MARCELLA, Marceil, Marcele, Marcelia, Marcelle, Marcilla, Marcille, Marselle

Language/Cultural Origin: **Latin**

Inherent Meaning: **Warlike**

Spiritual Connotation: **Steadfast in Spirit**
Scripture: **Psalm 27:1** NKJV
*The LORD is my light and my salvation;
whom shall I fear? The LORD is the
strength of my life; of whom shall I be
afraid?*

**MARCIA, Marcee, Marci, Marciana,
Marcianna, Marcie, Marcy,
Marsey, Marsha, Marsi, Marsie,
Marsy**
Language/Cultural Origin: **Latin**
Inherent Meaning: **Fearless**
Spiritual Connotation: **Excellent Worth**
Scripture: **1 John 3:2** NKJV
*Beloved, now we are children of
God. . . . We shall be like Him, for we
shall see Him as He is.*

MARCUS, MARCO, see Mark

MAREN, Marin, Miren
Language/Cultural Origin: **Aramaic**
Inherent Meaning: **Longed-For**
Spiritual Connotation: **Holy**
Scripture: **Isaiah 26:9** RSV
*My soul yearns for thee in the night, my
spirit within me earnestly seeks thee.*

**MARGARET, Margara, Margarett,
Margarita, Margaux, Marge,
Margeret, Margerite, Margi,
Margie, Margo, Margot, Margret,
Marguerite (see also Maggie,
Marjorie)**
Language/Cultural Origin: **Greek**
Inherent Meaning: **Pearl**
Spiritual Connotation: **Gift of God**
Scripture: **Psalm 18:32** NKJV
*It is God who arms me with strength,
and makes my way perfect.*

**MARIA, Marea, Mareah, Marija,
Mariya, Mariyah, Marja, Marya
(see also Mara, Marie)**
Language/Cultural Origin: **Italian**
Inherent Meaning: **Bitterness**
Spiritual Connotation: **Delivered**
Scripture: **Isaiah 38:17** NKJV
*Indeed it was for my own peace that
I had great bitterness; but You have
lovingly delivered my soul . . . For You
have cast all my sins behind Your back.*

**MARIAH, Maraia, Maraya, Mariyah,
Marriah (see also Moriah)**
Language/Cultural Origin: **English**
Inherent Meaning: **Bitterness**
Spiritual Connotation: **Comforted**
Scripture: **1 Samuel 1:27** NKJV
*For this child I prayed, and the LORD has
granted me my petition which I asked of
Him.*

**MARIAN, Mariana, Mariane,
Mariann, Marianna, Marianne,
Mariene, Marion, Marrian,
Marrianne, Maryana, Maryanna**
Language/Cultural Origin: **English**
Inherent Meaning: **Bitterness**
Spiritual Connotation: **Grace**
Scripture: **Isaiah 60:19** NRSV
*The sun shall no longer be your light
by day . . . but the LORD will be your
everlasting light, and your God will be
your glory.*

**MARIE, Maree (see also Maria,
Mary)**
Language/Cultural Origin: **French**
Inherent Meaning: **Bitterness**
Spiritual Connotation: **Consoled**
Scripture: **Isaiah 2:11** NCV
*Proud people will be made humble, and
they will bow low with shame. At that
time only the LORD will still be praised.*

**MARIEL, Marial, Mariela, Mariele,
Mariella, Marielle (see also
Maurelle, Merial, Muriel)**
Language/Cultural Origin: **English**
Inherent Meaning: **Bitterness**
Spiritual Connotation: **Exonerated**
Scripture: **Romans 8:30** NRSV
*And those whom he predestined he also
called; and those whom he called he also
justified; and those whom he justified he
also glorified.*

**MARIKA, Marica, Marrika, Maryka,
Merika**
Language/Cultural Origin: **Greek**
Inherent Meaning: **Bitterness**

Spiritual Connotation: **Vindicated**
Scripture: **Micah 5:9** NCV
So you will raise your fist in victory over your enemies, and all your enemies will be destroyed.

MARIKO, Meriko

Language/Cultural Origin: **Japanese**
Inherent Meaning: **Circle**
Spiritual Connotation: **Believer**
Scripture: **Isaiah 40:22** NCV
God sits on his throne above the circle of the earth, and compared to him, people are like grasshoppers.

MARILEE, Marrilee, Merrilee, Merrily

Language/Cultural Origin: **English**
Inherent Meaning: **Bitterness**
Spiritual Connotation: **Vindicated**
Scripture: **Job 13:18** NLT
I have prepared my case; I will be proved innocent.

MARILU, Marilow, Marylou

Language/Cultural Origin: **American**
Inherent Meaning: **Bitter Grace**
Spiritual Connotation: **Blessed**
Scripture: **Ephesians 1:6** TLB
Now all praise to God for his wonderful kindness to us and his favor that he has poured out upon us, because we belong to his dearly loved Son.

MARILYN, Maralin, Maralyn, Maralyne, Maralynn, Marillyn, Marilynn, Marralin, Marrilyn, Marrilynn, Marylin

Language/Cultural Origin: **English**
Inherent Meaning: **Bitterness**
Spiritual Connotation: **Sacrifice of Praise**
Scripture: **Psalm 69:30** NASB
I will praise the name of God with song, and shall magnify Him with thanksgiving.

MARINA, Marena, Marrina, Merina

Language/Cultural Origin: **Russian**
Inherent Meaning: **From the Sea**
Spiritual Connotation: **Wonder of God**
Scripture: **Psalm 93:4** NRSV
More majestic than the thunders of mighty waters, more majestic than the waves of the sea, majestic on high is the LORD!

MARIO, Marios, Marrio

Language/Cultural Origin: **Italian**
Inherent Meaning: **Sailor**
Spiritual Connotation: **Regenerated**
Scripture: **John 6:63** NRSV
It is the spirit that gives life; the flesh is useless. The words that I have spoken to you are spirit and life.

MARION, see Marian

MARISSA, Maressa, Maris, Marisa, Marise, Marisha, Marishka, Mariska, Marisse, Marris, Marrisa, Marrissa, Marrissia, Marysa, Maryssa, Meris, Merisa, Merissa

Language/Cultural Origin: **English**
Inherent Meaning: **Bitterness**
Spiritual Connotation: **Eternally Steadfast**
Scripture: **Job 13:15** NKJV
Though He slay me, yet will I trust Him. Even so, I will defend my own ways before Him.

MARIT, Marita, Merit

Language/Cultural Origin: **Aramaic**
Inherent Meaning: **Lady**
Spiritual Connotation: **Righteous**
Scripture: **Proverbs 31:10** TLB
If you can find a truly good wife, she is worth more than precious gems!

MARIUS, Mariano, Marino

Language/Cultural Origin: **Latin**
Inherent Meaning: **Warlike**
Spiritual Connotation: **Powerful**
Scripture: **Joel 2:7** NRSV
Like warriors they charge, like soldiers they scale the wall. Each keeps to its own course, they do not swerve from their paths.

MARJORIE, Margerie, Marjarie, Marjerie, Marji, Marjie, Marjorey, Marjori, Marjory

Language/Cultural Origin: **Latin**
Inherent Meaning: **Pearl**
Spiritual Connotation: **Gift of Praise**
Scripture: **Psalm 104:24** NASB
O LORD, how many are Your works!

In wisdom You have made them all; the earth is full of Your possessions.

MARK, Marc, Marciano, Marcio, Marco, Marcos, Marcus, Marek, Marke, Markeese, Markei, Markey, Markice, Marko, Markos, Markques, Markus, Márkus, Marqes, Marques, Marquez, Marqui, Marquis, Marx
Language/Cultural Origin: **Latin**
Inherent Meaning: **Martial**
Spiritual Connotation: **Servant of God**
Scripture: **John 4:24** RSV
God is spirit, and those who worship him must worship in spirit and truth.

MARKITA, Markeeta
Language/Cultural Origin: **Bulgarian**
Inherent Meaning: **Pearl**
Spiritual Connotation: **Wise**
Scripture: **Job 28:18** NKJV
No mention shall be made of coral or quartz, for the price of wisdom is above rubies.

MARLAND, Marlan
Language/Cultural Origin: **Old Englilsh**
Inherent Meaning: **From the Lake Land**
Spiritual Connotation: **Destined**
Scripture: **Ephesians 2:10** NKJV
For we are His workmanship, created in Christ Jesus for good works, which God prepared beforehand that we should walk in them.

MARLENE, Marla, Marlah, Marlaina, Marlaine, Marlana, Marlanna, Marlayne, Marlea, Marleah, Marlee, Marleen, Marleena, Marleigh, Marlena, Marli, Marlie, Marlina, Marline, Marlis, Marlo, Marlow, Marly, Marlys, Marlysa, Marlyssa
Language/Cultural Origin: **Slavic**
Inherent Meaning: **High Fortress**
Spiritual Connotation: **Shielded**
Scripture: **Psalm 61:3** TLB
For you are my refuge, a high tower where my enemies can never reach me.

MARLON, Marlin
Language/Cultural Origin: **Welsh**
Inherent Meaning: **From the Hill by the Sea**
Spiritual Connotation: **Victorious Spirit**
Scripture: **Psalm 8:6** NKJV
You have made him to have dominion over the works of Your hands; You have put all things under his feet.

MARNINA, Marna, Marne, Marnee, Marney, Marni, Marnia, Marnie, Marnja, Marnya
Language/Cultural Origin: **Hebrew**
Inherent Meaning: **Rejoice**
Spiritual Connotation: **Content**
Scripture: **Philippians 4:4** NKJV
Rejoice in the Lord always. Again I will say, rejoice!

MARSDEN, Marsdon
Language/Cultural Origin: **English**
Inherent Meaning: **From the Boundary Valley**
Spiritual Connotation: **Preserved**
Scripture: **Psalm 46:1** NKJV
God is our refuge and strength, a very present help in trouble.

MARSHA, see Marcia

MARSHALL, Marschal, Marshal, Marshel, Marshell
Language/Cultural Origin: **Old French**
Inherent Meaning: **Caretaker**
Spiritual Connotation: **Faithful**
Scripture: **Psalm 40:4** NKJV
Blessed is that man who makes the LORD his trust, and does not respect the proud, nor such as turn aside to lies.

MARTHA, Marta, Marti, Martie, Martika, Marty, Mattie
Language/Cultural Origin: **Aramaic**
Inherent Meaning: **Mistress of the House**
Spiritual Connotation: **Helpful Spirit**
Scripture: **Proverbs 31:27** NKJV
She watches over the ways of her household, and does not eat the bread of idleness.

MARTIN, Martan, Marten, Martinez, Marton, Marty, Martyn
Language/Cultural Origin: **Latin**

Inherent Meaning: **Warlike**
Spiritual Connotation: **Seeker of Truth**
Scripture: **John 15:7** NKJV
If you abide in Me, and My words abide in you, you will ask what you desire, and it shall be done for you.

MARTINA, Martel, Martelle, Marthina, Martinia, Martiza, Martoya, Martrina, Martyna
Language/Cultural Origin: **Hispanic**
Inherent Meaning: **Lady of the House**
Spiritual Connotation: **Virtuous**
Scripture: **1 Timothy 2:10** NLT
For women who claim to be devoted to God should make themselves attractive by the good things they do.

MARVEL, Marvelle
Language/Cultural Origin: **Latin**
Inherent Meaning: **Miracle**
Spiritual Connotation: **Sustained**
Scripture: **2 Corinthians 12:9** NKJV
My grace is sufficient for you, for My strength is made perfect in weakness.

MARVIN, Marv, Marven, Merv, Mervin
Language/Cultural Origin: **Welsh**
Inherent Meaning: **Lover of the Sea**
Spiritual Connotation: **Trusting Spirit**
Scripture: **Psalm 91:2** NLT
This I declare of the LORD: He alone is my refuge, my place of safety; he is my God, and I am trusting him.

MARY, Mari, Marietta, Meri (see also ☞ Mara, Maria, Marie)
Language/Cultural Origin: **Hebrew**
Inherent Meaning: **Sea of Bitterness**
Spiritual Connotation: **Blessed**
Scripture: **Luke 1:28** NKJV
And having come in, the angel said to her, "Rejoice, highly favored one, the Lord is with you; blessed are you among women!"

MARYLOU, see Marilu

MASADA, Massada
Language/Cultural Origin: **Hebrew**
Inherent Meaning: **Foundation**
Spiritual Connotation: **Enlightened**

Scripture: **Matthew 21:42** NKJV
The stone which the builders rejected has become the chief cornerstone. This was the Lord's doing, and it is marvelous in our eyes.

MASLIN, Maslen
Language/Cultural Origin: **French**
Inherent Meaning: **Little Twin**
Spiritual Connotation: **Bold**
Scripture: **John 11:16** NRSV
Thomas, who was called the Twin, said to his fellow disciples, "Let us also go, that we may die with him."

MASON, Maison
Language/Cultural Origin: **Old French**
Inherent Meaning: **Stoneworker**
Spiritual Connotation: **Overcomer**
Scripture: **Revelation 2:17** NRSV
To everyone who conquers . . . I will give a white stone, and on the white stone is written a new name that no one knows except the one who receives it.

MATANA, Matanna
Language/Cultural Origin: **Hebrew**
Inherent Meaning: **Gift**
Spiritual Connotation: **Blessed**
Scripture: **Ephesians 4:7** NKJV
But to each one of us grace was given according to the measure of Christ's gift.

MATHER, Mathre
Language/Cultural Origin: **English**
Inherent Meaning: **Conqueror**
Spiritual Connotation: **Intuitive**
Scripture: **Luke 6:45** TLB
A good man produces good deeds from a good heart. . . . Whatever is in the heart overflows into speech.

MATHILDA, Tilda, Tillie
Language/Cultural Origin: **German**
Inherent Meaning: **Noble Lady**
Spiritual Connotation: **Beloved**
Scripture: **Luke 12:32** NKJV
Do not fear, little flock, for it is your Father's good pleasure to give you the kingdom.

MATRIKA, Matreika
Language/Cultural Origin: **Indo-Pakastani**

Inherent Meaning: **Mother**
Spiritual Connotation: **Nurturing**
Scripture: **1 Timothy 5:2** NLT
Treat the older women as you would your mother, and treat the younger women with all purity as your own sisters.

MATSUKO, Metsuko
Language/Cultural Origin: **Japanese**
Inherent Meaning: **Evergreen**
Spiritual Connotation: **Perpetual**
Scripture: **Isaiah 55:13** NIV
Instead of the thornbush will grow the pine tree, and instead of briers the myrtle will grow. This will be . . . an everlasting sign.

MATTEA, Matea, Mathea
Language/Cultural Origin: **Hebrew**
Inherent Meaning: **Gift of God**
Spiritual Connotation: **Blessed**
Scripture: **Ephesians 2:8-9** RSV
For by grace you have been saved through faith; . . . it is the gift of God— not because of works, lest any man should boast.

MATTHEW, Mateo, Mathew, Mathias, Mathieux, Matt, Matthias
Language/Cultural Origin: **Hebrew**
Inherent Meaning: **Gift of God**
Spiritual Connotation: **Honor to God**
Scripture: **Psalm 104:1** KJV
Bless the LORD, O my soul. O LORD my God, thou art very great; thou art clothed with honour and majesty.

MAUDE, Maud
Language/Cultural Origin: **English**
Inherent Meaning: **Noble Lady**
Spiritual Connotation: **Victorious**
Scripture: **Isaiah 25:8** NKJV
He will swallow up death forever, and the Lord GOD will wipe away tears from all faces.

MAUREEN, Maura, Maurene, Maurine
Language/Cultural Origin: **Irish**
Inherent Meaning: **Wished-for Child**
Spiritual Connotation: **Beloved**
Scripture: **Psalm 139:17** NASB

How precious also are Your thoughts to me, O God! How vast is the sum of them!

MAURELLE, Maurial, Mauriall, Mauriel, Mauriell, Maurielle (see also Mariel, Merial, Muriel)
Language/Cultural Origin: **French**
Inherent Meaning: **Dark**
Spiritual Connotation: **Peaceful**
Scripture: **James 3:17** NKJV
But the wisdom that is from above is first pure, then peaceable, gentle, willing to yield, full of mercy and good fruits, without partiality and without hypocrisy.

MAURICE, Maury, Morrice, Morrie, Morris, Morry
Language/Cultural Origin: **Latin**
Inherent Meaning: **From the Marshland**
Spiritual Connotation: **Conciliatory**
Scripture: **Proverbs 16:7** NKJV
When a man's ways please the LORD, he makes even his enemies to be at peace with him.

MAVIS, Mayvis
Language/Cultural Origin: **French**
Inherent Meaning: **Songbird**
Spiritual Connotation: **Praise**
Scripture: **Psalm 138:2** NCV
I will bow down facing your holy Temple, and I will thank you for your love and loyalty. You have made your name and your word greater than anything.

MAXIMILLIAN, Max, Maximilian, Maxx
Language/Cultural Origin: **Latin**
Inherent Meaning: **Greatest in Excellence**
Spiritual Connotation: **Teachable Spirit**
Scripture: **Isaiah 64:8** NRSV
Yet, O LORD, you are our Father; we are the clay, and you are our potter; we are all the work of your hand.

MAXINE, Maxeen, Maxene
Language/Cultural Origin: **Latin**
Inherent Meaning: **Greatest in Excellence**
Spiritual Connotation: **Secure in Truth**
Scripture: **Philippians 3:15** NKJV
Therefore let us, as many as are mature, have this mind; and if in anything you

think otherwise, God will reveal even this to you.

MAXWELL, Max, Maxx
Language/Cultural Origin: **Scottish**
Inherent Meaning: **From the Great Spring**
Spiritual Connotation: **Righteous**
Scripture: **Matthew 6:22** NASB
The eye is the lamp of the body; so then if your eye is clear, your whole body will be full of light.

MAY, Mae, Maye
Language/Cultural Origin: **Hebrew**
Inherent Meaning: **Gift of God**
Spiritual Connotation: **Blessed**
Scripture: **Psalm 92:4** KJV
For thou, Lord, hast made me glad through thy work: I will triumph in the works of thy hands.

MAYA, Mayah (see also Maia, Maija, Mia, Miya)
Language/Cultural Origin: **Latin**
Inherent Meaning: **Esteemed**
Spiritual Connotation: **Honored**
Scripture: **Psalm 143:8** TLB
Let me see your kindness to me in the morning, for I am trusting you. Show me where to walk, for my prayer is sincere.

MAYER, Mayor (see also Meyer)
Language/Cultural Origin: **Latin**
Inherent Meaning: **Renowned**
Spiritual Connotation: **Enlightened**
Scripture: **Romans 12:2** NRSV
Do not be conformed to this world, but be transformed by the renewing of your minds.

MAYHEW, Maihew
Language/Cultural Origin: **Latin**
Inherent Meaning: **Gift of God**
Spiritual Connotation: **United in Spirit**
Scripture: **2 Corinthians 13:11** NKJV
Be of good comfort, be of one mind, live in peace; and the God of love and peace will be with you.

MAYNARD, Ménard
Language/Cultural Origin: **Old English**
Inherent Meaning: **Powerful**
Spiritual Connotation: **Spirit of Praise**

Scripture: **1 Corinthians 14:15** NLT
Well then, what shall I do? I will pray in the spirit, and I will also pray in words I understand.

MAYO, Maiyo
Language/Cultural Origin: **Irish**
Inherent Meaning: **From the Yew-Tree Plain**
Spiritual Connotation: **Heart of Praise**
Scripture: **Psalm 96:1** KJV
O sing unto the LORD a new song: sing unto the LORD, all the earth.

MEARA, Mearah (see also Meira, Mira, Mura)
Language/Cultural Origin: **Irish**
Inherent Meaning: **Mirthful**
Spiritual Connotation: **Gift of Discernment**
Scripture: **Psalm 119:18** NKJV
Open my eyes, that I may see wondrous things from Your law.

MEDINA, Medaena, Medaina, Medinah
Language/Cultural Origin: **Hebrew**
Inherent Meaning: **State/country**
Spiritual Connotation: **Intercessor**
Scripture: **Exodus 33:13** NCV
If I have truly pleased you, show me your plans so that I may know you and continue to please you. Remember that this nation is your people.

MEDORA, Medorra
Language/Cultural Origin: **English**
Inherent Meaning: **Mother's Gift**
Spiritual Connotation: **Blessing**
Scripture: **Luke 2:7** NRSV
And she gave birth to her firstborn son and wrapped him in bands of cloth, and laid him in a manger, because there was no place for them in the inn.

MEGAN, Maegan, Maeghan, Magan, Magen, Meagan, Meagann, Meagen, Meaghan, Meaghann, Meg, Megen, Meggan, Meggen, Meggie, Meghan, Meghann
Language/Cultural Origin: **Welsh**
Inherent Meaning: **Mighty**
Spiritual Connotation: **Victorious Spirit**

Scripture: **Isaiah 2:5** NRSV
O house of Jacob, come, let us walk in the light of the LORD!

MEIRA, Meera (see also Meara, Mira, Mura)
Language/Cultural Origin: **Hebrew**
Inherent Meaning: **Light**
Spiritual Connotation: **Exalted**
Scripture: **Isaiah 60:1** RSV
Arise, shine; for your light has come, and the glory of the LORD has risen upon you.

MELANIE, Melainie, Melanee, Melaney, Melani, Mélanie, Melaniya, Melanney, Melannie, Melanya, Mellanie
Language/Cultural Origin: **Greek**
Inherent Meaning: **Dark**
Spiritual Connotation: **Child of God**
Scripture: **Ezekiel 37:13** NASB
Then you will know that I am the LORD, when I have opened your graves and caused you to come up out of your graves, My people.

MELINDA, Mellinda, Melynda (see also Malinda)
Language/Cultural Origin: **Greek**
Inherent Meaning: **Honey**
Spiritual Connotation: **Cherished**
Scripture: **Isaiah 58:11** NKJV
The LORD will guide you continually, and satisfy your soul in drought, and strengthen your bones; you shall be like a watered garden.

MELISSA, Malissa, Mallissa, Melisa, Mélisa, Mélissa, Mellisa, Mellissa, Milissa, Millisa, Millissa, Missi, Missie, Missy, Mylis, Mylissa
Language/Cultural Origin: **Greek**
Inherent Meaning: **Honey Bee**
Spiritual Connotation: **Industrious, Creative**
Scripture: **James 2:22** NASB
You see that faith was working with his works, and as a result of the works, faith was perfected.

MELITA, Malita
Language/Cultural Origin: **Greek**
Inherent Meaning: **Sweetened With Honey**

Spiritual Connotation: **Content**
Scripture: **Psalm 145:16** NASB
Thou dost open Thy hand, and dost satisfy the desire of every living thing.

MELODY, Melodee, Melodey, Melodi, Melodie
Language/Cultural Origin: **English**
Inherent Meaning: **Song**
Spiritual Connotation: **Joyful**
Scripture: **Psalm 63:5** NRSV
My soul is satisfied as with a rich feast, and my mouth praises you with joyful lips.

MELORA, Melorra
Language/Cultural Origin: **Latin**
Inherent Meaning: **Improved**
Spiritual Connotation: **Sanctified**
Scripture: **Philippians 1:6** NRSV
I am confident of this, that the one who began a good work among you will bring it to completion by the day of Jesus Christ.

MELVIN, Malvin, Mel
Language/Cultural Origin: **Middle English**
Inherent Meaning: **Reliable Friend**
Spiritual Connotation: **Excellent Virtue**
Scripture: **Ephesians 3:19** TLB
And so at last you will be filled up with God himself.

MENDEL, Mendell
Language/Cultural Origin: **Hebrew**
Inherent Meaning: **Wisdom**
Spiritual Connotation: **Studious**
Scripture: **Proverbs 19:8** NLT
To acquire wisdom is to love oneself; people who cherish understanding will prosper.

MENORA, Manora
Language/Cultural Origin: **Hebrew**
Inherent Meaning: **Candelabrum**
Spiritual Connotation: **Witness**
Scripture: **Matthew 5:14** NASB
You are the light of the world. A city set on a hill cannot be hidden.

MERCEDES, Mersade
Language/Cultural Origin: **Latin**
Inherent Meaning: **Gift**
Spiritual Connotation: **Esteemed**

Scripture: **Isaiah 52:7** NRSV
How beautiful upon the mountains are the feet of the messenger who announces peace, who brings good news.

MEREDITH, Meredithe, Meredyth, Merideth, Meridith, Merridith, Merry

Language/Cultural Origin: **Welsh**
Inherent Meaning: **Guardian of the Sea**
Spiritual Connotation: **Faithful Friend**
Scripture: **Proverbs 2:10-11** NKJV
When wisdom enters your heart, and knowledge is pleasant to your soul, discretion will preserve you; understanding will keep you.

MERIAL, Meriel, Meriol (see also Mariel, Maurelle, Muriel)

Language/Cultural Origin: **Irish**
Inherent Meaning: **Shining Sea**
Spiritual Connotation: **Cherished**
Scripture: **Psalm 139:9-10** RSV
If I take the wings of the morning and dwell in the uttermost parts of the sea, even there thy hand shall lead me, and thy right hand shall hold me.

MERLIN, Merle, Merlen

Language/Cultural Origin: **Old English**
Inherent Meaning: **Falcon**
Spiritual Connotation: **Courageous**
Scripture: **Deuteronomy 31:6** RSV
Be strong and of good courage, do not fear or be in dread of them: for it is the LORD your God who goes with you; he will not fail you or forsake you.

MERRILL, Meril, Merill, Merril (see also Meryl)

Language/Cultural Origin: **French**
Inherent Meaning: **Famous**
Spiritual Connotation: **Honored**
Scripture: **Ecclesiastes 2:26** NASB
For to a person who is good in His sight He has given wisdom and knowledge and joy.

MERRILY, see Marilee

MERTON, Murton

Language/Cultural Origin: **Middle English**
Inherent Meaning: **From the Town by the Sea**

Spiritual Connotation: **Child of God**
Scripture: **Romans 8:16** NKJV
The Spirit Himself bears witness with our spirit that we are children of God.

MERVIN, see Marvin

MERYL, Meral, Merel, Merrall, Merryl, Meryll (see also Merrill)

Language/Cultural Origin: **German**
Inherent Meaning: **Famous**
Spiritual Connotation: **Chosen**
Scripture: **Isaiah 52:13** NASB
Behold, My servant will prosper, he will be high and lifted up and greatly exalted.

MEYER, Meier, Myer (see also Mayer)

Language/Cultural Origin: **German**
Inherent Meaning: **Farmer**
Spiritual Connotation: **Blessed**
Scripture: **Isaiah 28:26** NLT
The farmer knows just what to do, for God has given him understanding.

MIA, Meah, Miah (see also Maia, Maija, Maya, Miya)

Language/Cultural Origin: **English**
Inherent Meaning: **Wished-For**
Spiritual Connotation: **Devout**
Scripture: **Psalm 27:4** RSV
One thing have I asked of the LORD: . . . that I may dwell in the house of the LORD all the days of my life, to behold the beauty of the LORD, and to inquire in his temple.

MICAH, Mica, Micaiah, Michah, ☞Mycah

Language/Cultural Origin: **Hebrew**
Inherent Meaning: **Who Is Like God?**
Spiritual Connotation: **Reverent**
Scripture: **Psalm 113:5** NKJV
Who is like the LORD our God, who dwells on high?

MICHAEL, Mekhail, Micael, Mical, ☞Michale, Micheal, Michel, Mick, Mickey, Mickie, Micky, Mikael, Mikáele, Mikal, Mike, Mikhael, Mikhail, Miki, Mikki, Mychal, Mychael, Mycheal, Mykael, Mykal

Language/Cultural Origin: **Hebrew**

Inherent Meaning: **Who Is Like God?**
Spiritual Connotation: **Esteemed**
Scripture: **Exodus 15:11** NKJV
Who is like You, O LORD, among the gods? Who is like You, glorious in holiness, fearful in praises, doing wonders?

MICHAL, Machelle, Makayla, Mekaela, Mekala, Mekayla, Meshelle, Micaela, Michaela, Michaele, Michaelle, Michala, Michayla, Michayle, Michele, Michèle, Michelle, Mikaela, Mikalya, Mikyla, Mischel, Mishayle, Mychaela, Mykaela, Mykala
Language/Cultural Origin: **Hebrew**
Inherent Meaning: **Who Is Like God?**
Spiritual Connotation: **Godliness**
Scripture: **Psalm 71:19** NASB
For Your righteousness, O God, reaches to the heavens, You who have done great things; O God, who is like You?

MIDORI, Midoree
Language/Cultural Origin: **Japanese**
Inherent Meaning: **Green**
Spiritual Connotation: **Restful**
Scripture: **Psalm 23:2** RSV
He makes me lie down in green pastures. He leads me beside still waters.

MIGUEL, Migel
Language/Cultural Origin: **Portuguese**
Inherent Meaning: **Who Is Like God?**
Spiritual Connotation: **Victorious Spirit**
Scripture: **Philippians 2:13** RSV
For God is at work in you, both to will and to work for his good pleasure.

MILADA, Miladah, Milady
Language/Cultural Origin: **Czech**
Inherent Meaning: **My Love**
Spiritual Connotation: **Beloved**
Scripture: **1 Corinthians 16:24** NKJV
My love be with you all in Christ Jesus. Amen.

MILAN, Milen, Mylan, Mylen, Mylon
Language/Cultural Origin: **Italian**
Inherent Meaning: **From Milan**
Spiritual Connotation: **Witness**

Scripture: **Romans 1:16** NKJV
For I am not ashamed of the gospel of Christ, for it is the power of God to salvation for everyone who believes, for the Jew first and also for the Greek.

MILANA, Milani, Milania, Milanna (see also Malina)
Language/Cultural Origin: **Italian**
Inherent Meaning: **From Milan**
Spiritual Connotation: **Blessed**
Scripture: **Romans 2:10** NLT
But there will be glory and honor and peace from God for all who do good—for the Jew first and also for the Gentile.

MILDRED, Midge, Mildrid
Language/Cultural Origin: **Old English**
Inherent Meaning: **Gentle Spirit**
Spiritual Connotation: **Loving**
Scripture: **1 John 4:7** NLT
Dear friends, let us continue to love one another, for love comes from God. Anyone who loves is born of God and knows God.

MILENA, Milèna, Milenia, Milenya (see also Malina)
Language/Cultural Origin: **Slavic**
Inherent Meaning: **Dark**
Spiritual Connotation: **Prepared**
Scripture: **1 Thessalonians 5:2** NRSV
For you yourselves know very well that the day of the Lord will come like a thief in the night.

MILES, Myles
Language/Cultural Origin: **German**
Inherent Meaning: **Merciful**
Spiritual Connotation: **Heart of Compassion**
Scripture: **Proverbs 18:16** NRSV
A gift opens doors; it gives access to the great.

MILIANI, Milianni
Language/Cultural Origin: **Hawaiian**
Inherent Meaning: **Caress**
Spiritual Connotation: **Treasured**
Scripture: **Song of Songs 4:7** NCV
My darling, everything about you is beautiful, and there is nothing at all wrong with you.

MILLARD, Miller, Myller
Language/Cultural Origin: **Latin**
Inherent Meaning: **Caretaker**
Spiritual Connotation: **Excellent Worth**
Scripture: **1 Chronicles 29:12** NCV
Riches and honor come from you. You rule everything. You have the power and strength to make anyone great and strong.

MILLICENT, Melisenda, Mellicent, Millee, Millie, Milly
Language/Cultural Origin: **Old German**
Inherent Meaning: **Industrious**
Spiritual Connotation: **Strong Spirit**
Scripture: **1 Corinthians 1:25** NKJV
Because the foolishness of God is wiser than men, and the weakness of God is stronger than men.

MILO, Mylo
Language/Cultural Origin: **Old German**
Inherent Meaning: **Generous**
Spiritual Connotation: **Helpful Spirit**
Scripture: **Isaiah 30:29** NKJV
You shall have a song as in the night when a holy festival is kept, and gladness of heart.

MILTON, Milt, Mylton
Language/Cultural Origin: **English**
Inherent Meaning: **From the Mill Town**
Spiritual Connotation: **Blessed of God**
Scripture: **Romans 12:6** NKJV
Having then gifts differing according to the grace that is given to us, let us use them.

MIMI, Mimee, Mimie, Mimii
Language/Cultural Origin: **English**
Inherent Meaning: **Wished-for**
Spiritual Connotation: **Spiritual Passion**
Scripture: **Psalm 27:4** NKJV
One thing I have desired of the LORD . . . that I may dwell in the house of the LORD all the days of my life, to behold the beauty of the LORD, and to inquire in His temple.

MINDY, Mindee, Mindi, Mindie, Myndee, Myndie
Language/Cultural Origin: **English**

Inherent Meaning: **Sweet as Honey**
Spiritual Connotation: **Genuine**
Scripture: **Revelation 10:10** NRSV
So I took the little scroll from the hand of the angel and ate it; it was sweet as honey in my mouth.

MINGAN, Mingen
Language/Cultural Origin: **Native American**
Inherent Meaning: **Gray Wolf**
Spiritual Connotation: **Vigilant**
Scripture: **1 Peter 5:8** NRSV
Discipline yourselves, keep alert. Like a roaring lion your adversary the devil prowls around, looking for someone to devour.

MINH, Min
Language/Cultural Origin: **Vietnamese**
Inherent Meaning: **Light**
Spiritual Connotation: **Enlightened**
Scripture: **John 8:12** NRSV
Again Jesus spoke to them, saying, I am the light of the world. Whoever follows me will never walk in darkness but will have the light of life.

MINNA, Meena, Mena, Mina, Mini, Minni, Minnie, Minny
Language/Cultural Origin: **Old German**
Inherent Meaning: **Love**
Spiritual Connotation: **Cherished**
Scripture: **Isaiah 35:1** NASB
The wilderness and the desert will be glad, and the Arabah will rejoice.

MIRA, Mirah, Mirra (see also Meara, Meira, Mura)
Language/Cultural Origin: **English**
Inherent Meaning: **Wonderful**
Spiritual Connotation: **Worshipful**
Scripture: **1 Chronicles 16:9** TLB
Sing to him; yes, sing his praises and tell of his marvelous works.

MIRANDA, Maranda, Meranda, Mirranda, Myranda
Language/Cultural Origin: **Latin**
Inherent Meaning: **Admirable**
Spiritual Connotation: **Beloved**
Scripture: **Proverbs 3:6** TLB
In everything you do, put God first, and

he will direct you and crown your efforts with success.

MIRIAM, Mariam, Mariame, ☞ Mariamne, Miriame, Mirriam, Myriam, Myriame
Language/Cultural Origin: **Hebrew**
Inherent Meaning: **Bitterness**
Spiritual Connotation: **Discerning**
Scripture: **Jeremiah 30:3** NRSV
For the days are surely coming, says the LORD, when I will restore the fortunes of my people.

MIRON, Miran (see also Myron)
Language/Cultural Origin: **Polish**
Inherent Meaning: **Peace**
Spiritual Connotation: **Commissioned**
Scripture: **John 20:21** NASB
Jesus therefore said to them again, "Peace be with you; as the Father has sent Me, I also send you."

MISHA, Mischa, Mishka
Language/Cultural Origin: **Russian**
Inherent Meaning: **Who Is Like God?**
Spiritual Connotation: **Disciple**
Scripture: **Psalm 71:19** NASB
For Thy righteousness, O God, reaches to the heavens, Thou who hast done great things; O God, who is like Thee?

MISHAN, Mishán, Mishaun, Mishawn, Mishon
Language/Cultural Origin: **Hebrew**
Inherent Meaning: **Support**
Spiritual Connotation: **Helpful**
Scripture: **Galatians 6:2** TLB
Share each other's troubles and problems, and so obey our Lord's command.

MITCHELL, Mitch, Mitchall, Mytch, Mytchell
Language/Cultural Origin: **English**
Inherent Meaning: **Who Is Like God?**
Spiritual Connotation: **Consecrated to God**
Scripture: **Numbers 6:8** NKJV
All the days of his separation he shall be holy to the LORD.

MITZI, Mitzee, Mitzie
Language/Cultural Origin: **German**
Inherent Meaning: **Bitterness**

Spiritual Connotation: **Vindicated**
Scripture: **Acts 3:21** NCV
But Jesus must stay in heaven until the time comes when all things will be made right again.

MIYA, Miyana, Miyanna (see also Maia, Maija, Maya, Mia)
Language/Cultural Origin: **Japanese**
Inherent Meaning: **Temple**
Spiritual Connotation: **Pure**
Scripture: **1 Corinthians 6:19** TLB
Haven't you yet learned that your body is the home of the Holy Spirit God gave you? . . . Your own body does not belong to you.

MIYO, Miyoko, Miyuko
Language/Cultural Origin: **Japanese**
Inherent Meaning: **Beautiful Generation**
Spiritual Connotation: **Spirit of Praise**
Scripture: **Psalm 79:13** NRSV
Then we your people, the flock of your pasture, will give thanks to you forever; from generation to generation we will recount your praise.

MOHALA, Moala
Language/Cultural Origin: **Hawaiian**
Inherent Meaning: **Blooming**
Spiritual Connotation: **Destined**
Scripture: **Hosea 14:7** NCV
The people of Israel will again live under my protection. They will grow like the grain, they will bloom like a vine.

MOIRA, Moirah, Moyra, Moyrah (see also Mora)
Language/Cultural Origin: **Irish**
Inherent Meaning: **Wished-For**
Spiritual Connotation: **Zealous**
Scripture: **Psalm 119:20** NRSV
My soul is consumed with longing for your ordinances at all times.

MOISES, see Moses

MOLLY, Mollee, Molley, Molli, Mollie
Language/Cultural Origin: **English**
Inherent Meaning: **Desired**
Spiritual Connotation: **Righteous**
Scripture: **Isaiah 26:9** NRSV
My soul yearns for you in the night. . . .

For when your judgments are in the earth, the inhabitants of the world learn righteousness.

MONA, Monna, Moyna
Language/Cultural Origin: Irish
Inherent Meaning: Noble
Spiritual Connotation: Reflection of Wisdom
Scripture: Proverbs 2:6 NKJV
For the LORD gives wisdom; from His mouth come knowledge and understanding.

MONICA, Moneka, Moni, Monicka, Monika, Monique, Monnica, Monnika
Language/Cultural Origin: Latin
Inherent Meaning: Advisor
Spiritual Connotation: Consecrated
Scripture: 2 Corinthians 1:21 NRSV
But it is God who establishes us with you in Christ and has anointed us.

MONROE, Munroe
Language/Cultural Origin: Irish
Inherent Meaning: From the Hill
Spiritual Connotation: Trusting
Scripture: Mark 9:23 NRSV
All things can be done for the one who believes.

MONTANA, Montanna
Language/Cultural Origin: Spanish
Inherent Meaning: Mountain
Spiritual Connotation: Joyful
Scripture: Psalm 48:1 NASB
Great is the LORD, and greatly to be praised, in the city of our God, His holy mountain.

MONTGOMERY, Montaé, Monte, Montee, Monty
Language/Cultural Origin: Old English
Inherent Meaning: From the Mountain of the Wealthy One
Spiritual Connotation: Prosperous
Scripture: Psalm 37:5 NKJV
Commit your way to the LORD, trust also in Him, and He shall bring it to pass.

MORA, Morra (see also Moira)
Language/Cultural Origin: Spanish
Inherent Meaning: Blueberry
Spiritual Connotation: Lovely
Scripture: Genesis 1:11 NASB
*Then God said, "Let the earth sprout vegetation, plants yielding seed, and fruit trees bearing fruit after their kind . . .";
and it was so.*

MORASHA, Morascha, Morrasha
Language/Cultural Origin: Hebrew
Inherent Meaning: Legacy
Spiritual Connotation: Heritage
Scripture: Isaiah 54:17 RSV
No weapon that is fashioned against you shall prosper. . . . This is the heritage of the servants of the LORD and their vindication from me, says the LORD.

MORDECAI, Mordechai
Language/Cultural Origin: Persian
Inherent Meaning: Warlike
Spiritual Connotation: Reknowned
Scripture: Esther 9:4 NKJV
For Mordecai was great in the king's palace, and his fame spread throughout all the provinces; for this man Mordecai became increasingly prominent.

MORGAN, Morgana, Morgann, Morganna, Morganne, Morgen, Morgun, Morrgan, Morrgana
Language/Cultural Origin: Welsh
Inherent Meaning: White Sea
Spiritual Connotation: Bright
Scripture: Isaiah 12:2 NLT
See, God has come to save me. I will trust in him and not be afraid. The LORD GOD is my strength and my song; he has become my salvation.

MORRELL, Morell
Language/Cultural Origin: French
Inherent Meaning: Dark
Spiritual Connotation: Redeemed
Scripture: Isaiah 9:2 RSV
The people who walked in darkness have seen a great light; those who dwelt in a land of deep darkness, on them has light shined.

MORIAH, Moria, Moriel, Moriya, Morriah (see also Mariah)
Language/Cultural Origin: Hebrew

Inherent Meaning: **God Is My Teacher**
Spiritual Connotation: **Privileged**
Scripture: **John 1:49** RSV
*Nathanael answered him, Rabbi, you
are the Son of God! You are the King of
Israel!*

MORRIS, see Maurice

MORTON, Mort, Mortey
Language/Cultural Origin: **English**
Inherent Meaning: **From the Town Near
the Moor Estate**
Spiritual Connotation: **Empowered**
Scripture: **Matthew 28:18** NASB
*And Jesus came up and spoke to them,
saying, "All authority has been given to
Me in heaven and on earth."*

MOSELLE, Mozelle
Language/Cultural Origin: **Hebrew**
Inherent Meaning: **Drawn From the Water**
Spiritual Connotation: **Rescued**
Scripture: **Acts 20:28** NRSV
*Keep watch over yourselves and over all
the flock . . . to shepherd the church of
God that he obtained with the blood of
his own Son.*

MOSES, Moe, Moïse, Moisei, Moises,
☞ **Moisés, Moishe, Moisis, Mose,**
Moshe, Moyses, Mozes
Language/Cultural Origin: **Hebrew**
Inherent Meaning: **Drawn From the Water**
Spiritual Connotation: **Delivered**
Scripture: **Ecclesiastes 3:11** NRSV
*He has made everything suitable for its
time; moreover he has put a sense of past
and future into their minds.*

MOYA, Moia
Language/Cultural Origin: **English**
Inherent Meaning: **Wished-For**
Spiritual Connotation: **Hopeful**
Scripture: **Psalm 119:81** NLT
*I faint with longing for your salvation;
but I have put my hope in your word.*

MURA, Murah (see also Meara,
Meira, Mira)
Language/Cultural Origin: **Japanese**
Inherent Meaning: **Village**
Spiritual Connotation: **High Praise**

Scripture: **Daniel 4:3** NASB
*How great are His signs, and how mighty
are His wonders! His kingdom is an
everlasting kingdom, and His dominion is
from generation to generation.*

MURIEL, Murial, Muriell, Murielle
(see also Mariel, Maurelle, Merial)
Language/Cultural Origin: **Middle Eastern**
Inherent Meaning: **Myrrh**
Spiritual Connotation: **Fragrant**
Scripture: **Ephesians 5:2** NKJV
*And walk in love, as Christ also has
loved us and given Himself for us, an
offering and a sacrifice to God for a
sweet-smelling aroma.*

MURPHY, Murfey
Language/Cultural Origin: **Irish**
Inherent Meaning: **Sea Warrior**
Spiritual Connotation: **Full of Praise**
Scripture: **Psalm 100:4** RSV
*Enter his gates with thanksgiving, and his
courts with praise! Give thanks to him,
bless his name!*

MURRAY, Murrey
Language/Cultural Origin: **Gaelic**
Inherent Meaning: **Sailor**
Spiritual Connotation: **Discerning**
Scripture: **1 Kings 3:9** NRSV
*Give your servant therefore an under-
standing mind to govern your people,
able to discern between good and evil.*

MUSTAFA, Mostafa, Mustafah,
Mustapha
Language/Cultural Origin: **Middle Eastern**
Inherent Meaning: **Chosen**
Spiritual Connotation: **Destined**
Scripture: **Luke 18:7** NRSV
*And will not God grant justice to his cho-
sen ones who cry to him day and night?
Will he delay long in helping them?*

MYISHA, Miyesha, Myeisha,
Myeishia, Myesha, Myeshia,
Language/Cultural Origin: **Middle Eastern**
Inherent Meaning: **Woman**
Spiritual Connotation: **Invaluable**
Scripture: **Proverbs 31:10** NRSV

A capable wife who can find? She is far more precious than jewels.

MYLA, Mylah, Mylea, Mylie
Language/Cultural Origin: **English**
Inherent Meaning: **Merciful**
Spiritual Connotation: **Compassionate**
Scripture: **Hosea 6:6** NIV
For I desire mercy, not sacrifice, and acknowledgment of God rather than burnt offerings.

MYLES, see Miles

MYLON, see Milan

MYRA, Myrah, Myria
Language/Cultural Origin: **Latin**
Inherent Meaning: **Fragrant**
Spiritual Connotation: **Abundant Praise**
Scripture: **Psalm 32:11** NKJV
Be glad in the LORD and rejoice, you righteous; and shout for joy, all you upright in heart!

MYRNA, Mirna
Language/Cultural Origin: **Scottish**
Inherent Meaning: **Gentle**
Spiritual Connotation: **Beloved**
Scripture: **Isaiah 55:12** NKJV
The mountains and the hills shall break

forth into singing before you, and all the trees of the field shall clap their hands.

MYRON, Myran (see also Miron)
Language/Cultural Origin: **Greek**
Inherent Meaning: **Fragrant Ointment**
Spiritual Connotation: **Peaceful Praise**
Scripture: **Philippians 4:7** RSV
And the peace of God, which passes all understanding, will keep your hearts and your minds in Christ Jesus.

MYSIE
Language/Cultural Origin: **Scottish**
Inherent Meaning: **Pearl**
Spiritual Connotation: **Treasured**
Scripture: **Matthew 13:45** NKJV
Again, the kingdom of heaven is like a merchant seeking beautiful pearls.

MYSTIQUE, Mistique
Language/Cultural Origin: **French**
Inherent Meaning: **Intriguing**
Spiritual Connotation: **Reverent**
Scripture: **Psalm 33:8** NRSV
Let all the earth fear the LORD; let all the inhabitants of the world stand in awe of him.

N

NAARAN, Naaren, Naran, Naren
Language/Cultural Origin: **Hebrew**
Inherent Meaning: **Young Man**
Spiritual Connotation: **Temperate**
Scripture: **Titus 2:6** NRSV
Likewise, urge the younger men to be self-controlled.

NAARIA, Naarya, Naria (see also Nara, Narah)
Language/Cultural Origin: **Hebrew**
Inherent Meaning: **Child of God**
Spiritual Connotation: **Heir**
Scripture: **John 1:12** TLB
But to all who received him, he gave the right to become children of God. All they needed to do was to trust him to save them.

NADIA, Nadea, Nadiya, Nadja, Nadya (see also Nydia)
Language/Cultural Origin: **Slavic**
Inherent Meaning: **Hopeful**
Spiritual Connotation: **Blessed**
Scripture: **Deuteronomy 16:15** NKJV
The LORD your God will bless you in all your produce and in all the work of your hands, so that you surely rejoice.

NADIM, Nadeem, Nadím
Language/Cultural Origin: **Middle Eastern**
Inherent Meaning: **Friend**
Spiritual Connotation: **Friend of God**
Scripture: **Luke 12:8** TLB
I, the Messiah, will publicly honor you in the presence of God's angels if you publicly acknowledge me here on earth as your Friend.

NADINE, Nadean, Nadeen
Language/Cultural Origin: **French**
Inherent Meaning: **Hope**
Spiritual Connotation: **Spiritual Potential**
Scripture: **Psalm 18:28** TLB
You have turned on my light! The Lord my God has made my darkness turn to light.

NAIDA, Nayda
Language/Cultural Origin: **Greek**
Inherent Meaning: **Water Nymph**
Spiritual Connotation: **Gifted**
Scripture: **Psalm 90:17** NRSV
Let the favor of the Lord our God be upon us, and prosper for us the work of our hands—O prosper the work of our hands!

NAJILA, Naiyila, Najah
Language/Cultural Origin: **Middle Eastern**
Inherent Meaning: **Has Beautiful Eyes**
Spiritual Connotation: **Anointed**
Scripture: **1 Samuel 16:12** NASB
Now he was ruddy, with beautiful eyes and a handsome appearance. And the LORD said, "Arise, anoint him; for this is he."

NAKITA, see Nikita

NALANI, Nalanee
Language/Cultural Origin: **Hawaiian**
Inherent Meaning: **Calm as the Heavens**
Spiritual Connotation: **Discerning**
Scripture: **Isaiah 55:9** RSV
For as the heavens are higher than the earth, so are my ways higher than your ways and my thoughts than your thoughts.

NANCY, Nan, Nana, Nancee, Nanci, Nancie, Nanette, Nanna
Language/Cultural Origin: **English**
Inherent Meaning: **Grace**
Spiritual Connotation: **Gracious**
Scripture: **Psalm 145:9** NRSV
The LORD is good to all, and his compassion is over all that he has made.

NANI, Nanie

Language/Cultural Origin: Hawaiian
Inherent Meaning: Beautiful
Spiritual Connotation: Lovely
Scripture: Romans 10:15 NRSV
How beautiful are the feet of those who bring good news!

NAOMI, Naomie, Neomi

☞ Language/Cultural Origin: Hebrew
Inherent Meaning: Delightful Renewal
Spiritual Connotation: Trusting
Scripture: Psalm 52:8 NKJV
But I am like a green olive tree in the house of God; I trust in the mercy of God forever and ever.

NAPHTALI, Naftali, Naftalie, ☞ Naphtalie

Language/Cultural Origin: Hebrew
Inherent Meaning: Struggle
Spiritual Connotation: Seeker of Truth
Scripture: Genesis 32:24 NASB
Then Jacob was left alone, and a man wrestled with him until daybreak.

NAPOLEON, Nap, Napoléon

Language/Cultural Origin: Greek
Inherent Meaning: Lion of the Woodland
Spiritual Connotation: Bold
Scripture: Proverbs 28:1 NKJV
The wicked flee when no one pursues, but the righteous are bold as a lion.

NARA, Narra (see also Naaria, Narah)

Language/Cultural Origin: Japanese
Inherent Meaning: Oak
Spiritual Connotation: Holy
Scripture: Joshua 24:26 NKJV
Then Joshua wrote these words in the Book of the Law of God. And he took a large stone, and set it up there under the oak that was by the sanctuary of the LORD.

NARAH, Naara, Naari (see also ☞ Naaria, Nara)

Language/Cultural Origin: Hebrew
Inherent Meaning: Young Woman
Spiritual Connotation: Respectful
Scripture: 1 Timothy 5:2 NLT
Treat the older women as you would your mother, and treat the younger women with all purity as your own sisters.

NARI, Naree

Language/Cultural Origin: Japanese
Inherent Meaning: Thunder
Spiritual Connotation: Attentive
Scripture: Job 37:2 NCV
Listen! Listen to the thunder of God's voice and to the rumbling that comes from his mouth.

NARIKO, Nareeko

Language/Cultural Origin: Japanese
Inherent Meaning: Humble Child
Spiritual Connotation: Righteous
Scripture: Proverbs 23:24 NRSV
The father of the righteous will greatly rejoice; he who begets a wise son will be glad in him.

NASSER, Nassar, Nassor

Language/Cultural Origin: Middle Eastern
Inherent Meaning: Victorious
Spiritual Connotation: Delivered
Scripture: Psalm 60:5 NRSV
Give victory with your right hand, and answer us, so that those whom you love may be rescued.

NATALIE, Natalea, Natalee, Natali, Natalia, Nataliana, Natalina, Natallia, Natalya, Nattalie

Language/Cultural Origin: Latin
Inherent Meaning: Christmas Child
Spiritual Connotation: God's Gift of Joy
Scripture: Psalm 9:2 NKJV
I will be glad and rejoice in You; I will sing praise to Your name, O Most High.

NATANIA, Nathania

Language/Cultural Origin: Hebrew
Inherent Meaning: Gift of God
Spiritual Connotation: Righteous
Scripture: Psalm 119:11 NASB
Thy word I have treasured in my heart, that I may not sin against Thee.

NATARA, Natarra (see also Nitara)

Language/Cultural Origin: Middle Eastern
Inherent Meaning: Sacrifice
Spiritual Connotation: Generous
Scripture: Philippians 4:18 NKJV

*I am full, having received . . . the things
sent from you, a sweet-smelling aroma, an
acceptable sacrifice, well pleasing to God.*

**NATASHA, Natachia, Natacia,
Natascha, Natashah, Natashia,
Natasia, Nathasha, Nitasha (see
also Tasha)**
Language/Cultural Origin: **Russian**
Inherent Meaning: **Christmas Child**
Spiritual Connotation: **Innocent**
Scripture: **Matthew 18:3** NRSV
*Truly I tell you, unless you change and
become like children, you will never enter
the kingdom of heaven.*

NATHANIEL, Nat, Natan, Nataniel,
☞ **Nate, Nathan, Nathanael,
Nathaneal, Nathanial, Nathann,
Nathanyal, Nathanyel, Nathen,
Nathon, Natt, Naython,
Nethanial, Nethanyal**
Language/Cultural Origin: **Hebrew**
Inherent Meaning: **Gift of God**
Spiritual Connotation: **Victorious**
Scripture: **1 Corinthians 15:57** NRSV
*But thanks be to God, who gives us the
victory through our Lord Jesus Christ.*

NATIFA, Nateefah, Natifah
Language/Cultural Origin: **Middle Eastern**
Inherent Meaning: **Untainted**
Spiritual Connotation: **Pure**
Scripture: **Ephesians 5:27** NCV
*He died so that he could give the church
to himself like a bride in all her beauty.
He died so that the church could be pure
and without fault.*

**NAVIN, Navan, Naven (see also
Nevan)**
Language/Cultural Origin: **Indo-Pakistani**
Inherent Meaning: **New**
Spiritual Connotation: **Regenerated**
Scripture: **2 Corinthians 5:17** NRSV
*So if anyone is in Christ, there is a new
creation: everything old has passed away;
see, everything has become new!*

NED, Nedd, Nedra
Language/Cultural Origin: **English**
Inherent Meaning: **Guardian**

Spiritual Connotation: **Preserved**
Scripture: **Philippians 4:7** RSV
*And the peace of God, which passes all
understanding, will keep your hearts and
your minds in Christ Jesus.*

NEHEMIAH, Nehmiah
☞ Language/Cultural Origin: **Hebrew**
Inherent Meaning: **God Comforts**
Spiritual Connotation: **Righteous**
Scripture: **2 Corinthians 1:4** NCV
*He comforts us every time we have
trouble, so when others have trouble, we
can comfort them with the same comfort
God gives us.*

**NEIL, Neal, Neale, Nealon, Neile,
Neill, Neilon**
Language/Cultural Origin: **Irish**
Inherent Meaning: **Champion**
Spiritual Connotation: **Beloved**
Scripture: **1 John 4:7** NKJV
*Beloved, let us love one another, for love
is of God; and everyone who loves is
born of God and knows God.*

**NELLIE, Nel, Nell, Nelle, Nellee,
Nelley, Nelli**
Language/Cultural Origin: **English**
Inherent Meaning: **Shining**
Spiritual Connotation: **Witness**
Scripture: **Isaiah 60:3** NKJV
*The Gentiles shall come to your light,
and kings to the brightness of your rising.*

NELSON, Neilson, Nelsen, Nilsson
Language/Cultural Origin: **English**
Inherent Meaning: **Son of the Champion**
Spiritual Connotation: **Honored**
Scripture: **Isaiah 33:15-16** NASB
*He who walks righteously, and speaks
with sincerity, He who rejects unjust
gain . . . His bread will be given him;
His water will be sure.*

**NERIAH, Neri, Neria, Neriya,
Nerriah (see also Nuria)**
Language/Cultural Origin: **Hebrew**
Inherent Meaning: **Light of the Lord**
Spiritual Connotation: **Witness**
Scripture: **Matthew 5:14** NKJV

You are the light of the world. A city that is set on a hill cannot be hidden.

NERISSA, Narissa
Language/Cultural Origin: **English**
Inherent Meaning: **Sea Nymph**
Spiritual Connotation: **Expectant**
Scripture: **Luke 21:31** NKJV
So you also, when you see these things happening, know that the kingdom of God is near.

NESS, Nes
Language/Cultural Origin: **Hebrew**
Inherent Meaning: **Miracle**
Spiritual Connotation: **Act of God**
Scripture: **Acts 14:3** NKJV
Therefore they stayed there a long time, speaking boldly in the Lord, who was . . . granting signs and wonders to be done by their hands.

NEVA, Neyva
Language/Cultural Origin: **English**
Inherent Meaning: **New**
Spiritual Connotation: **Obedient Spirit**
Scripture: **Psalm 119:2** NKJV
Blessed are those who keep His testimonies, who seek Him with the whole heart!

NEVAN, Neven, Nevin, Nevon (see also Navin)
Language/Cultural Origin: **Irish**
Inherent Meaning: **Holy**
Spiritual Connotation: **Righteous**
Scripture: **2 Corinthians 7:1** NRSV
Let us cleanse ourselves from every defilement of body and of spirit, making holiness perfect in the fear of God.

NEVILLE, Nevil, Nevile, Nevill
Language/Cultural Origin: **Old French**
Inherent Meaning: **From the New Town**
Spiritual Connotation: **Compassionate Spirit**
Scripture: **Zechariah 7:9** TLB
Tell them to be honest and fair—and not to take bribes—and to be merciful and kind to everyone.

NEWELL, Newall
Language/Cultural Origin: **Middle English**
Inherent Meaning: **From the New Hall**
Spiritual Connotation: **Sincere**

Scripture: **Isaiah 58:14** NRSV
Then you shall take delight in the LORD, and I will make you ride upon the heights of the earth.

NEWTON, Newtyn
Language/Cultural Origin: **Middle English**
Inherent Meaning: **From the New Town**
Spiritual Connotation: **Helpful Counselor**
Scripture: **Proverbs 20:5** NKJV
Counsel in the heart of man is like deep water, but a man of understanding will draw it out.

NEYLAN, Neyla, Neylen
Language/Cultural Origin: **Turkish**
Inherent Meaning: **Granted Wish**
Spiritual Connotation: **Made Whole**
Scripture: **Luke 9:11** NCV
But the people learned where Jesus went and followed him. He welcomed them and talked with them about God's kingdom and healed those who needed to be healed.

NICHOLAS, see Nicolas

NICOLE, Nichola, Nichole, Nicholette, Nicholle, Nicki, Nickie, Nickola, Nickole, Nicky, Nicolette, Nicolle, Nicolyn, Niki, Nikkey, Nikki, Nikkie, Nikkola, Nikkole, Nikkolette, Nikky, Nikola, Nikole, Nikolette, Nikolle, Nikolyn, Niquole, Nykola (see also Colette, Nikita)
Language/Cultural Origin: **French**
Inherent Meaning: **Victory of the People**
Spiritual Connotation: **Overcomer**
Scripture: **Revelation 2:7** NRSV
To everyone who conquers, I will give permission to eat from the tree of life that is in the paradise of God.

NICOLAS, Nic, Niccolas, Nichalas, ☞**Nicholas, Nicholsen, Nicholson, Nick, Nickey, Nickolas, Nickolaus, Nickolus, Nicky, Nicolaas, Nicolai, Nicolás, Nicolo, Nik, Niki, Nikk, Nikki, Niklas, Niklaus, Niklos, Nikolaas, Nikolai, Nikolas, Nikolaus,**

Nikoli, Nikolos, Nycholas, Nykolas

Language/Cultural Origin: **Greek**
Inherent Meaning: **Victory of the People**
Spiritual Connotation: **Triumphant Spirit**
Scripture: **1 Corinthians 15:57** RSV
But thanks be to God, who gives us the victory through our Lord Jesus Christ.

NIESHA, Neisha, Neishia, Nesha, Neshia, Nisha

Language/Cultural Origin: **Hebrew**
Inherent Meaning: **Sign**
Spiritual Connotation: **Glorious Manifestation**
Scripture: **Luke 2:12** NRSV
This will be a sign for you: you will find a child wrapped in bands of cloth and lying in a manger.

NIGEL, Niegel, Nigell, Nijel, Nygel

Language/Cultural Origin: **Latin**
Inherent Meaning: **Champion**
Spiritual Connotation: **Adventurous Spirit**
Scripture: **2 Corinthians 2:14** NASB
But thanks be to God, who always leads us in His triumph in Christ.

NIKA, Neika

Language/Cultural Origin: **Russian**
Inherent Meaning: **Belonging to God**
Spiritual Connotation: **Purchased**
Scripture: **1 Corinthians 6:19** NRSV
Or do you not know that your body is a temple of the Holy Spirit within you, which you have from God, and that you are not your own?

NIKITA, Nakeeta, Nakita, Nakkita, Nakyta, Nikkita, Naquita, Niquita

Language/Cultural Origin: **Russian**
Inherent Meaning: **Victory of the People**
Spiritual Connotation: **Eternal Hope**
Scripture: **1 Thessalonians 4:17** NKJV
Then we . . . shall be caught up together with them in the clouds to meet the Lord in the air. And thus we shall always be with the Lord.

NILS, Niels, Niles

Language/Cultural Origin: **Scandinavian**
Inherent Meaning: **Champion**

Spiritual Connotation: **Triumphant**
Scripture: **Zechariah 9:9** TLB
Rejoice greatly, O my people! Shout with joy! For look—your King is coming! He is the Righteous One, the Victor!

NIMROD

☞ Language/Cultural Origin: **Hebrew**
Inherent Meaning: **Rebel**
Spiritual Connotation: **Mighty**
Scripture: **Genesis 10:9** NRSV
He was a mighty hunter before the LORD.

NINA, Neena, Neenah, Ninah

Language/Cultural Origin: **English**
Inherent Meaning: **Grace of God**
Spiritual Connotation: **Delivered**
Scripture: **2 Corinthians 2:14** RSV
But thanks be to God, who in Christ always leads us in triumph, and through us spreads the fragrance of the knowledge of him everywhere.

NIRAN, Nieran

Language/Cultural Origin: **Thai**
Inherent Meaning: **Eternal**
Spiritual Connotation: **Gift of Faith**
Scripture: **2 Corinthians 4:18** NCV
We set our eyes not on what we see but on what we cannot see. . . . What we cannot see will last forever.

NISHAN, Nishana, Nissim

Language/Cultural Origin: **Armenian**
Inherent Meaning: **Miracle**
Spiritual Connotation: **Spirit-Filled**
Scripture: **Galatians 3:5** NASB
Does He then, who provides you with the Spirit and works miracles among you, do it by the works of the Law, or by hearing with faith?

NITA, Nitika (see also Anita)

Language/Cultural Origin: **Hebrew**
Inherent Meaning: **Planter**
Spiritual Connotation: **Sower of Truth**
Scripture: **Luke 8:15** NCV
And the seed that fell on the good ground is like those who hear God's teaching with good, honest hearts and obey it and patiently produce good fruit.

NITARA, Nitarah (see also Natara)
Language/Cultural Origin: **Indo-Pakistani**
Inherent Meaning: **Deeply Rooted**
Spiritual Connotation: **Steadfast**
Scripture: **Psalm 1:3** NRSV
They are like trees planted by streams of water, which yield their fruit in its season, and their leaves do not wither.

NIXON, Nickson, Nikson, Nixson
Language/Cultural Origin: **English**
Inherent Meaning: **Son of the Victor**
Spiritual Connotation: **Overcomer**
Scripture: **Romans 8:37** RSV
No, in all these things we are more than conquerors through him who loved us.

NIZANA, Nizanna
Language/Cultural Origin: **Hebrew**
Inherent Meaning: **Flower Bud**
Spiritual Connotation: **Joyful**
Scripture: **Isaiah 35:1** NKJV
The wilderness and the wasteland shall be glad for them, and the desert shall rejoice and blossom as the rose.

NOAH, Noé
Language/Cultural Origin: **Hebrew**
Inherent Meaning: **Peaceful**
Spiritual Connotation: **Provider of Comfort**
Scripture: **Nahum 1:7** NASB
The LORD is good, a stronghold in the day of trouble, and He knows those who take refuge in Him.

NOAM, Noame
Language/Cultural Origin: **Hebrew**
Inherent Meaning: **Friend**
Spiritual Connotation: **Chosen**
Scripture: **Isaiah 41:8** TLB
But as for you, O Israel, you are mine, my chosen ones; for you are Abraham's family, and he was my friend.

NOEL, Noél, Noël, Noela, Noele, Noelia, Noell, Noella, Noelle
Language/Cultural Origin: **Latin**
Inherent Meaning: **Christmas Child**
Spiritual Connotation: **Precious Gift**
Scripture: **Isaiah 9:6** NKJV
For unto us a Child is born, unto us a Son is given. . . . And His name will be called Wonderful, Counselor, Mighty God, Everlasting Father, Prince of Peace.

NOKOMIS, Nokomas
Language/Cultural Origin: **Dakota**
Inherent Meaning: **Moon Child**
Spiritual Connotation: **Great Promise**
Scripture: **Isaiah 30:26** NRSV
Moreover the light of the moon will be like the light of the sun . . . on the day when the LORD binds up the injuries of his people.

NOLA, Nuala
Language/Cultural Origin: **Latin**
Inherent Meaning: **Small Bell**
Spiritual Connotation: **Harmonious**
Scripture: **Proverbs 25:11** TLB
Timely advice is as lovely as gold apples in a silver basket.

NOLAN, Noland, Nolyn
Language/Cultural Origin: **Gaelic**
Inherent Meaning: **Noble**
Spiritual Connotation: **Honorable**
Scripture: **Micah 6:8** NKJV
He has shown you, O man, what is good; and what does the LORD require of you but to do justly, to love mercy, and to walk humbly with your God?

NONA, Nonah, Noni, Nonie, Nonna, Nony, Nonya
Language/Cultural Origin: **Latin**
Inherent Meaning: **Ninth**
Spiritual Connotation: **Full of Wisdom**
Scripture: **Proverbs 2:6** NRSV
For the LORD gives wisdom; from his mouth come knowledge and understanding.

NORA, Norah, Nordia
Language/Cultural Origin: **Greek**
Inherent Meaning: **Light**
Spiritual Connotation: **Esteemed**
Scripture: **Isaiah 30:21** NASB
Your ears will hear a word behind you [that says], "This is the way, walk in it."

NORI, Noria
Language/Cultural Origin: **Japanese**
Inherent Meaning: **Tradition**

Spiritual Connotation: **Honored**

Scripture: **Exodus 31:16** TLB

Work six days only, for the seventh day is a special day to remind you of my covenant—a weekly reminder forever of my promises to the people of Israel.

NORMA, Noma

Language/Cultural Origin: **Latin**

Inherent Meaning: **Perfection**

Spiritual Connotation: **Model of Excellence**

Scripture: **1 Timothy 4:14** NRSV

Do not neglect the gift that is in you, which was given to you through prophecy with the laying on of hands by the council of elders.

NORMAN, Norm, Normand, Normen, Normie

Language/Cultural Origin: **Old English**

Inherent Meaning: **Man From the North**

Spiritual Connotation: **Courageous Spirit**

Scripture: **Psalm 17:7** NLT

Show me your unfailing love in wonderful ways. You save with your strength those who seek refuge from their enemies.

NORRIS, Noris

Language/Cultural Origin: **Old English**

Inherent Meaning: **Northerner**

Spiritual Connotation: **Wise**

Scripture: **Psalm 111:10** RSV

The fear of the LORD is the beginning of wisdom; a good understanding have all those who practice it. His praise endures for ever!

NORTON, Nortan

Language/Cultural Origin: **Middle English**

Inherent Meaning: **From the North Town**

Spiritual Connotation: **Integrity**

Scripture: **Psalm 42:8** KJV

Yet the LORD will command his lovingkindness in the daytime, and in the night his song shall be with me, and my prayer unto the God of my life.

NORWOOD, Norrwood

Language/Cultural Origin: **Middle English**

Inherent Meaning: **From the North Forest**

Spiritual Connotation: **Noble**

Scripture: **Philippians 3:14** TLB

I strain to reach the end of the race and receive the prize for which God is calling us up to heaven because of what Christ Jesus did for us.

NOVIA, Nuvia

Language/Cultural Origin: **Spanish**

Inherent Meaning: **Sweetheart**

Spiritual Connotation: **Beloved**

Scripture: **1 John 3:1** NKJV

Behold what manner of love the Father has bestowed on us, that we should be called children of God!

NURI, Nurie, Nury

Language/Cultural Origin: **Hebrew**

Inherent Meaning: **Fire of God**

Spiritual Connotation: **Guided of God**

Scripture: **Exodus 13:21** NASB

The LORD was going before them in a pillar of cloud by day to lead them on the way, and in a pillar of fire by night to give them light.

NURIA, Noura, Nura, Nuriah, Nuriel, Nuriya (see also Neriah)

Language/Cultural Origin: **Aramaic**

Inherent Meaning: **Fire of God**

Spiritual Connotation: **Dependent Upon God**

Scripture: **Numbers 14:14** NCV

The Egyptians will tell this to those who live in this land. . . . They know that . . . you lead your people . . . with fire at night.

NYDIA, Nydya (see also Nadia)

Language/Cultural Origin: **Latin**

Inherent Meaning: **Nest**

Spiritual Connotation: **Spiritual Potential**

Scripture: **Colossians 3:12** NASB

And so, as those who have been chosen of God, holy and beloved, put on a heart of compassion, kindness, humility, gentleness and patience.

NYUSHA, Nyasha

Language/Cultural Origin: **Russian**

Inherent Meaning: **Pure**

Spiritual Connotation: **Patient**

Scripture: **1 Peter 1:7** NLT

These trials are only to test your faith, to show that it is strong and pure.

O

OAKLEY, Oaklee, Oakleigh
Language/Cultural Origin: **Old English**
Inherent Meaning: **From the Oak Trees**
Spiritual Connotation: **Immovable**
Scripture: **Psalm 1:3** NASB
And he will be like a tree firmly planted by streams of water. . . . And in whatever he does, he prospers.

OBADIAH, Obediah
Language/Cultural Origin: **Hebrew**
Inherent Meaning: **Servant of God**
Spiritual Connotation: **Discerning**
Scripture: **Romans 12:2** NRSV
Do not be conformed to this world, but be transformed by the renewing of your minds.

OCEANA, Ocean
Language/Cultural Origin: **Greek**
Inherent Meaning: **Sea**
Spiritual Connotation: **Praise**
Scripture: **Psalm 65:5** NASB
By awesome deeds You answer us in righteousness, O God of our salvation, You who are the trust of all the ends of the earth and of the farthest sea.

OCTAVIA, Octivia
Language/Cultural Origin: **Latin**
Inherent Meaning: **Eighth**
Spiritual Connotation: **Abiding Place of God**
Scripture: **Psalm 23:6** KJV
Surely goodness and mercy shall follow me all the days of my life: and I will dwell in the house of the LORD for ever.

OCTAVIUS, Octavian, Octavien, Octavio, Octavious
Language/Cultural Origin: **Latin**
Inherent Meaning: **Eighth**
Spiritual Connotation: **Abiding Place of God**
Scripture: **Psalm 18:28** NKJV
For You will light my lamp; the LORD my God will enlighten my darkness.

ODELIA, Odeleya
Language/Cultural Origin: **Hebrew**
Inherent Meaning: **I Will Praise God**
Spiritual Connotation: **Thankful Spirit**
Scripture: **Luke 19:40** RSV
I tell you, if these were silent, the very stones would cry out.

ODELL, Odie
Language/Cultural Origin: **Middle English**
Inherent Meaning: **From the Wooded Hill**
Spiritual Connotation: **Hopeful**
Scripture: **Psalm 119:114** NRSV
You are my hiding place and my shield; I hope in your word.

ODESSA, Odyssa
Language/Cultural Origin: **Greek**
Inherent Meaning: **Long Voyage**
Spiritual Connotation: **Preserved**
Scripture: **2 Corinthians 11:26** TLB
I have traveled many weary miles. . . . I have faced grave dangers from mobs in the cities and from death in the deserts and in the stormy seas and from men who claim to be brothers in Christ but are not.

ODYSSEUS, Odesseus
Language/Cultural Origin: **Greek**
Inherent Meaning: **Wrathful**
Spiritual Connotation: **Righteous**
Scripture: **Isaiah 26:20** NLT
Go home, my people, and lock your doors! Hide until the Lord's anger against your enemies has passed.

OGDEN, Ogdan
Language/Cultural Origin: **Old English**
Inherent Meaning: **From the Oak Valley**
Spiritual Connotation: **One of Dignity**
Scripture: **Psalm 92:12** KJV
The righteous shall flourish like the palm tree: he shall grow like a cedar in Lebanon.

OKALANI, Okilani
Language/Cultural Origin: **Hawaiian**
Inherent Meaning: **Heavenly**
Spiritual Connotation: **Eternal**
Scripture: **Colossians 3:2** NKJV
Set your mind on things above, not on things on the earth.

OLAF, Olav, Ole, Olie, Olle
Language/Cultural Origin: **Old Norse**
Inherent Meaning: **Ancestor**
Spiritual Connotation: **Protector**
Scripture: **Psalm 18:2** RSV
The LORD is my rock, and my fortress, and my deliverer, my God, my rock, in whom I take refuge, my shield, and the horn of my salvation, my stronghold.

OLAJUWON, Olajuwan
Language/Cultural Origin: **Nigerian**
Inherent Meaning: **Honor of God**
Spiritual Connotation: **Reverent**
Scripture: **Daniel 2:20** NLT
Praise the name of God forever and ever, for he alone has all wisdom and power.

OLEG, Olleg
Language/Cultural Origin: **Latvian**
Inherent Meaning: **Holy**
Spiritual Connotation: **Unending Praise**
Scripture: **Revelation 4:8** NRSV
Day and night without ceasing they sing, Holy, holy, holy, the Lord God the Almighty, who was and is and is to come.

OLESIA, Olesha, Olésya
Language/Cultural Origin: **Polish**
Inherent Meaning: **Defender**
Spiritual Connotation: **Protector of Truth**
Scripture: **1 Timothy 6:20** NRSV
Guard what has been entrusted to you. Avoid the profane chatter and contradictions of what is falsely called knowledge.

OLGA, Olya
Language/Cultural Origin: **Scandinavian**
Inherent Meaning: **Holy**
Spiritual Connotation: **Wise**
Scripture: **Proverbs 15:33** NKJV
The fear of the LORD is the instruction of wisdom, and before honor is humility.

OLIANA, Olianna
Language/Cultural Origin: **Hawaiian**
Inherent Meaning: **Flowering Evergreen**
Spiritual Connotation: **Preserved**
Scripture: **Hosea 14:8** TLB
I look after you and care for you. I am like an evergreen tree, yielding my fruit to you throughout the year. My mercies never fail.

OLIVER, Olley, Ollie, Olliver
Language/Cultural Origin: **Old Norse**
Inherent Meaning: **Kind and Affectionate**
Spiritual Connotation: **Bringer of Peace**
Scripture: **Psalm 23:1** KJV
The LORD is my shepherd; I shall not want. He maketh me to lie down in green pastures: he leadeth me beside the still waters.

OLIVIA, Olive, Olivea, Olyvia (see also Livia)
Language/Cultural Origin: **Latin**
Inherent Meaning: **Peace**
Spiritual Connotation: **Walks With God**
Scripture: **Matthew 13:44** NCV
The kingdom of heaven is like a treasure hidden in a field. One day a man found the treasure. . . . He was so happy that he went and sold everything he owned to buy that field.

OLUJIMI, Oluyimi
Language/Cultural Origin: **Nigerian**
Inherent Meaning: **Given by God**
Spiritual Connotation: **Righteous**
Scripture: **Isaiah 42:6** NRSV
I am the LORD, I have called you in righteousness, I have taken you by the hand and kept you; I have given you as a covenant to the people, a light to the nations.

OLYA, Ollya
Language/Cultural Origin: **Russian**
Inherent Meaning: **Holy**

Spiritual Connotation: **High Praise**
Scripture: **Isaiah 6:3** NLT
In a great chorus they sang, Holy, holy, holy is the LORD Almighty! The whole earth is filled with his glory!

OLYMPIA, Olympa
Language/Cultural Origin: **Greek**
Inherent Meaning: **Heavenly**
Spiritual Connotation: **Beloved**
Scripture: **Psalm 103:11** NKJV
For as the heavens are high above the earth, so great is His mercy toward those who fear Him.

OMA, Omah
Language/Cultural Origin: **Hebrew**
Inherent Meaning: **Eloquent**
Spiritual Connotation: **Voice of God**
Scripture: **1 Corinthians 1:17** NIV
For Christ did not send me to baptize, but to preach the gospel—not with words of human wisdom.

OMAR, Omarr
☞ Language/Cultural Origin: **Hebrew**
Inherent Meaning: **Eloquent**
Spiritual Connotation: **Successful**
Scripture: **Romans 8:37** NKJV
Yet in all these things we are more than conquerors through Him who loved us.

ONA
Language/Cultural Origin: **Lithuanian**
Inherent Meaning: **Grace of God**
Spiritual Connotation: **Viewed With Favor**
Scripture: **Matthew 13:43** NRSV
Then the righteous will shine like the sun in the kingdom of their Father. Let anyone with ears listen!

ONI, Onii
Language/Cultural Origin: **Nigerian**
Inherent Meaning: **Born on Holy Ground**
Spiritual Connotation: **Sacred**
Scripture: **Exodus 3:5** NRSV
Then he said, "Come no closer! Remove the sandals from your feet, for the place on which you are standing is holy ground."

OONA, see Una

OPAL, Opall
Language/Cultural Origin: **Sanskrit**
Inherent Meaning: **Jewel**
Spiritual Connotation: **Treasure**
Scripture: **Malachi 3:17** NKJV
"They shall be Mine," says the LORD of hosts, "On the day that I make them My jewels."

OPHELIA, Ophilia
Language/Cultural Origin: **Greek**
Inherent Meaning: **Helper**
Spiritual Connotation: **Consecrated**
Scripture: **2 Corinthians 3:18** NKJV
But we all, with unveiled face, beholding as in a mirror the glory of the Lord, are being transformed into the same image from glory to glory.

OPRAH, see Orpah

ORA, Orah
Language/Cultural Origin: **Latin**
Inherent Meaning: **Prayerful**
Spiritual Connotation: **Precious**
Scripture: **1 John 4:7** NKJV
Beloved, let us love one another, for love is of God; and everyone who loves is born of God and knows God.

ORAN, Orane (see also Orin)
Language/Cultural Origin: **Irish**
Inherent Meaning: **Green**
Spiritual Connotation: **Fruitful**
Scripture: **Jeremiah 17:8** NKJV
For he shall be like a tree planted by the waters, which spreads out its roots by the river. . . . Its leaf will be green.

OREN, Oreen (see also Orin)
☞ Language/Cultural Origin: **Hebrew**
Inherent Meaning: **Ash Tree**
Spiritual Connotation: **Blessed**
Scripture: **Psalm 1:3** NASB
And he will be like a tree firmly planted by streams of water, which yields its fruit in its season, and its leaf does not wither; and in whatever he does, he prospers.

ORESTES, Orastes
Language/Cultural Origin: **Greek**

Inherent Meaning: **From the Mountain**
Spiritual Connotation: **Peaceful**
Scripture: **Isaiah 56:7** NLT
I will bring them also to my holy mountain of Jerusalem and will fill them with joy in my house of prayer.

ORIANA, Orania, Oriane, Oriann, Orianna

Language/Cultural Origin: **Latin**
Inherent Meaning: **Dawning Sun**
Spiritual Connotation: **Enlightened for Service**
Scripture: **Ephesians 6:7** NKJV
Whatever good anyone does, he will receive the same from the Lord, whether he is a slave or free.

ORIN, Orinn, Orrie, Orrin (see also Oran, Oren)

Language/Cultural Origin: **Greek**
Inherent Meaning: **Mountain**
Spiritual Connotation: **God-Revealed Insight**
Scripture: **2 Peter 1:18** NKJV
And we heard this voice which came from heaven when we were with Him on the holy mountain.

ORION, Orien

Language/Cultural Origin: **Greek**
Inherent Meaning: **Son of Fire**
Spiritual Connotation: **Zealous**
Scripture: **Psalm 104:4** NCV
You make the winds your messengers, and flames of fire are your servants.

ORLANDO, Orlanda, Orlondo

Language/Cultural Origin: **Italian**
Inherent Meaning: **Famous Throughout the Land**
Spiritual Connotation: **Reknowned**
Scripture: **James 4:10** NASB
Humble yourselves in the presence of the Lord, and He will exalt you.

ORLI, Ori, Orlie

Language/Cultural Origin: **Hebrew**
Inherent Meaning: **My Light**
Spiritual Connotation: **Fearless**
Scripture: **Psalm 27:1** NKJV
The LORD is my light and my salvation; whom shall I fear? The LORD is the strength of my life; of whom shall I be afraid?

ORPAH, Ophra, Opra, Oprah

☞ Language/Cultural Origin: **Hebrew**
Inherent Meaning: **Runaway**
Spiritual Connotation: **Chaste**
Scripture: **1 Corinthians 6:18** NKJV
Flee sexual immorality. Every sin that a man does is outside the body, but he who commits sexual immorality sins against his own body.

ORRICK, Orric, Orrik

Language/Cultural Origin: **English**
Inherent Meaning: **Aged Oak Tree**
Spiritual Connotation: **Great Joy**
Scripture: **Isaiah 55:12** NRSV
For you shall go out in joy, and be led back in peace . . . and all the trees of the field shall clap their hands.

ORSON, Orsen

Language/Cultural Origin: **Latin**
Inherent Meaning: **Little Bear**
Spiritual Connotation: **Loyal, Steadfast**
Scripture: **1 Corinthians 15:58** RSV
Be steadfast, immovable, always abounding in the work of the Lord, knowing that in the Lord your labor is not in vain.

ORVILLE, Orv, Orval

Language/Cultural Origin: **French**
Inherent Meaning: **From the Golden Town**
Spiritual Connotation: **Benevolent**
Scripture: **2 Corinthians 9:6** NKJV
But this I say: He who sows sparingly will also reap sparingly, and he who sows bountifully will also reap bountifully.

OSANNA, Osana (see also Hosanna)

Language/Cultural Origin: **Hebrew**
Inherent Meaning: **Save Us**
Spiritual Connotation: **Remnant**
Scripture: **Psalm 102:18** NRSV
Let this be recorded for a generation to come, so that a people yet unborn may praise the LORD.

OSBORN, Osborne

Language/Cultural Origin: **English**
Inherent Meaning: **Divine Warrior**

Spiritual Connotation: **Victorious in Truth**
Scripture: **Isaiah 61:2-3** NRSV
*To proclaim the year of the Lord's
favor . . . to comfort all who mourn . . .
to give them the oil of gladness instead
of mourning. . . . They will . . . display
his glory.*

OSCAR, Oskar
Language/Cultural Origin: **Old English**
Inherent Meaning: **Divine Spearman**
Spiritual Connotation: **Appointed of God**
Scripture: **Colossians 3:23** RSV
*Whatever your task, work heartily, as
serving the Lord and not men.*

OSMOND, Osmund
Language/Cultural Origin: **Old English**
Inherent Meaning: **Divine Protector**
Spiritual Connotation: **God's Warrior**
Scripture: **Psalm 5:11** NRSV
*But let all who take refuge in you rejoice;
let them ever sing for joy. Spread your
protection over them, so that those who
love your name may exult in you.*

OSWALD, Osvaldo, Oswaldo
Language/Cultural Origin: **English**
Inherent Meaning: **God's Power**
Spiritual Connotation: **Honored**
Scripture: **Psalm 77:11** NRSV
*I will call to mind the deeds of the LORD;
I will remember your wonders of old.*

OTHELLO, Othella
Language/Cultural Origin: **Spanish**
Inherent Meaning: **Wealthy**
Spiritual Connotation: **Obedient**
Scripture: **Joshua 1:8** NKJV
*This Book of the Law shall not depart
from your mouth, but you shall meditate
in it day and night. . . . For then you will
make your way prosperous. . . .*

OTIS, Ottis
Language/Cultural Origin: **Greek**
Inherent Meaning: **Keen of Hearing**
Spiritual Connotation: **Open to Divine
Inspiration**
Scripture: **Psalm 46:10** NKJV
*Be still, and know that I am God; I will
be exalted among the nations, I will be
exalted in the earth!*

OTTO, Oto
Language/Cultural Origin: **German**
Inherent Meaning: **Prosperous**
Spiritual Connotation: **Esteemed**
Scripture: **Jeremiah 29:11** NLT
*For I know the plans I have for you, says
the LORD. They are plans for good and
not for disaster, to give you a future and
a hope.*

OURAY, Orray
Language/Cultural Origin: **Cherokee**
Inherent Meaning: **Arrow**
Spiritual Connotation: **Guardian of Truth**
Scripture: **Isaiah 54:17** NKJV
*No weapon formed against you shall
prosper, and every tongue which rises
against you in judgment You shall
condemn.*

OWEN, Owens
Language/Cultural Origin: **Greek**
Inherent Meaning: **Distinguished**
Spiritual Connotation: **Pleasant to
Look Upon**
Scripture: **2 Samuel 23:4** NKJV
*And he shall be like the light of the morn-
ing when the sun rises, a morning with-
out clouds, like the tender grass springing
out of the earth, by clear shining after
rain.*

OXFORD, Oxforde
Language/Cultural Origin: **Old English**
Inherent Meaning: **From the Place Where
the Oxen Cross the River**
Spiritual Connotation: **Restful**
Scripture: **Matthew 11:28, 30** NRSV
*Come to me, all you that are weary and
are carrying heavy burdens, and I will
give you rest. For my yoke is easy, and
my burden is light.*

OYA, Oiya
Language/Cultural Origin: **Miwok**
Inherent Meaning: **Called Forth**
Spiritual Connotation: **Witness**
Scripture: **Acts 10:42** NLT
*And he ordered us to preach everywhere
and to testify that Jesus is ordained of
God to be the judge of all—the living and
the dead.*

OZ, Ozz, Ozzey, Ozzi, Ozzie

Language/Cultural Origin: **Hebrew**
Inherent Meaning: **Courage**
Spiritual Connotation: **Overcomer**
Scripture: **John 16:33** NRSV
I have said this to you, so that in me you may have peace. In the world you face persecution. But take courage; I have conquered the world!

OZARA, Ozarra

Language/Cultural Origin: **Hebrew**
Inherent Meaning: **Treasure**
Spiritual Connotation: **Divine Perspective**
Scripture: **Matthew 6:21** KJV
For where your treasure is, there will your heart be also.

P

PABLO, Paublo

Language/Cultural Origin: **Spanish**
Inherent Meaning: **Small**
Spiritual Connotation: **Great Faith**
Scripture: **Mark 4:31-32** NCV
The kingdom of God is like a mustard seed, the smallest seed you plant in the ground. But when planted, this seed grows and becomes the largest of all garden plants.

PAIGE, Page, Payge

Language/Cultural Origin: **French**
Inherent Meaning: **Young Assistant**
Spiritual Connotation: **Blessed Helper**
Scripture: **Philippians 2:13** RSV
For God is at work in you, both to will and to work for his good pleasure.

PALANI, Pallani

Language/Cultural Origin: **Hawaiian**
Inherent Meaning: **Free**
Spiritual Connotation: **Unchained**
Scripture: **John 8:36** NKJV
Therefore if the Son makes you free, you shall be free indeed.

PALASHA, Pasha, Pelasha

Language/Cultural Origin: **Russian**
Inherent Meaning: **From the Sea**
Spiritual Connotation: **Protected**
Scripture: **Psalm 139:9-10** RSV
If I take the wings of the morning and dwell in the uttermost parts of the sea, even there thy hand shall lead me, and thy right hand shall hold me.

PALMER, Palmar

Language/Cultural Origin: **Old English**
Inherent Meaning: **Peaceful Pilgrim**
Spiritual Connotation: **Bringer of Peace**
Scripture: **Zechariah 4:6** NASB
Not by might nor by power, but by My Spirit, says the LORD of hosts.

PALOMA, Palloma

Language/Cultural Origin: **Spanish**
Inherent Meaning: **Dove**
Spiritual Connotation: **Symbol**
Scripture: **Luke 3:22** NKJV
And the Holy Spirit descended in bodily form like a dove upon Him, and a voice came from heaven which said, "You are My beloved Son; in You I am well pleased."

PAMELA, Pam, Pamala, Pamella, Pammela

Language/Cultural Origin: **Greek**
Inherent Meaning: **Honey**
Spiritual Connotation: **Righteous**
Scripture: **Matthew 13:43** NRSV
Then the righteous will shine like the sun in the kingdom of their Father. Let anyone with ears listen!

PANCHO, Poncho

Language/Cultural Origin: **Spanish**
Inherent Meaning: **Frenchman**
Spiritual Connotation: **God's Witness**
Scripture: **Daniel 7:27** NKJV
His kingdom is an everlasting kingdom, and all dominions shall serve and obey Him.

PANDORA, Pandorra, Panndora

Language/Cultural Origin: **Greek**
Inherent Meaning: **Skilled**
Spiritual Connotation: **Gifted**
Scripture: **1 Corinthians 12:4-5** NRSV
Now there are varieties of gifts, but the same Spirit; and there are varieties of services, but the same Lord.

PANYA, Pania
Language/Cultural Origin: **Russian**
Inherent Meaning: **Crowned**
Spiritual Connotation: **Wise**
Scripture: **Proverbs 14:18** NASB
The naive inherit folly, but the prudent are crowned with knowledge.

PARI, Pári, Parri
Language/Cultural Origin: **Persian**
Inherent Meaning: **Eagle**
Spiritual Connotation: **Renewed**
Scripture: **Isaiah 40:31** RSV
But they who wait for the LORD shall renew their strength, they shall mount up with wings like eagles, they shall run and not be weary, they shall walk and not faint.

PARIS, Parras, Parris
Language/Cultural Origin: **Greek**
Inherent Meaning: **Attractive**
Spiritual Connotation: **Godly**
Scripture: **Psalm 27:4** NKJV
One thing I have desired of the LORD . . . that I may dwell in the house of the LORD all the days of my life, to behold the beauty of the LORD, and to inquire in His temple.

PARK, Parke
Language/Cultural Origin: **Chinese**
Inherent Meaning: **Cyprus Tree**
Spiritual Connotation: **Blessed**
Scripture: **Isaiah 41:19-20** NKJV
I will set in the desert the cypress tree and the pine and the box tree together, that they may see and know . . . that the hand of the LORD has done this.

PARKER, Parkker
Language/Cultural Origin: **Middle English**
Inherent Meaning: **Guardian of the Park**
Spiritual Connotation: **Spiritual Light**
Scripture: **Matthew 5:14** NASB
You are the light of the world. A city set on a hill cannot be hidden.

PARNELL, Parnel, Pernell
Language/Cultural Origin: **French**
Inherent Meaning: **Little Peter**
Spiritual Connotation: **Faithfulness**
Scripture: **Lamentations 3:23** NLT
Great is his faithfulness; his mercies begin afresh each day.

PARRISH, Parish
Language/Cultural Origin: **English**
Inherent Meaning: **From the Church District**
Spiritual Connotation: **Devout**
Scripture: **Hebrews 10:25** NCV
You should not stay away from the church meetings, as some are doing, but you should meet together and encourage each other.

PARRY, Parrey, Perry
Language/Cultural Origin: **Welsh**
Inherent Meaning: **Son of the Leader**
Spiritual Connotation: **Humble**
Scripture: **Psalm 37:11** RSV
But the meek shall possess the land, and delight themselves in abundant prosperity.

PASCAL, Pascale, Paschale, Pascual, Pascuale
Language/Cultural Origin: **French**
Inherent Meaning: **Easter Child**
Spiritual Connotation: **Resurrected**
Scripture: **Mark 16:6** NKJV
But he said to them, "Do not be alarmed. You seek Jesus of Nazareth, who was crucified. He is risen! He is not here. See the place where they laid Him."

PATIENCE, Paishence
Language/Cultural Origin: **English**
Inherent Meaning: **Endurance, Fortitude**
Spiritual Connotation: **Firmness of Spirit**
Scripture: **Psalm 77:12** NASB
I will meditate on all Thy work, and muse on Thy deeds.

PATRICIA, Pat, Patreice, Patrice, Patriece, Patrisha, Patsey, Patsi, Patsy, Patti, Pattrice, Patty
Language/Cultural Origin: **Latin**
Inherent Meaning: **Noble**
Spiritual Connotation: **Victorious**
Scripture: **Romans 8:37** NKJV
Yet in all these things we are more than conquerors through Him who loved us.

PATRICK, Pat, Patric, Patrik, Patrique, Patryck, Patryk
Language/Cultural Origin: **Welsh**
Inherent Meaning: **Nobleman**
Spiritual Connotation: **Obedient**
Scripture: **Romans 12:2** RSV
Do not be conformed to this world but be transformed by the renewal of your mind.

PATTON, Patten
Language/Cultural Origin: **Old English**
Inherent Meaning: **From the Warrior's Town**
Spiritual Connotation: **Immovable**
Scripture: **Psalm 147:5** NRSV
Great is our Lord, and abundant in power; his understanding is beyond measure.

PAUL, Pasha, Paolo, Pauley, Pauli, ☞ Paulis, Paulo, Paulus, Pavel
Language/Cultural Origin: **Latin**
Inherent Meaning: **Small**
Spiritual Connotation: **Dynamo of Energy and Faith**
Scripture: **2 Timothy 1:11** NRSV
For this gospel I was appointed a herald and an apostle and a teacher, and for this reason I suffer as I do.

PAULA, Paola, Paolina, Paulette, Paulina, Pauline, Paulla
Language/Cultural Origin: **Latin**
Inherent Meaning: **Small**
Spiritual Connotation: **Loving**
Scripture: **John 15:12** NKJV
This is My commandment, that you love one another as I have loved you.

PAXTON, Paxon, Paxten
Language/Cultural Origin: **Old English**
Inherent Meaning: **From the Peaceful Town**
Spiritual Connotation: **Prepared**
Scripture: **Ephesians 6:15** NLT
For shoes, put on the peace that comes from the Good News, so that you will be fully prepared.

PAYNE, Paine
Language/Cultural Origin: **Latin**
Inherent Meaning: **From the Country**
Spiritual Connotation: **Sacred**

Scripture: **Psalm 99:9** NKJV
Exalt the LORD our God, and worship at His holy hill; for the LORD our God is holy.

PAYTON, see Peyton

PEARL, Pearle
Language/Cultural Origin: **Latin**
Inherent Meaning: **Priceless Jewel**
Spiritual Connotation: **Health and Long Life**
Scripture: **Jeremiah 29:11** NKJV
For I know the thoughts that I think toward you, says the LORD, thoughts of peace and not of evil, to give you a future and a hope.

PEARSON, Pierson
Language/Cultural Origin: **English**
Inherent Meaning: **Son of the Rock**
Spiritual Connotation: **Joyful Praise**
Scripture: **Deuteronomy 32:4** NKJV
He is the Rock, His work is perfect; for all His ways are justice, a God of truth and without injustice; righteous and upright is He.

PEDRO, Pédro
Language/Cultural Origin: **Spanish**
Inherent Meaning: **Rock**
Spiritual Connotation: **Steadfast in Christ**
Scripture: **1 Corinthians 15:58** NRSV
Be steadfast, immovable, always excelling in the work of the Lord, because you know that in the Lord your labor is not in vain.

PEGGY, Peg, Pegg, Peggi
Language/Cultural Origin: **English**
Inherent Meaning: **Pearl**
Spiritual Connotation: **Promise**
Scripture: **Revelation 21:21** NASB
And the twelve gates were twelve pearls; each one of the gates was a single pearl. And the street of the city was pure gold, like transparent glass.

PELE, Pelé, Peleh
Language/Cultural Origin: **Hebrew**
Inherent Meaning: **Miracle**
Spiritual Connotation: **Strong Faith**
Scripture: **Micah 7:15** NASB
As in the days when you came out

from the land of Egypt, I will show you miracles.

PELI, Pelí
Language/Cultural Origin: **Basque**
Inherent Meaning: **Happy**
Spiritual Connotation: **Filled With Joy**
Scripture: **Psalm 84:4** NRSV
Happy are those who live in your house, ever singing your praise.

PENELOPE, Pennelope, Penney, Penni, Pennie, Penny
Language/Cultural Origin: **Greek**
Inherent Meaning: **Industrious Weaver**
Spiritual Connotation: **Creative Spirit**
Scripture: **Deuteronomy 28:12** RSV
The LORD will open to you his good treasury the heavens . . . to bless all the work of your hands.

PERCIVAL, Percie, Percivall, Percy, Purcell
Language/Cultural Origin: **Old French**
Inherent Meaning: **Pierce the Veil**
Spiritual Connotation: **Miracle**
Scripture: **Matthew 27:51** NLT
At that moment the curtain in the temple was torn in two, from top to bottom. The earth shook, rocks split apart.

PERKIN, Perkins, Perkyn, Perkyns
Language/Cultural Origin: **English**
Inherent Meaning: **Little Rock**
Spiritual Connotation: **Joyful**
Scripture: **Psalm 95:1** NASB
O come, let us sing for joy to the LORD, let us shout joyfully to the rock of our salvation.

PERRY, see Parry

PERVIS, Purvis
Language/Cultural Origin: **Latin**
Inherent Meaning: **Passage**
Spiritual Connotation: **Messenger**
Scripture: **Isaiah 40:3** NRSV
A voice cries out: In the wilderness prepare the way of the LORD, make straight in the desert a highway for our God.

PETER, Peder, Petar, Pete, Péter, Petey, Petr, Petras, Petros, Pietro
Language/Cultural Origin: **Greek**
Inherent Meaning: **Rock**
Spiritual Connotation: **Powerful Faith**
Scripture: **Matthew 16:18** RSV
And I tell you, you are Peter, and on this rock I will build my church, and the powers of death shall not prevail against it.

PETRA, Petrina, Pietra
Language/Cultural Origin: **Greek**
Inherent Meaning: **Small Rock**
Spiritual Connotation: **Strong and Everlasting**
Scripture: **John 14:27** NRSV
Peace I leave with you. . . . Do not let your hearts be troubled, and do not let them be afraid.

PEYTON, Paiton, Payden, Payton
Language/Cultural Origin: **Middle English**
Inherent Meaning: **From the Leader's Town**
Spiritual Connotation: **Christlike**
Scripture: **Isaiah 11:6** NLT
In that day the wolf and the lamb will live together; the leopard and the goat will be at peace . . . and a little child will lead them all.

PHEBE, Phoebe
Language/Cultural Origin: **Greek**
Inherent Meaning: **Bright**
Spiritual Connotation: **Cherished**
Scripture: **Matthew 5:14** KJV
Ye are the light of the world. A city that is set on an hill cannot be hid.

PHELAN, Phaelan
Language/Cultural Origin: **Irish**
Inherent Meaning: **Little Wolf**
Spiritual Connotation: **Exalted**
Scripture: **James 4:10** RSV
Humble yourselves before the Lord and he will exalt you.

PHELPS, Phellps
Language/Cultural Origin: **Middle English**
Inherent Meaning: **Son of Phillip**
Spiritual Connotation: **Loving Spirit**
Scripture: **2 Peter 1:3** NASB
His divine power has granted to us

everything pertaining to life and godliness, through the true knowledge of Him who called us by His own glory and excellence.

PHILANA, Philina
Language/Cultural Origin: **Greek**
Inherent Meaning: **Lover of Humankind**
Spiritual Connotation: **Gracious**
Scripture: **Matthew 22:39** NKJV
You shall love your neighbor as yourself.

PHILANTHA, Phillantha
Language/Cultural Origin: **Greek**
Inherent Meaning: **Lover of Flowers**
Spiritual Connotation: **Seeker of Truth**
Scripture: **Proverbs 4:9** NCV
[Wisdom] will be like flowers in your hair and like a beautiful crown on your head.

PHILEMON, Philémon
✍ Language/Cultural Origin: **Greek**
Inherent Meaning: **Kiss**
Spiritual Connotation: **Affectionate**
Scripture: **Romans 16:16** NASB
Greet one another with a holy kiss. All the churches of Christ greet you.

PHILLIP, Felipe, Felípe, Filip, Fillip, ✍ Phil, Philip, Philipp, Philippe, Phill, Phillipp
Language/Cultural Origin: **Greek**
Inherent Meaning: **Lover of Horses**
Spiritual Connotation: **Transformed**
Scripture: **2 Corinthians 3:18** NKJV
But we all, with unveiled face, beholding as in a mirror the glory of the Lord, are being transformed into the same image from glory to glory.

PHINEAS, Phinehas
✍ Language/Cultural Origin: **Hebrew**
Inherent Meaning: **Face of Compassion**
Spiritual Connotation: **Merciful**
Scripture: **Nehemiah 9:31** NASB
Nevertheless, in Your great compassion You did not make an end of them or forsake them, for You are a gracious and compassionate God.

PHOEBE, see Phebe

PHYLICIA, see Felicia

PHYLLIS, Philyss, Phylis, Phyllis, Phylliss
Language/Cultural Origin: **Greek**
Inherent Meaning: **Green Branch**
Spiritual Connotation: **Youthful Trust**
Scripture: **Psalm 86:11** NKJV
Teach me Your way, O LORD; I will walk in Your truth; unite my heart to fear Your name.

PIA, Piya
Language/Cultural Origin: **Italian**
Inherent Meaning: **Devoted**
Spiritual Connotation: **Focused**
Scripture: **1 Corinthians 7:35** NKJV
And this I say for your own profit, not that I may put a leash on you, but for what is proper, and that you may serve the Lord without distraction.

PIERCE, Pearce, Peerce, Peirce
Language/Cultural Origin: **English**
Inherent Meaning: **Stone**
Spiritual Connotation: **Strong in Spirit**
Scripture: **Psalm 18:32** NRSV
The God who girded me with strength, and made my way safe. He made my feet like the feet of a deer, and set me secure on the heights.

PIERRE, Peirre, Piere, Piero, Pierro
Language/Cultural Origin: **French**
Inherent Meaning: **Rock**
Spiritual Connotation: **Dependent Upon God**
Scripture: **Psalm 62:7** NKJV
In God is my salvation and my glory; the rock of my strength, and my refuge, is in God.

PILAR, Pillar
Language/Cultural Origin: **Latin**
Inherent Meaning: **Pillar**
Spiritual Connotation: **Strong in Faith**
Scripture: **Matthew 17:20** NKJV
If you have faith as a mustard seed, you will say to this mountain, move from here to there, and it will move; and nothing will be impossible for you.

PIPER
Language/Cultural Origin: **English**
Inherent Meaning: **Pipe Player**
Spiritual Connotation: **Joyous Spirit**
Scripture: **Isaiah 61:11** NCV
*The Lord GOD will make goodness and
praise come from all the nations.*

PIPPI, Pippen, Pippie, Pippin
Language/Cultural Origin: **English**
Inherent Meaning: **Lover of Horses**
Spiritual Connotation: **Eternal**
Scripture: **1 Corinthians 15:52** NKJV
*For the trumpet will sound, and the dead
will be raised incorruptible, and we shall
be changed.*

PIRAN, Pieran
Language/Cultural Origin: **Irish**
Inherent Meaning: **Prayer**
Spiritual Connotation: **Supplicant**
Scripture: **Philippians 4:6** NRSV
*Do not worry about anything, but in
everything by prayer and supplication
with thanksgiving let your requests be
made known to God.*

PITNEY, Pittnee, Pittney
Language/Cultural Origin: **English**
Inherent Meaning: **Strong-Willed**
Spiritual Connotation: **Act of God**
Scripture: **John 1:12** NKJV
*But as many as received Him, to them
He gave the right to become children of
God, to those who believe in His name.*

PLACIDO, Placydo
Language/Cultural Origin: **Spanish**
Inherent Meaning: **Tranquil**
Spiritual Connotation: **Serene**
Scripture: **Philippians 4:7** NRSV
*And the peace of God, which surpasses
all understanding, will guard your hearts
and your minds in Christ Jesus.*

PLATO, Plaeto, Platón
Language/Cultural Origin: **Greek**
Inherent Meaning: **Broad-Shouldered**
Spiritual Connotation: **Wise**
Scripture: **Proverbs 19:8** NLT
*To acquire wisdom is to love oneself;
people who cherish understanding will
prosper.*

POLLY, Pollee, Polli, Pollyana, Pollyanna
Language/Cultural Origin: **English**
Inherent Meaning: **Gentle**
Spiritual Connotation: **Loving Spirit**
Scripture: **Psalm 149:1** NCV
*Praise the LORD! Sing a new song to the
LORD; sing his praise in the meeting of
his people.*

PONCE, Poncé
Language/Cultural Origin: **Spanish**
Inherent Meaning: **Fifth**
Spiritual Connotation: **Increase**
Scripture: **Acts 6:7** NASB
*And the word of God kept on spreading;
and the number of the disciples continued
to increase greatly in Jerusalem.*

POPPY, Poppey, Poppi, Poppie
Language/Cultural Origin: **Latin**
Inherent Meaning: **Poppy Flower**
Spiritual Connotation: **Nourished**
Scripture: **Isaiah 35:2** NKJV
*It shall blossom abundantly and rejoice,
even with joy and singing. . . . They
shall see the glory of the LORD, the excel-
lency of our God.*

PORTER, Port
Language/Cultural Origin: **Latin**
Inherent Meaning: **Gatekeeper**
Spiritual Connotation: **Watchful Spirit**
Scripture: **Isaiah 12:2** RSV
*Behold, God is my salvation; I will trust,
and will not be afraid; for the LORD GOD
is my strength and my song, and he has
become my salvation.*

PORTIA, Porsché, Porschia, Porsha
Language/Cultural Origin: **Latin**
Inherent Meaning: **Offering**
Spiritual Connotation: **Gift of God**
Scripture: **Psalm 37:5** NKJV
*Commit your way to the LORD, trust also
in Him, and He shall bring it to pass.*

POWELL, Powel
Language/Cultural Origin: **English**
Inherent Meaning: **Prepared**
Spiritual Connotation: **Purified**
Scripture: **James 1:2** NKJV

My brethren, count it all joy when you
fall into various trials, knowing that the
testing of your faith produces patience.

PRENTICE, Prentis, Prentiss
Language/Cultural Origin: **Middle English**
Inherent Meaning: **Learner**
Spiritual Connotation: **Seeker of Truth**
Scripture: **Isaiah 30:21** NRSV
And when you turn to the right or when
you turn to the left, your ears shall hear
a word behind you, saying, "This is the
way; walk in it."

PRESCOTT, Prescot
Language/Cultural Origin: **Old English**
Inherent Meaning: **From the Priest's**
Dwelling
Spiritual Connotation: **Blessed**
Scripture: **1 John 5:11** NASB
And the witness is this, that God has
given us eternal life, and this life is in
His Son.

PRESLEY, Presleigh
Language/Cultural Origin: **Old English**
Inherent Meaning: **From the Priest's**
Meadow
Spiritual Connotation: **Peaceful Spirit**
Scripture: **Psalm 146:5** NASB
How blessed is he whose help is the God of
Jacob, whose hope is in the LORD his God.

PRESTON, Prestan
Language/Cultural Origin: **Old English**
Inherent Meaning: **From the Priest's Home**
Spiritual Connotation: **Consecrated to God**
Scripture: **Psalm 50:14** NRSV
Offer to God a sacrifice of thanksgiving,
and pay your vows to the Most High.

PRICE, Pryce
Language/Cultural Origin: **Welsh**
Inherent Meaning: **Son of the Ardent One**
Spiritual Connotation: **Eager**

Scripture: **Psalm 69:9** NRSV
It is zeal for your house that has con-
sumed me; the insults of those who insult
you have fallen on me.

PRIEL, Poriel, Priela, Priella
Language/Cultural Origin: **Hebrew**
Inherent Meaning: **Fruit of God**
Spiritual Connotation: **Righteous**
Scripture: **Galatians 5:22-23** NRSV
By contrast, the fruit of the Spirit is love,
joy, peace, patience, kindness, generosity,
faithfulness, gentleness, and self-control.

PRISCILLA, Prescilla, Pricilla,
☞ **Priscila, Prisilla, Prissilla, Prysilla**
Language/Cultural Origin: **Latin**
Inherent Meaning: **Primitive, Ancient**
Spiritual Connotation: **Eternal Value**
Scripture: **Philippians 4:8** NCV
Think about the things that are good and
worthy of praise. Think about the things
that are true and honorable and right and
pure and beautiful and respected.

PRUDENCE, Prudy
Language/Cultural Origin: **Latin**
Inherent Meaning: **Discretion**
Spiritual Connotation: **Awareness of God**
Scripture: **Psalm 19:8** NKJV
The statutes of the LORD are right, rejoic-
ing the heart; the commandment of the
LORD is pure, enlightening the eyes.

PRYOR, Prior
Language/Cultural Origin: **Latin**
Inherent Meaning: **Head of the Monastery**
Spiritual Connotation: **Respected**
Scripture: **1 Timothy 5:17** NASB
Let the elders who rule well be considered
worthy of double honor, especially those
who work hard at preaching and teaching.

Q

QABIL, Qabial, Qabiel, Qabiele, Qabielle
Language/Cultural Origin: **Middle Eastern**
Inherent Meaning: **Able**
Spiritual Connotation: **Strength of God**
Scripture: **Hebrews 2:18** RSV
For because he himself has suffered and been tempted, he is able to help those who are tempted.

QADIM, Qadeem, Qadím (see also Kadim)
Language/Cultural Origin: **Middle Eastern**
Inherent Meaning: **Ancient**
Spiritual Connotation: **Eternal**
Scripture: **Revelation 21:6** NKJV
It is done! I am the Alpha and the Omega, the Beginning and the End. I will give of the fountain of the water of life freely to him who thirsts.

QADIR, Qadeer
Language/Cultural Origin: **Middle Eastern**
Inherent Meaning: **Powerful**
Spiritual Connotation: **Witness**
Scripture: **Psalm 106:8** RSV
Yet he saved them for his name's sake, that he might make known his mighty power.

QADIRA, Qadeera
Language/Cultural Origin: **Middle Eastern**
Inherent Meaning: **Powerful**
Spiritual Connotation: **Power of God**
Scripture: **Ephesians 1:19** TLB
I pray that you will begin to understand how incredibly great his power is to help those who believe him.

QAMAR, Quamar
Language/Cultural Origin: **Middle Eastern**
Inherent Meaning: **Moon**
Spiritual Connotation: **Glorious Joy**
Scripture: **Isaiah 60:20** TLB
Your sun shall never set; the moon shall not go down—for the Lord will be your everlasting light; your days of mourning all will end.

QITARAH, Qitara
Language/Cultural Origin: **Middle Eastern**
Inherent Meaning: **Fragrance**
Spiritual Connotation: **Pleasing**
Scripture: **2 Corinthians 2:15** RSV
For we are the aroma of Christ to God among those who are being saved and among those who are perishing.

QUANAH, Quan, Quanh (see also Khan)
Language/Cultural Origin: **Comanche**
Inherent Meaning: **Fragrance**
Spiritual Connotation: **Beloved**
Scripture: **Song of Songs 1:12** NASB
While the king was at his table, my perfume gave forth its fragrance.

QUANEISHA, Quanesha, Quanisha, Quanishia, Quenisha, Quenishia (see also Keneisha)
Language/Cultural Origin: **American**
Inherent Meaning: **Beautiful**
Spiritual Connotation: **Righteous**
Scripture: **Proverbs 31:30** NLT
Charm is deceptive, and beauty does not last; but a woman who fears the LORD will be greatly praised.

QUBILAH, Quabilah
Language/Cultural Origin: **Middle Eastern**
Inherent Meaning: **Conciliatory**
Spiritual Connotation: **Peacemaker**
Scripture: **Hebrews 12:14** NIV
Make every effort to live in peace with all

men and to be holy; without holiness no one will see the Lord.

QUEISHA, Queshia, Quisha (see also Keisha)

Language/Cultural Origin: **American**
Inherent Meaning: **Beautiful**
Spiritual Connotation: **Unblemished**
Scripture: **Ecclesiastes 11:9** NCV
Young people, enjoy yourselves while you are young. . . . But remember that God will judge you for everything you do.

QUENBY, Quenbie

Language/Cultural Origin: **Swedish**
Inherent Meaning: **Feminine**
Spiritual Connotation: **Holy**
Scripture: **1 Timothy 5:2** NLT
Treat the older women as you would your mother, and treat the younger women with all purity as your own sisters.

QUENNELL, Quenell, Quennel

Language/Cultural Origin: **Old French**
Inherent Meaning: **From by the Oak Tree**
Spiritual Connotation: **Steadfast**
Scripture: **Psalm 1:3** NLT
They are like trees planted along the riverbank, bearing fruit each season without fail. Their leaves never wither.

QUENTIN, Quenton, Qwentin

Language/Cultural Origin: **Middle English**
Inherent Meaning: **From the Queen's Town**
Spiritual Connotation: **Forgiven**
Scripture: **Romans 8:1** NRSV
There is therefore now no condemnation for those who are in Christ Jesus.

QUERIDA, Queridah

Language/Cultural Origin: **Spanish**
Inherent Meaning: **Beloved**
Spiritual Connotation: **Loving**
Scripture: **1 John 4:7** NRSV
Beloved, let us love one another, because love is from God; everyone who loves is born of God and knows God.

QUIANA, Quianna (see also Keianna, Kiana, Kiona)

Language/Cultural Origin: **American**
Inherent Meaning: **Gracious**
Spiritual Connotation: **Blessed**
Scripture: **Numbers 6:24-25** KJV
The LORD bless thee, and keep thee: The LORD make his face shine upon thee, and be gracious unto thee.

QUILLAN, Quillen, Quillon

Language/Cultural Origin: **Gaelic**
Inherent Meaning: **Little Cub**
Spiritual Connotation: **Beloved**
Scripture: **Psalm 91:15** RSV
When he calls to me, I will answer him; I will be with him in trouble, I will rescue him and honor him.

QUIMBY, Quinby

Language/Cultural Origin: **Scandinavian**
Inherent Meaning: **From the Queen's Estate**
Spiritual Connotation: **Vigilant Spirit**
Scripture: **Matthew 24:42** NASB
Therefore be on the alert, for you do not know which day your Lord is coming.

QUINCY, Quincey, Quinci, Quincie

Language/Cultural Origin: **Old French**
Inherent Meaning: **From the Fifth Son's Estate**
Spiritual Connotation: **Freedom in Christ**
Scripture: **Romans 8:2** NRSV
For the law of the Spirit of life in Christ Jesus has set you free from the law of sin and of death.

QUINN, Quin

Language/Cultural Origin: **Gaelic**
Inherent Meaning: **Intelligent**
Spiritual Connotation: **Godly Insight**
Scripture: **1 John 3:2** NKJV
Beloved, now we are children of God; and . . . we shall be like Him, for we shall see Him as He is.

QUINTANA, Quinta, Quintanna, Quintara, Quintarah, Quintina

Language/Cultural Origin: **English**
Inherent Meaning: **Fifth**
Spiritual Connotation: **Compassionate**
Scripture: **Galatians 6:1** KJV
If a man be overtaken in a fault, ye which are spiritual, restore such an one in the spirit of meekness; considering thyself, lest thou also be tempted.

QUINTESSA, Quintesa
Language/Cultural Origin: **English**
Inherent Meaning: **Efficiency**
Spiritual Connotation: **Steward**
Scripture: **Ephesians 5:15** NRSV
Be careful then how you live, not as unwise people but as wise, making the most of the time, because the days are evil.

QUINTIN, Quint, Quintan, Quinten, Quinton, Quintus, Qwinton
Language/Cultural Origin: **Latin**
Inherent Meaning: **Fifth**
Spiritual Connotation: **Brave**
Scripture: **1 Corinthians 16:13** NRSV
Keep alert, stand firm in your faith, be courageous, be strong.

QUON, Quonn
Language/Cultural Origin: **Chinese**
Inherent Meaning: **Bright**
Spiritual Connotation: **Righteous**
Scripture: **Daniel 12:3** NRSV
Those who are wise shall shine like the brightness of the sky, and those who lead many to righteousness, like the stars forever and ever.

R

RAANAN, Ranaan, Ranan (see also Rhiannon, Ranon)
Language/Cultural Origin: **Hebrew**
Inherent Meaning: **Luxuriant**
Spiritual Connotation: **Sacrifice**
Scripture: **John 12:3** NASB
Mary therefore took a pound of very costly perfume . . . and anointed the feet of Jesus, and wiped His feet with her hair; and the house was filled with the fragrance.

RABIAH, Rabiya
Language/Cultural Origin: **Middle Eastern**
Inherent Meaning: **Breeze**
Spiritual Connotation: **Miracle**
Scripture: **John 3:8** NLT
Just as you can hear the wind but can't tell where it comes from or where it is going, so you can't explain how people are born of the Spirit.

RACHEL, Rachael, Rachaele, Rachal, Rachele, Racquel, Raechel, Raechele, Raquel, Raquela, Riquelle, Rashel
Language/Cultural Origin: **Hebrew**
Inherent Meaning: **Lamb**
Spiritual Connotation: **Innocence**
Scripture: **Hosea 14:9** NRSV
Those who are wise understand these things; those who are discerning know them. For the ways of the LORD are right, and the upright walk in them.

RACHELLE, see Rochelle

RADLEY, Radlee, Radleigh
Language/Cultural Origin: **English**
Inherent Meaning: **From the Reed Meadow**
Spiritual Connotation: **Spirit-Filled**
Scripture: **John 14:16** NLT
And I will ask the Father, and he will give you another Counselor, who will never leave you.

RAE, Ralina (see also Ray)
Language/Cultural Origin: **English**
Inherent Meaning: **Doe**
Spiritual Connotation: **Full of Grace**
Scripture: **Psalm 50:23** NKJV
Whoever offers praise glorifies Me; and to him who orders his conduct aright I will show the salvation of God.

RAEANN, Raeanna, Raeanne, Rayana, Rayann, Rayanna, Reana, Reane, Reann, Reanna, Reanne, Reonne, Reyanna, Reyanne, (see also Rhian)
Language/Cultural Origin: **English**
Inherent Meaning: **Gracious**
Spiritual Connotation: **Gentle**
Scripture: **Matthew 12:20** NRSV
He will not break a bruised reed or quench a smoldering wick until he brings justice to victory.

RAELENE, Raeleen, Raelina, Raelle, Raelyn, Raelynn, Rayele, Rayelle, Rayleen, Raylene, Raylynn
Language/Cultural Origin: **English**
Inherent Meaning: **Lovely**
Spiritual Connotation: **Compassionate**
Scripture: **Jeremiah 12:15** NASB
I will again have compassion on them; and I will bring them back, each one to his inheritance and each one to his land.

RAFAEL, RAFAELA, see Raphael, Raphaela

RAFER, Rafar
Language/Cultural Origin: **Gaelic**
Inherent Meaning: **Prosperous**
Spiritual Connotation: **Gifted**
Scripture: **Jeremiah 29:11** NRSV
For surely I know the plans I have for you, says the LORD, plans for your welfare and not for harm, to give you a future with hope.

RAGHIB, Raquib
Language/Cultural Origin: **Middle Eastern**
Inherent Meaning: **Desirous**
Spiritual Connotation: **Ardent**
Scripture: **Psalm 69:9** NKJV
Because zeal for Your house has eaten me up, and the reproaches of those who reproach You have fallen on me.

RAHIM, Raheem, Rahiim, Rahím
Language/Cultural Origin: **Middle Eastern**
Inherent Meaning: **Compassionate**
Spiritual Connotation: **Merciful**
Scripture: **James 5:11** NKJV
Indeed we count them blessed who endure. . . . The Lord is very compassionate and merciful.

RAINA, Raenah, Rainna (see also Rana, Rayna)
Language/Cultural Origin: **Russian**
Inherent Meaning: **Queenly**
Spiritual Connotation: **Gracious**
Scripture: **Psalm 143:8** RSV
Let me hear in the morning of thy steadfast love, for in thee I put my trust. Teach me the way I should go, for to thee I lift up my soul.

RAINEY, Rainée, Raini, Rainie
Language/Cultural Origin: **English**
Inherent Meaning: **Regal**
Spiritual Connotation: **Praised**
Scripture: **Esther 6:9** NCV
Let the robe and the horse be given to [him]. Let . . . the servants . . . lead him on the horse through the city streets. . . . Let them announce: "This is what is

done for the man whom the king wants to honor!"

RAINIER, Ráinier, Rainios, Ranios (see also Rainor)
Language/Cultural Origin: **Old German**
Inherent Meaning: **Mighty Army**
Spiritual Connotation: **Strength of God**
Scripture: **Psalm 66:7** NASB
He rules by His might forever; His eyes keep watch on the nations; let not the rebellious exalt themselves.

RAINOR, Rainar, Rainer, Rainos, Ranos (see also Rainier)
Language/Cultural Origin: **Greek**
Inherent Meaning: **Counselor**
Spiritual Connotation: **Promise**
Scripture: **Isaiah 9:6** NKJV
For unto us a Child is born, unto us a Son is given. . . . And His name will be called Wonderful, Counselor, Mighty God, Everlasting Father, Prince of Peace.

RAIZA, Raissa, Raisza
Language/Cultural Origin: **Russian**
Inherent Meaning: **Rose**
Spiritual Connotation: **Lovely**
Scripture: **Isaiah 35:1** NKJV
The wilderness and the wasteland shall be glad for them, and the desert shall rejoice and blossom as the rose.

RAIZEL, Raisel (see also Rasia)
Language/Cultural Origin: **Yiddish**
Inherent Meaning: **Rose**
Spiritual Connotation: **Adorned**
Scripture: **Isaiah 35:2** NKJV
It shall blossom abundantly and rejoice, even with joy and singing.

RAJA, Raija, Raiya
Language/Cultural Origin: **Middle Eastern**
Inherent Meaning: **Hopeful**
Spiritual Connotation: **Gift of Faith**
Scripture: **Romans 4:18** NRSV
Hoping against hope, he believed that he would become the father of many nations.

RALEIGH, Rawley
Language/Cultural Origin: **Old English**

Inherent Meaning: **From the Deer Meadow**
Spiritual Connotation: **Excellent Worth**
Scripture: **2 Corinthians 9:8** TLB
There will not only be enough for your
own needs but plenty left over to give joy-
fully to others.

RALPH, Ralf (see also Rolf)
Language/Cultural Origin: **Anglo-Saxon**
Inherent Meaning: **Counselor**
Spiritual Connotation: **Discerning**
Scripture: **Psalm 13:5** KJV
But I have trusted in thy mercy; my heart
shall rejoice in thy salvation.

RAMA, Ramah
Language/Cultural Origin: **Hebrew**
Inherent Meaning: **Praised**
Spiritual Connotation: **Glory to God**
Scripture: **Psalm 86:12** RSV
I give thanks to thee, O Lord my God,
with my whole heart, and I will glorify
thy name for ever.

RAMIRO, Rami, Ramierez, Ramieros, Ramos
Language/Cultural Origin: **Spanish**
Inherent Meaning: **Judge**
Spiritual Connotation: **Accountable**
Scripture: **Deuteronomy 16:20** NASB
Justice, and only justice, you shall pursue,
that you may live and possess the land
which the LORD your God is giving you.

RAMON, Raimon, Ramón, Ramone (see also Raymond)
Language/Cultural Origin: **Spanish**
Inherent Meaning: **Mighty Protector**
Spiritual Connotation: **Vigilant**
Scripture: **Habakkuk 2:1** NCV
I will stand like a guard to watch and
place myself at the tower. I will wait to
see what he will say to me.

RAMONA, Ramonda, Rimona, Romona
Language/Cultural Origin: **Old German**
Inherent Meaning: **Protector**
Spiritual Connotation: **Virtuous**
Scripture: **Proverbs 31:10** NKJV
Who can find a virtuous wife? For her
worth is far above rubies.

RAMSEY, Ramsay, Ramzee
Language/Cultural Origin: **Old English**
Inherent Meaning: **From the Wooded Island**
Spiritual Connotation: **Believer**
Scripture: **Matthew 16:16** NKJV
Simon Peter answered and said, "You are
the Christ, the Son of the living God."

RANA, Rahna, Rahni, Ranee, Rania (see also Raina, Rayna)
Language/Cultural Origin: **Sanskrit**
Inherent Meaning: **Regal**
Spiritual Connotation: **Noble**
Scripture: **James 4:10** NKJV
Humble yourselves in the sight of the
Lord, and He will lift you up.

RANDALL, Rand, Randal, Randel, Randell, Randle, Randy, Ranndy
Language/Cultural Origin: **English**
Inherent Meaning: **Shield**
Spiritual Connotation: **Protected**
Scripture: **Psalm 3:3** NASB
But Thou, O LORD, art a shield about
me, my glory, and the One who lifts my
head.

RANDI, Randalin, Randalyn, Randee, Randie, Randii
Language/Cultural Origin: **English**
Inherent Meaning: **Shield**
Spiritual Connotation: **Guarded**
Scripture: **Proverbs 30:5** RSV
Every word of God proves true; he is a
shield to those who take refuge in him.

RANDOLPH, Randolf
Language/Cultural Origin: **Old English**
Inherent Meaning: **Shield**
Spiritual Connotation: **Established in Peace**
Scripture: **Matthew 6:33** KJV
But seek ye first the kingdom of God,
and his righteousness; and all these things
shall be added unto you.

RANGER, Rainger, Range
Language/Cultural Origin: **French**
Inherent Meaning: **Keeper of the Forest**
Spiritual Connotation: **Covenant**
Scripture: **Isaiah 32:15** NCV
This will continue until God pours his
Spirit from above upon us. Then the

desert will be like a fertile field and the fertile field like a forest.

RANITA, Ranata, Ranitta (see also Renata)

Language/Cultural Origin: **Hebrew**
Inherent Meaning: **Song**
Spiritual Connotation: **Filled With Joy**
Scripture: **Isaiah 55:12** RSV
The mountains and the hills before you shall break forth into singing, and all the trees of the field shall clap their hands.

RANKIN, Randkin

Language/Cultural Origin: **Old English**
Inherent Meaning: **Small Shield**
Spiritual Connotation: **Valiant Spirit**
Scripture: **Psalm 27:14** RSV
Wait for the LORD; be strong, and let your heart take courage; yea, wait for the LORD!

RANON, Ranen, Rani, Ranie

Language/Cultural Origin: **Hebrew**
Inherent Meaning: **My Song**
Spiritual Connotation: **Praise**
Scripture: **Psalm 9:2** NKJV
I will be glad and rejoice in You; I will sing praise to Your name, O Most High.

RANSOM, Randsom, Ransome

Language/Cultural Origin: **Latin**
Inherent Meaning: **Redeemer**
Spiritual Connotation: **Hopeful**
Scripture: **Job 19:25** NRSV
For I know that my Redeemer lives, and that at the last he will stand upon the earth.

RAOUL, Raul, Raúl

Language/Cultural Origin: **French**
Inherent Meaning: **Counselor**
Spiritual Connotation: **Divine Wisdom**
Scripture: **Romans 11:34** TLB
For who among us can know the mind of the Lord? Who knows enough to be his counselor and guide?

RAPHAEL, see Rephael

RAPHAELA, Rafaela, Rafaell, Rafaelle, Raphaéla

Language/Cultural Origin: **Hebrew**
Inherent Meaning: **Healed by God**
Spiritual Connotation: **God's Anointed**
Scripture: **2 Chronicles 1:12** NKJV
Wisdom and knowledge are granted to you; and I will give you riches and wealth and honor.

RAQUEL, see Rachel

RASHA, Rahsha, Rashia

Language/Cultural Origin: **Middle Eastern**
Inherent Meaning: **Little Gazelle**
Spiritual Connotation: **Freedom**
Scripture: **Proverbs 6:5** NKJV
Deliver yourself like a gazelle from the hand of the hunter, and like a bird from the hand of the fowler.

RASHAD, Raashad, Rashaad, Reshaad, Rhashad, Rishaad

Language/Cultural Origin: **Middle Eastern**
Inherent Meaning: **Wise Leader**
Spiritual Connotation: **Discerning**
Scripture: **Proverbs 4:7** NRSV
The beginning of wisdom is this: Get wisdom, and whatever else you get, get insight.

RASHAWNA, Rashana, Rashanda, Rashaunda, Rashona, Rashonda, Reshana, Reshanna, Reshaunda, Reshawnda, Reshonda

Language/Cultural Origin: **American**
Inherent Meaning: **God Is Gracious**
Spiritual Connotation: **Preserved**
Scripture: **2 Chronicles 30:9** NLT
For if you return to the LORD, your relatives and your children . . . will be able to return to this land. For the LORD your God is gracious and merciful.

RASHID, Rasheed, Rasheid, Rashied, Rausheed

Language/Cultural Origin: **Turkish**
Inherent Meaning: **Well-Directed**
Spiritual Connotation: **Humble**
Scripture: **Proverbs 3:5-6** NKJV
Trust in the LORD with all your heart, and lean not on your own understanding; in all your ways acknowledge Him, and He shall direct your paths.

RASHIDA, Rahsheda, Rasheda, Rasheeda, Rasheida
Language/Cultural Origin: **Swahili**
Inherent Meaning: **Well-Directed**
Spiritual Connotation: **Discerning**
Scripture: **John 16:13** NRSV
When the Spirit of truth comes, he will guide you into all the truth.

RASIA, Rasha, Rasya (see also Raizel)
Language/Cultural Origin: **Greek**
Inherent Meaning: **Rose**
Spiritual Connotation: **Joyful**
Scripture: **Isaiah 35:1** NKJV
The wilderness and the wasteland shall be glad for them, and the desert shall rejoice and blossom as the rose.

RATANA, Ratania, Ratanya
Language/Cultural Origin: **Thai**
Inherent Meaning: **Made of Crystal**
Spiritual Connotation: **Priceless**
Scripture: **Revelation 21:11** NCV
It was shining with the glory of God and was bright like a very expensive jewel, like a jasper, clear as crystal.

RAUL, see Raoul

RAVEN, Ravan, Ravin, Ravon, Ravyn
Language/Cultural Origin: **Old German**
Inherent Meaning: **Blackbird**
Spiritual Connotation: **Cherished**
Scripture: **Matthew 6:26** TLB
Look at the birds! They don't worry about what to eat . . . for your heavenly Father feeds them. And you are far more valuable to him than they are.

RAY, Raye (see also Rae)
Language/Cultural Origin: **French**
Inherent Meaning: **Royal**
Spiritual Connotation: **Wise**
Scripture: **Proverbs 9:10** NASB
The fear of the LORD is the beginning of wisdom, and the knowledge of the Holy One is understanding.

RAYAH, Raia, Raya (see also Rhea)
Language/Cultural Origin: **Hebrew**
Inherent Meaning: **Companion**
Spiritual Connotation: **Friend of God**
Scripture: **Hebrews 13:6** TLB
That is why we can say without any doubt or fear, the Lord is my Helper, and I am not afraid of anything that mere man can do to me.

RAYANNE, see Raeann

RAYLEEN, see Raelene

RAYMOND, Raimond, Ramond, Raymon, Raymont (see also Ramon)
Language/Cultural Origin: **Old German**
Inherent Meaning: **Mighty Protector**
Spiritual Connotation: **Sanctified**
Scripture: **Philippians 1:6** NRSV
I am confident of this, that the one who began a good work among you will bring it to completion by the day of Jesus Christ.

RAYNA, Reyna (see also Raina, Rana)
Language/Cultural Origin: **Yiddish**
Inherent Meaning: **Pure**
Spiritual Connotation: **Virtuous**
Scripture: **Philippians 4:8** NKJV
Finally, brethren, whatever things are true, . . . noble, . . . just, . . . pure, . . . lovely, . . . [and] of good report, if there is any virtue and if there is anything praiseworthy; meditate on these things.

REA, Reah, Reha (see also Rayah, Rhea, Ria)
Language/Cultural Origin: **Greek**
Inherent Meaning: **Poppy Flower**
Spiritual Connotation: **Firmly Grounded**
Scripture: **Hosea 14:5** NLT
I will be to Israel like a refreshing dew from heaven. It will blossom like the lily; it will send roots deep into the soil like the cedars in Lebanon.

REAGAN, see Regan

REANNE, see Raeann

REBA, Reva, Rheba
Language/Cultural Origin: **English**
Inherent Meaning: **Bound**

Spiritual Connotation: **Witness**
Scripture: **Acts 4:20** NCV
*We cannot keep quiet. We must speak
about what we have seen and heard.*

REBECCA, Rebacca, Rebeca, ☞ Rébecca, Rebeccah, Rebecka, Rebeckah, Rebeka, Rebekah, Rebekka (see also Becky)
Language/Cultural Origin: **Hebrew**
Inherent Meaning: **Bound**
Spiritual Connotation: **Refreshed**
Scripture: **Psalm 23:1-2** KJV
*The LORD is my shepherd; I shall not
want. He maketh me to lie down in green
pastures: he leadeth me beside the still
waters.*

REED, see Reid

REENA, Rena (see also Rina)
Language/Cultural Origin: **Greek**
Inherent Meaning: **Peaceful**
Spiritual Connotation: **Abiding in God**
Scripture: **Philippians 4:7** RSV
*And the peace of God, which passes all
understanding, will keep your hearts and
your minds in Christ Jesus.*

REESA, Reesha, Resa, Risa, Risha, Rysha, Ryssa
Language/Cultural Origin: **Latin**
Inherent Meaning: **Laughter**
Spiritual Connotation: **Blessed**
Scripture: **Psalm 126:2** NLT
*We were filled with laughter, and we
sang for joy. And the other nations said,
"What amazing things the LORD has done
for them."*

REESE, Reece, Rhys
Language/Cultural Origin: **Welsh**
Inherent Meaning: **Enthusiastic**
Spiritual Connotation: **Dedicated**
Scripture: **Numbers 25:13** NLT
*In this covenant, he and his descendants
will be priests for all time, because he was
zealous for his God and made atonement
for the people of Israel.*

REEVE, Reaves, Reeves
Language/Cultural Origin: **Middle English**
Inherent Meaning: **Steward**

Spiritual Connotation: **Servant**
Scripture: **1 Peter 4:10** NRSV
*Like good stewards of the manifold grace
of God, serve one another with whatever
gift each of you has received.*

REGAN, Raegan, Reagan, Reaganne, Reegan, Reegen, Reganne
Language/Cultural Origin: **Irish**
Inherent Meaning: **Ruler**
Spiritual Connotation: **Spiritual Strength**
Scripture: **Proverbs 24:5** NCV
*Wise people have great power, and those
with knowledge have great strength.*

REGINA, Regeena, Reggi, Reggie, Regi, Regie, Reginia, Reginna
Language/Cultural Origin: **Latin**
Inherent Meaning: **Queen**
Spiritual Connotation: **Gracious**
Scripture: **Psalm 19:14** NKJV
*Let the words of my mouth and the
meditation of my heart be acceptable in
Your sight, O LORD, my strength and my
Redeemer.*

REGINALD, Reg, Reggie, Reginauld, Reginault
Language/Cultural Origin: **Middle English**
Inherent Meaning: **Powerful Counselor**
Spiritual Connotation: **Humble**
Scripture: **Micah 6:8** RSV
*He has showed you, O man, what is
good; and what does the LORD require of
you but to do justice, and to love kind-
ness, and to walk humbly with your God?*

REGIS, Reggis
Language/Cultural Origin: **Latin**
Inherent Meaning: **Regal**
Spiritual Connotation: **Honored**
Scripture: **Esther 6:9** NCV
*Let the robe and the horse be given to one
of the king's most important men. . . .
Let them announce: This is what is done
for the man whom the king wants to
honor!*

REID, Raed, Reade, Reed, Reide, Ried
Language/Cultural Origin: **Old English**
Inherent Meaning: **Fair Countenance**

Spiritual Connotation: **Blessed**
Scripture: **Psalm 118:14** NKJV
The LORD is my strength and song, and He has become my salvation.

REIKO, Reyko
Language/Cultural Origin: **Japanese**
Inherent Meaning: **Pleasant Child**
Spiritual Connotation: **Blessing**
Scripture: **Proverbs 23:24** NLT
The father of godly children has cause for joy. What a pleasure it is to have wise children.

REMEZ, Rémez
Language/Cultural Origin: **Hebrew**
Inherent Meaning: **Sign**
Spiritual Connotation: **Miraculous**
Scripture: **Luke 2:12** NRSV
This will be a sign for you: you will find a child wrapped in bands of cloth and lying in a manger.

REMI, Remee, Rémi, Remie, Remmie, Remmy, Remy,
Language/Cultural Origin: **French**
Inherent Meaning: **From Rheims**
Spiritual Connotation: **Obedient**
Scripture: **Psalm 119:105** KJV
Thy word is a lamp unto my feet, and a light unto my path.

REMINGTON, Remingten
Language/Cultural Origin: **Old English**
Inherent Meaning: **From the Home of the Raven**
Spiritual Connotation: **Devoted**
Scripture: **2 Timothy 3:16** NRSV
All scripture is inspired by God and is useful for teaching, for reproof, for correction, and for training in righteousness.

REMUS, Reemus
Language/Cultural Origin: **Latin**
Inherent Meaning: **Speedy**
Spiritual Connotation: **Joyful**
Scripture: **Matthew 28:7** NASB
Go quickly and tell His disciples that He has risen from the dead.

RENATA, Ranata, Renada, Reneeta, Renita, Rinata (see also Ranita)
Language/Cultural Origin: **Latin**

Inherent Meaning: **Reborn**
Spiritual Connotation: **Quickened Spirit**
Scripture: **Romans 12:2** NASB
And do not be conformed to this world, but be transformed by the renewing of your mind.

RENDOR, Renndor
Language/Cultural Origin: **Hungarian**
Inherent Meaning: **Police Officer**
Spiritual Connotation: **Trusted**
Scripture: **1 Peter 2:13** NIV
Submit yourselves for the Lord's sake to every authority instituted among men.

RENÉ, Raenée, Rainato, Ranato, Renato, Rene, Renne, Rennie
Language/Cultural Origin: **Latin**
Inherent Meaning: **Reborn**
Spiritual Connotation: **Forgiven**
Scripture: **John 3:3** NLT
Jesus replied, "I assure you, unless you are born again, you can never see the Kingdom of God."

RENEE, Renae, Renay, Renée
Language/Cultural Origin: **French**
Inherent Meaning: **Born Again**
Spiritual Connotation: **Joyful**
Scripture: **Galatians 2:20** RSV
I have been crucified with Christ; it is no longer I who live, but Christ who lives in me.

REPHAEL, Rafael, Rafeal, Raffael, ☞ Raffeal, Raphaél
Language/Cultural Origin: **Hebrew**
Inherent Meaning: **Healed by God**
Spiritual Connotation: **God's Anointed**
Scripture: **1 Samuel 2:10** NASB
Those who contend with the LORD will be shattered. . . . He will give strength to His king, and will exalt the horn of His anointed.

RESEDA, Resada
Language/Cultural Origin: **Spanish**
Inherent Meaning: **Fragrant Blossom**
Spiritual Connotation: **Pleasing Aroma**
Scripture: **2 Corinthians 2:15** NASB
For we are a fragrance of Christ to God

among those who are being saved and among those who are perishing.

RESEL, Reisel
Language/Cultural Origin: **German**
Inherent Meaning: **Summer**
Spiritual Connotation: **Blessing**
Scripture: **Psalm 74:17** NASB
You have established all the boundaries of the earth; You have made summer and winter.

RESHAWNA, see Rashawna

REUBEN, Reuban, Reubin,
☞**Rheuben, Rube, Rubin**
Language/Cultural Origin: **Hebrew**
Inherent Meaning: **Behold, a Son**
Spiritual Connotation: **Wondrous Recognition**
Scripture: **Psalm 119:16** NKJV
I will delight myself in Your statutes; I will not forget Your word.

REX, Rexx
Language/Cultural Origin: **Latin**
Inherent Meaning: **King**
Spiritual Connotation: **Leadership**
Scripture: **1 Peter 5:3** NLT
Don't lord it over the people assigned to your care, but lead them by your good example.

REYNARD, Reinhart, Renárd, Rennard, Rey, Reynardo
Language/Cultural Origin: **German**
Inherent Meaning: **Courageous**
Spiritual Connotation: **Brave**
Scripture: **Joshua 1:9** NKJV
Have I not commanded you? Be strong and of good courage; do not be afraid, nor be dismayed, for the LORD your God is with you wherever you go.

REYNOLD, Reinhold, Renaldo, Renault, Rey, Reynald, Reynaldo, Reynolds
Language/Cultural Origin: **German**
Inherent Meaning: **Counselor**
Spiritual Connotation: **Wise**
Scripture: **Proverbs 13:10** NASB
Through insolence comes nothing but

strife, but wisdom is with those who receive counsel.

RHEA, Rhaya, Rhéa, Rhia (see also Rayah, Rea, Ria)
Language/Cultural Origin: **Greek**
Inherent Meaning: **Flowing Stream**
Spiritual Connotation: **Refreshing**
Scripture: **Isaiah 35:6** NRSV
For waters shall break forth in the wilderness, and streams in the desert.

RHETT, Rhet
Language/Cultural Origin: **Welsh**
Inherent Meaning: **Ardent**
Spiritual Connotation: **Shepherd**
Scripture: **1 Peter 5:2** TLB
Feed the flock of God; care for it willingly, not grudgingly; not for what you will get out of it but because you are eager to serve the Lord.

RHIAN, Rhiana, Rhianna, Rhiauna, Rhyan, Rhyanna, Rian, Riana, Riann, Rianna, Rihana, Rihanna (see also Raeann, Ryan)
Language/Cultural Origin: **Welsh**
Inherent Meaning: **Maiden**
Spiritual Connotation: **Joyful**
Scripture: **Isaiah 62:5** NCV
As a young man marries a woman, so your children will marry your land. As a man rejoices over his new wife, so your God will rejoice over you.

RHIANNON, Rhianen, Rhiannan, Rhiannen, Rhianon, Riannon (see also Raana, Ranon)
Language/Cultural Origin: **Welsh**
Inherent Meaning: **Goddess**
Spiritual Connotation: **Mortal**
Scripture: **John 6:40** NRSV
This is indeed the will of my Father, that all who see the Son and believe in him may have eternal life; and I will raise them up on the last day.

RHODA, Rhodi, Rhody
☞ Language/Cultural Origin: **Greek**
Inherent Meaning: **From the Island of Roses**
Spiritual Connotation: **God's Unfolded Love**

Scripture: **Isaiah 35:1** NKJV
The wilderness and the wasteland shall be
glad for them, and the desert shall rejoice
and blossom as the rose.

RHODES, Rhoads
Language/Cultural Origin: **Greek**
Inherent Meaning: **From the Island**
of Roses
Spiritual Connotation: **Formed of God**
Scripture: **Isaiah 24:15** NCV
People in the east, praise the LORD.
People in the islands of the sea, praise the
name of the LORD, *the God of Israel.*

RHONDA, Ronda
Language/Cultural Origin: **Welsh**
Inherent Meaning: **Grand**
Spiritual Connotation: **Beloved**
Scripture: **Jeremiah 15:16** NRSV
Your words became to me a joy and the
delight of my heart; for I am called by
your name, O LORD, *God of hosts.*

RIA, Ría, Riah (see also Rayah, Rea, Rhea)
Language/Cultural Origin: **Spanish**
Inherent Meaning: **River**
Spiritual Connotation: **Sacred**
Scripture: **Psalm 46:4** NCV
There is a river that brings joy to the city
of God, the holy place where God Most
High lives.

RICHARD, Ric, Ricardo, Ricardos, Ricci, Rich, Richards, Richie, Rick, Rickey, Ricki, Rickie, Ricky, Rico, Ricqui, Ricquie, Rik, Riki, Rikk, Rikki, Rikky, Riks, Riq, Riqee, Riqui, Riquie, Ritch, Ritchard, Ritchie, Rykk (see also Dick)
Language/Cultural Origin: **Old German**
Inherent Meaning: **Powerful Ruler**
Spiritual Connotation: **Benevolent**
Scripture: **Psalm 111:10** NKJV
The fear of the LORD *is the beginning of*
wisdom; a good understanding have all
those who do His commandments. His
praise endures forever.

RICHELLE, Richela, Richele, Richella (see also Rochelle)
Language/Cultural Origin: **German**
Inherent Meaning: **Strong Ruler**
Spiritual Connotation: **Hand of God**
Scripture: **Psalm 68:28** NRSV
Summon your might, O God; show your
strength, O God, as you have done for
us before.

RICHMOND, Richmon
Language/Cultural Origin: **French**
Inherent Meaning: **From the Hill of**
Wealthy Vegetation
Spiritual Connotation: **Nourished**
Scripture: **Isaiah 27:6** NCV
Israel will grow like a plant beginning to
bloom. Then the world will be filled with
their children.

RIDER, Ryder
Language/Cultural Origin: **English**
Inherent Meaning: **Travels by Horse**
Spiritual Connotation: **Great Faith**
Scripture: **Psalm 20:7** NKJV
Some trust in chariots, and some in
horses; but we will remember the name
of the LORD *our God.*

RIGEL, Reigel, Reigell, Rigell
Language/Cultural Origin: **Middle Eastern**
Inherent Meaning: **Foot**
Spiritual Connotation: **Secure**
Scripture: **John 11:9** NRSV
Those who walk during the day do not
stumble, because they see the light of this
world.

RILEY, Reilly, Rileigh, Rylee, Rylie
Language/Cultural Origin: **Irish**
Inherent Meaning: **Valiant**
Spiritual Connotation: **Protected**
Scripture: **Psalm 36:7** NASB
How precious is Your lovingkindness,
O God! And the children of men take
refuge in the shadow of Your wings.

RINA, Rinnah (see also Reena)
Language/Cultural Origin: **Hebrew**
Inherent Meaning: **Song of Joy**
Spiritual Connotation: **Filled With Gladness**
Scripture: **Psalm 47:1** KJV

*O clap your hands, all ye people; shout
unto God with the voice of triumph.*

RINGO, Rengo
Language/Cultural Origin: **Japanese**
Inherent Meaning: **Apple**
Spiritual Connotation: **Beloved**
Scripture: **Psalm 17:8** NKJV
*Keep me as the apple of Your eye; hide
me under the shadow of Your wings.*

RIORDAN, Reardon
Language/Cultural Origin: **Irish**
Inherent Meaning: **Poet/Singer**
Spiritual Connotation: **Full of Wisdom**
Scripture: **Isaiah 50:4** RSV
*The Lord GOD has given me the tongue
of those who are taught, that I may know
how to sustain with a word him that is
weary.*

RIPLEY, Rip, Ripleigh
Language/Cultural Origin: **English**
Inherent Meaning: **From the Meadow of
the One Who Shouts**
Spiritual Connotation: **Thankful**
Scripture: **Psalm 32:11** NASB
*Be glad in the LORD and rejoice, you
righteous ones, and shout for joy, all you
who are upright in heart.*

RISHON, Rishán, Rishaun, Rishawn
Language/Cultural Origin: **Hebrew**
Inherent Meaning: **First**
Spiritual Connotation: **Servant**
Scripture: **Mark 10:45** NKJV
*For even the Son of Man did not come to
be served, but to serve, and to give His
life a ransom for many.*

RITA, Reeta, Rheta
Language/Cultural Origin: **Spanish**
Inherent Meaning: **Pearl**
Spiritual Connotation: **Priceless**
Scripture: **Matthew 13:45** NRSV
*Again, the kingdom of heaven is like a
merchant in search of fine pearls.*

RIVER, Rivers
Language/Cultural Origin: **English**
Inherent Meaning: **Large Stream**
Spiritual Connotation: **Vessel of God**
Scripture: **Psalm 74:15** NASB

*You broke open springs and torrents; You
dried up ever-flowing streams.*

ROANNA, Roana, Roann, Roanne, Rohana, Rohanna (see also Ruana)
Language/Cultural Origin: **Hebrew**
Inherent Meaning: **Reminder of Sweet
Incense**
Spiritual Connotation: **Spiritual Under-
standing**
Scripture: **Psalm 51:6** NKJV
*Behold, You desire truth in the inward
parts, and in the hidden part You will
make me to know wisdom.*

ROARKE, Rourke
Language/Cultural Origin: **Irish**
Inherent Meaning: **Famous Ruler**
Spiritual Connotation: **Courageous Spirit**
Scripture: **Psalm 31:24** NKJV
*Be of good courage, and He shall
strengthen your heart, all you who hope
in the LORD.*

ROBERT, Bob, Bobb, Bobby, Rob, Robb, Robbert, Robbie, Robby, Roberto, Roberts, Robertson, Robinson, Rupert
Language/Cultural Origin: **Old English**
Inherent Meaning: **Bright in Counsel**
Spiritual Connotation: **Abiding in God**
Scripture: **1 John 4:13** TLB
*And he has put his own Holy Spirit into
our hearts as a proof to us that we are
living with him and he with us.*

ROBERTA, Bertie, Birdee, Birdie, Bobbi, Robbi
Language/Cultural Origin: **English**
Inherent Meaning: **Famous Brilliance**
Spiritual Connotation: **Excellent Worth**
Scripture: **Ephesians 2:10** NASB
*For we are His workmanship, created
in Christ Jesus for good works, which
God prepared beforehand, that we should
walk in them.*

ROBIN, Robbin, Robbyn, Robyn, Robynn
Language/Cultural Origin: **English**
Inherent Meaning: **Shining Fame**

Spiritual Connotation: **Victorious Spirit**
Scripture: **Psalm 18:32** NKJV
*It is God who arms me with strength,
and makes my way perfect.*

ROCCO, Rock, Rocko, Rocky, Rokko, Roque
Language/Cultural Origin: **Italian**
Inherent Meaning: **Rest**
Spiritual Connotation: **Restored**
Scripture: **Psalm 23:2-23** KJV
*He maketh me to lie down in green
pastures: he leadeth me beside the still
waters. He restoreth my soul.*

ROCHELLE, Rachalle, Raechell, Raeshelle, Rochell, Rochella, Rochette, Roshele, Roshell, Roshelle (see also Richelle)
Language/Cultural Origin: **French**
Inherent Meaning: **Little Rock**
Spiritual Connotation: **Established**
Scripture: **Psalm 62:2** NIV
*He alone is my rock and my salvation; he
is my fortress, I will never be shaken.*

RODERICK, Rodderick, Roderic, Roderigo, Roderique, Rodric, Rodrigo, Rodriguez, Rodrik, Rodrique, Rodriquez (see also Broderick)
Language/Cultural Origin: **Old German**
Inherent Meaning: **Famous Ruler**
Spiritual Connotation: **Arm of God**
Scripture: **Psalm 33:16** NASB
*The king is not saved by a mighty army;
a warrior is not delivered by great
strength.*

RODMAN, Rodmond, Rodmund
Language/Cultural Origin: **Old English**
Inherent Meaning: **Heroic**
Spiritual Connotation: **Famous**
Scripture: **Isaiah 19:20** NLT
*It will be a sign and a witness to the
LORD Almighty in the land of Egypt. . . .
He will send them a savior who will
rescue them.*

RODNEY, Rod, Rhodney, Rodnee
Language/Cultural Origin: **Anglo-Saxon**

Inherent Meaning: **From the Clearing on
the Island**
Spiritual Connotation: **Joyful**
Scripture: **Psalm 40:3** NKJV
*He has put a new song in my mouth;
praise to our God; many will see it and
fear, and will trust in the LORD.*

ROGAN, Rogann
Language/Cultural Origin: **Irish**
Inherent Meaning: **Redhead**
Spiritual Connotation: **Persevering**
Scripture: **Hebrews 12:1** NKJV
*Let us lay aside every weight, and the sin
which so easily ensnares us, and let us
run with endurance the race that is set
before us.*

ROGER, Rodger, Rog, Rogers, Rutger
Language/Cultural Origin: **Old German**
Inherent Meaning: **Famous Warrior**
Spiritual Connotation: **Strong in Counsel**
Scripture: **Isaiah 48:17** NKJV
*I am the LORD your God, who teaches
you to profit, who leads you by the way
you should go.*

ROLAND, Rolando, Rolland, Rollando, Rolle, Rollie, Rowland
Language/Cultural Origin: **Old German**
Inherent Meaning: **Famous Throughout
the Land**
Spiritual Connotation: **Full of Wisdom**
Scripture: **Psalm 106:3** NKJV
*Blessed are those who keep justice, and
he who does righteousness at all times!*

ROLANDA, Rollanda
Language/Cultural Origin: **German**
Inherent Meaning: **Famous Throughout
the Land**
Spiritual Connotation: **Peaceful**
Scripture: **Numbers 6:26** NKJV
*The LORD lift up His countenance upon
you, and give you peace.*

ROLF, Rolfe, Rolph (see also Ralph)
Language/Cultural Origin: **Scandinavian**
Inherent Meaning: **Counselor**
Spiritual Connotation: **Wise**
Scripture: **Psalm 90:12** NASB

So teach us to number our days, that we may present to Thee a heart of wisdom.

ROMAINE, Romana, Romanda, Romayne, Romi, Romy
Language/Cultural Origin: **French**
Inherent Meaning: **From Rome**
Spiritual Connotation: **Blessed**
Scripture: **Romans 1:7** RSV
To all God's beloved in Rome, who are called to be saints: Grace to you and peace from God our Father and the Lord Jesus Christ.

ROMAN, Román
Language/Cultural Origin: **Latin**
Inherent Meaning: **From Rome**
Spiritual Connotation: **Protector of Truth**
Scripture: **Ephesians 6:10** NKJV
Finally, my brethren, be strong in the Lord and in the power of His might.

ROMEO, Roméo
Language/Cultural Origin: **Italian**
Inherent Meaning: **Pilgrim to Rome**
Spiritual Connotation: **Steadfast**
Scripture: **Hebrews 11:13** NKJV
These all died in faith, not having received the promises, but having seen them afar off were assured of them, embraced them and confessed that they were strangers and pilgrims on the earth.

RONALD, Ron, Ronny
Language/Cultural Origin: **Old English**
Inherent Meaning: **Mighty Power**
Spiritual Connotation: **Authority**
Scripture: **Micah 6:8** NKJV
He has shown you, O man, what is good; and what does the LORD require of you but to do justly, to love mercy, and to walk humbly with your God?

RONAN, Ronán, Rónán (see also Raanan, Rhiannon)
Language/Cultural Origin: **Irish**
Inherent Meaning: **Little Seal**
Spiritual Connotation: **Playful**
Scripture: **Zechariah 8:5** NLT
And the streets of the city will be filled with boys and girls at play.

RONDEL, Rondell, Rondrell
Language/Cultural Origin: **French**
Inherent Meaning: **Poem**
Spiritual Connotation: **Gifted**
Scripture: **Psalm 40:3** RSV
He put a new song in my mouth, a song of praise to our God. Many will see and fear, and put their trust in the LORD.

RONNI, Ronee, Roni, Ronia, Ronnee, Ronney, Ronnie, Ronny, Ronya
Language/Cultural Origin: **English**
Inherent Meaning: **Power**
Spiritual Connotation: **Strength**
Scripture: **Zechariah 4:6** NKJV
Not by might nor by power, but by My Spirit, Says the LORD of hosts.

ROOSEVELT, Rosevelt
Language/Cultural Origin: **Dutch**
Inherent Meaning: **From the Field of Roses**
Spiritual Connotation: **Blessed**
Scripture: **Isaiah 35:1** NKJV
The wilderness and the wasteland shall be glad for them, and the desert shall rejoice and blossom as the rose.

RORY, Roari, Rorey, Rori
Language/Cultural Origin: **Gaelic**
Inherent Meaning: **King**
Spiritual Connotation: **Worthy of Honor**
Scripture: **Psalm 97:11** TLB
Light is sown for the godly and joy for the good.

ROSALIND, Rosalea, Rosalee, Rosalia, Rosalin, Rosalina, Rosalinda, Rosalyn, Rosalynn, Roselynn, Rosetta, Rosette, Rosilyn, Roslyn, Rozália, Rozalee, Rozalie, Rozalin, Rozalyn, Rozlyn
Language/Cultural Origin: **Spanish**
Inherent Meaning: **Beautiful Rose**
Spiritual Connotation: **Wise**
Scripture: **Psalm 49:3** NKJV
My mouth shall speak wisdom, and the meditation of my heart shall give understanding.

ROSAMOND, Rosamund
Language/Cultural Origin: **Old German**

Inherent Meaning: **Guardian**
Spiritual Connotation: **Protector of Truth**
Scripture: **1 Timothy 6:20** NASB
*Guard what has been entrusted to you,
avoiding worldly and empty chatter and
the opposing arguments of what is falsely
called knowledge.*

ROSCOE, Rosco
Language/Cultural Origin: **Old Norse**
Inherent Meaning: **From the Deer Forest**
Spiritual Connotation: **Discerning**
Scripture: **Proverbs 2:11** NLT
*Wise planning will watch over you.
Understanding will keep you safe.*

ROSE, Rosa, Rosey, Rosi, Rosie, Rosy, Roza, Rozee, Rozy
Language/Cultural Origin: **Latin**
Inherent Meaning: **Rose**
Spiritual Connotation: **God's Gracious Gift**
Scripture: **Isaiah 35:1** NKJV
*The wilderness and the wasteland shall be
glad for them, and the desert shall rejoice
and blossom as the rose.*

ROSEANNA, Rosana, Rosangela, Rosannah, Rose Ann, Rose Anne, Roseann, Roseannah, Rossana, Rossanna, Rozana, Rozangela, Rozanna, Rozeanne
Language/Cultural Origin: **English**
Inherent Meaning: **Rose**
Spiritual Connotation: **Gracious**
Scripture: **Psalm 111:4** NASB
*He has made His wonders to be remem-
bered; the LORD is gracious and compas-
sionate.*

ROSEMARY, Rosemaria, Rosemarie
Language/Cultural Origin: **Latin**
Inherent Meaning: **Dew of the Sea**
Spiritual Connotation: **Crowned**
Scripture: **Psalm 121:1-2** NASB
*I will lift up my eyes to the mountains;
from whence shall my help come? My
help comes from the LORD, who made
heaven and earth.*

ROSINE, Rosina
Language/Cultural Origin: **Italian**
Inherent Meaning: **Cherished**

Spiritual Connotation: **Bold**
Scripture: **Isaiah 41:13** NRSV
*For I, the LORD your God, hold your
right hand; it is I who say to you, "Do
not fear, I will help you."*

ROSS, Roess
Language/Cultural Origin: **Gaelic**
Inherent Meaning: **Knight**
Spiritual Connotation: **Victorious Spirit**
Scripture: **1 Corinthians 15:57** NKJV
*But thanks be to God, who gives us the
victory through our Lord Jesus Christ.*

ROWEN, Rowan
Language/Cultural Origin: **Irish**
Inherent Meaning: **Red**
Spiritual Connotation: **Purchased**
Scripture: **1 Peter 1:18-19** NKJV
*You were not redeemed with corruptible
things, . . . but with the precious blood of
Christ, as of a lamb without blemish and
without spot.*

ROWENA, Rowina
Language/Cultural Origin: **Welsh**
Inherent Meaning: **Peaceful**
Spiritual Connotation: **Wise**
Scripture: **Proverbs 24:3** NKJV
*Through wisdom a house is built, and by
understanding it is established.*

ROXANNE, Roxana, Roxane, Roxann, Roxanna, Roxi, Roxie, Roxy
Language/Cultural Origin: **Persian**
Inherent Meaning: **Sunrise**
Spiritual Connotation: **Heavenly Light**
Scripture: **Psalm 113:3** NRSV
*From the rising of the sun to its setting
the name of the LORD is to be praised.*

ROY, Roi
Language/Cultural Origin: **French**
Inherent Meaning: **King**
Spiritual Connotation: **Seeker of Wisdom**
Scripture: **Psalm 119:34** NRSV
*Give me understanding, that I may keep
your law and observe it with my whole
heart.*

ROYCE, Roice
Language/Cultural Origin: **Old English**

Inherent Meaning: **Son of the King**
Spiritual Connotation: **Tranquil Spirit**
Scripture: **Matthew 5:9** NKJV
Blessed are the peacemakers, for they shall be called sons of God.

ROZEN, Roszen
Language/Cultural Origin: **Hebrew**
Inherent Meaning: **Ruler**
Spiritual Connotation: **Gifted**
Scripture: **Proverbs 28:2** NRSV
When a land rebels it has many rulers; but with an intelligent ruler there is lasting order.

RUANA, Ruanna (see also Roanna)
Language/Cultural Origin: **Indo-Pakistani**
Inherent Meaning: **Stringed Instrument**
Spiritual Connotation: **Joyful Praise**
Scripture: **Psalm 108:2** NASB
Awake, harp and lyre; I will awaken the dawn!

RUBY, Rubey, Rubi, Rubia, Rubie
Language/Cultural Origin: **French**
Inherent Meaning: **Beautiful Jewel**
Spiritual Connotation: **Full of Grace**
Scripture: **Psalm 26:3** NKJV
For Your lovingkindness is before my eyes, and I have walked in Your truth.

RUDOLPH, Rudi, Rudy
Language/Cultural Origin: **Old German**
Inherent Meaning: **Great and Famous**
Spiritual Connotation: **Resourceful**
Scripture: **Exodus 31:3** NKJV
And I have filled him with the Spirit of God, in wisdom, in understanding, in knowledge, and in all manner of workmanship.

RUFUS, Ruffus
☞ Language/Cultural Origin: **Latin**
Inherent Meaning: **Red-Haired**
Spiritual Connotation: **Excellent Virtue**
Scripture: **Zechariah 7:9** NLT
This is what the LORD Almighty says: Judge fairly and honestly, and show mercy and kindness to one another.

RUNE, Roone
Language/Cultural Origin: **Swedish**
Inherent Meaning: **Secret**

Spiritual Connotation: **Guarded of God**
Scripture: **Psalm 91:4** TLB
He will shield you with his wings! They will shelter you. His faithful promises are your armor.

RUPERT, see Robert

RURI, Rurika, Ruriko
Language/Cultural Origin: **Japanese**
Inherent Meaning: **Emerald**
Spiritual Connotation: **Future Hope**
Scripture: **Revelation 21:19** NASB
The foundation stones of the city wall were adorned with every kind of precious stone.

RUSH, Rusch
Language/Cultural Origin: **English**
Inherent Meaning: **Redhead**
Spiritual Connotation: **Strength**
Scripture: **Genesis 25:25** NASB
Now the first came forth red, all over like a hairy garment; and they named him Esau.

RUSSELL, Russ, Russel, Rusty
Language/Cultural Origin: **French**
Inherent Meaning: **Redhead**
Spiritual Connotation: **Trusting**
Scripture: **Psalm 143:8** RSV
Let me hear in the morning of thy steadfast love, for in thee I put my trust. Teach me the way I should go, for to thee I lift up my soul.

RUTH, Ruthann, Ruthanne, Ruthe, ☞ Ruthey, Ruthie
Language/Cultural Origin: **Hebrew**
Inherent Meaning: **Companion**
Spiritual Connotation: **Faithful**
Scripture: **Psalm 119:73** NKJV
Your hands have made me and fashioned me; give me understanding, that I may learn Your commandments.

RUTHERFORD, Rutherforde
Language/Cultural Origin: **Scottish**
Inherent Meaning: **From the Cattle Ford**
Spiritual Connotation: **Vigilant**
Scripture: **Proverbs 22:12** NKJV
The eyes of the LORD preserve knowl-

edge, but He overthrows the words of the faithless.

RUTLEDGE, Rutlege
Language/Cultural Origin: **Scandinavian**
Inherent Meaning: **From the Red Land**
Spiritual Connotation: **Loyal**
Scripture: **Isaiah 38:3** NKJV
Remember now, O LORD, I pray, how I have walked before You in truth and with a loyal heart, and have done what is good in Your sight.

RUZA, Runzena, Ruzenka, Ruzina, Ruzsa
Language/Cultural Origin: **Czech**
Inherent Meaning: **Rose**
Spiritual Connotation: **Lovely**
Scripture: **Isaiah 35:1** NKJV
The wilderness and the wasteland shall be glad for them, and the desert shall rejoice and blossom as the rose.

RYAN, Rhyan, Rhyne, Rian, Riann, Ryann, Ryanne, Ryen, Ryne, Ryon (see also Rhian)
Language/Cultural Origin: **Irish**
Inherent Meaning: **Little Ruler**
Spiritual Connotation: **Youthful Heart**
Scripture: **Zechariah 8:5** NLT
And the streets of the city will be filled with boys and girls at play.

S

SABA, Sabah, Sabbah (see also Shaba)
Language/Cultural Origin: **English**
Inherent Meaning: **Oath of God**
Spiritual Connotation: **Promise**
Scripture: **Romans 11:27** NLT
And then I will keep my covenant with them and take away their sins.

SABER, Sabre
Language/Cultural Origin: **French**
Inherent Meaning: **Sword**
Spiritual Connotation: **Spiritual Warrior**
Scripture: **Ephesians 6:17** NKJV
And take the helmet of salvation, and the sword of the Spirit, which is the word of God.

SABINA, Sabinna, Sebina, Sebinah
Language/Cultural Origin: **Latin**
Inherent Meaning: **Planter of Vines**
Spiritual Connotation: **Spiritual Discernment**
Scripture: **Philippians 1:9** NRSV
And this is my prayer, that your love may overflow more and more with knowledge and full insight.

SABIYA, Sabaya
Language/Cultural Origin: **Middle Eastern**
Inherent Meaning: **Morning**
Spiritual Connotation: **Lovely**
Scripture: **Psalm 50:1** NRSV
The mighty one, God the LORD, speaks and summons the earth from the rising of the sun to its setting.

SABLE, Sabel
Language/Cultural Origin: **English**
Inherent Meaning: **Sleek**
Spiritual Connotation: **Prudent**
Scripture: **Ephesians 5:16** NCV
Use every chance you have for doing good, because these are evil times.

SABRA, Sabrah, Sabriya
Language/Cultural Origin: **Hebrew**
Inherent Meaning: **Cactus**
Spiritual Connotation: **Joyful**
Scripture: **Isaiah 35:1** NKJV
The wilderness and the wasteland shall be glad for them, and the desert shall rejoice and blossom as the rose.

SABRINA, Sabreena, Sabrinna, Sebrina, Zabreena, Zabrina
Language/Cultural Origin: **Latin**
Inherent Meaning: **Boundary**
Spiritual Connotation: **Protected, Guarded**
Scripture: **Psalm 104:9** NCV
You set borders for the seas that they cannot cross, so water will never cover the earth again.

SADANNA, Sadana, Sadhana
Language/Cultural Origin: **Indo-Pakistani**
Inherent Meaning: **Devotion**
Spiritual Connotation: **Persistent**
Scripture: **Psalm 119:97** NRSV
Oh, how I love your law! It is my meditation all day long.

SADIE, Sáde, Sadé, Sadee, Saydee
Language/Cultural Origin: **English**
Inherent Meaning: **Princess**
Spiritual Connotation: **Beautiful**
Scripture: **Psalm 45:13** NIV
All glorious is the princess within her chamber; her gown is interwoven with gold.

SADIYA, Sadeea, Sadia, Sadya
Language/Cultural Origin: **Middle Eastern**
Inherent Meaning: **Fortunate**

Spiritual Connotation: **Blessed**
Scripture: **Isaiah 3:10** RSV
Tell the righteous that it shall be well with them, for they shall eat the fruit of their deeds.

SAFARI, Safáree, Safaria, Safarya
Language/Cultural Origin: **Swahili**
Inherent Meaning: **Born While Traveling**
Spiritual Connotation: **Promise**
Scripture: **Jeremiah 31:8** NASB
And I will gather them from the remote parts of the earth . . . The woman with child and she who is in labor with child, together; a great company, they will return here.

SAFFORD, Saford
Language/Cultural Origin: **Middle English**
Inherent Meaning: **From the Place of the Willow-River Crossing**
Spiritual Connotation: **Beloved**
Scripture: **1 John 4:9** NCV
This is how God showed his love to us: He sent his one and only Son into the world so that we could have life through him.

SAFFRON, Saffrón
Language/Cultural Origin: **English**
Inherent Meaning: **Flower**
Spiritual Connotation: **Valuable Spice**
Scripture: **Proverbs 4:9** NCV
[Wisdom] will be like flowers in your hair and like a beautiful crown on your head.

SAGE, Saige
Language/Cultural Origin: **English**
Inherent Meaning: **Wise**
Spiritual Connotation: **Discerning**
Scripture: **Proverbs 14:8** NRSV
It is the wisdom of the clever to understand where they go, but the folly of fools misleads.

SAHARA, Saharah
Language/Cultural Origin: **Middle Eastern**
Inherent Meaning: **Wilderness**
Spiritual Connotation: **Strengthened**
Scripture: **Isaiah 32:16** NLT
Justice will rule in the wilderness and righteousness in the fertile field.

SAKARI, Sakaree
Language/Cultural Origin: **Indo-Pakistani**
Inherent Meaning: **Heart of Sweetness**
Spiritual Connotation: **Forgiving**
Scripture: **Job 42:10** NASB
And the LORD restored the fortunes of Job when he prayed for his friends, and the LORD increased all that Job had twofold.

SAKURA, Sakhura
Language/Cultural Origin: **Japanese**
Inherent Meaning: **Cherry Blossom**
Spiritual Connotation: **Promise**
Scripture: **Deuteronomy 1:25** NLT
They picked some of its fruit and brought it back to us. And they reported that the land the LORD our God had given us was indeed a good land.

SALAAM, see Selam

SALIM, Saleem, Salím
Language/Cultural Origin: **Middle Eastern**
Inherent Meaning: **Safe**
Spiritual Connotation: **Shielded**
Scripture: **Psalm 28:9** TLB
Defend your people, Lord; defend and bless your chosen ones. Lead them like a shepherd and carry them forever in your arms.

SALINA, Salena, Saleena (see also Selena)
Language/Cultural Origin: **French**
Inherent Meaning: **Dignified**
Spiritual Connotation: **Delivered**
Scripture: **Leviticus 26:13** TLB
For I am the Lord your God. . . . I have broken your chains so that you can walk with dignity.

SALLY, Sallee, Salley, Salli, Sallie
Language/Cultural Origin: **Old English**
Inherent Meaning: **Princess**
Spiritual Connotation: **Beloved**
Scripture: **1 Peter 2:9** NRSV
But you are a chosen race, a royal priesthood, a holy nation, God's own people, in order that you may proclaim the mighty acts of him who called you out of darkness into his marvelous light.

SALMAN, Salamen, Salmun (see also Solomon)
Language/Cultural Origin: **Czech**
Inherent Meaning: **Serenity**
Spiritual Connotation: **Strong in Character**
Scripture: **Hebrews 12:11** RSV
For the moment all discipline seems painful rather than pleasant; later it yields the peaceful fruit of righteousness to those who have been trained by it.

SALOME, Saloma, Salomé
☞ Language/Cultural Origin: **Hebrew**
Inherent Meaning: **Peaceful**
Spiritual Connotation: **Restful**
Scripture: **Mark 4:39** NIV
He got up, rebuked the wind and said to the waves, "Quiet! Be still!" Then the wind died down and it was completely calm.

SALVADOR, Sal, Salvadore, Salvatore
Language/Cultural Origin: **Italian**
Inherent Meaning: **Savior**
Spiritual Connotation: **Faithful**
Scripture: **Hosea 13:4** NIV
You shall acknowledge no God but me, no Savior except me.

SAMANTHA, Sam, Samanthia, Sami, Sammantha, Semantha, Simantha, Symantha
Language/Cultural Origin: **Aramaic**
Inherent Meaning: **Listener**
Spiritual Connotation: **Attentive to God's Voice**
Scripture: **Job 22:28** NLT
Whatever you decide to do will be accomplished, and light will shine on the road ahead of you.

SAMARA, Samarra, Samira, Sammara, Samora
Language/Cultural Origin: **Hebrew**
Inherent Meaning: **Guarded by God**
Spiritual Connotation: **Proven Faithful**
Scripture: **Revelation 3:10** TLB
Because you have patiently obeyed me despite the persecution, therefore I will protect you from the time of Great Tribulation.

SAMINA, Sameena, Samayna
Language/Cultural Origin: **Middle Eastern**
Inherent Meaning: **Praised**
Spiritual Connotation: **Honorable**
Scripture: **1 Peter 2:17** TLB
Show respect for everyone. Love Christians everywhere. Fear God and honor the government.

SAMONA, see Simona

SAMSON, Sam, Sampson
☞ Language/Cultural Origin: **Hebrew**
Inherent Meaning: **Like the Sun**
Spiritual Connotation: **Strength of Spirit**
Scripture: **Psalm 33:16** NASB
The king is not saved by a mighty army; a warrior is not delivered by great strength.

SAMUEL, Sam, Samm, Sammie, ☞ Sammuel, Sammy, Samuele
Language/Cultural Origin: **Hebrew**
Inherent Meaning: **God Has Heard**
Spiritual Connotation: **Instructed of God**
Scripture: **1 Samuel 1:20** NASB
Hannah . . . gave birth to a son; and she named him "Samuel," saying, "Because I have asked him of the LORD."

SANBORN, Sanborne, Sandbourne
Language/Cultural Origin: **English**
Inherent Meaning: **From the Sandy Brook**
Spiritual Connotation: **Defender of the Faith**
Scripture: **1 Corinthians 8:6** NLT
But we know that there is only one God, the Father. . . . And there is only one Lord, Jesus Christ.

SANCHO, Sanchez
Language/Cultural Origin: **Latin**
Inherent Meaning: **Sanctified**
Spiritual Connotation: **Appointed of God**
Scripture: **Nehemiah 9:6** NKJV
You alone are the LORD; You have made heaven . . . with all their host, the earth and everything on it.

SANCIA, Sancha, Sanchia, Sancie, Sanzia
Language/Cultural Origin: **Spanish**
Inherent Meaning: **Holy**
Spiritual Connotation: **Chosen**

Scripture: **Leviticus 20:26** NRSV
*You shall be holy to me; for I the LORD
am holy, and I have separated you from
the other peoples to be mine.*

**SANDERS, Sander, Sándor, Sandey,
Sandy, Saunder, Saunders**
Language/Cultural Origin: **English**
Inherent Meaning: **Defender**
Spiritual Connotation: **Beloved**
Scripture: **Psalm 119:18** NRSV
*Open my eyes, so that I may behold
wondrous things out of your law.*

**SANDRA, Sahndra, Sandee, Sandi,
Sandie, Sandrea, Sandreea,
Sandreia, Sandria, Sandy, Saundra,
Sondra, Sonndra (see also Xandra,
Zandra)**
Language/Cultural Origin: **English**
Inherent Meaning: **Defender**
Spiritual Connotation: **Guardian of Truth**
Scripture: **1 Timothy 6:20** NLT
*Guard what God has entrusted to you.
Avoid godless, foolish discussions with
those who oppose you with their so-called
knowledge.*

SANFORD, Sandford
Language/Cultural Origin: **Old English**
Inherent Meaning: **From the Place of the
Sandy River Crossing**
Spiritual Connotation: **Gentle**
Scripture: **Matthew 11:29** NKJV
*Take My yoke upon you and learn from
Me, for I am gentle and lowly in heart,
and you will find rest for your souls.*

SANTIAGO, Sántiago
Language/Cultural Origin: **Spanish**
Inherent Meaning: **Saint**
Spiritual Connotation: **Gifted**
Scripture: **Ephesians 4:12** NCV
*Christ gave those gifts to prepare God's
holy people for the work of serving, to
make the body of Christ stronger.*

SANYA, Sania, Saniya
Language/Cultural Origin: **Indo-Pakistani**
Inherent Meaning: **Born on Saturday**
Spiritual Connotation: **Believer**
Scripture: **John 14:6** NKJV

*Jesus said to him, "I am the way, the
truth, and the life. No one comes to the
Father except through Me."*

SAPPHIRA, Safire, Saffire, Sapphire
Language/Cultural Origin: **Greek**
Inherent Meaning: **Gem**
Spiritual Connotation: **Precious**
Scripture: **Proverbs 8:11** NKJV
*For wisdom is better than rubies, and all
the things one may desire cannot be com-
pared with her.*

**SARAH, Saara, Saarah, Sahra, Sara,
Sarai, Sarra, Sarrah, Sharai,
Sharaiah, Sharaya, Sharayah (see
also Soraya, Zara)**
Language/Cultural Origin: **Hebrew**
Inherent Meaning: **Princess**
Spiritual Connotation: **Beloved**
Scripture: **Psalm 45:13** NIV
*All glorious is the princess within her
chamber; her gown is interwoven with
gold.*

SARIYA, Sareeya
Language/Cultural Origin: **Middle Eastern**
Inherent Meaning: **Night Clouds**
Spiritual Connotation: **Guided of God**
Scripture: **Exodus 13:22** NLT
*And the LORD did not remove the pillar
of cloud or pillar of fire from their sight.*

**SASHA, Sacha, Sascha, Sashah,
Sashana, Sashia, Sashka, Sausha,
Shasha, Shashia, Zasha**
Language/Cultural Origin: **Russian**
Inherent Meaning: **Defender of Mankind**
Spiritual Connotation: **Heart of God**
Scripture: **Deuteronomy 10:18** TLB
*He gives justice to the fatherless and wid-
ows. He loves foreigners and gives them
food and clothing.*

SASON, Sasóne, Sassón
Language/Cultural Origin: **Hebrew**
Inherent Meaning: **Delight**
Spiritual Connotation: **Godly**
Scripture: **Psalm 37:4** NKJV
*Delight yourself also in the LORD, and He
shall give you the desires of your heart.*

SATIN, Sattin

Language/Cultural Origin: **French**
Inherent Meaning: **Smooth**
Spiritual Connotation: **Freedom**
Scripture: **John 8:32** KJV
And ye shall know the truth, and the truth shall make you free.

SAUL, Saül, Sol

Language/Cultural Origin: **Hebrew**
Inherent Meaning: **Asked-For**
Spiritual Connotation: **God's Blessing**
Scripture: **Isaiah 44:3** NCV
I will pour out water for the thirsty land and make streams flow on dry land. I will pour out my Spirit into your children and my blessing on your descendants.

SAVANNAH, Sahvannah, Savana, Savanah, Savanna, Savauna, Sevana, Sevanah, Sevanna

Language/Cultural Origin: **Spanish**
Inherent Meaning: **From the Treeless Plain**
Spiritual Connotation: **Cherished**
Scripture: **James 4:8** NKJV
Draw near to God and He will draw near to you.

SAVILLE, Savill, Seville, Sevilla

Language/Cultural Origin: **French**
Inherent Meaning: **From the Willow Village**
Spiritual Connotation: **Trusting**
Scripture: **Psalm 143:8** NLT
Let me hear of your unfailing love to me in the morning, for I am trusting you. Show me where to walk, for I have come to you in prayer.

SAWYER, Soiyer

Language/Cultural Origin: **English**
Inherent Meaning: **Wood Worker**
Spiritual Connotation: **Gifted**
Scripture: **Exodus 31:3** NKJV
And I have filled him with the Spirit of God, in wisdom, in understanding, in knowledge, and in all manner of workmanship.

SAXON, Sax, Saxen

Language/Cultural Origin: **Middle English**
Inherent Meaning: **Swordsman**
Spiritual Connotation: **Valorous**
Scripture: **Ephesians 6:17** NCV
Accept God's salvation as your helmet, and take the sword of the Spirit, which is the word of God.

SCHAFER, Schaefer, Shäffer, Shayfer

Language/Cultural Origin: **German**
Inherent Meaning: **Shepherd**
Spiritual Connotation: **Leader**
Scripture: **John 10:14** NKJV
I am the good shepherd; and I know My sheep, and am known by My own.

SCHUYLER, see Skyler

SCOTT, Scot, Scottie, Scotty

Language/Cultural Origin: **Old English**
Inherent Meaning: **From Scotland**
Spiritual Connotation: **Temple of God**
Scripture: **1 Corinthians 3:16** NRSV
Do you not know that you are God's temple and that God's Spirit dwells in you?

SEAN, Séan, Seán, Seane, Shaan (see also Shane, Shawn)

Language/Cultural Origin: **Irish**
Inherent Meaning: **God Is Gracious**
Spiritual Connotation: **Servant**
Scripture: **1 Peter 4:10** NRSV
Like good stewards of the manifold grace of God, serve one another with whatever gift each of you has received.

SEANA, see Shauna

SEBASTIAN, Sabastien, Sébastien

Language/Cultural Origin: **Greek**
Inherent Meaning: **Venerable**
Spiritual Connotation: **Esteemed**
Scripture: **Philippians 2:13** NLT
For God is working in you, giving you the desire to obey him and the power to do what pleases him.

SEELEY, see Ceeley

SELAM, Saalam, Salaam, Selaam

Language/Cultural Origin: **Ethiopian**
Inherent Meaning: **Peaceful**
Spiritual Connotation: **Content**
Scripture: **Philippians 4:7** RSV
And the peace of God, which passes all understanding, will keep your hearts and your minds in Christ Jesus.

SELBY, Selby

Language/Cultural Origin: **English**
Inherent Meaning: **From the Mansion**
Spiritual Connotation: **Child of God**
Scripture: **Acts 17:28** NRSV
*For in him we live and move and have
our being; as even some of your own
poets have said, for we too are his off-
spring.*

SELENA, Selenia, Selina, Selyna, Sylena, Sylina (see also Salina)

Language/Cultural Origin: **Greek**
Inherent Meaning: **Fair as the Moon**
Spiritual Connotation: **Full of Wisdom**
Scripture: **Matthew 10:20** NLT
*For it won't be you doing the talking—it
will be the Spirit of your Father speaking
through you.*

SELMA, Selmah, Zelma

Language/Cultural Origin: **Celtic**
Inherent Meaning: **Divinely Protected**
Spiritual Connotation: **Enlightened Spirit**
Scripture: **Luke 12:31** NKJV
*But seek the kingdom of God, and all
these things shall be added to you.*

SEQUOIA, Seqora, Sequora, Sequoya

Language/Cultural Origin: **Cherokee**
Inherent Meaning: **Redwood Tree**
Spiritual Connotation: **Filled With Praise**
Scripture: **Psalm 96:12** NCV
*Let the fields and everything in them
rejoice. Then all the trees of the forest
will sing for joy.*

SERAPHINA, Sarafina, Saraphina, Serafina, Syrafina

Language/Cultural Origin: **Hebrew**
Inherent Meaning: **Ardent**
Spiritual Connotation: **Zealous**
Scripture: **Psalm 42:8** NRSV
*By day the LORD commands his steadfast
love, and at night his song is with me, a
prayer to the God of my life.*

SERENA, Sarina, Sereena, Serenah, Serenna, Serenity

Language/Cultural Origin: **Latin**
Inherent Meaning: **Secure**
Spiritual Connotation: **Content**

Scripture: **1 Corinthians 2:12** NCV
*Now we did not receive the spirit of the
world, but we received the Spirit that is
from God so that we can know all that
God has given us.*

SERGEI, Serg, Serge, Sergey, Sergio, Sergios, Sirgio, Sirgios

Language/Cultural Origin: **Russian**
Inherent Meaning: **Servant**
Spiritual Connotation: **Humble**
Scripture: **Mark 10:43** NKJV
*Whoever desires to become great among
you shall be your servant.*

SETH, Sethe

Language/Cultural Origin: **Hebrew**
Inherent Meaning: **Appointed of God**
Spiritual Connotation: **Chosen**
Scripture: **James 2:5** NLT
*Hasn't God chosen the poor in this world
to be rich in faith? Aren't they the ones
who will inherit the kingdom God prom-
ised to those who love him?*

SHABA, Shahba (see also Saba)

Language/Cultural Origin: **Hispanic**
Inherent Meaning: **Rose**
Spiritual Connotation: **Virtuous**
Scripture: **Isaiah 35:1** NKJV
*The wilderness and the wasteland shall be
glad for them, and the desert shall rejoice
and blossom as the rose.*

SHAE, see Shea

SHAELA, Shaila, Shalah, Shaylah, Shaylan, Shaylea, Shaylee, Shaylie, Shaylin, Shaylyn, Shaylynn

Language/Cultural Origin: **Afghani**
Inherent Meaning: **Lovely Eyes**
Spiritual Connotation: **Beautiful**
Scripture: **Song of Songs 4:1** RSV
*Behold, you are beautiful, my love,
behold, you are beautiful! Your eyes are
doves behind your veil.*

SHAINA, Shaena, Shainah, Shainna, Shayna

Language/Cultural Origin: **Yiddish**
Inherent Meaning: **Beautiful**
Spiritual Connotation: **Witness**

Scripture: **Romans 10:15** NRSV
How beautiful are the feet of those who bring good news!

SHAKARA, Shacara, Shaccara, Shakkara
Language/Cultural Origin: **American**
Inherent Meaning: **Pure**
Spiritual Connotation: **Innocent**
Scripture: **Titus 1:15** NKJV
To the pure all things are pure.

SHAKIA, Shakeeya, Shakeya, Shakiya, Shaqiya, Shaquiya, Shekeeya, Shekia
Language/Cultural Origin: **American**
Inherent Meaning: **Season's Beginning**
Spiritual Connotation: **Miraculous**
Scripture: **Genesis 1:14** NCV
Let there be lights in the sky to separate day from night. These lights will be used for signs, seasons, days, and years.

SHAKILA, Shakaela, Shakeela, Shaquilla, Shekaela, Shequilla, Shikeela, Shiquilla
Language/Cultural Origin: **Middle Eastern**
Inherent Meaning: **Pretty**
Spiritual Connotation: **Beautiful**
Scripture: **Proverbs 31:30** NRSV
Charm is deceitful, and beauty is vain, but a woman who fears the LORD is to be praised.

SHAKIRA, Shaakira, Shakeira, Shakira, Shakiria
Language/Cultural Origin: **Middle Eastern**
Inherent Meaning: **Grateful**
Spiritual Connotation: **Unifier**
Scripture: **Colossians 3:15** NASB
And let the peace of Christ rule in your hearts, to which indeed you were called in one body; and be thankful.

SHALANA, Shalaina, Shalauna, Shelanna, Shilauna
Language/Cultural Origin: **American**
Inherent Meaning: **Attractive**
Spiritual Connotation: **Peaceful**
Scripture: **Isaiah 26:3** NLT
You will keep in perfect peace all who trust in you, whose thoughts are fixed on you!

SHALMAN, Shalmon
Language/Cultural Origin: **Hebrew**
Inherent Meaning: **Peacemaker**
Spiritual Connotation: **Pure**
Scripture: **2 Peter 3:14** NCV
Dear friends, since you are waiting for this to happen, do your best to be without sin and without fault. Try to be at peace with God.

SHALOM, Salóm, Shalum, Sholome
Language/Cultural Origin: **Hebrew**
Inherent Meaning: **Peace**
Spiritual Connotation: **Hopeful**
Scripture: **Romans 12:18** NKJV
If it is possible, as much as depends on you, live peaceably with all men.

SHAMARA, Shamarah, Shamarra, Shammara
Language/Cultural Origin: **Middle Eastern**
Inherent Meaning: **Prepared for Battle**
Spiritual Connotation: **Vigilant**
Scripture: **1 Corinthians 14:8** NLT
And if the bugler doesn't sound a clear call, how will the soldiers know they are being called to battle?

SHAMIR, Shahmir, Shameer
Language/Cultural Origin: **Hebrew**
Inherent Meaning: **Precious Stone**
Spiritual Connotation: **Invaluable**
Scripture: **2 Chronicles 32:27** NCV
He made treasuries for his silver, gold, gems, spices, shields, and other valuable things.

SHAMIRA, Shamiria
Language/Cultural Origin: **Hebrew**
Inherent Meaning: **Precious Stone**
Spiritual Connotation: **Destined**
Scripture: **Zechariah 9:16** RSV
On that day the LORD their God will save them for they are the flock of his people; for like the jewels of a crown they shall shine on his land.

SHAMMAI, Shamai, Shammae, Shammay, Shammei
Language/Cultural Origin: **Hebrew**
Inherent Meaning: **Appraiser**
Spiritual Connotation: **Discerning**

Scripture: **Revelation 4:11** NASB
*Worthy are You, our Lord and our God,
to receive glory and honor and power; for
You created all things.*

SHANA, SHANAE, see Shauna

SHANAHAN, Shannahan
Language/Cultural Origin: **Irish**
Inherent Meaning: **Wise**
Spiritual Connotation: **Gifted**
Scripture: **1 Kings 3:28** NRSV
*All Israel heard of the judgment that the
king had rendered; and they stood in awe
of the king, because they perceived that
the wisdom of God was in him.*

SHANDRA, see Chandra

**SHANE, Shaine, Shayne (see also
Sean, Shawn)**
Language/Cultural Origin: **Irish**
Inherent Meaning: **God Is Gracious**
Spiritual Connotation: **Redeemed**
Scripture: **Hebrews 2:9** NCV
*But we see Jesus . . . wearing a crown of
glory and honor because he suffered and
died. And by God's grace, he died for
everyone.*

**SHANEISHA, Shaneesha, Shanesha,
Shaneshia, Shanisha, Shannisa**
Language/Cultural Origin: **American**
Inherent Meaning: **Beautiful**
Spiritual Connotation: **Witness**
Scripture: **Romans 10:15** NLT
*How beautiful are the feet of those who
bring good news!*

SHANEL, see Chanel

SHANEQUA, Shaneequa, Shaniqua
Language/Cultural Origin: **American**
Inherent Meaning: **God Is Gracious**
Spiritual Connotation: **Anointed**
Scripture: **Colossians 1:6** TLB
*The same Good News that came to you
is going out all over the world and chang-
ing lives everywhere.*

**SHANLEY, Shanlea, Shanlee,
Shanleigh, Shanly**
Language/Cultural Origin: **Irish**
Inherent Meaning: **Child of the Hero**

Spiritual Connotation: **Mature**
Scripture: **Proverbs 23:24** NRSV
*The father of the righteous will greatly
rejoice; he who begets a wise son will be
glad in him.*

SHANNA, see Shauna

**SHANNON, Shanan, Shannan,
Shannen, Shannin, Shannyn,
Shanon**
Language/Cultural Origin: **Irish**
Inherent Meaning: **Wise**
Spiritual Connotation: **Inspired of God**
Scripture: **Matthew 10:20** TLB
*For it won't be you doing the talking—it
will be the Spirit of your heavenly Father
speaking through you!*

**SHANTAE, Jhontae, Jhontay, Jontae,
Jontáe, Jonté, Jontée, Shanta,
Shantai, Shantay, Shantaya,
Shanté, Shantée (see also Chante)**
Language/Cultural Origin: **American**
Inherent Meaning: **Singer**
Spiritual Connotation: **Joyful**
Scripture: **Psalm 101:1** NLT
*I will sing of your love and justice. I will
praise you, LORD, with songs.*

**SHANTEL, Shantell, Shanntell,
Shantal, Shantrell, Shauntel,
Shauntell, Shauntelle (see also
Chantal)**
Language/Cultural Origin: **American**
Inherent Meaning: **Song**
Spiritual Connotation: **Spirit of Worship**
Scripture: **Psalm 13:6** NLT
*I will sing to the LORD because he has
been so good to me.*

**SHAQUANDA, Shaquana,
Shaquandra, Shaquani, Shaquanna**
Language/Cultural Origin: **American**
Inherent Meaning: **Wanderer**
Spiritual Connotation: **Seeker of Truth**
Scripture: **Matthew 6:33** KJV
*But seek ye first the kingdom of God,
and his righteousness; and all these things
shall be added unto you.*

SHAQUILLE, Shaquile
Language/Cultural Origin: **Middle Eastern**

Inherent Meaning: **Handsome**
Spiritual Connotation: **Attractive**
Scripture: **Song of Songs 1:16** NKJV
Behold, you are handsome, my beloved!

SHAREEF, Sharéf, Sharíf, Shariff
Language/Cultural Origin: **Middle Eastern**
Inherent Meaning: **Honest**
Spiritual Connotation: **Eternal**
Scripture: **Proverbs 12:19** RSV
Truthful lips endure for ever, but a lying tongue is but for a moment.

SHARI, Sharaé, Sharee, Shareen, Sharene, Sharie, Sharree, Sharrie, Sheeree, Sheree, Sheri, Sherie, Sherri, Sherrie (see also Cherie)
Language/Cultural Origin: **American**
Inherent Meaning: **Dearest**
Spiritual Connotation: **Cherished**
Scripture: **1 Thessalonians 2:8** TLB
We loved you dearly—so dearly that we gave you not only God's message, but our own lives too.

SHARICE, see Cherise

SHARISSA, see Charissa

SHARLEEN, see Charleen

SHARMAIN, see Charmain

SHARON, Shaara, Shaaron, Sharen, ☞**Sharona, Sharone, Sharonna, Sharra, Sharran, Sharren, Sharron, Sharyn, Sheronna, Sherryn (see also Cheran)**
Language/Cultural Origin: **Hebrew**
Inherent Meaning: **Floral Plain**
Spiritual Connotation: **Vision of Beauty**
Scripture: **Song of Songs 2:1** NASB
I am the rose of Sharon, the lily of the valleys.

SHAULA, Shaola, Shala
Language/Cultural Origin: **Hebrew**
Inherent Meaning: **Borrowed**
Spiritual Connotation: **Dedicated**
Scripture: **1 Samuel 1:28** NLT
Now I am giving him to the LORD, and he will belong to the LORD his whole life.

SHAUNA, Seana, Seandra, Seanna,

Shaana, Shana, Shanea, Shanna, Shannah, Shannay, Shannea, Shaunah, Shaundel, Shaundell, Shaundelle, Shaunelle, Shaunia, Shaunna, Shauntrel, Shauntrell, Shaunya, Shawna, Shawndel, Shawndelle, Shawndrelle, Shawnelle, Shawnna, Shawntel, Shawntelle, Shawntreice, Shona, Shonah, Shonda, Shondel, Shondelle, Shonelle, Shonna, Shonnika, Shonta, Shontá, Shontara, Shontasya, Shonte, Shonté, Shontel, Shontelle, Shontrail, Shontreece, Shunna, Shunnel, Shunnelle, Shunta, Shuntel, Shuntelle, Shuntia
Language/Cultural Origin: **English**
Inherent Meaning: **God Is Gracious**
Spiritual Connotation: **Accountable**
Scripture: **1 Peter 4:10** NRSV
Like good stewards of the manifold grace of God, serve one another with whatever gift each of you has received.

SHAVON, see Chavon

SHAWN, Shaughn, Shaune, Shaunn, Shawne, Shawnn, Shawon (see also Sean, Shane)
Language/Cultural Origin: **American**
Inherent Meaning: **God Is Gracious**
Spiritual Connotation: **Forgiven**
Scripture: **2 Chronicles 30:9** NKJV
For the LORD your God is gracious and merciful, and will not turn His face from you if you return to Him.

SHAY, see Shea

SHAYLA, see Shaela

SHAYNA, see Shaina

SHEA, Shae, Shaelea, Shaelee, Shaeleigh, Shaelyn, Shaena, Shaeya, Shaia, Shay, Shaya, Shaye, Shayia, Shealy, Shéana, Sheanna, Shey
Language/Cultural Origin: **Irish**
Inherent Meaning: **From the Fairy Palace**
Spiritual Connotation: **Blessed**

Scripture: **Ephesians 3:20** NCV
With God's power working in us, God can do much, much more than anything we can ask or imagine.

SHEENA, Sheenah, Sheenna, Sheina, Shena
Language/Cultural Origin: **Scottish**
Inherent Meaning: **God Is Gracious**
Spiritual Connotation: **Instrument of Grace**
Scripture: **Joel 2:13** TLB
Let your remorse tear at your hearts and not your garments. Return to the Lord your God, for he is gracious and merciful.

SHEILA, Sheela, Sheelah, Sheilah, Shiela, Shyla
Language/Cultural Origin: **English**
Inherent Meaning: **Blind**
Spiritual Connotation: **Wise**
Scripture: **Psalm 111:10** RSV
The fear of the LORD is the beginning of wisdom.

SHELBY, Shelbee, Shelbey, Shelbie, Shellby
Language/Cultural Origin: **Old English**
Inherent Meaning: **From the Estate on the Slope**
Spiritual Connotation: **Faithful Steward**
Scripture: **1 Corinthians 4:2** NCV
Now in this way those who are trusted with something valuable must show they are worthy of that trust.

SHELDON, Shelden, Sheldin
Language/Cultural Origin: **Middle English**
Inherent Meaning: **From the Steep Valley**
Spiritual Connotation: **Man of Virtue**
Scripture: **Ezekiel 36:27** NRSV
I will put my spirit within you, and make you follow my statutes and be careful to observe my ordinances.

SHELLEY, Shelee, Sheley, Shellee, Shelli, Shellie, Shelly
Language/Cultural Origin: **Old English**
Inherent Meaning: **From the Meadow on the Slope**
Spiritual Connotation: **Walks With God**
Scripture: **John 15:5** NRSV
I am the vine, you are the branches.

Those who abide in me and I in them bear much fruit, because apart from me you can do nothing.

SHELTON, Shelten
Language/Cultural Origin: **Middle English**
Inherent Meaning: **From the Edge of Town**
Spiritual Connotation: **Divinely Bestowed**
Scripture: **1 Corinthians 2:12** RSV
Now we have received not the spirit of the world, but the Spirit which is from God.

SHEM, Shemm
Language/Cultural Origin: **Hebrew**
Inherent Meaning: **Reputation**
Spiritual Connotation: **Honest**
Scripture: **2 Corinthians 8:21** NRSV
We intend to do what is right not only in the Lord's sight but also in the sight of others.

SHERIDAN, Sherridan
Language/Cultural Origin: **Irish**
Inherent Meaning: **Ambitious**
Spiritual Connotation: **Free in Spirit**
Scripture: **Job 33:4** NKJV
The Spirit of God has made me, and the breath of the Almighty gives me life.

SHERIKA, Shereka, Sherica, Shericka, Sherrika
Language/Cultural Origin: **Middle Eastern**
Inherent Meaning: **Easterner**
Spiritual Connotation: **Stranger**
Scripture: **Isaiah 43:5** NKJV
Fear not, for I am with you; I will bring your descendants from the east.

SHERMAN, Scherman, Shermann
Language/Cultural Origin: **Anglo-Saxon**
Inherent Meaning: **Sheepshearer**
Spiritual Connotation: **Gifted of God**
Scripture: **James 1:17** NASB
Every good thing given and every perfect gift is from above.

SHERROD, Sherod, Sherrard, Sherrodd
Language/Cultural Origin: **Anglo-Saxon**
Inherent Meaning: **Clearer of Land**
Spiritual Connotation: **Messenger**
Scripture: **John 4:35** TLB
Look around you! Vast fields of human

*souls are ripening all around us, and are
ready now for reaping.*

SHERWIN, Sherwyn
Language/Cultural Origin: **Anglo-Saxon**
Inherent Meaning: **Swift Runner**
Spiritual Connotation: **Steady Judgment**
Scripture: **Psalm 103:6** NLT
*The LORD gives righteousness and justice
to all who are treated unfairly.*

SHERYL, Sharilyn, Sharyl, Sherey, Sheri, Sheril, Sherill, Sherleen, Sherrey, Sherri, Sherrie, Sherril, Sherrilynn, Sherryl (see also Cheryl, Shari)
Language/Cultural Origin: **English**
Inherent Meaning: **Dearest**
Spiritual Connotation: **Treasured**
Scripture: **1 Peter 5:7** NRSV
*Cast all your anxiety on him, because he
cares for you.*

SHIANTE, Shianda, Shianna, Shianne, Shianta, Shianté, Shyanna, Shyanne, Shyenna, Shyenne (see also Cheyenne, Shantae)
Language/Cultural Origin: **Native American**
Inherent Meaning: **Tribe**
Spiritual Connotation: **Regenerated**
Scripture: **Ezekiel 11:19** NLT
*And I will give them singleness of heart
and put a new spirit within them. I will
take away their hearts of stone and give
them tender hearts instead.*

SHILO, Shiloh
☞ Language/Cultural Origin: **Hebrew**
Inherent Meaning: **God's Gift**
Spiritual Connotation: **Precious Sacrifice**
Scripture: **Genesis 49:10** NASB
*The scepter shall not depart from Judah,
nor the ruler's staff from between his feet,
until Shiloh comes.*

SHIONA, Shéona, Sheyona
Language/Cultural Origin: **Scottish**
Inherent Meaning: **God Is Gracious**
Spiritual Connotation: **Redeemed**
Scripture: **Titus 2:11** NLT

*For the grace of God has been revealed,
bringing salvation to all people.*

SHIRLEY, Sherlee, Shirlee
Language/Cultural Origin: **Old English**
Inherent Meaning: **From the Bright
Meadow**
Spiritual Connotation: **Happiness of Heart**
Scripture: **1 John 4:12** NRSV
*No one has ever seen God; if we love
one another, God lives in us, and his love
is perfected in us.*

SHONA, Shonda, see Shauna

SIBLEY, Siblee, Sibleigh, Syblie
Language/Cultural Origin: **Middle English**
Inherent Meaning: **Friendly**
Spiritual Connotation: **Reverent**
Scripture: **Psalm 25:14** NRSV
*The friendship of the LORD is for those
who fear him, and he makes his covenant
known to them.*

SIDNEY, Cyd, Cydna, Cydnee, Cydney, Sidanni, Sidona, Sidonia, Sidonio, Sidony, Sydna, Sydnee, Sydney, Sydnie, Sydonia (see also Cid)
Language/Cultural Origin: **Old French**
Inherent Meaning: **From St. Denis, France**
Spiritual Connotation: **Righteous**
Scripture: **Psalm 32:11** RSV
*Be glad in the LORD, and rejoice, O righ-
teous, and shout for joy, all you upright
in heart!*

SIEGFRIED, Seifert, Siegfred, Sig (see also Zigfrid)
Language/Cultural Origin: **German**
Inherent Meaning: **Victorious Peace**
Spiritual Connotation: **Grateful**
Scripture: **Colossians 3:15** NASB
*And let the peace of Christ rule in your
hearts, to which indeed you were called
in one body; and be thankful.*

SIERRA, Ciaara, Ciara, Ciera, Siaara, Siara, Siarra, Sieara, Siera
Language/Cultural Origin: **Irish**
Inherent Meaning: **Black**
Spiritual Connotation: **Pure**
Scripture: **1 John 1:9** RSV

If we confess our sins, he is faithful and just, and will forgive our sins and cleanse us from all unrighteousness.

SIGMUND
Language/Cultural Origin: **Old German**
Inherent Meaning: **Victorious Protector**
Spiritual Connotation: **Guardian**
Scripture: **Psalm 3:3** RSV
But thou, O LORD, art a shield about me, my glory, and the lifter of my head.

SIGOURNEY, Sigourny
Language/Cultural Origin: **Old English**
Inherent Meaning: **Conqueror**
Spiritual Connotation: **Victor**
Scripture: **Romans 8:37** NKJV
Yet in all these things we are more than conquerors through Him who loved us.

SILAS, Sylas
☞ Language/Cultural Origin: **Latin**
Inherent Meaning: **From the Forest**
Spiritual Connotation: **Steadfast in Trust**
Scripture: **Proverbs 29:25** TLB
Fear of man is a dangerous trap, but to trust in God means safety.

SILVIA, see Sylvia

SIMBA, Symba
Language/Cultural Origin: **Swahili**
Inherent Meaning: **Lion**
Spiritual Connotation: **Blessed**
Scripture: **Numbers 24:9** NIV
Like a lion they crouch and lie down, like a lioness—who dares to rouse them? May those who bless you be blessed and those who curse you be cursed!

SIMON, Shimon, Shimóne, Simeon,
☞ **Simion, Simmons, Symon**
Language/Cultural Origin: **Hebrew**
Inherent Meaning: **God Heard**
Spiritual Connotation: **Diligent**
Scripture: **Psalm 61:5** NASB
For You have heard my vows, O God; You have given me the inheritance of those who fear Your name.

SIMONE, Samona, Simmona,

Simmone, Simoane, Simona,
Simonne, Symone
Language/Cultural Origin: **French**
Inherent Meaning: **God Hears**
Spiritual Connotation: **Steadfast**
Scripture: **John 8:26** NKJV
He who sent Me is true; and I speak to the world those things which I heard from Him.

SINCLAIR, Sinclaire
Language/Cultural Origin: **French**
Inherent Meaning: **Prayer**
Spiritual Connotation: **Heavenly Minded**
Scripture: **1 Thessalonians 5:16-17** NCV
Always be joyful. Pray continually.

SINEAD, Sineád
Language/Cultural Origin: **Irish**
Inherent Meaning: **God Is Gracious**
Spiritual Connotation: **Blessed**
Scripture: **Psalm 67:1** NRSV
May God be gracious to us and bless us and make his face to shine upon us.

SIONA, Siauna, Siaunna, Sionna
Language/Cultural Origin: **Hebrew**
Inherent Meaning: **Apex**
Spiritual Connotation: **Productive**
Scripture: **Colossians 3:23** NLT
Work hard and cheerfully at whatever you do, as though you were working for the Lord rather than for people.

SKEETER, Skeet
Language/Cultural Origin: **English**
Inherent Meaning: **Fast**
Spiritual Connotation: **Efficient**
Scripture: **2 Kings 1:11** NKJV
Man of God, thus has the king said, "Come down quickly!"

SKELLY, Skelley
Language/Cultural Origin: **Gaelic**
Inherent Meaning: **Storyteller**
Spiritual Connotation: **Treasurer of Knowledge**
Scripture: **Exodus 10:2** NLT
You will be able to tell wonderful stories to your children and grandchildren about the marvelous things I am doing . . . to prove that I am the LORD.

SKIPPER, Skip, Skipp
Language/Cultural Origin: **Old Norse**
Inherent Meaning: **Master of a Ship**
Spiritual Connotation: **Leader**
Scripture: **Psalm 104:26** NLT
See the ships sailing along, and Leviathan, which you made to play in the sea.

SKYE, Sky
Language/Cultural Origin: **Middle Eastern**
Inherent Meaning: **Supplier of Water**
Spiritual Connotation: **Miraculous Creation**
Scripture: **Psalm 19:1** NCV
The heavens tell the glory of God, and the skies announce what his hands have made.

SKYLER, Schuyler, Schylar, Schyler, Skyelar, Skyla, Skylah, Skylar, Skylee, Skylie, Skyllar, Skyller, Skylor
Language/Cultural Origin: **Dutch**
Inherent Meaning: **Scholar**
Spiritual Connotation: **Wise**
Scripture: **Romans 15:4** RSV
For whatever was written in former days was written for our instruction, that by steadfastness and by the encouragement of the scriptures we might have hope.

SLADE, Slayde
Language/Cultural Origin: **Old English**
Inherent Meaning: **Child of the Valley**
Spiritual Connotation: **Fearless**
Scripture: **Psalm 23:4** NASB
Even though I walk through the valley of the shadow of death, I fear no evil; for Thou art with me; Thy rod and Thy staff, they comfort me.

SLATER, Slaeter
Language/Cultural Origin: **English**
Inherent Meaning: **Roof Slater**
Spiritual Connotation: **Skilled**
Scripture: **Exodus 31:3** NKJV
And I have filled him with the Spirit of God, in wisdom, in understanding, in knowledge, and in all manner of workmanship.

SLOAN, Sloane
Language/Cultural Origin: **Irish**

Inherent Meaning: **Warrior**
Spiritual Connotation: **Victorious Spirit**
Scripture: **1 John 5:4** RSV
For whatever is born of God overcomes the world; and this is the victory that overcomes the world, our faith.

SOCRATES, Socratis
Language/Cultural Origin: **Greek**
Inherent Meaning: **Learned**
Spiritual Connotation: **Brilliant**
Scripture: **1 Corinthians 1:21** NCV
In the wisdom of God the world did not know God through its own wisdom. So God chose to use the message that sounds foolish to save those who believe.

SOLANA, Solanna, Soliana, Solianna
Language/Cultural Origin: **Spanish**
Inherent Meaning: **Sunshine**
Spiritual Connotation: **Righteous**
Scripture: **Proverbs 4:18** NKJV
But the path of the just is like the shining sun, that shines ever brighter unto the perfect day.

SOLOMON, Salamun, Sol, Solaman, Sulaiman (see also Salman)
Language/Cultural Origin: **Hebrew**
Inherent Meaning: **Peaceful**
Spiritual Connotation: **Where God Dwells**
Scripture: **Job 22:26** NKJV
For then you will have your delight in the Almighty, and lift up your face to God.

SOMMER, Summar, Summer
Language/Cultural Origin: **English**
Inherent Meaning: **Summer**
Spiritual Connotation: **Ordained**
Scripture: **Psalm 74:17** NIV
It was you who set all the boundaries of the earth; you made both summer and winter.

SONYA, Sonia, Sonja, Sonjia, Sunya
Language/Cultural Origin: **Russian**
Inherent Meaning: **Wisdom**
Spiritual Connotation: **Spiritual Discernment**
Scripture: **Hebrews 5:14** NLT
Solid food is for those who are mature, who have trained themselves to recognize the difference between right and wrong and then do what is right.

SOPHIA, Sofi, Soffi, Sofia, Sofie, Sofiya, Sofya, Sophey, Sophi, Sophie, Zofia, Zophia

Language/Cultural Origin: **Greek**
Inherent Meaning: **Wisdom**
Spiritual Connotation: **Excellent Virtue**
Scripture: **James 1:5** NASB
But if any of you lacks wisdom, let him ask of God, who gives to all men generously and without reproach, and it will be given to him.

SORAYA, Sorayah, Suraya, Surayah

Language/Cultural Origin: **Persian**
Inherent Meaning: **Princess**
Spiritual Connotation: **Beautiful**
Scripture: **Psalm 45:13** NIV
All glorious is the princess within her chamber; her gown is interwoven with gold.

SOREN, Sören

Language/Cultural Origin: **Danish**
Inherent Meaning: **Thunder**
Spiritual Connotation: **Power of God**
Scripture: **Revelation 14:2** RSV
And I heard a voice from heaven like the sound of many waters and like the sound of loud thunder.

SORREL, Sorel, Sorell

Language/Cultural Origin: **French**
Inherent Meaning: **Reddish Brown**
Spiritual Connotation: **Witness**
Scripture: **Acts 4:12** TLB
There is salvation in no one else! Under all heaven there is no other name for men to call upon to save them.

SPENCER, Spence, Spenser

Language/Cultural Origin: **English**
Inherent Meaning: **Dispenser of Provisions**
Spiritual Connotation: **Faithful Steward**
Scripture: **1 Corinthians 4:1** NRSV
Think of us in this way, as servants of Christ and stewards of God's mysteries.

SPIKE, Spyke

Language/Cultural Origin: **English**
Inherent Meaning: **Ear of Grain**
Spiritual Connotation: **Content**
Scripture: **Psalm 4:7** NLT
You have given me greater joy than those who have abundant harvests of grain and wine.

SPIRO, Spiros, Spyros

Language/Cultural Origin: **Greek**
Inherent Meaning: **Breath**
Spiritual Connotation: **One of Integrity**
Scripture: **Job 27:3-4** NLT
As long as I live, while I have breath from God, my lips will speak no evil, and my tongue will speak no lies.

SPRING

Language/Cultural Origin: **English**
Inherent Meaning: **Springtime**
Spiritual Connotation: **Renewed**
Scripture: **Psalm 72:6** NLT
May his reign be as refreshing as the springtime rains—like the showers that water the earth.

STACEY, Stacee, Stacia, Stacie, Stacy, Stasha, Stashia, Stasia, Stasya

Language/Cultural Origin: **English**
Inherent Meaning: **Resurrection**
Spiritual Connotation: **Strengthened**
Scripture: **Isaiah 40:31** NKJV
But those who wait on the LORD shall renew their strength; they shall mount up with wings like eagles, they shall run and not be weary, they shall walk and not faint.

STAFFORD, Stafforde

Language/Cultural Origin: **English**
Inherent Meaning: **From the Riverbank Landing**
Spiritual Connotation: **High Praise**
Scripture: **Psalm 98:8** NASB
Let the rivers clap their hands, let the mountains sing together for joy.

STAMOS, Staemos, Stémos

Language/Cultural Origin: **Greek**
Inherent Meaning: **Crowned**
Spiritual Connotation: **Exalted**
Scripture: **Hebrews 2:9** NCV
But we see Jesus . . . wearing a crown of glory and honor because he suffered and died. And by God's grace, he died for everyone.

STANA, Stano, Stas, Stasik, Stasio
Language/Cultural Origin: **Czech**
Inherent Meaning: **Stand of Glory**
Spiritual Connotation: **Rewarded**
Scripture: **1 Peter 5:4** NRSV
And when the chief shepherd appears, you will win the crown of glory that never fades away.

STANFORD, Stamford
Language/Cultural Origin: **English**
Inherent Meaning: **From the Rocky Riverbank**
Spiritual Connotation: **Voice of God**
Scripture: **Proverbs 21:1** RSV
The king's heart is a stream of water in the hand of the LORD; he turns it wherever he will.

STANLEY, Stan, Stanlee
Language/Cultural Origin: **English**
Inherent Meaning: **From the Rocky Meadow**
Spiritual Connotation: **Sincere Devotion**
Scripture: **Colossians 1:23** NCV
You must not be moved away from the hope brought to you by the Good News that you heard.

STANTON, Stanten
Language/Cultural Origin: **English**
Inherent Meaning: **From the Stony Farm**
Spiritual Connotation: **Excellent Worth**
Scripture: **1 John 2:10** NRSV
Whoever loves a brother or sister lives in the light, and in such a person there is no cause for stumbling.

STARLING, Starrling
Language/Cultural Origin: **English**
Inherent Meaning: **Bird**
Spiritual Connotation: **Treasured**
Scripture: **Matthew 6:26** NLT
Look at the birds. . . . Your heavenly Father feeds them. And you are far more valuable to him than they are.

STASHA, see Stacey

STEADMAN, Stedman
Language/Cultural Origin: **English**
Inherent Meaning: **Landowner**
Spiritual Connotation: **Generous**

Scripture: **Acts 2:45** NLT
They sold their possessions and shared the proceeds with those in need.

STEFAN, Stefane, Stéfane, Stefano, Stefanos, Steffan, Steffon, Stefon, Stefón, Stefone, Stefóne (see also Stephen)
Language/Cultural Origin: **Polish/Swedish**
Inherent Meaning: **Crowned**
Spiritual Connotation: **Wise**
Scripture: **Proverbs 14:18** RSV
The prudent are crowned with knowledge.

STELLA, Stellar
Language/Cultural Origin: **Latin**
Inherent Meaning: **Star**
Spiritual Connotation: **Esteemed**
Scripture: **Psalm 91:11** NRSV
For he will command his angels concerning you to guard you in all your ways.

STEPHEN, Steeve, Steeven, Stephan, ☞ Stephán, Stephon, Stephón, Stephone, Stevan, Steve, Steven, Stevens, Stevie (see also Stefan)
Language/Cultural Origin: **Greek**
Inherent Meaning: **Crowned**
Spiritual Connotation: **Blessed**
Scripture: **2 Timothy 2:5** NASB
Also if anyone competes as an athlete, he does not win the prize unless he competes according to the rules.

STEPHANIE, Stafani, Stafanie, Staffany, Stefaney, Stefani, Stefany, Stefenie, Steffani, Steffanie, Steffi, Steffie, Stephana, Stephaney, Stephani, Stephania, Stephany, Stephanya, Stephenie, Stephi, Stephie, Stephney, Stephnie
Language/Cultural Origin: **Greek**
Inherent Meaning: **Crowned**
Spiritual Connotation: **Illuminated**
Scripture: **1 Corinthians 2:9** NRSV
What no eye has seen, nor ear heard, nor the human heart conceived, what God has prepared for those who love him.

STERLING, Stirling
Language/Cultural Origin: **Middle English**

Inherent Meaning: **Of Genuine Value**
Spiritual Connotation: **Excellent Worth**
Scripture: **1 Corinthians 2:12** RSV
Now we have received not the spirit of the world, but the Spirit which is from God, that we might understand the gifts bestowed on us by God.

STEVEN, see Stephen

STING
Language/Cultural Origin: **English**
Inherent Meaning: **Spike of Grain**
Spiritual Connotation: **Blessed**
Scripture: **Psalm 4:7** NLT
You have given me greater joy than those who have abundant harvests of grain and wine.

STOCKTON, Stokkton
Language/Cultural Origin: **English**
Inherent Meaning: **From the Town Full of Tree Stumps**
Spiritual Connotation: **Thankful**
Scripture: **Psalm 96:12** TLB
Praise him for the growing fields, for they display his greatness. Let the trees of the forest rustle with praise.

STORM, Stormy
Language/Cultural Origin: **Middle English**
Inherent Meaning: **Turbulent**
Spiritual Connotation: **Courageous**
Scripture: **Psalm 145:18** RSV
The LORD is near to all who call upon him, to all who call upon him in truth.

STRATFORD, Strattford
Language/Cultural Origin: **Old English**
Inherent Meaning: **Bridge Over the River**
Spiritual Connotation: **Comforted**
Scripture: **Job 11:16** NLT
You will forget your misery. It will all be gone like water under the bridge.

STROM, Stromm
Language/Cultural Origin: **German**
Inherent Meaning: **Stream**
Spiritual Connotation: **Seeker of Truth**
Scripture: **Psalm 42:1** NCV
As a deer thirsts for streams of water, so I thirst for you, God.

STUART, Steward, Stewart, Stu
Language/Cultural Origin: **Old English**
Inherent Meaning: **Caretaker**
Spiritual Connotation: **Helpful Spirit**
Scripture: **Galatians 6:2** NCV
By helping each other with your troubles, you truly obey the law of Christ.

SUKE, Sukee, Sukée
Language/Cultural Origin: **Hawaiian**
Inherent Meaning: **Lily**
Spiritual Connotation: **Adorned**
Scripture: **Luke 12:27** NLT
Look at the lilies and how they grow. They don't work or make their clothing, yet Solomon in all his glory was not dressed as beautifully as they are.

SUKI, Sukie, Suky
Language/Cultural Origin: **Japanese**
Inherent Meaning: **Beloved**
Spiritual Connotation: **Image of Christ**
Scripture: **1 John 4:7** NCV
Dear friends, we should love each other, because love comes from God. Everyone who loves has become God's child and knows God.

SULLIVAN, Sulley, Sullie, Sully
Language/Cultural Origin: **Irish**
Inherent Meaning: **Black-Eyed or Hawk-Eyed**
Spiritual Connotation: **Deep Wisdom**
Scripture: **Proverbs 13:14** NASB
The teaching of the wise is a fountain of life, to turn aside from the snares of death.

SULTAN, Sultaan
Language/Cultural Origin: **Swahili**
Inherent Meaning: **Ruler**
Spiritual Connotation: **Kind**
Scripture: **Proverbs 22:9** NRSV
Those who are generous are blessed, for they share their bread with the poor.

SUMIKO, Sumyko
Language/Cultural Origin: **Japanese**
Inherent Meaning: **Lovely Child**
Spiritual Connotation: **Pleasing**
Scripture: **Proverbs 10:1** NRSV
A wise child makes a glad father.

SUMMER, see Sommer

SUMMIT, Summet
Language/Cultural Origin: **English**
Inherent Meaning: **Peak**
Spiritual Connotation: **Righteous**
Scripture: **Luke 12:3** NLT
Whatever you have said in the dark will be heard in the light, and what you have whispered behind closed doors will be shouted from the housetops for all to hear!

SUNI, Sunni
Language/Cultural Origin: **Zuni**
Inherent Meaning: **Native**
Spiritual Connotation: **Restored**
Scripture: **Zephaniah 3:20** TLB
At that time, I will gather you together and bring you home again, and give you a good name.

SUNNY, Sunney, Sunnie
Language/Cultural Origin: **English**
Inherent Meaning: **Cheerful**
Spiritual Connotation: **Peaceful**
Scripture: **Psalm 98:6** NLT
Make a joyful symphony before the LORD, the King!

SUSANNA, Suanne, Sue, Sueanne, ☞ **Susan, Susana, Susanah, Susann, Susannah, Susanne, Susette, Susi, Susie, Suzan, Suzana, Suzann, Suzanna, Suzanne, Suzette, Suzi, Suzie, Suzy**
Language/Cultural Origin: **Hebrew**
Inherent Meaning: **Graceful Lily**
Spiritual Connotation: **Purity**
Scripture: **Proverbs 4:18** NRSV
But the path of the righteous is like the light of dawn, which shines brighter and brighter until full day.

SUTHERLAND, Sutherlend
Language/Cultural Origin: **Scandinavian**
Inherent Meaning: **Southern Land**
Spiritual Connotation: **Blessed**
Scripture: **Psalm 85:1** NLT
LORD, you have poured out amazing blessings on your land! You have restored the fortunes of Israel.

SVEN, Svein, Swen
Language/Cultural Origin: **Scandinavian**
Inherent Meaning: **Youth**
Spiritual Connotation: **Loving**
Scripture: **Proverbs 5:18** NKJV
Let your fountain be blessed, and rejoice with the wife of your youth.

SVETLANA, Sveta, Svetlania, Svetlanna, Svetlanya
Language/Cultural Origin: **Russian**
Inherent Meaning: **Bright Light**
Spiritual Connotation: **Image of Christ**
Scripture: **Matthew 4:16** NCV
These people who live in darkness will see a great light. They live in a place covered with the shadows of death, but a light will shine on them.

SWALEY, Swailee, Swailey
Language/Cultural Origin: **Old English**
Inherent Meaning: **Winding Stream**
Spiritual Connotation: **Expectant**
Scripture: **Psalm 126:4** NLT
Restore our fortunes, LORD, as streams renew the desert.

SWINDEL, Swindell
Language/Cultural Origin: **Old English**
Inherent Meaning: **From the Valley of the Pigs**
Spiritual Connotation: **Beloved**
Scripture: **1 John 3:1** NKJV
Behold what manner of love the Father has bestowed on us, that we should be called children of God!

SYBIL, Cybel, Cybele, Cybil, Cybill, Sibbel, Sibbill, Sibel, Sibyl, Sybille
Language/Cultural Origin: **Latin**
Inherent Meaning: **Prophet**
Spiritual Connotation: **Chosen**
Scripture: **Joel 2:28** NRSV
Your sons and your daughters shall prophesy, your old men shall dream dreams, and your young men shall see visions.

SYDNEY, see Sidney

SYLVESTER, Silvester, Sylvain, Sylvestre
Language/Cultural Origin: **Latin**

Inherent Meaning: **From the Forest**

Spiritual Connotation: **Strong in Spirit**

Scripture: **1 Kings 8:61** NRSV
Therefore devote yourselves completely to the LORD our God, walking in his statutes and keeping his commandments.

SYLVIA, Silva, Silvana, Silvanna, Silvia, Sylvana, Sylvania, Sylvanna, Sylvanya, Sylvya

Language/Cultural Origin: **Latin**

Inherent Meaning: **From the Forest**

Spiritual Connotation: **Dwelling in Spirit**

Scripture: **Psalm 138:8** NRSV
The LORD will fulfill his purpose for me; your steadfast love, O LORD, endures forever. Do not forsake the work of your hands.

T

TABER, Tabor, Taibor, Tayber
Language/Cultural Origin: **Persian**
Inherent Meaning: **Drummer**
Spiritual Connotation: **Merry of Heart**
Scripture: **Proverbs 15:13** NASB
A joyful heart makes a cheerful face.

TABITHA, Tabatha, Tabathia, Tabby, ☞ Tabytha
Language/Cultural Origin: **Aramaic**
Inherent Meaning: **Gazelle**
Spiritual Connotation: **Graceful**
Scripture: **Psalm 90:16** NCV
Show your servants the wonderful things you do; show your greatness to their children.

TACI, Tace, Tacee, Tacey, Tacia, Taciana, Tacianna, Tacie, Taceya
Language/Cultural Origin: **Zuni**
Inherent Meaning: **Washtub**
Spiritual Connotation: **Forgiven**
Scripture: **Psalm 51:2** NKJV
Wash me thoroughly from my iniquity, and cleanse me from my sin.

TADAN, Taedan, Taidan
Language/Cultural Origin: **Native American**
Inherent Meaning: **Plenty**
Spiritual Connotation: **Nourished**
Scripture: **Psalm 72:16** NLT
May there be abundant crops throughout the land, flourishing even on the mountaintops.

TAESHA, Taheisha, Tahisha, Taiesha, Taisha, Teisha, Tyeisha, Tyeshia, Tyishia (see also Tisha)
Language/Cultural Origin: **American**
Inherent Meaning: **Beautiful**
Spiritual Connotation: **Testimony**
Scripture: **Romans 10:15** NRSV
How beautiful are the feet of those who bring good news!

TAGGERT, Taggart
Language/Cultural Origin: **Gaelic**
Inherent Meaning: **Son of the Priest**
Spiritual Connotation: **Full of Life**
Scripture: **John 6:63** NLT
It is the Spirit who gives eternal life. Human effort accomplishes nothing. And the very words I have spoken to you are spirit and life.

TAJA, Taeja, Taija, Teijah, Tiájara
Language/Cultural Origin: **Indo-Pakistani**
Inherent Meaning: **Crown**
Spiritual Connotation: **Child of God**
Scripture: **Zechariah 9:16** TLB
The Lord their God will save his people in that day, as a Shepherd caring for his sheep. They shall shine in his land as glittering jewels in a crown.

TAKENYA, Takenia
Language/Cultural Origin: **Moquelumnan**
Inherent Meaning: **Swooping Hawk**
Spiritual Connotation: **Humble**
Scripture: **Job 39:26** NRSV
Is it by your wisdom that the hawk soars, and spreads its wings toward the south?

TAKARA, Takaria, Takarya, Taqara, Taqaria
Language/Cultural Origin: **Japanese**
Inherent Meaning: **Beloved Jewel**
Spiritual Connotation: **Discerning**
Scripture: **Proverbs 20:15** NASB
There is gold, and an abundance of jewels; but the lips of knowledge are a more precious thing.

TAKIA, Takéya, Takía, Takiya, Taquiia
Language/Cultural Origin: **Middle Eastern**
Inherent Meaning: **Worshiper**
Spiritual Connotation: **True Believer**
Scripture: **John 4:24** RSV
God is spirit, and those who worship him must worship in spirit and truth.

TAL, Talley, Tally
Language/Cultural Origin: **Hebrew**
Inherent Meaning: **Rain**
Spiritual Connotation: **Blessing**
Scripture: **Acts 14:17** NCV
Yet he proved he is real by showing kindness, by giving you rain from heaven and . . . by giving you food and filling your hearts with joy.

TALA, Tallah
Language/Cultural Origin: **Native American**
Inherent Meaning: **Stalking Wolf**
Spiritual Connotation: **Tamed**
Scripture: **Isaiah 11:6** NKJV
The wolf also shall dwell with the lamb . . . And a little child shall lead them.

TALBOT, Talbott
Language/Cultural Origin: **Old German**
Inherent Meaning: **Bright Valley**
Spiritual Connotation: **Promise**
Scripture: **Isaiah 40:4** NKJV
Every valley shall be exalted and every mountain and hill brought low; the crooked places shall be made straight and the rough places smooth.

TALIA, Tahila, Talaya, Talea, Taliah, Taliya, Tallia, Tallie, Tally, Talya, Thalia, Tylia
Language/Cultural Origin: **Hebrew**
Inherent Meaning: **Heaven's Dew**
Spiritual Connotation: **Richly Blessed**
Scripture: **Genesis 27:28** NIV
May God give you of heaven's dew and of earth's richness—an abundance of grain and new wine.

TALITHA, Talétha
Language/Cultural Origin: **Aramaic**
Inherent Meaning: **Little/Young Girl**
Spiritual Connotation: **Heavenly Vision**

Scripture: **Zechariah 8:5** NLT
And the streets of the city will be filled with boys and girls at play.

TALLIS, Tallys
Language/Cultural Origin: **French**
Inherent Meaning: **From the Forest**
Spiritual Connotation: **Thankful**
Scripture: **Psalm 96:12** NASB
Let the field exult, and all that is in it. Then all the trees of the forest will sing for joy.

TALMAN, Talmon
Language/Cultural Origin: **Aramaic**
Inherent Meaning: **Oppressed**
Spiritual Connotation: **Vindicated**
Scripture: **Psalm 146:7** NCV
He does what is fair for those who have been wronged. He gives food to the hungry. The LORD sets the prisoners free.

TALON, Talan, Talin, Tallin, Tallon, Tallyn, Talyn
Language/Cultural Origin: **French**
Inherent Meaning: **Claw**
Spiritual Connotation: **Eternal**
Scripture: **Isaiah 40:31** NCV
But the people who trust the LORD will become strong again. They will rise up as an eagle in the sky; they will run and not need rest; they will walk and not become tired.

TAMAR, Tamara, Tamarah, Tamaria, Tamarra, Tamarria, Tamary, Tamera, Tamerai, Tamerey, Tameriás, Tamia, Tamie, Tamiya, Tammara, Tammee, Tammera, Tammey, Tammi, Tammie, Tammra, Tammy, Tamra, Tamy, Tamya
Language/Cultural Origin: **Hebrew**
Inherent Meaning: **Palm Tree**
Spiritual Connotation: **Victorious Spirit**
Scripture: **Micah 5:9** RSV
Your hand shall be lifted up over your adversaries, and all your enemies shall be cut off.

TANI, Tahnee, Tahni, Tahnie, Tanee,

Taney, Tanie, Tany (see also Tawny)
Language/Cultural Origin: **Japanese**
Inherent Meaning: **Valley**
Spiritual Connotation: **Secure**
Scripture: **Psalm 23:4** NKJV
Yea, though I walk through the valley of the shadow of death, I will fear no evil; for You are with me; Your rod and Your staff, they comfort me.

TANIA, Tahnia, Tahniya, Tahnya, Taina, Tana, Tanae, Tanalia, Tanasha, Tanaya, Tanea, Taneia, Taneya, Tanija, Taniya, Tanna, Tannia, Tannis, Tanniya, Tannya, Tanya, Taunia, Tauniya, Taunya, Tawnia, Tawnya, Tonasha, Tonaya, Tonia, Tonja, Tonnia, Tonniya, Tonnya, Tonya (see also Tatiana)
Language/Cultural Origin: **Russian**
Inherent Meaning: **Queen**
Spiritual Connotation: **Honorable**
Scripture: **1 Corinthians 3:16** NRSV
Do you not know that you are God's temple and that God's Spirit dwells in you?

TANNER, Tannar, Tannor
Language/Cultural Origin: **Old English**
Inherent Meaning: **Leather Worker**
Spiritual Connotation: **Diligent**
Scripture: **Colossians 3:23** NLT
Work hard and cheerfully at whatever you do, as though you were working for the Lord rather than for people.

TAPANI, Tapánee, Tapáney
Language/Cultural Origin: **Finnish**
Inherent Meaning: **Crowned**
Spiritual Connotation: **Partaker in Grace**
Scripture: **Hebrews 2:9** NCV
But we see Jesus, who . . . is wearing a crown of glory and honor because he suffered and died. And by God's grace, he died for everyone.

TARAH, Taira, Tairra, Tara, Tarai, ☞ Taran, Tarasha, Taraya, Tari, Taria, Tarin, Taris, Tarisa, Tarise, Tarissa, Tarra, Tarren, Tarrin,

Tarron, Tarryn, Taryn, Tayra (see also Tera)
Language/Cultural Origin: **Hebrew**
Inherent Meaning: **Wild Goat**
Spiritual Connotation: **Excellent Worth**
Scripture: **1 Corinthians 2:12** NRSV
Now we have received not the spirit of the world, but the Spirit that is from God, so that we may understand the gifts bestowed on us by God.

TARIQ, Tareek, Tarék, Tarick, Tarik, Táriq, Tarreq
Language/Cultural Origin: **Middle Eastern**
Inherent Meaning: **Conqueror**
Spiritual Connotation: **Victorious**
Scripture: **Romans 8:37** NKJV
Yet in all these things we are more than conquerors through Him who loved us.

TARRANT, Terrant (see also Terrence)
Language/Cultural Origin: **Welsh**
Inherent Meaning: **Thunder**
Spiritual Connotation: **Mighty Power**
Scripture: **1 Samuel 12:18** TLB
So Samuel called to the Lord, and the Lord sent thunder and rain.

TARVER, Tarvar
Language/Cultural Origin: **English**
Inherent Meaning: **Leader**
Spiritual Connotation: **Dependent Upon God**
Scripture: **Isaiah 11:6** NKJV
The wolf also shall dwell with the lamb. . . . And a little child shall lead them.

TASHA, Tacha, Tachia, Tachiana, Tachianna, Tahsha, Tashana, Tashanna, Tashi, Tashia, Tashiana, Tashianna, Tashina, Tashira, Tashiya, Thasha (see also Natasha)
Language/Cultural Origin: **Russian**
Inherent Meaning: **Christmas Child**
Spiritual Connotation: **Glorious Gift**
Scripture: **Matthew 1:21** NCV
She will give birth to a son, and you will name him Jesus, because he will save his people from their sins.

TASHANA, Tashanda, Tashanna, Tashauna, Tashaunna, Tashawna, Tashonda, Tashondra, Tiashauna, Tyshanna, Tyshauna, Tyshawna
Language/Cultural Origin: **American**
Inherent Meaning: **Christmas Child**
Spiritual Connotation: **Miraculous**
Scripture: **Matthew 1:23** NRSV
Look, the virgin shall conceive and bear a son, and they shall name him Emmanuel, which means, God is with us.

TASIA, Tasiana, Tasianna, Tasiya, Tasiyana, Tasja, Tassiana, Tassianna, Tassie, Tasya (see also Anastasia)
Language/Cultural Origin: **Slavic**
Inherent Meaning: **Resurrection**
Spiritual Connotation: **Eternal Hope**
Scripture: **Luke 24:5-6** NKJV
Why do you seek the living among the dead? He is not here, but is risen!

TASMINE, Tasmin
Language/Cultural Origin: **English**
Inherent Meaning: **Twin**
Spiritual Connotation: **Worthy**
Scripture: **Galatians 3:28** NASB
There is neither Jew nor Greek, there is neither slave nor free man, there is neither male nor female; for you are all one in Christ Jesus.

TATIANA, Taitiana, Taitianna, Tatanya, Tatia, Tatiania, Tatianya, Tatjana, Tatyana, Tatyanna (see also Tania)
Language/Cultural Origin: **Slavic**
Inherent Meaning: **Queen**
Spiritual Connotation: **Lovely**
Scripture: **Psalm 45:11** NKJV
So the King will greatly desire your beauty; because He is your Lord, worship Him.

TATUM, Taetum, Taitum, Tate, Tayte, Taytum
Language/Cultural Origin: **Middle English**
Inherent Meaning: **Cheerful**
Spiritual Connotation: **Happy**
Scripture: **Proverbs 15:13** NASB

A joyful heart makes a cheerful face.

TAWNY, Tahnee, Tauna, Tauni, Tawnee, Tawney, Tawni, Tawnie (see also Tani)
Language/Cultural Origin: **Gypsy**
Inherent Meaning: **Little One**
Spiritual Connotation: **Trusting**
Scripture: **Matthew 10:42** NCV
Those who give one of these little ones a cup of cold water because they are my followers will truly get their reward.

TAYLOR, Tailor, Talor, Taya, Tayana, Tayanna, Tayla, Taylar, Tayler, Taylore, Taylour, Tayna, Taynie, Tayny, Teylar, Teyler, Teylor
Language/Cultural Origin: **English**
Inherent Meaning: **Tailor**
Spiritual Connotation: **Gifted**
Scripture: **Exodus 31:3** RSV
I have filled him with the Spirit of God, with ability and intelligence, with knowledge and all craftsmanship.

TEAGAN, Taegan, Teaghen, Teegan, Teégan, Tegan, Teigen, Tiegan
Language/Cultural Origin: **Welsh**
Inherent Meaning: **Attractive**
Spiritual Connotation: **Faithful**
Scripture: **Titus 2:10** NCV
They . . . should show their masters they can be fully trusted so that in everything they do they will make the teaching of God our Savior attractive.

TEMPEST, Tempestt
Language/Cultural Origin: **Latin**
Inherent Meaning: **Stormy**
Spiritual Connotation: **Serene**
Scripture: **Psalm 89:9** NKJV
You rule the raging of the sea; when its waves rise, You still them.

TERA, Terra (see also Tarah)
Language/Cultural Origin: **Latin**
Inherent Meaning: **Earth**
Spiritual Connotation: **Miraculous**
Scripture: **Daniel 6:27** NASB
He delivers and rescues and performs signs and wonders in heaven and on earth.

TERESA, see Theresa

**TERRELL, Tarell, Terel, Terell,
Terral, Terrell, Terrelle, Terriel,
Terryl, Tyrel, Tyrell, Tyrelle**
Language/Cultural Origin: **English**
Inherent Meaning: **Thunder Ruler**
Spiritual Connotation: **Mighty Protector**
Scripture: **Psalm 5:11** NRSV
*Spread your protection over them, so
that those who love your name may exult
in you.*

**TERRENCE, Tarrence, Tarry, Teran,
Teren, Terence, Terin, Terran,
Terrance, Terren, Terri, Terry (see
also Tarrant)**
Language/Cultural Origin: **Latin**
Inherent Meaning: **Tender**
Spiritual Connotation: **Gently Formed**
Scripture: **Job 33:4** NRSV
*The spirit of God has made me, and the
breath of the Almighty gives me life.*

**TESSA, Tesia, Tessey, Tessi, Tessia,
Tessie, Tessy**
Language/Cultural Origin: **English**
Inherent Meaning: **Reaper**
Spiritual Connotation: **Servant**
Scripture: **Luke 10:2** TLB
*Plead with the Lord of the harvest to send
out more laborers to help you, for the
harvest is so plentiful and the workers
so few.*

**THADDEUS, Tad, Tadd, Thad,
☞ Thadd, Thaddaeus**
Language/Cultural Origin: **Aramaic**
Inherent Meaning: **Loving**
Spiritual Connotation: **Joyful**
Scripture: **Psalm 28:7** NKJV
*The LORD is my strength and my shield;
my heart trusted in Him, and I am
helped; therefore my heart greatly rejoices,
and with my song I will praise Him.*

THALIA, see Talia

THANE, Thain, Thaine, Thayne
Language/Cultural Origin: **Old English**
Inherent Meaning: **Follower**
Spiritual Connotation: **Loyal**
Scripture: **Psalm 40:8** RSV

*I delight to do thy will, O my God; thy
law is within my heart.*

THATCHER, Thaxter
Language/Cultural Origin: **Old English**
Inherent Meaning: **Repairer of Roofs**
Spiritual Connotation: **Diligent**
Scripture: **Deuteronomy 33:11** NIV
*Bless all his skills, O LORD, and be
pleased with the work of his hands.*

THAYER, Thayor
Language/Cultural Origin: **French**
Inherent Meaning: **National Army**
Spiritual Connotation: **Brave Defender**
Scripture: **Isaiah 19:20** NRSV
*When they cry to the LORD because of
oppressors, he will send them a savior,
and will defend and deliver them.*

THELMA, Thellma
Language/Cultural Origin: **Greek**
Inherent Meaning: **Willful**
Spiritual Connotation: **Strong in Spirit**
Scripture: **2 Timothy 1:7** NKJV
*For God has not given us a spirit of fear,
but of power and of love and of a sound
mind.*

**THEODORE, Ted, Teddie, Teddy,
Theo, Theódore**
Language/Cultural Origin: **Greek**
Inherent Meaning: **Divine Gift**
Spiritual Connotation: **Gift of God**
Scripture: **Ecclesiastes 2:26** TLB
*For God gives those who please him wis-
dom, knowledge, and joy.*

**THERESA, Taresa, Tarisa, Tarise,
Tarissa, Teree, Tereese, Teresa,
Terese, Teresea, Terezia, Teri,
Terie, Terisa, Terise, Terisha,
Teriza, Terree, Terresa, Terri,
Terrie, Terry, Therese, Thérese,
Theressa, Thereza, Thressa,
Trescha, Tresa, Tresha, Treshana,
Tressa, Treysa, Treyssa**
Language/Cultural Origin: **Greek**
Inherent Meaning: **Harvester**
Spiritual Connotation: **Bountiful Spirit**
Scripture: **John 4:35** NLT
Look around you! Vast fields are ripening

*all around us and are ready now for the
harvest.*

THERON, Theran, Therron
Language/Cultural Origin: **Greek**
Inherent Meaning: **Hunter**
Spiritual Connotation: **Efficient**
Scripture: **2 Thessalonians 3:10** NRSV
*For even when we were with you, we
gave you this command: Anyone unwill-
ing to work should not eat.*

THOMAS, Thom, Thompson, Tom, ☞ Tomás, Tomm, Tommie, Tommy
Language/Cultural Origin: **Aramaic**
Inherent Meaning: **Twin**
Spiritual Connotation: **Divinely Preserved**
Scripture: **Proverbs 2:11** NASB
*Discretion will guard you, understanding
will watch over you.*

THOR, Thorin
Language/Cultural Origin: **Old Norse**
Inherent Meaning: **Thunder**
Spiritual Connotation: **God's Warrior**
Scripture: **Exodus 15:3** NASB
*The LORD is a warrior; the LORD is His
name.*

THORNTON, Thorntin
Language/Cultural Origin: **Old English**
Inherent Meaning: **From the Town Near
the Thorns**
Spiritual Connotation: **Wise**
Scripture: **Proverbs 22:5** TLB
*The rebel walks a thorny, treacherous
road; the man who values his soul will
stay away.*

TIA, Téa, Teeya, Teia, Tialeigh, Tiamarie, Tiandria, Tianika, Tiia
Language/Cultural Origin: **Spanish**
Inherent Meaning: **Aunt**
Spiritual Connotation: **Pure**
Scripture: **1 Timothy 5:2** NLT
*Treat the older women as you would your
mother, and treat the younger women
with all purity as your own sisters.*

TIANA, Teana, Teanna, Tianna
Language/Cultural Origin: **Greek**
Inherent Meaning: **Princess**
Spiritual Connotation: **Praised**

Scripture: **Psalm 45:13** NIV
*All glorious is the princess within her
chamber; her gown is interwoven with
gold.*

TIARA, Tearra, Teira, Teirra, Tiára, Tiaria, Tiarra, Tiárra, Tiera, Tiéra, Tierra, Tyara, Tyarra
Language/Cultural Origin: **Latin**
Inherent Meaning: **Crowned**
Spiritual Connotation: **Thankful**
Scripture: **Hebrews 2:9** RSV
*But we see Jesus . . . crowned with
glory and honor because of the suffering
of death, so that by the grace of God he
might taste death for every one.*

TIERNEY, Tiernan
Language/Cultural Origin: **Irish**
Inherent Meaning: **Lordly**
Spiritual Connotation: **Gracious Spirit**
Scripture: **Ephesians 4:7** NKJV
*But to each one of us grace was given
according to the measure of Christ's gift.*

TIFARA, Tifára, Tifaria, Tifarra, Tiffarya
Language/Cultural Origin: **Hebrew**
Inherent Meaning: **Splendor**
Spiritual Connotation: **Reverent**
Scripture: **Isaiah 2:10** NASB
*Enter the rock and hide in the dust from
the terror of the LORD and from the
splendor of His majesty.*

TIFFANY, Tifanee, Tifaney, Tifani, Tifanie, Tifany, Tiff, Tiffanee, Tiffaney, Tiffani, Tiffanie, Tiffanny, Tiffeney, Tiffeni, Tiffenie, Tiffennie, Tiffinee, Tiffiney, Tiffini, Tiffinie, Tiffiny, Tiffney, Tifnee, Tifnie, Tifny, Tiphanee, Tiphaney, Tiphani, Tiphanie, Tiphany, Tyfanny, Tyffani, Tyffini, Typhanee, Typhany
Language/Cultural Origin: **English**
Inherent Meaning: **Divine Showing**
Spiritual Connotation: **Beloved**
Scripture: **1 John 4:7** NKJV
Beloved, let us love one another, for love

is of God; and everyone who loves is born of God and knows God.

TIGER, Tig, Tige, Tyger
Language/Cultural Origin: **English**
Inherent Meaning: **Powerful**
Spiritual Connotation: **Strength of God**
Scripture: **Psalm 106:8** NRSV
Yet he saved them for his name's sake, so that he might make known his mighty power.

TILDA, TILLIE, see Matilda

TILDEN, Tildan
Language/Cultural Origin: **Old English**
Inherent Meaning: **From the Blessed Valley**
Spiritual Connotation: **Peaceful Spirit**
Scripture: **Psalm 23:6** KJV
Surely goodness and mercy shall follow me all the days of my life: and I will dwell in the house of the LORD for ever.

TILTAN, Tilton
Language/Cultural Origin: **Hebrew**
Inherent Meaning: **Clover**
Spiritual Connotation: **Blossom**
Scripture: **Isaiah 27:6** NLT
The time is coming when my people will take root. Israel will bud and blossom and fill the whole earth with her fruit!

TIMOTHY, Tim, Timmie, Timmothy, ☞ **Timmy, Timothé, Timothée, Timothi, Tymothee, Tymothy**
Language/Cultural Origin: **Greek**
Inherent Meaning: **Honor to God**
Spiritual Connotation: **Blessed of God**
Scripture: **1 Timothy 1:2** RSV
To Timothy, my true child in the faith: Grace, mercy, and peace from God the Father and Christ Jesus our Lord.

TINA, Teena, Téna, Tyna
Language/Cultural Origin: **English**
Inherent Meaning: **Anointed**
Spiritual Connotation: **Protected**
Scripture: **Psalm 20:6** NKJV
Now I know that the LORD saves His anointed; He will answer him from His holy heaven with the saving strength of His right hand.

TINO, Tíno
Language/Cultural Origin: **Hispanic**
Inherent Meaning: **Venerable**
Spiritual Connotation: **Promised Hope**
Scripture: **2 Thessalonians 1:10** NCV
This will happen on the day when the Lord Jesus comes to receive glory because of his holy people.

TIPPER, Typper
Language/Cultural Origin: **Gaelic**
Inherent Meaning: **Water Pourer**
Spiritual Connotation: **Generous**
Scripture: **Matthew 10:42** NASB
And whoever in the name of a disciple gives to one of these little ones even a cup of cold water to drink, truly I say to you, he shall not lose his reward.

TIRA, Teara, Teera (see also Tyra)
Language/Cultural Origin: **Hebrew**
Inherent Meaning: **Small Village**
Spiritual Connotation: **Treasured**
Scripture: **Romans 5:8** NRSV
But God proves his love for us in that while we still were sinners Christ died for us.

TIRZA, Thira, Tirsa, Tirzah, Tirzha, ☞ **Tyrza, Tyrzah**
Language/Cultural Origin: **Hebrew**
Inherent Meaning: **Pleasant**
Spiritual Connotation: **Gentle**
Scripture: **Psalm 133:1** NCV
It is good and pleasant when God's people live together in peace!

TISHA, Tiesha, Tieshia, Tish, Tishia, Tysha, Tyshia (see also Taesha)
Language/Cultural Origin: **English**
Inherent Meaning: **Joy**
Spiritual Connotation: **Thankful**
Scripture: **Psalm 66:1** NKJV
Make a joyful shout to God, all the earth!

TISHREY, Tishrae, Tishray, Tishreigh
Language/Cultural Origin: **Akkadian**
Inherent Meaning: **Beginning**
Spiritual Connotation: **Wise**
Scripture: **Proverbs 8:23** NKJV
I have been established from everlasting,

from the beginning, before there was ever an earth.

TITUS, Tito, Titos, Tytus
Language/Cultural Origin: **Greek**
Inherent Meaning: **Of the Giants**
Spiritual Connotation: **Honorable**
Scripture: **Matthew 12:35** NKJV
A good man out of the good treasure of his heart brings forth good things.

TOBIAS, Tobee, Tobey, Tobi, Tobiah, Tobie, Toby
Language/Cultural Origin: **Hebrew**
Inherent Meaning: **The Lord Is Good**
Spiritual Connotation: **God's Workmanship**
Scripture: **Matthew 5:16** NKJV
Let your light so shine before men, that they may see your good works and glorify your Father in heaven.

TODD, Tod
Language/Cultural Origin: **Scottish**
Inherent Meaning: **Fox Hunter**
Spiritual Connotation: **Divine Ingenuity**
Scripture: **Genesis 25:27** NCV
When the boys grew up, Esau became a skilled hunter. He loved to be out in the fields.

TONI, Tonee, Tonie
Language/Cultural Origin: **English**
Inherent Meaning: **Priceless**
Spiritual Connotation: **Lovely**
Scripture: **Psalm 36:7** NRSV
How precious is your steadfast love, O God! All people may take refuge in the shadow of your wings.

TONY, Toney
Language/Cultural Origin: **English**
Inherent Meaning: **Praiseworthy**
Spiritual Connotation: **Pure**
Scripture: **Philippians 4:8** NKJV
Whatever things are true . . . noble . . . just . . . pure . . . lovely . . . [and] of good report, if there is any virtue and if there is anything praiseworthy; meditate on these things.

TONYA, see Tania

TOPAZ
Language/Cultural Origin: **Latin**
Inherent Meaning: **Gem**
Spiritual Connotation: **Fidelity**
Scripture: **Revelation 2:10** NKJV
Do not fear any of those things which you are about to suffer. . . . Be faithful until death, and I will give you the crown of life.

TOPHER, Tofer
Language/Cultural Origin: **Greek**
Inherent Meaning: **Bearer**
Spiritual Connotation: **Helper**
Scripture: **Galatians 6:2** NRSV
Bear one another's burdens, and in this way you will fulfill the law of Christ.

TORI, Toria, Torian, Toriana, Torianna, Torie, Torii, Torri, Torria, Torriana, Torrianna, Torrie (see also Tory)
Language/Cultural Origin: **Japanese**
Inherent Meaning: **Bird**
Spiritual Connotation: **Great Worth**
Scripture: **Matthew 6:26** NKJV
Look at the birds of the air . . . your heavenly Father feeds them. Are you not of more value than they?

TORRANCE, Torance
Language/Cultural Origin: **Irish**
Inherent Meaning: **From the Knolls**
Spiritual Connotation: **Man of Peace**
Scripture: **Psalm 91:15** NKJV
He shall call upon Me, and I will answer him; I will be with him in trouble; I will deliver him and honor him.

TORY, Torey, Torre, Torrey, Torry (see also Tori)
Language/Cultural Origin: **English**
Inherent Meaning: **Tower**
Spiritual Connotation: **Preserved**
Scripture: **Proverbs 18:10** NKJV
The name of the LORD is a strong tower; the righteous run to it and are safe.

TOWNSEND, Townshend
Language/Cultural Origin: **English**
Inherent Meaning: **From the Edge of Town**

Spiritual Connotation: **Industrious**
Scripture: **1 Corinthians 12:4** RSV
Now there are varieties of gifts, but the same Spirit.

TRACEY, Trace, Tracee, Traci, Tracia, Tracie, Traciya, Tracy, Tracya, Traecee, Traecey, Traicey, Trasee, Trasey (see also Taci)
Language/Cultural Origin: **Latin**
Inherent Meaning: **Warrior**
Spiritual Connotation: **Noble Spirit**
Scripture: **2 Corinthians 8:21** NLT
We are careful to be honorable before the Lord, but we also want everyone else to know we are honorable.

TRAVERS, Travis
Language/Cultural Origin: **Old French**
Inherent Meaning: **From the Crossroads**
Spiritual Connotation: **Courageous**
Scripture: **Psalm 29:11** NKJV
The LORD will give strength to His people; the LORD will bless His people with peace.

TRAYTON, Traeton, Traiton
Language/Cultural Origin: **Old French**
Inherent Meaning: **From the Settlement Near the Forest**
Spiritual Connotation: **Treasured**
Scripture: **Psalm 121:8** NASB
The LORD will guard your going out and your coming in from this time forth and forever.

TREMAINE, Tremain, Tremayne
Language/Cultural Origin: **Celtic**
Inherent Meaning: **From the House by the Rock**
Spiritual Connotation: **High Praise**
Scripture: **2 Samuel 22:47** NKJV
The LORD lives! Blessed be my Rock! Let God be exalted, the Rock of my salvation!

TRENT, Trente
Language/Cultural Origin: **English**
Inherent Meaning: **Rapid Stream**
Spiritual Connotation: **Renewed**
Scripture: **Isaiah 65:17** NKJV
For behold, I create new heavens and a

new earth; and the former shall not be remembered or come to mind.

TRENTON, Trendon, Trenten, Trentin
Language/Cultural Origin: **Old English**
Inherent Meaning: **From the Town by the Rapid Stream**
Spiritual Connotation: **Rooted in Faith**
Scripture: **Psalm 1:3** NRSV
They are like trees planted by streams of water, which yield their fruit in its season, and their leaves do not wither. In all that they do, they prosper.

TREVOR, Trev, Trevar, Trever
Language/Cultural Origin: **Irish**
Inherent Meaning: **Prudent and Discreet**
Spiritual Connotation: **Righteous**
Scripture: **Psalm 84:11** NKJV
For the LORD God is a sun and shield; the LORD will give grace and glory; no good thing will He withhold from those who walk uprightly.

TREY, Trae, Trai
Language/Cultural Origin: **Middle English**
Inherent Meaning: **Third**
Spiritual Connotation: **Sacrifice**
Scripture: **1 Chronicles 16:29** RSV
Ascribe to the LORD the glory due his name; bring an offering, and come before him!

TRILBY, Trilbee, Trilbey, Trilbie
Language/Cultural Origin: **English**
Inherent Meaning: **Hat**
Spiritual Connotation: **Covered**
Scripture: **Psalm 36:7** RSV
How precious is thy steadfast love, O God! The children of men take refuge in the shadow of thy wings.

TRINA, Treena, Treina, Tria, Triana, Trianna, Trinette, Trinice, Triniece, Trinique, Triya
Language/Cultural Origin: **English**
Inherent Meaning: **Pure**
Spiritual Connotation: **Gentle**
Scripture: **Proverbs 22:11** NRSV
Those who love a pure heart and are

gracious in speech will have the king as a friend.

TRISHA, Tricha, Tricia, Trisa, Trish, Trishana, Trishanna, Trishara, Trissa, Tryssa
Language/Cultural Origin: **English**
Inherent Meaning: **Noble**
Spiritual Connotation: **Honest**
Scripture: **Proverbs 3:3** NRSV
Do not let loyalty and faithfulness forsake you; bind them around your neck, write them on the tablet of your heart.

TRISTEN, Trista, Tristan, Tristia, Tristian, Tristiana, Tristianna, Tristin, Tristina, Triston, Tristya, Trystan, Trysten, Trystia, Trystian, Trystin (see also Trusten)
Language/Cultural Origin: **Welsh**
Inherent Meaning: **Bold**
Spiritual Connotation: **Valiant**
Scripture: **Deuteronomy 31:6** NRSV
Be strong and bold; have no fear or dread of them, because it is the LORD your God who goes with you; he will not fail you or forsake you.

TRIXIE, Trix, Trixi
Language/Cultural Origin: **American**
Inherent Meaning: **Bringer of Joy**
Spiritual Connotation: **Peaceful**
Scripture: **Psalm 46:4** NASB
There is a river whose streams make glad the city of God, the holy dwelling places of the Most High.

TROY, Troi, Troye
Language/Cultural Origin: **Irish Gaelic**
Inherent Meaning: **Foot Soldier**
Spiritual Connotation: **Steadfast**
Scripture: **2 Corinthians 9:8** NASB
And God is able to make all grace abound to you, that always having all sufficiency in everything, you may have an abundance for every good deed.

TRUMAN, Trumann
Language/Cultural Origin: **English**
Inherent Meaning: **Honest**
Spiritual Connotation: **Faithful**

Scripture: **Proverbs 19:22** NLT
Loyalty makes a person attractive. And it is better to be poor than dishonest.

TRUSTEN, Trustan, Trustin (see also Tristen)
Language/Cultural Origin: **English**
Inherent Meaning: **Trustworthy**
Spiritual Connotation: **Reliable**
Scripture: **Psalm 101:1** NRSV
I will sing of loyalty and of justice; to you, O LORD, I will sing.

TRYGVE, Trigve, Trygvee
Language/Cultural Origin: **Norwegian**
Inherent Meaning: **Victor**
Spiritual Connotation: **Triumphant**
Scripture: **1 John 5:4** NCV
Everyone who is a child of God conquers the world. And this is the victory that conquers the world—our faith.

TUCKER
Language/Cultural Origin: **Old English**
Inherent Meaning: **Folder of Cloth**
Spiritual Connotation: **Efficient**
Scripture: **Colossians 3:23** NLT
Work hard and cheerfully at whatever you do, as though you were working for the Lord rather than for people.

TULLIS, Tullias, Tullius
Language/Cultural Origin: **Latin**
Inherent Meaning: **Rank**
Spiritual Connotation: **Admirable**
Scripture: **1 Peter 2:17** NCV
Show respect for all people: Love the brothers and sisters of God's family, respect God, honor the king.

TURNER, Turnar
Language/Cultural Origin: **English**
Inherent Meaning: **Woodworker**
Spiritual Connotation: **Infinite Creativity**
Scripture: **Exodus 35:35** TLB
God has filled them both with unusual skills as jewelers, carpenters . . . and as weavers—they excel in all the crafts we will be needing in the work.

TUSHIYA, Tuschiya
Language/Cultural Origin: **Hebrew**
Inherent Meaning: **Wisdom**

Spiritual Connotation: **Righteous**
Scripture: **Proverbs 4:11** RSV
I have taught you the way of wisdom; I have led you in the paths of uprightness.

TWAIN, Twaine, Twayne
Language/Cultural Origin: **English**
Inherent Meaning: **Divided in Two**
Spiritual Connotation: **Renewed**
Scripture: **2 Corinthians 7:1** RSV
Since we have these promises, beloved, let us cleanse ourselves from every defilement of body and spirit, and make holiness perfect in the fear of God.

TWYLA, Twila, Twilla, Twylla
Language/Cultural Origin: **English**
Inherent Meaning: **Doubly Woven**
Spiritual Connotation: **Strong**
Scripture: **Proverbs 31:25** NLT
She is clothed with strength and dignity, and she laughs with no fear of the future.

TYLER, Ty, Tylar, Tyller, Tylor
Language/Cultural Origin: **Middle English**
Inherent Meaning: **Tile Maker**
Spiritual Connotation: **Resourceful**
Scripture: **Mark 11:24** NRSV
So I tell you, whatever you ask for in prayer, believe that you have received it, and it will be yours.

TYRA, Tyraa, Tyrah, Tyresa, Tyrina, Tyrinia, Tyrisa (see also Tira)
Language/Cultural Origin: **Scandinavian**
Inherent Meaning: **Warrior**
Spiritual Connotation: **Blessed**
Scripture: **Psalm 127:4** NRSV
Like arrows in the hand of a warrior are the sons of one's youth.

TYREL, see Terrell

TYRONE, Ty, Tyronne
Language/Cultural Origin: **Greek**
Inherent Meaning: **Sovereign**
Spiritual Connotation: **Steadfast**
Scripture: **Psalm 1:3** NKJV
He shall be like a tree planted by the rivers of water, that brings forth its fruit in its season, whose leaf also shall not wither; and whatever he does shall prosper.

TYSON, Tison, Tyce, Tysen
Language/Cultural Origin: **French**
Inherent Meaning: **Son of the Ruler**
Spiritual Connotation: **Gifted**
Scripture: **1 Timothy 4:14** NASB
Do not neglect the spiritual gift within you.

U

ULANI, Ulana, Ulanna, Ulanni
Language/Cultural Origin: **Hawaiian**
Inherent Meaning: **Cheerful**
Spiritual Connotation: **Filled With Joy**
Scripture: **Isaiah 12:5** NIV
Sing to the LORD, for he has done glorious things; let this be known to all the world.

ULRIC, Ulrik
Language/Cultural Origin: **Old German**
Inherent Meaning: **Ruler of All**
Spiritual Connotation: **Regenerated**
Scripture: **Colossians 3:10** NRSV
[Clothe] yourselves with the new self, which is being renewed in knowledge according to the image of its creator.

ULRICA, Ulrika
Language/Cultural Origin: **Old German**
Inherent Meaning: **Ruler**
Spiritual Connotation: **Strong in Virtue**
Scripture: **Proverbs 31:10** NKJV
Who can find a virtuous wife? For her worth is far above rubies.

ULYSSES, Ulisses
Language/Cultural Origin: **Latin**
Inherent Meaning: **One Who Detests Deceit or Injustice**
Spiritual Connotation: **Seeker of truth**
Scripture: **Jeremiah 29:12** NASB
Then you will call upon Me and come and pray to Me, and I will listen to you.

UMA, Ooma, Umah
Language/Cultural Origin: **Indo-Pakistani**
Inherent Meaning: **Mother**
Spiritual Connotation: **Blessed**
Scripture: **Genesis 17:16** RSV
I will bless her, and she shall be a mother of nations; kings of peoples shall come from her.

UMI, Umee
Language/Cultural Origin: **Yao**
Inherent Meaning: **Life**
Spiritual Connotation: **Energetic**
Scripture: **Isaiah 43:19** TLB
For I'm going to do a brand new thing. See, I have already begun!

UNA, Oona
Language/Cultural Origin: **Hopi**
Inherent Meaning: **Strong Memory**
Spiritual Connotation: **Humble**
Scripture: **Isaiah 41:13** NRSV
Do not fear, I will help you.

UNIQUE
Language/Cultural Origin: **Latin**
Inherent Meaning: **One**
Spiritual Connotation: **Incomparable**
Scripture: **Psalm 139:14** NRSV
I praise you, for I am fearfully and wonderfully made.

UNITY
Language/Cultural Origin: **Latin**
Inherent Meaning: **Togetherness**
Spiritual Connotation: **Harmonious**
Scripture: **Psalm 133:1** NRSV
How very good and pleasant it is when kindred live together in unity!

UPTON, Uptonn
Language/Cultural Origin: **Old English**
Inherent Meaning: **From the Hill Town**
Spiritual Connotation: **Honorable**
Scripture: **Deuteronomy 8:3** NIV
Man does not live on bread alone but on every word that comes from the mouth of the LORD.

URBAN, Urbain
Language/Cultural Origin: **Latin**
Inherent Meaning: **From the City**
Spiritual Connotation: **Peaceful**
Scripture: **Psalm 46:4** RSV
There is a river whose streams make glad the city of God, the holy habitation of the Most High.

URBANA, Urbanna
Language/Cultural Origin: **Latin**
Inherent Meaning: **From the City**
Spiritual Connotation: **Majestic**
Scripture: **Psalm 87:3** NLT
O city of God, what glorious things are said of you!

URI, Uree, Urii (see also Yuri)
Language/Cultural Origin: **Hebrew**
Inherent Meaning: **My Light**
Spiritual Connotation: **Righteous**
Scripture: **2 Samuel 22:29** NLT
O LORD, you are my light; yes, LORD, you light up my darkness.

URIAH, Urias, Uriyah
Language/Cultural Origin: **Hebrew**
Inherent Meaning: **God Is My Light**
Spiritual Connotation: **Excellent Virtue**
Scripture: **Proverbs 12:28** NRSV
In the path of righteousness there is life, in walking its path there is no death.

URIEL, Uriela, Uriell, Uriella, Urielle (see also Ariel)
Language/Cultural Origin: **Hebrew**
Inherent Meaning: **Flame of God**
Spiritual Connotation: **Transformed**
Scripture: **Deuteronomy 4:24** NASB
For the LORD your God is a consuming fire.

URIKA, Uraeka, Uriqua
Language/Cultural Origin: **Omaha**
Inherent Meaning: **Universally Useful**
Spiritual Connotation: **Student of the Word**
Scripture: **2 Timothy 3:16** NRSV
All scripture is inspired by God and is useful for teaching, for reproof, for correction, and for training in righteousness.

URSULA, Ursa
Language/Cultural Origin: **Latin**
Inherent Meaning: **Little Bear**
Spiritual Connotation: **Courageous**
Scripture: **Deuteronomy 31:6** NKJV
Be strong and of good courage, do not fear nor be afraid of them; for the LORD your God, He is the One who goes with you.

UZIEL, Uzziah, Uzziel
Language/Cultural Origin: **Hebrew**
Inherent Meaning: **God Is My Strength**
Spiritual Connotation: **God's Servant**
Scripture: **Psalm 18:1** NRSV
I love you, O LORD, my strength.

VAIL, Vael, Vaile, Vale, Vayle
Language/Cultural Origin: **English**
Inherent Meaning: **Valley**
Spiritual Connotation: **Praise**
Scripture: **Isaiah 40:4** NKJV
Every valley shall be exalted and every mountain and hill brought low.

VALERIE, Val, Valarae, Valaree, Valarie, Valeree, Valeri, Valery, Vallerie, Vallery, Vallory
Language/Cultural Origin: **Latin**
Inherent Meaning: **Strength**
Spiritual Connotation: **Spiritual Purpose**
Scripture: **Ecclesiastes 3:1** NKJV
To everything there is a season, a time for every purpose under heaven:

VALESKA, Valisha, Valishia
Language/Cultural Origin: **Slavic**
Inherent Meaning: **Glorious Ruler**
Spiritual Connotation: **Esteemed**
Scripture: **Psalm 92:4** NKJV
For You, LORD, have made me glad through Your work; I will triumph in the works of Your hands.

VALIN, Vaylin (see also Balin)
Language/Cultural Origin: **Indo-Pakistani**
Inherent Meaning: **Mighty Warrior**
Spiritual Connotation: **Arm of God**
Scripture: **Deuteronomy 9:29** RSV
For they are thy people and thy heritage, whom thou didst bring out by thy great power and by thy outstretched arm.

VALLI, Vallee, Valley, Vallie, Vally
Language/Cultural Origin: **Latin**
Inherent Meaning: **Strong**
Spiritual Connotation: **God's Leader**
Scripture: **Micah 5:4** NASB

And He will arise and shepherd His flock in the strength of the LORD.

VAN, Vann
Language/Cultural Origin: **Dutch**
Inherent Meaning: **Water Dam**
Spiritual Connotation: **Forgiving**
Scripture: **Ecclesiastes 1:15** TLB
What is wrong cannot be righted; it is water over the dam; and there is no use thinking of what might have been.

VANCE, Vanse
Language/Cultural Origin: **English**
Inherent Meaning: **Thresher**
Spiritual Connotation: **Hard Worker**
Scripture: **Deuteronomy 16:15** NASB
The LORD your God will bless you in all your produce and in all the work of your hands, so that you shall be altogether joyful.

VANDA, Vandelia, Vandi, Vandie, Vannda (see also Wanda)
Language/Cultural Origin: **Slavic**
Inherent Meaning: **Wanderer**
Spiritual Connotation: **Redeemed**
Scripture: **Ephesians 2:19** TLB
Now you are no longer strangers to God and foreigners to heaven, but you are members of God's very own family, citizens of God's country.

VANESSA, Vanesa, Vanissa, Venessa
Language/Cultural Origin: **Greek**
Inherent Meaning: **Butterfly**
Spiritual Connotation: **Free Spirit**
Scripture: **John 8:36** NKJV
Therefore if the Son makes you free, you shall be free indeed.

VANNA, Vana, Vania, Vannah, Vanya
Language/Cultural Origin: **English**
Inherent Meaning: **Butterfly**
Spiritual Connotation: **Liberated**
Scripture: **Galatians 5:1** NASB
It was for freedom that Christ set us free; therefore keep standing firm and do not be subject again to a yoke of slavery.

VARINA, Vareena, Vareyna, Varia, Varya (see also Verena)
Language/Cultural Origin: **Slavic**
Inherent Meaning: **Foreigner**
Spiritual Connotation: **Sanctified**
Scripture: **Ephesians 2:13** NCV
But now in Christ Jesus, you who were far away from God are brought near through the blood of Christ's death.

VASHAWN, Vashaun, Vashon, Vishaun, Vishawn, Voshan, Voshaun, Voshawn, Voshon
Language/Cultural Origin: **American**
Inherent Meaning: **God Is Gracious**
Spiritual Connotation: **Blessed**
Scripture: **Numbers 6:25** NKJV
The LORD make His face shine upon you, and be gracious to you.

VASHTI, Vashtee, Vashtie
☞ Language/Cultural Origin: **Persian**
Inherent Meaning: **Lovely**
Spiritual Connotation: **Beautiful**
Scripture: **Esther 1:11** NCV
He commanded them to bring him Queen Vashti . . . because she was very beautiful.

VAUGHN, Von
Language/Cultural Origin: **Welsh**
Inherent Meaning: **Small**
Spiritual Connotation: **Compassionate**
Scripture: **Matthew 9:13** NKJV
I desire mercy and not sacrifice. For I did not come to call the righteous, but sinners, to repentance.

VEGA, Veyga
Language/Cultural Origin: **Middle Eastern**
Inherent Meaning: **Falling Star**
Spiritual Connotation: **Prophetic**
Scripture: **Matthew 24:29** NLT
The sun will be darkened, the moon will not give light, the stars will fall from the sky, and the powers of heaven will be shaken.

VELMA, Valma, Vellma
Language/Cultural Origin: **Old German**
Inherent Meaning: **Determined Protector**
Spiritual Connotation: **Watchful**
Scripture: **Matthew 25:13** NCV
So always be ready, because you don't know the day or the hour the Son of Man will come.

VENUS, Veenus
Language/Cultural Origin: **Latin**
Inherent Meaning: **Love**
Spiritual Connotation: **Greatest Power**
Scripture: **Titus 3:4** NLT
But then God our Savior showed us his kindness and love.

VERA, Vara, Vira
Language/Cultural Origin: **Latin**
Inherent Meaning: **Truth**
Spiritual Connotation: **Strong in Virtue**
Scripture: **Psalm 32:11** NLT
So rejoice in the LORD and be glad, all you who obey him! Shout for joy, all you whose hearts are pure!

VERENA, Verasha, Verasia, Vereena, Verina, Verity (see also Varina)
Language/Cultural Origin: **Latin**
Inherent Meaning: **Truthful**
Spiritual Connotation: **Forthright**
Scripture: **Proverbs 12:19** NLT
Truth stands the test of time; lies are soon exposed.

VERNON, Vern, Verne
Language/Cultural Origin: **Latin**
Inherent Meaning: **Youthful**
Spiritual Connotation: **Vigorous**
Scripture: **Colossians 3:23** NLT
Work hard and cheerfully at whatever you do, as though you were working for the Lord rather than for people.

VERONICA, Varonica, Veronika, Véronique, Vonnie, Vonny, Vronica
Language/Cultural Origin: **Latin**

Inherent Meaning: **True Image**
Spiritual Connotation: **In God's Reflection**
Scripture: **1 Corinthians 13:12** NCV
Now we see a dim reflection, as if we were looking into a mirror, but then we shall see clearly.

VIANNA, Viana (see also Vienna)
Language/Cultural Origin: **American**
Inherent Meaning: **Gracious**
Spiritual Connotation: **Blessed**
Scripture: **2 Chronicles 30:9** NKJV
For the LORD your God is gracious and merciful, and will not turn His face from you if you return to Him.

VICTOR, Vic, Victer, Vik, Viktor
Language/Cultural Origin: **Latin**
Inherent Meaning: **Conqueror**
Spiritual Connotation: **Triumphant Spirit**
Scripture: **Mark 11:24** RSV
Therefore I tell you, whatever you ask in prayer, believe that you have received it, and it will be yours.

VICTORIA, Vicci, Vickee, Vicki, Vickie, Vicky, Victori, Victoriana, Victorianna, Victorina, Victorya, Viki, Vikki, Vikkie, Vikky, Viktori, Viktoria, Viktoriana, Viktorianna, Viktorina, Viktory, Viktorya
Language/Cultural Origin: **Latin**
Inherent Meaning: **Conqueror**
Spiritual Connotation: **Triumphant Spirit**
Scripture: **Philippians 4:13** NKJV
I can do all things through Christ who strengthens me.

VIENNA, Viena (see also Vianna)
Language/Cultural Origin: **Latin**
Inherent Meaning: **Capital of Austria**
Spiritual Connotation: **Chosen**
Scripture: **Psalm 106:5** NCV
Let me be happy along with your happy nation; let me join your own people in praising you.

VINCENT, Vicente, Vince, Vincente, Vinnie, Vinny
Language/Cultural Origin: **Latin**
Inherent Meaning: **Conquering**

Spiritual Connotation: **Strength Through Faith**
Scripture: **Matthew 9:29** NASB
It shall be done to you according to your faith.

VINSON, Vinnson
Language/Cultural Origin: **English**
Inherent Meaning: **Son of the Victor**
Spiritual Connotation: **Redeemed**
Scripture: **Romans 5:8** NKJV
But God demonstrates His own love toward us, in that while we were still sinners, Christ died for us.

VIOLET, Vi, Viola, Violette, Vyolet
Language/Cultural Origin: **Latin**
Inherent Meaning: **Modest Flower**
Spiritual Connotation: **Humble**
Scripture: **James 4:10** NASB
Humble yourselves in the presence of the Lord, and He will exalt you.

VIRGIL, Vergil
Language/Cultural Origin: **Latin**
Inherent Meaning: **Staff Bearer**
Spiritual Connotation: **Loyal Spirit**
Scripture: **Isaiah 41:13** NKJV
For I, the LORD your God, will hold your right hand. . . . Fear not, I will help you.

VIRGILIA, Virgillia
Language/Cultural Origin: **Latin**
Inherent Meaning: **Staff Bearer**
Spiritual Connotation: **Protector**
Scripture: **Psalm 23:4** NLT
Your rod and your staff protect and comfort me.

VIRGINIA, Virg, Virgenia
Language/Cultural Origin: **Latin**
Inherent Meaning: **Pure**
Spiritual Connotation: **Unblemished**
Scripture: **2 Corinthians 5:17** NRSV
So if anyone is in Christ, there is a new creation: everything old has passed away; see, everything has become new!

VIVIAN, Viv, Vivia, Viviana, Viviane, Vivianna, Vivianne, Vivien, Vivienne
Language/Cultural Origin: **Latin**
Inherent Meaning: **Lively**

Spiritual Connotation: **Joyous Spirit**
Scripture: **Psalm 37:4** NRSV
Take delight in the LORD, and he will give you the desires of your heart.

VLADIMIR, Vladamir, Vlade, Vladé
Language/Cultural Origin: **Russian**
Inherent Meaning: **Famous Prince**
Spiritual Connotation: **Upright**
Scripture: **Jeremiah 29:13** NCV
When you search for me with all your heart, you will find me!

VONDRA, Vonda, Vondraea, Vondrea, Vondraya
Language/Cultural Origin: **Czech**
Inherent Meaning: **Loving**
Spiritual Connotation: **Reborn**
Scripture: **1 John 4:7** RSV
Beloved, let us love one another; for love is of God, and he who loves is born of God and knows God.

VOSHAWN, see Vashawn

W

WADE, Wayde
Language/Cultural Origin: **Old English**
Inherent Meaning: **One Who Advances**
Spiritual Connotation: **Generous Spirit**
Scripture: **Matthew 10:8** TLB
Give as freely as you have received!

WAGNER, Waggner
Language/Cultural Origin: **Old German**
Inherent Meaning: **Wagon Maker**
Spiritual Connotation: **Trusting Spirit**
Scripture: **Isaiah 26:3** NKJV
You will keep him in perfect peace, whose mind is stayed on You, because he trusts in You.

WAKANDA, Wakandra
Language/Cultural Origin: **Dakota**
Inherent Meaning: **Power**
Spiritual Connotation: **Faithful**
Scripture: **2 Corinthians 6:7** NLT
God's power has been working in us. We have righteousness as our weapon, both to attack and to defend ourselves.

WALDEN, Waldon
Language/Cultural Origin: **Old English**
Inherent Meaning: **From the Forest Valley**
Spiritual Connotation: **Calm Spirit**
Scripture: **Psalm 73:26** NCV
My body and my mind may become weak, but God is my strength. He is mine forever.

WALDO, Wald
Language/Cultural Origin: **German**
Inherent Meaning: **Strong**
Spiritual Connotation: **Thankful**
Scripture: **Philippians 4:6** NASB
Be anxious for nothing, but in everything by prayer and supplication with thanks-

giving let your requests be made known to God.

WALKER, Wallker
Language/Cultural Origin: **English**
Inherent Meaning: **Cloth Cleaner**
Spiritual Connotation: **Diligent**
Scripture: **Colossians 3:23** NCV
In all the work you are doing, work the best you can. Work as if you were doing it for the Lord, not for people.

WALLACE, Wallach, Wallis, Wally, Walsh, Welsh
Language/Cultural Origin: **English**
Inherent Meaning: **From Wales**
Spiritual Connotation: **Man of Peace**
Scripture: **Isaiah 26:3** NCV
You, LORD, give true peace to those who depend on you, because they trust you.

WALTER, Walt
Language/Cultural Origin: **Old German**
Inherent Meaning: **Powerful Ruler**
Spiritual Connotation: **Strong Protector**
Scripture: **Psalm 121:8** RSV
The LORD will keep your going out and your coming in from this time forth and for evermore.

WALTON, Walten
Language/Cultural Origin: **English**
Inherent Meaning: **From the Fortified Town**
Spiritual Connotation: **Freedom of Spirit**
Scripture: **John 8:32** NKJV
And you shall know the truth, and the truth shall make you free.

WANDA, Wahnda, Wannda (see also Vanda, Wendy)
Language/Cultural Origin: **Old German**
Inherent Meaning: **Wanderer**

Spiritual Connotation: **Seeker of Truth**
Scripture: **Psalm 139:17** NASB
*How precious also are Thy thoughts to
me, O God! How vast is the sum of
them!*

WARD, Warde
Language/Cultural Origin: **Old English**
Inherent Meaning: **Guardian**
Spiritual Connotation: **Watchful Spirit**
Scripture: **Luke 21:36** NCV
*So be ready all the time. Pray that you
will be strong enough to escape all these
things that will happen.*

WARDELL, Wardel
Language/Cultural Origin: **Old English**
Inherent Meaning: **From the
Watchman's Hill**
Spiritual Connotation: **Protector**
Scripture: **Isaiah 40:29** NASB
*He gives strength to the weary, and to
him who lacks might He increases power.*

WARNER (see also Werner)
Language/Cultural Origin: **Old French**
Inherent Meaning: **Defender**
Spiritual Connotation: **Courageous Spirit**
Scripture: **Luke 12:32** NKJV
*Do not fear, little flock, for it is your
Father's good pleasure to give you the
kingdom.*

WARREN, Warrin
Language/Cultural Origin: **German**
Inherent Meaning: **Protecting Friend**
Spiritual Connotation: **Righteous**
Scripture: **Psalm 112:4** NIV
*Even in darkness light dawns for the
upright, for the gracious and compassion-
ate and righteous man.*

WARWICK, Warick, Warrick
Language/Cultural Origin: **Old English**
Inherent Meaning: **From Near the Dam**
Spiritual Connotation: **Led by the Spirit**
Scripture: **Psalm 23:3** NKJV
*He restores my soul; He leads me in the
paths of righteousness for His name's
sake.*

WASHINGTON
Language/Cultural Origin: **English**

Inherent Meaning: **From the Town
Near the Water**
Spiritual Connotation: **Witness**
Scripture: **Psalm 71:18** NRSV
*So even to old age and gray hairs, O
God, do not forsake me, until I proclaim
your might to all the generations to come.*

WAVA, Waiva
Language/Cultural Origin: **Slavic**
Inherent Meaning: **Foreigner**
Spiritual Connotation: **Child of God**
Scripture: **Ephesians 2:19** NRSV
*So then you are no longer strangers and
aliens, but you are citizens with the saints
and also members of the household of God.*

WAYMAN, Waymon
Language/Cultural Origin: **Middle English**
Inherent Meaning: **Traveler**
Spiritual Connotation: **Shielded**
Scripture: **Deuteronomy 23:14** NKJV
*For the LORD your God walks in the
midst of your camp, to deliver you and
give your enemies over to you.*

WAYNE, Waiyne
Language/Cultural Origin: **English**
Inherent Meaning: **Wagon Maker**
Spiritual Connotation: **Industrious**
Scripture: **Philippians 2:16** NRSV
*It is by your holding fast to the word of
life that I can boast on the day of Christ
that I did not run in vain or labor in vain.*

WEBSTER, Web
Language/Cultural Origin: **Old English**
Inherent Meaning: **Weaver**
Spiritual Connotation: **Example**
Scripture: **Titus 2:7** NIV
*In everything set them an example by
doing what is good. In your teaching
show integrity.*

WELBY, Wellby
Language/Cultural Origin: **Old English**
Inherent Meaning: **From Near the Well**
Spiritual Connotation: **Trusting Spirit**
Scripture: **Psalm 36:7** NKJV
*How precious is Your lovingkindness,
O God! Therefore the children of men
put their trust under the shadow of
Your wings.*

WELDON, Welden
Language/Cultural Origin: **Old English**
Inherent Meaning: **From the Hill Near the Well**
Spiritual Connotation: **Preserved**
Scripture: **Isaiah 42:6** NASB
I am the LORD, I have called you in righteousness, I will also hold you by the hand and watch over you.

WELLINGTON, Wellingtun
Language/Cultural Origin: **Old English**
Inherent Meaning: **Prosperous**
Spiritual Connotation: **Conquering Spirit**
Scripture: **Acts 2:25** NKJV
I foresaw the LORD always before my face, for He is at my right hand, that I may not be shaken.

WENDELL, Wendal, Wendall, Wendel
Language/Cultural Origin: **Old German**
Inherent Meaning: **Wanderer**
Spiritual Connotation: **Messenger of Truth**
Scripture: **1 Corinthians 2:9** NRSV
No eye has seen, nor ear heard, nor the human heart conceived, what God has prepared for those who love him.

WENDY, Wenda, Wendee, Wendey, Wendi, Wendie (see also Wanda)
Language/Cultural Origin: **Welsh**
Inherent Meaning: **Wanderer**
Spiritual Connotation: **Redeemed**
Scripture: **Ephesians 2:13** NCV
But now in Christ Jesus, you who were far away from God are brought near through the blood of Christ's death.

WERNER (see also Warner)
Language/Cultural Origin: **Old German**
Inherent Meaning: **Protector**
Spiritual Connotation: **Peaceful**
Scripture: **John 14:27** NRSV
Peace I leave with you; my peace I give to you. Do not let your hearts be troubled, and do not let them be afraid.

WESLEY, Wes, Weslee, Westlee, Westley
Language/Cultural Origin: **English**
Inherent Meaning: **From the Western Meadow**
Spiritual Connotation: **Steadfast**
Scripture: **Proverbs 3:23** RSV
Then you will walk on your way securely and your foot will not stumble.

WHEATLEY, Wheatleigh
Language/Cultural Origin: **English**
Inherent Meaning: **From the Wheat Field**
Spiritual Connotation: **Witness**
Scripture: **John 4:35** NLT
Look around you! Vast fields are ripening all around us and are ready now for the harvest.

WHITLEY, Whitlee, Whitleigh
Language/Cultural Origin: **English**
Inherent Meaning: **From the White Field**
Spiritual Connotation: **Joyful**
Scripture: **Psalm 96:12** NASB
Let the field exult, and all that is in it. Then all the trees of the forest will sing for joy.

WHITNEY, Whitnee, Whitnée, Whitneigh, Whitnie, Whittany, Whittney, Witney, Wittney
Language/Cultural Origin: **Old English**
Inherent Meaning: **From the White Island**
Spiritual Connotation: **Protected**
Scripture: **Psalm 91:11** NKJV
For He shall give His angels charge over you, To keep you in all your ways.

WILBUR, Wilber
Language/Cultural Origin: **Old German**
Inherent Meaning: **Resolute**
Spiritual Connotation: **Obedient**
Scripture: **James 1:25** NRSV
But those who look into the perfect law, the law of liberty, and persevere . . . they will be blessed in their doing.

WILDER, Willder
Language/Cultural Origin: **Old English**
Inherent Meaning: **From the Wilderness**
Spiritual Connotation: **Sower**
Scripture: **Isaiah 40:3** NRSV
In the wilderness prepare the way of the LORD, make straight in the desert a highway for our God.

WILHELM, Willhelm
Language/Cultural Origin: **Old German**
Inherent Meaning: **Determined Guardian**
Spiritual Connotation: **Wise**
Scripture: **Proverbs 2:11** NASB
Discretion will guard you, understanding will watch over you.

WILLARD, Wilard
Language/Cultural Origin: **Old English**
Inherent Meaning: **Resolute and Brave**
Spiritual Connotation: **Champion**
Scripture: **Romans 8:28** KJV
And we know that all things work together for good to them that love God, to them who are the called according to his purpose.

WILLIAM, Bill, Billy, Wil, Wiley, Will, Willey, Willie, Willy, Wilson
Language/Cultural Origin: **Old German**
Inherent Meaning: **Resolute Protector**
Spiritual Connotation: **Noble Spirit**
Scripture: **Deuteronomy 5:33** NKJV
You shall walk in all the ways which the LORD your God has commanded you . . . that you may prolong your days in the land which you shall possess.

WILLIS, Willus
Language/Cultural Origin: **English**
Inherent Meaning: **Son of the Guardian**
Spiritual Connotation: **Cautious**
Scripture: **Psalm 141:3** RSV
Set a guard over my mouth, O LORD, keep watch over the door of my lips!

WILLOW, Wilow
Language/Cultural Origin: **English**
Inherent Meaning: **Willow Tree**
Spiritual Connotation: **Great Hope**
Scripture: **Ezekiel 17:5** TLB
There he planted it in fertile ground beside a broad river, where it would grow as quickly as a willow tree.

WILONA, Willona
Language/Cultural Origin: **English**
Inherent Meaning: **Desired**
Spiritual Connotation: **Seeker of Truth**
Scripture: **Psalm 42:1** NCV

As a deer thirsts for streams of water, so I thirst for you, God.

WINIFRED, Winn, Winnie, Winny, Wyn, Wynnie
Language/Cultural Origin: **German**
Inherent Meaning: **Peaceful Friend**
Spiritual Connotation: **Cheerful Heart**
Scripture: **Psalm 4:7** NKJV
You have put gladness in my heart.

WINONA, Wenonah, Winonah, Wynnona, Wynona
Language/Cultural Origin: **Sioux**
Inherent Meaning: **First-Born Daughter**
Spiritual Connotation: **Peaceful**
Scripture: **Philippians 4:7** NRSV
And the peace of God, which surpasses all understanding, will guard your hearts and your minds in Christ Jesus.

WINSTON, Winsten, Wynston
Language/Cultural Origin: **Old English**
Inherent Meaning: **From the Friendly Town**
Spiritual Connotation: **Trusting**
Scripture: **Proverbs 3:5-6** NKJV
Trust in the LORD with all your heart, and lean not on your own understanding; in all your ways acknowledge Him, and He shall direct your paths.

WINTHROP, Wynthrop
Language/Cultural Origin: **Old English**
Inherent Meaning: **From the Friend's Home**
Spiritual Connotation: **Benevolent**
Scripture: **Proverbs 18:24** NASB
A man of too many friends comes to ruin, but there is a friend who sticks closer than a brother.

WOLFGANG, Wolfgong
Language/Cultural Origin: **Old German**
Inherent Meaning: **Quarrel of the Wolves**
Spiritual Connotation: **Faithful**
Scripture: **1 Timothy 6:12** NKJV
Fight the good fight of faith, lay hold on eternal life, to which you were also called.

WOODROW, Woodson, Woody
Language/Cultural Origin: **Old English**
Inherent Meaning: **From the Woods**
Spiritual Connotation: **Excellent Worth**

Scripture: **John 3:33** NKJV
He who has received His testimony has
certified that God is true.

WOODWARD, Woodard
Language/Cultural Origin: **Old English**
Inherent Meaning: **Forest Warden**
Spiritual Connotation: **Guardian**
Scripture: **Isaiah 26:3** NKJV
You will keep him in perfect peace, whose
mind is stayed on You, because he trusts
in You.

WORRELL, Worrel
Language/Cultural Origin: **Old English**
Inherent Meaning: **From the Honest Home**
Spiritual Connotation: **Faith**
Scripture: **Mark 9:23** NCV
All things are possible for the one who
believes.

WORTH, Worthington
Language/Cultural Origin: **Old English**
Inherent Meaning: **Farmstead**
Spiritual Connotation: **Steadfast**
Scripture: **Psalm 1:3** NKJV
He shall be like a tree planted by the riv-
ers of water, that brings forth its fruit in
its season.

WYATT, Wyat, Wyatte
Language/Cultural Origin: **Old French**
Inherent Meaning: **Little Warrior**
Spiritual Connotation: **Immoveable**
Scripture: **2 Timothy 4:7** NKJV
I have fought the good fight, I have
finished the race, I have kept the faith.

WYMAN, Wymon
Language/Cultural Origin: **Old English**
Inherent Meaning: **Warrior**
Spiritual Connotation: **Determined**
Scripture: **1 Corinthians 9:26** TLB
So I run straight to the goal with purpose
in every step. I fight to win.

WYNN, Wyn, Wynette, Wynne
Language/Cultural Origin: **Welsh**
Inherent Meaning: **Fair**
Spiritual Connotation: **Righteous**
Scripture: **Proverbs 4:18** RSV
But the path of the righteous is like the
light of dawn, which shines brighter and
brighter until full day.

WYNONNA, see Winona

X

XANDRA, Xandraea, Xandraya, Xandrea, Xandria, Xandriana (see also Sandra, Zandra)
Language/Cultural Origin: **English**
Inherent Meaning: **Defender**
Spiritual Connotation: **Protector**
Scripture: **Isaiah 19:20** NRSV
He will send them a savior, and will defend and deliver them.

XANTHE, Xantha, Xanthia, Zantha, Zanthe, Zanthia
Language/Cultural Origin: **Greek**
Inherent Meaning: **Blond**
Spiritual Connotation: **Lovely**
Scripture: **Song of Songs 1:15** NKJV
Behold, you are fair, my love! Behold, you are fair!

XAVIER, Xaven, Xavian, Xavion, Xavon, Zavier, Zavon
Language/Cultural Origin: **Arabic**
Inherent Meaning: **Bright**
Spiritual Connotation: **Wise**
Scripture: **Proverbs 2:10-11** NKJV
When wisdom enters your heart, and knowledge is pleasant to your soul, discretion will preserve you; understanding will keep you.

XENIA, Xena (see also Zena, Zina)
Language/Cultural Origin: **Greek**
Inherent Meaning: **Hospitable**
Spiritual Connotation: **Blessed**
Scripture: **1 Peter 4:9** NLT
Cheerfully share your home with those who need a meal or a place to stay.

XERXES, Xerxus
Language/Cultural Origin: **Persian**
Inherent Meaning: **Ruler**
Spiritual Connotation: **Benevolent**
Scripture: **2 Peter 1:7** NCV
To your service for God, add kindness for your brothers and sisters in Christ; and to this kindness, add love.

XIMINES, Ximenes
Language/Cultural Origin: **Spanish**
Inherent Meaning: **God Heard**
Spiritual Connotation: **Vindicated**
Scripture: **Psalm 66:19** NKJV
But certainly God has heard me; He has attended to the voice of my prayer.

XUAN, Xuann
Language/Cultural Origin: **Vietnamese**
Inherent Meaning: **Spring**
Spiritual Connotation: **Refreshed**
Scripture: **Isaiah 58:11** NCV
The LORD will always lead you. . . . You will be like a garden that has much water, like a spring that never runs dry.

XUXA, Xúxa
Language/Cultural Origin: **Brazilian**
Inherent Meaning: **Lily**
Spiritual Connotation: **Beautiful**
Scripture: **Song of Songs 2:2** NIV
Like a lily among thorns is my darling among the maidens.

XYLIA, Xyleah, Xyliana, Xylina
Language/Cultural Origin: **Greek**
Inherent Meaning: **Wood**
Spiritual Connotation: **One of Integrity**
Scripture: **Proverbs 26:20** TLB
Fire goes out for lack of fuel, and tensions disappear when gossip stops.

XYLON, Xylen
Language/Cultural Origin: **Greek**
Inherent Meaning: **From the Forest**
Spiritual Connotation: **Joyful**
Scripture: **Psalm 96:12** NCV
Let the fields and everything in them rejoice. Then all the trees of the forest will sing for joy.

Y

YADIN, Yadeen, Yadín
Language/Cultural Origin: **Hebrew**
Inherent Meaning: **God Will Judge**
Spiritual Connotation: **Righteous**
Scripture: **Psalm 98:9** NCV
Let them sing before the LORD, because he is coming to judge the world. He will judge the world fairly; he will judge the peoples with fairness.

YAEL, Yaella, Yaelle (see also Jael)
Language/Cultural Origin: **Hebrew**
Inherent Meaning: **Strength of God**
Spiritual Connotation: **Arm of God**
Scripture: **Psalm 68:28** NRSV
Summon your might, O God; show your strength, O God, as you have done for us before.

YAGO, see Iago

YALE, Yail, Yayle
Language/Cultural Origin: **Old English**
Inherent Meaning: **From the Hill**
Spiritual Connotation: **Prosperous**
Scripture: **Psalm 72:3** NIV
The mountains will bring prosperity to the people, the hills the fruit of righteousness.

YAMILA, see Jamila

YAMINAH, Yamina
Language/Cultural Origin: **Middle Eastern**
Inherent Meaning: **Proper**
Spiritual Connotation: **Respectful**
Scripture: **1 Timothy 5:2** NLT
Treat the older women as you would your mother, and treat the younger women with all purity as your own sisters.

YANA, Yanah, Yanna, Yannah,
Yannam, Yannica, Yannick, Yannika (see also Jana)
Language/Cultural Origin: **Polish**
Inherent Meaning: **Gift of God**
Spiritual Connotation: **Purchased**
Scripture: **Romans 6:23** NKJV
For the wages of sin is death, but the gift of God is eternal life in Christ Jesus our Lord.

YARDAN, Yarden
Language/Cultural Origin: **Middle Eastern**
Inherent Meaning: **King**
Spiritual Connotation: **Victorious**
Scripture: **2 Chronicles 20:15** NKJV
Do not be afraid nor dismayed because of this great multitude, for the battle is not yours, but God's.

YARINA, Yariana, Yarianna, Yaryna
Language/Cultural Origin: **Russian**
Inherent Meaning: **Peace**
Spiritual Connotation: **Secure**
Scripture: **Philippians 4:7** NRSV
And the peace of God, which surpasses all understanding, will guard your hearts and your minds in Christ Jesus.

YARON, Yairon, Yaróne (see also Jaron)
Language/Cultural Origin: **Hebrew**
Inherent Meaning: **He Will Sing; He Will Cry Out**
Spiritual Connotation: **High Praise**
Scripture: **Romans 15:9** TLB
I will praise you among the Gentiles and sing to your name.

YASMINE, Yasmen, Yasmon,

Yazmen, Yazmin, Yazmine (see also Jasmine)
Language/Cultural Origin: **Persian**
Inherent Meaning: **Jasmine Flower**
Spiritual Connotation: **Blossom**
Scripture: **Isaiah 35:2** TLB
Yes, there will be an abundance of flowers and singing and joy!

YEIRA, Yeirah
Language/Cultural Origin: **Hebrew**
Inherent Meaning: **Light**
Spiritual Connotation: **Witness**
Scripture: **Matthew 5:14** KJV
Ye are the light of the world. A city that is set on an hill cannot be hid.

YELINA, Yelana, Yelanna (see also Jelena)
Language/Cultural Origin: **Russian**
Inherent Meaning: **Shining**
Spiritual Connotation: **Glory of God**
Scripture: **Exodus 34:30** NASB
So when Aaron and all the sons of Israel saw Moses, behold, the skin of his face shone, and they were afraid to come near him.

YEMENA, Yemina
Language/Cultural Origin: **Hebrew**
Inherent Meaning: **Capable**
Spiritual Connotation: **Exalted**
Scripture: **Proverbs 22:29** NKJV
Do you see a man who excels in his work? He will stand before kings; he will not stand before unknown men.

YERIEL, Yeriell, Yerielle (see also Jeriel)
Language/Cultural Origin: **Hebrew**
Inherent Meaning: **Taught by God**
Spiritual Connotation: **Wise**
Scripture: **John 7:16** NCV
The things I teach are not my own, but they come from him who sent me.

YOHANN, see Johann

YOHANNA, see Johanna

YOKO, Yoki
Language/Cultural Origin: **Japanese**
Inherent Meaning: **Good Girl**

Spiritual Connotation: **Justified**
Scripture: **Romans 3:10** NKJV
There is none righteous, no, not one.

YOLANDA, Yalonda, Yolana, Yolanna, Yolonda, Yulonda
Language/Cultural Origin: **Greek**
Inherent Meaning: **Violet Flower**
Spiritual Connotation: **Sign of Life**
Scripture: **Psalm 36:9** NKJV
For with You is the fountain of life; in Your light we see light.

YONINA, Yonita
Language/Cultural Origin: **Hebrew**
Inherent Meaning: **Dove**
Spiritual Connotation: **Graceful**
Scripture: **Song of Songs 4:1** NRSV
How beautiful you are, my love, how very beautiful! Your eyes are doves behind your veil.

YORDANA, Jordana, Jordanna, Yordanna
Language/Cultural Origin: **Hebrew**
Inherent Meaning: **Descender**
Spiritual Connotation: **Praise**
Scripture: **Psalm 25:1** NKJV
To You, O LORD, I lift up my soul.

YORI, Yoriko
Language/Cultural Origin: **Japanese**
Inherent Meaning: **Trustworthy**
Spiritual Connotation: **Honest**
Scripture: **Psalm 25:21** NLT
May integrity and honesty protect me, for I put my hope in you.

YORIANNA, see Jorianna

YORK, Yorick, Yorke, Yorrick
Language/Cultural Origin: **Celtic**
Inherent Meaning: **From the Yew-Tree Estate**
Spiritual Connotation: **Vigilant**
Scripture: **Proverbs 3:23** NKJV
Then you will walk safely in your way, and your foot will not stumble.

YOSHI, Yóshi, Yoshie
Language/Cultural Origin: **Japanese**
Inherent Meaning: **Respectful**
Spiritual Connotation: **Obedient**

Scripture: **Ephesians 6:5** NCV
Slaves, obey your masters here on earth
with fear and respect and from a sincere
heart, just as you obey Christ.

YUKI, Yukie

Language/Cultural Origin: **Japanese**
Inherent Meaning: **Snow**
Spiritual Connotation: **Cleansed**
Scripture: **Isaiah 1:18** NKJV
Though your sins are like scarlet, they
shall be as white as snow.

YUL, Yule, Yuul

Language/Cultural Origin: **Mongolian**
Inherent Meaning: **Beyond the Horizon**
Spiritual Connotation: **Worshiper**
Scripture: **Psalm 113:3** NASB
From the rising of the sun to its setting
the name of the LORD is to be praised.

YUMA, Yumia

Language/Cultural Origin: **Native American**
Inherent Meaning: **Son of the Chief**
Spiritual Connotation: **Beloved**
Scripture: **Proverbs 17:6** NRSV
Grandchildren are the crown of the aged,
and the glory of children is their parents.

YURI, Juri, Jurii, Jurri, Yurii, Yurri, Yury (see also Uri)

Language/Cultural Origin: **Russian**
Inherent Meaning: **Farmer**

Spiritual Connotation: **Gifted**
Scripture: **Isaiah 28:26** NLT
The farmer knows just what to do, for
God has given him understanding.

YURIKO, Yuríko

Language/Cultural Origin: **Japanese**
Inherent Meaning: **Lily Child**
Spiritual Connotation: **Blessed**
Scripture: **Hosea 14:5** TLB
She will blossom as the lily and root
deeply in the soil.

YVANNA, see Ivana

YVES, Ives

Language/Cultural Origin: **French**
Inherent Meaning: **Little Archer**
Spiritual Connotation: **Trusting Spirit**
Scripture: **Psalm 37:5** RSV
Commit your way to the LORD; trust in
him, and he will act.

YVONNE, Ivette, Ivonne, Yavonne, Yevette, Yvette

Language/Cultural Origin: **French**
Inherent Meaning: **Young Archer**
Spiritual Connotation: **Shielded**
Scripture: **Leviticus 25:18** NRSV
You shall observe my statutes and faith-
fully keep my ordinances, so that you
may live on the land securely.

Z

ZABRINA, see Sabrina

ZACHARIAH, Zac, Zacariah,
Zacarias, Zacary, Zacc, Zaccari,
Zaccary, Zach, Zacharee,
Zacharey, Zacharia, Zacharias,
Zacharie, Zachary, Zacherey,
Zacherie, Zachery, Zachrey,
Zachry, Zack, Zackari, Zackarie,
Zackary, Zackery, Zackory,
Zacory, Zak, Zakarey, Zakari,
Zakarie, Zakary, Zakery, Zakree,
Zakry, Zaqary
Language/Cultural Origin: **Hebrew**
Inherent Meaning: **God Has Remembered**
Spiritual Connotation: **Humble Before God**
Scripture: **Psalm 25:14** RSV
*The friendship of the LORD is for those
who fear him, and he makes known to
them his covenant.*

ZADA, Zaida, Zayda
Language/Cultural Origin: **Middle Eastern**
Inherent Meaning: **Fortunate**
Spiritual Connotation: **Faithful**
Scripture: **Matthew 10:22** TLB
*Everyone shall hate you because you
belong to me. But all of you who endure
to the end shall be saved.*

ZADOK, Zaydok
Language/Cultural Origin: **Hebrew**
Inherent Meaning: **Righteous**
Spiritual Connotation: **Rewarded**
Scripture: **Matthew 25:34** NKJV
*Come, you blessed of My Father, inherit
the kingdom prepared for you from the
foundation of the world.*

ZAFINA, Zafeena
Language/Cultural Origin: **Middle Eastern**

Inherent Meaning: **Victorious**
Spiritual Connotation: **Strength of God**
Scripture: **1 Corinthians 15:57** NKJV
*But thanks be to God, who gives us the
victory through our Lord Jesus Christ.*

ZAIM, Zaime, Zaimee, Zayme,
Zaymee
Language/Cultural Origin: **Middle Eastern**
Inherent Meaning: **Brigadier General**
Spiritual Connotation: **Leader**
Scripture: **Psalm 127:4** NKJV
*Like arrows in the hand of a warrior, so
are the children of one's youth.*

ZAMIR, Zameer, Zameir
Language/Cultural Origin: **Hebrew**
Inherent Meaning: **Song**
Spiritual Connotation: **Joyful**
Scripture: **Psalm 40:3** RSV
*He put a new song in my mouth, a song
of praise to our God.*

ZANDRA, Zahndra, Zandraea,
Zandrea, Zandria, Zanndra,
Zondra (see also Sandra, Xandra)
Language/Cultural Origin: **English**
Inherent Meaning: **Defender**
Spiritual Connotation: **Protector**
Scripture: **Jeremiah 51:36** NASB
*Behold, I am going to plead your case
and exact full vengeance for you.*

ZANE, Zain, Zayne
Language/Cultural Origin: **English**
Inherent Meaning: **God Is Gracious**
Spiritual Connotation: **Blessed**
Scripture: **Numbers 6:25** NASB
*The LORD make His face shine on you,
and be gracious to you.*

ZANNA, Zana (see also Zaynah)
Language/Cultural Origin: **English**
Inherent Meaning: **Lily**
Spiritual Connotation: **Beautiful**
Scripture: **Song of Songs 2:2** NKJV
Like a lily among thorns, so is my love among the daughters.

ZANTHA, see Xanthe

ZARA, Zaira, Zarah, Zaria, Zariana, Zarya
Language/Cultural Origin: **Middle Eastern**
Inherent Meaning: **Princess**
Spiritual Connotation: **Beloved**
Scripture: **Psalm 45:13** NIV
All glorious is the princess within her chamber; her gown is interwoven with gold.

ZAVIER, see Xavier

ZAYNAH, Zayna (see also Zanna)
Language/Cultural Origin: **Middle Eastern**
Inherent Meaning: **Lovely**
Spiritual Connotation: **Beautiful**
Scripture: **Song of Songs 2:14** NKJV
Let me see your face, let me hear your voice; for your voice is sweet, and your face is lovely.

ZEBEDIAH, Zebedee
Language/Cultural Origin: **Hebrew**
Inherent Meaning: **God's Gift**
Spiritual Connotation: **Redeemed**
Scripture: **Romans 1:16** NIV
I am not ashamed of the gospel, because it is the power of God for the salvation of everyone who believes: first for the Jew, then for the Gentile.

ZEBULON, Zebulun
Language/Cultural Origin: **Hebrew**
Inherent Meaning: **Exalted**
Spiritual Connotation: **Wise**
Scripture: **James 4:10** NKJV
Humble yourselves in the sight of the Lord, and He will lift you up.

ZEDEKIAH, Zedekias
Language/Cultural Origin: **Hebrew**
Inherent Meaning: **God Is Mighty and Just**
Spiritual Connotation: **Glory to God**

Scripture: **Proverbs 3:6** NKJV
In all your ways acknowledge Him, and He shall direct your paths.

ZEKE, see Ezekiel

ZELDA, Zellda
Language/Cultural Origin: **German**
Inherent Meaning: **Warrior**
Spiritual Connotation: **Gifted**
Scripture: **Ecclesiastes 2:26** NRSV
For to the one who pleases him God gives wisdom and knowledge and joy.

ZELENKA, Zelenkia
Language/Cultural Origin: **Czech**
Inherent Meaning: **Budding Blossom**
Spiritual Connotation: **Nurtured**
Scripture: **Isaiah 35:2** NKJV
It shall blossom abundantly and rejoice, even with joy and singing.

ZENA, Zeena, Zeenia, Zeenya, Zeina, Zenah, Zenia (see also Xenia, Zina)
Language/Cultural Origin: **Persian**
Inherent Meaning: **Woman**
Spiritual Connotation: **Cherished**
Scripture: **Genesis 2:22** NKJV
Then the rib which the LORD God had taken from man He made into a woman, and He brought her to the man.

ZEPHANIAH, Zephan, Zephania
Language/Cultural Origin: **Hebrew**
Inherent Meaning: **Protected by God**
Spiritual Connotation: **Precious**
Scripture: **Proverbs 4:6** NLT
Don't turn your back on wisdom, for she will protect you. Love her, and she will guard you.

ZEPHYR, Zephria, Zephriana
Language/Cultural Origin: **Greek**
Inherent Meaning: **West Wind**
Spiritual Connotation: **Reborn**
Scripture: **John 3:8** NRSV
The wind blows where it chooses, and you hear the sound of it, but you do not know where it comes from or where it goes.

ZERLINA, Zerleyna
Language/Cultural Origin: **Spanish**

Inherent Meaning: **Dawn**
Spiritual Connotation: **Blessed**
Scripture: **Psalms 139:9-10** NASB
*If I take the wings of the dawn, if I dwell
in the remotest part of the sea, even there
Thy hand will lead me, and Thy right
hand will lay hold of me.*

ZIA, Zea, Zeah, Zeya

Language/Cultural Origin: **Middle Eastern**
Inherent Meaning: **Light**
Spiritual Connotation: **Fearless**
Scripture: **Psalm 27:1** NKJV
*The LORD is my light and my salvation;
whom shall I fear?*

ZIGFRID, Ziggy (see also Siegfried)

Language/Cultural Origin: **Latvian**
Inherent Meaning: **Victorious Peace**
Spiritual Connotation: **Secure in Christ**
Scripture: **Philippians 4:7** NRSV
*And the peace of God, which surpasses
all understanding, will guard your hearts
and your minds in Christ Jesus.*

ZIMRA, Zamora, Zemora

Language/Cultural Origin: **Hebrew**
Inherent Meaning: **Song of Praise**
Spiritual Connotation: **Thankful**
Scripture: **Psalm 147:1** NRSV
*Praise the LORD! How good it is to sing
praises to our God; for he is gracious,
and a song of praise is fitting.*

ZIMRAAN, Zimran

Language/Cultural Origin: **Middle Eastern**
Inherent Meaning: **Praise**
Spiritual Connotation: **Reverent**
Scripture: **Psalm 145:21** NIV
*My mouth will speak in praise of the
LORD. Let every creature praise his holy
name for ever and ever.*

ZINA, Zinah (see also Xenia, Zena)

Language/Cultural Origin: **English**
Inherent Meaning: **Hospitable**
Spiritual Connotation: **Radiant Love**
Scripture: **1 Peter 4:9** NLT
*Cheerfully share your home with those
who need a meal or a place to stay.*

ZOE, Zoa, Zöe, Zoé, Zoë, Zoee, Zoey, Zoia, Zoie, Zoya

Language/Cultural Origin: **Greek**
Inherent Meaning: **Life**
Spiritual Connotation: **Delivered**
Scripture: **Psalm 91:14** NRSV
*Those who love me, I will deliver; I will
protect those who know my name.*

ZORA, Zorah, Zorana, Zoranna, Zoriana, Zorianna, Zorya

Language/Cultural Origin: **Slavic**
Inherent Meaning: **Dawn**
Spiritual Connotation: **Bringer of Light**
Scripture: **Isaiah 60:1** RSV
*Arise, shine; for your light has come, and
the glory of the LORD has risen upon you.*

ZORINA, Zori, Zoriana, Zorianna, Zorie, Zory (see also Czarina)

Language/Cultural Origin: **Slavic**
Inherent Meaning: **Golden**
Spiritual Connotation: **Attractive**
Scripture: **Song of Songs 6:10** NKJV
*Who is she who looks forth as the morn-
ing, fair as the moon, clear as the sun.*

ZSA ZSA, Zha Zha

Language/Cultural Origin: **Hungarian**
Inherent Meaning: **Lily**
Spiritual Connotation: **Lovely**
Scripture: **Song of Songs 2:2** NASB
*Like a lily among the thorns, so is my
darling among the maidens.*

ZULEMA, Zulima

Language/Cultural Origin: **Middle Eastern**
Inherent Meaning: **Peace**
Spiritual Con notation: **Secure**
Scripture: **Philippians 4:7** NASB
*And the peace of God, which surpasses
all comprehension, will guard your hearts
and your minds in Christ Jesus.*

ZURI, Zuria, Zuriya

Language/Cultural Origin: **Swahili**
Inherent Meaning: **Beautiful**
Spiritual Connotation: **Messanger**
Scripture: **Romans 10:15** NRSV
*How beautiful are the feet of those who
bring good news!*

LIST OF
BIBLE NAMES

WOMEN'S NAMES

Abi
Abia
Abiah
Abigail
Abihail
Abijah
Abishag
Achsa
Achsah
Agar
Ahinoam
Ahlai
Aholibamah
Anah
Anna
Apphia
Asenath
Atarah
Athaliah
Azubah

Baara
Bashemath
Basmath
Bathsheba
Bernice
Bilhah
Bithiah

Candace
Chloe
Claudia
Cozbi

Damaris
Deborah
Delilah
Dinah
Dorcas

Drusilla

Eglah
Elisabeth
Elisheba
Elizabeth
Ephah
Ephrath
Esther
Eunice
Euodias
Eve

Gomer

Hadassah
Hagar
Haggith
Hammoleketh
Hamutal
Hannah
Hazelelponi
Helah
Hephzibah
Herodias
Hodesh
Hodiah
Hoglah
Huldah
Hushim

Iscah

Jael
Jecholiah
Jecoliah
Jedidah
Jehoaddan
Jehoshabeath
Jehosheba

Jehudijah
Jemima
Jerioth
Jerusha
Jerushah
Jezebel
Joanna
Jochebed
Judith
Julia

Keren-Happuch
Keturah
Kezia

Leah
Lois
Lo-Ruhamah
Lydia

Maachah
Mahalah
Mahlah
Mara
Martha
Mary
Mary Magdalene
Matred
Mehetabel
Merab
Meshullemeth
Michaiah
Michal
Milcah
Miriam
Naamah
Naomi
Narah
Nehushta

Noadiah
Noah

Orpah

Peninnah
Persis
Phanuel
Phebe
Prisca
Priscilla
Puah

Rachel
Rahab
Rebecca
Rebekah
Reumah
Rhoda
Rizpah
Ruth

Salome
Sapphira
Sara
Sarah
Sarai
Serah
Shelomith
Sherah
Shimeath
Shimrith
Shiphrah
Shomer
Shua
Susanna
Syntyche

Tabitha
Tahpenes

Tamar
Taphath
Thamar
Timma

Tirzah
Tryphena
Tryphosa
Vashti

Zebudah
Zeresh
Zeruah
Zeruiah

Zibiah
Zillah
Zilpah
Zipporah

MEN'S NAMES

Aaron
Abagtha
Abda
Abdeel
Abdi
Abdiel
Abdon
Abednego
Abel
Abia
Abiah
Abialbon
Abiasaph
Abiathar
Abida
Abidah
Abidan
Abiel
Abiezer
Abihail
Abihu
Abihud
Abijah
Abijam
Abimael
Abimelech
Abinadab
Abinoam
Abiram
Abishai
Abishalom
Abishua
Abishur
Abitub
Abiud
Abner
Abraham
Abram
Absalom
Achaicus
Achan
Achar

Achaz
Achbor
Achim
Achish
Adaiah
Adalia
Adam
Adar
Adbeel
Addar
Addi
Ader
Adiel
Adin
Adina
Adino
Adlai
Admatha
Adna
Adnah
Adoni-Bezek
Adonijah
Adonikam
Adoniram
Adonizedek
Adoram
Adrammelech
Adriel
Aeneas
Agabus
Agag
Agee
Agrippa
Agur
Ahab
Aharah
Aharhel
Ahasai
Ahasbai
Ahasuerus
Ahaz
Ahaziah

Ahban
Aher
Ahi
Ahiah
Ahiam
Ahian
Ahiezer
Ahihud
Ahijah
Ahikam
Ahilud
Ahimaaz
Ahiman
Ahimelech
Ahimoth
Ahinadab
Ahio
Ahira
Ahiram
Ahisamach
Ahishahar
Ahishar
Ahithophel
Ahitub
Ahlai
Ahoah
Aholah
Aholiab
Aholibah
Aholibamah
Ahumai
Ahuzam
Ahuzzath
Aiah
Ajah
Akan
Akkub
Alameth
Alemeth
Alexander
Aliah
Alian

Allon
Almodad
Alphaeus
Alvah
Alvan
Amal
Amalek
Amariah
Amasa
Amasai
Amashai
Amasiah
Amaziah
Ami
Aminadab
Amittai
Ammiel
Ammihud
Amminadab
Amminadib
Ammishaddai
Ammizabad
Ammon
Amnon
Amok
Amon
Amos
Amoz
Amplias
Amram
Amraphel
Amzi
Anah
Anaiah
Anak
Anan
Anani
Ananiah
Ananias
Anath
Anathoth
Andrew

Andronicus
Aner
Aniam
Annas
Antipas
Antothijah
Anub
Apelles
Aphiah
Aphses
Apollos
Appaim
Aquila
Ara
Arad
Arah
Aram
Aran
Araunah
Arba
Archelaus
Archippus
Ard
Ardon
Areli
Aretas
Argob
Aridai
Aridatha
Arieh
Ariel
Arioch
Arisai
Aristarchus
Aristobulus
Armoni
Arnan
Arod
Arphaxad
Artaxerxes
Artemas
Arza
Asa
Asahel
Asahiah
Asaiah
Asaph
Asareel
Asarelah
Ashbea

Ashbel
Ashchenaz
Asher
Ashkenaz
Ashpenaz
Ashriel
Ashur
Ashvath
Asiel
Asnah
Asnapper
Aspatha
Asriel
Asshur
Asshurim
Assir
Assur
Asyncritus
Ater
Athaiah
Athaliah
Athlai
Attai
Augustus
Azaliah
Azaniah
Azarael
Azareel
Azariah
Azaz
Azaziah
Azbuk
Azel
Azgad
Aziel
Aziza
Azmaveth
Azor
Azriel
Azrikam
Azur
Azzan
Azzur

Baal
Baal-Hanan
Baalis
Baana
Baanah
Baaseiah

Baasha
Bakbakkar
Bakbuk
Bakbukiah
Balaam
Balac
Baladan
Balak
Bani
Barabbas
Barachel
Barak
Bariah
Bar-Jesus
Barkos
Barnabas
Barsabas
Barsabbas
Bartholomew
Bartimaeus
Baruch
Barzillai
Bavai
Bazlith
Bazluth
Bealiah
Bebai
Becher
Bechorath
Bedad
Bedan
Bedeiah
Beeliada
Beera
Beerah
Beeri
Bela
Belah
Belshazzar
Belteshazzar
Benaiah
Ben-Ammi
Ben-Hadad
Ben-Hail
Ben-Hanan
Beninu
Benjamin
Beno
Benoni
Ben-Zoheth

Beor
Bera
Berachah
Berachiah
Beraiah
Berechiah
Bered
Beri
Beriah
Berodach-Baladan
Besai
Besodeiah
Beth-Gader
Bethlehem
Beth-Rapha
Bethuel
Beth-Zur
Bezai
Bezaleel
Bezer
Bichri
Bidkar
Bigtha
Bigthan
Bigthana
Bigvai
Bildad
Bilgah
Bilgai
Bilhan
Bilshan
Bimhal
Binea
Binnui
Birsha
Birzavith
Bishlam
Biztha
Blastus
Boaz
Bocheru
Booz
Bukki
Bukkiah
Bunah
Bunni
Buz
Buzi

Caesar

Caiaphas
Cain
Cainan
Calcol
Caleb
Canaan
Carcas
Careah
Carmi
Carpus
Carshena
Cephas
Chalcol
Chedorlaomer
Chelluh
Chelub
Chelubai
Chenaanah
Chenani
Chenaniah
Cheran
Chesed
Chileab
Chilion
Chimham
Chislon
Chushan-
  Rishathaim
Chuza
Cis
Claudius
Clement
Cleopas
Cleophas
Colhozeh
Conaniah
Coniah
Cononiah
Core
Cornelius
Cosam
Coz
Crescens
Crispus
Cush
Cushi
Cyrenius
Cyrus

Dalaiah

Dalphon
Dan
Daniel
Dara
Darda
Darius
Darkon
Dathan
David
Debir
Dedan
Dekar
Delaiah
Demas
Demetrius
Deuel
Diblaim
Dibri
Didymus
Diklah
Dionysius
Diothephes
Dishan
Dishon
Dodai
Dodanim
Dodavah
Dodo
Doeg
Dumah

Ebal
Ebed
Ebed-Melech
Eber
Ebiasaph
Eden
Eder
Edom
Eglon
Ehi
Ehud
Eker
Eladah
Elah
Elam
Elasah
Eldaah
Eldad
Elead

Eleasah
Eleazar
Elhanan
Eli
Eliab
Eliada
Eliadah
Eliah
Eliahba
Eliakim
Eliam
Elias
Eliasaph
Eliashib
Eliathah
Elidad
Eliel
Elienai
Eliezer
Elihoenai
Elihoreph
Elihu
Elijah
Elika
Elimelech
Elioenai
Eliphal
Eliphalet
Eliphaz
Elipheleh
Eliphelet
Eliseus
Elisha
Elishah
Elishama
Elishaphat
Elishua
Eliud
Elizaphan
Elizur
Elkanah
Elmodam
Elnaam
Elnathan
Elon
Elpaal
Elpalet
Eluzai
Elymas
Elzabad

Elzaphan
Emmor
Enan
Enoch
Enos
Enosh
Epaenetus
Epaphras
Epaphroditus
Ephah
Ephai
Epher
Ephlal
Ephod
Ephraim
Ephron
Er
Eran
Erastus
Eri
Esaias
Esar-Haddon
Esau
Eshbaal
Eshban
Eshcol
Eshek
Eshtemoa
Eshtemoh
Eshton
Esli
Esrom
Etam
Ethan
Ethbaal
Ethnan
Ethni
Eubulus
Eutychus
Evi
Evil-Merodach
Ezar
Ezbai
Ezbon
Ezekias
Ezekiel
Ezer
Ezra
Ezri

Felix
Festus
Fortunatus

Gaal
Gabbai
Gad
Gaddi
Gaddiel
Gadi
Gaham
Gahar
Gaius
Galal
Gallio
Gamaliel
Gamul
Gareb
Gashmu
Gatam
Gazez
Gazzam
Geber
Gedaliah
Gedeon
Gedor
Gehazi
Gemalli
Gemariah
Genubath
Gera
Gershom
Gershon
Gesham
Geshem
Gether
Geuel
Gibbar
Gibea
Giddalti
Giddel
Gideon
Gideoni
Gilalai
Gilead
Ginath
Ginnetho
Gennethon
Gispa
Gog

Goliath
Gomer
Guni

Haahashtari
Habaiah
Habakkuk
Habaziniah
Hachaliah
Hachmoni
Hadad
Hadadezer
Hadarezer
Hadlai
Hadoram
Hagab
Hagaba
Hagabah
Haggai
Haggeri
Haggi
Haggiah
Hakkatan
Hakkoz
Hakupha
Hallohesh
Halohesh
Ham
Haman
Hammath
Hammedatha
Hammelech
Hamor
Hammuel
Hamuel
Hamul
Hanameel
Hanamel
Hanan
Hananeel
Hanani
Hananiah
Haniel
Hanniel
Hanoch
Hanun
Haran
Harbona
Harbonah
Hareph

Harhaiah
Harhas
Harhur
Harim
Hariph
Harnepher
Haroeh
Harum
Harumaph
Haruz
Hasadiah
Hasenuah
Hashabiah
Hashabnah
Hashabniah
Hashbadana
Hashem
Hashub
Hashubah
Hashum
Hashupha
Hasrah
Hassenaah
Hasshub
Hasupha
Hatach
Hathath
Hatipha
Hatita
Hattil
Hattush
Havilah
Hazael
Hazaiah
Hazarmaveth
Haziel
Hazo
Heber
Hebron
Hegai
Hege
Heldai
Heleb
Heled
Helek
Helem
Helez
Heli
Helkai
Helon

Hemam
Heman
Hemath
Hemdan
Hen
Hendad
Henoch
Hepher
Heresh
Hermas
Hermes
Hermogenes
Herod
Herodion
Hesed
Heth
Hezeki
Hezekiah
Hezion
Hezir
Hezrai
Hezro
Hezron
Hiddai
Hiel
Hilkiah
Hille
Hinnom
Hirah
Hiram
Hizkiah
Hizkijah
Hobab
Hod
Hodaiah
Hodaviah
Hodevah
Hodiah
Hodijah
Hoham
Homam
Hophni
Horam
Hori
Hosah
Hosea
Hoshaiah
Hoshama
Hoshea
Hotham

Hothan
Hothir
Hul
Hupham
Huppah
Huppim
Hur
Hurai
Huram
Huri
Hushah
Hushai
Husham
Hushim
Huz
Hymenaeus
Ibhar
Ibneiah
Ibnijah
Ibri
Ibzan
Ichabod
Idbash
Iddo
Igal
Igdaliah
Igeal
Ikkesh
Ilai
Imla
Imlah
Imma
Immer
Imnah
Imrah
Imri
Iphedeiah
Ir
Ira
Irad
Iram
Iri
Irijah
Irnahash
Iru
Isaac
Isaachar
Isaiah
Ishbah

Ishbak
Ishbi-Benob
Ishbosheth
Ishi
Ishiah
Ishijah
Ishma
Ishmael
Ishmaiah
Ishmerai
Ishod
Ishpan
Ishuah
Ishuai
Ishui
Ismachiah
Ismaiah
Ispah
Israel
Isshiah
Isuah
Isui
Ithai
Ithamar
Ithiel
Ithmah
Ithra
Ithran
Ithream
Ittai
Izehar
Izhar
Izrahiah
Izri
Jaakan
Jaakobah
Jaala
Jaalah
Jaalam
Jaanai
Jaare-Oregim
Jaasau
Jaasiel
Jaazaniah
Jaaziah
Jaaziel
Jabal
Jabesh
Jabez

Jabin
Jachan
Jachin
Jacob
Jada
Jadau
Jaddua
Jadon
Jahath
Jahaziah
Jahaziel
Jahdai
Jahdiel
Jahdo
Jahleel
Jahmai
Jahzeel
Jahzerah
Jahziel
Jair
Jairus
Jakan
Jakeh
Jakim
Jalon
Jambres
James
Jamin
Jamlech
Janna
Jannes
Japheth
Japhia
Japhlet
Jarah
Jareb
Jared
Jaresiah
Jarha
Jarib
Jaroah
Jashen
Jashobeam
Jashub
Jashubi-Lehem
Jason
Jathniel
Javan
Jaziz
Jeaterai

Jeberechiah
Jecamiah
Jechonias
Jeconiah
Jedaiah
Jediael
Jedidiah
Jeduthun
Jeezer
Jehaleleel
Jehalelel
Jehdeiah
Jehezekel
Jehiah
Jehiel
Jehieli
Jehizkiah
Jehoadah
Jehoahaz
Jehoash
Jehohanan
Jehoiachin
Jehoiada
Jehoiakim
Jehoiarib
Jehonadab
Jehonathan
Jehoram
Jehoshaphat
Jehoshua
Jehoshuah
Jehozabad
Jehozadak
Jehu
Jehubbah
Jehucal
Jehudi
Jehush
Jeiel
Jekameam
Jekamiah
Jekuthiel
Jemuel
Jephthae
Jephthah
Jephunneh
Jerah
Jerahmeel
Jered
Jeremai

Jeremiah
Jeremias
Jeremoth
Jeremy
Jeriah
Jeribai
Jeriel
Jerijah
Jerimoth
Jeroboam
Jeroham
Jerubbaal
Jerubbesheth
Jesaiah
Jese
Jeshaiah
Jesharelah
Jeshebeab
Jesher
Jeshishai
Jeshohaiah
Jeshua
Jeshuah
Jesiah
Jesimiel
Jesui
Jesus
Jether
Jetheth
Jethro
Jetur
Jeuel
Jeush
Jeuz
Jezaniah
Jezer
Jeziah
Jeziel
Jezliah
Jezoar
Jezrahiah
Jezreel
Jibsam
Jidlaph
Jimna
Jimnah
Joab
Joah
Joahaz
Joash

Joatham
Job
Jobab
Joed
Joel
Joelah
Joezer
Jogli
Joha
Johanan
John
Joiada
Joiakim
Joiarib
Jokim
Jokshan
Joktan
Jona
Jonadab
Jonah
Jonan
Jonas
Jonathan
Jorah
Joram
Jorim
Jorkoam
Josabad
Josaphat
Jose
Josedech
Joseph
Joses
Joshah
Joshaphat
Joshaviah
Joshbekashah
Joshua
Josiah
Josias
Josibiah
Josiphiah
Jotham
Jozabad
Jozachar
Jozadak
Jubal
Jucal
Juda
Judah

Judas
Jude
Julius
Junia
Jushab-Hesed
Justus

Kadmiel
Kallai
Kanan
Kareah
Kedar
Kedemah
Keilah
Kelaiah
Kelita
Kemuel
Kenaz
Keros
Kirjath-Jearim
Kish
Kishi
Kittim
Kohath
Kolaiah
Korah
Kore
Koz
Kushaiah

Laadah
Laadan
Laban
Lael
Lahad
Lahmi
Laish
Lamech
Lapidoth
Lazarus
Lebana
Lebanah
Lebbaeus
Lecah
Lehabim
Lemuel
Letushim
Leummim
Levi
Libni
Likhi

Linus
Lo-Ammi
Lot
Lotan
Lucas
Lucifer
Lucius
Lud
Ludim
Luke
Lysanias
Lysias

Maacah
Maachah
Maadai
Maadiah
Maai
Maaseiah
Maasiai
Maath
Maaz
Maaziah
Machbanai
Machi
Machir
Machnadebai
Madai
Madmannah
Magbish
Magdiel
Magog
Magor-Missabib
Magpiash
Mahalah
Mahalaleel
Mahali
Maharai
Mahath
Mahazioth
Maher-Shalal-
  Hash-Baz
Mahlah
Mahli
Mahlon
Mahol
Malachi
Malcham
Malchiah
Malchiel

Malchijah
Malchiram
Malchi-Shua
Malchus
Maleleel
Mallothi
Maluch
Mamre
Manaen
Manahath
Manasseh
Manasses
Manoah
Maoch
Maon
Marcus
Mareshah
Mark
Marsena
Mash
Massa
Mathusala
Matri
Mattan
Mattaniah
Mattatha
Mattathah
Mattathias
Mattenai
Matthan
Matthat
Matthew
Matthias
Mattithiah
Mebunnai
Medad
Medan
Mehetabeel
Mehetabel
Mehida
Mehir
Mehujael
Mehuman
Mehunim
Melatiah
Melchi
Melchiah
Melchisedec
Melchishua
Melchizedek

Melea
Melech
Melicu
Melzar
Memucan
Menahem
Menan
Meonothai
Mephibosheth
Meraiah
Meraioth
Merari
Mered
Meremoth
Meres
Merib-Baal
Merodach-
   Baladan
Mesech
Mesha
Meshach
Meshech
Meshelemiah
Meshezabeel
Meshillemith
Meshillemoth
Meshobab
Meshullam
Methusael
Methuselah
Meunim
Mezahab
Miamin
Mibhar
Mibsam
Mibzar
Micah
Micaiah
Micha
Michael
Michah
Michaiah
Michri
Midian
Mijamin
Mikloth
Mikneiah
Milalai
Miniamin
Mirma

Mishael
Misham
Mishma
Mishmannah
Mispereth
Mithredath
Mizpar
Mizraim
Mizzah
Mnason
Moab
Moadiah
Molid
Mordecai
Moses
Moza
Muppim
Mushi

Naam
Naaman
Naarai
Naashon
Naasson
Nabal
Naboth
Nachon
Nachor
Nadab
Nagge
Naham
Nahamani
Naharai
Nahari
Nahash
Nahath
Nahbi
Nahor
Nahshon
Nahum
Naphish
Naphtali
Narcissus
Nathan
Nathanael
Nathan-Melech
Naum
Neariah
Nebai
Nebaioth

Nebajoth
Nebat
Nebo
Nebuchadnezzar
Nebuchadrezzar
Nebushasban
Nebuzar-Adan
Necho
Nedabiah
Nehemiah
Nehum
Nekoda
Nemuel
Nepheg
Nephish
Nephthalim
Ner
Nereus
Nergal-Sharezer
Neri
Neriah
Nethaneel
Nethaniah
Neziah
Nicanor
Nicodemus
Nicolas
Niger
Nimrod
Nimshi
Noadiah
Noah
Nobah
Nogah
Nohah
Non
Nun
Nymphas

Obadiah
Obal
Obed
Obed-Edom
Obil
Ocran
Oded
Og
Ohad
Ohel
Olympas

Omar
Omri
On
Onam
Onan
Onesimus
Onesiphorus
Ophir
Ophrah
Oreb
Oren
Ornan
Osee
Oshea
Othni
Othniel
Ozem
Ozias
Ozni

Paarai
Padon
Pagiel
Pahath-Moab
Palal
Pallu
Palti
Paltiel
Parmashta
Parmenas
Parnach
Parosh
Parshandatha
Paruah
Pasach
Paseah
Pashur
Pathrusim
Patrobas
Paul
Pedahel
Pedahzur
Pedaiah
Pekah
Pekahiah
Pelaiah
Pelaliah
Pelatiah
Peleg
Pelet

Peleth
Peniel
Penuel
Peresh
Perez
Perida
Persis
Peter
Pethahiah
Pethuel
Peulthai
Phalec
Phallu
Phalti
Phaltiel
Phanuel
Pharaoh
Pharaoh-Hophra
Pharaoh-Necho
Phares
Pharez
Pharosh
Phaseah
Phichol
Philemon
Philetus
Philip
Philologus
Phinehas
Phlegon
Phurah
Phut
Phuvah
Phygellus
Pilate
Pildash
Pileha
Piltai
Pinon
Piram
Pispah
Pithon
Pochereth
Poratha
Porcius
Potiphar
Poti-Pherah
Prochorus
Pua
Puah

Publius
Pudens
Pul
Put
Putiel

Quartus

Raamah
Raamiah
Rabmag
Rabsaris
Rabshakeh
Raddai
Ragau
Raguel
Raham
Rakem
Ram
Ramiah
Ramoth
Rapha
Raphah
Raphu
Reaia
Reaiah
Reba
Rechab
Reelaiah
Regem
Regem-Melech
Rehabiah
Rehob
Rehoboam
Rehoboth
Rehum
Rei
Rekem
Remaliah
Rephael
Rephah
Rephaiah
Resheph
Reu
Reuben
Reuel
Rezia
Rezin
Rezon
Rhesa
Ribai

Rimmon
Riphath
Roboam
Rohgah
Romamti-Ezer
Rosh
Rufus

Sabta
Sabtah
Sabtecha
Sabtechah
Sacar
Sadoc
Sala
Salah
Salathiel
Sallai
Salma
Salmon
Salu
Samgar-Nebo
Samlah
Samson
Samuel
Sanballat
Saph
Saraph
Sargon
Sarsechim
Saruch
Saul
Sceva
Seba
Secundus
Segub
Seir
Seled
Sem
Semachiah
Semei
Senaah
Sennacherib
Senuah
Seorim
Seraiah
Sered
Sergius Paulus
Serug
Seth

Sethur
Shaaph
Shaashgaz
Shabbethai
Shachia
Shadrach
Shage
Shaharaim
Shallum
Shallun
Shalmai
Shalman
Shalmaneser
Shama
Shamed
Shamer
Shamgar
Shamhuth
Shamir
Shamma
Shammah
Shammai
Shammoth
Shammua
Shammuah
Shamsherai
Shapham
Shaphan
Shaphat
Sharai
Sharar
Sharezer
Shashai
Shashak
Shaul
Shavsha
Sheal
Shealtiel
Sheariah
Shear-Jashub
Sheba
Shebaniah
Sheber
Shebna
Shebuel
Shecaniah
Shechaniah
Shechem
Shedeur
Shehariah

Shelah
Shelemiah
Sheleph
Shelesh
Shelomi
Shelomith
Shelomoth
Shelumiel
Shem
Shema
Shemaah
Shemaiah
Shemariah
Shemember
Shemer
Shemida
Shemidah
Shemiramoth
Shemuel
Shenazar
Shephatiah
Shephi
Shepho
Shephupham
Shephuphan
Sherebiah
Sheresh
Sherezer
Sheshai
Sheshan
Sheshbazzar
Shetar-Boznai
Sheth
Shethar
Sheva
Shilhi
Shillem
Shiloni
Shilshah
Shimea
Shimeah
Shimeam
Shimei
Shimeon
Shimhi
Shimi
Shimma
Shimon
Shimrath
Shimri

Shimrom
Shimron
Shimshai
Shinab
Shiphi
Shiphtan
Shisha
Shishak
Shitrai
Shiza
Shobab
Shobach
Shobai
Shobal
Shobek
Shobi
Shoham
Shomer
Shophach
Shua
Shuah
Shual
Shubael
Shuham
Shuni
Shupham
Shuppim
Shuthelah
Sia
Siaha
Sibbecai
Sibbechai
Sichem
Sidon
Sihon
Silas
Silvanus
Simeon
Simon
Simri
Sippai
Sisamai
Sisera
So
Socho
Sodi
Solomon
Sopater
Sophereth
Sosipater

Sosthenes
Sotai
Stachys
Stephanas
Stephen
Suah
Susi
Sychar
Sychem

Tabbaoth
Tabeal
Tabeel
Tabrimon
Tahan
Tahath
Tahrea
Talmai
Talmon
Tamah
Tanhumeth
Tappuah
Tarah
Tarea
Tarshish
Tartan
Tatnai
Tebah
Tebaliah
Tehinnah
Tekoa
Telah
Telem
Tema
Teman
Temani
Temeni
Terah
Teresh
Tertius
Tertullus
Thaddaeus
Thahash
Thamah
Thara
Tharshish
Theophilus
Theudas
Thomas
Tiberius

Tibni
Tidal
Tiglath-Pileser
Tikvah
Tikvath
Tilgath-Pilneser
Tilon
Timaeus
Timna
Timnah
Timon
Timotheus
Timothy
Tiras
Tirhakah
Tirhanah
Tiria
Tirshatha
Titus
Toah
Tob-Adonijah
Tobiah
Tobijah
Togarmah
Tohu
Toi
Tola
Tou
Trophimus
Tubal
Tubal-Cain
Tychicus
Tyrannus

Ucal
Uel
Ulam
Ulla

Unni
Ur
Urbane
Uri
Uriah
Urias
Uriel
Urijah
Uthai
Uz
Uzai
Uzal
Uzza
Uzzah
Uzzi
Uzzia
Uzziah
Uzziel

Vajezatha
Vaniah
Vashni
Vophsi

Zaavan
Zabad
Zabbai
Zabbud
Zabdi
Zabdiel
Zabud
Zaccai
Zacchaeus
Zacchur
Zaccur
Zachariah
Zacharias
Zacher
Zadok

Zaham
Zalaph
Zalmon
Zalmunna
Zanoah
Zaphnath-
 Paaneah
Zaphon
Zara
Zarah
Zatthu
Zattu
Zavan
Zaza
Zebadiah
Zebah
Zebedee
Zebina
Zebul
Zebulun
Zechariah
Zecher
Zedekiah
Zeeb
Zelek
Zelophehad
Zelotes
Zemira
Zenas
Zephaniah
Zephi
Zepho
Zephon
Zerah
Zerahiah
Zereth
Zeri

Zeror
Zerubbabel
Zetham
Zethan
Zethar
Zia
Ziba
Zibeon
Zibia
Zichri
Zidkijah
Zidon
Ziha
Zilthai
Zimmah
Zimran
Zimri
Zina
Ziph
Ziphah
Ziphion
Zippor
Zithri
Ziza
Zizah
Zohar
Zoheth
Zophah
Zophai
Zophar
Zorobabel
Zuar
Zuph
Zur
Zuriel
Zurishaddai

BIRTHSTONES AND FL●WERS

January
Birthstone: Garnet
Flower: Carnation

February
Birthstone: Amethyst
Flower: Violet

March
Birthstone: Aquamarine
Flower: Jonquil

April
Birthstone: Diamond
Flower: Sweet Pea

May
Birthstone: Emerald
Flower: Lily of the Valley

June
Birthstone: Pearl
Flower: Rose

July
Birthstone: Ruby
Flower: Larkspur

August
Birthstone: Peridot
Flower: Gladiolus

September
Birthstone: Sapphire
Flower: Aster

October
Birthstone: Opal
Flower: Calendula

November
Birthstone: Topaz
Flower: Chrysanthemum

December
Birthstone: Turquoise
Flower: Narcissus

MOTHER'S
HERITAGE OF NAMES

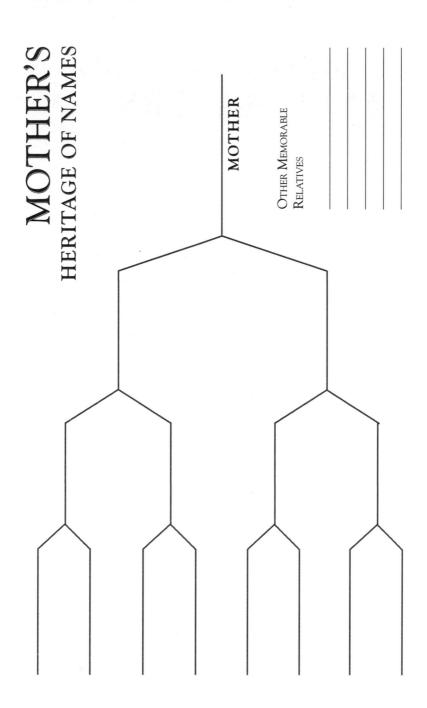

MOTHER

OTHER MEMORABLE
RELATIVES

FATHER'S
HERITAGE OF NAMES

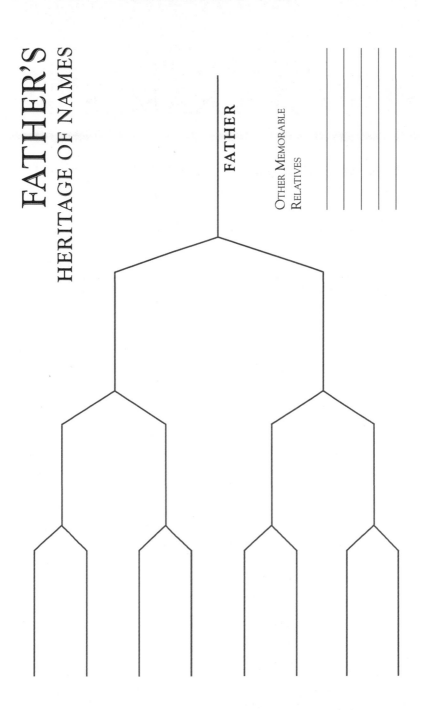

FATHER

OTHER MEMORABLE
RELATIVES

OUR FAVORITE
GIRL NAMES

Rank Mother's Choices

_____ _____
_____ _____
_____ _____
_____ _____
_____ _____
_____ _____
_____ _____
_____ _____
_____ _____
_____ _____

Rank Father's Choices

_____ _____
_____ _____
_____ _____
_____ _____
_____ _____
_____ _____
_____ _____
_____ _____
_____ _____
_____ _____

OUR FAVORITE
B●Y NAMES

Rank Mother's Choices

——— ————————————————
——— ————————————————
——— ————————————————
——— ————————————————
——— ————————————————
——— ————————————————
——— ————————————————
——— ————————————————
——— ————————————————
——— ————————————————

Rank Father's Choices

——— ————————————————
——— ————————————————
——— ————————————————
——— ————————————————
——— ————————————————
——— ————————————————
——— ————————————————
——— ————————————————
——— ————————————————
——— ————————————————